Abortion under State Constitutions

ABORTION UNDER STATE CONSTITUTIONS

A State-by-State Analysis

Paul Benjamin Linton

CAROLINA ACADEMIC PRESS
Durham, North Carolina

Library of Congress Cataloging-in-Publication Data

Linton, Paul Benjamin.
  Abortion under state constitutions : a state-by-state analysis / by Paul Benjamin Linton.
      p. cm.
  ISBN 978-1-59460-604-5 (alk. paper)
  1. Abortion--Law and legislation--United States--States. 2. Constitutional law--United States--States. I. Title.
  KF3771.L56 2008
  342.7308'4--dc22

                                                                  2008028709

Carolina Academic Press
700 Kent Street
Durham, North Carolina 27701
Telephone (919) 489-7486
Fax (919) 493-5668

www.cap-press.com

Printed in the United States of America

Dedication

This book is dedicated to the memory of my late friend, Thomas J. Marzen, Esq., who, in the almost twenty years that I knew him, was a constant source of encouragement, insight, advice and, not the least, humor.

CONTENTS

FOREWORD

When we think of Constitutional Law, we typically think only of the United States Constitution. Indeed, turn to the typical college or law school text on Constitutional Law, and you will find a collection of cases from just one Court, the United States Supreme Court.

Yet the state courts make Constitutional Law all the time. And, often, what the state courts say is different from what the United States Supreme Court says. Of course, the United States Supreme Court long ago decided that it is the supreme expositor of what the United States Constitution means. But state courts have their own state constitutions, which they may interpret to grant more rights or different rights than what the federal constitution offers. As Justice Brennan remarked over thirty years ago, "state courts no less than federal are and ought to be the guardians of our liberties."[1] State jurists[2] and commentators[3] have echoed this refrain.

The law governing abortions, like other laws, is subject to the state constitutions as well as the federal constitution. Lawyers who engage in the litigation in the trial level know that state constitutions matter. In the area of abortion law, the Supreme Court recently has taken to writing decisions that are less expansive and require that litigants have standing instead of hypothesizing circumstances that may never occur.[4] The modern Court does not embrace facial attacks.[5] This restraint creates a partial vacuum, which state courts rush to fill.

---

1. William Brennan, *State Constitutions and the Protection of Individual Rights*, 90 HARV. L. REV. 489, 491 (1977).

2. *E.g.*, Stanley Mosk, *The New States Rights*, 10 CALIF. L. ENFORCEMENT 81, 81 (1976). Stanley Mosk was Justice of the California Supreme Court at the time he wrote this article.

3. A.E. Dick Howard, *State Courts and Constitutional Rights in the Day of the Burger Court*, 62 VA. L. REV. 873 (1976). *See also,* 1 RONALD D. ROTUNDA & JOHN E. NOWAK, TREATISE ON CONSTITUTIONAL LAW: SUBSTANCE AND PROCEDURE §1.6(c) State Court Review of State Laws (Thomson-West, 4th ed. 2007).

4. *Ayotte v. Planned Parenthood of Northern New England*, 546 U.S. 320, 126 S.Ct. 961, 163 L.Ed. 812 (2006).

5. *Gonzales v. Carhart*, 550 U.S. ___, 127 S.Ct. 1610, 1631, 167 L.Ed.2d 480 (2007).

Consequently, litigants, whether they embrace or oppose a right to abortion, are turning to state constitutions. Not only do state courts interpret their constitutions without the need to follow federal law, they also need not follow federal law of standing, case or controversy, and other procedural restrictions.[6]

We cannot understand what state courts may do in the future regarding abortion unless we know what they are doing now. To find that, we must turn to Paul Linton's new book, ABORTION UNDER STATE CONSTITUTIONS: *A STATE-BY-STATE ANALYSIS*. He is specially qualified to write this book, for he has labored in this area for decades, publishing a dozen articles on abortion and related topics, such as sex discrimination, equal rights amendments under state law, the history of abortion regulation, and abortion case law.

Law review articles sometimes refer to abortion law under state constitutional provisions, but they discuss the state constitutional issues only in passing, not systematically. This book is the first full-length treatment of this issue in book form, and it meets a longstanding need by canvassing and analyzing the law of every State. Paul Linton's book is comprehensive in scope, thorough in research, and detailed in analysis. Mr. Linton covers all plausible (and even some implausible) grounds on which a litigant might assert an abortion right under various state constitutional provisions.

Only a dozen state courts, by Mr. Linton's count, explicitly recognize a constitutional right to abortion based only on state law and independent of federal law. Since the Supreme Court decided *Roe v. Wade* in 1973, several States (in Arkansas, Colorado and Rhode Island) have adopted new state constitutions (or constitutional amendments) that do not embrace *Roe*. For example, Rhode Island added the following language to Article I, §2, of the Rhode Island Declaration of Rights: "Nothing in this section shall be construed to grant or secure any right relating to abortion or the funding thereof."

Abortion is a controversial topic. Right to Life supporters are on one side while Abortion Rights groups are on the other. Everyone else is at some point in the continuum between these two sides. It is difficult to approach this topic with intellectual distance and objectivity. Mr. Linton manages this feat, although he is presently Special Counsel for the Thomas More Society (Chicago, Illinois), the former general counsel of Americans United for Life, and, for two decades, has submitted amicus briefs in the landmark Supreme Court cases. His book is not a brief arguing for a particular position. Instead, it of-

---

6. See discussion in 1 RONALD D. ROTUNDA & JOHN E. NOWAK, TREATISE ON CONSTITUTIONAL LAW §§2.13(c)(iv), 2.13(f)(i)(3), 2.13(f)(vi) (Thomson-West, 4th ed. 2007). See also, 4 RONALD D. ROTUNDA & JOHN E. NOWAK, TREATISE ON CONSTITUTIONAL LAW §§18.29(a) to 18.29(e) (Thomson-West, 5th ed. 2008).

fers analyses of what are the state constitutional rights regarding abortion and what the law may come to be. The presentation strives to be objective and evenhanded.

His book should be of interest and value, to not only lawyers on both sides of the abortion debate, but also to judges considering abortion rights claims, and lawyers and non-lawyers interested in the legal issues surrounding abortion. Although this book is a work of scholarship, Mr. Linton writes in a clear style that nonlawyers should find accessible.

The Good Book tells us that there is nothing new under the sun. When it comes to abortion litigation, under the present state of the law, there is probably no argument that some litigant has not raised in some state court, and, as Mr. Linton explains in his Introduction, he discusses them all, plus others that litigants may raise in the future. His goal is to provide an informed judgment about what state courts are likely to do, after examining the state constitution text, its history, interpretation and the historical and contemporary treatment of abortion and the rights of unborn children outside the context of abortion, such as laws governing fetal homicide, wrongful death, health care laws, property law, etc.

The law's movement is sometimes difficulty to predict—and those who make them tend to offer evidence of their fallibility. But, that does not mean that we should not try. The law is not random. Even if we cannot predict with confidence what a court will do, we should be able to predict with some confidence the arguments that a court will find more persuasive. Mr. Linton excels in exploring these arguments.

Ronald D. Rotunda
Professor of Law
Chapman University School of Law
Orange, California

Acknowledgments

This book could not have been written without the support and assistance of others. Principal funding for the research and writing was provided by the Thomas More Society, Chicago, Illinois. Their Board of Directors, chaired by Jennifer Craigmile Neubauer, and their President and Chief Counsel, Thomas Brejcha, had the vision to see the need for this book and the analysis it provides. I very much appreciate their support. Appreciation is also due to Denise Mackura, the former director of the Center for Life and Hope, who arranged for the Center to provide a mechanism by which interested individuals and organizations were able to contribute to the work. Ms. Mackura is now Executive Director and Counsel for the Thomas More Society.

Individual chapters have been reviewed by government attorneys, attorneys in private practice, law professors and retired state supreme court justices. I appreciate their suggestions. I particularly want to thank Michael Moses, Associate General Counsel, Office of the General Counsel, National Conference of Catholic Bishops. Michael kindly offered to read much of the manuscript and his thoughtful, measured comments greatly improved the tone, the substance and the style of the entire book. I also thank Diane Pietrzak for her meticulous review of some early chapters and helpful suggestions on style and organization.

Most of the research for this book was done at three Chicago law libraries-the Cook County Law Library, Northwestern University School of Law and DePaul University College of Law. The Cook County Law Library is an extraordinary public law library that has extensive (and relatively complete) collections of out-of-date, as well as current, state statutes, and state session laws, which needed to be consulted on a regular basis in the course of researching this book. I appreciate the friendliness of their entire staff and, in particular, the assistance of one of their reference librarians, Montell Davenport, in helping me find materials in their collections. Northwestern University's Law School library is beautifully situated on Lake Shore Drive overlooking Lake Michigan immediately north of downtown Chicago. I found their library to be especially useful in researching texts on state constitutional law and state constitutional convention proceedings. Special thanks are due to Marcia Lehr and Pegeen Bassett, who helped me locate materials in the law school's collections as well as referring me to other libraries which had materials that were not available at Northwestern. Both Northwestern and DePaul make their law libraries available to practitioners who are neither students nor alumni of their schools. I also benefitted from using the collections at the Newberry Library, a research library in Chicago. Finally, the staff of the reference and inter-library loan departments of my local public library (the Northbrook Public Library) was able to obtain materials for me from out-of-State libraries. I appreciate their help, as well.

ABORTION UNDER STATE CONSTITUTIONS

Introduction

The United States Supreme Court's decision in *Roe v. Wade*,[1] recognizing a federal constitutional right to abortion, has understandably overshadowed efforts to persuade state courts to recognize an equivalent right on state constitutional grounds. The Court, after all, effectively nullified the abortion laws of all fifty States and permitted abortion for any reason before viability,[2] and for virtually any reason after viability, as well.[3] Given the scope and impact of the

---

1. 410 U.S. 113 (1973).

2. *Id*. at 162–65. Viability is that stage of pregnancy when the unborn child is capable of sustained survival outside of the mother's womb, with or without medical assistance.

3. *Roe* held that, after viability, "the State in promoting its interest in the potentiality of human life may, if it chooses, regulate, and even proscribe, abortion except where it is necessary, in appropriate medical judgment, for the preservation of the life or health of the mother." 410 U.S. at 164–65. In *Roe*, the Court did not define the scope of the mandated health exception. In the companion case of *Doe v. Bolton*, 410 U.S. 197 (1973), however, the Court held that whether an abortion is "necessary" is a professional judgment that "may be exercised in the light of all factors-physical, emotional, psychological, familial, and the woman's age-relevant to the well-being of the patient. *All these factors may relate to health.*" *Id* at 192 (emphasis added); *see also Roe*, 410 U.S. at 154 (stating that *Doe* and *Roe* "are to be read together"). Although the Supreme Court has not yet considered the constitutionality of a statute prohibiting (subject to narrow exceptions) post-viability abortions (and the statute at issue in *Doe* did not make a distinction between pre- and post-viability abortions), at least three lower federal courts have held that the broad and open-ended definition of "health" in *Doe* limits the authority of the States to restrict post-viability abortions. *See Women's Medical Professional Corp. v. Voinovich*, 130 F.3d 187, 206–10 (6th Cir. 1997) (striking down statute that prohibited post-viability abortions except for narrow physical health reasons); *Margaret S. v. Edwards*, 488 F. Supp. 181 (E.D. La. 1980) (striking down statute that prohibited post-viability abortions unless the procedure was necessary "to prevent permanent impairment to [the pregnant woman's] health"); *Schulte v. Douglas*, 567 F. Supp. 522 (D. Neb. 1981), *aff'd per curiam, sub nom. Women's Services, P.C. v. Douglas*, 710 F.2d 465 (8th Cir. 1983) (striking down statute that prohibited post-viability abortions unless the procedure was "necessary to preserve the woman from an imminent peril that substantially endangers her life or health"). *See also American College of Obstetricians & Gynecologists v. Thornburgh*, 737 F.2d 283, 298–99 (3d Cir. 1984) (stating in dictum that had Pennsylva-

Supreme Court's decision in *Roe*, and the Court's subsequent invalidation of statutes and ordinances requiring parental consent,[4] spousal consent,[5] detailed informed consent,[6] short waiting periods[7] and a variety of other measures regulating the practice of abortion,[8] it is not surprising that abortion litigation under state constitutions has received so little attention, both in the public square and in the legal community. And yet, even before *Roe* was decided, statutes prohibiting abortion had been challenged in state court, usually on federal grounds, but sometimes on state grounds, too, with mixed results.[9]

---

nia attempted to prohibit post-viability abortions performed for psychological or emotional reasons, such a limitation would have been unconstitutional under *Doe v. Bolton*), *aff'd*, 476 U.S. 747 (1986). *But see Planned Parenthood of Southeastern Pennsylvania v. Casey*, 505 U.S. 833, 850–51(1992) (characterizing as "rare" those circumstances in which an abortion is a danger to a woman's life or health); *Voinovich v. Women's Medical Professional Corp.*, 523 U.S. 1036 (1998) (Thomas, J., dissenting from denial of certiorari) (distinguishing *Doe* and stating that it does not articulate the relevant constitutional standard for a ban on post-viability abortions).

4. *Planned Parenthood of Central Missouri v. Danforth*, 428 U.S. 52, 72–75 (1976); *City of Akron v. Akron Center for Reproductive Rights*, 462 U.S. 416, 439–42 (1983).

5. *Danforth*, 428 U.S. at 67–72.

6. *City of Akron*, 462 U.S. at 442–49; *Thornburgh v. American College of Obstetricians & Gynecologists*, 476 U.S. 747, 759–65 (1986).

7. *City of Akron*, 462 U.S. at 449–51; *Thornburgh*, 476 U.S. at 759–65.

8. *Danforth*, 428 U.S. at 75–79 (striking down statute prohibiting saline amniocentesis method of abortion); *City of Akron*, 462 U.S. at 431–39 (striking down ordinance requiring all abortions after the first trimester to be performed in hospitals); *Planned Parenthood Ass'n of Kansas City, Missouri, Inc. v. Ashcroft*, 462 U.S. 476, 481–82 (1983) (striking down statute requiring all abortions after the first twelve weeks of pregnancy to be performed in hospitals); *Thornburgh*, 476 U.S. at 768–71 (striking down statute imposing standard of care for post-viability abortions).

9. Prior to *Roe*, state reviewing courts in fifteen States considered state and/or federal constitutional challenges to their abortion statutes in twenty separate opinions. For the most part, those challenges were rejected and the statutes upheld. *See Nelson v. Planned Parenthood Center of Tucson*, 505 P.2d 580 (Ariz. Ct. App. 1972); *Cheaney v. State*, 285 N.E.2d 265 (Ind. 1972), *cert. denied for want of standing of petitioner*, 410 U.S. 991 (1973); *State v. Abodeely*, 179 N.W.2d 347, 354–55 (Iowa 1970), *appeal dismissed, cert. denied*, 402 U.S. 936 (1971); *Sasaki v. Commonwealth*, 485 S.W.2d 897 (Ky. 1972), *vacated and remanded*, 410 U.S. 951 (1973); *State v. Campbell*, 270 So.2d 506 (La. 1972); *State v. Scott*, 255 So.2d 736 (La. 1971); *State v. Shirley*, 237 So.2d 676, 678 (La. 1970); *State v. Pesson*, 235 So.2d 568, 573–74 (La. 1970); *Kudish v. Board of Registration in Medicine*, 248 N.E.2d 264 (Mass. 1969); *Commonwealth v. Brunelle*, 171 N.E.2d 850 (Mass. 1961); *Spears v. State*, 257 So.2d 876 (Miss. 1972) (*per curiam*); *Rodgers v. Danforth*, 486 S.W.2d 258 (Mo. 1972), *vacated and remanded*, 410 U.S. 949 (1973); *State v. Kruze*, No. 72-11 (Ohio March 10, 1972), *vacated and remanded*, 410 U.S. 951 (1973); *State v. Munson*, 201 N.W.2d 123 (S.D. 1972), *vacated and remanded*, 410 U.S. 950 (1973); *Thompson v. State*, 493 S.W.2d 913, 917–20 (Tex. Crim.

The pace of such litigation accelerated dramatically after the Supreme Court began to uphold some modest limitations on abortion, including statutes restricting public funding of abortions (or the availability of public facilities for the performance of abortions)[10] and statutes requiring, subject to a valid judicial bypass mechanism, parental consent or notice.[11] Following these decisions, more than two dozen lawsuits were brought in state courts challenging, on state constitutional grounds alone, statutes and regulations restricting public funding of abortion and statutes requiring parental consent or notice. And, despite the fact that such statutes had been upheld by the Supreme Court, most that were challenged in state court were struck down.[12] After the Supreme

---

App. 1971), *vacated and remanded*, 410 U.S. 950 (1973); *but see People v. Barksdale*, 503 P.2d 257 (Cal. 1972) (striking down the California Therapeutic Abortion Act); *People v. Belous*, 458 P.2d 194 (Cal. 1969) (striking down nineteenth-century statute prohibiting all abortions except those necessary to save the life of the pregnant woman); *State v. Barquet*, 262 So. 431 (Fla. 1972) (same); *Beacham v. Leahy*, 287 A.2d 836 (Vt. 1972) (same). *See also People v. Nixon*, 201 N.W.2d 635, 640–41 & n. 17 (Mich. Ct. App. 1972) (upholding physician's conviction for abortion but suggesting in dictum that the prohibition could not constitutionally be applied to the performance of an early abortion by a licensed physician in a hospital), *remanded*, 389 Mich. 809 (1973).

10. *Beal v. Doe*, 432 U.S. 438 (1977) (federal Medicaid statute does not require States to pay for nontherapeutic abortions); *Maher v. Roe*, 432 U.S. 464 (1977) (Constitution does not require States participating in Medicaid program to pay for nontherapeutic abortions); *Poelker v. Doe*, 432 U.S. 519 (1977) (upholding municipal policy prohibiting the performance of abortions in city hospitals except when there was a threat of grave physiological injury or death to the pregnant woman); *Harris v. McRae*, 448 U.S. 297 (1980) (upholding Hyde Amendment prohibiting the use of federal funds to pay for abortions except those necessary to save the life of the pregnant woman); *Williams v. Zbaraz*, 448 U.S. 358 (1980) (upholding Illinois statute containing the same restriction); *Webster v. Reproductive Health Services*, 492 U.S. 490, 507–11 (1989) (upholding statute prohibiting public employees from performing abortions and prohibiting the use of public facilities for the performance of abortions except those necessary to save the life of the pregnant woman).

11. *Bellotti v. Baird*, 443 U.S. 622 (1979) (setting forth, in context of decision striking down state parental consent statute, criteria under which such statutes would be upheld); *H.L. v. Matheson*, 450 U.S. 398 (1981) (upholding Utah's parental notice statute); *Planned Parenthood Ass'n of Kansas City, Missouri v. Ashcroft*, 462 U.S. at 490–93 (upholding Missouri's parental consent statute); *Hodgson v. Minnesota*, 497 U.S. 417 (1990) (upholding Minnesota's parental notice statute); *Ohio v. Akron Center for Reproductive Rights*, 497 U.S. 502 (1990) (upholding Ohio's parental notice statute); *Casey*, 505 U.S. at 899–900 (upholding Pennsylvania's parental consent statute); *Lambert v. Wicklund*, 520 U.S. 292 (1997) (upholding Montana's parental notice statute).

12. Public funding restrictions were struck down in *State of Alaska, Dep't of Health & Human Services v. Planned Parenthood of Alaska, Inc.*, 28 P.3d 904 (Alaska 2001); *Simat Corp. v. Arizona Health Care Cost Containment System*, 56 P.3d 28 (Ariz. 2002); *Committee to De-*

Court, in *Planned Parenthood of Southeastern Pennsylvania v. Casey*, modified *Roe v. Wade*, at least with respect to its impact on the regulation of abortion,[13]

---

fend Reproductive Rights v. Myers, 625 P.2d 779 (Cal. 1981); *Humphreys v. Clinic for Women, Inc.*, 796 N.E.2d 247 (Ind. 2003) (limited partial invalidity); *Moe v. Secretary of Administration & Finance*, 417 N.E.2d 387 (Mass. 1981); *Women of the State of Minnesota v. Gomez*, 542 N.W.2d 17 (Minn. 1995); *Right to Choose v. Byrne*, 450 A.2d 925 (N.J. 1982); *New Mexico Right to Choose/NARAL v. Johnson*, 975 P.2d 841 (N.M. 1998); *Planned Parenthood Ass'n, Inc. v. Dep't of Human Resources of the State of Oregon*, 663 P.2d 1247 (Or. Ct. App. 1983), *aff'd on other grounds*, 687 P.2d 785 (Or. 1984); *Women's Health Center of West Virginia, Inc. v. Panepinto*, 446 S.E.2d 658 (W. Va. 1993). In addition to the foregoing decisions, two state supreme courts held that quasi-public, non-denominational hospitals could not refuse to make their facilities available for the performance of elective abortions. *Valley Hospital Ass'n v. Mat-Su Coalition for Choice*, 948 P.2d 963 (Alaska 1997); *Doe v. Bridgeton Hospital Ass'n*, 366 A.2d 641 (N.J. 1976). Funding restrictions were upheld in *Renee B. v. Florida Agency for Health Care Administration*, 790 So.2d 1036 (Fla. 2001); *A Choice for Women, Inc. v. Florida Agency for Health Care Administration*, 872 So.2d 970 (Fla. Dist. Ct. App. 2004): *Doe v. Dep't of Social Services*, 487 N.W.2d 166 (Mich. 1992); *Hope v. Perales*, 634 N.E.2d 183 (N.Y. 1994): *Rosie J. v. North Carolina Dep't of Human Resources*, 491 S.E.2d 535 (N.C. 1997); *Fischer v. Dep't of Public Welfare*, 502 A.2d 114 (Pa. 1985); and *Bell v. Low-Income Women of Texas*, 95 S.W.3d 253 (Tex. 2002). In addition to these reviewing court decisions, funding restrictions were challenged in unreviewed trial court decisions in half a dozen other States with mixed results (where relevant, those decisions are discussed in the respective state analyses). Statutes mandating parental consent or notice (subject to a judicial bypass mechanism) were struck down in *State of Alaska v. Planned Parenthood of Alaska*, 171 P.3d 577 (Alaska 2007); *American Academy of Pediatrics v. Lungren*, 940 P.2d 797 (Cal. 1997); *In re T.W.*, 551 So.2d 1186 (Fla. 1989); *North Florida Women's Health and Counseling Services, Inc. v. State of Florida*, 866 So.2d 612 (Fla. 2003) (later overturned by state constitutional amendment); and *Planned Parenthood of Central New Jersey v. Farmer*, 762 A.2d 620 (N.J. 2000). Parental consent or notice statutes were upheld in *Planned Parenthood League of Massachusetts, Inc. v. Attorney General*, 677 N.E.2d 101 (Mass. 1997) (limited to one-parent consent); and *Pro-Choice Mississippi v. Fordice*, 716 So.2d 645 (Miss. 1998).

13. *Casey* overruled, in part, the Court's earlier decisions in *City of Akron* and *Thornburgh*, upheld a detailed informed consent requirement, a twenty-four hour waiting period, a requirement that the physician, not his agent, apprise the woman considering an abortion of specific information relating to the abortion, as well as a parental consent statute. 505 U.S. at 881–87, 899–900. *Casey* is notable for three doctrinal changes from *Roe*. First, in *Casey*, the Court rooted the right to abortion in the "liberty" language of the Fourteenth Amendment, *Casey*, 505 U.S. at 846–53, not, as in *Roe*, in an implied right of privacy. *Roe*, 410 U.S. at 153. Second, unlike *Roe*, 410 U.S. at 152–56, the Court in *Casey* did not characterize the right to abortion as "fundamental." Third, in reaffirming *Roe*, the Court never held that *Roe* had been correctly decided as a matter of original constitutional interpretation. *See, e.g.*, 505 U.S. at 871 ("the immediate question is not the soundness of *Roe*'s resolution of the issue [the weight to be given the State's interest in protecting the "potentiality" of human life], but the precedential force that must be accorded to its holding"). Instead, the Court relied heavily on the rule of *stare decisis* (the doctrine

lawsuits were brought in state court challenging the same kind of informed consent and waiting periods that had been upheld in *Casey*. Only one of those lawsuits succeeded, however.[14]

State challenges to abortion regulations have been brought with two objectives in mind: First, and most immediately, to invalidate statutes and administrative rules that would otherwise survive (and in many instances had survived) federal constitutional review. Second, to establish a right to abortion on *state* constitutional grounds that would outlive the overruling of *Roe v. Wade*. With few exceptions, state lawsuits that succeeded in the first effort typically succeeded in the second. Indeed, prevailing on the second argument usually was the condition necessary of prevailing on the first.[15] As of this writing, almost one-fourth of the state supreme courts in the United States have recognized a right to abortion under their state constitution that is separate from, and independent of, the right to abortion recognized in *Roe*.[16]

---

that courts should follow their own precedents) and the perceived need to protect its "institutional integrity." *Id.* at 854–69.

14. *Planned Parenthood of Middle Tennessee v. Sundquist*, 38 S.W.3d 1 (Tenn. 2000). Similar challenges were rejected in six other States. *See State of Florida v. Presidential Women's Center*, 937 So.2d 114 (Fla. 2006); *Clinic for Women, Inc. v. Brizzi*, 837 N.E.2d 973 (Ind. 2005); *Mahaffey v. Attorney General*, 564 N.W.2d 104 (Mich. Ct. App. 1997); *Pro-Choice Mississippi v. Fordice*, 716 So.2d 645 (Miss. 1998); *Reproductive Health Services of Planned Parenthood of the St. Louis Region, Inc. v. Nixon*, 185 S.W.3d 685 (Mo. 2006); *Preterm Cleveland v. Voinovich*, 627 N.E.2d 570 (Ohio Ct. App. 1993).

15. *But see Simat Corp. v. Arizona Health Care Cost Containment System*, 56 P.3d 28 (Ariz. 2002) (striking down, on the basis of the equal privileges and immunities provision of the state constitution, art. II, §13, restrictions on public funding of abortion, without deciding whether the Arizona Constitution confers a right to abortion); *Humphreys v. Clinic for Women, Inc.*, 796 N.E.2d 247 (Ind. 2003) (partially invalidating, on the basis of the equal privileges and immunities clause of the state constitution, art. I, §23, restrictions on public funding of abortion, without deciding whether the Indiana Constitution confers a right to abortion); *Women's Health Center of West Virginia, Inc. v. Panepinto*, 446 S.E.2d 658 (W.Va. 1993) (striking down, on the basis of the "common benefit" provision of the state constitution, art. III, §3, restrictions on public funding of abortion, without deciding whether the West Virginia Constitution confers a right to abortion).

16. *State of Alaska v. Planned Parenthood of Alaska*, 35 P.3d 30 (Alaska 2001); *State of Alaska, Dep't of Health & Human Services v. Planned Parenthood of Alaska, Inc.*, 28 P.3d 904 (Alaska 2001); *Valley Hospital Ass'n v. Mat-Su Coalition for Choice*, 948 P.2d 963 (Alaska 1997); *Committee to Defend Reproductive Rights v. Myers*, 625 P.2d 779 (Cal. 1981); *In re T.W.*, 551 So.2d 1186 (Fla. 1989); *Moe v. Secretary of Administration & Finance*, 417 N.E.2d 387 (Mass. 1981); *Women of the State of Minnesota v. Gomez*, 542 N.W.2d 17 (Minn. 1995); *Pro-Choice Mississippi v. Fordice*, 716 So.2d 645 (Miss. 1998); *Armstrong v. State*, 989 P.2d 364 (Mont. 1999); *Right to Choose v. Byrne*, 450 A.2d 925 (N.J. 1982); *New Mexico Right to*

The purpose of this book is to provide a comprehensive legal analysis of the status of abortion as a state constitutional right in all fifty States. With respect to the minority of state supreme courts that already have recognized a state right to abortion, the analysis is *descriptive*, setting forth the relevant case law and summarizing the court holdings. With respect to the overwhelming majority of state supreme courts that have *not* addressed this issue, the analysis is intended to be *predictive*, offering an informed judgment as to whether a given state supreme court would likely recognize a state right to abortion.[17] The need for such an analysis, which has never been undertaken by anyone on either side of the abortion debate, should be obvious.[18] Regardless of whether *Roe*, as modified by *Casey*, remains the law of the land, the authority of the States to *regulate* abortions consistent with federal constitutional doctrine will continue to be litigated as a state constitutional issue. And, if *Roe* is ultimately overruled, the authority of the States, under their state constitutions, to *prohibit* abortion would become an immediate and pressing issue.

The reader may be interested in the methodology that underlies the research and analysis contained herein. The point of departure was a review of all of the state court cases, both trial courts and reviewing courts, that have considered state constitutional challenges to abortion statutes and regulations, as well as related arguments that have been raised in federal courts. Those decisions, regardless of outcome, yielded a rich harvest of state constitutional provisions that have been held (or have been alleged) to support a state right to abortion, including, as one familiar with constitutional law would expect, guarantees of due process of law, privacy, inherent and natural rights, unenumerated (or retained) rights, equal protection and equal rights, and prohibiting unequal privileges and immunities. Court decisions addressing asserted abortion rights claims have also involved provisions that one unfamiliar with the case law might not expect, such as those guaranteeing free exercise of religion and rights of conscience, free speech, a right to a remedy for personal injuries and the

----

Choose/NARAL v. Johnson, 975 P.2d 841 (N.M. 1998); *Hope v. Perales*, 634 N.E.2d 183 (N.Y. 1994); *Planned Parenthood of Middle Tennessee v. Sundquist*, 38 S.W.3d 1 (Tenn. 2000); *Beacham v. Leahy*, 287 A.2d 836 (Vt. 1972).

17. This judgment, needless to say, is limited to a *legal* analysis of the relevant sources of state constitutional law. It is not intended (nor could it reasonably be expected) to be an assessment of the *politics* of a given state supreme court or the members thereof at any given time.

18. A recent law review article presents, in a highly abbreviated form, some of the arguments discussed herein, but without attempting to develop the arguments in depth, much less evaluate the likely counter-arguments. *See* Scott A. Moss and Douglas M. Raines, *The Intriguing Federalist Future of Reproductive Rights*, 88 Boston U. Law Rev. 175 (2008).

right of the people to abolish or alter the form of government; emphasizing the importance of a frequent recurrence to fundamental principles; and prohibiting the establishment of a religion, involuntary servitude and unreasonable searches and seizures. The case law interpreting each of these provisions was reviewed for each State, along with the relevant constitutional history (where available). In some States, this included as many as a dozen or more distinct constitutional provisions. There is no argument discussed in this book that has not been raised at some time in a state or federal court.

In addition, for each State where there is no state supreme court opinion recognizing a state right to abortion, the history of the State's treatment of abortion, both pre-*Roe* and post-*Roe*, is surveyed. This research required the review of hundreds of abortions statutes, some dating back to the early nineteenth century, and an even greater number of state court decisions applying and/or interpreting these statutes. In each of the foregoing States (where the state supreme court has not recognized a state constitutional right to abortion), research was also undertaken to ascertain what rights, if any, the law has extended to unborn children outside the context of abortion, including criminal law, tort law, health care law, property law and guardianship law. Does a given State make it a crime to cause the death of (or injury) to an unborn child (apart from a legal abortion)? In States that have retained capital punishment, does the State suspend imposition of a death sentence during a woman's pregnancy? Does the State recognize a statutory cause of action for the wrongful death of an unborn child? Or a common law cause of action for prenatal injuries? Does the State recognize wrongful life and wrongful birth causes of action? Do the State's laws on advance directives (living wills and durable powers of attorney for health care) limit their implementation during a woman's pregnancy? Do children conceived before but born after the death of a decedent qualify as the heirs of an intestate (a person who dies without a will) or the beneficiaries under a will of a person who dies testate (with a will)? And may guardianship proceedings be brought on behalf of (or a guardian *ad litem* appointed for) an unborn child?

Finally, a few words about the structure of the book. Following this Introduction is Part I, consisting of three preliminary chapters addressing the relationship between state and federal constitutional rights (Chapter 1); a review of state constitutional provisions guaranteeing freedom of religion and prohibiting the establishment of a religion that are interpreted in a manner that is consistent with the Free Exercise and Establishment Clauses of the First Amendment (Chapter 2); and a brief consideration of three of the more unusual arguments that have been raised (in state or federal courts) against statutes prohibiting or regulating abortion, based on constitutional provisions prohibiting involuntary servitude, guaranteeing freedom of speech and prohibiting unreasonable searches and seizures (Chapter 3).

Part II, the principal part of the book, provides detailed analyses of the constitutions of all fifty States, describing the existing case law on abortion rights claims in the minority of States whose supreme courts have addressed such issues, and predicting, on the basis of the research and analysis described in the preceding paragraphs, how state supreme courts in the remaining States (the overwhelming majority) would likely resolve such claims. Each state chapter begins with a short summary, indicating whether the state supreme court has recognized a state constitutional right to abortion and, if not, whether the court would likely recognize such a right in the future. In addition to indicating whether the State may *prohibit* abortion under the state constitution (assuming that *Roe,* as modified by *Casey,* is overruled), the summary also indicates whether the State may *regulate* abortion within current federal constitutional limits. The summary is followed by the analysis section, which describes the pre-*Roe* abortion laws and whether they have been repealed; identifies possible sources of an abortion right under the state constitution; and provides an in-depth review of the relevant legal materials with respect to each provision of the state constitution discussed. Each state analysis ends with a brief conclusion, offering an informed judgment as to whether, under the state constitution, the State would have the authority to *prohibit* abortion in the future and whether it presently has the authority to *regulate* abortion to the extent permitted by the federal constitution. Part II is followed by a Conclusion recapitulating the results of the foregoing analysis.

This book has been written so that, for the most part, a reader interested in the law of a particular State need refer only to the analysis for that State and not to any analysis that appears elsewhere in the book. With the exception of the specific arguments discussed in Chapters 2 and 3, each state analysis is intended to be self-contained.[19] The decision to make each state analysis "stand on its own" results in a certain amount of repetition from State to State with respect to similar constitutional arguments. That repetition is the price that must be paid to enable a reader to obtain all of the relevant analysis for a given State in one place. With a few minor modifications adopted for stylistic reasons (*e.g.,* the italicization of all case names), the citation format generally follows that of THE BLUEBOOK[:] A UNIFORM SYSTEM OF CITATION (18th ed.).

---

19. Where appropriate, Chapters 2 and 3 are cross-referenced in the individual state chapters.

PART I
PRELIMINARY CONSIDERATIONS
AND ANCILLARY ARGUMENTS

CHAPTER 1

FEDERAL FLOORS AND STATE CEILINGS

There are two principled approaches in considering the relationship between similar state and federal constitutional guarantees (*e.g.*, due process and equal protection). A state court may conclude, after a careful analysis of the relevant constitutional text, history of its adoption and judicial interpretation, that a given state constitutional guarantee should be construed consistently with the corresponding federal guarantee. Under this approach, often referred to as "lockstep" analysis (because the state constitution is said to march in "lockstep" with the federal constitution), a state constitutional right would not be recognized unless there is a corresponding federal constitutional right; and if there is such a right, the state right would be coextensive with the federal right, neither broader nor narrower. Alternatively, a state court may conclude, in light of its text, history and interpretation, that the state guarantee should be construed independently of the federal guarantee. Under this approach, known as independent state constitutionalism, whether a state right would be recognized (and its scope) would not depend upon whether there is a corresponding federal right. The asserted right might not exist at all under the state constitution and, if it does, it could be broader or narrower than the federal right. What is *not* principled, however, is to *combine* the two approaches and to say, on the one hand, that federal constitutional law will be controlling in determining whether a given right is protected by the state constitution (thereby establishing, as a matter of state law, a federal "floor" of protection), but, on the other hand, that federal law will not be controlling in determining the scope of that same right (allowing for a higher state "ceiling" of protection). That hybrid approach results in what may be called "cafeteria constitutionalism" which is unprincipled in theory and unsound in practice, as Professor Earl Maltz has recognized:

> The image of federal constitutional law as a "floor" in state court litigation pervades most commentary on state constitutional law. Commentators contend that in adjudicating cases, state judges must not adopt

state constitutional rules which fall below this floor; courts may, however, appeal to the relevant state constitution to establish a higher "ceiling" of rights for individuals....

Certainly, as a matter of federal law, state courts are bound not to apply any rule which is inconsistent with decisions of the Supreme Court; the Supremacy Clause of the Federal Constitution clearly embodies this mandate. It would be a mistake, however, to view federal law as a floor for state constitutional analysis; principles of federalism prohibit the Supreme Court from dictating the content of state law. In other words, state courts are not required to incorporate federally-created principles into their state constitutional analysis; the only requirement is that in the event of an irreconcilable conflict between federal law and state law principles, the federal principles must prevail

* * *

[S]uch courts [*i.e.*, those state courts which do not follow the lock-step analysis] must undertake an independent determination of the merits of each claim based solely on principles of state constitutional law. If the state court begins its analysis with the view that the federal practice establishes a "floor," the state court is allowing a federal governmental body—the United States Supreme Court—to define, at least in part, rights guaranteed by the state constitution. Thus, to avoid conflict with fundamental principles of state autonomy, a state court deciding whether to expand federally recognized rights as a matter of state law must employ a two-stage process. The court first must determine whether the federally recognized rights themselves are incorporated into the state constitution and *only then* must determine whether those protections are more expansive under state law.[1]

Other commentators have also recognized that "[i]ndependent interpretation, as a matter of constitutional principle, must be a two-way street."[2]

[T]here is no constitutional impediment preventing state courts from granting a lesser degree of protection under state law, *provided* only that these courts then proceed to apply the command of the Federal Constitution as interpreted by the United States Supreme Court. In other words, the logic of principled interpretation at the state level ... de-

---

1. Earl M. Maltz, *False Prophet-Justice Brennan and the Theory of State Constitutional Law*, 15 Hastings Const. L. Q. 429, 443–44 (1988) (emphasis in original).

2. Ronald K.L. Collins, *Reliance on State Constitutions-Away From a Reactionary Approach*, 9 Hastings Const. L. Q. 1, 10 (1981).

mands that any given argument be tested on its own merits independently of what level of constitutional protection could result. In some instances, it may well be that the logical scope of a state constitutional premise does not extend so far as to afford an equivalent or greater measure of protection than that allotted under the Bill of Rights.

.... Considerations of text, logic, history and consistency may prompt [state] judges to reject [certain] federally protected "rights," but only as questions of state law. These federal "rights" would not suffer in that the same state judges would then have to yield to the dictates of federal law and acknowledge the claims presented. Accordingly, the constitutional premises upon which the state law is grounded would not be sacrificed merely because federal decisional law pointed in another direction.[3]

State reviewing courts are increasingly recognizing that, under an independent state constitutional analysis (as opposed to "lockstep" analysis), *federal* constitutional rights are not necessarily incorporated into *state* constitutions. In *Ex parte Tucci*,[4] the Texas Supreme Court recognized the distinction between independent state constitutional analysis and the command of the Supremacy Clause:

When both federal and state constitutional claims are raised, a state court may not, under the supremacy clause, U.S. Const. art. VI, cl. 2, afford less protection to individual rights than that guaranteed by our national Bill of Rights. In that sense, the prior writings of this court are fully accurate regarding a "federal safety net"—a floor for our liberties and a potentially higher state ceiling. *It is also true that an independent state judiciary may interpret its fundamental law as affording less protection than our federal charter.*[5]

The Michigan Supreme Court has explained that,

Where a right is given to a citizen under federal law, it does not follow that the organic instrument of state government must be interpreted as conferring the identical right. Nor does it follow that where a right given by the federal constitution is not given by a state constitution, the state constitution offends the federal constitution. It is only where the organic instrument of government purports to deprive a citizen of

---

3. *Id.* at 15–16 (emphasis in original).
4. 859 S.W.2d 1 (Tex. 1993).
5. *Id.* at 13 (plurality opinion) (emphasis added).

a right granted by the federal constitution that the instrument can be said to violate the [federal] constitution.[6]

"[A]ppropriate analysis of our constitution does not begin from the conclusive premise of a federal floor.... As a matter of simple logic, because the texts were written at different times by different people, the protections afforded may be greater, lesser, or the same."[7] The Indiana Court of Appeals has said "Indiana courts have the obligation to determine whether an act is protected by the Indiana Constitution, independently of whether the act is protected by federal constitutional guarantees."[8] Accordingly, "The protections provided by the Indiana Constitution may be more extensive than those provided by its federal constitutional counterparts. [Citations omitted]. Those protections may be less extensive; or they may be coterminous."[9] Other state courts are in accord with these views.[10]

An understanding of the proper relationship between state and federal constitutional analysis, with respect to state courts that interpret their state constitutions (or provisions thereof) independently of the federal constitution (or corresponding provisions thereof) leads to but one conclusion: That a right is protected by the federal constitution does *not* require a state court, *as a matter of state law*, to extend protection to the same right. This conclusion should hold true for analysis of abortion rights, as it does of other asserted rights.[11]

---

6. *Sitz v. Dep't of State Police*, 506 N.W.2d 209, 216–17 (Mich. 1993).

7. *Id.* at 217.

8. *Taylor v. State*, 639 N.E.2d 1052, 1053–54 (Ind. Ct. App. 1994).

9. *Id.* at 1053. "Questions arising under the Indiana Constitution are to be resolved by examining the language of the text in the context of the history surrounding its drafting and ratification, the purpose and structure of our Constitution, and case law interpreting the specific provisions." *Ratliff v. Cohn*, 693 N.E.2d 530, 534 (Ind. 1998) (citations and internal quotation marks omitted).

10. *See, e.g., State v. Schwartz*, 689 N.W.2d 430, 438 (S.D. 2004) ("[a]t a minimum, citizens have the rights guaranteed by the federal provisions, but some of our state constitutional guarantees might afford only equal or less protection than the Federal Constitution"); *West v. Thompson Newspapers*, 872 P.2d 999, 1004 n. 4 (Utah 1994) ("[t]he scope of state constitutional protection for expression may be broader or narrower than the federal, depending on the state constitution's language, history, and interpretation").

11. Presumably, state courts that apply "lockstep" analysis to their state due process (or equivalent) guarantees would recognize a *state* right to abortion so long as the Supreme Court continues to recognize a *federal* right to abortion, but not if *Roe v. Wade*, 410 U.S. 113 (1973), as modified by *Planned Parenthood of Southeastern Pennsylvania v. Casey*, 505 U.S. 833 (1992), were overruled. Courts employing this mode of analysis would not recognize a right to abortion that is separate from, and independent of, the right recognized in *Roe*. Not one of the state supreme courts that have recognized a state constitutional right to abortion, however, has applied lockstep analysis.

In a decision rejecting a state constitutional challenge to Ohio's abortion informed consent statute, the Ohio Court of Appeals noted that although a state court is "not free to find constitutional a statute that violates the United States Constitution, as interpreted by *Planned Parenthood* on the basis that the [state] [c]onstitution is not violated," it need not "follow the undue burden test of *Planned Parenthood* [in construing] the [state] [c]onstitution."[12] "Instead, the state may use either a lesser or greater standard."[13] In a similar vein, the Massachusetts Supreme Judicial Court, in interpreting the Massachusetts Constitution, refused to employ the Supreme Court's (now abandoned) "rigid formulation" of balancing the interests at stake in the abortion debate, preferring instead a "more flexible approach to the weighing of interests that must take place."[14] Finally, both the Mississippi Supreme Court and the Michigan Court of Appeals have conducted independent analyses of their state constitutions, the former concluding, without reference to Supreme Court precedent, that the Mississippi Constitution confers a state right to abortion,[15] the latter concluding otherwise under the Michigan Constitution.[16]

In sum, depending upon text, history and interpretation, a state court may reasonably and legitimately either follow Supreme Court precedent construing a federal constitutional guarantee in construing a similar guarantee in the state constitution, with all the limitations that implies, or it may construe the state

---

12. *Preterm Cleveland v. Voinovich*, 627 N.E.2d 570, 577 n. 9 (Ohio Ct. App. 1993), *rev. denied*, 624 N.E.2d 194 (Ohio 1993).

13. *Id.* at 575 n. 5. In *Preterm Cleveland*, the Ohio Court of Appeals recognized a state constitutional right to abortion under art. I, § 1, of the Ohio Constitution. *Id.* at 575. Although denying review of the lower court's judgment (which upheld the informed consent statute), the Ohio Supreme Court, in a later, unrelated case, undermined the basis for the court of appeals decision. *See State v. Williams*, 728 N.E.2d 342 (Ohio 2000). In *Williams*, the Ohio Supreme Court held that the language of art. I, § 1, "is not an independent source of [judicially enforceable] self-executing protections. Rather, it is a statement of fundamental ideals upon which a limited government is created." *Id.* at 354. Both *Preterm Cleveland* and *Williams* are discussed in Chapter 38 (Ohio), *infra*.

14. *Moe v. Secretary of Administration & Finance*, 417 N.E.2d 387, 402–04 (Mass. 1981) (striking down restrictions on public funding of abortion). *See also Planned Parenthood League of Massachusetts, Inc. v. Attorney General*, 677 N.E.2d 101, 103 (Mass. 1997) (upholding parental consent statute, but limiting statute to one-parent consent). *Moe* and *Planned Parenthood League* are discussed in Chapter 24 (Massachusetts), *infra*.

15. *Pro-Choice Mississippi, v. Fordice*, 716 So.2d 645, 650–54 (Miss. 1998).

16. *Mahaffey v. Attorney General*, 564 N.W.2d 104, 109–11 (Mich. Ct. App. 1997). Both *Pro-Choice Mississippi* and *Mahaffey* are discussed in Chapter 27 (Mississippi) and Chapter 25 (Michigan), respectively, *infra*.

constitution independently of the federal constitution. But, if it chooses the latter course, then Supreme Court precedents should not dictate the interpretation of the state constitution.

CHAPTER 2

Religion Clause Arguments

All state constitutions contain provisions that guarantee religious freedom and prohibit the establishment of (or preference for) religion. Notwithstanding differences in wording, most (although not all) of these provisions have been construed consistently with Supreme Court precedents interpreting the Free Exercise and Establishment Clauses of the First Amendment.[1] For that reason, state constitutional challenges to abortion prohibitions are considered together in this chapter.

In any challenge to a statute prohibiting abortion, abortion advocates may raise either or both of two arguments under the religion clauses of a state constitution. First, they may argue that an abortion prohibition interferes with the "free exercise" of a woman's religious beliefs by forbidding her from obtaining an abortion that would be allowed by her religion. Second, they may argue in the alternative (or in addition) that an abortion prohibition constitutes an "establishment of religion" because it reflects sectarian beliefs regarding when human life begins and the sinfulness of abortion. In light of Supreme Court precedent, neither argument would likely prevail.

Free Exercise

A free exercise challenge to a statute prohibiting abortion would probably fail in light of the Supreme Court's decision in *Employment Division, Dep't of Human Resources of Oregon v. Smith.*[2] In *Smith*, the Court held that the Free Exercise Clause may not be invoked to "relieve an individual of the obligation to comply with a 'valid and neutral law of general applicability on the ground that the law proscribes (or prescribes) conduct that his religion prescribes (or

---

1. To the extent these provisions have been construed independently of the Religion Clauses of the First Amendment, they are discussed in the individual state chapters.

2. 494 U.S. 872 (1990).

proscribes).'"[3] Three years later, the Court reiterated this principle, stating that "a law that is neutral and of general applicability need not be justified by a compelling governmental interest even if the law has the incidental effect of burdening a particular religious practice."[4] A statute prohibiting abortion would be a "valid and neutral law of general applicability" that would not be subject to challenge on free exercise grounds.

Establishment of Religion

An establishment of religion challenge to a statute prohibiting abortion would be foreclosed by the Supreme Court's decision in *Harris v. McRae*, which rejected an Establishment Clause challenge to the Hyde Amendment. In *Harris*, the Court held that the Establishment Clause is not violated merely because "a statute 'happens to coincide or harmonize with the tenets of some or all religions.'"[5] Noting that the Hyde Amendment "is as much a reflection of 'traditionalist' values toward abortion, as it is an embodiment of the views of any particular religion," the Court held that "the fact that the funding restrictions in the Hyde Amendment may coincide with the religious tenets of the Roman Catholic Church does not, without more, contravene the Establishment Clause."[6] For the same reason, the fact that an abortion prohibition may "coincide with" the "religious tenets" of the Catholic Church (or any other church) does not, by itself, violate the Establishment Clause.

---

3. *Id.* at 879 (quoting *United States v. Lee*, 455 U.S. 252, 263 n. 3 (1982) (Stevens, J., concurring in the judgment)). It is doubtful that anyone would even have standing to bring such a challenge. In *Harris v. McRae*, 448 U.S. 297 (1980), the Court rejected a free exercise challenge to the constitutionality of the Hyde Amendment, which restricts federal funding of abortion for indigent women, because there were no Medicaid-eligible pregnant women plaintiffs who claimed that they sought an abortion "under compulsion of religious belief." *Id.* at 320. A prohibition of abortion except to save the life of the pregnant woman would not "burden" any woman in the "free exercise" of her religion, however, because there is no doctrine in any religion that *requires* (as opposed to *permits*) a woman to undergo an abortion in circumstances when her life is not in danger. Whether a particular religious doctrine *permits* abortion for reasons which are not recognized by law does not present a justiciable free exercise issue.

4. *Church of the Lukumi Babalu Aye, Inc. v. City of Hialeah*, 508 U.S. 520, 531 (1993).

5. 448 U.S. at 319.

6. *Id.* at 319–20. It should be noted that no state or federal court has accepted an Establishment Clause challenge against an abortion statute, and two courts have rejected such arguments brought under state constitutions. *See Right to Choose v. Byrne*, 450 A.2d 923, 938–39 (N.J. 1982); *Jane L. v. Bangerter*, 794 F. Supp. 1528, 1534–35 (D. Utah 1992) (interpreting Utah law).

CHAPTER 3

INVOLUNTARY SERVITUDE, FREEDOM OF SPEECH, SEARCH AND SEIZURE

Approximately one-half of American state constitutions prohibit involuntary servitude and all state constitutions guarantee freedom of speech and prohibit unreasonable searches and seizures. Statutes prohibiting or regulating abortion have occasionally, if rarely, been challenged on each of these grounds. Because arguments based on these provisions are seldom raised and have never succeeded, they are addressed, briefly, in this chapter.

Involuntary Servitude

There are relatively few cases interpreting state prohibitions of involuntary servitude, and what cases do exist tend to apply federal precedents interpreting the Thirteenth Amendment.[1] The argument has been made that an abortion prohibition constitutes "involuntary servitude" because it compels a woman to "work" or "provide services" for another (the unborn child). This rather fanciful argument is not likely to be given any credence by either a state or federal court and was rejected in the only case in which it has been raised.

"Involuntary servitude" has been defined in federal case law as "the coerced service of one person for another through the use, or threatened use, of law, physical force, or some other method that causes the laborer to believe that [he] has no alternative to performing the service."[2] "Where the laborer has

---

1. *See, e.g., Akers v. Handley*, 149 N.E.2d 692, 693 (Ind. 1958); *Stone v. City of Paducah*, 86 S.W. 531, 534 (Ky. 1905); *Blair v. Checker Cab. Co.*, 558 N.W.2d 439, 441–42 (Mich. Ct. App. 1996).

2. *Blair*, 558 N.W.2d at 442, citing *United States v. Mussry*, 726 F.2d 1448, 1453 (9th Cir. 1984).

some alternative to performing the service, even if distasteful or less attractive than the service, there is no involuntary servitude."[3]

As an initial matter, except in the cases of rape and incest, the conduct that results in "labor" is voluntarily assumed by the woman who becomes pregnant. But even with respect to involuntary pregnancies, the burdens of pregnancy simply do not fall within the scope of the prohibition against involuntary servitude.

In *Jane L. v. Bangerter*,[4] a federal district court rejected an involuntary servitude challenge to a Utah abortion prohibition (which was later struck down on other grounds). The court noted that, in an early case interpreting the Thirteenth Amendment, the Supreme Court said that the amendment " 'was not intended to introduce any novel doctrine with respect to certain descriptions of service which have always been treated as exceptional; such as military and naval enlistments, or to disturb the rights of parents and guardian to the custody of their minor children or wards.' "[5] At the time the Thirteenth Amendment was ratified, on December 18, 1865, twenty-seven of the thirty-six States had enacted statutes prohibiting abortion, including twenty-one of the twenty-seven ratifying States.[6] "Given this historical context, the contention that one of the purposes of the Thirteenth Amendment was to secure the right of elective abortion totally lacks merit."[7] In *Jane L.*, the district court said that "[i]t strains credulity to equate the carrying of a child to term with 'compulsory labor,' and the argument borders on the frivolous."[8]

There is yet another reason why an abortion prohibition does not constitute "involuntary servitude." In every case in which the Supreme Court has found a condition of involuntary servitude, "the victim has no available choice but to work or be subject to legal sanction."[9] But, as the district court in *Jane L.* observed, "the Utah statute does not create a situation where the woman has no available choice but to bear the child or be subject to legal sanction. No crim-

---

3. *Id.* (citing *Brogan v. San Mateo County*, 901 F.2d 762, 763–64 (9th Cir. 1990)). *See also Jefferson County Teachers Ass'n v. Board of Education of Jefferson County, Kentucky*, 463 S.W.2d 627, 630 (injunction preventing teachers from going out on strike did not subject them to involuntary servitude because they retained the option of terminating their employment contracts).

4. 794 F. Supp. 1537 (D. Utah 1992).

5. *Id.* at 1548, quoting *Robertson v. Baldwin*, 165 U.S. 275, 282 (1897).

6. *Id.*

7. *Id.* at 1548–49.

8. *Id.* at 1549.

9. *United States v. Kozminski*, 487 U.S. 931, 943 (1988).

inal penalties at all apply to a woman who chooses to abort by going to another state that permits abortion."[10]

It should be noted that one of the *amicus* briefs submitted in *Roe v. Wade*[11] and *Doe v. Bolton*[12] argued that laws restricting or regulating abortion as a special procedure violate the Thirteenth Amendment by imposing involuntary servitude without due conviction for a crime.[13] Under that reasoning, no State could forbid abortion at any stage of pregnancy without running afoul of the Thirteenth Amendment. Yet, the States may prohibit abortion after viability, except when the procedure is necessary to preserve the life or health of the pregnant woman.[14] The Supreme Court has repeatedly held that the State's interest in the "potential" life of the unborn child grows throughout pregnancy,[15] even though the physical burdens of pregnancy are growing at the same time.[16] Recognition of that interest suggests that an involuntary servitude argument is baseless.

Finally, in *Webster v. Reproductive Health Services*,[17] the Court upheld the validity of a fetal viability testing requirement that arguably conflicted with the trimester framework of *Roe v. Wade*.[18] Notwithstanding the plurality's decision to abandon the "rigid trimester analysis" of *Roe v. Wade*,[19] the Court up-

---

10. 794 F. Supp. at 1549 n. 16.

11. 410 U.S. 113 (1973).

12. 410 U.S. 179 (1973).

13. *See* Brief *Amici Curiae* on Behalf of Organizations and Named Women in Support of Appellants in Each Case.

14. *Roe v. Wade*, 410 U.S. at 163–65; *Planned Parenthood of Southeastern Pennsylvania v. Casey*, 505 U.S. 833, 846, 879 (1992).

15. *Roe*, 410 U.S. at 162–63 (State's interest in "protecting the potentiality of human life…. grows in substantiality as the woman approaches term and, at a point during pregnancy [viability] becomes 'compelling'"); *Casey*, 505 U.S. at 869 ("[t]he woman's liberty is not so unlimited … that from the outset the State cannot show its concern for the life of the unborn, and at a later point in fetal development [viability] the State's interest in life has sufficient force so that the right of the woman to terminate the pregnancy can be restricted"). *See also Thornburgh v. American College of Obstetricians & Gynecologists*, 476 U.S. 747, 778 (1986) (Stevens, J., concurring) ("I should think it obvious that the State's interest in the protection of the embryo … increases progressively and dramatically as the organism's capacity to feel pain, to experience pleasure, to survive, and to react to its surroundings increases day by day").

16. *Roe*, 410 U.S. at 150 (noting that "the risk to the woman increases as her pregnancy continues"); *Casey*, 505 U.S. at 852 ("[t]he mother who carries a child to full term is subject to anxieties, to physical constraints, to pain that only she must bear").

17. 492 U.S. 490 (1989).

18. *Id*. at 513–21.

19. *Id*. at 517.

held the viability testing requirement,[20] implicitly denying appellees' request to remand the cause for "consideration of what other constitutional principles can support the right recognized in *Roe*," including "the right to be free of involuntary servitude."[21] If, as the foregoing analysis suggests, an abortion prohibition does not constitute "involuntary servitude" for purposes of the Thirteenth Amendment, then it would not constitute involuntary servitude under state constitutional provisions that are construed consistently with the Thirteenth Amendment.

Freedom of Speech

State courts generally interpret their free speech guarantees consistently with the interpretation the Supreme Court has given the First Amendment, although, at least in certain circumstances, some of these courts will give their state guarantees a broader reading. On occasion, abortion advocates have argued that statutes prohibiting or regulating abortion, as opposed to statutes purporting to regulate the advertising of abortion services,[22] interfere with their right to communicate with their patients, and their patients' right to communicate with them. These arguments have been uniformly rejected.

Nothing in the First Amendment (or, by extension, a state free speech guarantee) prohibits the evidentiary use of speech to establish the elements of a crime.[23] In *Giboney v. Empire Storage & Ice Co.*,[24] the Supreme Court said: "It rarely has been suggested that the constitutional freedom for speech and press extends its immunity to speech or writing used as an integral part of conduct in violation of a valid criminal statute."[25] Free speech challenges against abortion prohibitions have been rejected.[26] Indeed both the Supreme Court and state courts have rejected free speech claims raised against informed consent statutes, which actually *mandate* speech, as opposed to abortion prohibitions, which forbid conduct.[27] Accordingly, it is unlikely that a free speech challenge

---

20. *Id.* at 522.

21. Brief of Appellees at 18–19.

22. *See Bigelow v. Virginia*, 421 U.S. 809 (1975) (striking down, as applied, Virginia statute that made it a misdemeanor, by the sale or circulation of any publication, to encourage or prompt the procuring of an abortion).

23. *See Stromberg v. California*, 283 U.S. 359, 368–69 (1931).

24. 336 U.S. 490 (1949).

25. *Id.* at 498. *See also New York v. Ferber*, 458 U.S. 747, 761–62 (1982) (citing *Giboney*).

26. *See Jane L. v. Bangerter*, 794 F. Supp. at 1548.

27. *See Planned Parenthood v. Casey*, 505 U.S. at 884; *Preterm Cleveland v. Voinovich*, 627 N.E.2d 570, 579–80 (Ohio Ct. App. 1993); *Planned Parenthood of Mid-Michigan, Inc.*

to a statute prohibiting or regulating abortion (other than one purporting to regulate advertising) would succeed.

Search and Seizure

Abortion advocates occasionally cite search and seizure provisions, along with other state constitutional provisions, in support of an asserted state right to abortion. They argue that the prohibition of unreasonable searches and seizures protects a zone of privacy which includes abortion. Such arguments, however, fundamentally misapprehend the purpose and scope of state search and seizure provisions.[28] Search and seizure analysis is concerned with the *means* by which suspected criminal activity is investigated, not on the *end* to which that activity is directed. Whether one has a reasonable expectation of privacy in avoiding unlawful disclosure of criminal activity is obviously unrelated to whether the activity is criminal and may be punished, if detected by lawful means.[29]

More than forty years ago, the Supreme Court held that the Fourth Amendment, which "protects individual privacy against certain kinds of governmental intrusions," "cannot be translated into a general constitutional 'right to privacy.'"[30] The Fourth Amendment is aimed at "unwarranted governmental

---

v. Attorney General, Case No. D 91-0571 AZ, Order and Opinion of April 29, 1994, at 4–9 (Michigan Circuit Court, Kalamazoo County)

28. State search and seizure provisions that contain explicit privacy language, as well as freestanding privacy provisions, are considered in the individual state chapters.

29. The converse is also true. That criminal activity has been detected by lawful means has no bearing on whether the activity itself is constitutionally protected. In *Lawrence v. Texas*, 539 U.S. 558 (2003), the Supreme Court struck down, on due process grounds, the Texas sodomy statute, even though, as the Court recognized at the outset of its opinion, "[t]he right of the police to enter [Lawrence's apartment in response to a reported weapons disturbance] does not seem to have been questioned." *Id*. at 563.

30. *Katz v. United States*, 389 U.S. 347, 350 (1967). In *Griswold v. Connecticut*, 381 U.S. 479 (1965), the Supreme Court struck down a state statute prohibiting the use of contraceptives by married couples, holding that the statute impermissibly invaded a "zone of privacy created by several fundamental constitutional guarantees," including the First, Third, Fourth, Fifth and Ninth Amendments. *Id*. at 484-85. *Katz*, as noted in the text, implicitly rejected *Griswold's* suggestion that the Fourth Amendment confers a general right of privacy. Moreover, *Roe v. Wade* rooted the right of privacy in the Due Process Clause of the Fourteenth Amendment, not in the Fourth Amendment or any other provision of the Bill of Rights. 410 U.S. at 153. Furthermore, in a marked departure from the rationale of *Roe*, 410 U.S. at 153 ("[t]his right of privacy ... is broad enough to encompass a woman's decision whether or not to terminate her pregnancy"), the Court no longer analyzes substantive due process claims under the rubric of "privacy," either in the area of abortion, *see Casey*, 505 U.S. at 846-53 (reaffirming *Roe* on the basis of the liberty language of the Due Process

intrusion" into private affairs, not whether the private affairs themselves involve constitutionally protected conduct.[31]

> What the Fourth Amendment protects is the security a man relies upon when he places himself or his property within a constitutionally protected area, be it his home or his office, his hotel room or his automobile. There he is protected from unwarranted governmental intrusion. And when he puts something in his filing cabinet, in his desk drawer, or in his pocket, he has the right to know that it will be secure from *an unreasonable search or an unreasonable seizure.*[32]

The United States Court of Appeals for the District of Columbia expounded on this in *Reporters Committee for Freedom of the Press v. American Telephone & Telegraph.*[33] The court explained:

> The Fourth Amendment strikes a balance between the individual citizen's interest in conducting certain affairs in private, and the general public's interest in subjecting possible criminal activity to intensive investigation. It strikes this balance by securing for each individual a private enclave-a "zone" bounded by the individual's own reasonable expectations of privacy. So long as the individual acts within this "zone of privacy", his activities are shielded from unreasonable Government investigation; any attempt by the Government to search for or seize evidence from *within* this zone must be based on "probable cause" and usually must be preceded by a judicial determination that "probable cause" exists. However, the protections afforded the privacy interests of the individual by the Fourth Amendment are necessarily limited by the public's interest in effective law enforcement; the Fourth Amendment does not insulate *all* personal activity from official scrutiny. Just as it creates "zones of privacy", it also demarcates appropriate areas for investigation, in the sense that it allows the Government relatively free access to evidence located *outside* the individual's "zone of privacy."[34]

Clause without relying on privacy theory), or elsewhere. *See Cruzan v. Director, Missouri Dep't of Health*, 497 U.S. 261, 279 n. 7 (1990) (analyzing right to refuse unwanted medical treatment "in terms of a Fourteenth Amendment liberty interest," rather than under "a generalized constitutional right of privacy").

31. *Hoffa v. United States*, 385 U.S. 293, 301 (1966).

32. *Id.* (emphasis added).

33. 593 F.2d 1030 (D.C. Cir. 1978).

34. *Id.* at 1042–43 (emphasis in original).

Just as the Supreme Court and lower federal courts have recognized that the Fourth Amendment is concerned with the means by which criminal activity is detected, and not whether the activity itself is constitutionally protected, so, too, have state reviewing courts recognized that state search and seizure provisions are concerned with investigative methods, not whether what is being investigated is constitutionally protected. For example, the fact that a homeowner has a reasonable expectation that his house will not be searched except upon a warrant issued upon probable cause or in exigent circumstances does not confer upon him a right to keep contraband in his home or use his home for other illegal purposes. In *State ex rel. Zander v. District Court for the Fourth Judicial District*,[35] the Montana Supreme Court held that the right of privacy in one's home did not preclude prosecution for possession of marijuana, where marijuana plants were discovered by police who entered defendant's unlocked home in response to a burglary-in-progress call from a neighbor. In *Zander,* the state supreme court distinguished between whether certain conduct could be made illegal (a legislative judgment) and whether its discovery was lawful (a judicial determination). On the first question, the court stated:

> We do not reach a determination of whether the cultivation or use of marijuana is or should be criminalized. This is patently a matter of state law to be determined by the legislature. The legislature has determined this by enactment of statutes making sale or possession of marijuana a criminal offense. This Court will not intrude upon this legislative prerogative under the questionable theory that there is no evidence or policy basis for the statutes and that the legislature had no rational or reasonable basis for enacting them.[36]

On the second question, the court held that the police had a valid reason to enter the defendant's home (to respond to a burglary-in-progress call).[37]

The Arizona Supreme Court reached a similar conclusion in *State v. Murphy*,[38] in which it upheld a defendant's conviction for possession of marijuana. In *Murphy,* the state supreme court recognized that "the right of an individual to be free from unreasonable searches and seizures is more strictly applied to home situations."[39] Nevertheless, "that extra protection we rightfully give to the home does not restrict the power of the legislature to make possession

---

35. 591 P.2d 656 (Mont. 1979).
36. *Id.* at 660.
37. *Id.* at 660–61.
38. 570 P.2d 1070 (Ariz. 1977).
39. *Id.* at 1073.

of marijuana in or out of the home a crime. *It goes only to the power of the police to enter a home in search of evidence of that crime.*"[40] In *City of Sherman v. Henry,*[41] the Texas Supreme Court held that a police officer could be denied promotion for engaging in an adulterous affair with the wife of another police officer. The court cautioned, however, that in upholding the municipality's authority to consider the officer's conduct in denying him a promotion, it did not mean to suggest "that the government is free to engage in intrusive investigation methods to determine the sexual practices of individuals."[42] Finally, in *Lawrence v. State,*[43] the Texas Court of Appeals noted that "[t]he fact that unlawful behavior is conducted in private between consenting adults may complicate detection and prosecution, but it does not, *ipso facto,* render its statutory prohibition unconstitutional."[44]

In sum, provisions in state constitutions prohibiting unreasonable searches and seizures, like the Fourth Amendment, place no limitations on what conduct the State may define and punish as criminal. Such limitations must be found, if they exist at all, in other provisions of state Bills of Rights.

---

40. *Id.* (emphasis added).

41. 928 S.W.2d 464 (Tex. 1996).

42. *Id.* at 474.

43. 41 S.W.2d 349 (Tex. App. 2001, *writ ref'd*) (*en banc*), *rev'd, Lawrence v. Texas,* 539 U.S. 558 (2003).

44. *Id.* at 362 n. 39. That remains true, notwithstanding the Supreme Court's decision in *Lawrence* striking down the Texas sodomy statute. There are a variety of acts that may be performed "in private between consenting adults" that are not constitutionally protected, including adult incest, prostitution and adultery.

PART II
STATE ANALYSES

CHAPTER 4

ALABAMA

Summary

The Alabama Supreme Court has not yet decided whether the Alabama Constitution protects a right to abortion separate from, and independent of, the right to abortion recognized under the United States Constitution.[1] A careful examination of the state constitution, in light of its history and interpretation, as well as other relevant legal sources, however, suggests that the state supreme court probably would not recognize a state constitutional right to abortion. Thus, if *Roe v. Wade*,[2] as modified by *Planned Parenthood of Southeastern Pennsylvania v. Casey*,[3] were overruled, Alabama could enforce its pre-*Roe* abortion statute. Moreover, nothing in the state constitution, properly understood, precludes the State from enacting and enforcing reasonable measures regulating abortion within current federal constitutional limits.

Analysis

The pre-*Roe* statute prohibited performance of an abortion upon a pregnant woman unless the procedure was "necessary to preserve her life or health

---

1. The Alabama Supreme Court has referred to the right to abortion solely as a matter of *federal*, not *state*, constitutional law. *See, e.g., In re Anonymous*, 720 So.2d 497, 500 (Ala. 1998) (holding that it was only because of United States Supreme Court precedents and the Supremacy Clause that the state legislature "could not constitutionally confer upon a non-viable fetus the right to appeal, through a guardian *ad litem*, an order granting a minor's request to have an abortion"); *Ex parte Anonymous*, 618 So.2d 722, 725 (Ala. 1993) (right to abortion based on *Roe v. Wade*); *Ex parte Anonymous*, 810 So.2d 786, 793 (Ala. 2001) (same, referring to "federal constitutional law").

2. 410 U.S. 113 (1973).

3. 505 U.S. 833 (1992).

and done for that purpose."[4] The statute, which is not currently enforceable, has not been repealed.[5]

Based upon arguments that have been raised in other States with similar constitutional provisions, possible sources for an asserted abortion right could include provisions of the Declaration of Rights guaranteeing religious freedom (art. I, §§3, 3.01), a remedy by due process of law (§13), due process of law (§§6, 13) and equal protection (§§1, 6, 22); recognizing inalienable rights (§1) and inherent political power in the people (§2); limiting the legitimate ends of government (§35); and retaining rights (§36).[6] The analysis that follows addresses each of these provisions.

Religious Freedom

Article I, §3, of the Alabama Constitution provides, in part, that "no religion shall be established by law; that no preference shall be given by law to any religious sect, society, denomination, or mode of worship; … and … the civil rights, privileges, and capacities of any citizen shall not be in any manner affected by his religious principles."[7] In 1998, the People of the State of Alabama adopted the "Alabama Religious Freedom Amendment," a detailed, seven-part amendment to the Alabama Constitution which provides greater protection for religious freedom than is provided by the Free Exercise Clause of the First Amendment.[8] Under Section V of §3.01, government may not "burden a person's freedom of religion, even if the burden results from a rule of general applicability," unless application of the burden to the person promotes a "compelling governmental interest" and is the "least restrictive means" of promoting that interest.[9]

In any state constitutional challenge to a statute prohibiting abortion (either the pre-*Roe* statute, if *Roe* is overruled, or any other abortion prohibition Alabama may enact), abortion advocates may raise either or both of two arguments under art. I, §§3 and 3.01. First, they may argue that an abortion

---

4. ALA. CODE tit. 14, §9 (1958).

5. *See* ALA. CODE §13A-13-7 (2005).

6. Three other more unlikely sources of an abortion right under the Alabama Constitution—art. I, §4 (guaranteeing freedom of speech), §5 (prohibiting unreasonable searches and seizures) and §32 (prohibiting involuntary servitude)—are discussed generally in Chapter 3, *supra*.

7. ALA. CONST. art. I, §3 (2006).

8. *Id.* art. I, §3.01.

9. *Id.* art. I, §3.01 (Section V).

prohibition burdens the free exercise of a woman's religious beliefs by forbidding her from obtaining an abortion that would be allowed by her religion. Second, they may argue in the alternative (or in addition) that an abortion prohibition constitutes a "preference given by law" to a "religious sect" because it reflects sectarian beliefs regarding when human life begins and the sinfulness of abortion. Neither argument would likely prevail.

With respect to the latter argument, the Alabama Supreme Court has held that "the Alabama constitutional provisions concerning the establishment of religion are not more restrictive than the Federal Establishment of Religion Clause in the First Amendment to the United States Constitution."[10] In light of that congruence of interpretation, a challenge to an abortion statute that would not succeed under the Establishment Clause of the First Amendment would not succeed under art. I, §3, either. For the reasons set forth in Chapter 2, *supra*, an abortion statute could not be successfully challenged on Establishment Clause grounds. Accordingly, a similar challenge under art. I, §3, would not likely be successful.

With respect to the former argument, the adoption of the Alabama Religious Freedom Amendment clearly provides greater protection to free exercise claims than is provided by the Free Exercise Clause, as interpreted by the Supreme Court in *Employment Division, Dep't of Human Resources of Oregon v. Smith*.[11] In *Employment Division*, the Court held that the Free Exercise Clause may not be invoked to "relieve an individual of the obligation to comply with a 'valid and neutral law of general applicability on the ground that the law proscribes (or prescribes) conduct that his religion prescribes (or proscribes).'"[12] Section 3.01 of the Alabama Declaration of Rights, however, imposes the pre-*Smith* standard, under which burdens on the free exercise of religion can be justified only by a compelling governmental interest.[13] Notwithstanding that more rigorous standard, an abortion prohibition would not violate either §3 or §3.01.

A prohibition of abortion except to save the life of the pregnant woman does not "burden" any woman in the "free exercise" of her religion because there is no doctrine in any religion that *requires* (as opposed to *permits*) a woman to undergo an abortion in circumstances when her life is not in danger. Whether a particular religious doctrine *permits* abortion for reasons which are not recognized by law does not present a justiciable free exercise issue even under pre-*Smith* precedents. To have the standing necessary to raise such an

10. *Alabama Education Ass'n v. James*, 373 So.2d 1076, 1081 (Ala. 1979).
11. 494 U.S. 872 (1990).
12. *Id.* at 879 (quoting *United States v. Lee*, 455 U.S. 252, 263 n. 3 (1982) (Stevens, J., concurring in the judgment)).
13. ALA. CONST. art. I, §3.01 (Section V).

issue (with respect to a law that does not single out religious practices for regulation), one must allege that one seeks an abortion "under compulsion of religious belief."[14] Although the Alabama reviewing courts have not yet interpreted § 3.01, their earlier decisions rejecting free exercise claims in other contexts suggest that they would reject a free exercise claim under the Alabama Religious Freedom Amendment.[15]

Even assuming, however, that a prohibition of abortion could be said to "burden" a pregnant woman's free exercise of religion, within the meaning of § 3.01, such prohibition would satisfy the test set forth in Section V(b). The State has a compelling interest in protecting and preserving the life of the unborn child and there is no less restrictive means available to the State, short of an outright prohibition, that would adequately promote and safeguard that interest. An example, not involving abortion, that illustrates this principle is the line of cases authorizing compulsory blood transfusions on pregnant women (typically, Jehovah's Witnesses) to save the lives of their unborn children.[16] The prohibition of abortion, for the same end, stands on even firmer ground, however, because it does not implicate the federal constitutional right to refuse unwanted medical treatment.[17] Moreover, unlike an order authorizing a blood transfusion of a pregnant woman, which is intended to *save* the life of the unborn child (and very possibly the mother's life as well), the intent in an abortion is to *destroy* the unborn child's life. The prohibition of abortion does not violate either art. I, § 3, or art. I, § 3.01, of the Alabama Constitution.

---

14. *Harris v. McRae*, 448 U.S. 297, 320 (1980).

15. *See, e.g., Rheuark v. State*, 601 So.2d 135, 139–40 (Ala. Crim. App. 1992) (state and federal guarantees of free exercise of religion did not entitle defendant to use marijuana or other illegal drugs); *Hill v. State*, 88 So.2d 880, 883–85 (Ala. Ct. App. 1956) (upholding conviction of person under statute prohibiting the display, handling or exhibition of poisonous snakes in a manner endangering the life and health of another, even though statute infringed upon religious practices of some groups).

16. *See Fosmire v. Nicoleau*, 536 N.Y.S.2d 492, 496 (App. Div. 1989) (dictum) (when "a pregnant adult woman refuses medical treatment and, as a result of that refusal, places the life of her unborn baby in jeopardy," "the State's interest, as *parens patriae*, in protecting the health and welfare of the child is determined to be paramount") (citing *In the Matter of Application of Jamaica Hospital*, 491 N.Y.S.2d 898 (Sup. Ct. 1985) (blood transfusion) (18 weeks gestation); and *Crouse Irving Memorial Hospital, Inc. v. Paddock*, 485 N.Y.S.2d 443 (Sup. Ct. 1985) (blood transfusion) (premature delivery)). *See also Raleigh Fitkin-Paul Morgan Memorial Hospital v. Anderson*, 201 A.2d 537 (N.J. 1964) (same with respect to blood transfusion at 32 weeks gestation); *but see In re Brown*, 689 N.E.2d 397 (Ill. App. Ct. 1997) (*contra*) (blood transfusion).

17. *See, e.g., Cruzan v. Director, Missouri Dep't of Health*, 497 U.S. 261, 278–79 & n. 7 (1990); *Washington v. Glucksberg*, 521 U.S. 702, 719–26 & n. 17 (1997).

Remedy by Due Process of Law

Article I, § 13, of the Alabama Constitution provides, in part, that "every person, for any injury done him, in his lands, goods, person, or reputation, shall have a remedy by due process of law...."[18] Abortion advocates might argue that any statute prohibiting abortion interferes with a woman's control over her own body, and that such interference causes an "injury" to her "person," as those terms are used in § 13, for which there must be a "remedy by due process of law." That "remedy," in turn, would be invalidation of the statute. This argument assumes that art. I, § 13, confers substantive rights. The case law is clear, however, that it does not.

"The injury mentioned in Section 13 is damage resulting from breach of a legal duty. Whatever damage results from doing that which is lawful does not lay the foundation of an action."[19] In other words, "[t]here can be no legal claim for damages to the person or property of any one except as it follows from the breach of a legal duty."[20] Legal duties, however, are established by other sources of law (statutory or common law), not § 13. Section 13 merely guarantees, subject to broad exceptions,[21] a remedy for breach of those duties. Thus, if the Legislature determines that certain conduct (*e.g.*, abortion) shall be illegal, then the prevention of that conduct (by a criminal prohibition) cannot be regarded as the breach of a "legal duty." Because art. I, § 13, is not a source of substantive rights, it could not provide a basis for invalidating an otherwise constitutional statute of the State.

Inalienable Rights, Due Process of Law

Article I, § 1, of the Alabama Constitution provides, in pertinent part, that "all men ... are endowed by their Creator with certain inalienable rights; that among these are life, liberty and the pursuit of happiness."[22] And art. I, § 6,

---

18. ALA. CONST. art. I, § 13 (2006).

19. *Randle v. Payne*, 107 So.2d 907, 911 (Ala. 1958).

20. *Pickett v. Matthews*, 192 So. 261, 263 (Ala. 1939).

21. Section 13 places no limits on the authority of the Legislature to modify, limit or repeal causes of action created by statute, except with respect to those causes of action which have already accrued. *Slagle v. Parker*, 370 So.2d 947, 949 (Ala. 1979), *appeal dismissed*, 444 U.S. 804 (1979). Even common law causes of action may be abolished (without providing an equivalent statutory remedy) if the Legislature believes that such action is necessary to "eradicate[] or ameliorate[] a perceived social evil...." *Baugher v. Beaver Construction Co.*, 791 So.2d 932, 935 (Ala. 2000) (citation and internal quotation marks omitted).

22. ALA. CONST. art. I, § 1 (2006).

provides, in part, that "the accused ... shall not ... be deprived of life, liberty, or property, except by due process of law...."[23]

In any state constitutional challenge to Alabama's pre-*Roe* abortion statute, abortion advocates are most likely to rely upon these two provisions to argue that the statutes interfere with a pregnant woman's "liberty" interest in obtaining an abortion. That reliance would be misplaced.

As an initial matter, it is not apparent that the due process guarantee of art. I, §6, has any application outside the context of criminal prosecutions, as the Alabama Supreme Court has noted on more than one occasion.[24] Although the state supreme court has recognized that there is a substantive, as well as a procedural, component to the due process guarantee,[25] the court has not developed a methodology for identifying what liberty interests are protected by art. I, §6 (or art. I, §1) or for determining whether an asserted liberty interest should be deemed to be "fundamental" for purposes of state constitutional analysis.[26] Given Alabama's history and tradition of prohibiting abortion, however, as well as the rights the State of Alabama extends to unborn children outside the context of abortion, it is unlikely that there is a liberty interest in obtaining an abortion.

Alabama enacted its first abortion statute in 1840, more than sixty years before the present state constitution was adopted in 1901. The statute prohibited the performance of an abortion upon a pregnant woman for any reason at any stage of pregnancy "unless the same shall be necessary to preserve her life, or shall have been advised by a respectable physician to be necessary for that purpose...."[27] In 1923, the exception for abortions "advised by a respectable

---

23. *Id.* art. I, §6. Due process language also appears in art. I, §13. That language, however, is tied to the availability of remedies for injuries, which is discussed in the preceding section of this analysis, *supra*.

24. *See Fuller v. Associates Commercial Corp.*, 389 So.2d 506, 509 (Ala. 1980) (Section 6 "deals with the rights of persons in criminal prosecutions"); *Ex parte Frazier*, 562 So.2d 560, 565 (Ala. 1989) (same).

25. *See Alabama Power Co. v. Citizens of the State of Alabama*, 740 So.2d 371, 377–82 (Ala. 1999).

26. To the extent that the Alabama Supreme Court considers federal precedent in determining whether an asserted liberty interest (or right) is "fundamental" under the state due process guarantee, abortion would not qualify as a "fundamental" right. Although the Supreme Court characterized the right to choose abortion as "fundamental" in *Roe*, 410 U.S. at 152–53, it tacitly abandoned that characterization in *Casey*, 505 U.S. at 869–79 (Joint Op. of O'Connor, Kennedy and Souter, JJ., replacing *Roe's* "strict scrutiny" standard of review with the more relaxed "undue burden" standard, allowing for a broader measure of abortion regulation).

27. Ala. Acts, ch. 6, §2 (1840–41), *codified at* ALA. PENAL CODE, ch. VI, §2 (Meek Supp. 1841), *recodified at* ALA CODE §3230 (1852), *recodified at* ALA. REV. CODE §3605

physician" to be necessary to preserve the pregnant woman's life was deleted.[28] In 1951, the legislature amended the statute to allow abortions to preserve the pregnant woman's "life or health."[29] The statute has not been repealed.[30]

Prior to *Roe v. Wade*, the Alabama reviewing courts affirmed abortion convictions without any hint that either the prosecutions or convictions were barred by the state constitution.[31] In *Trent v. State*, the Alabama Court of Appeals stated that the "manifest purpose" of the abortion statute was "to restrain after conception an unwarranted interference with the course of nature in the propagation and reproduction of human kind...."[32] The court quoted with approval the following excerpt from a paper presented to the Alabama Medical Association five years earlier by the state health officer:

> "[W]e are forced to concede that when ... two germs, male and female, are brought together, that fuse themselves into one, a new being, crowned with humanity and mentality, comes into life. If this be true, does not the new being, from the first day of its uterine life, acquire a legal and moral status that entitles it to the same protection as that guaranteed to human beings in extrauterine life? Indeed, should it not receive a greater protection for the reason that to the nature of a human being it adds the condition of utter helplessness, a condition that should appeal in mute, but sublime, eloquence to the manhood, the womanhood, and above all, to the motherhood, of those who can shield and protect it? Lives there a man or woman who would assault a little, laughing, prattling babe? If that be a crime from which the coldest-blooded villain would recoil, how much more a crime to assault and slay an innocent babe quietly sleeping in what should be an impregnable fortress—a babe whose voice is hushed and cannot be raised in piteous cry for mercy or for help!"[33]

(1866–67), *recodified at* ALA. CODE §4192 (1876), *recodified at* ALA. CODE §4022 (1887), *recodified at* ALA. CODE §4305 (1897), *recodified at* ALA. CODE §6215 (1907).

28. ALA. CODE §3191 (1923), *recodified at* ALA. CODE tit. 14, §9 (1940).

29. 1951 Ala. Acts 1630, *codified at* ALA. CODE tit. 14, §9 (1958).

30. ALA. CODE 13A-13-7 (2005).

31. *Thomas v. State*, 47 So. 257 (Ala. 1908); *Trent v. State*, 73 So. 834 (Ala. Ct. App. 1916); *Dykes v. State*, 1 So.2d 754 (Ala. Ct. App. 1941). *See also Lingle v. State*, 283 So.2d 660 (Ala. Crim. App. 1973) (affirming conviction of non-physician for performing abortion).

32. 73 So. at 836.

33. *Id.* (quoting Paper of Dr. Sanders, State Health Officer of Alabama, on "Physiological and Legal Status of the Fetus in Utero," Transactions of Medical Association of Alabama

More recently, a majority of the Alabama Supreme Court joined a concurring opinion which took issue with the use of the word "fetus" to describe an unborn child in a wrongful death case.[34] That term, which "has come to occupy a position in the cultural debate on abortion," connotes that the unborn child is "not entitled to the full panoply of rights to which a 'person' is entitled."[35] "[I]t is not surprising," Justice See continued, "that this connotation—that the unborn child does not have full human rights—is taken as a statement that the unborn child is somehow less than fully human, and it is therefore not surprising that the use of the term 'fetus' often evokes a visceral reaction."[36] The Alabama Legislature, however, has redefined the word "person" to describe the victim of a homicide or assault to include an "unborn child."[37] "The legislature has thus recognized under that statute that, when an 'unborn child' is killed, a 'person' is killed."[38] Given that amendment, Justice See would have used the term "unborn child" to describe the wrongful death victim at the time of his death.[39]

The concurring opinion of Justice See in *Ziade*, which a majority of the court joined, appears to recognize that the unborn child is "fully human," and is "entitled to the full panoply of rights to which a 'person' is entitled." Recognition of the unborn child as a rights bearing entity, however, suggests that the court would not readily recognize a right to abortion under the state constitution.

"The public policy of the State of Alabama is to protect life, both born and unborn."[40] Consistent with that policy, the Alabama Legislature has enacted a comprehensive scheme of abortion regulation.[41] The Alabama courts have repeatedly rejected federal constitutional challenges to those statutes and rules.[42] And the Alabama Supreme Court has held that "a parent's [statutory] right to be

---

262–72 (1911)). Twenty-five years later, the court of appeals quoted this passage with approval. *See Dykes v. State*, 1 So.2d at 757.

34. *Ziade v. Koch*, 952 So.2d 1072, 1081–82 (Ala. 2006) (See, J., specially concurring).

35. *Id.*

36. *Id.* at 1082.

37. ALA. CODE § 13A-6-1 (Supp. 2007).

38. *Ziade*, 952 So.2d at 1082 (See, J., specially concurring).

39. *Id.*

40. ALA. CODE § 26-22-1(a) (Supp. 2007).

41. *See, e.g.,* ALA. CODE § 26-23A-1 *et seq.* (Supp. 2007) (mandating informed consent); *id.,* § 26-21-1 *et seq.* (1992) (requiring parental consent); *id.,* § 26-22-1 *et seq.* (Supp. 2007) (restricting post-viability abortions); *id.,* § 22-21-20 *et seq.* (2006) (clinic regulations). *See also* ALA. ADMIN. CODE ch. 560-X-6-.09(1), −6.13(25)(b) (Supp. 2006) (limiting public funding of abortion for indigent women to those circumstances for which federal reimbursement is available, currently life-of-the-mother, rape and incest).

42. *Ex parte Anonymous*, 531 So.2d 901, 903–05 (Ala. 1988) (upholding constitutionality of the parental consent statute); *Tucker v. State Dep't of Public Health*, 650 So.2d 910

informed regarding a minor child's intended abortion creates a right of action on the part of the parents against any person who performs an abortion on the minor child without having obtained parental consent or the required court-ordered waiver of consent, despite the minor's intentional misrepresentation of her age."[43]

Alabama has recognized the rights of unborn children in a variety of contexts outside of abortion, including criminal law, tort law, health care law and property law. Under the criminal law, Alabama includes unborn children within the category of persons who may be the victims of homicide and assault.[44] And a woman convicted of a capital offense may not be executed while she is pregnant.[45]

In tort law, a statutory cause of action for wrongful death may be brought on behalf of an unborn child who was viable (capable of sustained survival outside the mother's womb, with or without medical assistance) at the time of its death.[46] A common law cause of action for (nonlethal) prenatal injuries may be brought without regard to the stage of pregnancy when the injuries were inflicted.[47] The Alabama Supreme Court has refused to recognize a cause of action for wrongful life, explaining that "a legal right not to be born is alien to the public policy of this State to protect and preserve human life."[48]

Under Alabama's health care laws, an agent acting under a durable power of attorney for health care may not authorize an abortion to be performed on

---

(Ala. Civ. App. 1994) (upholding constitutionality of statutes and rules regulating abortion clinics).

43. *Boykin v. Magnolia Bay, Inc.*, 570 So.2d 639, 642 (Ala. 1990).

44. ALA. CODE § 13A-6-1 (Supp. 2007).

45. *Id.* § 15-18-86 (1995).

46. *Eich v. Town of Gulf Shores*, 300 So.2d 354 (Ala. 1974), interpreting what is now codified at ALA. CODE § 6-5-391 (2005). In the absence of legislative reform, however, the court has declined to extend the wrongful death act to *non*viable children who are stillborn. *See Gentry v. Gilmore*, 613 So.2d 1241, 1243–44 (Ala. 1993); *Lollar v. Tankersley*, 613 So.2d 1249, 1250–53 (Ala. 1993).

47. *Wolfe v. Isbell*, 280 So.2d 758, 760–64 (Ala. 1973).

48. *Elliott v. Brown*, 361 So.2d 546, 548 (Ala. 1978). The state supreme court has recognized a cause of action for wrongful birth, however. *Keel v. Banach*, 624 So.2d 1022, 1023–29 (Ala. 1993). A "wrongful life" cause of action is a claim brought on behalf of child who is born with a physical or mental disability or disease that could have been discovered before the child's birth by genetic testing, amniocentesis or other medical screening. The gravamen of the action is that, as a result of a physician's failure to inform the child's parents of the child's disability or disease (or at least of the availability of tests to determine the presence of the disability or disease), they were deprived of the opportunity to abort the child, thus resulting in the birth of a child suffering permanent physical or mental impairment. A "wrongful birth" cause of action, on the other hand, is a claim, based on the same facts, brought by the parents of the impaired child on their own behalf.

his or her principal unless the procedure is necessary to save the principal's life.[49] And life-sustaining treatment may not be withheld or withdrawn from a pregnant patient pursuant to an advance directive.[50]

In property law, a child conceived before the death of a relative who dies intestate (without a will), but born thereafter, inherits as if he had been born in the lifetime of the decedent.[51] And, with certain exceptions, if a person fails to provide in his will for any of his children born after the execution of his will, the omitted child receives a share in the state equal in value to what he would have received if the testator had died intestate.[52] Where a future estate is limited to "heirs," "issue" or "children," posthumous children (children conceived before but born after the death of a parent) are entitled to take a share of the estate in the same manner as if they had been born before the death of the parent.[53]

In light of Alabama's longstanding tradition of prohibiting abortion, as well as the State's solicitude for the rights of the unborn child in other areas of law, it cannot reasonably be said that the liberty guaranteed by art. I, §1, or art. I, §6, encompasses a right to abortion. More generally, a right to abortion cannot be found in the text or structure of the Alabama Constitution. There is no evidence that either the framers or ratifiers of the Alabama Constitution intended the Declaration of Rights to limit the Legislature's authority to prohibit abortion.[54] Such an intent would have been remarkable in light of the contemporaneous prohibition of abortion except to save the life of the pregnant woman.

Equal Protection

Article I, §1, of the Alabama Constitution provides, in part, that "all men are equally free and independent...."[55] Article I, §6, provides, in part, that the accused in a criminal prosecution shall not be "deprived of life, liberty, or

---

49. Ala. Code §26-1-2(g)(1) (Supp. 2007).

50. Id. §22-8A-4(h) "Advance Directive for Health Care," §3: "If I am pregnant, or if I become pregnant, the choices I have made on this form will not be followed until after the birth of the baby."

51. Id. §43-8-47 (1991).

52. Id. §43-8-91.

53. Id. §35-4-8 (1991).

54. See I Official Proceedings of the Alabama Constitutional Convention of 1901 (hereinafter Proceedings) 784–91 (Report of the Committee on Preamble and Declaration of Rights); II Proceedings 1622–34, 1639–89, 1697–1727, 1729–67 (second reading); id at 2254–60 (third reading); IV Proceedings 4673–82 (final adoption) (University of Alabama, Birmingham, Alabama 1948).

55. Ala. Const. art. I, §1 (2006).

property, except by due process of law...."[56] And art. I, § 22, prohibits the legislature from "making any irrevocable or exclusive grants of special privileges or immunities...."[57] Taken together, art. I, §§ 1, 6 and 22 "have been interpreted to guarantee equal protection of the laws."[58] In 1999, however, the Alabama Supreme Court held that this was a misinterpretation of *Pickett v. Matthews*, and concluded that the state constitution contains no guarantee of equal protection.[59] In light of that holding, a state equal protection challenge could not be raised against the unrepealed pre-*Roe* abortion statute (§ 13A-13-7) or any other abortion prohibition the legislature may enact.

Inherent Political Power

Article I, § 2, of the Alabama Constitution provides:

> That all political power is inherent in the people, and all free governments are founded on their authority, and instituted for their benefit; and that, therefore, they have at all times an inalienable and indefeasible right to change their form of government in such manner as they may deem expedient.[60]

In any challenge to the pre-*Roe* Alabama abortion statute (or any other abortion prohibition), abortion advocates might argue that the statute interferes with the "inherent" political power of the people because it does not promote their "benefit." Given the purpose of § 2, this argument would not likely prevail.

Section 2 has seldom been cited by the Alabama reviewing courts, and never in support of striking down a state statute. The right of the people to "change their form of government in such manner as they may deem expedient" secures to the people themselves, through the amendment process, the right to decide whether, how and to what extent the organic instrument of government should be changed.[61] Section 2, thus, is not a source of substantive

---

56. *Id.* art. I, § 6.

57. *Id.* art. I, § 22.

58. *Cooley v. Knapp*, 607 So.2d 146, 148 n. 5 (Ala. 1992) (citing *Pickett v. Matthews*, 192 So. 261 (Ala. 1939)). *See also City of Hueytown v. Jiffy Chek Co. of Alabama*, 342 So.2d 761, 762 (Ala. 1977) ("Sections 1, 6, and 22 of the Alabama Constitution combine to guarantee equal protection of the laws").

59. *Ex parte Melof*, 735 So.2d 1172, 1181–86 (Ala. 1999).

60. ALA. CONST. art. I, § 2 (2006).

61. *See Opinion of the Justices*, 81 So.2d 881, 883 (Ala. 1955) (recognizing that, under § 2, "ultimate sovereignty" resides with the people, and "they can legally and lawfully remove any provision from the Constitution which they previously put in or ratified, even to

rights (other than the right to change the state constitution). Rather, it recognizes the people as the ultimate source of authority in a republican form of government. As such, it could not serve as a basis for asserting a right to abortion. Whether a given law promotes the "benefit" of the people, as that term in used in art. I, § 2, presents a political question for the legislature (and, ultimately, the people) to decide, not a constitutional question for the judiciary.

Limiting the Legitimate Ends of Government

Article I, § 35, of the Alabama Constitution provides that "the sole object and only legitimate end of government is to protect the citizen in the enjoyment of life, liberty, and property, and when the government assumes other functions it is usurpation and oppression."[62]

In any challenge to Alabama's pre-*Roe* abortion statute (or any other abortion prohibition), abortion advocates may argue that the statute violates § 35 because it is not related to a "legitimate end of government." Such an argument would not likely prevail.

Along with § 1 of the Declaration of Rights, § 35 has been cited in two lines of cases. In the first, the Alabama Supreme Court has held that the Legislature may not regulate competitive prices or prohibit *bona fide* competitive price cutting in businesses not affected with a public interest, merely in the interest of promoting fairness in competition.[63] In the second, the state supreme court has construed § 35 (along with § 1) "to prohibit the state or its subdivisions from engaging in a business venture 'solely for the purpose of raising revenues.'"[64] Neither of these two lines of cases, which limit the government's power to regulate prices and to engage in business, would lend any support to a challenge to an abortion prohibition.[65] Moreover, the prohibition of abortion has an obvious relationship to the protection of the *life* of its unborn citizens.

---

the extent of amending or repealing one of the sections comprising our Declaration of Rights").

62. ALA. CONST. art. I, § 35 (2006).

63. *Rabren v. City Wholesale Grocery Co.*, 266 So.2d 882, 886 (Ala. 1972).

64. *Taxpayers & Citizens of the City of Foley v. City of Foley*, 527 So.2d 1261, 1264 (Ala. 1988) (quoting *Churchill v. Board of Trustees of University of Alabama in Birmingham*, 409 So.2d 1382, 1386 (Ala. 1982)).

65. Section 35 has also been given a procedural gloss. *See Ex parte Weeks*, 611 So.2d 259, 262 (Ala. 1992) (it would constitute "usurpation and oppression" by the state judiciary to deny an appeal to a defendant who had not been notified that his case had been dismissed until after the time for appeal had expired).

Retained Rights

Article I, § 36, of the Alabama Constitution provides:

> That this enumeration of certain rights shall not impair or deny others retained by the people; and to guard against any encroachments on the rights herein retained, we declare that everything in this Declaration of Rights is excepted out of the general powers of government, and shall forever remain violate.[66]

In any challenge to the pre-*Roe* statute prohibiting abortion (or any other abortion prohibition), abortion advocates may be expected to argue that abortion is a "retained right" under art. I, § 36. That argument would not likely succeed, however.

Article I, § 36, has been cited in very few Alabama decisions, and the focus of those decisions has been the second clause of § 36, not the first.[67] In an older decision, the Alabama Supreme Court held that "Section 36 is a mere reaffirmation of the reservation of the rights enumerated in the preceding thirty-five sections of the Constitution constituting the bill of rights,"[68] which suggests that § 36 is not an independent source of substantive rights under the state constitution.

An entirely plausible reading of the first clause of § 36 is that the enumeration of certain rights in the state constitution should not be construed to "impair or deny" other rights retained by the people under the common law or statutes. But even if § 36 is understood to retain unspecified *constitutional* rights (as opposed to *common law* or *statutory* rights), abortion could not plausibly be considered to be among such rights because, at the time the Alabama Constitution was adopted in 1901, abortion was a crime. The argument that the first clause of § 36 "retained" as an "unenumerated" right conduct that was criminal when the state constitution was adopted is, at the very least, counterintuitive.

The language of § 36 appears to be based on the Ninth Amendment, which provides: "The enumeration in the Constitution of certain rights, shall not be construed to deny or disparage others retained by the people."[69] In light of that equiv-

---

66. ALA. CONST. art. I, § 36 (2006).

67. *See, e.g., Ex parte Chapman*, 792 So.2d 392, 401 n. 12 (Ala. 2000) (physicians employed by state university to work at student health center were not entitled to state-agent immunity in medical malpractice action arising from their treatment of university student).

68. *Johnson v. Robinson*, 192 So. 412, 416 (Ala. 1939).

69. U.S. CONST. AMEND. IX (West 2006). Wm. H. Stewart, THE ALABAMA STATE CONSTITUTION[:] A REFERENCE GUIDE 38 (Westport, Conn. 1994) (Section 36 "parallels" the Ninth Amendment).

alence, §36 should be given a parallel interpretation. That, in turn, suggests that if no right to abortion exists under the Ninth Amendment, then none would be recognized under art. I, §36. The Supreme Court, however, has rooted the "abortion liberty" in the liberty language of the Due Process Clause of the Fourteenth Amendment, not in the unenumerated rights language of the Ninth Amendment.[70] Because abortion has not been recognized as a "retained right" under the Ninth Amendment, it should not be recognized as one under §36, either.

Conclusion

Based on the foregoing analysis, an argument that the Alabama Constitution protects a right to abortion that is separate from, and independent of, the right to abortion recognized in *Roe v. Wade* would not likely succeed. That, in turn, suggests that if *Roe*, as modified by *Casey*, is ultimately overruled, the State of Alabama could enforce its pre-*Roe* statute *prohibiting* abortion except to preserve the life or health of the pregnant woman (or enact and enforce a new statute prohibiting abortion). Moreover, nothing in the Alabama Constitution precludes Alabama from *regulating* abortion within federal constitutional limits in the meantime.

---

70. *See Roe*, 410 U.S. at 153; *Casey*, 505 U.S. at 846. In any event, the Ninth Amendment, standing alone, is not a source of substantive rights. *Gibson v. Matthews*, 926 F.2d 532, 537 (6th Cir. 1991). Although "[s]ome unenumerated rights may be of [c]onstitutional magnitude," that is only "by virtue of other amendments, such as the Fifth or Fourteenth Amendment. A person cannot claim a right that exists solely under the Ninth Amendment." *United States v. Vital Health Products, Ltd.*, 786 F. Supp. 761, 777 (E.D. Wis. 1992), *aff'd mem. op., sub nom. United States v. LeBeau*, 985 F.2d 563 (7th Cir. 1993). *See also Charles v. Brown*, 495 F. Supp. 862, 863 (N.D. Ala. 1980) (same).

CHAPTER 5

ALASKA

Summary

As the result of a series of decisions of the Alaska Supreme Court interpreting the Alaska Constitution, the State of Alaska could not prohibit any abortion before viability, or any abortion after viability that would be necessary to preserve the pregnant woman's life or health, even if *Roe v. Wade*,[1] as modified by *Planned Parenthood of Southeastern Pennsylvania v. Casey*,[2] were overruled, unless the state constitution is amended to overturn those decisions (or those decisions are overruled). Moreover, by virtue of those same decisions, Alaska has little or no authority to enact and enforce reasonable measures regulating abortion, even within current federal constitutional limits, because any such regulations would have to satisfy the "strict scrutiny" standard of judicial review.

Analysis

The pre-*Roe* statute allowed abortion on demand prior to viability,[3] and impliedly prohibited abortion after viability.[4] Section 18.16.010(d) was repealed in 1997.[5] As a result, an abortion may be performed for any reason at any stage of pregnancy.[6] Although it is not known at this time whether the Alaska Legislature would consider legislation prohibiting abortion if *Roe*, as modified by

---

1. 410 U.S. 113 (1973).

2. 505 U.S. 833 (1992).

3. ALASKA STAT. § 11.15.060 (1970), renumbered as § 18.16.010 in 1978 and reorganized in 1986. *See* ALASKA STAT. § 18.16.010 (Michie 1994).

4. *Id.* § 11.15.060(a) (second sentence), renumbered as § 18.16.010(a) (second sentence) in 1978, and reorganized as § 18.16.010(d) in 1986.

5. 1997 Alaska Sess. Laws ch. 14, § 6.

6. ALASKA STAT. §§ 18.16.010(a)(1), (2) (Michie 2006).

Casey, were overruled, it is virtually certain that the Alaska Supreme Court would declare unconstitutional an abortion prohibition, at least any prohibition that would apply before viability. And a prohibition of abortion after viability would have to contain exceptions for abortions performed to preserve the life or health of the pregnant woman. That is apparent from a review of the state supreme court's decisions striking down, on state constitutional grounds, the policy of a quasi-public hospital not to permit elective abortions to be performed at the hospital, a regulation restricting public funding of abortion and the state's parental consent law.

In *Valley Hospital Ass'n v. Mat-Su Coalition for Choice*,[7] the Alaska Supreme Court considered the constitutionality of a policy adopted by what the court regarded as a quasi-public hospital not to permit elective abortions to be performed at the hospital. A physician who performs abortions, and others, challenged the policy under the right of privacy guarantee of the Alaska Constitution, which provides, in part: "The right of the people to privacy is recognized and shall not be infringed."[8]

The state supreme court began its analysis of § 22 by noting that "[a] woman's control of her body, and the choice whether to bear children, involves the kind of decision-making that is 'necessary for ... civilized life and ordered liberty.'"[9] The court determined that "the right to an abortion is the kind of fundamental right and privilege encompassed within the intention and spirit of Alaska's constitutional language."[10] After reviewing earlier precedents involving personal autonomy, bodily integrity and privacy, the court concluded that "reproductive rights are fundamental, and that they are encompassed within the right to privacy expressed in article I, section 22 of the Alaska Constitution."[11] Because they are "fundamental," the court explained, "[t]hese rights may be legally constrained only when the constraints are justified by a compelling state interest, and no less restrictive means could advance that interest."[12] Finally, "[t]hese fundamental reproductive rights include the right to an abortion."[13] The scope of this "fundamental right to an abortion" is "similar to that expressed in *Roe v.*

---

7. 948 P.2d 963 (Alaska 1997).

8. ALASKA CONST. art. I, § 22 (Michie 2006).

9. *Valley Hospital Ass'n*, 948 P.2d at 968 (quoting *Baker v. City of Fairbanks*, 471 P.2d 386, 402 (Alaska 1970)).

10. *Id.*

11. *Id.* at 969.

12. *Id.*

13. *Id.*

Wade."[14] Significantly, for purposes of the State's authority to regulate abortion, the Alaska Supreme Court refused to adopt, as a matter of *state* constitutional interpretation, "the narrower definition of that right promulgated in the plurality opinion in [*Planned Parenthood of Southeastern Pennsylvania v.*] *Casey*."[15]

The court held that the Valley Hospital Association is a "quasi-public institution" and, as such, "its policies are subject to the limitations which the Alaska Constitution imposes on legislation and government regulations."[16] The hospital's policy against the performance of elective abortion "interferes with that right."[17] The hospital defended its policy as "a matter of conscience," and not on any "medical, safety, or economic" grounds.[18] In the absence of a free exercise claim, however, which the hospital could not raise as a "quasi-public" entity, "this does not amount to a compelling state interest."[19] The court also rejected the hospital's reliance on the Alaska right of conscience statute,[20] holding the statute unconstitutional to the extent that it applies to quasi-public institutions.[21]

The Alaska Supreme Court's decision in *Valley Hospital Association* and its endorsement of the strict scrutiny standard of judicial review adopted in *Roe v. Wade* leaves little doubt that the court would strike down any law attempting to prohibit pre-viability abortions or even post-viability abortions if such abortions were sought for reasons relating to a woman's life or health. That is

---

14. *Id.* Earlier in its opinion, the court stated that the Supreme Court's "articulation [in *Roe*] of the United States Constitution's protection of reproductive rights establishes the minimum protection provided to women in Alaska," a protection that includes "the right to an abortion." *Id.* at 966.

15. *Id.*

16. *Id.* at 971. In reaching this conclusion, the court relied upon the following factors: Valley Hospital Association (VHA) had received a "Certificate of Need" from the Alaska Department of Health and Social Services to operate a health care facility, which conferred upon VHA "a type of health care monopoly" for the community it served; VHA had received "construction funds, land, and operating funds from the State, local, and federal governments[;]" and a "significant portion" of the operating funds VHA receives for hospital services "comes from governmental sources." *Id.* at 970–71. The court also took into consideration that VHA is "a community hospital whose board is elected by a public membership." *Id.* at 971.

17. *Id.*

18. *Id.*

19. *Id.*

20. ALASKA STAT. § 18.16.010(b) (Michie 2006): "Nothing in this section requires a hospital or person to participate in an abortion, nor is a hospital or person liable for refusing to participate in an abortion under this section."

21. *Valley Hospital Ass'n*, 948 P.2d at 971–72.

confirmed by a review of a pair of decisions the state supreme court handed down four years after *Valley Hospital Association.*

In *State of Alaska, Dep't of Health & Human Services v. Planned Parenthood of Alaska, Inc.,*[22] the court held that a state regulation restricting public funding of abortion violated the "inherent rights" guarantee of the Alaska Constitution, art. I, § 1, which provides, in relevant part, that "all persons are equal and entitled to equal rights, opportunities, and protection under the law...."[23] The regulation in question prohibited Medicaid assistance for abortion unless the life of the mother would be endangered if the pregnancy were carried to term, or the pregnancy resulted from an act of rape or incest.[24] The court held that the regulation "affects the exercise of a constitutional right, the right to reproductive freedom," and, therefore, was subject to "the most searching judicial scrutiny, often called 'strict scrutiny.'"[25] Such scrutiny is also required "where the government, by selectively denying a benefit to those who exercise a constitutional right, effectively deters the exercise of that right."[26]

The court found that neither of the two interests advanced by the State justified either the burden on the exercise of a fundamental constitutional right or the difference in treatment between those women who choose to carry their pregnancies to term and those who choose abortion. Rejecting the State's argument that "medical and public welfare interests ... are served by the legislature's decision to fund childbirth," the court observed that "the regulation does not relate to funding for childbirth, and the State's decision to fund prenatal care and other pregnancy-related services has not been challenged."[27]

> [A] woman who carries her pregnancy to term and a woman who terminates her pregnancy exercise the same fundamental right to reproductive choice. Alaska's equal protection clause does not permit governmental discrimination against either woman; both must be granted access to state health care under the same terms as any similarly situated person. The State's undisputed interest in providing health care to women who carry pregnancies to term has no effect on the State's interest in providing medical care to Medicaid-eligible women who, for health reasons, require abortions.[28]

---

22. 28 P.3d 904 (Alaska 2001).
23. ALASKA CONST. art. I, § 1 (Michie 2006).
24. 7 ALASKA ADMIN. CODE § 43.140.
25. *State of Alaska, Dep't of Health & Human Services,* 28 P.3d at 909.
26. *Id.*
27. *Id.* at 913.
28. *Id.*

The State also asserted an interest in "minimizing health risks to mother and child," and argued that "these interests are often closely aligned."[29] The court rejected this interest, as well, noting that "those interests are not aligned ... when pregnancy threatens a woman's health."[30] Under the United States Constitution, "the State's interest in the life and health of the mother is paramount at every stage of pregnancy."[31] Under the Alaska Constitution, "'[t]he scope of the fundamental right to an abortion ... is similar to that expressed in *Roe v. Wade.*'"[32] "Thus," the court concluded, "although the State has a legitimate interest in protecting a fetus, *at no point does that interest outweigh the State's interest in the life and health of the pregnant woman.*"[33]

Given the Alaska Supreme Court's holding that the scope of the fundamental right to abortion under the state constitution is "similar" to the right recognized in *Roe v. Wade,* and that at no point in pregnancy does the State's interest in protecting a fetus outweigh the State's interest in the life and health of the pregnant woman, Alaska could not prohibit any abortion *before* viability, or an abortion performed *after* viability for reasons relating to the pregnant woman's life or health, even if *Roe,* as modified by *Casey,* were overruled.[34]

In *State of Alaska v. Planned Parenthood of Alaska,*[35] the Alaska Supreme Court considered the constitutionality of Alaska's parental consent statute.[36] The court reversed an order of the superior court granting summary judgment to the plaintiffs and remanded the cause for an evidentiary hearing on whether "the state has a compelling interest in enforcing the parental consent statute and whether the statute is properly tailored to promote the state's interest."[37]

---

29. *Id.*

30. *Id.*

31. *Id.* (citing *Roe,* 410 U.S. at 163–64).

32. *Id.* (quoting *Valley Hospital Ass'n,* 948 P.2d at 969).

33. *Id.* (emphasis added).

34. The Supreme Court has not yet decided whether a statute prohibiting post-viability abortions must make exceptions for mental, as well as physical, health. *See Voinovich v. Women's Medical Professional Corporation,* 523 U.S. 1036, 1039 (1998) (Thomas, J., dissenting from denial of *certiorari*) (noting that this issue was not addressed in *Doe v. Bolton,* 410 U.S. 179 (1973), the companion case to *Roe v. Wade*). As a result, it is not known whether, as a matter of *state* constitutional law, the Alaska Supreme Court would require a post-viability statute to contain a mental health exception.

35. 35 P.3d 30 (Alaska 2001).

36. ALASKA STAT. §§ 18.16.010(a)(3), (e)-(g); 18.16.020; 18.16.030 (Michie 2006).

37. *State of Alaska,* 35 P.3d at 32. On remand, the superior court again held the statute unconstitutional, and the supreme court affirmed. *See Planned Parenthood of Alaska v. State of Alaska,* Case No. 3AN-97-6014 CI, Alaska Superior Court, Third Judicial District, De-

In the parental consent case, the State argued that the privacy guarantee of the Alaska Constitution is not self-executing because the second sentence of art. I, § 22, provides: "The legislature shall implement this section."[38] The State recognized that its proposed reading of § 22 conflicted with the court's four-year old precedent in *Valley Hospital Association,* but urged the court to overrule that decision.[39] This the court declined to do. "[T]he legislative history of our privacy clause and three decades of cases interpreting the provision firmly establish that its basic guarantee—the people's right to privacy from unwarranted governmental intrusion—became fully effective upon the provision's adoption, without need for further implementation."[40] "With or without legislative action," the court concluded, "this guarantee has the usual attributes of a constitutional provision: its broad contours and particular applications fall within the judiciary's province and are subject to definition, interpretation, and refinement through the traditional course of adjudication, case by case."[41]

Having declined the State's invitation to overrule *Valley Hospital Association,* the court held that art. I, § 22, confers a right of privacy upon minors, as well as adults, which includes the right to choose abortion.[42] Because of the special vulnerability of minors, the State may assert interests with respect to them that would not apply to adults.[43] Nevertheless, the State may "constrain a minor's privacy right only when necessary to further a compelling state interest and only if no less restrictive means exist to advance that interest."[44]

The court then turned to an analysis of the equal protection issue presented. Alaska applies a "flexible, three-step sliding scale test" to state action challenged under the equal protection guarantee.[45]

> Under this test, we initially establish the nature of the right allegedly infringed by state action, increasing the state's burden to justify the action as the right it affects grows more fundamental: at the low end of the sliding scale the state needs only to show that it has a legitimate purpose; but at the high end—when its action directly infringes a fun-

---

cision on Remand, Oct. 13, 2003, *aff'd,* 171 P.3d 577 (Alaska 2007). The Alaska Supreme Court's decision is discussed below.

38. *Id.* at 35 (quoting ALASKA CONST. art. I, § 22 (Michie 2006)).

39. *Id.*

40. *Id.* at 38.

41. *Id.* at 38–39.

42. *Id.* at 39–41.

43. *Id.* at 39–40.

44. *Id.* at 41.

45. *Id.* at 42 (citing *State v. Erickson,* 574 P.2d 1 (Alaska 1978)).

damental right—the state must prove a compelling governmental interest. We next examine the importance of the state purpose served by the challenged action in order to determine whether it meets the requisite standard. We last consider the particular means that the state selects to further its purpose; a showing of substantial relationship between means and ends will suffice at the low end of the scale, but at the high end the state must demonstrate that no less restrictive alternative exists to accomplish its purpose.[46]

The supreme court determined that, although the superior court had properly applied the first step of the "sliding scale" test, it "undertook no second-step inquiry," and, therefore, had applied the third step, "without determining "whether the state actually does have a compelling interest in requiring parental consent or judicial authorization to abortion or what the exact nature of that interest is."[47] It was error for the superior court to declare the parental consent act unconstitutional "without allowing an evidentiary hearing on the issue of whether the act furthers compelling state interests using the least restrictive means possible."[48] Because it was at least possible that the State would be able to advance such interests, the order granting the plaintiffs summary judgment was reversed and the cause remanded for an evidentiary hearing.[49] On remand, the parental consent statute was again declared unconstitutional.[50] In another split decision, the state supreme court affirmed.[51]

The court reaffirmed its earlier holdings that "[i]ncluded within the broad scope of the Alaska Constitution's privacy clause is the fundamental right to reproductive choice," which right "extend[s] … to minors."[52] The majority acknowledged that the State has compelling interests in "protecting minors from their own immaturity and aiding parents in fulfilling their parental responsibilities."[53] Requiring parental consent, however, "does not represent the least restrictive means of achieving the State's asserted interests."[54] "There exists a less

---

46. *Id.*

47. *Id.* at 42–45

48. *Id.* at 43.

49. *Id.* at 44–46. Two justices would have reversed outright without a remand. *See id.* at 46–53 (Matthews, C.J., joined by Carpeneti, J., dissenting).

50. Decision on Remand, *Planned Parenthood of Alaska v. State of Alaska*, Case No. 3AN-97-6014 CI, Alaska Superior Court, Third Judicial District, Oct. 13, 2003.

51. *State of Alaska v. Planned Parenthood of Alaska*, 177 P.3d 577 (Alaska 2007).

52. *Id.* at 581–82.

53. *Id.* at 582.

54. *Id.* at 579.

burdensome and widely used means of actively involving parents in their minor children's abortion decisions: parental notification."[55]

Conclusion

Because of the Alaska Supreme Court's abortion decisions, it is apparent that the State of Alaska could not prohibit abortions, at least before viability, even if *Roe*, as modified by *Casey*, were overruled, unless the state constitution is amended to overturn the holdings in those decisions (or they are overruled). Moreover, by virtue of those same decisions, the State has little or no authority to regulate abortion, even within current federal constitutional limits, because any such regulations would have to satisfy the "strict scrutiny" standard of judicial review.

---

55. *Id.*

CHAPTER 6

ARIZONA

Summary

The Arizona Supreme Court has not yet decided whether the Arizona Constitution protects a right to abortion separate from, and independent of, the right to abortion recognized under the United States Constitution.[1] A careful examination of the state constitution, in light of its history and interpretation, as well as other relevant legal sources, however, suggests that the state supreme court probably would not recognize a state constitutional right to abortion. Thus, if *Roe v. Wade*,[2] as modified by *Planned Parenthood of Southeastern Pennsylvania v. Casey*,[3] were overruled, Arizona could enforce its pre-*Roe* statutes prohibiting abortion. Moreover, nothing in the state constitution, properly understood, precludes the State from enacting and enforcing reasonable measures regulating abortion within current federal constitutional limits (other than restrictions on public funding of abortion).

Analysis

The principal pre-*Roe* abortion statute prohibited performance of an abortion upon a pregnant woman unless the procedure was "necessary to save her life."[4] Another statute prohibited a woman from soliciting an abortion or allowing an abortion to be performed upon her (subject to the same exception).[5]

---

1. *See Simat Corp. v. Arizona Health Care Cost Containment System*, 56 P.3d 28, 37 (Ariz. 2002) ("[w]e reach no conclusion about whether the Arizona Constitution provides a right of choice, let alone one broader than that found in the federal constitution"). The state supreme court's decision striking down state restrictions on public funding of abortion is discussed later in this analysis.

2. 410 U.S. 113 (1973).

3. 505 U.S. 833 (1992).

4. ARIZ. REV. STAT. ANN. § 13-211 (1956).

5. *Id.* § 13-212. No prosecutions were reported under this statute.

Pursuant to *Roe*, §§ 13-211 and 13-212 were declared unconstitutional (on federal, not state, grounds) by the Arizona Court of Appeals in a pair of decisions.[6] The statutes have not been repealed.[7]

Based upon arguments that have been raised in Arizona and other States with similar constitutional provisions, possible sources for an asserted abortion right could include provisions of the Declaration of Rights guaranteeing due process of law (art. II, §4), privacy (§9), equal privileges and immunities (§13) and liberty of conscience (§12); recognizing inherent political power in the people (§2) and the importance of frequent recurrence to fundamental principles (§1); and retaining rights (§33), as well as the religious toleration guarantee of art. XX, §1.[8] The analysis that follows addresses each of these provisions.

Due Process of Law

Article II, §4 of the Arizona Constitution provides: "No person shall be deprived of life, liberty, or property without due process of law."[9] In any challenge to an Arizona statute prohibiting abortion (either the pre-*Roe* statutes, if *Roe* is overruled, or any other abortion prohibition Arizona may enact), abortion advocates will most likely rely upon art. II, §4 (due process of law), and art. II, §8 (privacy), in support of an asserted state right to abortion. For the reasons set forth in this section and the following section of the analysis, however, that reliance would be misplaced.

For purposes of state substantive due process analysis, "fundamental rights protected by [art. II, §4] are those firmly entrenched in our state's history and tradition and implicit in the concept of ordered liberty that may be, or may not be, shared with the rest of the country."[10] In light of Arizona's "history and

---

6. *Nelson v. Planned Parenthood Center of Tucson*, 505 P.2d 580, 590 (Ariz. Ct. App. 1973) (*on rehearing*); *State v. Wahlrab*, 509 P.2d 245 (Ariz. Ct. App. 1973). In its original opinion in *Nelson*, decided less than three weeks before *Roe v. Wade*, the Arizona Court of Appeals upheld the statute.

7. Ariz. Rev. Stat. Ann. §§ 13-3603, 13-3604 (West 2001).

8. One other more unlikely sources of an abortion right under the Arizona Constitution-§6 (guaranteeing freedom of speech)-is discussed generally in Chapter 3, *supra*.

9. Ariz. Const. art. II, §4 (West 2001).

10. *Standhardt v. Superior Court*, 77 P.3d 451, 456 (Ariz. Ct. App. 2003) (fundamental right to marry does not include the freedom to choose a same-sex spouse). To the extent that Arizona reviewing courts may consider federal precedent in determining whether an asserted liberty interest (or right) is "fundamental" under the state due process guarantee, abortion would not qualify as a "fundamental" right. Although the Supreme Court characterized the right to choose abortion as "fundamental" in *Roe*, 410 U.S. at 152–53, it tacitly abandoned that characterization in *Casey*, 505 U.S. at 869–79 (Joint Op. of O'Connor,

tradition," however, abortion could not be considered a "fundamental right" protected by the state due process guarantee.[11]

In enacting the Howell Code in 1864, the first legislative assembly of the Territory of Arizona prohibited the performance of an abortion at any stage of pregnancy for any reason, unless a physician deemed the procedure "necessary ... to save her [the pregnant woman's] life."[12] In 1887, the territorial legislature enacted a penal code which replaced the existing abortion provision with one that changed the life-of-the-mother exception from a subjective one (whether a physician "deems it necessary") to an objective one (whether the procedure was "necessary to preserve her life"),[13] and added another provision that made it a crime for the woman herself to solicit or submit to an abortion, unless the same was necessary "to preserve her life."[14] These provisions, recodified and renumbered from time to time, have never been repealed.[15]

Prior to the Supreme Court's decision in *Roe v. Wade*, the Arizona Supreme Court affirmed convictions for abortions, including criminal abortions performed by licensed physicians, without any suggestion that either the prosecutions or convictions violated the Arizona Constitution.[16] Less than three weeks before *Roe* was decided, the Arizona Court of Appeals rejected both federal *and* state constitutional challenges to the Arizona abortion statutes.[17] The court explained that the abortion statutes had been enacted for two reasons:

Kennedy and Souter, JJ., replacing *Roe's* "strict scrutiny" standard of review with the more relaxed "undue burden" standard, allowing for a broader measure of abortion regulation).

11. As previously noted, *see* n. 1, *supra*, the Arizona Supreme Court has not decided whether a state right to abortion is conferred by art. II, §4 (due process), or art. II, §8 (privacy), of the Arizona Constitution.

12. Ariz. (Terr.) Code ch. X, div. 5, §45 (1865).

13. Ariz. (Terr.) Rev. Stat. (Penal Code) Pt. I, tit. IX, ch. III, §454 (1887), *recodified at* Ariz. (Terr.) Rev. Stat. (Penal Code) Pt. I, tit. IX, ch. III, §243, (1901), *recodified at* Ariz. Rev. Stat. (Penal Code) Pt. I, tit. IX, ch. V, §273 (1913).

14. *Id.* Pt. I, tit. IX, ch. III, §455, *recodified at* Ariz. (Terr.) Rev. Stat. (Penal Code) Pt. I, tit. IX, ch. III, §244 (1901), *recodified at* Ariz. Rev. Stat. (Penal Code) Pt. I, tit. IX, ch. V, §274 (1913).

15. Ariz. Rev. Stat. (Penal Code) Pt. I, tit. IX, ch. V, §§273, 274 (1913), *combined in* Ariz. Rev. Code §4645 (1928), *recodified at* Ariz. Code Ann. §43-301 (1939), *separated and renumbered as* Ariz. Rev. Stat. Ann. §§13-211, 13-212 (West 1956), *recodified at* Ariz. Rev. Stat. Ann. §§13-3603, 13-3604 (West 2001).

16. *Hightower v. State*, 158 P.2d 156 (Ariz. 1945); *State v. Boozer*, 291 P.2d 786 (Ariz. 1955). *See also Kinsey v. State*, 65 P.2d 1141 (Ariz. 1937) (affirming second degree murder conviction based on a death resulting from an illegal abortion).

17. *Nelson v. Planned Parenthood Center of Tucson, Inc.*, 505 P.2d 580 (Ariz. Ct. App. 1973), *modified on rehearing*, Jan. 30, 1973, *review denied*, March 20, 1973.

To embody the belief in the right to life and the necessity of preserving human life even when the existence of "human life" is problematic to some degree, and to protect the health and life of pregnant women by keeping them from incompetent abortionists and restraining them from attempting dangerous self-induced abortions.[18]

In reference to the first reason, the State's interest "in preserving human life," the court noted that "[a] substantial case" could be made "for holding [that] the fetus is a 'person' within the due process clause of the Fourteenth Amendment."[19] Rejecting plaintiffs' privacy challenge to the statutes, the court stated:

Although there is a private realm of family life which the court may not enter…, one cannot seriously argue that parents are thereby free to abuse and neglect their children free of state control. One cannot gainsay a legislative determination that an embryonic or fetal organism is "life." Once begun, the inevitable result is a human being, barring prior termination of the pregnancy. Rhetorically, one may ask: Does the fundamental right to privacy … include a fundamental right to destroy life? We do not think so.[20]

In *Nelson*, the court of appeals expressed its agreement with those decisions that had rejected challenges to the abortion laws of other States, and held that "the subject of abortion is within the police power of the state," and that "there is no fundamental right to destroy life."[21] The court concluded that it was "within the province of the state legislature to weigh the competing interests and enact, as the legislature has done in this state, a statute which prohibits all abortions except those necessary to save the life of the mother."[22]

Subsequent to the Supreme Court's decision in *Roe*, Arizona enacted extensive abortion regulations, including statutes mandating parental consent,[23]

---

18. *Id.* at 582.

19. *Id.* at 585. Although *Roe* held otherwise, *see* 410 U.S. at 156–59, *Roe* "neither prohibits nor compels" the State of Arizona from treating the unborn child as a "person" in other contexts. *Summerfield v. Superior Court*, 698 P.2d 712, 723 (Ariz. 1985) (interpreting the word "person," as used in the wrongful death statute, ARIZ. REV. STAT. ANN. § 12-611 *et seq.* (West 2003), to include viable, unborn children).

20. *Id.* at 586.

21. *Id.* at 587.

22. *Id.* at 588.

23. ARIZ. REV. STAT. ANN. § 36-2152 (West 2003).

imposing clinic regulations,[24] and securing individual and institutional rights of conscience.[25] Arizona also prohibits the performance of an abortion at any facility under the jurisdiction of the Arizona Board of Regents,[26] and excludes abortion from family planning services offered under the Children's Health Insurance Program.[27]

Arizona has recognized the rights of unborn children in a variety of contexts outside of abortion, including criminal law, tort law and property law. Under the criminal code, the killing of an unborn child, other than in an abortion, may be prosecuted as a homicide.[28] Moreover, causing the death of an unborn child is an aggravating factor in sentencing for certain classes of felonies.[29] And a woman convicted of a capital offense may not be executed while she is pregnant.[30]

In tort law, a statutory cause of action for wrongful death may be brought on behalf of an unborn child who was viable (capable of sustained survival outside the mother's womb, with or without medical assistance) at the time of its death.[31] A common law action for (nonlethal) prenatal injuries may be brought without regard to the stage of pregnancy when the injuries were inflicted.[32] And the Arizona Supreme Court has refused to recognize wrongful life causes of action.[33]

---

24. *Id.* § 36-499 *et seq.*

25. *Id.* § 36-2151.

26. *Id.* § 15-1630 (West 2002).

27. *Id.* § 36-2989(A)(9) (West 2003).

28. *Id.* §§ 13-1105(A)(1), -(C) (first degree murder), 13-1104(A), -(B) (second degree murder, 13-1103(A)(5), -(B) (manslaughter), 13-1102(A), -(B) (negligent homicide) (West Supp. 2006).

29. *Id.* §§ 13-702(C)(10), 13-703(F)(9) (West Supp. 2006).

30. *Id.* §§ 13-4025, 13-4026 (West 2001).

31. *Summerfield v. Superior Court*, 698 P.2d 712 (Ariz. 1985), interpreting ARIZ. REV. STAT. ANN., § 12-611 *et seq.* (West 2003). In holding that the parents of twins, one of whom was stillborn, could recover "loss-of-society" damages for the baby's death caused by medical negligence, the Arizona Court of Appeals noted that "[b]efore the twins were born, [their parents] developed a relationship with them. They spoke, sang and read to them; they developed love for them and expectations for their future." *Burnham v. Miller*, 972 P.2d 645, 647 (Ariz. Ct. App. 1998).

32. *Id.* at 720.

33. *Walker by Pizano v. Mart*, 790 P.2d 735 (Ariz. 1990). A "wrongful life" cause of action is a claim brought on behalf of a child who is born with a physical or mental disability or disease that could have been discovered before the child's birth by genetic testing, amniocentesis or other medical screening. The gravamen of the action is that, as a result of a physician's failure to inform the child's parents of the child's disability or disease (or at least of the availability of tests to determine the presence of the disability or disease), they were deprived of the opportunity to abort the child, thus resulting in the birth of a child suffering permanent physical or mental impairment. Very few courts recognize "wrongful

In property law, a posthumous child (a child conceived before but born after the death of a parent) may inherit from an intestate (a person who dies without a will) if the child lives for at least 120 hours (five days) after birth.[34] Subject to certain exceptions, an afterborn child (a child conceived before the death of a parent but born after the parent executes a will) receives that share of the estate he would have received if the decedent had died intestate, or, if there are other children, an equal share.[35]

A right to abortion cannot be found in the text or structure of the Arizona Constitution. There is no evidence that the framers or ratifiers of the state constitution intended to limit the Legislature's authority to prohibit abortion.[36] Such an intent would have been remarkable in light of the contemporaneous and longstanding prohibition of abortion except to save the life of the pregnant woman. Moreover, recognition of an abortion right would be manifestly inconsistent with the history and traditions of the State, as well as the precedents of the Arizona reviewing courts. Taken together, these factors militate against recognition of a right to abortion as a "fundamental right" under the due process guarantee of the Arizona Constitution.

Privacy

Article II, § 8, of the Arizona Constitution provides: "No person shall be disturbed in his private affairs, or his home invaded, without authority of law."[37] Neither the Arizona Supreme Court nor the Arizona Court of Appeals has developed a methodology for determining whether given conduct is protected by this provision. Nevertheless, their decisions strongly suggest that art. II, § 8, embraces only that conduct which traditionally has enjoyed legal protection.

---

life" causes of action because an assessment of damages requires the courts to compare the value of life, albeit with some degree of physical or mental impairment, to nonexistence. The state supreme court has recognized wrongful birth actions, however. *Id.* at 738. A "wrongful birth" cause of action is a claim, based on the same facts, brought by the parents of an impaired child on their own behalf.

34. Ariz. Rev. Stat. Ann. § 14-2108 (West 2005).

35. *Id.* § 14-2302.

36. *See* John S. Goff, The Records of the Arizona Constitutional Convention of 1910 (hereinafter Records) 658–71, 673–81 (debate on Declaration of Rights in Committee of the Whole); 758–63, 893–98, 905–06 (debate on Declaration of Rights in Convention) (Phoenix, Arizona 1991).

37. Ariz. Const. art. II, § 8 (West 2001).

In *Rasmussen by Mitchell v. Fleming*,[38] the Arizona Supreme Court held that art. II, § 8, usually invoked in a search and seizure context,[39] also "encompass[es] an individual's right to refuse medical treatment."[40] The court held that a right to refuse medical treatment also existed under the federal constitution and the common law.[41] Regarding the latter, the court referred to the well-established common law right "to be free from non-consensual bodily invasions."[42]

By way of contrast, the Arizona Supreme Court has refused to recognize a state right of privacy to possession of marijuana for personal use in one's home.[43] "The right to possess marijuana in a person's own home," the court concluded, "is not a basic constitutional right and is not ... made so by invocation of the right of privacy provision[] of the Arizona Constitution."[44] There is, of course, no history or tradition of allowing a person to smoke marijuana in the privacy of his home.

In *Behavioral Health Agency of Central Arizona v. City of Casa Grande*,[45] the court of appeals held that a city's single-family ordinance, which prohibited the use of a residence as a facility to provide foster care to unrelated elderly persons, did not violate either federal or state constitutional rights to due process, equal protection, privacy or freedom of association. The court distinguished *Moore v. City of East Cleveland, Ohio*,[46] where the Supreme Court struck down an ordinance that prohibited first cousins from residing in the same home as their grandparents. In *Moore*, the court of appeals explained, the Supreme Court held that "the constitution's protection of the sanctity of the family was deeply rooted in the nation's history and its tradition, and that such tradition was not limited to respect for the bonds uniting the members of the nuclear family but extended as well to the sharing of their households with uncles, aunts, cousins and especially grandparents."[47] The lack of a comparable history and tradition

---

38. 741 P.2d 674 (Ariz. 1987).

39. *See, e.g., State v. Bolt*, 689 P.2d 519, 523–24 (Ariz. 1984) (holding that Arizona's privacy provision bestows greater privacy rights in a person's home than does the Fourth Amendment).

40. *Rasmussen*, 741 P.2d at 682.

41. *Id*. at 681–83.

42. *Id*. at 683 (citing *Union Pacific Railway Co. v. Botsford*, 141 U.S. 250, 251 (1891), and *Schloendorff v. Society of New York Hospital*, 105 N.E. 92, 93 (N.Y. 1914)).

43. *State v. Murphy*, 570 P.2d 1070, 1072–73 (Ariz. 1977).

44. *Id*. at 1073.

45. 708 P.2d 1317 (Ariz. Ct. App. 1985).

46. 431 U.S. 494 (1977).

47. *Behavioral Health Agency*, 708 P.2d at 1322.

of allowing unrelated adults to reside in the same household was deemed fatal to plaintiffs' state and federal constitutional challenge to the zoning ordinance.[48]

More recently, the Arizona Court of Appeals has held that neither the state due process guarantee (art. II, §4), nor the privacy guarantee (art. II, §8), requires the State to recognize marriages between members of the same sex.[49] With respect to its privacy holding, the court of appeals held that "it is unlikely [that] the framers intended to confer a right to enter [into] a same-sex marriage," pointing out that at the time the state constitution was drafted, "marriage" was "commonly defined as a civil status existing between one man and one woman."[50] It is even more unlikely that the framers intended to confer a right to abortion, which had been a crime under the laws of the Territory of Arizona for almost fifty years before the constitution was drafted.

The unifying principle that emerges from a review of the cases interpreting the due process and privacy guarantees of the Arizona Declaration of Rights is that there is no protected liberty or privacy interest in engaging in given conduct unless there is a well-established history and tradition of according legal protection to that conduct. But, as set forth in the previous section of this analysis, there is no history and tradition of protecting abortion in Arizona law. From the enactment of the Howell Code by the first territorial legislature down to the present day, it has been the public policy of the State of Arizona to prohibit abortion at any stage of pregnancy for any reason other than to save the life of the pregnant woman (a policy which, of course, is not currently enforceable).

For purposes of the due process and privacy provisions of the Arizona Constitution, a statute that does not implicate the exercise of a fundamental right is reviewed under the rational basis standard.[51] The prohibition of abortion, however, is rationally related to the legitimate state interest in protecting unborn human life. Accordingly, it would pass muster under art. II, §§4 and 8.

Liberty of Conscience

Article II, § 12, of the Arizona Constitution provides, in part:

> The liberty of conscience secured by the provisions of this Constitution shall not be so construed as to excuse acts of licentiousness, or

---

48. *Id.* at 1322–23.

49. *Standhardt v. Superior Court*, 77 P.3d 451.

50. *Id.* at 460.

51. *Large v. Superior Court*, 714 P.2d 399, 407 (Ariz. 1986) (using the rational basis test under the due process provision); *State v. Murphy*, 570 P.2d 1070, 1074 (Ariz. 1977) (applying rational basis analysis in deciding whether a statute violated the right of privacy).

justify practices inconsistent with the peace and safety of the State. No public money or property shall be appropriated for or applied to any religious worship, exercise, or instruction, or to the support of any religious establishment.[52]

Article XX, ¶ 1, of the Arizona Constitution provides: "Perfect toleration of religious sentiment shall be secured to every inhabitant of this State, and no inhabitant of this State shall ever be molested in person or property on account of his or her mode of religious worship, or lack thereof."[53]

In any state constitutional challenge to Arizona's pre-*Roe* abortion statutes (or any other abortion prohibition Arizona may enact), abortion advocates may argue that the statute interferes with the "liberty of conscience" guaranteed by II, § 12, and the "perfect toleration of religious sentiment" mandated by art. XX, ¶ 1, by forbidding a woman from obtaining an abortion that would be allowed by her religion.[54] There is very little case law interpreting the quoted language of either provision.

In an eighty-year old decision, however, the Arizona Supreme Court held that a Sunday closing law did not interfere with "religious freedom or liberty of conscience, but is based upon the undoubted right of the Legislature to pass laws for the preservation of health and the protection of the public welfare."[55] Key to the court's decision was that nothing in the defendant's religion *required* him to work on Sundays.[56] So, too, in the absence of a claim that a person's religious beliefs (or conscience) *requires* (as opposed to *permits*) her to obtain an abortion, a "liberty of conscience" claim could not be raised under art. II, § 12.[57]

---

52. ARIZ. CONST. art. II, § 12 (West 2001).

53. *Id.* art. XX, ¶ 1 (West 2001).

54. An argument based on the second sentence of art. II, § 12, forbidding the use of public funds or property to support a "religious establishment," would not appear to be available in a challenge to an abortion prohibition. That sentence "prohibits the use of public money for religious worship, exercise, instruction, or to support any religious establishment." *Kotterman v. Killian*, 972 P.2d 606, 620 (Ariz. 1999). *See also Pratt v. Arizona Board of Regents*, 520 P.2d 514, 516 (Ariz. 1974) (under second sentence of art. II, § 12, "public money or property may not be used to promote or favor any particular religious sect or denomination or religion generally"). A prohibition of abortion would not entail the use of "public money or property" for such proscribed purposes.

55. *Elliott v. State*, 242 P. 340, 341 (Ariz. 1926). The law was struck down on other grounds (privileges and immunities).

56. *Id.* at 340–31.

57. Whether a particular religious doctrine *permits* abortion under certain circumstances does not present a justiciable free exercise issue because, to have the standing necessary to raise such an issue (with respect to a law that does not single out religious practices for reg-

In a similar vein, the Arizona Court of Appeals has suggested that to state a claim under art. XX, ¶1, a person must establish, at a minimum, that he was "required to do or refrain from doing" something that his religion prohibited or commanded.[58] If a woman's religious beliefs do not *require* her to obtain an abortion, the mere fact that those beliefs would *permit* her to obtain an abortion under circumstances not allowed by law would not be sufficient to state a claim under art. XX, ¶1.[59]

Equal Privileges and Immunities

Article II, §13, of the Arizona Constitution provides: "No law shall be enacted granting to any citizen, class of citizens, or corporation other than municipal, privileges or immunities which, upon the same terms, shall not equally belong to all citizens or corporations."[60] The Arizona reviewing courts have characterized art. II, §13, as Arizona's "equal protection clause," and have construed it consistently with the Equal Protection Clause of the Fourteenth Amendment.[61]

For purposes of both state and federal equal protection analysis, there are three standards of judicial review. Under the first standard, which is known as rational basis scrutiny, "legislative regulation that results in disparate treatment of an affected class is upheld so long as there is a legitimate state interest to be served and the legislative classification rationally furthers that interest."[62] Under the second standard, intermediate (or heightened) scrutiny, which applies to "discriminatory regulations that affect classifications such as those based on

---

ulation), one must allege that one seeks an abortion "under compulsion of religious belief." *Harris v. McRae*, 448 U.S. 297, 320 (1980).

58. *Wagenseller v. Scottsdale Memorial Hospital*, 714 P.2d 412, 415 (Ariz. Ct. App. 1984), *vacated and remanded on other grounds*, 710 P.2d 1025 (Ariz. 1085).

59. *See generally* Chapter 2, *supra*.

60. ARIZ. CONST. art. II, §13 (West 2001).

61. *Valley Nat'l Bank of Phoenix v. Glover*, 159 P.2d 292, 299 (Ariz. 1945) ("[t]he equal protection clauses of the 14th Amendment and the state constitution [referring to art. II, §13] have for all practical purposes the same effect"). *See also Big D Construction Corp. v. Court of Appeals*, 789 P.2d 1061, 1066–67 (Ariz. 1990) (same). In *Standhardt*, the court of appeals held that §13 "provides the same benefits as its federal counterpart." 77 P.3d at 464 n. 19 (citing *Empress Adult Video & Bookstore v. Tucson*, 59 P.3d 814, 828 (Ariz. Ct. App. 2002)). A federal district court has also noted that "[t]he effects of the state equal protection clause and the federal equal protection clause are essentially the same [citation omitted], although the Arizona law has unique roots in a fear of overreaching by business entities [citations omitted]." *American Greyhound Racing, Inc. v. Hull*, 146 F. Supp.2d 1012, 1079 (D. Ariz. 2001), *vacated and remanded on other grounds*, 305 F.3d 1015 (9th Cir. 2002).

62. *Simat Corp. v. Arizona Health Care Cost Containment System*, 56 P.3d at 32 (citation omitted).

gender and illegitimacy of birth," a court must find that "the interest served by governmental action is important and the means adopted to achieve the state's goals are reasonable, not arbitrary, and have a fair relation to those goals."[63] Under the third standard, strict scrutiny, which applies to statutes that affect the exercise of a fundamental constitutional right or discriminate on the basis of a suspect classification, "discriminatory regulation will be upheld only if there is a compelling state interest to be served and the regulation is necessary and narrowly tailored to achieve the legislative objective."[64]

Strict scrutiny review would not apply to an abortion prohibition because, for the reasons set forth in the preceding sections of this analysis, neither the due process guarantee (art. II, §4), nor the privacy guarantee (art. II, §8), of the Arizona Constitution confers a "fundamental right" to abortion. Nor would the prohibition of abortion classify persons on the basis of a "suspect" personal characteristic. Abortion advocates may argue in the alternative, however, that a statute prohibiting abortion discriminates against women and is subject to intermediate scrutiny because only women are capable of becoming pregnant. An abortion prohibition would appear to satisfy this level of scrutiny because the prohibition would have a "fair relation" to the "important" goal of protecting unborn human life. Nevertheless, the standard applicable to sex-based discrimination (intermediate scrutiny) would not apply to an abortion prohibition. Abortion laws do not discriminate on the basis of sex.

First, the United States Supreme Court has reviewed restrictions on abortion funding under a rational basis standard of review, *not* under the heightened scrutiny required of gender-based classifications.[65] Indeed, the Court has held that "the disfavoring of abortion ... is not *ipso facto* sex discrimination," and, citing its decisions in *Harris* and other cases addressing abortion funding, stated that "the constitutional test applicable to government abortion-funding restrictions is not the heightened-scrutiny standard that our cases demand for sex discrimination, ... but the ordinary rationality standard."[66]

---

63. *Id.* (citations omitted).

64. *Id.* (citation omitted).

65. *Harris v. McRae*, 448 U.S. at 321–26.

66. *Bray v. Alexandria Women's Health Clinic*, 506 U.S. 263, 273 (1993). Several state supreme courts and individual state supreme court justices have recognized that abortion regulations and restrictions on abortion funding are not "directed at women as a class" so much as "abortion as a medical treatment, which, because it involves a potential life, has no parallel as a treatment method." *Bell v. Low Income Women of Texas*, 95 S.W.3d 253, 258 (Tex. 2002) (upholding funding restrictions) (citing *Harris*, 448 U.S. at 325). *See also Fischer v. Dep't of Public Welfare*, 502 A.2d 114, 125 (Pa. 1985) ("the basis for the distinction here is not sex, but abortion") (upholding funding restrictions); *Moe v. Secretary of Ad-*

Second, even assuming that an abortion prohibition differentiates between men and women on the basis of sex, and would otherwise be subject to a higher standard of review, the Supreme Court has held that biological differences between men and women may justify different treatment based on those differences. In upholding a statutory rape statute that applied only to males, the Supreme Court noted, "this Court has consistently upheld statutes where the gender classification is not invidious, but rather realistically reflects the fact that the sexes are not similarly situated in certain circumstances."[67] As one federal district court observed: "Abortion statutes are examples of cases in which the sexes are not biologically similarly situated" because only women are capable of becoming pregnant and having abortions.[68]

A statute prohibiting abortion quite obviously can affect only women because only women are capable of becoming pregnant.[69] Unlike laws that use women's ability to become pregnant (or pregnancy itself) to discriminate against them in *other* areas (*e.g.*, employment opportunities), abortion prohibitions cannot fairly be said to involve a distinction between men and women that is a "mere pretext[] designed to erect an invidious discrimination against [women]."[70]

A prohibition of abortion would not substantially interfere with the exercise of a fundamental state constitutional right, nor would it classify upon the basis of a suspect or quasi-suspect characteristic. Accordingly, it would be subject to rational basis review. A law prohibiting abortion would be rationally related to the State's legitimate interest in protecting unborn human life.

Nothing in the Arizona Supreme Court's decision in *Simat Corp. v. Arizona Health Care Cost Containment System* would dictate a contrary result. In *Simat*, a bare majority of the state supreme court struck down state statutes and regulations restricting public funding of abortion for poor women to circumstances where the procedure was necessary to save the life of the pregnant

---

ministration & Finance, 417 N.E.2d 387, 407 (Mass. 1981) (Hennessey, C.J., dissenting) (funding restrictions were "directed at abortion as a medical procedure, not women as a class"); *Right to Choose v. Byrne*, 450 A.2d 925, 950 (N.J. 1982) (O'Hern, J., dissenting) ("[t]he subject of the legislation is not the person of the recipient, but the nature of the claimed medical service"). Both *Moe* and *Right to Choose* were decided on other grounds. The dissenting justices were addressing alternative arguments raised by the plaintiffs, but not reached by the majority opinions.

67. *Michael M. v. Superior Court*, 450 U.S. 464, 469 (1981). *See City of Tucson v. Wolfe*, 917 P.2d 706, 708 (Ariz. Ct. App. 1995) (citing *Michael M.* with approval).

68. *Jane L. v. Bangerter*, 794 F. Supp. 1537, 1549 (D. Utah 1992).

69. *Geduldig v. Aiello*, 417 U.S. 484, 496 n. 20 (1974) ("[n]ormal pregnancy is an objectively, identifiable physical condition with unique characteristics").

70. *Id.*

woman or where the pregnancy resulted from rape or incest. The statutes and regulations did not allow public funds to be used to pay for health related abortions. Without characterizing the distinction between those abortions that would be paid for by the State and those that would not be as one based on sex,[71] the court held that the classification burdened the exercise of a fundamental *federal* right.[72] As such, it could be upheld only if it was narrowly tailored to promote a compelling state interest.[73] Although the court found that the State has a legitimate interest in protecting unborn human life and promoting childbirth, that interest is no greater than the State's interest in "promoting and actually saving the health and perhaps eventually the life of [the] mother...."[74] Moreover, the State's interest in the unborn child does not become compelling before viability.[75] Accordingly, the funding restrictions, which applied throughout pregnancy, could not be sustained.[76]

Simat would not preclude Arizona from enforcing its pre-*Roe* abortion prohibition (or enacting a new one) if *Roe*, as modified by *Casey*, were overruled. If *Roe* is overruled, there would no longer be a federal constitutional right to obtain an abortion, thus removing the underlying jurisprudential basis for the state supreme court's selection of the strict scrutiny standard of review (interference with the exercise of a fundamental federal constitutional right).[77]

Fundamental Principles

Article II, §1, of the Arizona Constitution provides: "A frequent recurrence to fundamental principles is essential to the security of individual rights and

---

71. For the reasons set forth in n. 66, *supra*, the restrictions were aimed at abortion as a medical procedure, not women, or even pregnant women, as a class.

72. *Simat Corp.*, 56 P.3d at 32.

73. *Id.* at 33.

74. *Id.*

75. *Id.* at 33 (citing *Roe*, 410 U.S. at 165–66).

76. *Id.* at 33–35.

77. The *Simat* majority failed to note that in reaffirming *Roe* in *Casey*, the Supreme Court never once referred to abortion as a "fundamental" right. *See* n. 10, *supra*. *Simat* is a curiosity in another respect. Without holding that the *state* constitution confers a right to abortion, the majority held that state equal protection principles require public funding of *all* therapeutic abortions where *some* therapeutic abortions are funded. The court arrived at this holding in order to vindicate a *federal*, not a *state*, constitutional right, even though the Supreme Court, in *Harris v. McRae*, had held that the federal constitution does *not* require the government to pay for all therapeutic abortions.

the perpetuity of free government."[78] In a challenge to Arizona's pre-*Roe* abortion statutes (or any other abortion prohibition), abortion advocates might argue that the statutes interfere with the "individual rights" referenced in art. II, § 1. That argument would not likely prevail.

Article II, § 1, is simply a reminder that no one should lose sight of the "fundamental principles" upon which both "individual rights" and "free government" are based. For example, "[i]n determining whether a defendant has had trial by 'an impartial jury,'" the Arizona Supreme Court "is admonished to consider fundamental principles."[79] Yet, art. II, § 1, is not the source of the right to trial by "an impartial jury," or, for that matter, any other substantive right.[80] A right to abortion cannot be derived from the language of art. II, § 1.

Inherent Political Power

Article II, § 2, of the Arizona Constitution provides:

> All political power is inherent in the people, and governments derive their just powers from the consent of the governed, and are established to protect and maintain individual rights.[81]

In any challenge to the pre-*Roe* statutes prohibiting abortion (or any other abortion prohibition) abortion advocates might argue that the prohibition interferes with the "inherent" political power of the people, and violates the obligation of the government to "protect and maintain [their] individual rights." Like the argument based on art. II, § 1, an argument based on art. II, § 2, would not likely prevail.

The Arizona Supreme Court has observed that "all powers of government are lodged in the people, ... exercised by the state subject to constitutional limitations."[82] Those limitations, however, are found in other sections of the Declaration of Rights and other articles of the state constitution, not art. II, § 2.

---

78. Ariz. Const. art. II, § 1 (West 2001).

79. *State v. Huerta*, 855 P.2d 776, 782 (Ariz. 1993) (Corcoran, J., dissenting) (citing art. II, § 1).

80. In debate on the floor of the 1910 Constitutional Convention, Delegate Crutchfield stated that the "purpose" of § 1 "is to emphasize the value of the fundamental principles and call attention to the fact that they are the real basis for all laws. It only gives emphasis to the fundamental and gives it preference." Records at 762.

81. Ariz. Const. art. II, § 2 (West 2001).

82. *City of Mesa v. Salt River Project Agricultural Improvement & Power District*, 373 P.2d 722, 730 (Ariz. 1962).

Section 2 itself is not a source of "individual rights." Accordingly, § 2 could not serve as a basis for a challenge to an abortion prohibition.

Retained Rights

Article II, § 33, of the Arizona Constitution provides: "The enumeration in this Constitution of certain rights shall not be construed to deny others retained by the people."[83] In any challenge to a law prohibiting abortion, abortion advocates may be expected to argue that abortion is a "retained right" under art. II, § 33.

There is virtually no Arizona case law interpreting art. II, § 33.[84] No Arizona reviewing court has ever recognized an unenumerated right under § 33. An entirely plausible reading of § 33 is that the enumeration of certain rights in the state constitution should not be construed to deny other rights retained by the people under the common law or statutes. But even if § 33 is understood to retain unspecified *constitutional* rights (as opposed to *common law* or *statutory* rights), abortion could not plausibly be considered to be among such rights.

In *State v. Cramer*,[85] the Arizona Court of Appeals, citing § 33, stated that the "the Arizona Constitution specifically reserved rights *already possessed by the people at the time the constitution was adopted*."[86] For the reasons set forth in the section of this analysis addressing the due process guarantee (art. II, § 4), there was no was no "right" to abortion at the time the Arizona Constitution was adopted. Indeed, abortion had been a statutory crime under the laws of the territory for almost fifty years before Arizona was admitted as a State. Accordingly, abortion may not be considered a "retained right" under § 33.

Conclusion

Based on the foregoing analysis, an argument that the Arizona Constitution protects a right to abortion that is separate from, and independent of, the

---

83. ARIZ. CONST. art. II, § 33 (West 2001).

84. "The Arizona courts have to date recognized [§ 33] as an essentially superfluous recognition of the plenary nature of state legislative power where not expressly limited by the constitution." John D. Leshy, THE ARIZONA STATE CONSTITUTION[:] A REFERENCE GUIDE 82 (Westport, Conn. 1993) (citing *Earhart v. Frohmiller*, 178 P.2d 436, 437–38 (Ariz. 1947); *Cox v. Superior Court*, 237 P.2d 820, 821–22 (Ariz. 1951) (following *Earhart*); *Adams v. Bolin*, 247 P.2d 617, 625–26 (Ariz. 1952) (same)).

85. 851 P.2d 147 (Ariz. Ct. App. 1992).

86. *Id.* at 148 (emphasis added).

right to abortion recognized in *Roe v. Wade* would not likely succeed. That, in turn, suggests that if *Roe*, as modified by *Casey*, is ultimately overruled, the State of Arizona could enforce its pre-*Roe* statutes *prohibiting* abortion (or enact and enforce new statutes prohibiting abortion). Moreover, nothing in the Arizona Constitution precludes Arizona from *regulating* abortion within federal constitutional limits in the meantime. Under the Arizona Supreme Court's decision in *Simat Corp.*, however, the State's restrictions on public funding of abortion are unconstitutional.

CHAPTER 7

ARKANSAS

Summary

As the result of an amendment to the Arkansas Constitution in 1988, a right to abortion may not be derived from any provision of the state constitution. The State of Arkansas may regulate abortion to the maximum extent permitted by the federal constitution and, if the authority of the States over abortion is restored by the United States Supreme Court, Arkansas may also prohibit abortion.

Analysis

The pre-*Roe* Arkansas abortion statute was based on § 230.3 of the Model Penal Code.[1] The statute prohibited abortion except when there was "substantial risk that continuance of the pregnancy would threaten the life or gravely impair the health of the ... woman," when there was "substantial risk that the child would be born with grave physical or mental defect," or when the pregnancy resulted from a promptly reported act of rape or incest.[2] As the result of a post-*Roe* codification of Arkansas law in 1987, all of the provisions of the pre-*Roe* abortion statute (including the exceptions allowing abortion for various reasons) were repealed other than the prohibition itself and a provision protecting the rights of conscience of physicians opposed to abortion.[3] Under

---

1. ARK. STAT. ANN. § 41-303 *et seq.* (Supp. 1969), renumbered as § 41-2553 in 1977. *See* ARK. REV. STAT. ANN. § 41-2553 (1977). The complete text of § 230.3 of the Model Penal Code is set out in Appendix B to the Supreme Court's decision in *Doe v. Bolton*, 410 U.S. 179, 205–07 (1973).

2. *Id.* §§ 41-303, 41-304, renumbered as §§ 41-2553, 41-2554 in 1977. *See* ARK. REV. STAT. ANN. § 41-2553, 41-2554 (1977).

3. *See* ARK. CODE ANN. §§ 5-61-102 (Michie 1997), 20-16-601 (Michie 2000). Whether the codification commission intended to retain the prohibition itself (without any of the exceptions) is unknown.

current federal constitutional doctrine, the prohibition is not enforceable. If *Roe v. Wade*,[4] as modified by *Planned Parenthood of Southeastern Pennsylvania v. Casey*,[5] were overruled, however, nothing in the Arkansas Constitution would preclude its enforcement.

In 1988, the people of the State of Arkansas approved an amendment to their constitution which effectively prevents an Arkansas state court from recognizing a right to abortion under the Arkansas Constitution. The amendment (Amendment 68) provides:

1. No public funds will be used to pay for any abortion, except to save the mother's life.
2. The policy of Arkansas is to protect the life of every unborn child from conception until birth, to the extent permitted by the Federal Constitution.
3. This amendment will not effect contraceptives or require an appropriation of public funds.[6]

The Arkansas Supreme Court has held that the public policy set forth in §2 is not self-executing, but requires implementing legislation.[7] By virtue of §2, however, such legislation, whether an abortion prohibition (once *Roe* is overruled) or an abortion regulation, could not be successfully challenged on the basis that the state constitution protects a right to abortion. Such challenges would be precluded by §2 of Amendment 68.[8]

---

4. 410 U.S. 113 (1973).

5. 505 U.S. 833 (1992).

6. ARK. CONST. AMEND. 68 (1988).

7. *See Knowlton v. Ward*, 889 S.W.2d 724, 726 (Ark. 1994); *Unborn Child Amendment Committee v. Ward*, 943 S.W.2d 591, 594–95 (Ark. 1997). The Arkansas Supreme Court, however, cited §2 in its decision recognizing a cause of action for the wrongful death of a viable unborn child. *See AKA v. Jefferson Hospital Ass'n., Inc.*, 42 S.W.3d 508, 517 (Ark. 2001); *id.* at 524–25 (Imber, J., concurring) (relying upon amendment 68).

8. The public funding restriction of §1 has been declared unconstitutional on federal grounds and its enforcement enjoined to the extent that it forbids state funds to be used to pay for part of the costs of those abortions for which reimbursement is available under the Hyde Amendment (currently, life-of-the-mother, rape and incest). *Little Rock Family Planning Services v. Dalton*, 860 F. Supp. 609 (E.D. Ark. 1994), *aff'd*, 60 F.3d 487 (8th Cir. 1995), *rev'd in part and remanded*, 516 U.S. 474 (1996) (*per curiam*); *Unborn Child Amendment Committee*, 943 S.W.2d at 594 (discussing effect of *Dalton* decision); *Hodges v. Huckabee*, 994 S.W.2d 341, 343–46 (Ark. 1999) (reciting history of litigation). That holding, based on the Supremacy Clause, would not affect the authority of Arkansas to prohibit abortion if *Roe*, as modified by *Casey*, is overruled. The State, it goes without saying, need not pay for those abortions which it has decided to criminalize.

Conclusion

If *Roe*, as modified by *Casey*, is overruled, the State of Arkansas may enforce §5-61-102. Because of Amendment 68, §5-61-102 (or any other abortion prohibition Arkansas may enact) could not be successfully challenged on the ground that the Arkansas Constitution protects a right to abortion. Moreover, Arkansas may regulate abortion within federal constitutional limits in the meantime.

CHAPTER 8

CALIFORNIA

Summary

As the result of a series of California Supreme Court decisions interpreting the California Constitution, the State of California could not prohibit any abortion before viability, or any abortion after viability that would be necessary to preserve the pregnant woman's life or health, even if *Roe v. Wade*,[1] as modified by *Planned Parenthood of Southeastern Pennsylvania v. Casey*,[2] were overruled, unless the state constitution is amended to overturn those decisions (or those decisions are overruled). Moreover, by virtue of those same decisions, California has little or no authority to enact and enforce reasonable measures regulating abortion within current federal constitutional limits.

Analysis

California does not currently have any law on the books restricting pre-viability abortions.[3] Moreover, it is unlikely that the California Legislature would consider enacting such a law even if *Roe*, as modified by *Casey*, were overruled.

---

1. 410 U.S. 113 (1973).

2. 505 U.S. 833 (1992).

3. *See* the "Reproductive Privacy Act," 2002 Cal. Stat. ch. 385, § 8, *codified at* CAL. HEALTH & SAFETY CODE § 123460 *et seq.* (West 2006). Under the Act, an abortion performed on a viable fetus is "unauthorized" only if, in the good faith medical judgment of the physician, "continuation of the pregnancy pose[s] no risk to [the] life or health of the pregnant woman." CAL. HEALTH & SAFETY CODE § 123468. Section 123468 does not define the scope of the health exception. The Supreme Court has not yet decided whether a statute prohibiting post-viability abortions must make exceptions for mental, as well as physical, health reasons. *See Voinovich v. Women's Medical Professional Corporation*, 523 U.S. 1036, 1039 (1998) (Thomas, J., dissenting from denial of *certiorari*) (noting that this issue was not addressed in *Doe v. Bolton*, 410 U.S. 179 (1973), the companion case to *Roe v. Wade*). As a result, it is not know whether, as a matter of *state* constitutional law, the California Supreme Court would require a post-viability statute to contain a mental health exception.

Assuming that the legislature *did* enact an abortion prohibition, however, it almost certainly would be struck down as unconstitutional under the California Constitution.

The California Supreme Court has been extremely receptive to abortion rights claims. In a pair of pre-*Roe*, 4-3 decisions issued over vigorous dissents,[4] the state supreme court struck down the longstanding nineteenth century abortion statute, first enacted in 1872, which prohibited abortion except when the procedure was necessary to preserve the pregnant woman's life,[5] and major portions of the Therapeutic Abortion Act, enacted in 1967 (based on § 230.3 of the Model Penal Code[6]), which allowed abortion through the twentieth week of pregnancy for physical or mental health reasons or when the pregnancy resulted from an act of rape or incest.[7]

In *Belous*, the supreme court relied upon the state and federal due process doctrine of vagueness and upon an implied right of privacy said to exist under both the state and federal constitutions.[8] With respect to privacy, the court said: "The fundamental right of the woman to choose whether to bear children follows from the Supreme Court's and this court's repeated acknowledgment of a 'right of privacy' or 'liberty' in matters related to marriage, family, and sex."[9] The court added, "The critical issue is not whether such rights exist, but whether the state has a compelling interest in the regulation of a subject which is within the police power of the state."[10] In *Belous*, the court held that the State's interest "in the protection of the embryo and fetus" was not sufficiently compelling to override "the pregnant woman's right to life...."[11] Accordingly, the court rejected suggestions that the phrase "necessary to preserve"

---

4. *See People v. Belous*, 458 P.2d 194 (Cal. 1969); *People v. Barksdale*, 503 P.2d 257 (Cal. 1972).

5. CAL. PENAL CODE § 274 (West 1955). Another statute prohibited a woman from soliciting an abortion or allowing an abortion to be performed upon her (subject to the same exception). *Id.* § 275. No prosecutions were reported under this statute.

6. The complete text of § 230.3 of the Model Penal Code is set out in Appendix B to the Supreme Court's decision in *Doe v. Bolton*, 410 U.S. 179, 205–07 (1973).

7. CAL. HEALTH & SAFETY CODE § 25950 *et seq.* (West 1984). The Act prohibited abortion after the twentieth week of pregnancy. In 2002, the Therapeutic Abortion Act was repealed, 2002 Cal. Stat. ch. 385, §§ 2-7, and replaced with the Reproductive Privacy Act, *id.* § 8, *codified at* CAL. HEALTH & SAFETY CODE § 123460 *et seq.* (West 2006). The latter act recognizes a woman's right to obtain an abortion for any reason before viability and for any reason relating to her life or health after viability.

8. *Belous*, 458 P.2d at 197–206.

9. *Id.* at 199 (citations omitted).

10. *Id.* (citations omitted).

11. *Id.* at 202–03.

life, as used in the abortion statute, should be interpreted to mean that death from childbirth would be "medically certain," "substantially certain" or "more likely than not." [12] Any of those suggested interpretations, the court determined, would constitute "an invalid infringement upon the woman's constitutional rights."[13]

The supreme court recognized in *Belous* that an interpretation that would permit an abortion "when the risk of death due to the abortion was less than the risk of death in childbirth" would serve to make the statute "certain."[14] The court declined to adopt such an interpretation, however, because "[t]he language of the statute ... does not suggest a relative safety test, and no case interpreting the statute has suggested that the statute be so construed."[15]

With respect to vagueness, the California Supreme Court held was that there was no reasonably precise definition of the term "necessary to preserve" life, consistent with the language of the statute as it had been interpreted over the years, that did not violate the pregnant's woman's right to life. In other words, California could not require any pregnant woman to run the risk of death as a condition precedent to obtaining an abortion. The court's opinion did not explain to what extent the woman's acknowledged right of privacy limited the State's authority to prohibit an abortion, other than in life threatening circumstances.

In *Barksdale*, the California Supreme Court considered a challenge to the Therapeutic Abortion Act. At the outset of its opinion, the majority declined to address the scope of the woman's right of privacy as it relates to abortion.[16] Instead, the supreme court held that the terminology used in two key provisions of the Act, to wit, "substantial risk that continuance of the pregnancy would gravely impair the physical or mental health of the mother" and the definition of "mental health," was impermissibly vague.[17] The court concluded that "the language establishing the medical criteria upon which abortions may be approved is not

---

12. *Id.* at 203.

13. *Id.*

14. *Id.* at 204.

15. *Id.* at 205.

16. 503 P.2d at 261–62.

17. *Id.* at 262–66. An abortion for "mental health" reasons was authorized if the pregnant woman "would be dangerous to herself or to the person or property of others or is in need of supervision or restraint." CAL. HEALTH & SAFETY CODE §25951 (West 1984). Despite this narrow definition (essentially the same standard as for civil commitment), more than 60,000 abortions were performed in California in 1970, 98.2% of which were performed for mental health reasons. *Barksdale*, 503 P.2d at 265. In *Barksdale*, the California Supreme Court expressed "[s]erious doubt ... that such a considerable number of pregnant women could have been committed to a mental institution" as the result of becoming

sufficiently certain to meet minimal standards of due process."[18] The court did not reach the constitutionality of the prohibition of abortion after the twentieth week of pregnancy because the case before it (a criminal prosecution) concerned a physician who performed an abortion at thirteen weeks.[19]

In a pair of post-*Roe* decisions,[20] also issued over vigorous dissents, the California Supreme Court struck down restrictions on public funding of abortion,[21] and the State's parental consent law.[22] In *Committee to Defend Reproductive Rights v. Myers*, the state supreme court noted that it had "first recognized the existence of [a] constitutional right of procreative choice" in its 1969 opinion in *Belous*.[23] Since then, art. I, § 1, of the California Constitution had been amended (in 1972) to included an express right of privacy.[24] In light of this amendment, the Attorney General conceded that "the state has no authority *directly* to prohibit rich or poor women from exercising their right of procreative choice as they see fit."[25] The question for the supreme court to decide in *Myers* was whether art. I, § 1, as amended, also disempowered the legislature from *indirectly* affecting the choice of an indigent woman to carry her child to term or undergo an abortion by funding the former and not funding the latter.

Upon reviewing the effect the funding restrictions would have on poor women, the court found that "the statutory restrictions in question will severely impair or totally deny the actual exercise of this intimate and fundamental constitutional right."[26] Under California fundamental rights

---

pregnant. *Id.* The experience in California strongly suggests that mental health exceptions in abortion statutes are inherently manipulable and subject to abuse.

18. *Barksdale*, 503 P.2d at 266 (citing U.S. Const. Amend. XIV, § 1, and what is now Cal. Const. art. 1, § 15 (West 2002)).

19. *Id.* at 268. After the United States Supreme Court's decision in *Roe v. Wade*, 410 U.S. 113 (1973), the California Attorney General ruled that the ban on post-20 week abortions was enforceable except at to nonviable fetuses and those abortions necessary to preserve the life or health of the mother. *See* 65 Op. Cal. Att'y Gen. 261 (1982).

20. *See Committee to Defend Reproductive Rights v. Myers*, 625 P.2d 779 (Cal. 1981); *American Academy of Pediatrics v. Lungren*, 940 P.2d 797 (Cal. 1997).

21. The challenged restrictions were contained in the annual budget acts for three consecutive years.

22. Cal. Health & Safety Code § 123450 (West 1996).

23. *Myers*, 625 P.2d at 784.

24. Article I, § 1, as amended, states: "All people are by nature free and independent and have inalienable rights. Among these are enjoying and defending life and liberty, acquiring, possessing and protecting property, and pursuing and obtaining safety, happiness and privacy." Cal. Const. art. I, § 1 (West 2002).

25. *Myers*, 625 P.2d at 784 (emphasis added).

26. *Id.* at 793.

jurisprudence, the issue was "whether the benefits the state derives from the restrictions 'manifestly outweigh' such significant impairment."[27] The majority
opinion held that "only the most compelling of state interests could possibly
satisfy this test."[28] After considering and rejecting other proposed state interests, the court addressed the State's argument that the funding restrictions were
necessary "to protect the life and health of the fetus."[29] The majority opinion
rejected this proffered defense of the restrictions, however, ruling that the
State's interest in "protecting the potential life of the fetus" was not compelling
before viability and that even after viability the State's interest was subordinate
to the woman's health.[30] In so ruling, the court held that "the protection afforded
the woman's right of procreative choice as an aspect of the right of privacy
under the explicit provisions of our Constitution is at least as broad as that
described in *Roe v. Wade.*"[31]

In one of its concluding paragraphs, the majority opinion stated:

> By virtue of the explicit protections afforded an individual's in-
> alienable right of privacy by article I, section 1 of the California Con-
> stitution, ... the decision whether to bear a child or have an abortion
> is so private and so intimate that each woman in this state-rich or
> poor-is guaranteed the constitutional right to make that decision *as an*
> *individual,* uncoerced by government intrusion. Because a woman's right
> to choose whether or not to bear a child is explicitly afforded this con-
> stitutional protection, in California the question of whether an indi-
> vidual woman should or should not terminate her pregnancy is not a
> matter that may be put to a vote of the Legislature.[32]

This passage suggests that, under *Myers,* the California General Assembly
has no authority to prohibit abortion, either directly or indirectly, at least before viability. Whether the legislature has any vestigial authority even to regulate abortion is doubtful. This was borne out in the supreme court's fractured
(and fractious) 2000 opinion striking down the state parental consent law.[33]
In *American Academy of Pediatrics v. Lungren,* the court reaffirmed *Myers* and

---

27. *Id.* (citation omitted).
28. *Id.*
29. *Id.* at 791.
30. *Id.* at 795–96.
31. *Id.* at 796.
32. *Id.* at 798 (emphasis in original).
33. *American Academy of Pediatrics v. Lungren* (hereinafter *AAP*) 940 P.2d at 848–65
(Mosk, J., dissenting); *id.* at 865–71 (Baxter, J., dissenting); *id.* at 871–91 (Brown, J., dissenting).

reiterated that "the protection afforded by the California Constitution of a pregnant woman's right of choice is broader than the constitutional protection afforded by the federal Constitution as interpreted by the United States Supreme Court...."[34] The court concluded that, "under the California constitutional privacy clause, a statute that impinges upon the fundamental autonomy privacy right of either a minor or an adult must be evaluated under the demanding 'compelling interest' test."[35] As previously noted, a bare majority of the court held that the parental consent law failed this test.[36]

Conclusion

Because of the California Supreme Court's abortion decisions, the State of California would have no authority to prohibit abortions, at least before viability, even if *Roe*, as modified by *Casey*, were overruled, unless the state constitution is amended to overturn those decisions (or they are overruled). Moreover, the State has little or no authority to regulate abortion within current federal constitutional limits.

---

34. *Id.* at 809–10.
35. *Id.* at 819.
36. *Id.* at 830 (plurality), 847–48 (Kennard, J., concurring in the judgment).

CHAPTER 9

COLORADO

Summary

The Colorado Supreme Court has not yet decided whether the Colorado Constitution protects a right to abortion separate from, and independent of, the right to abortion recognized under the United States Constitution.[1] A careful examination of the state constitution, in light of its history and interpretation, as well as other relevant legal sources, however, suggests that the state supreme court probably would not recognize a state constitutional right to abortion. Thus, if *Roe v. Wade*,[2] as modified by *Planned Parenthood of Southeastern Pennsylvania v. Casey*,[3] were overruled, Colorado could enforce its pre-*Roe* statute prohibiting abortion (subject to the exceptions provided therein) or enact a new prohibition. Moreover, nothing in the state constitution, properly understood, precludes the State from enacting and enforcing reasonable measures regulating abortion within current federal constitutional limits.

Analysis

The pre-*Roe* Colorado abortion statute was based on § 230.3 of the Model Penal Code.[4] Under the statute, an abortion could be performed at any stage

---

1. The Colorado Supreme Court has referred to the right to abortion solely as a matter of *federal*, not *state*, constitutional law. *See, e.g., People v. Rosburg*, 805 P.2d 432, 435–36 (Colo. 1991); *People v. Seven Thirty- Five East Colfax, Inc.*, 697 P.2d 348, 369 (Colo. 1985); *Lujan v. Colorado State Board of Education*, 649 P.2d 1005, 1015 (Colo. 1982) (plurality); *Chiappe v. State Personnel Board*, 622 P.2d 527, 531 (Colo. 1981); *Agustin v. Barnes*, 626 P.2d 625, 629–30 (Colo. 1981).

2. 410 U.S. 113 (1973).

3. 505 U.S. 833 (1992).

4. COLO. REV. STAT. § 40-6-101 *et seq.* (Perm. Supp. 1971). The complete text of § 230.3 of the Model Penal Code is set out in Appendix B to the Supreme Court's decision in *Doe v. Bolton*, 410 U.S. 179, 205–07 (1973).

of pregnancy (defined as "the implantation of an embryo in the uterus") when continuation of the pregnancy was likely to result in the death of the woman, "serious permanent impairment" of her physical or mental health, or the birth of a child with "grave and permanent physical deformity or mental retardation."[5] An abortion could be performed within the first sixteen weeks (gestational age) when the pregnancy resulted from rape (statutory or forcible) or incest, and the local district attorney confirmed in writing that there was probable cause to believe that the alleged offense had occurred.[6] Pursuant to *Roe*, the limitations on the circumstances under which abortions could be performed (and the requirement that all abortions be performed in hospitals) were declared unconstitutional (on federal, not state, grounds) by the Colorado Supreme Court in *People v. Norton*.[7] The statute has not been repealed.[8]

Based upon arguments that have been raised in other States with similar constitutional provisions, possible sources for an asserted abortion right could include provisions of the Bill of Rights guaranteeing religious freedom (art. II, §4), a speedy remedy (§6), due process of law and equal protection (§25) and equal rights (§29); recognizing political power in the people (§1), the right of the people to alter or abolish the form of government (§2) and inherent rights (§3); and retaining rights (§28).[9] The analysis that follows addresses each of these provisions.

Religious Freedom

Article II, §4, of the Colorado Constitution provides:

> The free exercise and enjoyment of religious profession and worship, without discrimination, shall forever hereafter be guaranteed; and no person shall be denied any civil or political right, privilege or capacity, on account of his opinions concerning religion; but the liberty of conscience hereby secured shall not be construed to dispense with oaths or affirmations, excuse acts of licentiousness or justify practices inconsistent with the good order, peace or safety of the state. No

---

5. *Id.* §40-6-101(3)(a).
6. *Id.* §40-6-101(3)(b).
7. 507 P.2d 862 (Colo. 1973).
8. COLO. REV. STAT. ANN. §18-6-101 *et seq.* (West 2004).
9. Three other more unlikely sources of an abortion right under the Colorado Constitution-art. II, §7 (prohibiting unreasonable searches and seizures), §10 (guaranteeing freedom of speech) and §26 (prohibiting involuntary servitude)-are discussed generally in Chapter 3, *supra*.

person shall be required to attend or support any ministry or place of religious worship, religious sect or denomination against his consent. Nor shall any preference be given by law to any religious denomination or mode of worship.[10]

In any challenge to a statute prohibiting abortion (either the pre-*Roe* statute, if *Roe* is ultimately overruled, or any other abortion prohibition Colorado may enact), abortion advocates may raise either or both of two arguments under art. II, §4. First, relying on the first clause of the first sentence of §4, they may argue that an abortion prohibition interferes with the "free exercise and enjoyment" of a woman's "religious profession" by forbidding her from obtaining an abortion that would be allowed by her religion. Second, relying on the last sentence of §4, they may argue in the alternative (or in addition) that an abortion prohibition gives a "preference" to a "religious denomination" because it reflects sectarian beliefs regarding when human life begins and the sinfulness of abortion. Neither argument would likely prevail.

The Colorado Supreme Court has observed that "the provisions of Article II, Section 4 ... embody the same values of free exercise and governmental non-involvement secured by the religious clauses of the First Amendment."[11] Because the state and federal provisions "embody the same values," the court "look[s] to the body of law that has developed in the federal courts with respect to the meaning and application of the First Amendment for useful guidance" in interpreting art. II, §4.[12] Although "determination of a first amendment challenge will not necessarily be dispositive of the state constitutional issue,"[13] the Colorado reviewing courts have consistently relied upon the interpretation given the federal Free Exercise Clause in construing the state "free exercise" clause,[14] and upon the interpretation given the federal Establishment Clause in

---

10. COLO. CONST. art. II, §4 (West 2001).

11. *Americans United for Separation of Church and State Fund, Inc. v. State*, 648 P.2d 1072, 1081–82 (Colo. 1982).

12. *Conrad v. City & County of Denver*, 656 P.2d 622, 670–71 (Colo. 1983). *See also Bishop & Diocese of Colorado v. Mote*, 716 P.2d 85, 91 n. 5 (Colo. 1986) (noting that "[t]here is no reason to believe that the limiting effect of article II, section 4, on the judicial resolution of church property disputes will differ from that of the first amendment").

13. *Bishop & Diocese of Colorado*, 716 P.2d at 91 n. 5.

14. *In re E.L.M.C.*, 100 P.3d 546, 563 (Colo. Ct. App. 2004) (free exercise provisions of state and federal constitutions "are subject to similar analysis") (citing *Young Life v. Division of Employment Training*, 650 P.2d 515, 525–26 (1982)); *People in Interest of D.L.E.*, 645 P.2d 271, 275–76 (Colo. 1982) (construing Free Exercise Clause of First Amendment and art. II, §4, together); *In re Marriage of McSoud*, 131 P.3d 1208, 1215 (Colo. Ct. App. 2006) (same). *See also Sanderson v. People*, 12 P.3d 851 (Colo. Ct. App. 2000) (no free exercise right to as-

construing the state "Preference Clause."[15] This reliance suggests that a challenge to an abortion statute that would not succeed under the Free Exercise or Establishment Clauses of the First Amendment would not succeed under the "free exercise" or "preference" clauses of art. II, §4, either. For the reasons set forth in Chapter 2, *supra*, an abortion statute could not be successfully challenged on First Amendment grounds. Accordingly, a similar challenge under art. II, §4, would not likely be successful, either.

Speedy Remedy

Article II, §6, of the Colorado Constitution provides: "Courts of justice shall be open to every person, and a speedy remedy afforded for every injury to person, property or character; and right and justice should be administered without sale, denial or delay."[16] Abortion advocates might argue that a statute prohibiting abortion interferes with a woman's control over her own body, and that such interference constitutes an "injury" to her "person," as those terms are used in §6, for which there must be a "speedy remedy." That "remedy," in turn, would be invalidation of the statute. This argument assumes that art. II, §6, confers substantive rights. The case law is clear, however, that it does not.

The Colorado Supreme Court has held that art. II, §6, "does not create a substantive right; it provides a procedural right to a judicial remedy whenever the General Assembly creates a substantive right that accrues under Colorado law."[17] "Thus, the 'access right' guarantees access to the courts only when an individual has a viable claim for relief."[18] Section 6 "applies only to injuries which may result from a breach of a legal duty or an invasion or infringement upon a legal right."[19] Legal duties and legal rights, however, are established by other sources of law, not

sistance in committing suicide); *People v. LaPorte Church of Christ*, 830 P.2d 1150, 1152, (Colo. Ct. App. 1992) (no free exercise right for non-attorney pastor to represent church in legal proceeding).

15. "In interpreting our Preference Clause we have looked to the Establishment Clause of the First Amendment to the United States Constitution and the body of federal cases that have construed it." *State v. Freedom from Religion Foundation, Inc.*, 898 P.2d 1013, 1019 (Colo. 1995) (citing *Conrad v. City & County of Denver*, 656 P.2d at 1313–16).

16. COLO. CONST. art. II, §6 (West 2001).

17. *Allison v. Industrial Claims Appeals Office*, 884 P.2d 1113, 1119 (Colo. 1994).

18. *Norsby v. Gensen*, 916 P.2d 555, 563 (Colo. Ct. App. 1995).

19. *Goldberg v. Musim*, 427 P.2d 698, 702 (Colo. 1967). In *Goldberg*, the state supreme court upheld a statute that abolished the common law causes of action for breach of promise to marry, alienation of affections, criminal conversation and seduction. Article II, §6, as the state court of appeals later recognized, "does not preserve pre-existing common law

§6. Section 6 merely guarantees a "speedy remedy" for breach of those duties and rights. Thus, if the Legislature determines that certain conduct (*e.g.*, abortion) shall be illegal, then the prevention of that conduct (by a criminal prohibition) cannot be regarded as the breach of a "legal duty" or a "legal right." Because art. II, §6, is not a source of substantive rights, it could not provide a basis for invalidating an otherwise constitutional statute of the State.[20]

Due Process of Law, Inalienable Rights

Article II, §25, of the Colorado Constitution provides: "No person shall be deprived of life, liberty or property, without due process of law."[21] Article II, §3, provides: "All persons have certain natural, essential and inalienable rights, among which may be reckoned the right of enjoying and defending their lives and liberties; of acquiring, possessing and protecting property; and of seeking and obtaining their safety and happiness."[22]

In any state constitutional challenge to Colorado's pre-*Roe* abortion statute (or any other abortion prohibition), abortion advocates are most likely to rely upon these provisions to argue that the statute interferes with a pregnant woman's "liberty" interest in obtaining an abortion. That reliance would be misplaced, however.

Due process, for purposes of the state and federal constitutions, has both substantive and procedural components. "Substantive due process prohibits the government in engaging in conduct that shocks the conscience or interferes with the rights implicit in the concept of ordered liberty."[23] "Procedural due process," on the other hand, "involves the manner in which state action occurs and requires notice and a fair opportunity to be heard."[24]

The Colorado Supreme Court has not clearly articulated a methodology for determining what liberty interests are protected by art. II, §§3 and 25, or for determining which of those interests should be regarded as "fundamental."[25]

---

remedies from legislative change." *Shoemaker v. Mountain States Tel. & Tel. Co.*, 559 P.3d 721, 723 (Colo. Ct. App. 1976).

20. It should not be surprising to note, therefore, that no criminal statute has ever been struck down on the authority of the "right to a remedy" language of art. II, §6.

21. COLO. CONST. art. II, §25 (West 2001).

22. *Id.* art. II, §3.

23. *People v. Garlotte*, 958 P.2d 469, 474 (Colo. Ct. App. 1997). *See also Coalition for Equal Rights, Inc. v. Owens*, 458 F. Supp. 1251, 1262 (D. Colo. 2006) (same).

24. *Garlotte*, 958 P.2d at 474.

25. To the extent that the Colorado Supreme Court may consider federal precedent in determining whether an asserted liberty interest (or right) is "fundamental" under the state

In a sixty-year old decision, the supreme court gave a broad reading to these provisions. In *Zavila v. Maisse*,[26] the court stated that the term "liberty," as used in these sections, "connotes far more than mere freedom from physical constraint; it is broad enough to protect one from governmental interference in the exercise of his intellect, in the formation of opinions, in the expression of them and in action or inaction dictated by his judgment, or choice in countless matters of purely personal concern."[27] "[A] law that restricts the freedom of the individual in matters of purely personal concern either by prohibiting action under penalty or enjoining upon him action for an avowed objective cannot be sustained unless there is some appropriate relation between the legislative command and the prescribed punishment on the one hand, and the avowed objective on the other."[28]

Despite its broad language, *Zavila* would not prevent the State from enforcing an abortion prohibition. In the first instance, abortion cannot be regarded as a matter of "purely personal concern," as it involves the intentional destruction of an unborn child. Moreover, the standard *Zavila* applies, an "appropriate relation between the legislative command and the prescribed punishment on the one hand, and the avowed objective on the other," is simply a more elaborate way of stating the rational basis standard of review,[29] which an abortion prohibition would clearly satisfy.

The Colorado reviewing courts have identified three fundamental liberty interests under art. II, §3 (inalienable rights) and art. II, §25 (due process) to date. First, the supreme court has noted that "[i]n interpreting constitutional provisions providing for the right to enjoy life and liberty [similar to

---

due process guarantee, abortion would not qualify as a "fundamental" right. Although the Supreme Court characterized the right to choose abortion as "fundamental" in *Roe*, 410 U.S. at 152–53, it tacitly abandoned that characterization in *Casey*, 505 U.S. at 869–79 (Joint Op. of O'Connor, Kennedy and Souter, JJ., replacing *Roe's* "strict scrutiny" standard of review with the more relaxed "undue burden" standard, allowing for a broader measure of abortion regulation).

26. 147 P.2d 823 (Colo. 1944).

27. *Id.* at 827.

28. *Id.* At issue in *Zavila* was whether children of Jehovah's Witnesses could be expelled from a public school for refusing to recite the Pledge of Allegiance.

29. *See, e.g., People v. Brown*, 485 P.2d 500, 503 (Colo. 1971) ("limitations may be placed upon an inalienable or inherent right based upon a proper exercise of the police power"), *appeal dismissed*, 404 U.S. 1007 (1972). "These 'natural, essential and inalienable rights' are not absolute and are subject to the reasonable exercise of the police power." *Trinen v. City & County of Denver*, 53 P.3d 754, 760 (Colo. Ct. App. 2002) (Roy, J., concurring in part and dissenting in part).

art. II, §3], courts have declared that the right of personal liberty consists in the power of locomotion [*i.e.*, freedom of movement]."[30] Second, the court of appeals has recognized, apparently on state as well as federal grounds, that "[p]arents have a fundamental right to make decisions concerning the care, custody, and control of their children."[31] And, third, the same court has recognized that involuntary commitment (for mental health reasons) implicates an individual's right to liberty.[32]

None of the foregoing liberty interests would be implicated by a statute prohibiting abortion. Of greater significance is that all three liberty interests are firmly rooted in English and American legal traditions and history. With respect to the first liberty interest, the power of locomotion, the right to freedom of movement has long been recognized in American law.[33] With respect to the second liberty interest, parental rights, the state court of appeals has noted that "the interest of parents in the care, custody, and control of their children is one of the oldest fundamental liberty interests recognized."[34] With respect to the third liberty interest, freedom from unwanted restraint, the Supreme Court recognized more than one hundred years ago that: "No right is held more sacred, is more carefully guaranteed by the common law, than the right of every individual to the possession and control of his own person, *free from all restraint or interference of others,* unless by clear and unquestioned authority of law."[35]

---

30. *Dominguez v. City & County of Denver*, 363 P.2d 661, 664 (Colo. 1961) (interpreting art. II, §3), *overruled on other grounds, Arnold v. City & County of Denver*, 464 P.2d 515, 517 (Colo. 1970). *See also People in Interest of J.M.*, 768 P.2d 219, 221 (Colo. 1989) (recognizing as "fundamental" liberty interests protected by the state and federal constitutions "the rights of freedom of movement and to use the public streets and facilities in a manner that does not interfere with the liberty of others").

31. *In re L.F.*, 121 P.3d 267, 270. Although there are many state supreme court cases recognizing this fundamental right, they all appear to be based solely upon the federal Due Process Clause, not the state due process guarantee (or art. II, §3).

32. *People v. Garlotte*, 958 P.2d at 474. It is clear from the context of the court's opinion that this right is fundamental.

33. "The rights of locomotion, freedom of movement, to go where one pleases, and to use the public streets in a way that does not interfere with the personal liberty of others are basic values 'implicit in the concept of ordered liberty' protected by the due process clause of the fourteenth amendment." *Bykofsky v. Borough of Middletown*, 401 F. Supp. 1242, 1254 (M.D. Pa. 1975) (citing cases), *aff'd* 535 F.2d 1245 (3d Cir. 1976) (mem. op.). *See also Williams v. Fears*, 179 U.S. 270, 274 (1900) (identifying the "right to remove from one place to another according to inclination" as "an attribute of personal liberty" protected by the Constitution).

34. *People in the Interest of A.R.D.*, 43 P.3d 632, 635 (Colo. Ct. App. 2001) (citing *Troxel v. Granville*, 530 U.S. 57, 65 (2000)).

35. *Union Pacific Railway Co. v. Botsford*, 141 U.S. 250, 251 (1891) (emphasis added).

Unlike these fundamental liberty interests, an asserted "right" to abortion has no pedigree in American or English law. The experience in Colorado is particularly instructive in this regard. The first territorial legislature enacted an abortion statute in 1861, fourteen years before Colorado adopted its present constitution and fifteen years before Colorado entered the Union. The statute prohibited performance of an abortion upon "any woman then being with child" without exception.[36] In 1868, the statute was amended to allow an abortion upon the advice of a physician or surgeon when it was performed "with intent to save the life of [the] woman, or to prevent serious and permanent bodily injury to her."[37] Other than changing the classification of the offense from manslaughter to murder if the woman died in the course of an illegal abortion, the statue remained unchanged until 1967.[38] In 1967, as previously noted, the Colorado Legislature enacted an abortion statute based on §230.3 of the Model Penal Code.[39]

Prior to *Roe*, the Colorado Supreme Court regularly affirmed abortion convictions (and homicide convictions based upon the death of the woman resulting from an illegal abortion) without any hint that the prosecutions or convictions were barred by the state constitution.[40] In a case decided before Colorado adopted its present constitution and was admitted to the Union, the territorial supreme court explained that the Territory's abortion statute was "intended specially to protect the mother and her unborn child from operations calculated and directed to the destruction of the one and the inevitable injury of the other."[41] More than seventy five years later, the state supreme court stated that the offense defined by the statute is "the criminal act of destroying the foetus at any time before birth."[42] Subsequent to *Roe*, the Colorado Supreme Court struck down portions of the 1967 statute on federal constitutional grounds only.[43]

---

36. Colo. (Terr.) Gen. Laws, 1st Sess. §42, at 296–97 (1861).

37. Colo. (Terr.) Rev. Stat., ch. XXII, §42 (1868).

38. Colo. (Terr.) Rev. Stat., ch. XXII, §42 (1868), *recodified at* Colo. Gen. Laws §637 (1877), *recodified at* Colo. Gen. Stat. §735 (1883), *recodified at* Mills Colo. Stat. Ann. §1209 (Supp. 1891–1896), *recodified at* Colo. Rev. Stat. §1646 (1908), *recodified at* Colo. Comp. Laws §6687 (1921), *recodified at* Colo. Stat. Ann. ch. 48, §56 (1935), *recodified at* Colo. Rev. Stat. Ann. §40-2-23 (1953).

39. *See* nn. 4–6 and accompanying text, *supra*.

40. *Dougherty v. People*, 1 Colo. 514 (1872); *Johnson v. People*, 80 P. 133 (Colo. 1905); *Fitch v. People*, 100 P. 1132 (Colo. 1909); *Marmaduke v. People*, 100 P. 337 (1909); *Hall v. People*, 201 P.2d 382 (Colo. 1948); *Palmer v. People*, 424 P.2d 766 (Colo. 1967); *Caraway v. People*, 486 P.2d 17 (Colo. 1971).

41. *Dougherty v. People*, 1 Colo. at 522.

42. *Hall v. People*, 201 P.2d at 383.

43. *People v. Norton*, 507 P.2d 862.

For more than one hundred years, from 1861, when the first abortion statute was enacted, until 1967, when the current statute was enacted, the State of Colorado strictly limited the circumstances under which an abortion could be performed. That history, along with the state supreme court's acknowledgment that the state legislature had enacted the abortion statute with the intent to protect unborn human life, strongly suggests that there is no fundamental interest in obtaining an abortion under the liberty clauses of art. II, §§ 3 and 25 of the Colorado Constitution. That suggestion is supported by other sources of law.

The interest of the People of Colorado in extending the protection of the law to unborn children is evidenced by their adoption of citizen-sponsored initiatives amending the state constitution to prohibit the expenditure of public funds for abortion,[44] and enacting a statute requiring parental notice of abortion.[45] Colorado recognizes the rights of unborn children in several areas outside of abortion, including tort law, health care law and property law.

In tort law, a statutory cause of action for wrongful death may be brought on behalf of an unborn child who was viable (capable of sustained survival outside the mother's womb, with or without medical assistance) at the time of its death.[46] A common law cause of action for (nonlethal) prenatal injuries may be brought on behalf of a viable unborn child.[47] Under the statute authorizing advance medical directives, life-sustaining procedures may not be withheld or withdrawn from a woman who is known to be pregnant if "the fetus is viable and could with a reasonable degree of medical certainty develop to live birth with continued application of life-sustaining procedures."[48]

In property law, a child conceived before the death of a relative, but born thereafter, may inherit from a deceased relative who dies without a will if the child survives for at least 120 hours (five days) after birth.[49] Subject to certain exceptions, a child who is born after a parent executes a will, and who is not otherwise provided for in the will, may receive that share he or she would have received if the parent had died without a will (or a share equal to that provided

---

44. Colo. Const. art. V, § 50 (West 2001). *See also* Colo. Rev. Stat. Ann. § 25.5-4-415 (West Supp. 2007) (implementing amendment).

45. Colo. Rev. Stat. Ann. § 12-37.5-101 *et seq.* (West Supp. 2007), as amended by the state legislature.

46. *Espadero v. Feld*, 649 F. Supp. 1480, 1483–85 (D. Colo. 1986), interpreting Colo. Rev. Stat. Ann. § 13-21-201 (West 2005).

47. *Id.* at 1484.

48. Colo. Rev. Stat. Ann. § 15-18-104(2) (West Supp. 2007).

49. *Id.* § 15-11-108 (West 2005).

to other children in the will).[50] A posthumous child (a child born after the death of a parent) may also receive "remainder" interests (a future interest in property).[51]

In light of the history of abortion regulation in Colorado, the Colorado Supreme Court's recognition that the abortion statute was intended to protect unborn children, the public referenda approving constitutional amendments and legislation regulating abortion and its funding, and the rights extended to unborn children outside the area of abortion, it cannot plausibly be said that the liberty clauses of the Colorado Constitution confer a right to abortion. More generally, a right to abortion cannot be found in the text or structure of the Colorado Constitution. There is no evidence that either the framers or ratifiers of the Colorado Constitution intended the Bill of Rights to limit the Legislature's authority to prohibit abortion.[52] Such an intent would have been remarkable in light of the contemporaneous prohibition of abortion except to save the life of the pregnant woman or to pervent serious and permanent bodily injury to her.

Equal Protection, Equal Rights

The Colorado Constitution "does not contain an explicit equal protection clause...."[53] Nevertheless, "equal treatment under the laws is a right constitutionally guaranteed to Colorado citizens under the due process clause of article II, section 25, of the Colorado Constitution."[54] Although the right to "equal treatment under the laws" guaranteed by the state constitution is "similar" to that provided by the federal Equal Protection Clause,[55] state courts are "free to construe the Colorado Constitution to afford greater protections than those recognized by the United States Constitution," and, therefore, may "extend the guarantee of equal protection of laws afforded by [the] state constitution further than that provided under the Fourteenth Amendment to the United States Constitution."[56] That being said, the state courts of Colorado "have applied

---

50. *Id.* § 15-11-302.

51. *Id.* § 38-30-119 (West 2007).

52. *See* Proceedings of the Constitutional Convention held in Denver, Dec. 20, 1875, to frame a Constitution for the State of Colorado 88–92, 137, 141–45 (proceedings in the Committee of the Whole); 200–11, 374–78, 486–89, 523–27 (proceedings in Convention) (Denver 1907).

53. *Mayo v. Nat'l Farmers Union*, 833 P.2d 54, 56 n. 4 (Colo. 1992).

54. *Id.*

55. *Nat'l Prohibition Party v. State*, 752 P.2d 80, 83 n. 4 (Colo. 1988).

56. *Millis v. Board of County Comm'rs of Larimar County*, 626 P.2d 652, 657 (Colo. 1981).

the same standards of strict scrutiny, intermediate scrutiny and rational basis developed by the United States Supreme Court in analyzing equal protection issues arising under the federal constitution."[57]

The Colorado Supreme Court has succinctly summarized these standards:

> In equal protection cases, we employ a three-tiered standard of review. We will subject classifications that affect a suspect class or a fundamental right to strict scrutiny. To survive strict scrutiny, the government must establish that the classification is necessarily related to a compelling state interest. Classifications based on gender, illegitimacy or alienage receive an intermediate level of scrutiny. This standard requires the government to establish that the classification is substantially related to achievement of an important governmental objective. All other classifications are subject to a rational basis test, the most deferential standard of judicial review. This standard requires that the statutory classification have a rational basis in fact and that it bear a reasonable relationship to a legitimate governmental objective. A presumption of constitutionality attaches to a statute analyzed under the rational basis standard, and the challenging party has the burden of establishing unconstitutionality beyond a reasonable doubt.[58]

Strict scrutiny would not apply to review of an abortion prohibition because, for the reasons set forth in the preceding section of this analysis, neither the recognition of inalienable rights (art. II, §3), nor the guarantee of due process (art. II, §25), confers a "fundamental right" to abortion. Nor would the prohibition of abortion classify persons on the basis of a "suspect" personal characteristic (*e.g.*, race).

Abortion advocates may argue in the alternative, however, that a statute prohibiting abortion discriminates against women and is subject to intermediate scrutiny under both art. II, §25, and art. II, §29,[59] because only women are capable of becoming pregnant.[60] An abortion prohibition would appear to satisfy this level of scrutiny because the prohibition would be "substantially re-

---

57. *Van Dorn Retail Management, Inc. v. City and County of Denver*, 902 P.2d 383, 387 (Colo. Ct. App. 1994).

58. *Mayo v. Nat'l Farmers Union*, 833 P.2d at 57 (citations omitted).

59. "Equality of rights under the law shall not be denied or abridged by the state of Colorado or any of its political subdivisions on account of sex." COLO. CONST. art. II, §29 (West 2001).

60. The same standard-intermediate scrutiny-applies to gender-based classifications under both sections. *See Austin v. Litvak*, 682 P.2d 41, 49 (Colo. 1984) (interpreting art. II, §25); *People In Interest of S.P.B.*, 651 P.2d 1213, 1215 (Colo. 1982) (same); *Lujan v. Col-*

lated" to the "important governmental objective" of protecting unborn human life. Nevertheless, the standard applicable to sex-based discrimination should not apply to an abortion prohibition. Abortion laws do not discriminate on the basis of sex.

First, the United States Supreme Court has reviewed restrictions on abortion funding under a rational basis standard of review, *not* under the intermediate (heightened) scrutiny required of gender-based classifications.[61] Indeed, the Court has held that "the disfavoring of abortion … is not *ipso facto* sex discrimination," and, citing its decisions in *Harris* and other cases addressing abortion funding, stated that "the constitutional test applicable to government abortion-funding restrictions is not the heightened-scrutiny standard that our cases demand for sex discrimination, … but the ordinary rationality standard."[62]

Second, even assuming that an abortion prohibition differentiates between men and women on the basis of sex, and would otherwise be subject to a higher standard of review, the Supreme Court has held that biological differences between men and women may justify different treatment based on those differences. In upholding a statutory rape statute that applied only to males, the Supreme Court noted, "this Court has consistently upheld statutes where the gender classification is not invidious, but rather realistically reflects the fact that the sexes are not similarly situated in certain circumstances."[63] As one federal district court observed: "Abortion statutes are examples of cases in which

---

orado State Board of Education, 649 P.2d 1005, 1015 (Colo. 1982) (interpreting art. II, §29); *Matter of Estate of Musso*, 932 P.2d 853, 855 (Colo. Ct. App. 1997) (same).

61. *Harris v. McRae*, 448 U.S. 297, 321–26 (1980).

62. *Bray v. Alexandria Women's Health Clinic*, 506 U.S. 263, 273 (1993). Several state supreme courts and individual state supreme court justices have recognized that abortion regulations and restrictions on abortion funding are not "directed at women as a class" so much as "abortion as a medical treatment, which, because it involves a potential life, has no parallel as a treatment method." *Bell v. Low Income Women of Texas*, 95 S.W.3d 253, 258 (Tex. 2002) (upholding funding restrictions) (citing *Harris*, 448 U.S. at 325). *See also Fischer v. Dep't of Public Welfare*, 502 A.2d 114, 125 (Pa. 1985) ("the basis for the distinction here is not sex, but abortion") (upholding funding restrictions); *Moe v. Secretary of Administration & Finance*, 417 N.E.2d 387, 407 (Mass. 1981) (Hennessey, C.J., dissenting) (funding restrictions were "directed at abortion as a medical procedure, not women as a class"); *Right to Choose v. Byrne*, 450 A.2d 925, 950 (N.J. 1982) (O'Hern, J., dissenting) ("[t]he subject of the legislation is not the person of the recipient, but the nature of the claimed medical service"). Both *Moe* and *Right to Choose* were decided on other grounds. The dissenting justices were addressing alternative arguments raised by the plaintiffs, but not reached by the majority opinions.

63. *Michael M. v. Superior Court*, 450 U.S. 464, 469 (1981).

the sexes are not biologically similarly situated" because only women are capable of becoming pregnant and having abortions.[64]

A statute prohibiting abortion quite obviously can affect only women because only women are capable of becoming pregnant.[65] Unlike laws that use women's ability to become pregnant (or pregnancy itself) to discriminate against them in *other* areas (*e.g.*, employment opportunities), abortion prohibitions cannot fairly be said to involve a distinction between men and women that is a "mere pretext[] designed to erect an invidious discrimination against [women]."[66]

The Colorado Supreme Court has stated that although the equal rights provision (art. II, § 29) "prohibits unequal treatment based exclusively on the circumstances of sex, social stereotypes connected with gender, and culturally induced dissimilarities," "it does not prohibit differential treatment [between] the sexes when ... that treatment is reasonably and genuinely based on physical characteristics unique to just one sex."[67] "In such a case, the sexes are not similarly situated and thus, equal treatment is not required."[68]

A prohibition of abortion would not substantially interfere with the exercise of a fundamental state constitutional right, nor would it classify upon the basis of a suspect or quasi-suspect characteristic. Accordingly, it would be subject to rational basis review. A law prohibiting abortion would be rationally related to the State's legitimate interest in protecting unborn human life.

Political Power

Article II, § 1, of the Colorado Constitution provides: "All political power is vested in and derived from the people; all government, of right, originates from the people, is founded upon their will only, and is instituted solely for the good of the whole."[69] In a challenge to a statute prohibiting abortion, abortion advocates might argue that the statute interferes with the "political power" of the people because it does not serve "the good of the whole." Given the purpose of § 1, however, this argument would not likely prevail.

---

64. *Jane L. v. Bangerter*, 794 F. Supp. 1537, 1549 (D. Utah 1992).
65. *Geduldig v. Aiello*, 417 U.S. 484, 496 n. 20 (1974) ("[n]ormal pregnancy is an objectively, identifiable physical condition with unique characteristics").
66. *Id.*
67. *People v. Salinas*, 551 P.2d 703, 706 (Colo. 1976) (upholding statutory rape statute that applied only to males).
68. *Id.*
69. Colo. Const. art. II, § 1 (West 2001).

Under art. II, § 1, "all political power is vested in the people and derives from them."[70] "An aspect of that power is the initiative, which is the power reserved by the people to themselves to propose laws by petition and to enact or reject them at the polls independent of the legislative assembly."[71] Apart from the initiative, however, the General Assembly "has plenary legislative powers, conferred by the people in their Constitution."[72] "These powers," of course, "are subject to express or implied restraints reflected in the Constitution itself."[73] The legislature, therefore, "cannot enact a law contrary to those constitutional constraints."[74] Article II, § 1, itself, however, imposes no restraints, express or implied, on the legislature's power. Such restraints as do exist are found in other provisions of the state constitution (principally, other sections of the Bill of Rights). Accordingly, § 1, which simply recognizes that political power rests in the people, would not prevent the General Assembly from enacting an abortion prohibition. Whether a given law serves "the good of the whole," within the meaning of art. II, § 1, presents a political question for the legislature (and, ultimately, the people) to decide, not a constitutional question for the judiciary.

Right to Alter or Abolish the Form of Government

Article II, § 2, of the Colorado Constitution provides:

> The people of this state have the sole and exclusive right of governing themselves, as a free, sovereign and independent state; and to alter or abolish their constitution and form of government whenever they may deem it necessary to their safety and happiness, provided, such change not be repugnant to the constitution of the United States.[75]

In any challenge to the pre-*Roe* abortion statute (or any other abortion prohibition), abortion advocates might argue that the statute interferes with the "sole and exclusive right" of the people to "govern[] themselves" because it does not promote their "safety and happiness." Given the purpose of § 2, this argument would not likely prevail.

---

70. *Colorado Project-Common Cause v. Anderson*, 495 P.2d 220, 221 (Colo. 1972).

71. *Id.* (citing art. V, § 1 (conferring initiative power on the people)). *See also Armstrong v. Mitten*, 37 P.2d 757, 759 (Colo. 1934) (same).

72. *Colorado Ass'n of Public Employees v. Lamm*, 677 P.2d 1350, 1353 (Colo. 1984) (citation omitted).

73. *Id.* (citation omitted).

74. *Id.* (citation omitted).

75. Colo. Const. art. II, § 2 (West 2001).

Although there is little case law authoritatively interpreting art. II, §2, its purpose would appear to be limited to securing to the people themselves, through the amendment process, the right to decide whether, how and to what extent the organic instrument of government should be changed. Section 2, thus, is not a source of substantive rights (other than the right to "alter or abolish" the state constitution). Rather, it recognizes the people as the ultimate source of authority in a republican form of government. As such, it could not serve as a basis for asserting a right to abortion. Whether a given law promotes the "safety and happiness" of the people, within the meaning of §2, is a political question for the legislature to decide, not a constitutional question for the judiciary.

Retained Rights

Article II, §28, of the Colorado Constitution provides: "The enumeration in this constitution of certain rights shall not be construed to deny, impair or disparage others retained by the people."[76] In any challenge to a statute prohibiting abortion (either the pre-*Roe* statute or any other abortion prohibition the State may enact), abortion advocates may be expected to argue that abortion is a "retained right" under art. II, §28.

Article II, §28, has been cited in very few Colorado decisions and authoritatively interpreted in none.[77] An entirely plausible reading of §28 is that the enumeration of certain rights in the state constitution should not be construed to "deny, impair or disparage" other rights retained by the people under the common law or statutes. But even if §28 is understood to retain unspecified *constitutional* rights (as opposed to *common law* or *statutory* rights), abortion could not plausibly be considered to be among such rights because, at the time the Colorado Constitution was adopted in 1876, abortion was a crime. The argument that §28 "retained" as an "unenumerated right" conduct that was criminal when the state constitution was adopted is, at the very least, counterintuitive.

The language of §28 appears to be based on the Ninth Amendment, which provides: "The enumeration in the Constitution of certain rights, shall not be construed to deny or disparage others retained by the people."[78] In light of that

---

76. *Id.* art. II, §28 (West 2001).

77. "No Colorado decision has depended on Section 28." Dale A. Oesterle and Richard B. Collins, THE COLORADO STATE CONSTITUTION[:] A REFERENCE GUIDE 63 (Westport, Conn. 2002).

78. U.S. CONST. AMEND. IX (West 2006). Oesterle and Collins, THE COLORADO STATE CONSTITUTION at 63 (Section 28 is "virtually identical to the Ninth Amendment").

equivalence, § 28 should be given a parallel interpretation.[79] That, in turn, suggests that if no right to abortion exists under the Ninth Amendment, then none would be recognized under art. II, § 28. The Supreme Court, however, has rooted the "abortion liberty" in the liberty language of the Due Process Clause of the Fourteenth Amendment, not in the unenumerated rights language of the Ninth Amendment.[80] Because abortion has not been recognized as a "retained right" under the Ninth Amendment, it should not be recognized as one under § 28, either.

Conclusion

Based on the foregoing analysis, an argument that the Colorado Constitution protects a right to abortion that is separate from, and independent of, the right to abortion recognized in *Roe v. Wade* would not likely succeed. That, in turn, suggests that if *Roe*, as modified by *Casey*, is ultimately overruled, the State of Colorado could enforce its pre-*Roe* statute *prohibiting* abortion (subject to the exceptions provided therein) or enact and enforce a new statute prohibiting abortion. Moreover, nothing in the Colorado Constitution precludes Colorado from *regulating* abortion within federal constitutional limits in the meantime.

---

79. *See Colorado Anti-Discrimination Comm'n v. Case*, 380 P.2d 34, 40 (Colo. 1962) (equating art. II, § 28, with the Ninth Amendment).

80. *See Roe*, 410 U.S. at 153; *Casey*, 505 U.S. at 846. In any event, the Ninth Amendment, standing alone, is not a source of substantive rights. *Gibson v. Matthews*, 926 F.2d 532, 537 (6th Cir. 1991). Although "[s]ome unenumerated rights may be of [c]onstitutional magnitude," that is only "by virtue of other amendments, such as the Fifth or Fourteenth Amendment. A person cannot claim a right that exists solely under the Ninth Amendment." *United States v. Vital Health Products, Ltd.*, 786 F. Supp. 761, 777 (E.D. Wis. 1992), *aff'd mem. op., sub nom. United States v. LeBeau*, 985 F.2d 563 (7th Cir. 1993). *See also Charles v. Brown*, 495 F. Supp. 862, 863 (N.D. Ala. 1980) (same).

CHAPTER 10

CONNECTICUT

Summary

The Connecticut Supreme Court has not yet decided whether the Connecticut Constitution protects a right to abortion separate from, and independent of, the right to abortion recognized under the United States Constitution.[1] A careful examination of the state constitution, in light of its history and interpretation, as well as other relevant legal sources, however, suggests that the state supreme court probably would not recognize a state constitutional right to abortion if *Roe v. Wade*,[2] as modified by *Planned Parenthood of Southeastern Pennsylvania v. Casey*,[3] were overruled. Accordingly,

---

1. The Connecticut Supreme Court has noted that the Connecticut Superior Court (a trial court whose decisions are not binding precedents) has recognized a state right to abortion, *see Ramos v. Town of Vernon*, 761 A.2d 705, 727 n. 10 (Conn. 2000), and *Perkins v. Freedom of Information Comm'n*, 635 A.2d 783, 789 n. 15 (Conn. 1993) (citing *Doe v. Maher*, 515 A.2d 134 (Conn. Super. Ct. 1986)), but the state supreme court neither reviewed the decision in *Maher* nor endorsed its reasoning. In *Maher*, the superior court struck down an administrative regulation restricting public funding of abortion. The court held that the regulation was inconsistent with the statutory provisions of the Medicaid program. 515 A.2d at 143–45. Although that holding effectively disposed the of the case, the superior court added an extended discussion of why the regulation violated the "civil" due process clause (art. first, § 10) of the state constitution, as well as the equal protection clauses (art. first, §§ 1, 20), and the state equal rights amendment added to § 20 in 1974. *Id.* at 146–62. That discussion, however, was unnecessary to the decision, which rested on administrative law grounds only. In two later decisions reversing attorney fee awards in *Maher*, the Connecticut Supreme Court noted that, although the defendants had not appealed the superior court's decision on the merits, the regulation in question "closely paralleled" one version of the Hyde Amendment which had been upheld by the Supreme Court in *Harris v. McRae*, 448 U.S. 297 (1980). *Doe v. State*, 579 A.2d 37, 39 n. 4 (Conn. 1990), *Doe v. Heintz*, 526 A.2d 1318, 1320 n. 3 (Conn. 1987). At a minimum, these two decisions raise some doubt as to whether the state supreme court would have agreed with the superior court's state constitutional analysis if the lower court's decision on the merits had been appealed.

2. 410 U.S. 113 (1973).

3. 505 U.S. 833 (1992).

Connecticut could prohibit abortion. Moreover, nothing in the state constitution, properly understood, precludes the State from enacting and enforcing reasonable measures regulating abortion within current federal constitutional limits.

Analysis

The principal pre-*Roe* abortion statutes, based upon an 1860 law, prohibited performance of an abortion upon a woman unless the procedure was "necessary to preserve her life or that of her unborn child,"[4] and made a woman's participation in her own abortion a criminal offense (subject to the same exception).[5] In a pre-*Roe* decision, those statutes were declared unconstitutional (on federal, not state, grounds) by a three-judge federal district court.[6] Enforcement of the statutes was not enjoined. After the district court entered its judgment and before the case was remanded by the Supreme Court, Connecticut enacted a new abortion statute with provisions similar to those previously invalidated by the federal district court.[7] Section 1 of the Act stated in part that it was "[t]he public policy of the state and the intent of the legislature ... to protect and preserve human life from the moment of conception...."[8] This statute was also declared unconstitutional (on federal, not state grounds) and permanently enjoined by the same three-judge federal district court.[9] On remand from the Supreme Court, the federal district court held that the older statutes had not been repealed with the enactment of the newer statute and declared both sets of statutes unconstitutional under *Roe* and permanently enjoined their enforcement.[10] The pre-*Roe* statutes were repealed in 1990.[11]

---

4. CONN. GEN. STAT. ANN. § 53-29 (West 1960).

5. *Id.* § 53-30. No prosecutions were reported under this statute.

6. *Abele v. Markle,* 342 F. Supp. 800 (D. Conn. 1972), *judgment vacated cause and remanded for consideration of question of mootness,* 410 U.S. 91 (1973).

7. 1972 Conn. Acts 1, § 1 (1st Spec. Sess.), *codified at* CONN. GEN. STAT. ANN. § 53-31a (West Supp. 1972).

8. *Id.*

9. *Abele v. Markle,* 351 F. Supp. 224 (D. Conn. 1972), *judgment vacated and cause remanded for further proceedings in light of Roe v. Wade,* 410 U.S. 951 (1973).

10. *Abele v. Markle,* 369 F. Supp. 807 (D. Conn. 1973).

11. 1990 Conn. Acts 90–113, § 4 (Reg. Sess.). In repealing its pre-*Roe* statutes, Connecticut enacted a new section which provides: "The decision to terminate a pregnancy prior to the viability of the fetus shall be solely that of the pregnant woman in consultation with her physician." *Id.* § 3(a), *codified at* CONN. GEN. STAT. § 19a-602(a) (West 2003).

Based upon arguments that have been raised in Connecticut and other States with similar constitutional provisions, possible sources for an asserted abortion right could include provisions of the Declaration of Rights guaranteeing religious liberty (art. first, §3), a remedy by due course of law (§10), due process of law (§§8(a), 10), personal liberty (§9), equal protection of the laws (§§1, 20); and recognizing inherent political power in the people (§2), as well as a separate provision of the state constitution prohibiting religious preferences (art. seventh).[12] The analysis that follows addresses each of these provisions.

Religious Liberty, Prohibition of Religious Preferences

Article first, §3, of the Connecticut Constitution provides, in part, that "[t]he exercise and enjoyment of religious profession and worship, without discrimination, shall forever be free to all persons on the state...."[13] Article seventh provides, in part, that "[n]o preference shall be given by law to any religious society or denomination in the state."[14]

In any challenge to a statute prohibiting abortion, abortion advocates may raise either or both of two arguments under art. first, §3, and art. seventh. First, relying upon art. first, §3, they may argue that an abortion prohibition interferes with the "free exercise" of a woman's "religious profession" by forbidding her from obtaining an abortion that would be allowed by her religion. Second, relying upon the anti-discrimination language of art. first, §3, and the anti-preference language of art. seventh, they may argue in addition (or in the alternative) that an abortion prohibition impermissibly "discriminates" between those religions that prescribe abortion and those that allow it, and gives a "preference" to a "religious ... denomination" because it reflects sectarian beliefs regarding when human life begins and the sinfulness of abortion. Neither argument would likely succeed.

The Connecticut reviewing courts have generally interpreted art. first, §3, and art. seventh consistently with Supreme Court precedent interpreting the Free Exercise and Establishment Clauses of the First Amendment.[15] This con-

---

12. Three other more unlikely sources of an abortion right under the Connecticut Constitution-§§4, 5 (guaranteeing freedom of speech) and §7 (prohibiting unreasonable searches and seizures)-are discussed generally in Chapter 3, *supra*.

13. CONN. CONST. art. 1, §3 (West 2007).

14. *Id.* art. 7.

15. *See First Church of Christ, Scientist v. Historic District Comm'n of the Town of Ridgefield*, 737 A.2d 989, 990 (Conn Ct. App. 1999), *adopting op.* in 738 A.2d 224, 230 (Conn. Super. Ct. 1998) (free exercise); *Grimm v. Grimm*, 844 A.2d 855, 859 (Conn. Ct. App. 2004), *aff'd in part, rev'd in part on other grounds and remanded with directions*, 886 A.2d 391

sistency of interpretation suggests that a challenge to an abortion statute that would not succeed under the Religion Clauses of the First Amendment would not succeed under art. first, §3, or art. seventh, either. For the reasons set forth in Chapter 2, *supra*, an abortion statute could not be successfully challenged on First Amendment grounds. Accordingly, a similar challenge under art. first, §3, and art. seventh would not likely be successful, either.

Remedy by Due Course of Law

Article first, §10, of the Connecticut Constitution provides: "All courts shall be open, and every person, for an injury done to him in his person, property or reputation, shall have remedy by due course of law, and right and justice administered without sale, denial or liberty."[16]

Abortion advocates might argue that a statute prohibiting abortion interferes with a woman's control over her own body, and that such interference constitutes an "injury" to her "person," as those terms are used in §10, for which there must be a "remedy by due course of law." That "remedy," in turn, would be invalidation of the statute. This argument assumes that, with respect to remedies, §10 confers substantive rights. That assumption, however, is mistaken.

As is apparent from its text and structure, §10 is concerned with *remedies* for tortiously inflicted injuries-it does not purport to establish what *constitutes* an injury to anyone's "person, property or reputation." Those remedies are derived from other sources of law (the common law and, in some cases, statutes codifying common law causes of action), not §10. Moreover, the remedies themselves redress injuries recognized by common law or statutory law, not constitutional "injuries." Section 10, in other words, does not *create* any causes of action-it merely *preserves* pre-existing causes of action. The case law interpreting §10 supports this understanding.

Article first, §10, "prohibits the legislature from abolishing or significantly limiting common law and certain statutory rights that were redressable in court

---

(Conn. 2005) (same); *Board of Education of Town of Stafford v. State Board of Education*, 709 A.2d 510, 517 (Conn. 1998) (noting that the First Amendment to the United States Constitution and article seventh of the Connecticut Constitution serve "similar purposes") (statute requiring school district to provide transportation to nonpublic school students, including parochial school students, even on days when public schools were not in session, did not violate either the Establishment Clause of the First Amendment or art. seventh of the Connecticut Constitution). As one commentator has noted, the Connecticut Supreme Court "has given §3 no significant independent meaning." Wesley W. Horton, The Connecticut State Constitution[:] A Reference Guide 44 (Westport, Conn. 1993).

16. Conn. Const. art. 1, §10 (West 2007).

as of 1818, when the constitution was first adopted, and which were incorporated in that provision by virtue of being established by law as right the breach of which precipitates a recognized injury."[17] "The legislature is precluded, therefore, from abolishing or substantially modifying any such right unless it enacts a reasonable alternative to the enforcement of that right."[18] Article first, § 10, however, "does not itself create new substantive rights, but instead, protects access to our state's courts."[19] Because § 10 does not create "new substantive rights," it could not serve as a source of an abortion right under the Connecticut Constitution.

The remedy language of § 10 is concerned with the availability of private civil causes of action and reasonable "access" to state courts to redress those injuries for which remedies were provided at the time the Connecticut Constitution was adopted in 1818. Section 10 places no limitation on the State's authority to define and punish crimes and has never been so interpreted.[20]

Due Process of Law

The Connecticut Declaration of Rights contains two provisions which have been construed to guarantee due process of law. Article first, § 8(a) provides, in relevant part, that "[n]o person shall ... be deprived of life, liberty or property without due process of law...."[21] And art. first, § 10, provides, in part, that "every person, for an injury done to him in his person, property or reputation, shall have remedy by due course of law...."[22] "Section 8," as one court has noted, "is generally applied to criminal matters and § 10 to civil matters."[23] Both § 8 and § 10 have been held to include substantive due process guarantees.[24]

In any state constitutional challenge to a statute Connecticut may enact prohibiting abortion, abortion advocates are most likely to rely upon art. first, §§ 8 and 10, arguing that the statute interferes with the "liberty" of a woman to obtain an abortion. Such an argument probably would not prevail, however.

---

17. *Moore v. Ganim*, 660 A.2d 742, 751 (Conn. 1995) (citation and internal quotation marks omitted).

18. *Binette v. Sabo*, 710 A.2d 688, 691 (Conn. 1998).

19. *Id.* at 691–92.

20. To the extent that § 10 has been construed as a "civil" due process guarantee, it is discussed in the next section of this analysis, *infra*.

21. Conn. Const. art. first, § 8(a) (West 2007).

22. *Id.* art. first, § 10.

23. *Doe v. Maher*, 515 A.2d at 148 n. 31.

24. *Ramos v. Town of Vernon*, 761 A.2d at 726 n. 30.

There is some authority in the decisions of the Connecticut Supreme Court supporting the view that art. first, §8, and art. first, §10, are to be construed consistently with the construction the United States Supreme Court has given the Due Process Clauses of the Fourteenth Amendment.[25] That similarity of construction would suggest that the Connecticut Supreme Court would recognize a state due process liberty interest in obtaining an abortion only so long as one was recognized under the federal due process guarantee, but not otherwise.[26] On the other hand, the court has stated that art. first, §8, and art. first, §10, do not necessarily have the same meaning and impose the same limitations as the Due Process Clause of the Fourteenth Amendment.[27]

In determining whether a provision of the state constitution affords greater protection with respect to an asserted right than does its federal counterpart, the Connecticut Supreme Court considers six factors: "(1) persuasive federal precedents; (2) the text of the operative constitutional provisions; (3) historical insights into the intent of our constitutional forebears; (4) related Connecticut precedents; (5) persuasive precedents of other state courts; and (6) contemporary understandings of applicable economic and sociological norms, or as otherwise described, relevant public policies."[28] A review of these factors suggests that the Connecticut Supreme Court probably would not recognize a state constitutional right to abortion under either art. first, §8, or art. first, §10.[29]

On the assumption that the Connecticut Supreme Court does not consider a state abortion rights claim unless and until *Roe*, as modified by *Casey*, has been overruled, the first factor, persuasive federal precedents, would be a negative one, not favoring recognition of a state constitutional right to abortion, because, on that assumption, the Supreme Court would have overruled *Roe*,

---

25. *See, e.g., State v. Brigandi*, 442 A.2d 927, 937 (Conn. 1982) ("the due process clauses of both the United States and Connecticut constitutions have the same meaning and impose similar limitations") (citing art. first, §8); *Roundhouse Construction Corp. v. Telesco Masons Supplies Co., Inc.*, 365 A.2d 393, 394 (Conn. 1976) (same statement in case citing art. first, §10).

26. The state supreme court, however, has not had occasion to pronounce on this issue, yet. *See* n. 1, *supra.*

27. *State v. Morales*, 657 A.2d 585, 590 (Conn. 1995) (interpreting art. first, §8); *Fair Cadillac-Oldsmobile Isuzu Partnership v. Bailey*, 640 A.2d 101, 104 (Conn. 1994) (same); *Ramos v. Town of Vernon*, 761 A.2d at 726–27 (interpreting §10).

28. *City Recycling, Inc. v. State*, 778 A.2d 77, 87 n. 12 (Conn. 2001). These factors were first identified in *State v. Geisler*, 610 A.2d 1225, 1231–32 (Conn. 1992), and are generally referred to as the *Geisler* factors.

29. This conclusion also applies to art. first, §9, to the extent that §9 places any limitations on conduct the State may proscribe.

removing any basis for a federal right to abortion. The second factor, the text of the operative constitutional provisions (due process), would also count against recognition of a state right to abortion, given the similarity of language between the state and federal due process guarantees.[30]

The third factor, which calls for an examination of how the asserted right has been treated in the State's history, particularly at or near the time the first state constitution was adopted in 1818,[31] would strongly count against recognition of a state right to abortion. In an early twentieth century case, the Connecticut Supreme Court observed that "[a]t common law an operation on the body of a woman quick with child, with intent thereby to cause her miscarriage, was an indictable offense...."[32] In 1796, Zephaniah Swift, later Chief Justice of the Connecticut Supreme Court of Errors (now the Connecticut Supreme Court), in his classic study of the laws of Connecticut, explained that "[t]o kill a child in its mother's womb, is not murder, but a great misdemeanor, but if the child be born alive, and then die by reason of the injury it suffered in the womb, it will be murder in him who caused it."[33] Significantly, his characterization of the offense of killing an unborn child *in utero* ("a great misdemeanor") did not turn on whether the child had "quickened." One scholar has concluded, on the basis of the report of a mid-eighteenth century prosecution and conviction, that "even pre-quickening abortions were considered serious crimes in colonial Connecticut."[34]

---

30. "The textual similarity between the federal and state due process clauses undermines the defendant's claim that the state constitution affords greater protection of the right of sexual privacy than the federal constitution and, instead, 'support[s] a common source and thus, a common interpretation of the provisions.'" *State v. McKenzie-Adams*, 915 A.2d 822, 839 (Conn. 2007) (quoting *State v. Ledbetter*, 881 A.2d 290, 309 (Conn. 2005)). In *McKenzie-Adams*, the Connecticut Supreme Court held that art. first, §8, of the Connecticut Constitution does not "confer[] a fundamental right of sexual privacy on an elementary or secondary schoolteacher to engage in consensual sexual intercourse with students over the age of consent enrolled in the school system in which the teacher is employed." 915 A.2d at 841.

31. With the exception of §20, a new equal protection clause, the Declaration of Rights "was largely unchanged" in the Connecticut Constitution of 1965. Horton, THE CONNECTICUT STATE CONSTITUTION at 18. Accordingly, this section focuses on the state of the law in or near 1818, when the first state constitution was adopted.

32. *State v. Carey*, 56 A. 632, 636 (Conn. 1904). "Quick," in this context, refers to "quickening," that stage of pregnancy, usually sixteen to eighteen weeks gestation, when the woman first detects fetal movement.

33. Zephaniah Swift, A SYSTEM OF THE LAWS OF THE STATE OF CONNECTICUT, Vol. II, Book Fifth, "Of Crimes and Punishments," ch. III, p. 299 (Arno Press, Inc. 1972) (1796).

34. Joseph W. Dellapenna, DISPELLING THE MYTHS OF ABORTION HISTORY 223 (Carolina Academic Press 2006), discussing the case of *Rex v. Hallowell*, 9 Super. Ct. Records Nos. 113, 173, 175 (Wyndham County Super. Ct. Files, box 171).

Connecticut enacted its first abortion statute in 1821, only three years after the first Connecticut Constitution was adopted.[35] The statute prohibited the use of "any deadly poison, or other noxious and destructive substance" with the intention "to cause or procure the miscarriage of any woman, then being quick with child," and punished the offense as a serious felony (natural life "or such other term as the court having cognizance of the offense shall determine").[36] This statute, the first one of its kind enacted in the United States, "was limited to attempts at abortion through administration of drugs, and was classed with attempts to murder by poison."[37] In 1830, the statute was amended to reach all methods of causing abortion.[38] Abortion "was made an entirely distinct offense, and extended to attempts at miscarriage through the employment of any instruments for physical operation."[39] Thirty years later, in 1860, the original abortion statute, as amended, was repealed and replaced with a new statute, one provision of which prohibited an abortion performed by any means at any time of pregnancy, "unless the same shall be necessary to preserve the life of such woman, or of her unborn child,"[40] and another prohibited a woman's participation in her own abortion (subject to the same exception).[41] These statutes differed from the former statute "only in omitting the limitation that the subject of the attempted abortion must be quick with child and in the extent of punishment."[42] With minor rewording, these statutes, codified in 1866, remained on the books until after *Roe* was decided.[43] In 1972, in response to

35. It should be noted that more than thirty delegates to the 1818 Constitutional Convention also served in the legislature that enacted the State's first abortion statute. 1822 Connecticut Register & Manual 19–23 (Connecticut State Library) (listing members of the Senate and House of Representatives as of May 1821); JOURNAL OF THE PROCEEDINGS OF THE CONVENTION OF DELEGATES CONVENED AT HARTFORD, AUGUST 27, 1818, FOR THE PURPOSE OF FORMING A CONSTITUTION OF CIVIL GOVERNMENT FOR THE PEOPLE OF THE STATE OF CONNECTICUT (hereinafter JOURNAL OF PROCEEDINGS) 7–10 (Hartford, Conn. 1907) (listing delegates). This suggests that delegates who later served in the legislature harbored no doubts about their authority to prohibit abortion

36. CONN. PUB. STAT. LAWS tit. 22, § 14 (1821).

37. *State v. Carey*, 56 A. at 636.

38. Conn. Laws, ch. 1, § 16, at 255 (1830), *codified at* CONN. STAT. tit. VI, ch. II, § 19, pp. 307–08 (1854).

39. *Carey*, 56 A. at 636.

40. Conn. Laws, ch. LXXVI, § 1, p. 65 (1860).

41. *Id.*, § 3, pp. 65–66. No prosecutions were reported under this section.

42. *Carey*, 56 A. at 636.

43. CONN. GEN. STAT. tit. XII, ch. II, §§ 22, 24 (1866), *recodified at* CONN. GEN. STAT. §§ 1155, 1156 (1902), *recodified at* CONN. GEN. STAT. §§ 6200, 6201 (1918), *recodified at* CONN. GEN. STAT. §§ 6056, 6057 (1930), *recodified at* CONN. GEN. STAT. §§ 8363, 8364

a federal district court decision, Connecticut reenacted the 1860 statutes, stating that it was "[t]he public policy of the state and the intent of the legislature to protect and preserve human life from the moment of conception...."[44] There is no evidence that the drafters of the 1818 Connecticut Constitution intended to recognize a right to obtain an abortion,[45] which, at the time, was a common law crime. The third *Geisler* factor, "historical insights into the intent of our constitutional forebears," would count against interpreting the state due process clauses to confer a right to abortion.

The fourth factor, related Connecticut precedents, would also count against recognition of a state constitutional right to abortion. Before *Roe* was decided, the Connecticut Supreme Court never questioned the constitutionality of the State's prohibition of abortion. The court regularly affirmed abortion convictions without any hint that the prosecutions or convictions violated the state constitution.[46] Moreover, in *State v. Lee*, the court implicitly recognized that the abortion statute had been enacted to protect unborn human life.[47] After *Roe* was decided, the state supreme court applied *Roe* without any discussion of the state constitution.[48]

The Connecticut Supreme Court has refused to give the state right of privacy (derived from the due process clauses) a broader reading than that given the federal right of privacy (derived from the Due Process Clause) by the United States Supreme Court.[49] The court's refusal to do so undermines the reason-

---

(1949), *recodified at* CONN. GEN. STAT. ANN. §§ 53-29, 53-30 (1960), *repealed by* 1990 Conn. Acts 90-113, § 4 (Reg. Sess.).

44. 1972 Conn. Acts 1, § 1 (1st Spec. Sess.).

45. *See* Wesley W. Horton, *Annotated Debates of the 1818 Constitutional Convention*, 65 CONN. BAR J. 1, 16–33 (Special Issue Jan. 1991). Although there is no official record of the debates of the 1818 Constitutional Convention, extensive notes were taken by two newspaper reporters and were published in the *Connecticut Courant* (Hartford) and the *Connecticut Journal* (New Haven). The reporters' notes, as published, provided the basis for Horton's article.

46. *State v. Lee*, 37 A. 75 (Conn. 1897); *State v. Carey*, 56 A. 632 (Conn. 1904); *State v. Horwitz*, 142 A. 470 (Conn. 1928); *State v. Itczak*, 149 A. 213 (Conn. 1930); *State v. Santoro*, 22 A.2d 793 (Conn. 1941); *State v. Orsini*, 232 A.2d 907 (Conn. 1967).

47. *Lee*, 37 A. at 80 (noting that, under the statute, an abortion could be performed only "to save the life of the woman or of the unborn child").

48. *See State v. Sulman*, 339 A.2d 62 (Conn. 1973) (reversing conviction of physician for performing an abortion); *State v. Menillo*, 368 A.2d 136 (Conn. 1976) (affirming conviction of non-physician for performing an abortion). *See also State v. Anthony*, 588 A.2d 214, 221–22 & n. 13 (Conn. Ct. App. 1991) (rejecting defenses of necessity and justification in prosecution for offenses related to abortion protest without any discussion of the state constitution).

49. *State v. McKenzie-Adams*, 915 A.2d at 839 ("the defendant has not pointed to any case law in which this court has construed the right of privacy protected by the due process

ing of the superior court in *Doe v. Maher*,[50] purporting to find a broader state right of privacy.[51] The fourth *Geisler* factor would not favor recognition of a state right to abortion.

At first blush, the fifth factor, persuasive precedents of other state courts, would appear to favor recognition of a right to abortion under the Connecticut Constitution. After all, since 1972, twelve state supreme courts have recognized a state constitutional right to abortion.[52] Upon closer examination, however, most of those decisions are distinguishable. In recognizing a state constitutional right to abortion, four state supreme courts (Alaska, California, Florida and Montana) relied upon an express right of privacy which does not exist under the Connecticut Constitution; in three other States (Mississippi, New Jersey and Tennessee), the state supreme court derived a state right to abortion from provisions (reserved rights, inalienable rights and, in the case of Tennessee, a veritable smorgasbord of rights) for which, again, there are no equivalents in the Connecticut Constitution;[53] in two more States (Minnesota and New York), the existence of a state right to abortion was conceded by the defendants; in one State (Vermont), it is not clear whether the state supreme court's decision was based on the state or the federal constitution and the rea-

---

clause of the state constitution to be broader than its federal counterpart"); *Ramos v. Town of Vernon*, 761 A.2d at 727–28 (although state constitution may provide greater substantive due process protection than the federal constitution, plaintiff failed to establish that "our state constitution contains greater rights of 'family autonomy' than does the federal constitution"). Indeed, prior to the Supreme Court's decision in *Griswold v. Connecticut*, 381 U.S. 479 (1965), the Connecticut Supreme Court repeatedly rejected both state and federal constitutional challenges (liberty and due process) to a statute proscribing the use of contraceptive drugs or instruments. *State v. Nelson*, 11 A.2d 856, 860–62 (Conn. 1940); *Tiletson v. Ullman*, 26 A.2d 582, 585–87 (Conn. 1942), *appeal dismissed*, 318 U.S. 44 (1943); *Buxton v. Ullman*, 156 A.2d 508, 514 (Conn. 1959), *appeal dismissed*, 367 U.S. 497 (1961); *Trubek v. Ullman*, 165 A.2d 158 (Conn. 1960), *appeal dismissed, cert. denied*, 367 U.S. 907 (1961); *State v. Griswold*, 200 A.2d 479 (Conn. 1964), *rev'd*, 381 U.S. 479 (1965).

50. *See* n. 1, *supra*.

51. 515 A.2d at 146–57. *Doe v. Maher* was decided before the Connecticut Supreme Court developed a methodology for determining whether a given state constitutional provision should be construed more broadly than the corresponding federal provision, *see State v. Geisler*, 610 A.2d at 1231–32, and does not take into account the *Geisler* factors. Consideration of those six factors, however, strongly militates against recognition of a state right to abortion.

52. *See* Introduction, n. 16, *supra* (collecting cases).

53. A proposal to amend the Connecticut Declaration of Rights to add a reservation of rights section was tabled and never taken up again by the convention. JOURNAL OF PROCEEDINGS at 20; Horton, *Annotated Debates of the 1818 Constitutional Convention*, 65 CONN. BAR J., Special Issue, at 33.

soning of the court is somewhat opaque. In only two States (Massachusetts and New Mexico) were the state supreme court decisions based solely on provisions (equal rights and due process, respectively) for which there *are* equivalents in the Connecticut Constitution. On the other side of the ledger is the decision of the Michigan Court of Appeals holding that the implied right of privacy under the Michigan Constitution does not extend to abortion.[54] Moreover, the overwhelming number of state courts that considered pre-*Roe* challenges to their abortion statutes rejected them.[55] Based on the number of state reviewing court decisions that have actually considered constitutional provisions similar to those that exist in Connecticut in the context of an abortion rights claim, the fifth factor is essentially neutral, neither favoring nor opposing recognition of a right to abortion under the Connecticut Constitution.[56]

The sixth factor requires an examination of "contemporary understandings of applicable economic and sociological norms," or, more simply, "relevant public policies."[57] "Community standards of acceptable legislative policy choices are necessarily reflected in the text of our constitutional document, in our history and in the teachings of the jurisprudence of our sister states as well as that of the federal courts."[58] For the reasons set forth in discussing the first five *Geisler* factors, *supra*, the sixth factor would not favor recognition of a state constitutional right to abortion under the due process clauses. Of particular significance is the fact that abortion was a common law crime (at least after quickening, and very likely without such a limitation) prior to 1821, when the State's

---

54. *Mahaffey v. Attorney General*, 564 N.W.2d 104 (Mich. Ct. App. 1997). The Ohio Court of Appeals recognized a state constitutional right to abortion in *Preterm Cleveland v. Voinovich*, 627 N.E.2d 570 (Ohio Ct. App. 1993). The constitutional underpinnings of that decision, however, were swept away in a later decision of the Ohio Supreme Court. *See State v. Williams*, 728 N.E.2d 342 (Ohio 2000), which is discussed in the Ohio state analysis, *infra*.

55. *See* Introduction, n. 9, *supra* (collecting cases). Most of these decisions, it must be noted, involved federal, not state, challenges.

56. *See State v. Ledbetter*, 881 A.2d at 310–11 (where two sister state courts decided a constitutional question relating to the reliability of eyewitness identification favorably to the prosecution, but one state court decided the same issue favorably to the defendant, "the scales remain balanced on this *Geisler* factor").

57. *City Recycling*, 778 A.2d at 87 n. 12. *See also State v. Diaz*, 628 A.2d 567, 582 (Conn. 1993) ("[i]n effect, [the sixth *Geisler*] factor directs our attention to considerations of public policy").

58. *State v. Ross*, 646 A.2d 1318, 1357 (Conn. 1994) (refusing to interpret the Connecticut Constitution to prohibit imposition of the death penalty).

first abortion statute was enacted, and a statutory crime for more than one hundred fifty years before *Roe v. Wade* was decided.[59]

Obviously, if *Roe*, as modified by *Casey*, were overruled and Connecticut enacted a statute prohibiting abortion, that statute would represent a "public policy" against abortion. That policy would not stand alone. Connecticut has recognized the rights of unborn children in several contexts outside of abortion, including tort law, health care law, property law and guardianship law. In tort law, a statutory cause of action for wrongful death may be brought on behalf of an unborn child who is viable (capable of sustained survival outside the mother's womb, with or without medical assistance) at the time of its death.[60] A common law cause of action for (nonlethal) prenatal injuries may be brought on behalf of a viable unborn child.[61] And, for purposes of the Workers' Compensation Act, an employee is entitled to a dependency allowance for a child conceived before but born after the date of the employee's injury.[62]

In health care law, life-sustaining medical treatment may not be withheld or withdrawn from a pregnant patient under either a living will or a durable power of attorney for health care.[63] In guardianship law, a guardian *ad litem* may be appointed to represent the interests of "unborn persons" in probate proceedings.[64] And in property law, subject to certain exceptions, a child who is born after a parent executes a will, and who is not otherwise provided for in the will, may receive that share he or she would have received if the parent had died without a will (or a share equal to that provided to other children in the will).[65]

In sum, none of the *Geisler* factors would weigh in favor of interpreting the due process clauses of the state constitution to confer a fundamental right of a woman to obtain an abortion. All but one of those factors (the fifth, persuasive precedents of other state courts, is neutral) would weigh against recognition of such a right. Accordingly, the Connecticut Supreme Court would probably not recognize a right to abortion under either art. first, §8, or art. first, §10, of the Connecticut Constitution if *Roe*, as modified by *Casey*, were overruled.

---

59. "In determining the scope our constitution's due process clauses, we have taken as a point of departure those constitutional or quasi-constitutional rights that were recognized at common law in this state prior to 1818." *State v. Ross*, 646 A.2d at 1354. There was no "constitutional or quasi-constitutional right[]" to abortion in Connecticut prior to 1818.

60. *Florence v. Town of Plainfield*, 849 A.2d 7, 15–19 (Conn. Super. Ct. 2004), interpreting CONN. GEN. STAT. ANN. §52-555 (West 2005). *See also Gorke v. Le Clerc*, 181 A.2d 448, 451 (Conn. Super. Ct. 1962) (same).

61. *Tursi v. New England Windsor Co.*, 111 A.2d 14, 17 (Conn. Super. Ct. 1955).

62. *Crook v. Academy Drywall Co.*, 591 A.2d 429 (Conn. 1991).

63. CONN. GEN. STAT. ANN. §19a-574 (West 2003).

64. *Id.* §§45a-132, 45a-164 (West 2004).

65. *Id.* §45a-257b.

Personal Liberty

Article first, §9, of the Connecticut Constitution provides: "No person shall be arrested, detained or punished, except in cases clearly warranted by law."[66] In any challenge to a statute Connecticut may enact prohibiting abortion, abortion advocates may argue that the statute interferes with the personal liberty guaranteed by §9. Such an argument, however, probably would not prevail.

As its text suggests, the focus of art. first, §9, is on the *procedure* (or method) by which a person is arrested,[67] detained[68] or punished,[69] *not* on whether the *substance* of the underlying criminal conduct with which he has been charged (or for which he has been punished) is constitutionally protected.[70] No criminal statute of the State has ever been struck down on the authority of art. first, §9. Because §9 is concerned solely with the *means* by which a person is arrested, detained or punished, not on the *end* to which the criminal conduct is directed, it would not support an asserted right to abortion.[71]

---

66. CONN. CONST. art. first, §9 (West 2007).

67. *State v. Bjorklund*, 830 A.2d 1141, 1147–49 (Conn. Ct. App. 2003) (defendant failed to prove that an arrest warrant based on probable cause that he had violated a condition of his probation was obtained as a pretext for securing evidence against him in an unrelated crime).

68. *State v. Lamme*, 579 A.2d 484, 489–90 (Conn. 1990) (art. first, §9, "permit[s] a brief investigatory detention, even in the absence of probable cause, if the police have a reasonable and articulable suspicion that a person has committed or is about to commit a crime"). *See also Ramos v. Town of Vernon*, 761 A.2d at 720–22 (rejecting a challenge under art. first, §9, to a curfew ordinance without discussing whether the ordinance violated any substantive rights of juveniles).

69. *State v. Ross*, 646 A.2d at 1354–59 (death penalty statutes do not violate art. first, §§8 and 9, of the state constitution). *See also Thomas v. Warden*, 891 A.2d 1016, 1028–31 (Conn. Super. Ct. 2005) (labeling of a prisoner as a sex offender, even though he had been acquitted of a sexual assault charge, constituted "punishment" without clear warrant of law in violation of art. first, §9).

70. For another opinion indicating that §9 is concerned with criminal procedure, not the substance of the criminal law, *see State v. Joyner*, 625 A.2d 791, 796–803 (Conn. 1993) (State may impose on the defendant the burden of proving his insanity by a preponderance of the evidence).

71. To the extent that §9 has been construed as a due process guarantee, *see State v. Rizzo*, 833 A.2d 363, 394 (Conn. 2003), it is discussed in the previous section of this analysis, *supra*.

Equal Protection

The Connecticut Declaration of Rights contains two provisions that guarantee (or have been construed to guarantee) equal rights. Article first, §1, provides: "All men when they form a social compact, are equal in rights; and no man or set of men are entitled to exclusive public emoluments or privileges from the community."[72] And art. first, §20, provides: "No person shall be denied the equal protection of the law nor be subjected to segregation or discrimination in the exercise or enjoyment of his or her civil or political rights because of religion, race, color, ancestry, national origin, sex or physical or mental disability."[73]

Although the state equal protection provisions *may* have "an independent meaning from the equal provision in the federal constitution,"[74] the Connecticut Supreme Court has generally held that they "provide[] the same limitations as the federal equal protection provision."[75] "We have held, in accordance with the federal frame of analysis, that state action concerning social and economic regulation will survive an equal protection challenge if it satisfies a rational basis test."[76] "If, however, state action invidiously discriminates against a suspect class or affects a fundamental right, the action passes constitutional muster under the state constitution only if it survives strict scrutiny."[77] "State action can survive [strict scrutiny review]," the court explained, "only if it (1) serves a compelling state interest, and (2) is narrowly tailored to serve that interest."[78]

For the reasons set forth in the section discussing state due process analysis, *supra*, a prohibition of abortion would not interfere with the exercise of a fundamental right under the Connecticut Constitution. Abortion advocates, however, would likely argue in the alternative that an abortion prohibition should be subject to "strict scrutiny" review because it discriminates against women in violation of the "equal rights" language of art. first, §20. In *Daly v. DelPonte*,

---

72. CONN. CONST. art. first, §1 (West 2007).

73. *Id.* art. first, §20.

74. *Barton v. Ducci Electrical Contractors, Inc.*, 730 A.2d 1149, 1161 n. 15 (Conn. 1999).

75. *City Recycling*, 778 A.2d at 87.

76. *Daly v. DelPonte*, 624 A.2d 876, 883 (Conn. 1993) (citation omitted). The Connecticut Supreme Court has refused to require more rigorous rational basis review under the state equal protection clause than that accorded under the federal equal protection clause. *Contractor's Supply of Waterbury, LLC v. Comm'r of Environmental Protection*, 925 A.2d 1071, 1079–84 (Conn. 2007).

77. *Daly*, 624 A.2d at 883.

78. *Id.* at 884.

the state supreme court held that § 20 defines several constitutionally protected classes of persons "whose rights are protected by requiring encroachments on these rights to pass a strict scrutiny test."[79] The protected classes are those defined by "religion, race, color, ancestry, national origin, sex or physical or mental disability."[80] Thus, under the reasoning of *Daly*, discrimination (or segregation) "because of ... sex" would be subject to strict scrutiny review.

There are several reasons, however, why a statute prohibiting abortion would not be subject to strict scrutiny review. First, § 20, as the state supreme court has noted, "prohibits ... sex discrimination in a person's exercise or enjoyment of his or her *civil or political rights*."[81] But abortion could not be said to be a "civil or political right" if it were prohibited. It would be a crime.[82]

Second, several state supreme courts and individual state supreme court justices have recognized that abortion regulations and restrictions on abortion funding are not "directed at women as a class" so much as "abortion as a medical treatment, which, because it involves a potential life, has no parallel as a treatment method."[83] Accordingly, a prohibition of abortion could not be said to "discriminate" against women.

Third, although there is no case law from the Connecticut Supreme Court on point,[84] reviewing courts in other States with "equal rights" language in their constitutions have consistently held that laws that differentiate between the sexes are permissible and do not violate the state guarantee of gender equality if they are based upon the unique physical characteristics of a particular

---

79. *Id.* at 883.

80. CONN. CONST. art. first, § 20.

81. *Thibodeau v. Desian Group One Architects*, 802 A.2d 731, 744 (Conn. 2002) (emphasis added).

82. For the reasons set forth in the preceding sections of this analysis, abortion could not be considered to be a "civil or political right[]."

83. *Bell v. Low Income Women of Texas*, 95 S.W.3d 253, 258 (Tex. 2002) (upholding funding restrictions) (citing *Harris*, 448 U.S. at 325). *See also Fischer v. Dep't of Public Welfare*, 502 A.2d 114, 125 (Pa. 1985) ("the basis for the distinction here is not sex, but abortion") (upholding funding restrictions); *Moe v. Secretary of Administration & Finance*, 417 N.E.2d 387, 407 (Mass. 1981) (Hennessey, C.J., dissenting) (funding restrictions were "directed at abortion as a medical procedure, not women as a class); *Right to Choose v. Byrne*, 450 A.2d 925, 950 (N.J. 1982) (O'Hern, J., dissenting) ("[t]he subject of the legislation is not the person of the recipient, but the nature of the claimed medical service"). Both *Moe* and *Right to Choose* were decided on other grounds. The dissenting justices were addressing alternative arguments raised by the plaintiffs, but not reached by the majority opinions.

84. *But see Dydyn v. Dep't of Liquor Control*, 531 A.2d 170, 175 (Conn. App. Ct. 1987) (upholding regulation barring women from dancing topless in establishments serving alcoholic beverages).

sex.[85] As one federal district court observed: "Abortion statutes are examples of cases in which the sexes are not biologically similarly situated" because only women are capable of becoming pregnant and having abortions.[86]

A statute prohibiting abortion quite obviously can affect only women because only women are capable of becoming pregnant.[87] Unlike laws that use women's ability to become pregnant (or pregnancy itself) to discriminate against them in *other* areas (*e.g.*, employment opportunities), abortion prohibitions cannot fairly be said to involve a distinction between men and women that is a "mere pretext[] designed to erect an invidious discrimination against [women]."[88] The failure to recognize that the regulation of abortion *qua* abortion does not constitute sex discrimination, and that abortion, unlike any other medical procedure, involves the intentional destruction of unborn human life, undermines the "equal rights" analysis of § 20 set forth in *Doe v. Maher*.[89]

A prohibition of abortion would not substantially interfere with the exercise of a fundamental state constitutional right, nor would it classify upon the basis of a suspect personal characteristic. Accordingly, it would be subject to rational basis review under both art. first, § 1, and art. first, § 20, of the Connecticut Constitution. A law prohibiting abortion would be rationally related to the State's legitimate interest in protecting unborn human life.

---

85. The cases have upheld rape statutes, *State v. Rivera*, 612 P.2d 526, 530–31 (Haw. 1980), *State v. Fletcher*, 341 So.2d 340, 348 (La. 1976), *Brooks v. State*, 330 A.2d 670, 672–73 (Md. Ct. Sp. App. 1975), *State v. Craig*, 545 P.2d 649 (Mont. 1976), *Finley v. State*, 527 S.W.2d 553, 555–57 (Tex. Crim. App. 1975); statutory rape statutes, *People v. Salinas*, 551 P.2d 703, 705–06 (Colo. 1976), *State v. Bell*, 377 So.2d 303 (La. 1979); an aggravated incest statute, *People v. Boyer*, 349 N.E.2d 50 (Ill. 1976); statutes governing the means of establishing maternity and paternity, *People v. Morrison*, 584 N.E.2d 509 (Ill. App. Ct. 1991), *A v. X, Y & Z*, 641 P.2d 1222, 1224–25 (Wyo. 1982); statutes barring female nudity in bars, *Messina v. State*, 904 S.W.2d 178, 181 (Tex. App.-Dallas 1995, *no pet.*); an ordinance prohibiting public exposure of female breasts, *City of Seattle v. Buchanan*, 584 P.2d 918, 919–21 (Wash. 1978); and limitations on public funding of abortion, *Fischer v. Dep't of Public Welfare*, 502 A.2d 114, 124–26 (Pa. 1985), *Bell v. Low Income Women of Texas*, 95 S.W.3d 253, 257–64 (Tex. 2002). The one exception is *New Mexico Right to Choose/NARAL v. Johnson*, 975 P.2d 841 (N.M. 1998), in which the New Mexico Supreme Court struck down a state regulation restricting public funding of abortion. In applying "heightened scrutiny," the court failed to recognize that the funding regulation did not use "the unique ability of women to become pregnant and bear children" as a pretext to discriminate against them in *other* respects, *e.g.*, "imposing restrictions on [their] ability to work and participate in public life." *Id.* at 855.

86. *Jane L. v. Bangerter*, 794 F. Supp. 1537, 1549 (D. Utah 1992).

87. *Geduldig v. Aiello*, 417 U.S. 484, 496 n. 20 (1974) ("[n]ormal pregnancy is an objectively, identifiable physical condition with unique characteristics").

88. *Id.*

89. 515 A.2d at 157–62. *See* n. 1, *supra.*

Inherent Political Power

Article first, §2, of the Connecticut Constitution provides:

All political power is inherent in the people, and all free governments are founded on their authority, and instituted for their benefit; and they have at all times an undeniable right to alter their form of government in such manner as they may think expedient.[90]

In a challenge to any statute prohibiting abortion that Connecticut may enact, abortion advocates might argue that the statute interferes with the "inherent" political power of the people because it does not promote their "benefit." Given the purpose of §2, this argument would not likely prevail.

Section 2 simply provides that "our government is to be responsible to the people."[91] The purpose of §2 is to secure to the people themselves, through the amendment process, the right to decide whether, how and to what extent the organic instrument of government should be changed. Section 2, thus, is not a source of substantive rights. Rather, it recognizes the people as the ultimate source of authority in a republican form of government. As such, it could not serve as a basis for asserting a right to abortion. Whether a given law promotes the "benefit" of the people, within the meaning of §2 is a political question for the legislature to decide, not a constitutional question for the judiciary.[92]

Conclusion

Based on the foregoing analysis, an argument that the Connecticut Constitution protects a right to abortion that is separate from, and independent of, the right to abortion recognized in *Roe v. Wade* would not likely succeed. That, in turn, suggests that if *Roe*, as modified by *Casey*, is ultimately overruled, the State of Connecticut could enact and enforce a statute *prohibiting* abortion. Moreover, nothing in the Connecticut Constitution precludes Connecticut from *regulating* abortion within federal constitutional limits in the meantime.

---

90. CONN. CONST. art. first, §2 (West 2007).

91. *Lieberman v. State Board of Labor Relations, Freedom of Information Comm'n*, 579 A.2d 505, 512 (Conn. 1990). Section 2 "reminds the government ... that the people are the ultimate source of all legislative power." Horton, THE CONNECTICUT STATE CONSTITUTION at 42.

92. *See In re Adoption of Baby Z.*, 724 A.2d 1035, 1064 (Conn. 1999) (McDonald, J., concurring).

CHAPTER 11

DELAWARE

Summary

The Delaware Supreme Court has not yet decided whether the Delaware Constitution protects a right to abortion separate from, and independent of, the right to abortion recognized under the United States Constitution.[1] A careful examination of the state constitution, in light of its history and interpretation, as well as other relevant legal sources, however, suggests that the state supreme court probably would not recognize a state constitutional right to abortion. Thus, if *Roe v. Wade*,[2] as modified by *Planned Parenthood of Southeastern Pennsylvania v. Casey*,[3] were overruled, Delaware could enforce its pre-*Roe* statutes prohibiting abortion (subject to the exceptions provided therein) or enact a new prohibition. Moreover, nothing in the state constitution, properly understood, precludes the State from enacting and enforcing reasonable measures regulating abortion within current federal constitutional limits.

Analysis

The principal pre-*Roe* Delaware abortion statutes were based on § 230.3 of the Model Penal Code.[4] The statutes prohibited the performance of an abor-

---

1. The Delaware Supreme Court has referred to the right to abortion solely as a matter of *federal*, not *state*, constitutional law. *See, e.g., In re Kennedy*, 442 A.2d 79, 90 (Del. 1982) ("[t]he Supreme Court set the parameters of the constitutional right to privacy in *Roe v. Wade*"); *State ex rel. State Board of Examiners in Pharmacy v. Kuhwald*, 389 A.2d 1277, 1280–81 (Del. 1978) ("[i]n *Roe*, the United States Supreme Court ruled that the decision by a physician and his patient as to whether an abortion should be performed is protected by the Federal Constitution under the right of privacy").

2. 410 U.S. 113 (1973).

3. 505 U.S. 833 (1992).

4. 57 Del. Laws, chapters 145, 235, 344, 58 Del. Laws, ch. 497, at 1623, *codified at* DEL. CODE ANN. tit. 11, §§ 222(21), 651–654 (1975); *id.* tit. 24, §§ 1766(b), 1790–1793 (1975).

tion upon a pregnant woman unless the procedure was a "therapeutic abortion,"[5] and made a woman's participation in her own abortion a criminal offense (subject to the same exception).[6] A "therapeutic abortion," in turn, was defined as "an abortion performed pursuant to the provisions of Title 24,..., Chapter 17, Subchapter VIII."[7]

Under that subchapter, an abortion could be performed at any stage of pregnancy when continuation of the pregnancy was "likely to result in the death of the mother."[8] An abortion could also be performed within the first twenty weeks of gestational age when there was "substantial risk of the birth of [a] child with grave and permanent physical deformity or mental retardation," the pregnancy resulted from incest or rape, or continuation of the pregnancy would involve "substantial risk of permanent injury to the physical or mental health of the mother."[9] The pre-*Roe* statues, which have not been repealed,[10] have not been declared unconstitutional nor has their enforcement been enjoined.[11]

Based upon arguments that have been raised in other States with similar constitutional provisions, possible sources for an asserted abortion right could include provisions of the Bill of Rights guaranteeing freedom of religion (art. I, §1) and a remedy "by the due course of law" (§9); and prohibiting anyone from being deprived of life, liberty or property, "unless by the judgment of his or her peers or by the law of the land" (§7).[12] The analysis that follows addresses each of these provisions.

The complete text of §230.3 of the Model Penal Code is set out in Appendix B to the Supreme Court's decision in *Doe v. Bolton*, 410 U.S. 179, 205–07 (1973).

5. DEL. CODE ANN. tit. 11, §651 (1975).

6. *Id.* tit. 11, §652. No prosecutions were reported under this statute.

7. *Id.* tit. 11, §222(21).

8. *Id.* tit. 24, §§1790(a)(1), -(b)(1).

9. *Id.* tit. 24, §1790(a)(2)-(4). The law imposed other conditions. An abortion could be performed only in an accredited hospital and had to be approved by a hospital abortion review authority. *Id.* §1790(a), -(c). Two physicians had to certify that the procedure was justified under one of the circumstances specified in the statute (except in cases where the pregnancy resulted from rape, in which case the Attorney General had to certify that there was probable cause to believe that the alleged rape had occurred). *Id.* §§1790(a)(3)(b), -(b)(2). In the case of an unmarried female under the age of eighteen or a mentally ill or incompetent woman, the written consent of her parents or guardian(s) was required. *Id.* §1790(b)(3)

10. *Id.* tit. 11, §§222(26), 651, 652 (2007); *id.* tit. 24, §1790 *et seq.* (2005).

11. Based upon an Attorney General opinion that the statutes were unconstitutional and a formal policy not to enjoin them, a challenge to the constitutionality of the statutes was dismissed for want of a "justiciable controversy." *Delaware Women's Health Organization, Inc. v. Weir*, 441 F. Supp. 497, 499 n. 9 (D. Del. 1997).

12. Two other more unlikely sources of an abortion right under the Delaware Consti-

Freedom of Religion

Article I, § 1, of the Delaware Constitution provides:

Although it is the duty of all persons frequently to assemble together for the public worship of Almighty God; and piety and morality, on which the prosperity of communities depends, are hereby
promoted; yet no person shall or ought to be compelled to attend any
religious worship, to contribute to the erection or support of any place
of worship, or to the maintenance of any ministry, against his or her
own free will and consent; and no power shall or ought to be vested
in or assumed by any magistrate that shall in any case interfere with,
or in any manner control the rights of conscience, in the free exercise
of religious worship, nor a preference given by law to any religious
societies, denominations, or modes of worship.[13]

In any challenge to statutes prohibiting abortion (either the pre-*Roe* statutes,
if *Roe* is overruled, or any other abortion prohibition Delaware may enact),
abortion advocates may raise either or both of two arguments under art. I, § 1.
First, relying on the fourth clause of § 1, they may argue that an abortion prohibition interferes with a woman's "rights of conscience, in the free exercise of
religious worship," by forbidding her from obtaining an abortion that would
be allowed by her religion. Second, relying on other language in the same
clause, they may argue in the alternative (or in addition) that an abortion prohibition gives a "preference" to a "religious societ[y]" or "denomination[]" because it reflects sectarian beliefs regarding when human life begins and the
sinfulness of abortion. Neither argument would likely prevail.

The Delaware Supreme Court has construed the "free exercise of worship"
and the "preference" language of art. I, § 1, consistently with the Free Exercise
and Establishment Clauses of the First Amendment.[14] Given that consistency

tution-art. I, § 5 (guaranteeing freedom of speech) and § 6 (prohibiting unreasonable searches
and seizures)-are discussed generally in Chapter 3, *supra*. The Delaware Constitution does
not contain express language guaranteeing equal protection of the law, nor has the Delaware
Supreme Court held that an equal protection guarantee is implicit in the Bill of Rights. *See
Hughes v. State*, 653 A.2d 241, 243 n. 3 (Del. 1994).

13. DEL. CONST. art. I, § 1 (2007).

14. *See East Lake Methodist Episcopal Church, Inc. v. Trustees of the Peninsula-Delaware Annual Conference of the United Methodist Church, Inc.*, 731 A.2d 798, 805 n. 2 (Del. 1999) (the
language of art. I, § 1, "enjoining 'nay magistrate ... in any case' from interfering with the free exercise of religious worship is of equal force" with the Free Exercise Clause of the First Amendment);
Newmark v. Williams, 588 A.2d 1108, 1112–13 & nn. 5–6 (Del. 1991) (considering the "preference" language of art. I, § 1, and the Establishment Clause of the First Amendment together).

of construction, a challenge to an abortion statute that would not succeed under the Religion Clauses of the First Amendment probably would not succeed under the "free exercise" or "preference" clauses of art. I, § 1, either. For the reasons set forth in Chapter 2, *supra*, an abortion statute could not be successfully challenged on First Amendment grounds. Accordingly, a similar challenge under art. I, § 1, would not likely be successful.

Remedy by Due Course of Law

Article I, § 9, of the Delaware Constitution provides, in part:

> All courts shall be open; and every person for an injury done him or her in his or her reputation, person, movable or immovable possessions, shall have remedy by the due course of the law, and justice administered according to the very right of the cause and the law of the land, without sale, denial, or unreasonable delay or expense.[15]

Abortion advocates might argue that a statute prohibiting abortion interferes with a woman's control over her own body, and that such interference constitutes an "injury" to her "person," as those terms are used in § 9, for which there must be a "remedy by the due course of law." That "remedy," in turn, would be invalidation of the statute. This argument assumes that art. I, § 9, confers substantive rights. The case law is clear, however, that it does not.

As is apparent from its text and structure, § 9 is concerned with *remedies* for injuries-it does not establish what *constitutes* an injury to anyone's "reputation, person, movable or immovable possessions." Those remedies, however, are derived from the common law and statutory law, not § 9. Moreover, the remedies themselves redress injuries recognized by the common law and statutory law, not constitutional "injuries." The language of art. I, § 9, that "every man for an injury done to him ... shall have remedy by the due course of law," the Delaware Supreme Court has explained, "does not require the courts to create a right of action unknown to the common law."[16] Indeed, even with respect to common law rights, the Legislature may limit or eliminate such rights so long as "this power [is] exercised in conformity with the dictates of due process."[17] "Thus, while no one has a vested interest in a rule of the common law, due process preserves a right of action which has accrued or vested be-

---

15. DEL. CONST. art. I, § 9 (2007).

16. *Alfree v. Alfree*, 410 A.2d 161, 163 (Del. 1979), *appeal dismissed*, 446 U.S. 931 (1980).

17. *Cheswold Volunteer Fire Co. v. Lambertson Construction Co.*, 489 A.2d 413, 418 (Del. 1984).

fore the effective date of the statute."[18] There was no common law "right" to abortion. In any event, §9 is concerned with the availability of private civil causes of action and reasonable access to the courts. It places no limitation on the State's power to define and punish crimes and has never been so interpreted.

Law of the Land (Due Process of Law)

Article I, §7, of the Delaware Constitution provides, in part, that no one "shall ... be deprived of life, liberty or property, unless by the judgment of his or her peers or by the law of the land."[19] The "law of the land" language of art. I, §7, means essentially the same as "due process of law."[20] In any state constitutional challenge to Delaware's pre-*Roe* abortion statutes (or any other statute prohibiting abortion the State may enact), abortion advocates are most likely to rely upon art. I, §7, arguing that the prohibition interferes with a woman's liberty in obtaining an abortion.[21] Such an argument probably would not prevail, however.

The "due process" clause of art. I, §7, has a substantive, as well as a procedural, component,[22] and "has 'substantially the same meaning' as the due process clause contained in its federal counterpart [referring to §1 of the Fourteenth Amendment]."[23] Accordingly, an argument might be made that the Delaware Supreme Court should recognize a *state* right to abortion corresponding to the *federal* right recognized in *Roe v. Wade* so long as *Roe* (as modified by *Casey*) has not been overruled. Whether the state supreme court would do so is uncertain because the Delaware Legislature has enacted little legislation regulating abortion, and such legislation as it has enacted is unlikely to be

---

18. *Id.*

19. DEL. CONST. art. I, §7 (2007).

20. *Opinion of the Justices*, 246 A.2d 90, 92 (Del. 1968).

21. To the extent that the language of art. I, §9, of the Delaware Constitution may be said to guarantee liberty interests, *see Cheswold Volunteer Fire Co.*, 489 A.2d at 416 ("terms 'due course of law' and 'law of the land' in ... Art. I, §9 are analogous to the term 'due process of law' in the Fourteenth Amendment"), it is subsumed in the discussion of art. I, §7, herein. It should be noted, however, that the Delaware Supreme Court has held that art. I, §9, does not provide a basis for "postulating broad liberty interest[s]." *Helman v. State*, 784 A.2d 1058, 1071 (Del. 2001).

22. *Tailor v. Becker*, 708 A.2d 626, 628 (Del. 1998).

23. *Helman*, 784 A.2d at 1070 (quoting *Opinion of the Justices*, 246 A.2d at 92). *See also Matter of Carolyn S.S.*, 498 A.2d 1095, 1098 (Del. 1984) (same); *Blinder, Robinson & Co., Inc. v. Bruton*, 552 A.2d 466, 472 (Del. 1989) ("[t]he due process protection of the Delaware Constitution is construed to be coextensive with the due process protection of the United States Constitution").

challenged. The state court's repeated holding that the state and federal due process clause have "substantially the same meaning," however, does suggest that the court would *not* recognize a state right to abortion if *Roe*, as modified by *Casey*, were overruled. Moreover, the court's refusal to recognize such a right would be consistent with its methodology for determining fundamental rights.[24]

In determining whether an asserted liberty interest (or right) should be regarded as "fundamental," the United States Supreme Court applies a two-prong test. First, there must be a "careful description" of the asserted fundamental liberty interest.[25] Second, the interest, so described, must be firmly rooted in "the Nation's history, legal traditions, and practices."[26] The Delaware Supreme Court employs the same test in evaluating state substantive due process claims.[27] A right to abortion cannot be regarded as "fundamental" under art. I, §7, because such a "right" is not firmly rooted in Delaware's "history, legal traditions, and practices."

Delaware enacted its first abortion statute in 1883, fourteen years before the present constitution was adopted.[28] Section 2 of the statute made it a felony

---

24. To the extent that the Delaware Supreme Court recognizes the same fundamental rights under the *state* due process guarantee as the Supreme Court does under the *federal* due process guarantee, abortion would not qualify as a "fundamental" right. Although the Supreme Court characterized the right to choose abortion as "fundamental" in *Roe*, 410 U.S. at 152–53, it tacitly abandoned that characterization in *Casey*, 505 U.S. at 869–79 (Joint Op. of O'Connor, Kennedy and Souter, JJ., replacing *Roe's* "strict scrutiny" standard of review with the more relaxed "undue burden" standard, allowing for a broader measure of abortion regulation).

25. *Washington v. Glucksberg*, 521 U.S. 702, 721 (1997) (citation and internal quotation marks omitted).

26. *Id.* at 710.

27. *Tailor v. Becker*, 708 A.2d at 628 (following *Glucksberg*). For example, the state supreme court has referred to " '[t]he fundamental liberty interest of natural parents in the care, custody, and management of their child....' " *Matter of Burns*, 519 A.2d 638, 645 (Del. 1986) (quoting *Santosky v. Kramer*, 455 U.S. 745, 753 (1982)). *See also Daber v. Div. of Child Protective Services*, 470 A.2d 723, 726 (Del. 1983) ("[f]ewer rights are more sacred than those which derive from the parent-child relationship"). Without relying upon the state constitution, the court has also recognized the right to refuse unwanted medical treatment. *Severns v. Wilmington Medical Center, Inc.*, 421 A.2d 1334, 1344 (Del. 1980). Both the right of parents to the "care, custody, and management of their child," and the right to refuse unwanted medical treatment have long been recognized in English and American common law. *See Wisconsin v. Yoder*, 406 U.S. 205, 232 (1972) (parental rights); *Cruzan v. Director, Missouri Dep't of Health*, 497 U.S. 261, 278–79 & n. 7 (1990) (right to refuse unwanted medical treatment); *Washington v. Glucksberg*, 521 U.S. 702, 719–26 & n. 17 (1997) (same).

28. An Act of Feb. 13, 1883, 17 Del. Laws, ch. 226.

to perform an abortion upon a pregnant woman at any stage of pregnancy by any means "unless the same be necessary to preserve her life...."[29] This statute remained on the books, essentially unchanged, until it was repealed in 1969 and replaced with the statutes based on the Model Penal Code.[30]

In an early case decided under the 1883 statute, the Delaware Court of General Sessions referred to the crime prohibited by § 2 thereof as the "unlawful destruction ... of the foetus or unborn offspring of a pregnant woman, at any time before birth according to the course of nature."[31] More than fifty years later, the Delaware Supreme Court noted that the crime of abortion was properly classified among "offenses against the lives and persons of individuals."[32] And, as late as 1960, the state supreme court affirmed a conviction for abortion, without any hint that the prosecution or conviction was barred by the state constitution.[33] Following the Supreme Court's decision in *Roe v. Wade*, the Delaware Legislature enacted legislation mandating informed consent and a twenty-four hour waiting period,[34] requiring parental notice (subject to numerous exceptions)[35] and recognizing individual and institutional rights of conscience.[36]

Delaware recognizes the rights of unborn children in several areas outside of abortion, including tort law, health care law and property law. In tort law, a statutory cause of action for wrongful death may be brought on behalf of an unborn child who was viable (capable of sustained survival outside the mother's womb, with or without medical assistance) at the time of its death.[37] A common law cause of action for (nonlethal) prenatal injuries may be brought on behalf of a viable unborn child.[38] And the Delaware Supreme Court has re-

---

29. *Id.*, ch. 226, § 2. Section 1 prohibited the advertising of abortion services.

30. 17 Del. Laws, ch. 226, § 2, *codified at* Del. Rev. Code § 4171 (1915), *recodified at* DEL. REV. CODE § 5171 (1935), *recodified at* DEL. CODE ANN. tit. 11, § 301 (1953), *repealed by* 57 Del. Laws, ch. 161, § 1 (eff. June 19, 1969). The statute prohibiting self-abortion (or soliciting an abortion) was repealed at the same time. *Id.*, ch 161, § 2.

31. *State v. Magnell*, 51 A. 606, 606 (Del. Ct. Gen. Sess. 1901).

32. *Scott v. State*, 117 A.2d 830, 835–36 (Del. 1955).

33. *Zatz. v. State*, 160 A.2d 727 (Del. 1960).

34. DEL. CODE ANN. tit. 24, § 1794 (2005).

35. *Id.* tit. 24, § 1780 *et seq.*

36. *Id.* tit. 24, § 1791. Delaware also limits public funding of abortions for indigent women to those circumstances for which federal reimbursement is available (currently, life-of-the mother, rape and incest). *See* Delaware State Medicaid Manual, Practitioner Provider Policy 2.7 (March 21, 2006).

37. *Luff v. Hawkins*, 551 A.2d 437, 438 n. 1 (Del. Super. Ct. 1988); *Worgan v. Greggo & Ferrara, Inc.*, 128 A.2d 557 (Del. Super. Ct. 1956), interpreting DEL. CODE ANN. tit. 10, § 3721 *et seq.* (1999 & Supp. 2006).

38. *Worgan*, 128 A.2d at 558 (by implication).

fused to recognize a cause of action for "wrongful life" because of the "impossible task of identifying damages based on a comparison between life in the child's impaired state and nonexistence."[39]

In health care law, a life-sustaining procedure may not be withheld or withdrawn from a patient known to be pregnant under an advance health-care directive, "so long as it is probable that the fetus will develop to be viable outside the uterus with the continued application of a life-sustaining procedure."[40]

In property law, a posthumous child (a child conceived before, but born after, the death of a parent) may inherit from a deceased parent who dies without a will if the child is born alive.[41] And, subject to certain exceptions, a child who is born after a parent executes a will, and who is not otherwise provided for in the will, may receive that share he or she would have received if the parent had died without a will.[42]

In light of the history of abortion regulation in Delaware, the Delaware Supreme Court's implicit recognition in *Scott v. State* that the 1883 abortion statute was intended to protect unborn children and the rights extended to unborn children outside the area of abortion, it cannot plausibly be said that the liberty clause of art. I, §7, of the Delaware Constitution confers a fundamental right to abortion.[43] More generally, a right to abortion cannot be found in the text or structure of the Delaware Constitution. There is no evidence that

---

39. *Garrison v. Medical Center of Delaware, Inc.*, 581 A.2d 288, 293 (Del. 1990). A "wrongful life" cause of action is a claim brought on behalf of a child who is born with a physical or mental disability or disease that could have been discovered before the child's birth by genetic testing, amniocentesis or other medical screening. The gravamen of the cause of action is that, as a result of a physician's failure to inform the child's parents of the child's disability or disease (or at least of the availability of tests to determine the presence of the disability or disease), they were deprived of the opportunity to abort the child, thus resulting in the birth of a child suffering permanent physical or mental impairment. The Delaware Supreme Court has recognized wrongful birth actions, however. *Garrison*, 581 A.2d at 290–93. A "wrongful birth" cause of action is a claim based upon the same facts, brought by the parents of the impaired child on their own behalf.

40. DEL. CODE ANN. tit. 16, §2503(j) (2003).

41. *Id.* tit. 12, §505 (2007).

42. *Id.* tit. 12, §§301, 310.

43. Apart from fundamental rights, the test for the constitutionality of legislation under art. I, §7, of the Delaware Constitution is "whether the end result and the method adopted bear a reasonable relation to the public health, safety, morals or general welfare." *Glendon v. State*, 461 A.2d 1004, 1006 (Del. 1983) (rejecting state and federal due process challenge to statute prohibiting the fraudulent delivery of a non-controlled substance). Moreover, "[a]ll doubts are resolved in favor of the challenged statute." *Id.* A statute prohibiting abortion would bear a "reasonable relation" to the State's legitimate interest in protecting unborn human life.

the framers of the Delaware Constitution of 1897 intended the Bill of Rights to limit the Legislature's authority to prohibit abortion.[44] Such an intent would have been remarkable in light of the contemporaneous prohibition of abortion except to save the life of the pregnant woman.

Conclusion

Based on the foregoing analysis, an argument that the Delaware Constitution protects a right to abortion that is separate from, and independent of, the right to abortion recognized in *Roe v. Wade* would not likely succeed. That, in turn, suggests that if *Roe*, as modified by *Casey*, is ultimately overruled, the State of Delaware could enforce its pre-*Roe* statutes *prohibiting* abortion (subject to the exceptions provided therein) or enact and enforce new statutes prohibiting abortion. Moreover, nothing in the Delaware Constitution precludes Delaware from *regulating* abortion within federal constitutional limits in the meantime.

---

44. *See* 4 DEBATES & PROCEEDINGS OF THE CONSTITUTIONAL CONVENTION OF THE STATE OF DELAWARE, COMMENCING DEC. 1, 1896, 2382–84 (Report of the Committee on the Bill of Rights); 2385–91 (debate on Bill of Rights in the Committee of the Whole); 2710–13 (debate on Bill of Rights in Convention).

CHAPTER 12

FLORIDA

Summary

As the result of a series of Florida Supreme Court decisions interpreting the Florida Constitution, the State of Florida could not prohibit any abortion before viability, or any abortion after viability that would be necessary to preserve the pregnant woman's life or health, even if *Roe v. Wade*,[1] as modified by *Planned Parenthood of Southeastern Pennsylvania v. Casey*,[2] were overruled, unless the state constitution is amended to overturn those decisions (or those decisions are overruled). The State's authority under the state constitution to regulate abortion within current federal constitutional limits is mixed.

Analysis

The pre-*Roe* abortion statute was based on §230.3 of the Model Penal Code.[3] The statute provided that an abortion could be performed at any stage of pregnancy when "continuation of the pregnancy would substantially impair the life or health of the female," there was "substantial risk that the continuation of the pregnancy would result in the birth of a child with a serious physical or mental defect," or there was "reasonable cause to believe that the pregnancy resulted from rape or incest."[4] The law was repealed in 1979.[5]

---

1. 410 U.S. 113 (1973).

2. 505 U.S. 833 (1992).

3. 1972 Fla. Laws 608, ch. 72-196. The complete text of §230.3 of the Model Penal Code is set out in Appendix B to the Supreme Court's decision in *Doe v. Bolton*, 410 U.S. 179, 205–07 (1973). The statute was enacted in response to a decision of the Florida Supreme Court the same year striking down, on vagueness grounds, older statutes that prohibited abortion unless the procedure was necessary to preserve the life of the pregnant woman. *State v. Barquet*, 262 So.2d 431 (Fla. 1972), invalidating FLA. STAT. ANN. §§782.10, 791.10 (West 1965).

4. 1972 Fla. Laws 608, ch. 72-196, §2.

5. 1979 Fla. Laws 1618, ch. 79-302, §5.

In light of the Florida Supreme Court's post-*Roe* abortion jurisprudence, it is unlikely that the state supreme court would uphold any statute prohibiting abortion, at least before viability, even if *Roe*, as modified by *Casey*, were overruled. The court's record on statutes regulating abortion and restricting public funding of abortion is more mixed.

In *In re T.W.*,[6] the Florida Supreme Court declared the state parental consent statute (which contained a judicial bypass mechanism)[7] unconstitutional under the state guarantee of privacy. Article I, §23, of the Florida Constitution provides, in part: "Every natural person has the right to be let alone and free from governmental intrusion into his private life...."[8]

Section 23, which was "intentionally phrased in strong terms," creates a right of privacy "much broader in scope than that of the Federal Constitution."[9] As a "fundamental right," the right of privacy "demands the compelling state interest standard."[10] The State can meet its burden of intruding upon privacy only if "the challenged regulation serves a compelling state interest and accomplishes its goal through the use of the least intrusive means."[11] In *In re T.W.*, the Florida Supreme Court observed that "this is a highly stringent standard," which "no [challenged] government intrusion in ... personal decisionmaking ... has survived."[12]

The privacy provision is "clearly implicated in a woman's decision of whether or not to continue her pregnancy."[13] "We can conceive of few more personal or private decisions concerning one's body that one can make in the course of a lifetime," the court commented, "except perhaps the decision of the terminally ill in their choice of whether to discontinue necessary medical treatment."[14] The court concluded that "this freedom of choice ... extends to minors" because §23 applies to "[e]very natural person," and minors are "natural persons in the eyes of the law."[15] The rights of minors, however, are not absolute and must be weighed against the interests of the State in maternal health and "the potentiality of life in the fetus.[16]

---

6. 551 So.2d 1186 (Fla. 1989).

7. FLA. STAT. ANN. §390.001(4)(a) (West 1986).

8. FLA. CONST. art. I, §23 (West 2004).

9. *Winfield v. Division of Pari-Mutuel Wagering*, 477 So.2d 544, 548 (Fla. 1985).

10. *Id.* at 547.

11. *Id.*

12. 551 So.2d at 1192.

13. *Id.*

14. *Id.* Later in its opinion, the court reaffirmed its determination that "a woman's right to decide whether or not to continue her pregnancy constitutes a fundamental constitutional right...." *Id.* at 1196.

15. *Id.* at 1193.

16. *Id.*

Adopting the reasoning of *Roe v. Wade*, the Florida Supreme Court determined that the former interest (maternal health) becomes compelling at the end of the first trimester of pregnancy, and the latter at viability.[17] Prior to the end of the first trimester, "no interest in maternal health could be served by significantly restricting the manner in which abortions are performed by qualified doctors."[18] Subsequent to that stage of pregnancy, "the [S]tate may impose significant restrictions only in the least intrusive manner designed to safeguard the health of the mother."[19] The court found that, before viability, "the fetus is a highly specialized set of cells that is entirely dependent upon the mother for sustenance," and concluded that the mother and the fetus "are so inextricably intertwined that their interests can be said to coincide."[20] After viability, however, "the [S]tate may protect its interest in the potentiality of life by regulating abortion, provided that the mother's health is not jeopardized."[21]

The supreme court determined that the parental consent statute could not be justified under either of the foregoing interests "because it intrudes upon the privacy of the pregnant minor from conception to birth. Such a substantial invasion of a pregnant female's privacy by the [S]tate for the full term of the pregnancy is not necessary for the preservation of maternal health or the potentiality of life."[22] The court acknowledged that "where parental rights over a minor child are concerned, society has recognized additional state interests- protection of the immature minor and preservation of the family unit."[23] Neither interest, however, is "sufficiently compelling under Florida law to override Florida's privacy amendment."[24] The court noted that where procedures other than abortion are concerned, Florida law does not require parental consent of an unwed pregnant minor.[25]

> In light of this wide authority that the [S]tate grants an unwed mother
> to make life-or-death decisions concerning herself or an existing child
> without parental consent, we are unable to discern a special com-

---

17. *Id.*

18. *Id.*

19. *Id.*

20. *Id.* Notwithstanding the court's equation of the mother's interests with those of the unborn child, it is doubtful that the mother's decision to abort her unborn child before viability could be said, in any meaningful sense, to "coincide[]" with the interests of the child.

21. *Id.* at 1194.

22. *Id.*

23. *Id.*

24. *Id.*

25. *Id.* at 1195 (citing Fla. Stat. Ann. §743.965 (West 2005)) (authorizing unwed pregnant minor or minor mother to consent to medical services for the minor or the minor's child).

pelling interest on the part of the [S]tate under Florida law in protecting the minor only where abortion is concerned. We fail to see the qualitative difference in terms of impact on the well-being of the minor between allowing the life of an existing child to come to an end and terminating a pregnancy, or between undergoing a highly dangerous medical procedure on oneself and undergoing a far less dangerous procedure to end one's pregnancy. If any qualitative difference exists, it certainly is insufficient in terms of state interest.[26]

The supreme court did not question that the State has an interest in protecting minors, but said that "the selective approach employed by the legislature evidences the limited nature of the ... interest being furthered by these provisions."[27] The court noted in this respect that the state adoption act does not require parental consent before a minor may place her child for adoption, "even though this decision clearly is fraught with intense emotional and societal consequences."[28]

The court held further that the parental consent statute failed the second prong of the *Winfield* test, *i.e.*, that the restriction is not "the least intrusive means of furthering the state interest."[29] The statute was defective for not providing the procedural safeguards of appointed counsel or a record hearing, and for not making any exceptions for emergency or therapeutic abortions.[30] In light of the foregoing, the court declared the parental consent statute unconstitutional, expressly basing its decision on state law grounds.[31]

What are the implications of the opinion in *In re T.W.* for abortion legislation in Florida? The court held that a woman's right to decide whether or not to continue her pregnancy constitutes a fundamental constitutional right protected by the right of privacy guarantee of the state constitution.[32] The court held further that the State's interest in the "potentiality of life" of the unborn child arises only after viability.[33] Regulation is permitted at that stage of pregnancy, "provided that the mother's health is not jeopardized."[34]

---

26. *Id.*

27. *Id.*

28. *Id.* (citing FLA. STAT. ANN. ch. 63 (West 2005)).

29. *Id.*

30. *Id.*

31. *Id.*

32. *Id.* at 1192, 1196.

33. *Id.* at 1193–94.

34. *Id.* at 1194. The Supreme Court has not yet decided whether a statute prohibiting post-viability abortions must make exceptions for mental, as well as physical, health. *See Voinovich v. Women's Medical Professional Corporation*, 523 U.S. 1036, 1039 (1998) (Thomas, J., dissenting from denial of *certiorari*) (noting that this issue was not addressed in *Doe v.*

In the absence of a state constitutional amendment, the State may not prohibit any pre-viability abortion. The State may prohibit an abortion performed after viability only if the statute contains exceptions for those circumstances in which an abortion is necessary to preserve the pregnant woman's life or health.

The Florida Supreme Court revisited the issue of parental involvement statutes in *North Florida Women's Health & Counseling Services, Inc. v. State*.[35] In that case, a majority of the state supreme court, relying upon the court's earlier decision in *In re T.W.*,[36] struck down a parental notice statute, which also contained a judicial bypass mechanism.[37]

The Florida Supreme Court has decided two other abortion cases and declined to review a third, none of which limited the scope of the *T.W.* opinion or the right to an abortion under the Florida Constitution. In *Renee B. v. Florida Agency for Health Care Administration*,[38] the supreme court rejected a state privacy challenge to state restrictions on public funding of abortion. In the course of its opinion, the court, citing *In re T.W.* held that "[t]he right of privacy in the Florida Constitution protects a woman's right to choose an abortion."[39] In *State v. Presidential Women's Center*,[40] the court upheld certain provisions of the Florida "Women's Right to Know Act."[41] Two years earlier, the supreme court denied a petition to review a decision of the district court of appeal rejecting an equal protection challenge to the State's restrictions on public funding of abortion.[42]

Bolton, 410 U.S. 179 (1973), the companion case to *Roe v. Wade*). As a result, it is not known whether, as a matter of *state* constitutional law, the Florida Supreme Court would require a post-viability statute to contain a mental health exception. Under current state law, an abortion may be performed after the twenty-fourth week of gestation if the procedure is necessary to save the life or preserve the health of the pregnant woman. FLA. STAT. ANN. §§ 390.011(8), 390.0111(1) (West 2007). The statutes do not define the scope of the health exception.

35. 866 So.2d 612 (Fla. 2003).

36. *Id.* at 620–22, 634–39.

37. FLA. STAT. ANN. § 390.01115 (West 2002). In response to the decision, the Florida Legislature proposed and the people of the State of Florida approved an amendment to the Florida Constitution expressly recognizing the Legislature's authority to enact a parental notice statute. *See* FLA. CONST. art. X, § 22 (West Supp. 2007). The amendment, however, does not otherwise affect the Florida Supreme Court's abortion jurisprudence.

38. 790 So.2d 1036 (Fla. 2001).

39. *Id.* at 1041.

40. 937 So.2d 114 (Fla. 2006).

41. FLA. STAT. ANN. § 390.0111(3)(a)(1) (West 2007).

42. *A Choice for Women, Inc. v. Florida Agency for Health Care Administration*, 872 So.2d 970 (Fla. Dist. Ct. App. 2004), *review denied*, 885 So.2d 386 (Fla. 2004).

Conclusion

Because of the Florida Supreme Court's decision in *In re T.W.*, the State of Florida would have no authority to prohibit abortions, at least before viability, even if *Roe*, as modified by *Casey*, were overruled, unless the state constitution is amended to overturn the holding in *In re T.W.* (or the latter is overruled). The State's authority to regulate abortion within current federal constitutional limits is mixed.

CHAPTER 13

GEORGIA

Summary

The Georgia Supreme Court has not yet decided whether the Georgia Constitution protects a right to abortion separate from, and independent of, the right to abortion recognized under the United States Constitution.[1] A careful examination of the state constitution, in light of its history and interpretation, as well as other relevant legal sources, however, suggests that the state supreme court probably would not recognize a state constitutional right to abortion. Thus, if *Roe v. Wade*,[2] as modified by *Planned Parenthood of Southeastern Pennsylvania v. Casey*,[3] were overruled, Georgia could enact and enforce a statute prohibiting abortion. Moreover, nothing in the state constitution, properly understood, precludes the State from enacting and enforcing reasonable measures regulating abortion within current federal constitutional limits.

Analysis

The pre-*Roe* Georgia abortion statute was based on § 230.3 of the Model Penal Code.[4] Under the statute, an abortion could not be performed unless

---

1. The Georgia Supreme Court has referred to the right to abortion solely as a matter of *federal*, not *state*, constitutional law. *See, e.g.*, *Etkind v. Suarez*, 519 S.E.2d 210, 212 (Ga. 1999); *Atlanta Obstetrics & Gynecology Group v. Abelson*, 398 S.E.2d 557, 561 (Ga. 1990) ("a woman has been recognized, under *Roe v. Wade*, ... to have a constitutional right to make an informed decision regarding the procreative options available to her") (citation and internal quotation marks omitted).

2. 410 U.S. 113 (1973).

3. 505 U.S. 833 (1992).

4. GA. CODE ANN. § 26-1201 *et seq.* (1972). The complete text of § 230.3 of the Model Penal Code is set out in Appendix B to the Supreme Court's decision in *Doe v. Bolton*, 410 U.S. 179, 205–07 (1973).

"continuation of the pregnancy would endanger the life of the pregnant woman or would seriously and permanently injure her health," the "fetus would very likely be born with a grave, permanent, and irremediable mental or physical defect," or the pregnancy resulted from forcible or statutory rape.[5] The statute did not place any express limits on the stage of pregnancy at which an authorized abortion could be performed. Major provisions of the statute were declared unconstitutional (on federal constitutional grounds) by a three-judge federal district court in *Doe v. Bolton*,[6] whose decision was affirmed, as modified, by the Supreme Court in the companion case to *Roe v. Wade*.[7] The statute was repealed in 1973.[8]

Based upon arguments that have been raised in Georgia and other States with similar constitutional provisions,[9] possible sources for an asserted abortion right could include provisions of the Bill of Rights guaranteeing due process of law (art. 1, §I, ¶I), equal protection (¶II), freedom of conscience (¶III),

---

5. *Id.* §§26-1202(a)(1), -(2), -(3). The law imposed other conditions. The abortion had to be performed in licensed and accredited hospital and had to be approved in advance by a majority vote of a medical and staff committee of the hospital. *Id.* §§26-1202(b)(4), -(5). In addition to the attending physician, two other physicians had to certify in writing that, based upon their separate personal examination of the pregnant woman, the abortion was, in their judgment, necessary because of one of the reasons specified in §26-1202(a). *Id.* §1202(b)(3). If the abortion was sought because the pregnancy resulted from rape, the rape had to be reported in writing under oath to a local law enforcement officer or agency and both a certified copy of the police report and a written statement by the solicitor general for the judicial circuit where the rape occurred (or allegedly occurred) that there was probable cause to believe that the rape had occurred had to be completed. *Id.* §26-1202(b)(6). The woman upon whom the abortion was performed had to certify in writing under oath that she was a bona fide resident of the State., *id.* §26-1202(b)(1), and the attending physician had to certify in writing that he believed that the woman was a bona fide resident of the State. *Id.* §26-1202(b)(2). The law also allowed the solicitor general of the judicial circuit in which an abortion was to be performed and any person who would be a relative of the child within the second degree of consanguinity to petition the superior court of the county in which the abortion was to be performed for a declaratory judgment to determine whether the performance of the abortion would violate the constitutional or other legal rights of the fetus. *Id.* §26-1202(c).

6. 319 F. Supp. 1048 (N.D. Ga. 1970).

7. 410 U.S. 179 (1973).

8. Ga. Laws No. 328, §1 (1973): Vol. I Ga. Acts & Resolutions 635, 636–37 (1973).

9. In *Feminist Women's Health Center v. Burgess*, 651 So.2d 36 (Ga. 2007), the Georgia Supreme Court reversed an order dismissing, for lack of standing and failure to exhaust administrative remedies, a complaint challenging, on state constitutional grounds, regulations restricting public funding of abortion. On remand, the plaintiffs dismissed their complaint without prejudice. *Feminist Women's Health Center v. Burgess*, Civ. Action File No. 2003-CV-78487, April 16, 2008 (Fulton County Superior Court).

and freedom of religion (¶ IV); and recognizing inherent rights (¶ XXIX).[10] The analysis that follows addresses each of these provisions.

Due Process of Law

Art. 1, § 1, ¶ 1, of the Georgia Constitution provides: "No person shall be deprived of life, liberty, or property except by due process of law."[11] In any state constitutional challenge to an abortion statute Georgia may enact if *Roe*, as modified by *Casey*, is overruled, abortion advocates are most likely to rely upon art. 1, § I, ¶ I. Such reliance probably would be misplaced.

More than one hundred years ago, the Georgia Supreme Court interpreted the state due process clause to confer a fundamental right of privacy.[12] That right has been broadly construed by the state supreme court to allow a quadriplegic to refuse unwanted life-sustaining medical treatment;[13] to prohibit correctional officials from force-feeding an inmate on a hunger strike;[14] to protect medical records from unauthorized disclosure without notice to the patient;[15] to bar prosecution of private, noncommercial acts of sodomy between consenting adults;[16] and to bar prosecution of minors for fornication where the minors could legally consent to acts of sexual intercourse.[17]

---

10. Three other more unlikely sources of an abortion right under the Georgia Constitution-art. 1, §I, ¶V (guaranteeing freedom of speech), ¶XIII (prohibiting unreasonable searches and seizures) and ¶XXII (prohibiting involuntary servitude)-are discussed generally in Chapter 3, *supra*.

11. GA. CONST. art. 1, §I, ¶I (2007).

12. *Pavesich v. New England Life Ins. Co.*, 50 S.E. 68, 79 (Ga. 1905) (publishing a person's picture in an advertisement without his consent violates his right to privacy).

13. *State v. McAfee*, 385 S.E.2d 651 (Ga. 1989).

14. *Zant v. Prevatte*, 286 S.E.2d 715 (Ga. 1982).

15. *King v. State*, 535 S.E.2d 492 (Ga. 2000). *But see King v. State*, 577 S.E.2d 764 (Ga. 2003) (the right of privacy does not require the State to give the target of a search warrant an opportunity to be heard before the State obtains private medical records).

16. *Powell v. State*, 510 S.E.2d 18 (Ga. 1998). *See also State v. Eastwood*, 535 S.E.2d 246 (Ga. Ct. App. 2000) (public school teacher could not be convicted of sodomy for engaging in consensual, unforced, private and noncommercial acts of sodomy with a student who was of legal age to consent to those acts). *But see Odett v. State*, 541 S.E.2d 29, 30 (Ga. 2001) ("*Powell* did not hold that the right to privacy protects sodomy generally") (upholding convictions for aggravated child molestation and child molestation); *Widner v. State*, 630 S.E.2d 675, 678 (Ga. 2006) (same); *Howard v. State*, 527 S.E.2d 194, 195–96 (Ga. 2000) (upholding conviction for solicitation of sodomy).

17. *In re J.M.*, 575 S.E.2d 441, 444 (Ga. 2003) ("the government may not reach into the bedroom of a private residence and criminalize the private, non-commercial, consensual sexual acts of the persons legally capable of consenting to those acts").

The state right of privacy has been given a broad construction, but it is subject to an important qualification. Conduct is *not* protected by the right of privacy if it "interfere[s] with the rights of another or of the public."[18] In *McAfee*, which involved a quadriplegic who wished to stop being maintained on a ventilator, the state supreme stated: "We note that we do not have before us a case where the state's interest is in preserving the life of an innocent third party, *such as the unborn child of a woman who wishes to refuse medical treatment.*"[19]

Taken together, the Georgia Supreme Court's opinions in *Pavesich*, *McAfee*, *Powell* and *In re J.M.* stand for the proposition that the state right of privacy ends where the rights of third parties, including unborn children, begin. And the State of Georgia has long recognized those rights in both statutory and case law.

Georgia enacted its first abortion statute in 1876. One section of the statute prohibited the use of any medical or surgical means upon a pregnant woman "with the intent thereby to destroy [the unborn] child, unless the same shall have been necessary to preserve the life of such mother, or shall have been advised by two physicians to be necessary for that purpose."[20] This section classified the offense as "assault with intent to murder," if either the unborn child or the mother resulted.[21] Another section of the statute prohibited the use of any means upon a pregnant woman "with the intent thereby to procure the miscarriage or abortion of any such mother," a misdemeanor.[22] A third section of the statute prohibited "the wilful killing of an unborn child, so far developed to be ordinarily called 'quick,' by any injury to the mother of such child, which would be murder if it resulted in the death of such mother," and classified the offense as a felony, "punishable by death or imprisonment for life...."[23] These statutes, amended from time to time, remained on the books

---

18. *Pavesich*, 50 S.E at 70. *See also Powell*, 510 S.E.2d at 22 (citing *Pavesich*); *In re J.M.*, 575 S.E.2d at 443 ("Georgia's right to privacy means that citizens have a fundamental constitutional right to 'be let alone,' provided [that] they are not interfering with the rights of other individuals or of the public").

19. *McAfee*, 385 S.E.2d at 652 (emphasis added) (citing *Jefferson v. Griffin Spalding County Hospital Authority*, 274 S.E.2d 457 (Ga. 1981)). *Jefferson* is discussed in the next section of this analysis, *infra*.

20. Ga. Laws No CXXX, §II (1876).

21. *Id.*

22. *Id.* No. CXXX, §III. The Georgia Supreme Court later interpreted §II to apply to a "quick" child, and §III to apply to a child who was not "quick." *Passley v. State*, 21 S.E.2d 230, 232 (Ga. 1942). A "quick" child meant a child who had "quickened." "Quickening" is that stage of pregnancy, usually sixteen to eighteen weeks gestation, when the woman first detects fetal movement.

23. Ga. Laws No. CXXX, §I (1876).

until Georgia enacted its abortion statute based on § 230.3 of the Model Penal Code.[24]

Prior to *Roe*, the Georgia reviewing courts regularly affirmed abortion convictions and homicide convictions (based upon the death of the pregnant woman as the result of an illegal abortion) without any hint that the prosecutions or convictions were precluded by the Georgia Constitution.[25] In *Passley v. State*,[26] the Georgia Supreme Court stated that it was "evident" that in enacting the original abortion statute in 1876 "the legislature was undertaking to provide by penal law appropriate penalties for the destruction of an unborn child."[27] In 1969, the Georgia Court of Appeals confirmed that "the protection of the unborn child and society," as well as "the protection of the woman," were "valid purposes of the [abortion] statute."[28] Subsequent to *Roe*, Georgia enacted a comprehensive scheme of abortion regulation.[29]

Georgia has recognized the rights of unborn children in a variety of contexts outside of abortion, including criminal law, tort law, health care law and property law. In criminal law, the killing of an unborn child, other than in an abor-

---

24. Ga. Laws, No. CXXX, §§ I, II, III (1876), *codified at* GA. CODE §§ 4337(a), -(b), -(c) (1882), *recodified at* GA. PENAL CODE §§ 80, 81, 82 (1895), *recodified at* GA. CODE §§ 26-1101, 26-1102, 26-1103 (1933), *carried forward as* GA. CODE ANN. §§ 26-1101, 26-1102, 26-1103 (1953), *amended by* 1968 Ga. Laws 1249, 1277 (1968). *See also* nn. 4–8 and accompanying text, *supra*.

25. *Sullivan v. State*, 48 S.E. 949 (Ga. 1904); *Barrow v. State*, 48 S.E. 950 (Ga. 1904); *Gullatt v. State*, 80 S.E. 340 (Ga. Ct. App. 1913); *Summerlin v. State*, 103 S.E. 461 (Ga. 1920); *Guiffrida v. State*, 7 S.E.2d 34 (Ga. Ct. App. 1940); *Soldaat v. State*, 57 S.E.2d 705 (Ga. Ct. App. 1950); *Biegun v. State*, 7 S.E.2d 34 (Ga. Ct. App. 1950); *Holloway v. State*, 82 S.E.2d 235 (Ga. Ct. App. 1954).

26. 21 S.E.2d 230 (Ga. 1942).

27. *Id.* at 232.

28. *Gaines v. Wolcott*, 167 S.E.2d 366, 369 (Ga. Ct. App. 1969), *aff'd* 169 S.E.2d 165 (Ga. 1969).

29. GA. CODE ANN. § 16-12-141 (2007) (adopting trimester framework of abortion regulation); § 31-9A-1 *et seq.* (2006 & Supp. 2007) (mandating informed consent and a twenty-four hour waiting period); § 15-11-110 *et seq.* (2005) (requiring parental notice and twenty-four hours actual notice or forty-eight hours constructive notice); § 16-12-142 (2007) (recognizing individual and institutional rights of conscience); § 16-12-144 (2007) (prohibiting partial birth abortion). *See also* Division of Medical Assistance, Georgia Dep't of Community Health, *Policies and Procedures for Physician Services*, § 9.04.2 (July 2004); *Policies and Procedures for Hospital Services*, § 911.1 (July 1, 2004); *Policies and Procedures for Family Planning Clinic Services*, § 903 (limiting public funding of abortion for indigent women to those circumstances for which federal reimbursement is available, currently life-of-the-mother, rape and incest).

tion, may be prosecuted as feticide.[30] An assault or battery of an unborn child may also be prosecuted as a distinct criminal offense.[31] And a woman convicted of a capital offense may not be executed while she is pregnant.[32]

In tort law, a statutory cause of action for wrongful death may be brought on behalf of an unborn child who was "quick" at the time of its death.[33] A common law action for (nonlethal) prenatal injuries may be brought without regard to the stage of pregnancy when the injuries were inflicted.[34] And the Georgia reviewing courts have refused to recognize wrongful birth and wrongful life causes of action.[35]

Under Georgia's health care statute, an advance directive (a living will or a durable power of attorney for health care) may not authorize the withholding or withdrawal of life-sustaining procedures from a woman who is pregnant

---

30. GA. CODE ANN. §§ 16-5-80 (2007) (feticide), 40.6-393.1 (2007) (feticide by vehicle), 52-7-12.3 (Supp. 2007) (feticide by vessel). The feticide statutes apply to the killing of an unborn child *in utero*. If the child is born alive, then dies as the result of prenatal injuries caused by criminal agency, the person who caused the injuries causing death may be prosecuted under the homicide statutes, regardless of when the injuries were inflicted. *State v. Hammett*, 384 S.E.2d 220, 221 (Ga. Ct. App. 1989).

31. GA. CODE ANN. §§ 16-5-28 (2007) (assault), 16-5-29 (2007) (battery).

32. *Id.* §§ 17-10-34, 17-10-39 (2004).

33. *Porter v. Lassiter*, 87 S.E.2d 100 (Ga. Ct. App. 1955), interpreting what is now codified at GA. CODE ANN. § 19-7-1 (Supp. 2007). *See also Shirley v. Bacon*, 267 S.E.2d 809, 810–11 (Ga. Ct. App. 1980) (following *Porter*). For purposes of applying this rule a "quick" unborn child refers to the stage in pregnancy when the fetus "is able to move in its mother's womb." *Porter*, 87 S.E.2d at 103.

34. *Hornbuckle v. Plantation Pipe Line Co.*, 93 S.E.2d 727, 728 (Ga. 1956) ("[i]f a child born after an injury sustained at any period of its prenatal life can prove the effect on it of a tort, it would have a right to recover"). *See also McAuley v. Wills*, 303 S.E.2d 258, 260 (Ga. 1983) (citing *Hornbuckle* with approval).

35. *Atlanta Obstetrics & Gynecology Group v. Abelson*, 398 S.E.2d at 558–63 (expressly rejecting wrongful birth actions and implicitly rejecting wrongful life actions); *Etkind v. Suarez*, 519 S.E.2d 210 (Ga. 1999) (following *Abelson*); *Spires v. Kim*, 416 S.E.2d 780, 781–82 (Ga. Ct. App. 1992) (rejecting wrongful life actions on authority of *Abelson*). A "wrongful life" cause of action is a claim brought on behalf of a child who is born with a physical or mental disability or disease that could have been discovered before the child's birth by genetic testing, amniocentesis or other medical screening. The gravamen of the cause of action is that, as a result of a physician's failure to inform the child's parents of the child's disability or disease (or at least of the availability of tests to determine the presence of the disability or disease), they were deprived of the opportunity to abort the child, thus resulting in the birth of a child suffering permanent physical or mental impairment. A "wrongful birth" cause of action is a claim based upon the same facts, brought by the parents of the impaired child on their own behalf.

with a viable unborn child.[36] And an advance directive may not authorize the performance of an abortion.[37]

In property law, a posthumous child (the child of a decedent conceived before but born after his or her death) may inherit from an intestate (a person who dies without a will) if the child lives for at least 120 hours (five days) after birth.[38] And an afterborn child (a child conceived before the death of a parent but born after the parent executes a will) receives that share of the parent's estate that he or she would have received if the parent had died without a will.[39]

In light of the foregoing authorities, the Georgia Court of Appeals concluded that "Georgia cases show a clear tendency toward placing a high premium on human life, and an unmistakable willingness to recognize a fetus as a person at a time prior to actual delivery."[40]

A right to abortion cannot be found in the text or structure of the Georgia Constitution. There is no evidence that the framers or ratifiers of the state constitution intended to limit the Legislature's authority to prohibit abortion. Recognition of an abortion right would be manifestly inconsistent with the history and traditions of the State, as well as with the precedents of the Georgia Supreme Court. Taken together, these factors militate against recognition of a right to abortion under the due process guarantee of the Georgia Constitution.

Freedom of Conscience, Freedom of Religion

Article 1, §I, ¶III, of the Georgia Constitution provides: "Each person has the natural and inalienable right to worship God, each according to the dictates of that person's own conscience; and no human authority should, in any case, control or interfere with such right of conscience."[41] Article 1, §I, ¶IV, provides:

---

36. GA. CODE ANN. §31-32-4 (Form, Part Two, ¶(9)) (Supp. 2007).
37. *Id.* §31-32-14(b).
38. *Id.* §53-2-1(b)(1) (Supp. 2007).
39. *Id.* §53-4-48.
40. *Gulf Life Ins. Co. v. Brown*, 351 S.E.2d 267, 269 (Ga. Ct. App. 1986).
41. GA. CONST. art. 1, §I, ¶III (2007). *See* STATE OF GEORGIA SELECT COMMITTEE ON CONSTITUTIONAL REVISION (1977–1981) TRANSCRIPTS OF MEETINGS, COMMITTEE TO REVISE ART. I, Oct. 4, 1979, pp. 6–10, 12–25, 29–33, 37–141; Oct. 5, 1979, pp. 5–137; Oct. 25, 1979, pp. 5–139; Oct. 26, 1979, pp. 4–10, 12–56, 58–114; Nov. 9, 1979, pp. 3–77, 80–143, 145–46; Nov. 30, 1979, pp. 4–31, 33–45, 48–51; SELECT COMMITTEE, Dec. 17, 1979, pp. 11–76; Jan. 9, 1980, pp. 14–55; LEGISLATIVE OVERVIEW COMMITTEE, June 4, 1981, pp. 25–26, 30–31, 35–39; June 17, 1981, pp. 18–70, 103–24; June 18, 1981, pp. 5–13; July 28, 1981, p. 46; Aug. 12, 1981, pp. 4–12; Aug. 20, 1981, pp. 86–87 (Atlanta, Georgia 1982).

> No inhabitant of this state shall be molested in person or property or be prohibited from holding any public office or trust on account of religious opinions; but the right of freedom of religion shall not be so construed as to excuse acts of licentiousness or justify practices inconsistent with the peace and safety of the state.[42]

In any challenge to a statute Georgia may enact prohibiting abortion, abortion advocates may argue that the statute interferes with the pregnant woman's "right of conscience" under art. 1, §I, ¶3, and her "freedom of religion" under art. I, §I, ¶4, by prohibiting her from obtaining an abortion that would be permitted by her religion. Such an argument would not likely succeed, however.

In *Jones v. City of Moultrie*,[43] the Georgia Supreme Court recognized that under both state and federal constitutional guarantees of freedom of religion, "the right to adopt, profess, entertain, or advocate any religious views, or to fail so to do, is unlimited, and cannot be controlled by any law."[44] "[A] person's sentiments and opinions upon this subject are controlled entirely by his own judgment and conscience," and, therefore, "[t]he courts will ever guard the right to a full and unlimited exercise of one's religious beliefs."[45] Nevertheless, "[w]hile there is no power to control what a person may believe about religion or the type of religion he may adopt or profess, yet there is a power under the law to limit his acts, even though to do such acts may be part of his religious belief."[46] The court then elaborated on this theme:

> The constitutional guarantee of the exercise of religious freedom does not extend to acts which are inimical to the peace, good order, and morals of society. Under the claim of a religious privilege one could not practice promiscuous sexual intercourse, or offer up a human sacrifice, or practice public nudeness; because the laws of society, designated to secure its peace, prosperity, and the morals of its people are affected. All of the foregoing are plain and well-recognized instances of curtailment of activities in furtherance of religious beliefs, and are so well implanted in the minds of our people that statutes prohibiting these acts may well be denominated as being based upon moral law. Yet limitations upon religious activities are not confined to instances where such acts are in contravention of moral law; as the right to ex-

---

42. *Id.* art. I, §I, ¶IV.
43. 27 S.E.2d 39 (Ga. 1943).
44. *Id.* at 42.
45. *Id.*
46. *Id.*

ercise these activities ends where the rights of others begin. A person's right to exercise religious freedom, which may be manifested by acts, ceases where it overlaps and transgresses the rights of others. Every one's rights must be exercised with due regard for the rights of others.... To construe this constitutional right as being unlimited, and to hold as privileged any act if based upon religious belief, would be to make the professed doctrine of religious faith superior to the law of the land, and in effect would permit every citizen to become a law unto himself.[47]

The Georgia Supreme Court's opinion in *Jones v. City of Moultrie* leaves little doubt that the state supreme court would not recognize a right to abortion under the freedom of conscience and freedom of religion guarantees of the state constitution. Regardless of the debate over the morality of abortion, a statute prohibiting abortion would clearly be intended to protect "the rights of others." That intention, and its implementation in a statute prohibiting abortion, would not contravene either art. 1, §I, ¶III, or art. 1, §I, ¶IV, of the Georgia Constitution. This conclusion is supported by a consideration of the Georgia Supreme Court's post-*Roe* decision in *Jefferson v. Griffin Spalding County Hospital Authority*.[48]

In *Jefferson*, a county hospital authority petitioned a state superior court for an order authorizing it to perform a caesarian section and any necessary blood transfusions upon a woman was in the thirty-ninth week of pregnancy, in the event that she presented herself to the hospital for delivery of her unborn child, despite the woman's (and her husband's) religious objections to surgery and blood transfusions. The basis for the petition was that the woman had "complete placenta previa, that the afterbirth is between the baby and the birth canal; that it is virtually impossible that this condition [would] correct itself prior to delivery; and that [there was] a 99% certainty that the child [could not] survive natural [vaginal] childbirth[;] [and that] [t]he chances of [the mother] surviving vaginal delivery are no better than 50%."[49] If the baby were delivered by caesarian section prior to the commencement of labor, there would be "an almost 100% chance of preserving the life of the child, along with that of defendant."[50] The superior court granted the petition, noting that, under *Roe v. Wade*, the State could recognize "legal right[s]" in a viable unborn child and, in fact had done so in enacting a statute prohibiting abortions after viability.[51]

---

47. *Id.*
48. *See* n. 19, *supra*.
49. 274 S.E.2d at 458.
50. *Id.*
51. *Id.* (citing GA. CODE ANN. §16-12-141(c) (2007)).

One day later, the state Department of Human Resources, acting through the local county Department of Children and Family Services, petitioned a juvenile court judge for temporary custody of the unborn child, alleging that the child "was a deprived child without proper parental care necessary for his or her physical care…, and praying for an order requiring the mother to submit to a caesarian section."[52] Following a joint hearing on both the superior court and juvenile court cases, the court granted the petition, finding that the "intrusion involved into the life of [the pregnant mother and her husband] [was] outweighed by the duty of the State to protect a living unborn human being from meeting his or her death before being given the opportunity to live."[53] The same day, the Georgia Supreme Court unanimously denied the parents motion for a stay of the lower court's order.[54]

Presiding Justice Hill concurred, stating: "In denying the stay of the trial court's order…, we weighed the right of the mother to practice her religion and to refuse surgery on herself, against her unborn child's right to live. We found in favor of the child's right to live."[55] Justice Smith also concurred:

> In the instant case, it appears that there is no less burdensome alternative for preserving the life of a fully developed fetus than requiring the mother to undergo surgery against her religious convictions. Such an intrusion by the state would be extraordinary, presenting some medical risk to both the mother and the fetus. However, the state's compelling interest in preserving the life of this fetus is beyond dispute [citing *Roe* and Georgia's post-viability statute]. Moreover, the medical evidence indicates that the risk to the fetus and the mother presented by a Caesarian section would be minimal, whereas, in the absence of surgery, the fetus would almost certainly die and the mother's chance of survival would be no better than 50 per cent. Under these circumstances, I must conclude that the trial court's order is not violative of the First Amendment, notwithstanding that it may require the mother to submit to surgery against her religious beliefs.[56]

The Georgia Supreme Court's decision in *Jefferson* suggests that, in the absence of some other state or federal constitutional impediment (as now exists

---

52. *Id.* at 459.
53. *Id.* at 460.
54. *Id.*
55. *Id.* (Hill, P.J., concurring).
56. *Id.* (Smith, J., concurring) (citations omitted).

under *Roe*), a statute prohibiting abortion would not violate the state constitutional rights to freedom of conscience and freedom of religion.[57]

Equal Protection

Article 1, §I, ¶II, of the Georgia Constitution provides: "Protection to person and property is the paramount duty of government and shall be impartial and complete. No person shall be denied the equal protection of the laws."[58] The Georgia Supreme Court has held that art. 1, §I, ¶II, "is construed to be consistent with its federal counterpart," the Equal Protection Clause of the Fourteenth Amendment.[59]

For purpose of both state and federal equal protection analysis, there are three standards of judicial review. Under the first standard, which is known as rational basis scrutiny, legislation "is presumed to be valid and will be sustained if the classification drawn by the statute is rationally related to a legitimate state interest."[60] Under the second standard, intermediate (or heightened) scrutiny, which applies to sex-based classifications, the classification must be "substantially related to a sufficiently important governmental interest."[61] Under the third standard, strict scrutiny, which applies to statutes that classify "by race, alienage, or national origin" or "impinge" on the exercise of fundamental "personal rights protected by the Constitution," the classification "will be sustained only if [it is] suitably tailored to serve a compelling state interest."[62]

Strict scrutiny review would not apply to an abortion prohibition because, for the reasons set forth in the first section of this analysis (due process of law), a prohibition of abortion would not "impinge" upon the exercise of a fundamental personal right. Nor would the prohibition of abortion classify persons on the basis of a "suspect" personal characteristic (race, alienage or national origin). Abortion advocates may argue in the alternative, however,

---

57. The state supreme court has acknowledged the continuing viability of *Griffin. See McAfee*, n. 13, *supra, In re Doe*, 418 S.E.2d 3, 6-7 n. 6 (Ga. 1992). *See also Anderson v. State*, 65 S.E.2d 848 (Ga. Ct. App. 1951) (rejecting state freedom of religion challenge to statute requiring vaccination of school children).

58. Ga. Const. art. 1, §I, ¶II (2007).

59. *City of Atlanta v. Watson*, 475 S.E.2d 896, 899 (Ga. 1996). *See also Etkind v. Suarez*, 519 S.E.2d at 213 (same).

60. *City of Cleburne, Texas v. Cleburne Living Center*, 473 U.S. 432, 440 (1985).

61. *Id.* at 441. A similar standard applies to classifications based on illegitimacy. *See Mills v. Habluetzel*, 456 U.S. 91, 99 (1982) (classification must be "substantially related to a legitimate state interest").

62. *City of Cleburne*, 473 U.S. at 440.

that a statute prohibiting abortion discriminates against women and is subject to intermediate scrutiny because only women are capable of becoming pregnant. An abortion prohibition would appear to satisfy this level of scrutiny because the prohibition would be "substantially related" to the "important governmental interest" in protecting unborn children. Nevertheless, the standard applicable to sex-based discrimination (intermediate scrutiny) would not apply to an abortion prohibition. Abortion laws do not discriminate on the basis of sex.

First, the United States Supreme Court has reviewed restrictions on abortion funding under a rational basis standard of review, *not* under the intermediate (heightened) scrutiny required of gender-based classifications.[63] Indeed, the Court has held that "the disfavoring of abortion ... is not *ipso facto* sex discrimination," and, citing its decisions in *Harris* and other cases addressing abortion funding, stated that "the constitutional test applicable to government abortion-funding restrictions is not the heightened-scrutiny standard that our cases demand for sex discrimination, ... but the ordinary rationality standard."[64]

Second, even assuming that an abortion prohibition differentiates between men and women on the basis of sex, and would otherwise be subject to a higher standard of review, the United States Supreme Court has held that biological differences between men and women may justify different treatment based on those differences. In upholding a statutory rape statute that applied only to males, the Supreme Court noted, "this Court has consistently upheld statutes where the gender classification is not invidious, but rather realistically reflects the fact that the sexes are not similarly situated in certain circumstances."[65]

---

63. *Harris v. McRae*, 448 U.S. 297, 321–26 (1980).

64. *Bray v. Alexandria Women's Health Clinic*, 506 U.S. 263, 273 (1993). Several state supreme courts and individual state supreme court justices have recognized that abortion regulations and restrictions on abortion funding are not "directed at women as a class" so much as "abortion as a medical treatment, which, because it involves a potential life, has no parallel as a treatment method." *Bell v. Low Income Women of Texas*, 95 S.W.3d 253, 258 (Tex. 2002) (upholding funding restrictions) (citing *Harris*, 448 U.S. at 325). *See also Fischer v. Dep't of Public Welfare*, 502 A.2d 114, 125 (Pa. 1985) ("the basis for the distinction here is not sex, but abortion") (upholding funding restrictions); *Moe v. Secretary of Administration & Finance*, 417 N.E.2d 387, 407 (Mass. 1981) (Hennessey, C.J., dissenting) (funding restrictions were "directed at abortion as a medical procedure, not women as a class"); *Right to Choose v. Byrne*, 450 A.2d 925, 950 (N.J. 1982) (O'Hern, J., dissenting) ("[t]he subject of the legislation is not the person of the recipient, but the nature of the claimed medical service"). Both *Moe* and *Right to Choose* were decided on other grounds. The dissenting justices were addressing alternative arguments raised by the plaintiffs, but not reached by the majority opinions.

65. *Michael M. v. Superior Court*, 450 U.S. 464, 469 (1981).

"Abortion statutes are examples of cases in which the sexes are not biologically similarly situated" because only women are capable of becoming pregnant and having abortions.[66]

A statute prohibiting abortion quite obviously can affect only women because only women are capable of becoming pregnant.[67] Unlike laws that use women's ability to become pregnant (or pregnancy itself) to discriminate against them in *other* areas (*e.g.*, employment opportunities), abortion prohibitions cannot fairly be said to involve a distinction between men and women that is a "mere pretext[] designed to erect an invidious discrimination against [women]."[68]

A prohibition of abortion would not interfere with the exercise of a fundamental state constitutional right, nor would it classify upon the basis of a suspect or quasi-suspect characteristic. Accordingly, it would be subject to rational basis review. Under that standard of review, the statute need only be "rationally related to a legitimate state interest."[69] A law prohibiting abortion would be "rationally related" to the "legitimate state interest" in protecting the lives of unborn children.

Inherent Rights

Article 1, §I, ¶XXIX, of the Georgia Constitution provides: "The enumeration of rights herein contained as a part of this Constitution shall not be construed to deny to the people any inherent rights which they may have hitherto enjoyed."[70] In any challenge to a statute Georgia may enact prohibiting abortion, abortion advocates may argue that the state interferes with an "inherent right[]" protected by art. 1, §I, ¶XXIX. Such an argument is not likely to succeed.

Paragraph XXIX has received relatively little attention from the Georgia Supreme Court. The court has held that the people do not have an inherent right "to make, sell, barter, give away, keep, and furnish [intoxicating] liquors."[71] In reaching that holding, the court relied upon the well-established authority of the State to regulate the possession, manufacturing and sale of alcoholic bever-

---

66. *Jane L. v. Bangerter*, 794 F. Supp. 1537, 1549 (D. Utah 1992).

67. *Geduldig v. Aiello*, 417 U.S. 484, 496 n. 20 (1974) ("[n]ormal pregnancy is an objectively, identifiable physical condition with unique characteristics").

68. *Id.*

69. *Cleburne*, 473 U.S. at 440.

70. GA. CONST. art. 1, §I, ¶XXIX (2007).

71. *Whitley v. State*, 68 S.E. 716, 724 (Ga. 1910).

ages, which authority antedated the adoption of the former constitution.[72] By a parity of reasoning, given that the State of Georgia prohibited abortion for more than one hundred years before the present constitution was adopted, it cannot be said that there is an "inherent right" to obtain an abortion under ¶XXIX.

One commentator has observed that art. I, §I, ¶XXIX is the "counterpart" of the Ninth Amendment to the United States Constitution and should be given a parallel interpretation.[73] That, in turn, suggests that if no right to abortion exists under the Ninth Amendment, then none would be recognized under ¶XXIX. The Supreme Court, however, has rooted the "abortion liberty" in the liberty language of the Due Process Clause of the Fourteenth Amendment, not in the unenumerated rights language of the Ninth Amendment.[74] Because abortion has not been recognized as a "retained right" under the Ninth Amendment, it should not be recognized as one under ¶XXIX, either.

Conclusion

Based on the foregoing analysis, an argument that the Georgia Constitution protects a right to abortion that is separate from, and independent of, the right to abortion recognized in *Roe v. Wade* would not likely succeed. That, in turn, suggests that if *Roe*, as modified by *Casey*, is ultimately overruled, the State of Georgia could enact and enforce a statute *prohibiting* abortion. Moreover, nothing in the Georgia Constitution precludes Georgia from *regulating* abortion within federal constitutional limits in the meantime.

---

72. *Id.* at 723–24.

73. Melvin B. Hill, Jr., THE GEORGIA STATE CONSTITUTION[:] A REFERENCE GUIDE 52 (Westport, Conn. 1994). The Ninth Amendment provides: "The enumeration in the Constitution of certain rights, shall not be construed to deny or disparage others retained by the people." U.S. CONST. AMEND. IX (West 2006).

74. *See Roe*, 410 U.S. at 153; *Casey*, 505 U.S. at 846. In any event, the Ninth Amendment, standing alone, is not a source of substantive rights. *Gibson v. Matthews*, 926 F.2d 532, 537 (6th Cir. 1991). Although "[s]ome unenumerated rights may be of [c]onstitutional magnitude," that is only "by virtue of other amendments, such as the Fifth or Fourteenth Amendment. A person cannot claim a right that exists solely under the Ninth Amendment." *United States v. Vital Health Products, Ltd.*, 786 F. Supp. 761, 777 (E.D. Wis. 1992), *aff'd mem. op., sub nom. United States v. LeBeau*, 985 F.2d 563 (7th Cir. 1993). *See also Charles v. Brown*, 495 F. Supp. 862, 863 (N.D. Ala. 1980) (same).

CHAPTER 14

HAWAII

Summary

The Hawaii Supreme Court has not yet decided whether the Hawaii Constitution protects a right to abortion separate from, and independent of, the right to abortion recognized under the United States Constitution. In light of the history of the state constitutional right of privacy,[1] however, the state supreme court probably would recognize a state right to abortion. Thus, even if *Roe v. Wade*,[2] as modified by *Planned Parenthood of Southeastern Pennsylvania v. Casey*,[3] were overruled, Hawaii could not prohibit any abortion before viability, or any abortion after viability that would be necessary to preserve the pregnant woman's life or health. Whether the State may regulate abortion within current federal constitutional limits has not been determined, but such regulations would be subject to rigorous judicial scrutiny.

Analysis

The pre-*Roe* abortion statute explicitly allowed abortion on demand *before* viability and implicitly allowed abortion *after* viability for any reason.[4] The statute, which has not been repealed, was recently amended to eliminate the hospitalization and residency requirements.[5]

---

1. HAW. CONST. art. I, §6 (Michie 2005).

2. 410 U.S. 113 (1973).

3. 505 U.S. 833 (1992).

4. HAW. REV. STAT. §453-16 (Supp. 1971). The statute prohibited "abortion" unless the procedure was performed by a licensed physician in a licensed hospital. *Id.* §453-16(a)(3). The term "abortion," however, was limited to the intentional termination of a pregnancy of a "*nonviable fetus*." *Id.* §453-16(b) (emphasis added). As a result, the "prohibition" set forth in the first sentence of the statute did not prohibit (and does not prohibit) an abortion of a viable fetus.

5. *Id.* §453-16 (Michie Supp. 2006). Those requirements were unenforceable under *Doe v. Bolton*, 410 U.S. 179 (1973).

Based upon the history of its adoption, the most likely source for an asserted abortion right under the Hawaii Constitution would be art. I, §6, which provides, in relevant part: "The right of the people to privacy is recognized and shall not be infringed without the showing of a compelling state interest."[6] Along with other amendments proposed by the Hawaii Constitutional Convention of 1978, art. I, §6, was adopted by the voters in 1978.

The Committee on Bill of Rights, Suffrage and Election proposed adding art. I, §6, to extend the right of privacy "beyond the criminal area," which was already protected by art. I, §5,[7] and "create a new section as it relates to privacy in the informational and personal autonomy sense."[8] To avoid uncertainty as to what the right of privacy would mean, the Committee explained in detail and at some length its intent regarding the "scope and nature of the right," with respect to both informational privacy and personal autonomy.[9] While acknowledging that it would be up to the courts" to decide "[w]hether an individual's desire to engage in a particular activity is protected by this aspect of the right to privacy (the right to personal autonomy)," the Committee noted that the courts had recognized "certain marital, sexual and *reproductive* matters within this right, thereby insuring freedom of choice in these matters."[10] If a given activity is protected by the right to personal autonomy, "it can be infringed upon only by the showing of a compelling state interest."[11] Moreover, "in view of the important nature of this right, the State must use the least restrictive means should it desire to interfere with the right."[12] The right of privacy should "be considered a fundamental right," and "interference with the activities protected by it [should] be minimal."[13]

The report of the Committee on Bill of Rights, Suffrage and Elections was referred to the Committee of the Whole. Following an extended debate, the Committee adopted a report reflecting the consensus of the Convention regarding the adoption of a "separate and distinct section on the right to privacy."[14]

---

6. HAW. CONST. art. I, §6.

7. *Id.* art. I, §5 (dealing with search and seizure).

8. Standing Committee Report No. 69, Committee on Bill of Rights, Suffrage and Elections, *reprinted in* PROCEEDINGS OF THE CONSTITUTIONAL CONVENTION OF HAWAII OF 1978 (hereinafter PROCEEDINGS), Vol. I, Journal & Documents, 674 (Honolulu, Hawaii 1980).

9. *Id.* at 674–76.

10. *Id.* at 675 (emphasis added).

11. *Id.*

12. *Id.*

13. *Id.*

14. Committee of the Whole Report No. 15, PROCEEDINGS, Vol. I, at 1024; Vol. II, at 697.

By amending the Constitution to include a separate and distinct privacy right, it is the intent of your Committee to insure that privacy is treated as a fundamental right for purposes of constitutional analysis. Privacy as used in this sense concerns the possible abuses in the use of highly personal and intimate information in the hands of government or private parties but is not intended to deter the government from the legitimate compilation and dissemination of data. More importantly, this privacy concept encompasses the notion that in certain highly personal and intimate matters, the individual should be afforded freedom of choice absent a compelling state interest. This right is similar to the privacy right discussed in cases such as *Griswold v. Connecticut*, 381 U.S. 479 (1965) [use of contraceptives by married couples], *Eisenstadt v. Baird*, 405 U.S. 438 (1972) [use of contraceptives by unmarried individuals], *Roe v. Wade*, 410 U.S. 113 (1973) [abortion], etc. It is a right that, though unstated in the federal Constitution, emanates from the penumbra of several guarantees of the Bill of Rights. Because of this, there has been some confusion as to the source of the right and the importance of it. As such, it is treated as a fundamental right subject to interference only when a compelling state interest is demonstrated. By inserting clear and specific language regarding this right into the Constitution, your Committee intends to alleviate any possible confusion over the source of the right and the existence of it.[15]

As previously noted, art. I, §6, was approved by the voters in 1978.

The constitutional history of Hawaii's right of privacy leaves little doubt that the framers of art. I, §6, intended to recognize abortion as a fundamental right under the state constitution. The Committee on Bill of Rights, Suffrage and Elections took note that the courts have held that "certain marital, sexual and reproductive matters" are protected by the right of privacy. And the Committee of the Whole acknowledged that the proposed state right of privacy, in affording "freedom of choice" in "certain highly and personal and intimate matters," is "similar" to the privacy right discussed in *Griswold*, *Eisenstadt* and *Roe*. Both Committees stated that the right of privacy is "fundamental," and may be infringed only by a "compelling state interest."

The Hawaii Supreme Court has held that the Hawaii Constitution "must be construed with due regard to the intent of the framers and the people adopt-

---

15. *Id.*

ing it."[16] Consistent with that rule of construction, the state supreme court has often relied upon the reports of the Committee on Bill of Rights, Suffrage and Elections and the Committee of the Whole in interpreting art. I, §6.[17] Indeed, in its "search for guidance on the intended scope of the privacy protected by the Hawaii Constitution," the court, quoting the Committee of the Whole Report No. 15, has cited *Griswold, Eisenstadt* and *Roe*.[18]

In light of the constitutional history of art. I, §6, the Hawaii Supreme Court would most likely recognize that the fundamental right of privacy includes a right to obtain an abortion that is at least as extensive as *Roe v. Wade*. Under *Roe*, as reaffirmed in relevant part by *Casey*, the States may not prohibit abortion *before* viability for any reason, nor may they prohibit abortion after *viability* if the procedure is necessary to preserve the life or health of the pregnant woman.[19]

Given the history of art. I, §6, only a "compelling interest" would be sufficient to override the exercise of a woman's right to obtain an abortion. There is no basis in Hawaii law to establish such an interest, however. Indeed, if statutory history is any guide to the likely interpretation of Hawaii's privacy guarantee, it is possible (though unknown at this time) that the state supreme court may give abortion even greater protection than is afforded by *Roe* and *Casey*. Hawaii adopted an abortion-on-demand statute in 1970, more than two years before *Roe* was decided. The Aloha State has enacted no post-*Roe* laws regulating abortion, and neither its statutes nor its court decisions extend the protection of the law to unborn children outside the context of abortion.

In sum, the Hawaii Supreme Court would probably construe art. I, §6, of the Hawaii Constitution to protect a right to abortion separate from, and in-

---

16. *State v. Kam*, 748 P.2d 372, 377 (Haw. 1988) (statute prohibiting possession of pornographic adult magazines infringed on the customers' state right to privacy).

17. *Id.* at 377–78; *State v. Mueller*, 671 P.2d 1351, 1356–1358 (Haw. 1983) (no fundamental privacy right to engage in prostitution). *See also State v. Mallan*, 950 P.2d 178, 222–29 (Haw. 1998) (Levinson, J., dissenting) (setting forth constitutional history). In *Mallan*, the court held that there is no fundamental privacy right to possess marijuana for personal recreational use).

18. *Mueller*, 671 P.2d at 1358.

19. The Supreme Court has not yet decided whether a statute prohibiting post-viability abortions must make exceptions for mental, as well as physical, health. *See Voinovich v. Women's Medical Professional Corporation*, 523 U.S. 1036, 1039 (1998) (Thomas, J., dissenting from denial of *certiorari*) (noting that this issue was not addressed in *Doe v. Bolton*, 410 U.S. 179 (1973), the companion case to *Roe v. Wade*). As a result, it is not known whether, as a matter of *state* constitutional law, the Hawaii Supreme Court would require a post-viability statute to contain a mental health exception.

dependent of, the right to abortion recognized in *Roe v. Wade*. That, in turn, suggests that if *Roe*, as modified by *Casey*, is ultimately overruled, Hawaii could not prohibit any abortion before viability, or any abortion after viability that was necessary to preserve the life or health of the pregnant woman.

Conclusion

The State of Hawaii probably could not prohibit abortions, at least before viability, even if *Roe*, as modified by *Casey*, were overruled. Whether the State may regulate abortion within current federal constitutional limits has not been determined, but such regulations would be subject to rigorous judicial scrutiny in the form of the "compelling interest" test.

CHAPTER 15

IDAHO

Summary

The Idaho Supreme Court has not yet decided whether the Idaho Constitution protects a right to abortion separate from, and independent of, the right to abortion recognized under the United States Constitution.[1] A careful examination of the state constitution, in light of its history and interpretation, as well as other relevant legal sources, however, suggests that the state supreme court probably would not recognize a state constitutional right to abortion. Thus, if *Roe v. Wade*,[2] as modified by *Planned Parenthood of Southeastern Pennsylvania v. Casey*,[3] were overruled, Idaho could prohibit abortion. Moreover, nothing in the state constitution, properly understood, precludes the State from enacting and enforcing reasonable measures regulating abortion within current federal constitutional limits.

Analysis

The principal pre-*Roe* abortion statute prohibited performance of an abortion upon a pregnant woman unless the procedure was "necessary to preserve

---

1. Without citing the Supreme Court's abortion decisions, the Idaho Supreme Court has repeatedly stated in dictum that procreation is a fundamental right under the Idaho Constitution. *See Van Valkenburgh v. Citizens for Term Limits*, 15 P.3d 1129, 1134 (Idaho 2000); *Idaho Schools for Equal Educational Opportunity v. Evans*, 850 P.2d 724, 732–33 (Idaho 1993); *Tarbox v. Tax Comm'n*, 695 P.2d 342, 345 n. 1 (Idaho 1984). All of these statements may be traced back to *Newlan v. State*, 535 P.2d 1348, 1350 (Idaho 1975), which cited neither the state constitution nor any cases interpreting the state constitution. *See also State v. Cantrell*, 496 P.2d 276, 279 n. 9 (Idaho 1972) (same). Even assuming that the state constitution protects a right to procreate-a right to *create* life-that right cannot be equated with a right to undergo an abortion, which *destroys* life.

2. 410 U.S. 113 (1973).

3. 505 U.S. 833 (1992).

her life."[4] Another statute prohibited a woman from soliciting an abortion or allowing an abortion to be performed upon her (subject to the same exception).[5] These statutes were repealed in 1973.[6]

Based upon arguments that have been raised in Idaho and other States with similar constitutional provisions,[7] possible sources for an asserted abortion right could include provisions of the Declaration of Rights guaranteeing due process of law and equal protection (art. I, §§2, 13), religious liberty (§4) and a speedy remedy (§18); recognizing inalienable rights (§1); and retaining rights (§21).[8] The analysis that follows addresses each of these provisions.

Inalienable Rights, Due Process of Law

Article I, §1, of the Idaho Constitution provides: "All men are by nature free and equal, and have certain inalienable rights, among which are enjoying and defending life and liberty; acquiring, possessing and protecting property; pursuing happiness and securing safety."[9] Article I, §13, provides, in part: "No person shall ... be deprived of life, liberty or property without due process of law."[10] In any challenge to a statute prohibiting abortion, abortion advocates are most likely to rely upon these two provisions. That reliance would be misplaced, however.

The Idaho Supreme Court has not developed a methodology for determining whether an asserted liberty interest is protected by the inalienable rights language of art. I, §1, or the due process guarantee of §13. The court has stated more generally that fundamental rights are "those expressed as a positive right" in the state constitution or are "implicit in our State's concept of ordered liberty."[11] The Idaho Constitution does not expressly protect a right to

---

4. IDAHO CODE §18-601 (Supp. 1972).

5. *Id.* §18-602. No prosecutions were reported under this statute.

6. 1973 Idaho Sess. Laws 443, ch. 197, §2.

7. *See Planned Parenthood of Idaho, Inc. v. Kurtz*, Case No. CV0C0103909D, Memorandum Decision, June 12, 2002 (Idaho Dist. Ct. Fourth Judicial District) (rejecting state constitutional challenge to statute restricting public funding of abortion).

8. Two other more unlikely sources of an abortion right under the Idaho Constitution-art. I, §9 (guaranteeing freedom of speech) and §17 (prohibiting unreasonable searches and seizures)-are discussed generally in Chapter 3, *supra.*

9. IDAHO CONST. art. I, §1 (2004).

10. *Id.* art. I, §13.

11. *Idaho Schools for Equal Educational Opportunity*, 850 P.2d at 732–33. To the extent that the Idaho Supreme Court considers federal precedent in determining whether an asserted liberty interest (or right) is "fundamental" under the state due process guaranteed, abortion would not qualify as a "fundamental" right. Although the Supreme Court characterized the right to choose abortion as "fundamental" in *Roe*, 410 U.S. at 152–53, it tac-

abortion, nor can it be said that such a right is "implicit in [Idaho's] concept of ordered liberty."[12]

Abortion has long been a serious criminal offense in Idaho. In 1864, twenty-five years before the Idaho Constitution was adopted, the first territorial legislature enacted a law prohibiting abortion, without respect to gestational age.[13] An abortion could be performed only by a physician "who ... deems it necessary to produce the miscarriage of any woman in order to save her life."[14] In 1887, this statute was replaced by two new statutes which prohibited both abortion and soliciting and/or submitting to an abortion.[15] Like the earlier statutes, those enacted in 1887 imposed no gestational requirement. Abortion at *any* stage of pregnancy was a crime.[16] These statutes remained on the books and were not repealed until after *Roe v. Wade* was decided.[17]

---

itly abandoned that characterization in *Casey*, 505 U.S. at 869–79 (Joint Op. of O'Connor, Kennedy and Souter, JJ., replacing *Roe's* "strict scrutiny" standard of review with the more relaxed "undue burden" standard, allowing for a broader measure of abortion regulation).

12. Apart from the specific privacy interests protected by the state guarantee against unreasonable searches and seizures (art. I, § 17), the Idaho reviewing courts have not recognized a general right of privacy under the state constitution. In *State v. Kincaid*, 566 P.2d 763 (Idaho 1977), the supreme court held that a person does not have a state or federal privacy interest in possessing marijuana in his home. The court noted that the defendant had failed to cite "any authority establishing a fundamental right of privacy in the home which is independent of a conjunctive first amendment or other constitutional protection." *Id.* at 765. In *State v. Holden*, 890 P.2d 341, 346–48 (Idaho Ct. App. 1995), the court of appeals invalidated, on *federal* constitutional grounds, the "infamous crime against nature" statute, IDAHO CODE § 18-6605 (2004), to the extent that it criminalizes private consensual acts of married couples. The state constitution was not cited in the opinion. Finally, it must be noted that in 1970, the electorate *rejected* a proposed revision of the state constitution which, among other changes, would have added an explicit "right to privacy" to art. I, § 1. *See* Idaho Secretary of State, PROPOSED REVISION OF THE IDAHO CONSTITUTION 2 (Boise, Idaho 1970).

13. An Act of Feb. 4, 1864, ch. IV, § 42, 1863–64 IDAHO (TERR.) LAWS 443, *repealed and reenacted by* an Act of Dec. 21, 1864, ch. III, pt. IV, § 42, 1864 IDAHO (TERR.) LAWS 305, *reenacted by* an Act of Jan. 14, 1875, ch. IV, § 42, 1874 IDAHO (TERR.) LAWS 328.

14. An Act of Feb. 4, 1864, ch. IV, § 42, 1863–64 IDAHO (TERR.) LAWS.

15. IDAHO REV. STAT. §§ 6794, 6795 (1887).

16. "At the common law an abortion [was not a crime] prior to the quickening of the foetus. This is not the case under our statutes." *State v. Alcorn*, 64 P. 1014, 1016 (1901). "Quickening" is that stage of pregnancy, usually sixteen to eighteen weeks gestation, when the woman first detects fetal movement.

17. IDAHO REV. CODE, §§ 6794, 6795 (1908), *recodified at* IDAHO COMP. STAT. §§ 17-1810, 17-1811 (1932), *recodified at* IDAHO CODE §§ 18-601, 18-602 (1948), *repealed by* an Act of March 17, 1973, ch. 197, § 2, 1973 Idaho Laws 443.

In *Nash v. Meyer*,[18] the Idaho Supreme Court held that the state abortion statutes had been enacted not "for the protection of the woman, but to discourage abortions because thereby the life of a human being, the unborn child, is taken."[19] And in *State v. Alcorn*, the supreme court stated that "[a]n unnatural abortion … is … destructive of a life unborn."[20]

Prior to *Roe*, the Idaho Supreme Court affirmed convictions for abortion (and manslaughter convictions based upon the death of the woman resulting from an illegal abortion) without any hint that either the prosecutions or convictions violated the Idaho Constitution.[21] Subsequent to *Roe*, Idaho reviewing courts have cited *Roe* in only eight cases, five of which concerned the mootness doctrine.[22] In none of the other three cases did either the Idaho Supreme Court or the Idaho Court of Appeals adopt the reasoning of or the result in *Roe* as a matter of state constitutional law. Thus, in *Newlan v. State*,[23] the Idaho Supreme Court distinguished *Roe* and other federal cases involving "fundamental constitutional rights" in rejecting a challenge to the notice of claim provisions of the Tort Claims Act.[24] In *Volk v. Baldazo*,[25] the supreme court cited *Roe* in the context of discussing the evolution of legal doctrine on the recognition of causes of action for prenatal injuries.[26] And in *Blake v. Cruz*,[27] the court cited *Roe* for the proposition that "public policy now supports, rather than militates against, the proposition that a woman may not be impermissibly denied a meaningful opportunity to make the decision whether to have an abortion."[28] At issue in *Blake* was whether Idaho would recognize a common law action for wrongful birth,[29] which presented a public policy question only,

---

18. 31 P.2d 273 (Idaho 1934).

19. *Id.* at 280.

20. 64 P. at 1019.

21. *State v. Alcorn*; *State v. Proud*, 262 P.2d 1016 (Idaho 1953); *State v. Rose*, 267 P.2d 109 (Idaho 1954).

22. *See Ellibee v. Ellibee*, 826 P.2d 462, 464 (Idaho 1992); *Mallery v. Lewis*, 678 P.2d 19, 26 (Idaho 1983); *State v. Hargis*, 889 P.2d 1117, 1120 (Idaho Ct. App. 1995); *State v. Henderson*, 808 P.2d 1324, 13254 (Idaho Ct. App. 1991); *Russell v. Fortney*, 722 P.2d 490, 492 (Idaho Ct. App. 1986).

23. 535 P.2d 1348.

24. *Id.* at 1351.

25. 651 P.2d 11 (Idaho 1982).

26. *Id.* at 13.

27. 698 P.2d 315 (Idaho 1984).

28. *Id.* at 318.

29. A "wrongful birth" cause of action is a claim brought by the parents of a child who is born with a physical or mental disability or disease that could have been discovered before the child's birth by genetic testing, amniocentesis or other medical screening. The

not a question of state constitutional law. The Idaho Legislature later enacted a statute abolishing any cause of action for either wrongful birth or wrongful life.[30]

The public policy of the State of Idaho prefers childbirth over abortion.[31] Consistent with that policy, Idaho has enacted a comprehensive scheme of abortion regulation.[32] The first comprehensive post-*Roe* law recited that nothing in the Legislature's attempt to comply with the trimester framework of *Roe* was intended to "condon[e] or approv[e] abortion or the liberalization of abortion laws generally...."[33]

Idaho has recognized the rights of unborn children in a variety of contexts outside of abortion, including criminal law, tort law, health care law, property law, family law and guardianship law. Under the penal code, the killing of an unborn child, other than in an abortion, may be prosecuted as a homicide.[34] A woman convicted of a capital offense may not be executed while she is pregnant.[35] And a pregnant woman who ingests illegal drugs causing harm to her unborn child may be charged with injury to children under state law.[36]

---

gravamen of the action is that, as a result of a physician's failure to inform the parents of the child's disability or disease (or at least of the availability of tests to determine the presence of the disability or disease), they were deprived of the opportunity to abort the child, thus resulting in the birth of a child suffering permanent physical or mental impairment. Most courts that have considered wrongful birth causes of action have recognized them, while denying wrongful life causes of action. A "wrongful life" cause of action is a claim, based on the same facts, brought on behalf of the impaired child.

30. An Act of March 21, 1985, ch. 147, §1, 1985 Idaho Laws 394, *codified at* IDAHO CODE §5-334 (2004) (abolishing causes of action based upon an act or omission preventing abortion). That *Blake* did not recognize a *constitutionally* based cause of action is apparent from the state supreme court's later decision in *VanVooren v. Astin*, 111 P.3d 125 (Idaho 2005), in which the court applied §5-334 to bar recovery of damages for emotional injuries based on an underlying action for wrongful birth.

31. IDAHO CODE §18-601 (2004) (declaring it to be the public policy of the State of Idaho that "all state statutes, rules and constitutional provisions shall be interpreted to prefer, by all legal means, live childbirth over abortion").

32. *Id.* §18-608 (2004) (codifying *Roe's* trimester framework); §18-609 (2004) (mandating informed consent and a 24-hour waiting period); §18-609A (2004 and Supp. 2006) (requiring parental consent of minors seeking abortions); §18-612 (2004) (recognizing individual and institutional rights of conscience); §56-209c (2002) (restricting public funding of abortion for indigent women).

33. An Act of March 17, 1973, ch. 197, §1, 1997 Idaho Laws 443.

34. IDAHO CODE §18-4016 (2004).

35. *Id.* §§19-2713, 19-2714, 19-2719a.

36. *See* IDAHO CODE §18-1501 (2004), as construed by *State of Idaho, Dep't of Health & Welfare v. Doe*, 992 P.2d 1226, 1228 (Idaho Ct. App. 1999).

Such conduct may also be taken into account in sentencing her for injuries inflicted after the child has been born.[37]

In tort law, a statutory cause of action for wrongful death may be brought on behalf of an unborn child who is viable (capable of sustained survival outside the mother's womb, with or without medical assistance) at the time of its death.[38] A common law cause of action for (nonlethal) prenatal injuries may be brought on behalf of a viable unborn child.[39] Finally, Idaho has refused to recognize a cause of action for wrongful life.[40] The state supreme court noted that the widespread "judicial resistance" to recognizing such an action "stems partially from the fact that the theory amounts to a repudiation of the value of human life."[41] The court joined the overwhelming majority of jurisdictions rejecting such a cause of action:

> Basic to our culture is the precept that life is precious. As a society, therefore, our laws have as their driving force the purpose of protecting, preserving and improving the quality of human existence. To recognize wrongful life as a tort would do violence to that purpose and is completely contradictory to the belief that life is precious.[42]

Under Idaho's health care statutes, a living will may not direct the withholding or withdrawal of artificial, life-sustaining procedures from a woman who is known to be pregnant.[43] Durable powers of attorney for health care are subject to the same limitation.[44]

In property law, a relative of an intestate (a person who dies without a will) conceived before his death but born thereafter inherits as if he had been born during the lifetime of the decedent.[45] A similar rule applies to afterborn children (children born after a parent executes a will but conceived before the par-

---

37. *State v. Reyes*, 826 P.2d 919, 923 (Idaho Ct. App. 1992).

38. *Volk v. Baldazo*, 651 P.2d at 14–15 (rejecting "live birth as the point of demarcation of the beginning of legal personality"), interpreting IDAHO CODE § 5-311 (2004).

39. *Id.* at 13–14.

40. *Blake v. Cruz*, 698 P.2d at 321–22.

41. *Id.* at 321.

42. *Id.* at 322. Although *Blake* recognized a common law cause of action for wrongful birth, *id.* at 317–21, that holding, as previously noted, was abrogated by the Legislature. *See* n. 30, *supra*, and accompanying text.

43. IDAHO CODE § 39-4504 (A Living Will, ¶ 4) (2002).

44. *Id.* § 39-4505 (A Durable Power of Attorney for Health Care, ¶ 4) ("the authority under this durable power of attorney for health care ... is subject to the special provisions and limitations stated in the living will") (2002).

45. *Id.* § 15-2-108 (Supp. 2006).

ent's death) of a person who dies testate (with a will).[46] For the purpose of inheriting future interests, posthumous children (children conceived before but born after the death of a parent) are treated as if living at the death of their parent(s).[47]

In domestic relations law, "[a] child conceived, but not yet born, is to be deemed an existing person so far as may be necessary for its interests, in the event of its subsequent birth."[48] This section was enacted "to protect the rights and interests of children 'conceived but not yet born' during divorce, custody, property settlement and similar types of proceedings."[49] Finally, a guardian *ad litem* may be appointed for an unborn child.[50]

A right to abortion cannot be found in the text, structure or history of the Idaho Constitution. There is no evidence that the framers or ratifiers of the Idaho Constitution intended to limit the Legislature's authority to prohibit abortion.[51] Such an intent would have been remarkable in light of the contemporaneous and long-standing prohibition of abortion except to save the life of the mother.

Equal Protection

Article I, § 1, of the Idaho Constitution provides, in pertinent part, "All men are by nature free and equal...."[52] And art. I, § 2, provides, in part, "All political power is inherent in the people. Government is instituted for their equal protection and benefit...."[53] Taken together, these provisions guarantee equal protection of the laws.

The Idaho Supreme Court has recognized three standards of equal protection review:

> Where the classification is based on a suspect classification, or involves a fundamental right we have employed the "strict scrutiny" test. Where the discriminatory character of a challenged statutory classification is apparent on its face and where there is also a patent indication

---

46. *Id.* § 15-2-302 (2001).

47. *Id.* § 55-108 (2003). *See also id.*, § 55-112 (2003).

48. *Id.* § 32-102 (2006).

49. *Volk v. Baldazo,* 651 P.2d at 15.

50. IDAHO CODE § 15-1-403(d) (2001).

51. *See* PROCEEDINGS & DEBATES OF THE CONSTITUTIONAL CONVENTION OF IDAHO, Vol. I, 127–46, 279–81, 287–88, 371–72, 392, 396–97 (debate on Declaration of Rights in Committee of the Whole); Vol. II, 1589, 1594–95, 1635–38, 1644 (debate on Declaration of Rights in Convention) (Boise, Idaho 1889).

52. IDAHO CONST. art. I, § 1 (2004).

53. *Id.* art. I, § 2.

of a lack of relationship between the classification and the declared purpose of the statute, the "means-focus" test is applicable. In other cases the "rational basis" test is employed.[54]

The appropriate standard for evaluating the constitutionality of an abortion prohibition under the Idaho Constitution would be the "rational basis" test. "Strict scrutiny" review would not apply because, for the reasons set forth in the previous section, an abortion prohibition does not "involve[] a fundamental right." And, even assuming that a prohibition of abortion classifies on the basis of gender, gender is not a suspect class under the Idaho Constitution.[55]

Nor is the "means-focus" test appropriate. The "means-focus" test is employed "where the discriminatory character of a statutory classification is apparent on its face and where there is also a patent indication of a lack of a relationship between the classification and the declared purpose of the statute."[56] "[T]he classification must be obviously invidiously discriminatory before the means-focus test will be used."[57] Before a classification may be considered "obviously invidiously discriminatory," the court emphasized, "it must distinguish between individuals or groups either odiously or on some other basis calculated to excite animosity or ill will."[58] To the extent that a prohibition of abortion may be said to "classify" between men and women,[59] it does not distinguish be-

---

54. *Olsen v. J.A. Freeman*, 791 P.2d 1285, 1289 (Idaho 1990) (citations and internal quotation marks omitted).

55. *Rudeen v. Cenarrusa*, 38 P.3d 598, 607 (Idaho 2001).

56. *Id.* (citation and internal quotation marks omitted). At one point in the development of Idaho's equal protection jurisprudence, the state supreme court appeared to apply the same intermediate standard of review to gender-based classifications under art. I, §2, of the Idaho Constitution that the United States Supreme Court has applied under the Equal Protection Clause. *Compare Murphey v. Murphey*, 653 P.2d 441, 444 (Idaho 1982) (striking down former statute allowing an award of alimony to the wife, but not the husband, in a divorce decree), *with State v. LaMere*, 655 P.2d 46, 49–50 (Idaho 1982) (upholding statutory rape statute which applied only to males). Under that standard, "classifications by gender must serve important governmental objectives and must be substantially related to achievement of those objectives." *Craig v. Boren*, 429 U.S. 190, 197 (1976). Under *Rudeen*, however, gender-based classifications are no longer singled out for special scrutiny under the Idaho Constitution.

57. *Rudeen*, 38 P.3d at 607 (citation and internal quotation marks omitted).

58. *Id.* (citation and internal quotation marks omitted).

59. Abortion regulations and restrictions on abortion funding are not "directed at women as a class" so much as "abortion as a medical treatment, which, because it involves a potential life, has no parallel as a treatment method." *Bell v. Low Income Women of Texas*, 95 S.W.3d 253, 258 (Tex. 2002) (upholding funding restrictions) (citing *Harris v. McRae*, 448 U.S. 297, 325 (1980)). *See also Fischer v. Dep't of Public Welfare*, 502 A.2d 114, 125 (Pa. 1985) ("the basis for the distinction here is not sex, but abortion") (upholding funding restrictions);

tween them "odiously or on some other basis calculated to excite animosity or ill will." Moreover, an abortion prohibition would have an obvious relationship between the "classification" and its purpose, *i.e.*, protecting unborn human life. Thus, the "means-focus" test would not be applicable.[60] "All other challenges are given low level or rational basis review."[61]

A prohibition of abortion would be reasonably related to the State's legitimate interest in protecting unborn human life. Accordingly, an abortion prohibition would not run afoul of the equal protection guarantees of the Idaho Constitution.

Religious Liberty

Article I, §4, of the Idaho Constitution provides:

> The exercise and enjoyment of religious faith and worship shall forever be guaranteed; and no person shall be denied any civil right or political right, privilege, or capacity on account of his religious opinions; but the liberty of conscience hereby secured shall not be construed to dispense with oaths or affirmations, or excuse acts of licentiousness or justify polygamous or other pernicious practices, inconsistent with morality or the peace and safety of the state; nor to

---

Moe v. Secretary of Administration & Finance, 417 N.E.2d 387, 407 (Mass. 1981) (Hennessey, C.J., dissenting) (funding restrictions were "directed at abortion as a medical procedure, not women as a class"); *Right to Choose v. Byrne*, 450 A.2d 925, 950 (N.J. 1982) (O'Hern, J., dissenting) ("[t]he subject of the legislation is not the person of the recipient, but the nature of the claimed medical service"). Both *Moe* and *Right to Choose* were decided on other grounds. The dissenting justices were addressing alternative arguments raised by the plaintiffs, but not reached by the majority opinions. The Supreme Court has held that "the disfavoring of abortion … is not *ipso facto* sex discrimination," and, citing its decisions in *Harris v. McRae* and other cases addressing abortion funding, stated that "the constitutional test applicable to government abortion-funding restrictions is not the heightened-scrutiny standard that our cases demand for sex discrimination, … but the ordinary rationality standard." *Bray v. Alexandria Women's Health Clinic*, 506 U.S. 263, 273 (1993).

60. The "means-focus" test applies only "when a two-part trigger has been satisfied. The statute must be discriminatory on its face *and* there must be a patent indication of a lack of relationship between the classification and the declared purpose of the statute." *Leliefeld v. Johnson*, 659 P.2d 111, 128 (Idaho 1983) (citation and internal quotation marks omitted) (emphasis added). In *Leliefeld*, the supreme court, "[w]ithout deciding the discriminatory effect of the recovery limitation [in the Idaho Tort Claims Act, which places caps on the tort liability of the State]," declined to apply the "means-focus" standard because it determined that there was "a valid relationship between the limitation and the avowed purpose of the statute which is to protect the public coffers." *Id.*

61. *Rudeen*, 38 P.3d at 607.

permit any person, organization, or association to directly or indirectly aid or abet, counsel or advise any person to commit the crime of bigamy or polygamy, or any other crime. No person shall be required to attend or support any ministry or place of worship, religious sect or denomination, or pay tithes against his consent; nor shall any preference be given by law to any religious denomination or mode of worship. Bigamy and polygamy are forever prohibited in the state, and the legislature shall provide by law for the punishment of such crimes.[62]

In any challenge to a statute prohibiting abortion, abortion advocates may raise either or both of two arguments under art. I, §4. First, relying on the first clause of the first sentence of §4, they may argue that an abortion prohibition interferes with the "exercise and enjoyment" of a woman's "religious faith" by forbidding her from obtaining an abortion that would be allowed by her religion. Second, relying upon the last clause of the second sentence of §4, they may argue in the alternative (or in addition) that an abortion prohibition gives a "preference" to a "religious denomination" because it reflects sectarian beliefs regarding when human life begins and the sinfulness of abortion. Neither argument would likely prevail.

The Ninth Circuit Court of Appeals has observed that the provisions of art. I, §4, "bear no resemblance to those found in the First Amendment and appear to be the product of Idaho's unique religious history."[63] The Idaho Supreme Court has suggested that, at least in certain contexts, art. I, §4, provides "an even greater guardian of religious liberty" than the First Amendment,[64] and, along with art. IX, §5,[65] "places a much greater restriction upon the power of State government to aid activities undertaken by religious sects than does [the Establishment Clause of] the First Amendment."[66] That being said, it is doubtful that an abortion prohibition could be successfully challenged under §4.

---

62. IDAHO CONST. art. I, §4 (2004).

63. *Harris v. Joint School District No. 241*, 41 F.3d 447, 450 (9th Cir. 1994). Presumably, the court was referring to the struggle to suppress polygamy in Idaho.

64. *Osteraas v. Osteraas*, 859 P.2d 948, 953 (Idaho 1993) ("denying a parent custody because of certain entertained religious beliefs, or lack thereof, clearly would be denying that parent a civil right because of such religious opinions or beliefs" which would violate art. I, §4, even if it did not violate the First Amendment). *See also Meredith v. Meredith*, 434 P.2d 116, 119 (Idaho 1967) (award of child custody could not be based on a parent's religious beliefs).

65. "Neither the legislature nor any … public corporation, shall ever make any appropriation, or pay from any public fund or moneys whatever, anything in aid of any church or sectarian or religious society,…." IDAHO CONST. art. IX, §5 (2004).

66. *Board of County Comm'rs of Twin Falls County, Idaho v. Idaho Health Facilities Authority*, 531 P.2d 588, 599 (Idaho 1974) (appropriation of public funds to public hospitals

As the text itself indicates, the "liberty of conscience" secured by § 4 "shall not be construed to … justify … pernicious practices, inconsistent with morality," nor "to permit any person … to directly or indirectly aid or abet, counsel or advise any person to commit the crime of bigamy or polygamy, *or any other crime*."[67] Prior to *Roe*, the Idaho Supreme Court consistently referred to abortion in condemnatory terms.[68] So described, there could be no "liberty of conscience" in obtaining an abortion under § 4 if the State were to prohibit it. And that conclusion would be consistent with the intent of § 4. In a leading early case interpreting § 4, the Idaho Supreme Court stated:

> Constitutions and statutes … do not deal with beliefs, but with acts and practices. They protect any man in believing anything he wants to believe…, but they prohibit him from acting or practicing any thing in any manner contrary to good morals or the public weal as prescribed by the laws of the land.[69]

The Idaho courts have continued to reject "liberty of conscience" claims against statutes that may incidentally regulate religiously based *acts* and *practices*, as opposed to religiously based *beliefs*.[70]

It also seems unlikely that the Idaho Supreme Court would strike down an abortion prohibition on the basis that it gives a "preference" to a "religious sect or denomination" by embodying a particular religion's view of the "sinfulness of abortion and the time at which life commences."[71] In *Harris v. McRae*, the

---

operated by religious sects violated the Idaho Constitution). The holding in *Twin Falls* was overturned by an amendment to art. IX, § 5, in 1980. *See* IDAHO CONST. art. IX, § 5 (last clause). Apart from art. IX. § 5, it is not clear that art. I, § 4, provides any broader protection for religious liberty than the Free Exercise Clause of the First Amendment or any narrower scope of legislative authority than the Establishment Clause. *See Epeldi v. Engelking*, 488 P.2d 860, 865 (Idaho 1971) (provisions of § 4 are "comparable" to the Free Exercise and Establishment Clauses of the First Amendment).

67. IDAHO CONST. art. I, § 4 (2004) (emphasis added).

68. *Nash v. Meyer*, 31 P.2d at 280 (in an abortion, "the life of a human being, the unborn child, is taken"); *State v. Alcorn*, 64 P. at 1019 (an abortion is "destructive of a life unborn").

69. *Toncray v. Budge*, 95 P. 26, 37 (Idaho 1908) (upholding statute disqualifying advocates of polygamy, bigamy and "plural marriage" from the electoral franchise).

70. *See Gregersen v. Blume*, 743 P.2d 88, 90–92 (Idaho Ct. App. 1987) (rejecting "liberty of conscience" challenge to statutes and rules requiring licensing and regulation of barbers); *Bissett v. State*, 727 P.2d 1293, 1295–96 (Idaho Ct. Ap. 1986) (rejecting "liberty of conscience" challenge to statutes requiring motorists to be licensed and insured and requiring motor vehicles to be registered and display license plates).

71. *Harris v. McRae*, 448 U.S. at 319.

Supreme Court held that the Establishment Clause is not violated merely because "a statute 'happens to coincide or harmonize with the tenets of some or all religions.'"[72] Noting that the Hyde Amendment "is as much a reflection of 'traditionalist' values toward abortion, as it is an embodiment of the views of any particular religion," the Court held that "the fact that the funding restrictions in the Hyde Amendment may coincide with the religious tenets of the Roman Catholic Church does not, without more, contravene the Establishment Clause."[73] There is no reason to believe that the Idaho Supreme Court would not follow the reasoning of *Harris* if confronted with a challenge to an abortion prohibition under art. I, § 4. The court, it must be noted, has never invalidated a criminal law on this basis.

Speedy Remedy

Article I, § 18, of the Idaho Constitution provides: "Courts of justice shall be open to every person, and a speedy remedy afforded for every injury of person, property or character, and right and justice shall be administered without sale, delay or prejudice."[74] Abortion advocates might argue that a statute prohibiting abortion interferes with a woman's control over her own body, and that such interference constitutes an "injury" to her "person," as those terms are used in § 18, for which there must be a "speedy remedy." That "remedy," in turn, would be invalidation of the statute. This argument assumes that art. I, § 18, confers substantive rights. The case law is clear, however, that it does not.

In *Hawley v. Green*,[75] the Idaho Supreme Court stated that § 18, "merely admonishes the Idaho courts to dispense justice and to secure citizens the rights and remedies afforded by the legislature or by the common law, *and ... [does] not create any substantive rights*."[76] Because art. I, § 18, does not "create any

---

72. *Id.* (citation omitted).

73. *Id.* at 319–20. It should be noted that no state or federal court has accepted an Establishment Clause argument against an abortion statute, and two courts have rejected such arguments brought under state constitutions. *See Right to Choose v. Byrne*, 450 A.2d 923, 938–39 (N.J. 1982); *Jane L. v. Bangerter*, 794 F. Supp. 1528, 1534–35 (D. Utah 1992) (interpreting Utah law).

74. IDAHO CONST. art. I, § 18 (2004).

75. 788 P.2d 1321 (Idaho 1990).

76. *Id.* at 1324 (emphasis added) (citing *Moon v. Bullock*, 151 P.2d 765, 769 (1944), *overruled on other grounds*, *Doggett v. Boiler Engineering & Supply Co., Inc.*, 477 P.2d 511, 513 (Idaho 1970)). *See also Venters v. Sorrento Delaware, Inc.*, 108 P.3d 392, 399 (Idaho 2005) (following *Hawley*).

substantive rights," it could not provide a basis for invalidating an otherwise constitutional statute of the State.[77]

Retained Rights

Article I, § 21, of the Idaho Constitution provides: "This enumeration of rights shall not be construed to impair or deny other rights retained by the people."[78] Abortion advocates may be expected to cite § 21 in support of an asserted right to abortion under the state constitution. Although there is little case law interpreting § 21, it does not appear that a proper interpretation of § 21 would support a right to abortion as a "retained right."

In *Murphy v. Pocatello School District # 25*,[79] the Idaho Supreme Court cited art. I, § 21, along with art. I, § 1, of the Idaho Constitution and the Ninth Amendment to the United States Constitution,[80] in support of its holding that "the right to wear one's hair in a manner of his choice [is] a protected right of personal taste not to be interfered with by the state unless the state can meet the 'substantial burden' criteria...."[81] The state supreme court's citation of § 21 in conjunction with the Ninth Amendment indicates that the court views § 21 as the state equivalent of the Ninth Amendment.[82] That, in turn, suggests that if there no right to abortion exists under the Ninth Amendment, then none would be recognized under art. I, § 24. The Supreme Court, however, has rooted the "abortion liberty" in the liberty language of the Due Process Clause of the Fourteenth Amendment, not in the unenumerated rights language of the Ninth Amendment.[83] Because abortion has not been recognized as a "retained right"

---

77. It should not be surprising to note, therefore, that no criminal statute has ever been struck down under the "speedy remedy" language of art. I, § 18.

78. IDAHO CONST. art. I, § 21 (2004).

79. 480 P.2d 878 (Idaho 1971).

80. "The enumeration in the Constitution of certain rights, shall not be construed to deny or disparage others retained by the people." U.S. CONST. AMEND. IX (West 2006).

81. *Id.* at 884. Section 21, it should be noted, has not been cited in any reported Idaho opinion since *Murphy* was decided more than 35 years ago.

82. As one state supreme court justice has observed. *See In re Petition of Idaho State Federation of Labor (AFL)*, 272 P.2d 707, 713 (Idaho 1954) (Taylor, J., dissenting) (section 21 is "a parallel to the Ninth Amendment to the federal constitution"). *See also* Donald Crowly & Florence Heffron, THE IDAHO STATE CONSTITUTION[:] A REFERENCE GUIDE 62 ("[a]lthough marginally different in wording from the Ninth Amendment..., this section was clearly intended to be its equivalent") (Westport, Conn. 1994).

83. *See Roe*, 410 U.S. at 153; *Casey*, 505 U.S. at 846. In any event, the Ninth Amendment, standing alone, is not a source of substantive rights. *Gibson v. Matthews*, 926 F.2d 532, 537 (6th Cir. 1991). Although "[s]ome unenumerated rights may be of [c]onstitutional

under the Ninth Amendment, it should not be recognized as one under §21, either.

More importantly, the Idaho Supreme Court has indicated that §21 retains rights that belonged to the people *"before the constitution was adopted."*[84] Abortion, however, was not a "right" that belonged to the people "before the constitution was adopted."[85] Accordingly, it should not be recognized as one by the Idaho Supreme Court.

Conclusion

Based on the foregoing analysis, an argument that the Idaho Constitution protects a right to abortion that is separate from, and independent of, the right to abortion recognized in *Roe v. Wade* would not likely succeed. That, in turn, suggests that if *Roe*, as modified by *Casey*, is ultimately overruled, the Idaho Legislature could enact and enforce a statute *prohibiting* abortion. Moreover, nothing in the Idaho Constitution precludes Idaho from *regulating* abortion within federal constitutional limitations in the meantime.

---

magnitude," that is only "by virtue of other amendments, such as the Fifth or Fourteenth Amendment. A person cannot claim a right that exists solely under the Ninth Amendment." *United States v. Vital Health Products, Ltd.*, 786 F. Supp. 761, 777 (E.D. Wis. 1992), *aff'd mem. op.*, *sub nom. United States v. LeBeau*, 985 F.2d 563 (7th Cir. 1993). *See also Charles v. Brown*, 495 F. Supp. 862, 863 (N.D. Ala. 1980) (same).

84. *Electors of Big Butte Area v. State Board of Education*, 308 P.2d 225, 231 (Idaho 1957) (emphasis added) (recognizing right of parents to participate in the supervision and control of the education of their children).

85. See the discussion of the history of abortion prohibition in Idaho set forth in the analysis of art. I, §§2, 13, *supra*.

CHAPTER 16

ILLINOIS

Summary

The Illinois Supreme Court has not yet decided whether the Illinois Constitution protects a right to abortion separate from, and independent of, the right to abortion recognized under the United States Constitution.[1] A careful examination of the state constitution, in light of its history and interpretation, as well as other relevant legal sources, however, suggests that the state supreme court probably would not recognize a state constitutional right to abortion. Thus, if *Roe v. Wade*,[2] as modified by *Planned Parenthood of Southeastern Pennsylvania v. Casey*,[3] were overruled, Illinois could prohibit abortion. Moreover, nothing in the state constitution, properly understood, precludes the State from enacting and enforcing reasonable measures regulating abortion within current federal constitutional limits.

Analysis

The pre-*Roe* abortion statute prohibited performance of an abortion unless the procedure was "necessary for the preservation of the woman's life."[4]

---

1. *In Family Life League v. Dep't of Public Aid*, 493 N.E.2d 1054 (1986), the Illinois Supreme Court noted that in *Roe v. Wade*, 410 U.S. 113 (1973), "the Supreme Court first recognized a fundamental constitutional right of privacy which encompasses a woman's decision of whether to terminate her pregnancy." *Id.* at 1057. "That right of privacy guaranteed by the penumbra of the Bill of Rights of the United States Constitution," the court added in dictum, "was also secured by the drafters of the 1970 Constitution of the State of Illinois." *Id.*, citing art. I, §§6 and 12 of the Illinois Constitution. Whether either §6 or §12 secures rights relating to privacy of conduct is discussed later in this analysis. No such issue was presented in *Family Life League*, which rejected an informational privacy defense raised on behalf of abortion providers and their patients to the disclosure of the names of physicians who received public funds for abortion services.

2. 410 U.S. 113 (1973).

3. 505 U.S. 833 (1992).

4. ILL. REV. STAT. ch. 38, ¶ 23-1 (1971).

Pursuant to *Roe*, ¶ 23-1 was declared unconstitutional by the Illinois Supreme Court (on federal, not state, grounds) in *People v. Frey*,[5] and was later repealed.[6]

Based upon arguments that have been raised in Illinois and other States with similar constitutional provisions,[7] possible sources for an asserted abortion right could include provisions of the Bill of Rights guaranteeing due process of law and equal protection (art. I, § 2), religious freedom (§ 3) and a certain remedy (§ 12); prohibiting unreasonable searches and seizures, invasions of privacy and interceptions of communications by eavesdropping devices (§ 6) and discrimination on account of sex (§ 18); recognizing inherent and inalienable rights (§ 1); and retaining rights (§ 24).[8] The analysis that follows addresses each of these provisions.

Inherent and Inalienable Rights

Article I, § 1, of the Illinois Constitution provides: "All men are by nature free and independent and have certain inherent and inalienable rights among which are life, liberty and the pursuit of happiness. To secure these rights and the protection of property, governments are instituted among men, deriving their just powers from the consent of the governed."[9] The official commentary

---

5. 294 N.E.2d 257 (Ill. 1973). Prior to the Supreme Court's decision in *Roe*, the Illinois Supreme Court rejected an attempt to engraft mental or psychiatric grounds onto the statute. *People ex rel. Hanrahan v. White*, 285 N.E.2d 129 (Ill. 1972). The pre-*Roe* statute was also struck down by a three-judge federal district court. *Doe v. Scott*, 321 F. Supp. 1385 (N.D. 1971) , *vacated and remanded sub nom. Hanrahan v. Doe*, 410 U.S. 950 (1973).

6. Ill. Public Act 78-225, § 10 (1973). The preamble to the Illinois Abortion Act of 1975 states that if the decisions of the United States Supreme Court recognizing a right to abortion are "ever reversed or modified or the United States Constitution is ever amended to allow protection of the unborn[,] then the former policy of this State to prohibit abortions unless necessary for the preservation of the mother's life shall be reinstated." 720 ILL. COMP. STAT. ANN. 510/1 (West 2003). In the absence of new legislation criminalizing abortion, the preamble would not, by its own terms, make abortion illegal. It contains no operative provisions and authorizes no punishment. Conduct is not criminal in Illinois unless a statute defines the particular conduct as criminal. *See* 720 ILL. COMP. STAT. ANN. 5/1-3 (West 2002). Moreover, one General Assembly cannot bind another to enact legislation. *See* ILLINOIS GENERAL ASSEMBLY LEGISLATIVE RESEARCH UNIT, EFFECTS ON ILLINOIS IF *ROE V. WADE* IS MODIFIED OR OVERRULED (Feb. 9, 1989).

7. *See Doe v. Wright*, No. 91 CH 1958, Order, Dec. 2, 1994 (Illinois Circuit Court, Cook County) (invalidating restrictions on public funding of abortion), *leave to file late appeal denied*, No. 78512 (Ill. Feb. 28, 1995).

8. One other more unlikely source of an abortion right under the Illinois Constitution-art. I, § 4 (guaranteeing freedom of speech)-is discussed generally in Chapter 3, *supra*.

9. ILL. CONST. art. I, § 1 (West 2006).

notes that art. I, § 1, "is generally not considered alone as a limitation upon the exercise of governmental power. Rather, it is considered with the due process and equal protection guarantees of Section 2."[10] In reference to almost identical language in the 1870 Illinois Constitution, the Illinois Supreme Court has said that "this section 'is not generally considered, of itself, an operative constitutional limitation upon the exercise of governmental powers. Rather, it is considered supplemental to and implicitly within [the due process clause]. There is thus little purpose in treating this section as an independent source of constitutional law.'"[11] Because the Illinois Supreme Court does not recognize art. I, § 1, as "an operative constitutional limitation on the exercise of governmental powers," it could not serve as a source of a right to abortion under the state constitution.

Due Process of Law, Equal Protection

Article I, § 2, of the Illinois Constitution provides: "No person shall be deprived of life, liberty or property without due process of law nor be denied the equal protection of the law."[12] In any challenge to a statute prohibiting abortion, abortion advocates are likely to rely upon art. I, § 2. That reliance would be misplaced, however.

The Illinois Supreme Court has held that it "may construe the state due process clause independently of its federal counterpart, and in appropriate cases will interpret the state due process clause to provide greater protections...."[13] Thus, the mere fact that the Supreme Court may overrule *Roe v. Wade* and hold that the liberty language of the Due Process Clause of the Fourteenth Amendment does not confer a right to abortion would not necessarily mean that the Illinois Supreme Court would follow suit in interpreting the due process clause of the Illinois Constitution. Nevertheless, there is little, if any, reason to believe that the state supreme court would recognize a right to abortion under the liberty language of the due process clause of the state constitution.

For purposes of state and federal substantive due process analysis, a statute is unconstitutional "if it impermissibly restricts a person's life, liberty or property interest."[14] "If the life, liberty or property interest is a fundamental right,

---

10. *Constitutional Commentary*, ILL. CONST. art. I, § 1 (West 2006).

11. *Kunkel v. Walton*, 689 N.E.2d 1047, 1056–57 (Ill. 1998) (quoting G. Braden & R. Cohn, THE ILLINOIS CONSTITUTION: AN ANNOTATED AND COMPARATIVE ANALYSIS 8 (1969)).

12. ILL. CONST. art. I, § 2 (West 2006).

13. *People v. Molnar*, 857 N.E.2d 209, 218 (Ill. 2006).

14. *People v. R.G.*, 546 N.E.2d 533, 540 (Ill. 1989).

then any statute limiting that right may be justified only by a compelling state interest, and must be narrowly drawn to express only the legitimate interests at stake."[15] "If," on the other hand, "the interest is not a fundamental right, then the statute need only have a rational relation to the purpose the legislature sought to accomplish by enacting the statute."[16] The Illinois Supreme Court has emphasized that "[n]ot every right secured by the State or Federal constitutions is fundamental, ... but only those which 'lie at the heart of the relationship between the individual and a republican form of government.'"[17] "Fundamental rights include the expression of ideas, participation in the political process, travel among the states and privacy with respect to the most intimate and personal aspects of one's life."[18]

The Illinois Supreme Court has not held that a right to abortion is a "fundamental right" under the *state* constitution.[19] Abortion is not mentioned in the text of §2. Moreover, a review of the proceedings of the Constitutional Convention indicates that a right to abortion cannot be derived from the liberty language of the due process clause of §2.[20] Ironically, that indication is based upon the Convention's *rejection* of language that would have included the unborn within the meaning of the word "person," as used in the due process clause.

The original draft of art. I, §2, proposed by the Bill of Rights Committee, added the phrase, "including the unborn," after the word "person."[21] The ad-

---

15. *Id.* (citation and internal quotation marks omitted).

16. Id. (citation omitted).

17. *Kalodimos v. Village of Morton Grove*, 470 N.E.2d 266, 277 (Ill. 1984) (quoting *People ex rel. Tucker v. Kotsos*, 368 N.E.2d 903, 907 (1977)).

18. *Committee for Educational Rights v. Edgar*, 672 N.E.2d 1178, 1194 (1996) (citing *Kotsos*, 368 N.E.2d at 907).

19. *See* n. 1, *supra.* To the extent that the Illinois Supreme Court considers federal precedent in determining whether an asserted liberty interest (or right) is "fundamental" under the state due process guarantee, abortion would not qualify as a "fundamental" right. Although the Supreme Court characterized the right to choose abortion as "fundamental" in *Roe*, 410 U.S. at 152–53, it tacitly abandoned that characterization in *Casey*, 505 U.S. at 869–79 (Joint Op. of O'-Connor, Kennedy and Souter, JJ., replacing *Roe's* "strict scrutiny" standard of review with the more relaxed "undue burden" standard, allowing for a broader measure of abortion regulation).

20. "The meaning which the delegates to the convention attached to a provision in the Constitution before sending it to the voters for ratification is relevant in resolving ambiguities which may remain after consulting the language of the provision." *Kalodimos*, 470 N.E.2d at 270 (citations omitted). "The reason is that it is only with the consent of the convention that such provisions are submitted to the voters in the first place." *Id. See also People v. Tisler*, 469 N.E.2d 147, 161 (Ill. 1984) (Ward, J., concurring) ("it is generally accepted that courts must look to the intent of the adopters and framers as controlling").

21. VI Record of Proceedings, Sixth Illinois Constitutional Convention (hereinafter Record of Proceedings) 18 (1969–1970).

ditional language was "meant to assure than an unborn person cannot be deprived of life, liberty or property by the State without due process of law."[22] A minority of committee members opposed inclusion of this language.[23] Their reasons for doing so are revealing on the question of whether the language, as ultimately adopted, embraces an abortion right.

The Minority Report stated that the chief, if not only, effect of including these words would be "to prohibit the General Assembly from enacting any laws to permit abortions, except presumably abortions which are now permitted under Illinois law where necessary to preserve the life of the mother."[24] The authors of the Minority Report argued that "the subject of abortion law should be left to the legislature, which can study and evaluate the pertinent medical and social facts and policy consideration[s]."[25] In presenting their arguments on the convention floor, the delegates who signed the Minority Report left no doubt regarding the legislature's authority to prohibit abortion. Delegate Wilson said:

> It is the position of the minority that the legislature should be left free to deal with the question of abortion under the due process clause as it now stands, and that no further impediments on the power of the legislature to act freely should be inserted in the due process clause in the form of these words. It is not the position of the minority that the constitution should speak to the question of abortion by putting into the constitution some provision that presumably would authorize or make more constitutional ... the enactment of what I will refer to as liberalized abortion laws. It is our position that the constitution should not address itself to the issue of abortion at all, but that this should be left to be acted upon by the legislature under the existing language of the due process clause.[26]

He emphasized that

> this whole matter should be left to the legislature to act upon.... The legislature, I think, has shown the capacity and the will to act in the field of abortion law; and we feel perfectly confident in leaving this

---

22. *Id.* at 19.

23. *Id.* at 127–36.

24. *Id.* at 130.

25. *Id.* at 131. *See also id.* at 134–35: "The subject of abortion law should be left to the legislature. This Constitutional Convention is not equipped to study the pertinent medical or social facts or weigh the competing policy considerations which bear on the question of what kind of abortion law Illinois should have."

26. III Record of Proceedings at 1504.

to the legislature and not trying to constitutionalize it. There are too many imponderables. The whole subject is too dynamic and too volatile.... [T]he world is changing; and we feel that this should be left to the legislature.[27]

Delegate Weisberg echoed these sentiments:

The minority believes ... that this subject is peculiarly appropriate and necessary to leave to the legislature. Thee are serious problems here. It has been pointed out more and more frequently in recent years that there are serious medical and social problems which the Constitutional Convention ... is not equipped to study and evaluate.[28]

Most of the delegates who spoke in favor of the Minority Report expressed the view that the Constitutional Convention should not attempt to deal with the question of abortion, but should leave it up to the legislature to act as it might deem appropriate.[29] After extended debate, the Convention adopted the Minority Report and deleted the phrase, "including the unborn," from proposed art. I, § 2.[30] No delegate suggested that art. I, § 2, shorn of this language, would constitutionalize a right to abortion. Delegate Kinney, who voted in favor of the Minority Report, spoke to this question:

If there is any mischief in the proposed phrase [*i.e.*, "including the unborn"] and its deletion, if it is to be deleted, it may lie in opening a line of argument that by [its] deletion this Convention has expressed itself in favor of unlimited legalized abortion. To foreclose that possibility, I wish to set the record straight on my vote. I do not adopt this position.[31]

And neither did the Convention. Three member proposals were submitted which would have limited the General Assembly's authority to prohibit abortion. Member Proposal No. 387 provided: "The State shall make no law decreeing

---

27. *Id.* at 1504–05.

28. *Id.* at 1505.

29. *Id.* at 1511–12 (remarks of Delegate Foster); 1513 (remarks of Delegate Pappas); 1514 (remarks of Delegate Raby); 1516–17 (remarks of Delegate Kelley), 1519 (remarks of Delegate Howard), and 1522 (remarks of Delegate MacDonald).

30. *Id.* at 1523.

31. *Id.* at 1521.

who is to be born and who is to die."[32] Member Proposal No. 407 provided: "No penalty may be imposed by law upon any person in connection with an abortion performed by a licensed physician with the consent of the woman upon whom it is performed and, if she is an unmarried minor, the consent of her parents or guardian."[33] And Member Proposal No. 506 provided: "That any female by giving her consent and approval shall not be denied the right to comply with advice given by qualified medical authorities. The General Assembly shall define qualified medical authorities."[34] None of these proposals was adopted by either the Bill of Rights Committee or the Convention itself. Several delegates, including Elmer Gertz, the Chairman of the Bill of Rights Committee, acknowledged that neither the Bill of Rights Committee nor the Convention would recognize abortion rights.[35] A review of the record of the proceedings of the 1970 Illinois Constitutional Convention leaves no doubt that the Convention did not intend to recognize abortion rights in the language of the due process clause of art. I, §2. To suggest that a constitutional convention that expressly *rejected* specific abortion rights proposals and left the issue of abortion up to the legislature impliedly *accepted* a right to abortion under the general language of *other* provisions of the constitution is, at best, disingenuous.

Unlike the Illinois Supreme Court's independent due process analysis, "in applying an equal protection analysis, we apply the same standard under both the United States Constitution and the Illinois Constitution."[36] This equivalency of interpretation suggests that if the Supreme Court does not construe the Equal Protection Clause of the Fourteenth Amendment to place limits on the State's authority to prohibit abortion (and it has not done so to date), then

---

32. VII Record of Proceedings at 3012.

33. *Id.* at 3021.

34. *Id.* at 3069.

35. III Record of Proceedings at 1514 ("[w]hile I would hope that this Convention would have faced this issue [abortion] squarely-would have included in the constitution a prevention from the legislature acting on this matter, ... I recognize that that is not possible") (remarks of Delegate Raby); 1516 ("[w]hereas this proposal [Member Proposal 407] reflects my philosophy in regard to abortion, I am not at this time suggesting that we adopt such. I am suggesting that we not preclude the General Assembly from enacting such legislation in the future") (remarks of Delegate Kelley); 1500 (remarks of Delegate Gertz). It is apparent from the remarks of Delegates Gertz (*id.* at 1500) and Wilson (*id.* at 1504) that the Bill of Rights Committee defeated a proposal to restrict the legislature's authority over abortion.

36. *General Motors Corp. v. State of Illinois Motor Vehicle Review Board*, 862 N.E.2d 209, 229 (Ill. 2007).

the Illinois Supreme Court will not so construe the equal protection clause of art. I, § 2, either.[37]

Religious Freedom

Article I, § 3, of the Illinois Constitution provides:

> The free exercise and enjoyment of religious profession and worship, without discrimination, shall forever be guaranteed, and no person shall be denied any civil or political right, privilege or capacity, on account of his religious opinions; but the liberty of conscience hereby secured shall not be construed to dispense with oaths or affirmations, excuse acts of licentiousness, or justify practices inconsistent with the peace or safety of the State. No person shall be required to attend or support any ministry or place of worship against his consent, nor shall any preference by given by law to any religious denomination or mode or worship.[38]

In any challenge to a statute prohibiting abortion, abortion advocates may raise either or both of two arguments under art. I, § 3. First, relying on the first clause of the first sentence of § 3, they may argue than an abortion prohibition interferes with the "free exercise and enjoyment" of a woman's "religious profession" by forbidding her from obtaining an abortion that would be allowed by her religion. Second, relying upon the second clause of the second sentence of § 3, they may argue in the alternative (or in addition) that an abortion prohibition gives a "preference" to a "religious denomination" because it reflects sectarian beliefs regarding when human life begins and the sinfulness of abortion. Neither argument would likely prevail.

The Illinois reviewing courts have that the rights secured by art. I, § 3, are no broader than those secured by the Free Exercise and Establishment Clauses of the First Amendment.[39] This equivalency of interpretation suggests that a challenge to an abortion statute that would not succeed under the Religion Clauses of the First Amendment would not succeed under art. I, § 3, either. For the reasons set forth in Chapter 2, *supra*, an abortion statute could not be successfully challenged on First Amendment grounds. Accordingly, a similar challenge under art. I, § 3, would not likely be successful.

---

37. Whether an abortion prohibition would run afoul of the state prohibition of discrimination on account of sex (art. I, § 18) is discussed below.

38. ILL. CONST. art. I, § 3 (West 2006).

39. *People v. Falbe*, 727 N.E.2d 200, 207 (Ill. 2000) ("any statute which is valid under the first amendment is also valid under the Illinois Constitution) (Establishment Clause); *Mefford v. White*, 770 N.E.2d 1251, 1260 (Ill. App. Ct. 2002) (same with respect to Free Exercise Clause).

Searches, Seizures, Invasions of Privacy and Interceptions of Communications

Article I, §6, of the Illinois Constitution provides, in pertinent part: "The people shall have the right to be secure in their persons, houses, papers and other possessions against unreasonable searches, seizures, invasions of privacy or interceptions of communications by eavesdropping devices or other means."[40] In addition to restating the right to be secure against unreasonable searches and seizures in "more modern usage," §6 "was substantively changed by inclusion of two new clauses, each of which created a right not expressly stated in the 1870 constitution-the right to be secure against unreasonable invasions of privacy by the state and the right to be secure against unreasonable interceptions of communications by the state."[41]

The first clause of §6, securing the right of the people against unreasonable searches and seizures, is concerned with the *means* by which evidence of criminal conduct is discovered,[42] not whether the underlying conduct is constitutionally protected.[43] Thus, although the first clause may protect aspects of privacy ("the right [of the people] to be secure in their persons, houses, papers and other possessions against unreasonable searches [and] seizures"), that privacy interest relates solely to the *means* by which incriminating evidence is obtained. The exclusionary rule, which has been adopted to enforce §6 and bars admission of illegally obtained evidence, is primarily directed at and is intended to deter police misconduct.[44] The third clause of §6, securing the right of the people against unreasonable interceptions of communications by

---

40. ILL. CONST. art. I, §6 (West 2006).

41. *People v. Caballes*, 851 N.E.2d 26, 33 (Ill. 2006).

42. *People v. McGee*, 644 N.E.2d 439, 446 (Ill. App. Ct. 1994) ("judiciary cannot, and should not, tolerate evidence-gathering practices [that] violate the constitution").

43. *See, e.g., People v. Ledesma*, 795 N.E.2d 253, 261 (Ill. 2003): The "fundamental purpose" of the Fourth Amendment and art. I, §6, of the Illinois Constitution "is to safeguard the privacy and security of individuals against arbitrary invasions by government officials. [Citation omitted]. We must carefully balance the legitimate aims of law enforcement against the right of our citizens to be free from unreasonable government intrusion." *See also In re Brewer*, 320 N.E.2d 340, 342 (Ill. App. Ct. 1974) ("the very purpose of the constitutional guarantee was to place obstacles in the way of a too permeating police surveillance thereby subjecting a free people to an even greater danger than the escape of some criminals"). Illinois generally follows the Supreme Court's construction of the Fourth Amendment in interpreting the search and seizure language of art. I, §6. *See People v. Caballes*, 851 N.E.2d at 31–45.

44. *People v. Madison*, 520 N.E.2d 374, 380 (Ill. 1998) (referring to "the central purpose of deterring police misconduct which underlies the exclusionary rule").

eavesdropping or other means, obviously has no bearing on determining what conduct may be deemed criminal.

The second clause of §6, however, secures the right of the people against unreasonable "invasions of privacy." This language, the Illinois Supreme Court has held, "recognizes a zone of privacy not found in the Fourth Amendment and, therefore, affords protections that go beyond the guarantees of the Federal Constitution."[45] Abortion advocates may be expected to argue that this language creates an independent right of privacy which, in turn, includes a right to choose abortion. There are several problems with this line of argument, however.

First, the overriding concern of the drafters of §6 was informational privacy and privacy in communication.[46] Review of the debate fails to reflect any intent on behalf of the drafters to limit the legislature's power to prohibit abortion or any other conduct not given express constitutional protection.

Second, although the Illinois Supreme Court has not held that the privacy language of §6 does not protect conduct, in each case in which it has upheld a privacy claim, the claim involved informational privacy (or privacy with respect to the gathering of physical evidence), not privacy of conduct.[47] The court has consistently rejected privacy of conduct claims under §6.[48] In *Longe-*

---

45. *King v. Ryan*, 607 N.E.2d 154, 162 (Ill. 1992). Both the Fourth Amendment and art. I, §6, of the Illinois Constitution prohibit "searches" and "seizures" that are "unreasonable." *People v. Watson*, 825 N.E.2d 257, 261 (Ill. 2005). Section 6, however, "extends the 'reasonableness' requirement to 'invasions of privacy' and, as a result, provides citizens of this state with broader protection from unreasonable intrusions than the [F]ourth [A]mendment." *Id.* (citing *In re May 1991 Will County Grand Jury*, 604 N.E.2d 929, 934 (Ill. 1992)).

46. III RECORD OF PROCEEDINGS at 1525, 1530 (remarks of Delegate Dvorak), 1529 (remarks of Delegate Foster), and 1535 (remarks of Delegate Gertz).

47. *See, e.g., Kunkel v. Walton*, 689 N.E.2d at 1055–56 (protecting confidentiality of personal medical information); *Best v. Taylor Machine Works*, 689 N.E.2d 1057, 1096–1100 (Ill. 1997) (same); *King v. Ryan*, 607 N.E.2d at 162 (statute authorizing chemical testing of driver without any indication that the driver had been drinking was unconstitutional); *In re May 1991 Will County Grand Jury*, 604 N.E.2d at 936–39 (in the absence of probable cause, hair samples could not be subpoenaed from an individual under investigation but not charged with any offense).

48. *See, e.g., In re C.E.*, 641 N.E.2d 345, 351 (Ill. 1994) (declining to decide whether there is a federal or state right to privacy that encompasses a right to refuse medical treatment); *In re Estate of Longeway*, 549 N.E.2d 292, 297 (Ill. 1989) (same); *People v. Geever*, 522 N.E.2d 1200, 1206–07 (Ill. 1988) (no privacy right to private possession of child pornography), *appeal dismissed, Geever v. Illinois*, 488 U.S. 920 (1988); *People v. Kohrig*, 498 N.E.2d 1158, 1162 (Ill. 1986) (no privacy right not to use seat belts). *See also Illinois NORML, Inc. v. Scott*, 383 N.E.2d 1330, 1332–34 (Ill. App. Ct. 1978) (no privacy right to private use and possession of cannabis).

way, the court said that, in the absence of "a clear expression of intent from the drafters of our 1970 State constitution, we ... abstain from expanding the privacy provision of our State constitution to embrace this right [to refuse life-sustaining medical treatment]."[49] There was no "clear expression of intent from the drafters" that the privacy provision "embrace[s]" a right to abortion.

Third, and most important, the drafters unequivocally disavowed any intent that the privacy language of art. I, § 6, would affect the legislature's authority with respect to abortion. This is evident from an exchange between Fr. Francis Lawlor, one of the delegates to the Convention, and Elmer Gertz, chairman of the Bill of Rights Committee, on the floor of the Convention. The exchange is brief, but illuminating:

> FR. LAWLOR: "Mr. Gertz—I would very much appreciate it if you would assure the entire delegation here that the right of the people to be secure in their persons against unreasonable invasions of their privacy ... has absolutely nothing to do with the question of abortion."
>
> MR. GERTZ: "It certainly has nothing to do with the question of abortion."[50]

In light of the Convention's repudiation of specific abortion rights language, Delegate Gertz's reply should come as no surprise to anyone. Nothing in the language of art. I, § 6, may be construed to confer a right to abortion.

Certain Remedy

Article I, § 12, of the Illinois Constitution provides: "Every person shall find a certain remedy in the laws for all injuries and wrongs which he receives to his person, privacy, property or reputation. He shall obtain justice by law, freely, completely, and promptly."[51] In any challenge to a law prohibiting abortion, abortion advocates may be expected to rely upon the privacy language in the first sentence of § 12 in support of a claim that the Illinois Constitution protects a right to abortion. Such reliance would be misplaced for a variety of reasons.

First, as is apparent from its text and structure, § 12 is concerned with *remedies* for tortiously inflicted injuries and wrongs—it does not establish what *constitutes* an injury or wrong to anyone's "person, privacy, property or reputation." Those remedies, however, are derived from the common law and statutes, not § 12. Moreover, the remedies themselves redress injuries and wrongs recognized

---

49. *Longeway*, 549 N.E.2d at 297.
50. III Record of Proceedings at 1537.
51. Ill. Const. art. I, § 12 (West 2006).

by the common law and statutory law, not constitutional "injuries." Section 12, in other words, does not *create* any new causes of action, but, at most, merely *preserves* existing common law and statutory remedies.

Second, although there is one older case in which the predecessor of §12 was used to strike down a statute eliminating certain common law remedies,[52] there are no modern cases so holding. The Illinois Supreme Court has held that "this constitutional provision is merely an expression of philosophy and not a mandate that a certain remedy be provided in any specific form."[53]

Third, with respect to remedies for "injuries and wrongs" to a person's privacy, the state supreme court has held that art. I, §12, "was intended to protect an individual's privacy from invasions or injuries caused by another *non-governmental* individual or company."[54] To the extent that a statute prohibiting abortion may be said to "invade" one's privacy, that "invasion" is caused by the State, not by a private actor, and, therefore, does not implicate the concerns underlying §12 as it has been interpreted by the supreme court.

Finally, even assuming, contrary to its purpose and interpretation, that §12 confers substantive rights, as opposed to guaranteeing remedies, §12 "does not create fundamental rights in the interests listed [therein]."[55] Accordingly, the proper test for statutes challenged under §12 is rational basis, not strict scrutiny.[56] A statute prohibiting abortion would clearly satisfy that test.

Taken as a whole, §12 is concerned with the availability of private civil causes of action (first sentence) and reasonable access to the courts (second sentence). It places no limitation on the State's authority to define and punish crimes and has never been so interpreted.

Prohibition of Sex Based Discrimination

Article I, §18, of the Illinois Constitution provides: "The equal protection of the laws shall not be denied or abridged on account of sex by the State or

---

52. *See Heck v. Schupp*, 68 N.E.2d 464 (Ill. 1946) (striking down statute abolishing causes of action for alienation of affection, criminal conversation and breach of promise to marry).

53. *Unzicker v. Kraft Food Ingredients Corp.*, 783 N.E.2d 1024, 1036 (Ill. 2002). *See also Best v. Taylor Machine Works*, 689 N.E.2d at 1100 ("the certain remedy provision has been referred to in general as a statement of philosophy rather than a guarantee of a specific remedy").

54. *In re A Minor*, 595 N.E.2d 1052, 1056 (Ill. 1992) (emphasis in original) (citing III RECORD OF PROCEEDINGS at 1531–32).

55. *Schultz v. Lakewood Electric Corp.*, 841 N.E.2d 37, 46 (Ill. App. Ct. 2005) (citing *Gavery v. Lake County*, 513 N.E.2d 1127, 1131 (Ill. App. Ct. 1987)).

56. *Id.* at 47.

its units of local government and school districts."[57] Section 18 was added to the Illinois Bill of Rights on the floor of the Constitutional Convention.[58] The chief sponsor of § 18, Delegate Nicholson, emphasized the problem of gender-based discrimination in employment, education and business.[59] She did not even allude to the issue of abortion. Moreover, Delegate Nicholson denied that adoption of the anti-discrimination provision would bring about "any significant change" in anyone's way of life,[60] which she could not have said if the proposed language would have limited the Legislature's authority over abortion.

Notwithstanding the absence of any mention of abortion in the debate over § 18, abortion advocates may challenge a law prohibiting abortion on the theory that such prohibitions, indeed, abortion regulations generally, affect only women and, therefore, are gender based and subject to the "strict scrutiny" standard of judicial review that applies to sex-based discrimination under § 18.[61] Such a challenge would not likely succeed. Even assuming, contrary to federal equal protection analysis, that a law affecting abortion warrants greater than rational basis scrutiny,[62] both the Illinois Supreme Court and the United States Supreme Court have held that biological differences between men and women may justify different treatment based on those differences.

In *People v. Boyer*,[63] the Illinois Supreme Court rejected a challenge to a state criminal statute that classified and punished incest between a father and his daughter (aggravated incest) more harshly than incest between a mother and her son or between siblings (simple incest). The court held that, regardless of the applicable standard of review (strict scrutiny or rational basis), the distinction did not violate § 18.

> That the State has an interest in protecting potential victims of incestuous relationships is obvious. It is also apparent that a female

---

57. ILL. CONST. art. I, § 18 (West 2006).

58. V RECORD OF PROCEEDINGS at 3669, 3677.

59. *Id.* at 3669–70.

60. *Id.* at 3672.

61. *See People v. Ellis,* 311 N.E.2d 98, 101 (Ill. 1974) (adopting the strict scrutiny standard for review of sex-based classifications).

62. The Supreme Court has held that "the disfavoring of abortion ... is not *ipso facto* sex discrimination," and, citing its decisions in *Harris v. McRae,* 448 U.S. 297, 321–26 (1980), and other cases addressing abortion funding, stated that "the constitutional test applicable to government abortion-funding restrictions is not the heightened-scrutiny standard that our cases demand for sex discrimination, ... but the ordinary rationality standard." *Bray v. Alexandria Women's Health Clinic,* 506 U.S. 263, 273 (1993).

63. 349 N.E.2d 50 (Ill. 1976).

victim of a father-daughter incestuous relationship is exposed to potential harm to which male victims of incestuous relationships are
not exposed.... [T]he psychological trauma that may result from incest is potentially severe whether the object of the incest is a male or
a female. The possibility that the female victim may become pregnant, however, adds considerably to the potential harm that may result from a father-daughter incestuous relationship. A female who is
impregnated by her father is confronted with a traumatic experience
beyond the experience of the incestuous act itself. The female must
either endure the pregnancy and give birth to a baby or make the decision to have an abortion. If a child is born as a result of the incest,
the female victim must either care for the child herself or give the
child up for adoption. The physical change in a female who becomes
pregnant could in itself be a source of trauma to the female. The potential psychological damage to the victim of a father-daughter incestuous relationship is admittedly difficult to estimate, but it is surely
existent and considerable. Additionally, a pregnant woman is exposed
to some physical dangers. While the statute prohibits deviate sexual
conduct, as well as intercourse, and such acts could not cause pregnancies, the legislature could reasonably conclude that enhanced
penalties were required to deter deviate sexual conduct, since such
actions if undeterred would normally lead to acts of intercourse. We
therefore agree with the State that the physical and psychological dangers of incest are greater with the offense is committed by a male and
the victim is his daughter.... [T]he State's interest in protecting potential victims of incestuous relationships justifies the statutory classification at issue.[64]

So, too, in upholding a statutory rape statute that applied only to males,
the Supreme Court noted, "this Court has consistently upheld statutes where
the gender classification is not invidious, but rather realistically reflects the
fact that the sexes are not similarly situated in certain circumstances."[65] As one
federal district court observed: "Abortion statutes are examples of cases in
which the sexes are not biologically similarly situated" because only women
are capable of becoming pregnant and having abortions.[66]

---

64. *Id.* at 51–52.
65. *Michael M. v. Superior Court*, 450 U.S. 464, 469 (1981).
66. *Jane L. v. Bangerter*, 794 F. Supp. 1537, 1549 (D. Utah 1992).

A statute prohibiting abortion quite obviously can affect only women because only women are capable of becoming pregnant.[67] Unlike laws that use women's ability to become pregnant (or pregnancy itself) to discriminate against them in *other* areas (*e.g.,* employment opportunities), abortion prohibitions cannot fairly be said to involve a distinction between men and women that is a "mere pretext[] designed to erect an invidious discrimination against [women]."[68]

Retained Rights

Article I, § 24, of the Illinois Constitution provides: "The enumeration in this Constitution of certain rights shall not be construed to deny or disparage others retained by the individual citizens of the State."[69] Abortion advocates may be expected to cite § 24 in support of an asserted right to abortion under the state constitution. A proper interpretation of § 24, however, would not appear to support a right to abortion as a "retained right."

The official commentary notes that the language of § 24 "is the same as that of the Ninth Amendment to the United States Constitution, except that 'people' has been replaced by 'individual citizen[s] of this State.' "[70] Given that the language of § 24 is essentially the same as that of the Ninth Amendment, it should be given a parallel interpretation, absent evidence to the contrary in the proceedings of the Constitutional Convention.[71] That, in turn, suggests that if no right to abortion exists under the Ninth Amendment, then none would be recognized under art. I, § 24. The Supreme Court, however, has rooted the "abortion liberty" in the liberty language of the Due Process Clause of the Fourteenth Amendment, not in the unenumerated rights language of the Ninth Amendment.[72] Because abortion has not been recognized as a "retained

---

67. *Geduldig v. Aiello,* 417 U.S. 484, 496 n. 20 (1974) ("[n]ormal pregnancy is an objectively, identifiable physical condition with unique characteristics").

68. *Id.*

69. Ill. Const. art. I, § 24 (West 2006).

70. *Constitutional Commentary,* Ill. Const. art. I, § 24 (West 2006). The Ninth Amendment provides: "The enumeration in the Constitution of certain rights, shall not be construed to deny or disparage others retained by the people." U.S. Const. amend. IX (West 2006).

71. To give § 24 a different interpretation, "there must be evidence in the language of the state constitution or in the debates and committee reports from its drafting that shows that the drafters intended the state constitution to be construed differently." *People v. Moss,* 842 N.E.2d 699, 705 (Ill. 2005). With respect to § 24, there is no such evidence.

72. *See Roe,* 410 U.S. at 153; *Casey,* 505 U.S. at 846. In any event, the Ninth Amendment, standing alone, is not a source of substantive rights. *Gibson v. Matthews,* 926 F.2d 532, 537 (6th Cir. 1991). Although "[s]ome unenumerated rights may be of [c]onstitutional

right" under the Ninth Amendment, it should not be recognized as one under §24, either. In the more than 35 years since the 1970 Illinois Constitution was adopted, §24 has never been interpreted by a state reviewing court or cited in favor of any decision recognizing a "retained right."[73]

Apart from the conscious decision of the drafters to model §24 on the Ninth Amendment,[74] which does not secure a right to abortion, the State's history of prohibiting abortion would appear to undermine any argument that abortion could be regarded as a "retained" right, that is, a right that existed at the time the state constitution was adopted in 1970. From 1827, only nine years after Illinois was admitted to the Union, until 1973, when *Roe v. Wade* was decided, it was the public policy of Illinois to protect unborn human life by prohibiting abortion.[75] More than 100 years ago, the Illinois Supreme Court recognized the purpose underlying this policy when it characterized abortion as "a grave crime, involving the destruction of an unborn child."[76] Except for a brief, seven-year period between 1867 and 1874, when abortion was allowed "for *bona fide* medical or surgical purposes,"[77] Illinois prohibited abortion at any stage of pregnancy unless the mother's life was endangered.[78] When, after *Roe*, the Illinois Supreme Court declared the state abortion law unconstitutional, it did so strictly on the basis of the Supremacy Clause, and not upon any independent state ground.[79] In light of the foregoing, there is no basis on which it fairly could be argued that the "retained rights" provision of the Illinois Bill of Rights secures a right to abortion.

---

magnitude," that is only "by virtue of other amendments, such as the Fifth or Fourteenth Amendment. A person cannot claim a right that exists solely under the Ninth Amendment." *United States v. Vital Health Products, Ltd.*, 786 F. Supp. 761, 777 (E.D. Wis. 1992), *aff'd mem. op., sub nom. United States v. LeBeau*, 985 F.2d 563 (7th Cir. 1993). *See also Charles v. Brown*, 495 F. Supp. 862, 863 (N.D. Ala. 1980) (same).

73. An entirely plausible alternative reading of §24 is that the enumeration of certain *constitutional* rights should not be construed to "deny or disparage" *common law* or *statutory* rights retained by the individual citizens of the State.

74. *See* VI Report of Proceedings at 66 (Bill of Rights Majority Report), III Report of Proceedings at 1613–14 (debate on floor of Convention).

75. Act of Jan. 30, 1827, §46, Ill. Rev. Code at 131 (1827), *repealed and replaced by* an Act of Feb. 26, 1833, §46, Ill. Rev. Code at 179 (1833).

76. *Earll v. People*, 99 Ill. 123, 132 (1881).

77. Act of Feb. 18, 1867, Ill. Laws §89 (1867).

78. Ill. Rev. Stat. ch. 38, §3 (1874), *carried forward as* Ill. Rev. Stat. ch. 38, ¶23-1 (1971).

79. *People v. Frey*, 54 Ill. 2d 28 (Ill. 1973).

Conclusion

Based on the foregoing analysis, an argument that the Illinois Constitution protects a right to abortion that is separate from, and independent of, the right to abortion recognized in *Roe v. Wade* would not likely succeed. That, in turn, suggests that if *Roe*, as modified by *Casey*, is ultimately overruled, the State of Illinois could enact and enforce a statute *prohibiting* abortion. Moreover, nothing in the Illinois Constitution precludes Illinois from *regulating* abortion within federal constitutional limits in the meantime.

CHAPTER 17

INDIANA

Summary

The Indiana Supreme Court has not yet decided whether the Indiana Constitution protects a right to abortion separate from, and independent of, the right to abortion recognized under the United States Constitution.[1] A careful examination of the state constitution, in light of its history and interpretation, as well as other relevant legal sources, however, suggests that the state supreme court probably would not recognize a state constitutional right to abortion. Thus, if *Roe v. Wade*,[2] as modified by *Planned Parenthood of Southeastern Pennsylvania v. Casey*,[3] were overruled, Indiana could prohibit abortion. Moreover, with the exception of restrictions on public funding of abortion,[4] nothing in

---

1. *See Clinic for Women, Inc. v. Brizzi*, 837 N.E.2d 973, 978 (Ind. 2005) (upholding statute mandating informed consent and an eighteen-hour waiting period without deciding whether the state constitution confers a right to abortion).

2. 410 U.S. 113 (1973).

3. 505 U.S. 833 (1992).

4. In *Humphreys v. Clinic for Women, Inc.*, 796 N.E.2d 247 (Ind. 2003), the Indiana Supreme Court considered the constitutionality of the State's restrictions on public funding of abortion for poor women. Indiana pays for an abortion only "if performed to preserve the life of the pregnant woman or in other circumstances if the abortion is required to be covered by Medicaid under federal law," which includes pregnancies caused by rape or incest. *Id.* at 250 (citations omitted). A majority of the court held that the funding restrictions are facially valid, but a differently constituted majority found them invalid as applied to women whose pregnancies create a serious risk of substantial and irreversible impairment of a major bodily function. *Id.* at 253–60. With respect to the latter holding, the court explained that there was no principled basis on which to distinguish cases where an abortion is performed because the woman was the victim of rape or incest, and the abortion is paid for, in part, with state funds, from those where "the pregnant woman faces substantial and irreversible impairment of a major bodily function," *id.* at 258, and no part of the cost of the abortion is paid for by the State. "The medical, moral, social, and ethical concerns are the same or at least the differences too insubstantial to be sustained by the State's classification." *Id.* The majority held that "[s]o long as the Indiana Medicaid program pays

the state constitution, properly understood, precludes the State from enacting and enforcing reasonable measures regulating abortion within current federal constitutional limits.

Analysis

The principal pre-*Roe* abortion statute prohibited performance of an abortion upon a pregnant woman unless the procedure was "necessary to preserve her life."[5] Another statute prohibited a woman from soliciting an abortion or allowing an abortion to be performed upon her (subject to the same exception).[6] Following *Roe*, §§ 35-1-58.1 and 35-1-58-2 were repealed in 1977.[7]

Based upon arguments that have been raised in Indiana and other States with similar constitutional provisions, possible sources for an asserted abortion right could include provisions of the Bill of Rights guaranteeing freedom of religious opinions and rights of conscience (art. I, § 3), a remedy by due course of law (§ 12) and equal privileges and immunities (§ 23); prohibiting religious preferences (§ 4); and recognizing inherent and inalienable rights (§ 1).[8] The analysis that follows addresses each of these provisions.

---

for abortions for Medicaid-eligible women where necessary to preserve the life of the pregnant woman or where the pregnancy was caused by rape or incest, … it must pay for abortions for Medicaid-eligible women whose pregnancies create serious risk of substantial and irreversible impairment of a major bodily function." *Id.* at 259. The constitutional provision on which the majority relied, art. I, § 23 (equal privileges), is discussed later in this analysis. What is important to note here is that the decision in *Humphreys* would not limit the State's authority to prohibit abortion so long as a rational distinction could be drawn between those abortions the law prohibited and those that it allowed. This is apparent from the majority's tacit recognition that if the funding restrictions had paid only for abortions to preserve the pregnant woman's life, and not in any other circumstances, they would have been upheld. *Id.* at 258 (the classification "includes abortions where the pregnancy was caused by rape or incest where there is no inherent threat to life").

5. IND. CODE ANN. § 35-1-58-1 (Burns 1971).

6. *Id.* § 35-1-58-2. No prosecutions were reported under this statute.

7. 1977 Ind. Acts 1513, 1524, Pub. L. No. 335, § 21.

8. Three other more unlikely sources of an abortion right under the Indiana Constitution-art. I, § 9 (guaranteeing freedom of speech), § 11 (prohibiting unreasonable searches and seizures) and § 37 (prohibiting involuntary servitude)-are discussed generally in Chapter 3, *supra*.

Inherent and Inalienable Rights

Article I, § 1, of the Indiana Constitution provides:

> WE DECLARE, That all people are created equal; that they are
> endowed by their CREATOR with certain inalienable rights; that
> among these are life, liberty, and the pursuit of happiness; that all
> power is inherent in the people; and that all free governments are,
> and of right ought to be, founded on their authority, and instituted
> for their peace, safety and well-being. For the advancement of these
> ends, the *people* have, at all times, an indefeasible right to alter and
> reform their government.[9]

The Indiana Supreme Court has questioned whether art. I, § 1, creates any
judicially enforceable rights. In *Doe v. O'Connor*,[10] the state supreme court
surveyed state court decisions interpreting similar language in other state constitutions. Virtually without exception, those decisions have held that provisions comparable to § 1 simply enunciate general fundamental principles to
guide the legislature and are not sufficiently specific to provide courts with a
judicially enforceable standard in the absence of implementing legislation.[11]
In *Doe*, the supreme court did not decide whether § 1 "presents any justiciable issues" because the plaintiff did not press "a substantive claim."[12] Nevertheless, the court's opinion leaves little doubt that, if squarely confronted with
the issue, it would hold that the language of art. I, § 1, is too vague and open-
ended to be capable of application without implementing legislation. That, in
turn, suggests that § 1 could not be a source of an abortion right under the
Indiana Constitution.

Even assuming, however, that § 1 creates judicially enforceable rights, a right
to abortion could not reasonably be considered to be among them. "Questions
arising under the Indiana Constitution are to be resolved by examining the
language of the text in the context of the history surrounding its drafting and
ratification, the purpose and structure of our Constitution, and case law interpreting the specific provisions."[13] Nothing in the language of § 1, considered in light of the history surrounding its drafting and ratification, the purpose

---

9. IND. CONST. art. I, § 1 (2007) (emphasis in original).

10. 790 N.E.2d 985 (Ind. 2003).

11. *Id*. at 990–91 (collecting cases).

12. *Id*. at 991.

13. *Ratliff v. Cohn*, 693 N.E.2d 530, 534 (Ind. 1998) (citations and internal quotation
marks omitted).

and structure of the constitution or the case law interpreting art. I, §1, supports a holding that the liberty language of §1 confers a right to abortion.

Indiana enacted its first abortion statute on February 7, 1835, only nine-
teen years after Indiana became a State and sixteen years before the present
constitution was adopted. The act prohibited abortion at any stage of pregnancy, except to save the mother's life.[14] After undergoing various changes in
1852 and 1859, the law was superseded in 1881 by an act which raised the
penalty from a misdemeanor to a felony and made solicitation of an abortion
by the pregnant woman herself a misdemeanor.[15] In 1905, a new criminal code
was enacted which restated the prohibitions in the 1881 act.[16] Those provisions remained on the books until *Roe v. Wade* was decided.[17] They were repealed
in 1977.[18]

In confronting claims brought under art. I, §1, the Indiana Supreme Court
has "examined text and history to determine whether a given interest is of such
a quality that the founding generation would have considered it fundamental
or 'natural.'"[19] Given the contemporaneous prohibition of abortion, the founding generation would not have considered an interest in obtaining an abortion
as "fundamental" or "natural." The history of the State's efforts to enforce that
prohibition only confirms that understanding.

Before the Supreme Court's decision in *Roe v. Wade*, the Indiana Supreme
Court routinely affirmed the criminal convictions of both laypersons and physicians for performing illegal abortions, without any hint that the prosecutions
or convictions were barred by the Indiana Constitution.[20] And less than six

---

14. Act of Feb. 7, 1835, ch. XLVII, §3, IND. GEN. LAWS, p. 66 (19th Sess.) (1835), *codified at* IND. REV. STAT. ch. XXVI (1838), *recodified at* IND. REV. STAT. ch. 53, §109 (1843).

15. Act of April 14, 1881, ch. 37, §§22, 23, p. 177, *codified at* IND. REV. STAT. ch. 5,
art. 2, §§1923, 1924 (1881), *recodified at* IND. ANN. STAT. Vol. I, ch. 5, art. 2, §§1996, 1997
(1901), *recodified at* IND. ANN. STAT. ch. 5, art. 2, §§2010, 2011 (Supp. 1905).

16. Act of March 10, 1905, ch. 169, §§367, 368, pp. 663–64, *codified at* IND. STAT. ANN.
ch. 5, art. 2, §§2256, 2257 (1908).

17. *Id., carried forward as* IND. STAT. ANN. §§35-1-58.1, 35-1-58.2 (Burns 1971).

18. *See* n. 7, *supra*.

19. *Price v. State*, 622 N.E.2d 954, 959 n. 4 (1993) (citing *In the Matter of Lawrence*, 579
N.E.2d 32, 39 (Ind. 1991)). Both *Price*, which dealt with a free speech issue, and *Lawrence*,
which dealt with the right to refuse unwanted medical treatment, were decided before *Doe
v. O'Connor*, discussed above, in which the court questioned whether art. I, §1, confers
any judicially enforceable rights.

20. *Hauk v. State*, 46 N.E. 126 (Ind. 1897); *McCaughey v. State*, 59 N.E. 169 (Ind. 1900);
Carter v. State, 87 N.E. 1081 (Ind. 1909); *Thain v. State*, 106 N.E. 690 (Ind. 1914); *Hill v.
State*, 141 N.E. 639 (Ind. 1924); *Pleak v. State*, 167 N.E. 524 (Ind. 1929); *Sharp v. State*, 19
N.E.2d 942 (Ind. 1939); *Waltermire v. State*, 59 N.E.2d 123 (Ind. 1945), *on rehearing*, 60 N.E.2d

months before *Roe* was decided, the Indiana Supreme Court rejected privacy, equal protection and vagueness challenges to the principal pre-*Roe* abortion statute (§ 35-1-58.1).[21]

In *Cheaney*, the court reviewed developments in law and medicine recognizing the independent existence of the unborn child from conception and extending legal rights to the unborn child in property, tort and other areas of the law.[22] The court noted that these developments "illustrate the existence of certain rights inhering in the unborn child independent of the mother, which the state may protect."[23] "The existence of the unborn child," the court explained, "distinguishes this case from *Griswold v. Connecticut* [381 U.S. 479 (1965)] or *Eisenstadt v. Baird* [405 U.S. 438 (1972)]."[24] "Those cases involved the right to receive contraceptives while this case involves abortion, the *fundamental distinction* being the difference *between prevention and destruction*."[25] "When the rights of the unborn child come in conflict with the rights of the mother, the State can and must strike a balance between these interests."[26] But striking this balance requires "a weighing of social values which is a legislative function and properly outside the ambit of the judiciary."[27] The state supreme court held that "a State interest in what is, at the very least, from the moment of conception a living being and potential human life, is both valid and compelling."[28]

No state constitutional arguments were raised in *Cheaney*. Nevertheless, the Indiana Supreme Court's acknowledgment that the unborn child has rights and that the State has a "valid and compelling" interest in the life of the child "from the moment of conception" cast doubt on any claim that an independ-

---

526 (Ind. 1945); *Grecu v. State*, 120 N.E.2d 179 (Ind. 1954); *Specht v. State*, 163 N.E.2d 581 (Ind. 1960). Most of the defendants in these cases were licensed physicians.

21. *Cheaney v. State*, 285 N.E.2d 265 (Ind. 1972), *cert. denied for want of standing of petitioner*, 410 U.S. 991 (1973).

22. *Id.* at 267–69.

23. *Id.* at 269.

24. *Id.*

25. *Id.* (emphasis in original). *See also Clinic for Women, Inc. v. Brizzi*, 837 N.E.2d at 990 (Dickson, J., concurring in the result) ("[e]very decision to terminate a pregnancy denies this right ["the inalienable right of 'life'"] recognized by art. I, §1] to an unborn child").

26. *Cheaeny*, 285 N.E.2d at 269.

27. *Id. See also Clinic for Women*, 837 N.E.2d at 990 (Dickson, J., concurring in the result) ("the individual rights protected by this section [art. I, §1] are each also expressly subject to the right and obligation of government to provide for 'the peace, safety, and well-being' of its citizens, often referred to as the 'police power'.... and ... such rights may be intruded upon when there is a valid reason to exercise the police power to do so") (citation and internal quotation marks omitted).

28. *Cheaney*, 285 NE2d at 270.

ent right of abortion exists under the state constitution. At the very least, *Cheaney* supports the conclusion that an abortion prohibition would bear a rational relationship to the legitimate goal of protecting unborn human life.

The State of Indiana places a high value on the life of the unborn child. Under Indiana law, "Childbirth is preferred, encouraged, and supported over abortion."[29] Consistent with that public policy, Indiana has enacted a comprehensive scheme of abortion regulation.[30]

Indiana has recognized the rights of unborn children in a variety of contexts outside of abortion, including criminal law, tort law, health care law and property law. Under the criminal code, the killing of a viable, unborn child may constitute murder, voluntary manslaughter or involuntary manslaughter.[31] The feticide statute makes it a crime for anyone knowingly or intentionally to terminate a human pregnancy (other than in a lawfully performed abortion) at any stage of pregnancy.[32] And a woman convicted of a capital offense may not be executed while she is pregnant.[33]

In tort law, Indiana recognizes a common law cause of action for prenatal injuries, regardless of the stage of pregnancy when the injuries are suffered.[34] In keeping with the legislative policy of promoting childbirth over abortion, Indiana prohibits wrongful life causes of action.[35] In health care law, "[t]he liv-

---

29. IND. CODE ANN. § 16-34-1-1 (West 2007).

30. *See* IND. CODE ANN. § 16-34-2-1(a) (West 2007) (codifying *Roe's* trimester framework); § 16-34-2-4 (West 2007) (requiring parental consent); §§ 12-15-5-1(3), 12-15-5-1(17), 12-15-5-2, 16-34-1-2 (West 2002), 405 IND. ADMIN. CODE 5-28-7 (prohibiting public funding of abortion and restricting state Medicaid payments to those services for which federal reimbursement is available); § 16-34-2-1.1 (West 2007) (mandating informed consent and an eighteen-hour waiting period); §§ 16-34-1-3 through 16-34-1-7 (West 2007) (recognizing individual and institutional rights of conscience and prohibiting discrimination against persons who object to abortion).

31. IND. CODE ANN. §§ 35-42-1-1(4), 35-42-1-3(a)(2), 35-42-1-4(d) (West 2004 & Supp. 2006).

32. *Id.* § 35-42-1-6.

33. *Id.* § 35-38-6-10.

34. *Cowe v. Forum Group, Inc.* 575 N.E.2d 630, 636–37 (Ind. 1991).

35. IND. CODE ANN. § 34-12-1-1 (West 1999). A "wrongful life" claim is a claim brought on behalf of a child who is born with an inherited physical or mental disability that could have been discovered before the child's birth by genetic testing or other medical screening. The gravamen of the cause of action is that, as a result of a physician's failure to inform the child's parents of the child's disability (or at least of the availability of tests to determine the presence of the disability), they were deprived of the opportunity to abort the child, thus resulting in the birth of a child suffering a lifetime of disability. Very few courts recognize "wrongful life" causes of action because an assessment of damages requires the courts

ing will declaration of a person diagnosed as pregnant by the attending physician has no effect during the person's pregnancy."[36]

Finally, in property law, afterborn heirs enjoy the same rights of inheritance under the probate code as heirs born during the lifetime of the intestate (a person who dies without a will), so long as they were begotten before the intestate's death.[37] A similar rule applies to the pretermitted children of a decedent who dies testate (with a will).[38]

A right to abortion cannot be found in the text, structure or history of the Indiana Constitution. There is no evidence that either the framers or ratifiers of the Indiana Constitution intended to limit the Legislature's authority to prohibit abortion.[39] Such an intent would have been remarkable in light of the contemporaneous and longstanding prohibition of abortion except to save the life of the mother. Assuming, contrary to the implications of *Doe v. O'Connor*, that art. I, § 1, confers judicially enforceable rights, a right to abortion cannot reasonably considered to be one of those rights.

Freedom of Religious Opinions and Rights of Conscience

Article I, § 3, of the Indiana Constitution provides: "No law shall, in any case whatever, control the free exercise and enjoyment of religious opinions, or interfere with the rights of conscience."[40] In any challenge to a statute prohibiting abortion, abortion advocates may argue that an abortion prohibition interferes with the "free exercise and enjoyment" of a pregnant woman's "religious opinions" and her "rights of conscience" by forbidding her from obtaining an abortion that would be allowed by her religion. This argument would not likely succeed.

---

to compare the value of life, albeit with some degree of physical or mental impairment, to nonexistence.

36. *Id.* § 16-36-4-8(d) (West 2007).

37. *Id.* § 29-1-2-6 (West 1999).

38. *Id.* § 29-1-3-8. A "pretermitted child" is a child who is born after the execution of a will and for whom the will makes no provision.

39. "There was no discussion at the 1850–51 Constitutional Convention suggesting or implying any intention to nullify, curtail, or limit this statute [referring to the 1835 act prohibiting abortion]. Significantly, several cases immediately after the adoption of Section 1 involved appeals following convictions for violation of the criminal abortion statute, and none of the resulting opinions even hinted at any concern that the statue violated Section 1 or any other provision in the Indiana Constitution. [Citations omitted]. Clearly, the framers and ratifiers of Section 1 did not intend to recognize a right to abortion, and their intention is of paramount importance." *Clinic for Women*, 837 N.E.2d at 990 (Dickson, J., concurring in the result).

40. IND. CONST. art. I, § 3 (West 2007).

The Indiana Supreme Court has held that the Supreme Court's interpretation of the Free Exercise and Establishment Clauses of the First Amendment does not necessarily control the interpretation of the multiple religion clauses in the Indiana Bill of Rights.[41] Nevertheless, the Indiana Court of Appeals *has* adopted the federal free exercise standard in interpreting art. I, §3.[42] Under that standard, "The right of free exercise of religion does not relieve an individual of the obligation to comply with a valid and neutral law of general applicability on the ground that the law proscribes (or prescribes) conduct that his religion prescribes (or proscribes)."[43] An Indiana law prohibiting abortion would be a "neutral law of general applicability" that could not be successfully challenged under §3.

Prohibiting Religious Preferences

Article I, §4, of the Indiana Constitution provides: "No preference shall be given, by law, to any creed, religious society, or mode of worship; and no person shall be compelled to attend, erect, or support, any place of worship, or to maintain any ministry, against his consent."[44] A challenge to an abortion prohibition brought under §4 would most likely be based on the argument that it gives a "preference" to a "creed" by reflecting sectarian beliefs regarding when human life begins and the sinfulness of abortion. There is relatively little case law addressing the "preference" language of §4, but precedent interpreting comparable language in the First Amendment suggests that such a challenge would not prevail.

In *Harris v. McRae*,[45] the Supreme Court held that the Establishment Clause is not violated merely because "a statute 'happens to coincide or harmonize with the tenets of some or all religions.'"[46] Noting that the Hyde Amendment "is as much a reflection of 'traditionalist' values toward abortion, as it is an embodiment of the views of any particular religion," the Court held that "the fact that the funding restrictions in the Hyde Amendment may coincide with the religious tenets of the Roman Catholic Church does not, without more,

---

41. *City Chapel Evangelical Free, Inc. v. City of South Bend*, 744 N.E.2d 443, 445–51 (Ind. 2001) (referring to art. I, §§2-8).

42. *Cosby v. State*, 738 N.E.2d 709, 711 (Ind. Ct. App. 2000).

43. *Id.* (citing *Employment Division, Dep't of Human Resources of Oregon v. Smith*, 494 U.S. 872, 879 (1990)). *See generally* Chapter 2, *supra*.

44. IND. CONST. art. I, §4 (West 2007).

45. *Harris v. McRae*, 448 U.S. 297 (1980).

46. *Id.* (citation omitted).

contravene the Establishment Clause."[47] Although the Indiana Supreme Court has held that the religion clauses of the Indiana Bill of Rights may be given an interpretation that differs from the Supreme Court's reading of the Free Exercise and Establishment Clauses,[48] there is no indication that the Indiana Supreme Court would give the language in art. I, §4, prohibiting a "preference" to "any creed," a different reading than the Supreme Court has given the Establishment Clause. And the state supreme court has never invalidated a criminal law on this basis.

In *John Malone Enterprises v. Schaeffer*,[49] the Indiana Court of Appeals held that the Alcoholic Beverage Commission's denial of a permit to operate a package liquor store in a predominantly Amish and Mennonite town (Shipshewana) did not confer a "preference" to the Amish and Mennonites who opposed granting the permit. "[O]ur review of the record reveals no preference given, by virtue of the Commission's action in denying the permit, to the Amish or Mennonite religions."[50] By a parity of reasoning, the legislature's enactment of a statute prohibiting abortion would not confer a "preference" to the Roman Catholic Church and other churches and religious bodies that oppose abortion.

Remedy by Due Course of Law

Article I, §12, of the Indiana Constitution provides, in relevant part, that "every person, for injury done to him in his person, property, or reputation, shall have remedy by due course of law."[51] Abortion advocates might argue that a statute prohibiting abortion interferes with a woman's control over her own body, and that such interference constitutes an "injury" to her "person," as those terms are used in §12, for which there must be a "remedy by due course of law." That "remedy," in turn, would be invalidation of the statute. This argument erroneously assumes that art. I, §12, confers substantive rights.

As is apparent from its text and structure, §12 is concerned with *remedies* for injuries-it does not establish what *constitutes* an injury to anyone's "per-

---

47. *Id.* at 319–20. It should be added that no state or federal court has accepted an Establishment Clause argument against an abortion statute, and two courts have rejected such arguments brought under state constitutions. *See Right to Choose v. Byrne*, 450 A.2d 923, 938–39 (N.J. 1982); *Jane L. v. Bangerter*, 794 F. Supp. 1528, 1534–35 (D. Utah 1992) (interpreting Utah law).

48. *City Chapel Evangelical Free, Inc.*, 744 N.E.2d at 445–51.

49. 674 N.E.2d 599 (Ind. Ct. App. 1996).

50. *Id.* at 606.

51. IND. CONST. art. I, §12 (West 2007).

son, property, or reputation." Article I, §12, "leaves the definition of wrongs and the specification of remedies to the legislature and the common law."[52]

The Indiana Supreme Court has recognized that "there is a strain of Article I, Section 12 doctrine that is analogous to federal substantive due process.... [I]n general this doctrine imposes the requirement that legislation interfering with a right bear a rational relationship to a legitimate legislative goal, but does not preserve any particular remedy from legislative repeal."[53] Section 12 guarantees a "remedy by due course of law" for injuries to "person, property, or reputation." Unlike the federal Due Process Clause, however, §12 "omits any reference to deprivation of 'life, liberty, or property.'"[54] In light of that omission, it is not at all clear that §12 has any application outside of tort law. *McIntosh* itself does not suggest a broader reading.[55] In any event, §12 does not "preserve ... substantive rule[s] of law," but requires only "that our courts be open to entertain claims based on established rules of law."[56] A right to abortion may not be derived from the language of art. I, §12.

Equal Privileges and Immunities

Article I, §23, of the Indiana Constitution provides: "The general assembly shall not grant to any citizen, or class of citizens, privileges or immunities, which, upon the same terms, shall not equally belong to all citizens."[57] In *Collins v Day*,[58] the Indiana Supreme Court articulated a new standard for evaluating claims brought under §23:

> ... Article 1, Section 23 of the Indiana Constitution imposes two requirements upon statutes that grant unequal privileges or immunities to different classes of persons. First, the disparate treatment accorded by the legislation must be reasonably related to inherent characteristics which distinguish the unequally treated classes. Sec-

---

52. *Cantrell v. Morris*, 849 N.E.2d 488, 499 (Ind. 2006).
53. *McIntosh v. Melroe Co.*, 729 N.E.2d 972, 976 (Ind. 2000). It is apparent that *McIntosh* was referring to common law and statutory rights, not constitutional rights. A prohibition of abortion would clearly "bear a rational relationship to a legitimate legislative goal," *i.e.*, protecting unborn human life.
54. *Id.* at 976.
55. *Id.* at 979 ("[s]ection 12 requires that legislation that deprives a person of a complete tort remedy must be a rational means to achieve a legitimate legislative goal").
56. *Id.*
57. IND. CONST. art. I, §23 (West 2007).
58. 644 N.E.2d 72 (Ind. 1994).

ond, the preferential treatment must be uniformly applicable and equally applicable to all persons similarly situated.[59]

Under this reformulated standard, "[t]he resolution of Section 23 claims does not require an analytical framework applying varying degrees of scrutiny for different protected interests."[60] Rather, "[t]he protections assured by Section 23 apply fully, equally, and without diminution to prohibit any and all improper grants of unequal privileges or immunities, including not only those grants involving suspect classes or impinging upon fundamental rights but other such grants as well."[61] Because "the same level of scrutiny is applied to analyze the constitutional propriety of 'any and all' grants of unequal privileges or immunities,"[62] it is immaterial for purposes of *state* constitutional analysis whether the challenged classification distinguishes on the basis of suspect classes or affects the exercise of a fundamental right. The constitutional calculus is the same.

Would a statute prohibiting abortion except to preserve the life of the pregnant woman pass muster under §23? The answer would appear to be yes. Abortion advocates might argue that such a statute creates three "unequal" classifications, one between men, who cannot become pregnant, and women, who can; between abortions, which would be generally prohibited, and all other medical services, which are allowed; and between women whose pregnancies pose a threat to their life and those whose pregnancies do not pose such a threat. None of these classifications would run afoul of §23.

The first requirement of *Collins*, that "the disparate treatment accorded by the legislation must be reasonably related to inherent characteristics which distinguish the unequally treated classes,"[63] would be satisfied with respect to each classification. First, pregnancy is an "inherent characteristic" peculiar to women. Men cannot become pregnant and, therefore, are not subject to an abortion statute. Second, "[a]bortion," as the Supreme Court has noted, "is inherently different from other medical procedures because no other procedure involves the purposeful termination of a potential human life."[64] Third, a life-threatening condition of pregnancy is distinct from those conditions that do not threaten the pregnant woman's life. A public policy decision to prohibit abortions, ex-

59. *Id*. at 80.

60. Id.

61. *Id*.

62. *Indiana High School Athletic Ass'n, Inc. v. Carlberg*, 694 N.E.2d 222, 239 (Ind. 1997) (quoting *Collins*).

63. *Collins*, 644 N.E.2d at 80.

64. *Harris v. McRae*, 448 U.S. at 325.

cept those necessary to preserve the pregnant woman's life, would be "reasonably related" to these characteristics.

The second requirement of *Collins*, that "the preferential treatment ... be uniformly applicable and equally available to all persons similarly situated,"[65] would also be satisfied. The classification (as to who could obtain an abortion) would be "open to any and all persons who share the inherent characteristic[] [*i.e.*, a life-threatening condition] which distinguish and justify the classification, with the special treatment accorded to any particular classification extended equally to all such persons."[66] The exception to the prohibition in this hypothetical abortion statute would be available to all women with a life-threatening condition.

The Indiana Court of Appeals has noted that "[t]he practical effect of *Collins* and cases following it is that statutes will survive Article 1, §23 scrutiny if they pass the most basic rational relationship test."[67] "No statute or ordinance has ever been declared facially invalid under the *Collins* test."[68] And neither, it is submitted, would a prohibition of abortion. An abortion prohibition would be rationally related to the State's legitimate, indeed, compelling, interest in protecting unborn human life.[69]

Conclusion

Based on the foregoing analysis, an argument that the Indiana Constitution protects a right to abortion that is separate from, and independent of, the right to abortion recognized in *Roe v. Wade* would not likely succeed. That, in turn, suggests that if *Roe*, as modified by *Casey*, is ultimately overruled, the State of Indiana could enact and enforce a statute *prohibiting* abortion. Moreover, nothing in the Indiana Constitution precludes Indiana from *regulating* abortion within federal constitutional limits in the meantime.

---

65. *Collins*, 644 N.E.2d at 80.

66. *Id*. at 79.

67. *Morrison v. Sadler*, 821 N.E.2d 15, 22 (Ind. Ct. App. 2005) (lead op.).

68. *Id*. As previously noted, in *Humphreys v. Clinic for Women, Inc.*, 796 N.E.2d 247 (Ind. 2003), Indiana's restrictions on public funding of abortion were found to be unconstitutional *as applied* to women who need an abortion to avoid a serious risk of substantial and irreversible impairment of a major bodily function.

69. *See Cheaney v. State*, 285 N.E.2d at 270 (recognizing State's interest as "both valid and compelling").

CHAPTER 18

IOWA

Summary

The Iowa Supreme Court has not yet decided whether the Iowa Constitution protects a right to abortion separate from, and independent of, the right to abortion recognized under the United States Constitution.[1] A careful examination of the state constitution, in light of its history and interpretation, as well as other relevant legal sources, however, suggests that the state supreme court probably would not recognize a state constitutional right to abortion. Thus, if *Roe v. Wade*,[2] as modified by *Planned Parenthood of Southeastern Pennsylvania v. Casey*,[3] were overruled, Iowa could prohibit abortion. Moreover, nothing in the state constitution, properly understood, precludes the State from enacting and enforcing reasonable measures regulating abortion within current federal constitutional limits.

Analysis

The principal pre-*Roe* abortion statute prohibited performance of an abortion on a pregnant woman unless the procedure was "necessary to preserve her life."[4] Pursuant to *Roe*, the statute was declared unconstitutional (on federal, not state, grounds) by a three-judge federal district court in *Doe v. Turner*,[5] and was repealed in 1976.[6]

---

1. The Iowa Supreme Court has referred to the right to abortion solely as a matter of *federal*, not *state*, constitutional law. *See State v. Campbell*, 633 N.W.2d 302, 305 (Ia. 2001) ("[a] woman has a limited constitutional right to an abortion") (citing *Roe v. Wade*).

2. 410 U.S. 113 (1973).

3. 505 U.S. 833 (1992).

4. IOWA CODE §701.1 (1950).

5. 361 F. Supp. 1288 (S.D. Iowa 1973).

6. 1976 Iowa Acts 549, 774, ch. 1245, §526.

Based upon arguments that have been raised in other States with similar constitutional provisions, possible sources for an asserted abortion right could include provisions of the Bill of Rights recognizing inalienable rights (art. I, §1) and inherent political power in the people (§2); retaining rights (§25); and guaranteeing religious rights (§3), due process of law (§9) and equal protection (§6).[7] The analysis that follows addresses each of these provisions.

Inalienable Rights, Retained Rights

Article 1, §1, of the Iowa Constitution provides: "All men and women are, by nature, free and equal, and have certain inalienable rights-among which are those of enjoying and defending life and liberty, acquiring, possessing and protecting property, and pursuing and obtaining safety and happiness."[8] And art. I, §25, provides: "This enumeration of rights shall not be construed to impair or deny others, retained by the people."[9]

In any challenge to an Iowa statute prohibiting abortion, abortion advocates are likely to argue that abortion is both an "inalienable right" protected by art. I, §1, and a "retained right" under §25. For the reasons that follow, neither section would support a state right to abortion.

The Iowa Supreme Court has held that "[b]oth the inalienable rights clause and the unenumerated rights clause secure to the people of Iowa *common law rights that pre-existed Iowa's Constitution*."[10] Abortion (after quickening), however, was a crime at common law,[11] as the Iowa Supreme Court recognized in one of its earliest decisions, before the current state constitution was adopted.[12] In a case decided shortly after the Civil War, the state supreme court noted the common law's "solicitude for the sacredness of human life and the personal safety of every human being," a solicitude that "not only extends to persons actually born, but, for some purposes, to infants *in* [sic] *ventre sa mere*."[13] Indeed, thirty years earlier, the first territorial legislature prohibited abortion at

---

7. Three other more unlikely sources of an abortion right under the Iowa Constitution- §7 (guaranteeing freedom of speech), §8 (prohibiting unreasonable searches and seizures) and §23 (prohibiting involuntary servitude)-are discussed generally in Chapter 3, *supra*.

8. IOWA CONST. art. 1, §1 (West 2000).

9. *Id.* art. I, §25.

10. *Atwood v. Vilsack*, 725 N.W.2d 641, 651 (Iowa 2006) (emphasis added).

11. "Quickening" is that stage of pregnancy, usually sixteen to eighteen weeks gestation, when the woman first detects fetal movement.

12. *Abrams v. Foshee*, 3 Iowa 274, 278–80 (1856) (whether an accusation that a pregnant woman had obtained an abortion constituted actionable slander).

13. *State v. Moore*, 25 Iowa 128, 135 (1868). The phrase, "*en ventre sa mere*," is Law

any stage of pregnancy for any reason.[14] Because there was no "right" to abortion at common law, abortion may not be considered as either an "inalienable right" protected by art. I, § 1, or an "unenumerated right" protected by § 25.

Even assuming that abortion was a common law right that pre-existed Iowa's Constitution, nothing in either § 1 or § 25 would bar the State from prohibiting abortion. The Iowa Supreme Court has explained that neither section prevents legislative action with respect to the exercise of an inalienable or unenumerated right; rather, these provisions prevent only arbitrary, unreasonable legislative action.[15] A prohibition of abortion, however, would be reasonably related to the State's legitimate interest in protecting unborn human life.

Inherent Political Power

Article I, § 2, of the Iowa Constitution provides: "All political power is inherent in the people. Government is instituted for the protection, security, and benefit of the people, and they have the right, at all times, to alter or reform the same, whenever the public good may require it."[16]

In any challenge to a statute prohibiting abortion, abortion advocates might argue that the statute interferes with the "inherent" political power of the people because it does not promote their "protection, security, and benefit...." Such an argument is not likely to be persuasive.

The first sentence of art. I, § 2, simply means that political power "exists in those who under the Constitution are privileged to exercise the elective franchise."[17] It is not a limitation on *how* that power is exercised. Thus, whether a given law promotes the "protection, security, and benefit of the people" presents a political question for the legislature to decide, not a constitutional question for the judiciary. The second sentence of § 2 secures to the people themselves, through the amendment process, the right to decide whether, how and to what extent the organic instrument of government should be changed. Section 2 is not a limitation on legislative power, other than reserving to the people the right "at all times, to alter or reform [the government], whenever the public good may require it."

French for "in its mother's womb." BLACK'S LAW DICTIONARY 534 (6th ed. 1990).

14. An Act defining Crimes and Punishments, Jan. 25, 1839, § 18, *reprinted in* IOWA (TERR.) LAWS 153–54 (1838-39).

15. *Atwood*, 725 N.W. 2d at 652.

16. IOWA CONST. art. I, § 2 (West 2000).

17. *Barr v. Cardell*, 155 N.W. 312, 314 (Iowa 1915).

Religious Rights

Article I, §3, of the Iowa Constitution provides:

> The general assembly shall make no law respecting an establish-
> ment of religion, or prohibiting the free exercise thereof; nor shall any
> person be compelled to attend any place of worship, pay tithes, taxes,
> or other rates for building or repairing places of worship, or the main-
> tenance of any minister, or ministry.[18]

In any challenge to a statute prohibiting abortion, abortion advocates may
raise either or both of two arguments under art. I, §3. First, they may argue
that an abortion prohibition interferes with the "free exercise" of a woman's
religious beliefs by forbidding her from obtaining an abortion that would be
allowed by her religion. Second, they may argue in the alternative (or in addition) that an abortion prohibition constitutes an "establishment of religion"
because it reflects sectarian beliefs regarding when human life begins and the
sinfulness of abortion. Neither argument would likely prevail.

The establishment and free exercise provisions set forth in the first clause
of art. I, §3, generally have been interpreted consistently with Supreme Court
precedent interpreting the Establishment and Free Exercise Clauses of the
First Amendment.[19] "To the extent [art. I, §3] differs from the First Amendment to the United States Constitution we think our framers were merely addressing the evils incident to the state church,"[20] which is addressed in the
second clause of §3, and would not be at issue in any challenge to an abortion prohibition.

In light of the foregoing, it would appear that a challenge to an abortion
statute that would not succeed under the Free Exercise and Establishment
Clauses of the First Amendment would not succeed under art. I, §3, either.
For the reasons set forth in Chapter 2, *supra*, an abortion statute could not be

---

18. IOWA CONST. art. I, §3 (West 2000).

19. *See Kliebenstein v. Iowa Conference of the United Methodist Church*, 663 N.W.2d 404,
406 (Iowa 2003) (analyzing the Establishment Clauses of the state and federal constitutions
simultaneously); *Hope Evangelical Lutheran Church v. Iowa Dep't of Revenue*, 463 N.W.2d
76-, 79–82 (Iowa 1990) (same with respect to Free Exercise Clauses). *See also Americans
United for Separation of Church and State v. Prison Fellowship Ministries*, 432 F. Supp.2d
862, 864 n. 1 (S.D. Iowa 2006) (construing state and federal Establishment Clauses together).

20. *Rudd v. Ray*, 248 N.W.2d 125, 132 (Iowa 1976).

successfully challenged on First Amendment grounds. Accordingly, a similar challenge under art. I, §3, would not likely be successful

Due Process of Law

Article I, §9, of the Iowa Constitution provides, in pertinent part, that "no person shall be deprived of life, liberty, or property, without due process of law."[21] In any challenge to an abortion prohibition, abortion advocates are most likely to rely upon art. I, §9, arguing that a pregnant woman has a substantive due process liberty interest in obtaining an abortion. The Iowa Supreme Court has recognized that §9 has both a substantive, as well as a procedural, component.[22] For purposes of substantive due process analysis, the state supreme court first determines the nature of the right involved. "If a fundamental right is implicated, we apply strict scrutiny analysis, which requires a determination of 'whether the government action infringing the fundamental right is narrowly tailored to serve a compelling government interest.'"[23] "If a fundamental right is not implicated," however, then "a statute need only survive a rational basis analysis, which requires us to consider whether there is 'a reasonable fit between the government interest and the means utilized to advance that interest.'"[24]

In determining whether an asserted liberty interest (or right) should be regarded as "fundamental," the United States Supreme Court applies a two-prong test. First, there must be a "careful description" of the asserted fundamental liberty interest.[25] Second, the interest, so described, must be firmly rooted in "the Nation's history, legal traditions, and practices."[26] The Iowa Supreme Court employs the same test in evaluating state substantive due process claims.[27] A

---

21. Iowa Const. art. I, §9 (West 2000).

22. *State v. Seering*, 701 N.W.2d 655, 662 (Iowa 2005).

23. *Id.* (quoting *State v. Hernandez-Lopez*, 639 N.W.2d 226, 238 (Iowa 2002)).

24. *Id.*

25. *Washington v. Glucksberg*, 521 U.S. 702, 721 (1997) (citation and internal quotation marks omitted). In *Seering*, the defendant was found guilty of violating a statute proscribing convicted sex offenders from living within 2,000 feet of an elementary or secondary school or child care facility. On appeal, the defendant challenged the residency restriction, arguing that the statute interfered with an asserted "fundamental right" to "the privacy and freedom of association in one's family." 701 N.W.2d at 662 (internal quotation marks omitted). The court rejected defendant's formulation of the interest at stake, defining the interest instead as "freedom of choice in residence," which is "not a fundamental interest entitled to the highest constitutional protection." *Id.* at 664.

26. *Id.* at 710.

27. *Seering*, 701 N.W.2d at 662–65. *See also Sanchez v. State*, 692 N.W.2d 812, 819–20 (Iowa 2005) (following *Glucksberg*); *Santi v. Santi*, 633 N.W.2d 312, 317 (Iowa 2001) (same).

right to abortion cannot be regarded as "fundamental" under art. I, § 9, because such a "right" is not firmly rooted in Iowa's "history, legal traditions, and
practices."[28]

Iowa enacted its first abortion prohibition in 1839, eight years before the State
was admitted to the Union. The statute prohibited abortion at any stage of
pregnancy for any reason.[29] In 1843, this statute was replaced by a statute that
prohibited abortion at any stage of pregnancy unless the procedure was "necessary to preserve the life of the mother...."[30] In 1851, the Legislature enacted
a new code of law which repealed all statutes (including the statute prohibiting abortion) not otherwise included in the new code.[31] Immediately following a state supreme court decision holding that, as a result of the enactment
of the 1851 code, abortion was punishable only as a common law offense (after
quickening) and not as a statutory offense,[32] the Legislature promptly responded
and enacted a new statute making abortion a crime at any stage of pregnancy
unless the procedure was "necessary to preserve of the life of [the pregnant]
woman."[33] This response suggests, at a minimum, that the legislature did not
believe that the due process clause of the 1846 state constitution (which was simply restated in art. I, § 9, of the 1857 constitution) precluded legislation prohibiting abortion.[34]

---

28. To the extent that the Iowa Supreme Court considers federal precedent in determining whether an asserted liberty interest (or right) is "fundamental" under the state due
process guarantee, abortion would not qualify as a "fundamental" right. Although the
Supreme Court characterized the right to choose abortion as "fundamental" in *Roe*, 410
U.S. at 152–53, it tacitly abandoned that characterization in *Casey*, 505 U.S. at 869–79
(Joint Op. of O'Connor, Kennedy and Souter, JJ., replacing *Roe's* "strict scrutiny" standard
of review with the more relaxed "undue burden" standard, allowing for a broader measure
of abortion regulation).

29. An Act defining Crimes and Punishments, Jan. 25, 1839, § 18, *reprinted in* Iowa
(Terr.) Laws 153–54 (1838-39).

30. Act of Feb. 16, 1843, *codified at* Iowa. (Terr.) Rev. Stat. ch. 49, § 10 (1843).

31. Act of Feb. 5, 1851, Iowa Code Part First, tit. I, ch. 4, § 28 (1850–51).

32. *Abrams v. Foshee*, 3 Iowa at 278–80.

33. Act of March 15, 1858, *codified at* Iowa Rev. Laws § 4221 (1860), *recodified at* Iowa
Code § 3864 (1873), *recodified at* McClain's Iowa Code Ann. § 5163 (1888), *recodified at*
Iowa Code Ann. § 4759 (1897), *amended by* Iowa Acts 1915, ch. 45, § 1 (eliminating requirement that woman was pregnant), *codified at* Iowa Code Supplemental Supplement
§ 4759 (1915), *recodified at* Iowa Code § 12973 (1924), *recodified at* Iowa Code § 701.1
(1950), *repealed by* 1976 Iowa Acts 549, 774, ch. 1245, § 526.

34. *See Rudd v. Ray*, 248 N.W.2d at 132 (legislature that enacted statute in 1855 ap-
pointing a paid chaplain for the state penitentiary obviously did not believe that the appointment of a chaplain was barred by the establishment clause of art. I, § 3, of the 1846
state constitution).

In *State v. Moore*, the Iowa Supreme Court quoted with approval the following language from the trial judge's charge to the jury in a prosecution for second degree murder based upon the performance of an illegal abortion:

> To attempt to produce a miscarriage, except when in proper professional judgment it is necessary to preserve the life of the woman, is an unlawful act. It is known to be a dangerous act, generally producing one and sometimes two deaths,—I mean the death of the unborn infant and the death of the mother.[35]

The supreme court then summarized its own view of the matter:

> The common law is distinguished, and is to be commended, for its all-embracing and salutary solicitude for the sacredness of human life and the personal safety of every human being. This protecting, paternal care, enveloping every individual like the air he breathes, not only extends to persons actually born, but, for some purposes, to infants *in* [*sic*] *ventre sa mere.*[36]

Prior to *Roe v. Wade*, the Iowa Supreme Court regularly affirmed the convictions of persons (including licensed physicians) for performing abortions, without any hint that the prosecutions or convictions violated the due process guarantee (or any other provision) of the Iowa Constitution.[37] Indeed, less than three years before *Roe* was decided, the Iowa Supreme Court rejected vagueness and equal protection challenges to the principal state abortion statute.[38]

Iowa recognizes the rights of unborn children in a variety of contexts outside of abortion. In tort law, the Iowa Supreme Court has refused to recognize a "wrongful pregnancy" cause of action for the birth of a normal, healthy baby.[39] In property law, a posthumous child (a child conceived before but born after the death of a person who dies without a will) may inherit from an in-

---

35. 25 Iowa at 132–33.

36. *Id.* at 135-36. The phrase, "*en ventre sa mere,*" means within the mother.

37. *State v. Stafford*, 123 N.W. 167 (Iowa 1909); *State v. Barrett*, 198 N.W. 36 (Iowa 1924); *State v. Rowley*, 198 N.W. 37 (Iowa 1924). The court also affirmed second degree murder convictions for causing the death of a pregnant woman by an illegal abortion. *State v. Moore*, 25 Iowa 128 (1868); *State v. Thurman*, 24 N.W. 511 (Iowa 1885). The defendant in *Moore* was a licensed physician.

38. *State v. Abodeely*, 179 N.W.2d 347, 354–55 (Iowa 1970), *appeal dismissed, cert. denied*, 402 U.S. 936 (1971).

39. *Nanke v. Napier*, 346 N.W.2d 520 (Iowa 1984).

testate (a person who dies without a will).[40] And, subject to certain exceptions, an afterborn child (a child born after a person executes a will but conceived before the death of the decedent) receives the same share of the estate that he would have received if the person had died intestate (without a will).[41] And, at any point in a judicial proceeding, the court may appoint a guardian *ad litem* "to represent and approve a settlement on behalf of the interest of … an … unborn … person."[42]

Under Iowa's health care statutes, life-sustaining medical care may not be withheld or withdrawn from a pregnant woman pursuant to a living will.[43] The same limitation applies to surrogate health care decision makers and, in certain instances (where the patient is terminally ill), agents acting under a durable power of attorney for health care.[44]

There is no evidence in the debates of the Iowa Constitutional Convention that the framers of the Bill of Rights intended to recognize a right to abortion, which was a crime at common law and under territorial and state statutes.[45]

In light of Iowa's longstanding tradition of prohibiting abortion, which goes back one hundred and thirty-five years before *Roe v. Wade* was decided and antedates the Iowa's first constitution, the absence of any indication that the framers of the present constitution intended to recognize a right to abortion, and the State's interest in protecting the rights of unborn children, it cannot plausibly be said that the due process guarantee of the Iowa Constitution (or any other provision of the Bill of Rights) secures a right to abortion.

Equal Protection

Article I, §6, of the Iowa Constitution provides, in relevant part: "All laws of a general nature shall have a uniform operation…."[46] Although in interpreting art. I, §6, the Iowa Supreme Court is not bound by the Supreme Court's

---

40. Iowa Code §633.220 (West 1992).
41. *Id.* §633.267.
42. *Id.* §633A.6306 (West Supp. 2007).
43. *Id.* §144A.6, ¶2 (West 2005).
44. *Id.* §144A.7, ¶¶1.a, -3 (West Supp. 2007).
45. *See* 1The Debates of the Constitutional Convention of the State of Iowa, Assembled at Iowa City, January 19, 1857 (hereinafter Debates) 98–115, 118–140 (debate on Bill of Rights in Committee of the Whole); *id.* at 141–215, 223–26, 2 Debates at 651–57, 732–41, 1006–08 (debate on Bill of Rights in Convention) (Davenport, Iowa 1857).
46. Iowa Const. art. I, §6 (West 2000).

decisions interpreting the Equal Protection Clause of the Fourteenth Amendment,[47] and, on occasion, has departed from them,[48] the court normally applies the same analysis as it does in considering federal equal protection claims.[49] Consistent with that equivalency of interpretation, the state supreme court has recognized that "[s]tate laws are subjected to various levels of scrutiny depending on the classification the laws draw and the kind of right the laws affect."[50]

> If a statute affects a fundamental right or classifies individuals on the basis of race, alienage, or national origin, it is subjected to strict scrutiny review. [Citation omitted]. The State must prove [that] it is narrowly tailored to the achievement of a compelling state interest. [Citation omitted]. If a statute classifies individuals on the basis of gender or legitimacy, it is subject to intermediate scrutiny and will only be upheld if it is substantially related to an important state interest.[51]

In all other cases, rational basis review applies.[52] Under this level of scrutiny, a statute "need only be rationally related to a legitimate state interest."[53]

---

47. *State v. Simmons*, 714 N.W.2d 264, 277 (Iowa 2006).

48. *See Racing Ass'n of Central Iowa v. Fitzgerald*, 675 N.E.2d 1, 4–7 (Iowa 2004) (striking down disparity in taxes imposed on slot machines located at racetracks and those on riverboats); *Bierkamp v. Rogers*, 293 N.W.2d 517, 580–82 (Iowa 1980) (striking down guest statute). The difference between state and federal equal protection analysis, to the extent that there is one, appears to be that "Iowa rational basis analysis is more searching than federal equal protection analysis in evaluating the relationship between the proposed purpose and the legislation as a means to achieve that purpose." *Johnson v. University of Iowa*, 408 F. Supp.2d 728, 750 (S.D. Iowa 2004). Given the State's strong interest in protecting unborn human life, and the obvious connection between that interest and a prohibition of abortion, the difference, if any, between state and federal equal protection analysis should not result in a difference in outcome.

49. "Generally, a statute that does not offend against the equal protection guarantees in the federal constitution does not offend against a similar provision in our State constitution." *Klein v. Dep't of Revenue & Finance*, 451 N.W.2d 837, 842 (Iowa 1990). *See also Bowers v. Polk County Board of Supervisors*, 638 N.W.2d 682, 689 (Iowa 2002) (provisions are "identical in scope, import, and purpose"); *Gilleland v. Armstrong Rubber*, 524 N.W.2d 404, 406 (Iowa 1994) (Iowa Constitution "puts substantially the same limitations on state legislation" as does the Equal Protection Clause of the Fourteenth Amendment); *Iowa Independent Bankers v. Board of Governors of the Federal Reserve System*, 511 F.2d 1288, 1297 (D.C. Cir. 1975) (art. I, §6, of the Iowa Constitution is not applied "more rigorously" than the Equal Protection Clause of the Fourteenth Amendment).

50. *Sanchez v. State*, 692 N.W.2d at 817.

51. *Id.* (citations omitted). Another term for "intermediate scrutiny" is "heightened scrutiny." The terms are used interchangeably in this section of the analysis.

52. *Id.*

53. *Id.* at 817–18.

Strict scrutiny review would not apply because, for the reasons set forth in the preceding section of this analysis, the state constitution does not confer a "fundamental right" to abortion. Nor would the prohibition of abortion classify persons on the basis of "race, alienage, or national origin." Abortion advocates may argue in the alternative that a statute prohibiting abortion discriminates against women and is subject to intermediate scrutiny because only women are capable of becoming pregnant. An abortion prohibition would appear to satisfy this level of scrutiny because the prohibition would be "substantially related" to the "important state interest" in protecting unborn human life. Nevertheless, the standard applicable to sex-based discrimination should not apply to an abortion prohibition. Abortion laws do not discriminate on the basis of sex.

First, the United States Supreme Court has reviewed restrictions on abortion funding under a rational basis standard of review, *not* under the heightened scrutiny required of gender-based classifications.[54] Indeed, the Court has held that "the disfavoring of abortion ... is not *ipso facto* sex discrimination," and, citing its decisions in *Harris* and other cases addressing abortion funding, stated that "the constitutional test applicable to government abortion-funding restrictions is not the heightened-scrutiny standard that our cases demand for sex discrimination, ... but the ordinary rationality standard."[55]

Second, even assuming that an abortion prohibition differentiates between men and women on the basis of sex, and would otherwise be subject to a higher standard of review, the Supreme Court has held that biological differences between men and women may justify different treatment based on those differ-

---

54. *Harris v. McRae*, 448 U.S. 297, 321–26 (1980).

55. *Bray v. Alexandria Women's Health Clinic*, 506 U.S. 263, 273 (1993). Several state supreme courts and individual state supreme court justices have recognized that abortion regulations and restrictions on abortion funding are not "directed at women as a class" so much as "abortion as a medical treatment, which, because it involves a potential life, has no parallel as a treatment method." *Bell v. Low Income Women of Texas*, 95 S.W.3d 253, 258 (Tex. 2002) (upholding funding restrictions) (citing *Harris*, 448 U.S. at 325). *See also Fischer v. Dep't of Public Welfare*, 502 A.2d 114, 125 (Pa. 1985) ("the basis for the distinction here is not sex, but abortion") (upholding funding restrictions); *Moe v. Secretary of Administration & Finance*, 417 N.E.2d 387, 407 (Mass. 1981) (Hennessey, C.J., dissenting) (funding restrictions were "directed at abortion as a medical procedure, not women as a class"); *Right to Choose v. Byrne*, 450 A.2d 925, 950 (N.J. 1982) (O'Hern, J., dissenting) ("[t]he subject of the legislation is not the person of the recipient, but the nature of the claimed medical service"). Both *Moe* and *Right to Choose* were decided on other grounds. The dissenting justices were addressing alternative arguments raised by the plaintiffs, but not reached by the majority opinions.

ences. In upholding a statutory rape statute that applied only to males, the Supreme Court noted, "this Court has consistently upheld statutes where the gender classification is not invidious, but rather realistically reflects the fact that the sexes are not similarly situated in certain circumstances."[56] As one federal district court observed: "Abortion statutes are examples of cases in which the sexes are not biologically similarly situated" because only women are capable of becoming pregnant and having abortions.[57]

A statute prohibiting abortion quite obviously can affect only women because only women are capable of becoming pregnant.[58] Unlike laws that use women's ability to become pregnant (or pregnancy itself) to discriminate against them in *other* areas (*e.g.*, employment opportunities), abortion prohibitions cannot fairly be said to involve a distinction between men and women that is a "mere pretext[] designed to erect an invidious discrimination against [women]."[59]

Because a prohibition of abortion would not infringe upon a fundamental state constitutional right and would not impermissibly classify on the basis of a suspect or quasi-suspect class, it would need to satisfy only the rational basis test. Under that test, the classification must be "rationally related to a legitimate state interest."[60] A prohibition of abortion would be "rationally related" to the "appropriate purpose" of protecting unborn human life. Accordingly, Iowa could enact an abortion prohibition without violating the equal protection guarantee of the Iowa Constitution.

Conclusion

Based on the foregoing analysis, an argument that the Iowa Constitution protects a right to abortion that is separate from, and independent of, the right to abortion recognized in *Roe v. Wade* would not likely succeed. That, in turn, suggests that if *Roe*, as modified by *Casey*, is ultimately overruled, the State of Iowa could enact and enforce a statute *prohibiting* abortion. Moreover, nothing in the Iowa Constitution precludes Iowa from *regulating* abortion within federal constitutional limits in the meantime.

---

56. *Michael M. v. Superior Court*, 450 U.S. 464, 469 (1981).

57. *Jane L. v. Bangerter*, 794 F. Supp. 1537, 1549 (D. Utah 1992).

58. *Geduldig v. Aiello*, 417 U.S. 484, 496 n. 20 (1974) ("[n]ormal pregnancy is an objectively, identifiable physical condition with unique characteristics").

59. *Id.*

60. *Sanchez v. State*, 692 N.W.2d at 817–18.

CHAPTER 19

KANSAS

Summary

The Kansas Supreme Court has not yet decided whether the Kansas Constitution protects a right to abortion separate from, and independent of, the right to abortion recognized under the United States Constitution.[1] A careful examination of the state constitution, in light of its history and interpretation, as well as other relevant legal sources, however, suggests that the state supreme court probably would not recognize a state constitutional right to abortion if *Roe v. Wade*,[2] as modified by *Planned Parenthood of Southeastern Pennsylvania v. Casey*,[3] were overruled. Accordingly, Kansas could prohibit abortion. Moreover, nothing in the state constitution, properly understood, precludes the State from enacting and enforcing reasonable measures regulating abortion within current federal constitutional limits.

Analysis

The pre-*Roe* Kansas abortion statute was based on § 230.3 of the Model Penal Code.[4] The statute allowed an abortion to be performed upon a pregnant woman at any stage of pregnancy when (1) there was "substantial risk that a

---

1. *See Alpha Medical Clinic v. Anderson*, 128 P.3d 364, 376–77 (Kan. 2006) (declining to decide whether the federal constitutional privacy interest in obtaining a lawful abortion without government imposition of an undue burden on that right "also exist[s] under the Kansas Constitution"). *See also City of Wichita v. Tilson*, 855 P.2d 911, 915 (Kan. 1993) (rejecting necessity defense offered by abortion protesters without any discussion of the state constitution as an independent source of an abortion liberty).

2. 410 U.S. 113 (1973).

3. 505 U.S. 833 (1992).

4. *See* KAN. STAT. ANN. § 21-3407 (Vernon 1971). The complete text of § 230.3 of the Model Penal Code is set out in Appendix B to the Supreme Court's decision in *Doe v. Bolton*, 410 U.S. 179, 205–07 (1973).

continuance of the pregnancy [would] impair the physical or mental health of the mother," (2) there was "substantial risk ... that the child would be born with physical or mental defect," or (3) "the pregnancy resulted from rape, incest or other felonious intercourse."[5] The statute was repealed in 1992.[6]

Based upon arguments that have been raised in Kansas and other States with similar constitutional provisions, possible sources for an asserted abortion right could include provisions of the Bill of Rights guaranteeing religious liberty (§ 7), a remedy by due course of law (§ 18), due process of law (§ 18) and equal protection (§§ 1, 2); and retaining rights (§ 20).[7] The analysis that follows addresses each of these provisions.

Religious Liberty

Section 7 of the Kansas Bill of Rights provides, in part:

> The right to worship God according to the dictates of conscience shall never be infringed; nor shall any person be compelled to attend or support any form of worship, nor shall any control of or interference with the rights of conscience be permitted, nor any preference be given by law to any religious establishment or mode of worship.[8]

In any state constitutional challenge to a statute prohibiting abortion, abortion advocates may raise either or both of two arguments under § 7. First, they may argue that an abortion prohibition interferes with a woman's "rights of conscience" by forbidding her from obtaining an abortion that would be allowed by her religion. Second, they may argue in addition (or in the alternative) that an abortion prohibition gives a "preference" to a "religious establishment" be-

---

5. *Id.* § 21-3407(2). The law imposed other conditions. Abortions could be performed only by licensed physicians in accredited hospitals. *Id.* §§ 21-3407(2), 65-444. Except in emergency cases, no abortion could be performed unless three physicians certified in writing the circumstances that existed that justified the abortion. *Id.* §§ 21-3407(2)(a), -(b), 65-444. The hospitalization and three-physician concurrence requirements were declared unconstitutional by a three-judge federal district court in a pre-*Roe* decision. *Poe v. Menghini*, 339 F. Supp. 986 (D. Kan. 1972).

6. 1992 Kan. Sess. Laws 723, 729, ch. 183, § 9.

7. Three other more unlikely sources of an abortion right under the Kansas Bill of Rights-§ 6 (prohibiting involuntary servitude), § 11 (prohibiting unreasonable searches and seizures) and § 15 (guaranteeing freedom of speech)-are discussed generally in Chapter 3, *supra*.

8. KAN. CONST., BILL OF RIGHTS, § 7 (1988).

cause it reflects sectarian beliefs regarding when human life begins and the sinfulness of abortion. Neither argument would likely succeed.

The Kansas Supreme Court has generally interpreted §7 consistently with Supreme Court precedent interpreting the Free Exercise and Establishment Clauses of the First Amendment. For example, in *State ex rel. Pringle v. Heritage Baptist Temple*,[9] the state supreme court stated:

> The First Amendment to the U.S. Constitution and Section 7 of the Kansas Bill of Rights embrace two concepts: the prohibition of establishment of religion by government, and the guarantee of the free exercise of religion by all persons. It [*sic*] thereby prevents state compulsory religion and also safeguards the free exercise of religion.[10]

This consistency of interpretation suggests that a challenge to an abortion statute that would not succeed under the Religion Clauses of the First Amendment would not succeed under §7, either. For the reasons set forth in Chapter 2, *supra*, an abortion statute could not be successfully challenged on First Amendment grounds. Accordingly, a similar challenge under §7 would not likely be successful, either.

Remedy by Due Course of Law

Section 18 of the Kansas Bill of Rights provides: "All persons, for injuries suffered in person, reputation or property, shall have remedy by due course of law, and justice administered without delay."[11]

Abortion advocates might argue that a statute prohibiting abortion interferes with a woman's control over her own body, and that such interference constitutes an "injury" to her "person," as those terms are used in §18, for which there must be a "remedy by due course of law." That "remedy," in turn, would be invalidation of the statute. This argument assumes that, with respect to remedies, §18, confers substantive rights.[12] The case law is clear, however, that it does not.

As is apparent from its text and structure, §18 is concerned with *remedies* for injuries-it does not establish what *constitutes* an injury to anyone's "per-

---

9. 693 P.2d 1163 (Kan. 1985).

10. *Id.* at 1165. *See also Lower v. Cemetery Board*, 56 P.3d 235, 245–46 (Kan. 2002) (construing Free Exercise Clause and §7 of the Kansas Bill of Rights together); *Corder v. Kansas Board of Healing Arts*, 889 P.2d 1127, 1137 (Kan. 1994) (same).

11. KAN. CONST., BILL OF RIGHTS, §18 (1988).

12. To the extent that §18 has been interpreted as a due process guarantee, it is discussed in the next section of this analysis, *infra*.

son, reputation or property." Those remedies, however, are derived from the common law, not § 18.[13] Moreover, the remedies themselves redress injuries recognized by the common law, not constitutional "injuries."[14] There was no "right" to abortion at common law. Abortion was a common law crime (at least after quickening) at the time the Kansas Constitution was adopted in 1859. Because there was no right to abortion at that time (either under the common law or under the statutes of the Kansas Territory), a woman who has been denied an abortion (by a statute prohibiting abortion) could not be said to have suffered an "injury" for which § 18 requires a "remedy."[15]

Due Process of Law

The Kansas Supreme Court has variously referred to § 1 and § 18 of the Kansas Bill of Rights as guaranteeing due process of law,[16] although neither provision actually refers to due process and the latter, as the previous section of this analysis indicates, appears to be concerned only with civil remedies for private injuries. Section 1 provides: "All men are possessed of equal and inalienable natural rights, among which are life, liberty, and the pursuit of happiness."[17] Section 18 provides, in part: "All persons, for injuries suffered in person, reputation or property, shall have remedy by due course of law...."[18]

Regardless of the source of due process under the Kansas Constitution, in any challenge to a statute prohibiting abortion, abortion advocates are

---

13. *Prager v. State of Kansas, Dep't of Revenue*, 20 P.3d 39, 66 (Kan. 2001) ("Section 18 does not create any new rights of action; it merely requires the Kansas courts to be open and afford a remedy for such rights as are recognized by law").

14. *Leiker by and through Leiker v. Gafford*, 778 P.2d 823, 848 (Kan. 1989) (the right to a remedy by due course of law applies "only ... as to civil causes of action that were recognized as justiciable by the common law as it existed at the time our constitution was adopted").

15. *See Noel v. Menninger Foundation*, 276 P.2d 934, 943 (Kan. 1954) (section 18 means that "for such wrongs that are recognized by the law of the land the court shall be open and afford a remedy, or that laws shall be enacted giving a certain remedy for all injuries or wrongs").

16. *State ex rel Tomasic v. Kansas City, Kansas Port Authority*, 636 P.2d 760, 777 (Kan. 1981) (stating that §§ 1 and 2 of the Kansas Bill of Rights "are given much the same effect as the clauses of the Fourteenth Amendment relating to due process and equal protection of the law"); *Alliance Mortgage Co. v. Pastine*, 136 P.3d 457, 463 (Kan. 2006) (identifying § 18 as a due process guarantee); *State v. Van Hoet*, 89 P.3d 606, 617 (Kan. 2004) (same); *Bonin v. Vannaman*, 929 P.2d 754, 768 (Kan. 1996) (same); *Wesley Medical Center v. McCain*, 597 P.2d 1088, 1091 (Kan. 1979) (same).

17. KAN. CONST., BILL OF RIGHTS, § 1 (1998).

18. *Id.* § 18.

likely to argue that a pregnant woman has a substantive due process liberty interest in obtaining an abortion. Such an argument probably would not prevail.

The Kansas Supreme Court has held that "[g]enerally, provisions of the Kansas Constitution which are similar to the Constitution of the United States have been applied in a similar manner."[19] More specifically, the state supreme court has held that state due process and equal protection principles do not "differ" from those under the Due Process and Equal Protection Clauses of the Fourteenth Amendment.[20] That equivalency of interpretation suggests that the Kansas Supreme Court would not recognize a state right to abortion under either § 1 or § 18 if the Supreme Court overrules *Roe*, as modified by *Casey*.

Apart from generally following Supreme Court precedent interpreting the Due Process Clause of the Fourteenth Amendment, the Kansas Supreme Court has not developed a methodology for evaluating asserted liberty interests under the state due process clause. The court has stated, however, that the primary guide in determining whether a principle in question is fundamental, for purposes of due process, is historical practice.[21] But there is no historical practice of recognizing a right to abortion in Kansas law.

Kansas enacted its first abortion statutes in 1855, four years before it adopted the present constitution and joined the Union. One statute prohibited the performance of an abortion upon a woman, "pregnant with a quick child," unless the procedure was "necessary to preserve the life of [the] mother, or shall have been advised by a physician to be necessary for that purpose," and punished the offense as manslaughter in the second degree.[22] Another statute prohibited the performance of an abortion upon a pregnant woman at any stage of pregnancy (subject to the same exception) and punished the offense as a misdemeanor.[23] A third statute made the "wilful killing of any unborn quick child, by any injury to the mother of such child, which would be murder if it resulted in the death of such mother," manslaughter in the first degree.[24] These statutes remained essentially unchanged (except for an increase in the offense for aborting a "quick" child from second to first degree manslaughter) until they were

---

19. *State v. Schoonover*, 133 P.3d 48, 77 (Kan. 2006).

20. *In re K.M.H.*, 169 P.3d 1025, 1033 (Kan. 2007).

21. *State v. Bethell*, 66 P.3d 840, 846 (Kan. 2003).

22. KAN. (TERR.) STAT. ch. 48, § 10 (1855). A "quick" child, in this context, refers to "quickening," that stage of pregnancy, usually sixteen to eighteen weeks gestation, when a woman first detects fetal movement.

23. *Id.* ch. 48, § 39.

24. *Id.* ch. 48, § 9.

repealed and replaced with the provision based upon the Model Penal Code in 1969.[25]

Prior to *Roe v. Wade*, the Kansas Supreme Court regularly affirmed convictions for abortion (and manslaughter convictions based upon the death of the woman resulting from an illegal abortion) under the nineteenth century statutes without any hint that the prosecutions or convictions were barred by the Kansas Constitution.[26] In an early decision, the state supreme court held that the principal abortion statute had been enacted "to protect the pregnant woman and the unborn child."[27] Forty years later, the court held that the next of kin of a woman who had died as a result of a negligently performed illegal abortion could sue the abortionist for damages.[28] Rejecting the defendant's argument that the deceased's consent to an illegal act barred recovery, the court said, "We are of the opinion that no person may lawfully and validly consent to any act the very purpose of which is to destroy human life."[29] Subsequent to the Supreme Court's decision in *Roe*, Kansas enacted a comprehensive scheme of abortion regulation.[30]

Kansas recognizes the rights of unborn children in several areas outside of abortion, including criminal law, tort law, health care law and property law.

---

25. *Id.* ch. 48, §§ 9, 10, 39 (1855), *recodified at* KAN. GEN. LAWS ch. 28, §§ 9, 10, 37 (1859), *recodified at* KAN. GEN. STAT. ch. 31, §§ 14, 15, 44 (1868), *recodified at* KAN. GEN. STAT. §§ 1952, 1953, 1982 (1899), *recodified at* KAN. GEN. STAT. §§ 1999, 2000, 2029 (1901), *recodified at* KAN. GEN. STAT. §§ 2090, 2091, 2120 (1905), *recodified at* KAN. GEN. STAT. §§ 3375, 3376, 3405 (1915), *recodified at* KAN. GEN. STAT. §§ 21-409, 21-410, 21-437 (1923), *carried forward as* KAN. STAT. ANN. §§ 21-409, 21-410, 21-437 (1964), *repealed by* 1969 Kan. Sess. Laws 503, ch. 180.

26. *See State v. Watson*, 1 P. 770 (Kan. 1883); *State v. Hatch*, 112 P. 149 (Kan. 1910); *State v. Harris*, 136 P. 264 (Kan. 1913); *State v. Patterson*, 181 P. 609 (Kan. 1919); *State v. Nossaman*, 243 P. 326 (Kan. 1926); *State v. Keester*, 4 P.2d 679 (Kan. 1931); *State v. Brown*, 236 P.2d 59 (Kan. 1951); *State v. Ledbetter*, 327 P.2d 1039 (Kan. 1958); *State v. Darling*, 493 P.2d 216 (Kan. 1972).

27. *State v. Miller*, 133 P. 878, 879 (Kan. 1913). Six years later, the court stated that "[a]ny human embryo which is not dead.... is no less endowed with life before reaching the stage of development known as quickening than after." *State v. Patterson*, 181 P. at 610.

28. *Joy v. Brown*, 252 P.2d 889 (1953).

29. *Id.* at 892.

30. KAN. STAT. ANN. § 65-6709 (2002) (mandating informed consent and a twenty-four hour waiting period); § 65-6705 (requiring parental notice); §§ 65-443, 65-444 (2002) (recognizing individual and institutional rights of conscience); § 65-6703(a) (2002) (prohibiting post-viability abortions unless two physicians determine that the procedure is "necessary to preserve the life of the pregnant woman," or "continuation of the pregnancy will cause a substantial and irreversible impairment of a major bodily function of the pregnant woman"). *See also* Kansas Medical Assistance Program, Professional Services Provider Manual, Benefits & Limitations, p. 8-3 (limiting public funding of abortion for indigent women to those

In criminal law, killing or injuring an unborn child may be prosecuted as a homicide or battery.[31] And a woman convicted of a capital offense may not be executed while she is pregnant.[32]

In tort law, a statutory cause of action for wrongful death may be brought on behalf of an unborn child who was viable (capable of sustained survival outside the mother's womb, with or without medical assistance) at the time of its death.[33] A common law cause of action for (nonlethal) prenatal injuries may be brought on behalf of a viable unborn child.[34] More recently, the Kansas Supreme Court has held that "a physician who has a doctor-patient relationship with a pregnant woman who intends to carry her fetus to term and deliver a healthy baby also has a doctor-patient relationship with the fetus," and may be held liable in negligence for injuries caused by failing to provide the pregnant woman and her unborn child with proper medical care during pregnancy.[35] And the state supreme court has refused to recognized a cause of action for "wrongful life."[36] The court explained:

> It has long been a fundamental principle of our law that human life is precious. Whether the person is in perfect health, in ill health, or has or does not have impairments or disabilities, the person's life is valuable, precious and worth of protection. A legal right not to be

---

circumstances for which federal reimbursement is available, currently life-of-the-mother, rape and incest).

31. *Id.* § 21-3452 (2007).

32. *Id.* § 22-4009 (Supp. 2006).

33. *Hale v. Manion*, 368 P.2d 1 (Kan. 1962), interpreting what is now codified at KAN. STAT. ANN. § 60-1901 *et seq.* (2005). In the absence of legislative reform, however, the court has declined to extend the wrongful death act to *non*viable unborn children who were stillborn. *Humes v. Clinton*, 792 P.2d 1032, 1035–37 (Kan. 1990).

34. *Id.* at 2.

35. *Nold ex rel. Nold v. Binyon*, 31 P.3d 274, 289 (Kan. 2000).

36. *Bruggemann by and through Bruggemann v. Schimke*, 718 P.2d 635 (Kan. 1986). A "wrongful life" cause of action is a claim brought on behalf of a child who is born with a physical or mental disability or disease that could have been discovered before the child's birth by genetic testing, amniocentesis or other medical screening. The gravamen of the cause of action is that, as a result of a physician's failure to inform the child's parents of the child's disability or disease (or at least of the availability of tests to determine the presence of the disability or disease), they were deprived of the opportunity to abort the child, thus resulting in the birth of a child suffering permanent physical or mental impairment. The Kansas Supreme Court has recognized wrongful birth actions, however. *Arche v. U.S. Dep't of the Army*, 798 P.2d 477, 478–80 (Kan. 1990). A "wrongful birth" cause of action is a claim based upon the same facts, brought by the parents of the impaired child on their own behalf.

born — to be dead, rather than to be alive with deformities — is completely contradictory to our law.[37]

In health care law, a living will may not direct the withholding or withdrawal of life-sustaining medical treatment from a woman who is known to be pregnant.[38] And in property law, posthumous children (children conceived before but born after the death of a parent) are considered as living at the death of their parents for purposes of inheritance.[39]

There is no evidence that either the framers or ratifiers of the Kansas Constitution intended the Bill of Rights to limit the Legislature's authority to prohibit abortion.[40] Such an intent would have been remarkable in light of the contemporaneous prohibition of abortion except to save the life of the pregnant woman. Because there is no right—fundamental or otherwise—to obtain an abortion under the Kansas due process guarantee, an abortion prohibition would be subject to the rational basis standard of review. For a statute to pass constitutional muster under that standard, "[i]t must implicate legitimate goals, and ... the means chosen by the legislature must bear a rational relationship to those goals."[41] A statute prohibiting abortion would be rationally related to the State's legitimate goal of protecting unborn human life.

Equal Protection

The Kansas Bill of Rights contains two provisions which have been interpreted as guaranteeing equal protection of the law. Section 1, as previously noted, provides: "All men are possessed of equal and inalienable natural rights, among which are life, liberty, and the pursuit of happiness."[42] And § 2 provides:

> All political power is inherent in the people, and all free governments are founded on their authority, and are instituted for their equal protection and benefit. No special privileges or immunities shall ever be granted by the legislature, which may not be altered, revoked or

---

37. *Bruggemann,* 718 P.2d at 642.

38. KAN. STAT. ANN. § 65-28,103(a) (last sentence) (2002).

39. *Id.* § 59-501(a) (2005).

40. *See* WYANDOTTE (KANSAS) CONSTITUTIONAL CONVENTION (1859) 184–89 (Report of the Committee on the Preamble and Bill of Rights), 271–91, 460–65, 535–37 (debate on Bill of Rights in Convention) (Topeka, Kansas 1920).

41. *Mudd v. Neosho*, 62 P.3d 236, 244 (Kan. 2003).

42. KAN. CONST., BILL OF RIGHTS, § 1 (1998).

repealed by the same body; and this power shall be exercised by no other tribunal or agency.[43]

Section 1 is the "counterpart" to the Equal Protection Clause of the Fourteenth Amendment,[44] and "is given much the same effect."[45] Section 2, on the other hand, applies "solely to political privileges, not to the personal or property rights of an individual,"[46] and thus would have no bearing on the constitutionality of an abortion prohibition.[47]

For purposes of both state and federal equal protection analysis, statutes that involve "suspect classifications" or infringe upon the exercise of "fundamental interests" are subject to strict scrutiny review; under that standard, "the presumption of constitutionality [is] displaced and the burden [is] placed on the party asserting constitutionality to demonstrate a compelling state interest which justifies the classification."[48] Suspect classes include "race, ancestry, and alienage."[49] An intermediate standard of review, known as "heightened scrutiny," applies to "quasi-suspect" classifications based on gender or illegitimacy.[50] Such classifications must be "substantially related" to the achievement of "important [state] objectives."[51] The lowest and most relaxed standard of review is rational basis. Under this standard, a statute will be upheld if it is "rationally related to a legitimate [state] purpose."[52]

Strict scrutiny review would not apply because, for the reasons set forth in the preceding section of this analysis, the state constitution does not confer a "fundamental right" to abortion. Nor would the prohibition of abortion clas-

---

43. *Id.* § 2.

44. *Sharples v. Roberts*, 816 P.2d 390, 393 (Kan. 1991); *Bair v. Peck*, 811 P.2d 1176, 1182 (Kan. 1991) (same).

45. *State ex rel. Tomasic v. Kansas City, Kansas*, 701 P.2d 1314, 1326 (Kan. 1985).

46. *Sharples*, 816 P.2d at 393. *See also Samsel v. Wheeler Transport Services*, 789 P.2d 541, 553 (Kan. 1990) (same); *Farley v. Engelken*, 740 P.2d 1058, 1061 (Kan. 1987) ("[w]hen an equal protection challenge is raised involving individual personal or property rights, not political rights, the proper constitutional section to be considered is Section 1 of the Kansas Bill of Rights").

47. On occasion, the Kansas Supreme Court has referred to both § 1 and § 2 as guaranteeing equal protection, without indicating that § 2 has a narrower scope of operation. *See State v. Gaudina*, 160 P.3d 854, 865 (Kan. 2007); *Leiker by and through Leiker v. Gafford*, 778 P.2d at 849. Whether § 2 is limited to "political privileges," as *Sharples* suggests, or extends to "the personal or property rights of an individual" is immaterial for purposes of state equal protection analysis, however, because § 2 has never been given a *broader* interpretation than has § 1.

48. *Farley v. Engelken*, 740 P.2d at 1061 (citation omitted).

49. *Id.* at 1063.

50. *Id.* at 1062–63.

51. *Craig v. Boren*, 429 U.S. 190, 197 (1976) (gender discrimination).

52. *Christopher v. State ex rel. Kansas Juvenile Justice Authority*, 143 P.3d 685, 692 (Kan. 2006) (citation and internal quotation marks omitted).

sify persons on the basis of "race, ancestry [or] alienage." Abortion advocates may argue in the alternative that a statute prohibiting abortion discriminates against women and is subject to intermediate scrutiny because only women are capable of becoming pregnant. An abortion prohibition would appear to satisfy this level of scrutiny because the prohibition would be "substantially related" to the "important [state] objective" in protecting unborn human life. Nevertheless, the standard applicable to sex-based discrimination should not apply to an abortion prohibition. Abortion laws do not discriminate on the basis of sex.

First, the United States Supreme Court has reviewed restrictions on abortion funding under a rational basis standard of review, *not* under the heightened scrutiny required of gender-based classifications.[53] Indeed, the Court has held that "the disfavoring of abortion ... is not *ipso facto* sex discrimination," and, citing its decisions in *Harris* and other cases addressing abortion funding, stated that "the constitutional test applicable to government abortion-funding restrictions is not the heightened-scrutiny standard that our cases demand for sex discrimination, ... but the ordinary rationality standard."[54]

Second, even assuming that an abortion prohibition differentiates between men and women on the basis of sex, and would otherwise be subject to a higher standard of review, the Supreme Court has held that biological differences between men and women may justify different treatment based on those differences. In upholding a statutory rape statute that applied only to males, the Supreme Court noted, "this Court has consistently upheld statutes where the gender classification is not invidious, but rather realistically reflects the fact

---

53. *Harris v. McRae*, 448 U.S. 297, 321–26 (1980).

54. *Bray v. Alexandria Women's Health Clinic*, 506 U.S. 263, 273 (1993). Several state supreme courts and individual state supreme court justices have recognized that abortion regulations and restrictions on abortion funding are not "directed at women as a class" so much as "abortion as a medical treatment, which, because it involves a potential life, has no parallel as a treatment method." *Bell v. Low Income Women of Texas*, 95 S.W.3d 253, 258 (Tex. 2002) (upholding funding restrictions) (citing *Harris*, 448 U.S. at 325). *See also Fischer v. Dep't of Public Welfare*, 502 A.2d 114, 125 (Pa. 1985) ("the basis for the distinction here is not sex, but abortion") (upholding funding restrictions); *Moe v. Secretary of Administration & Finance*, 417 N.E.2d 387, 407 (Mass. 1981) (Hennessey, C.J., dissenting) (funding restrictions were "directed at abortion as a medical procedure, not women as a class"); *Right to Choose v. Byrne*, 450 A.2d 925, 950 (N.J. 1982) (O'Hern, J., dissenting) ("[t]he subject of the legislation is not the person of the recipient, but the nature of the claimed medical service"). Both *Moe* and *Right to Choose* were decided on other grounds. The dissenting justices were addressing alternative arguments raised by the plaintiffs, but not reached by the majority opinions.

that the sexes are not similarly situated in certain circumstances."[55] As one federal district court observed: "Abortion statutes are examples of cases in which the sexes are not biologically similarly situated" because only women are capable of becoming pregnant and having abortions.[56]

A statute prohibiting abortion quite obviously can affect only women because only women are capable of becoming pregnant.[57] Unlike laws that use women's ability to become pregnant (or pregnancy itself) to discriminate against them in *other* areas (*e.g.*, employment opportunities), abortion prohibitions cannot fairly be said to involve a distinction between men and women that is a "mere pretext[] designed to erect an invidious discrimination against [women]."[58]

Because a prohibition of abortion would not infringe upon a fundamental state constitutional right and would not impermissibly classify on the basis of a suspect or quasi-suspect class, it would need to satisfy only the rational basis test. Under that test, the classification must be "rationally related to a legitimate [state] purpose."[59] A prohibition of abortion would be "rationally related" to the "legitimate [state] interest" in protecting unborn human life. Accordingly, Kansas could enact an abortion prohibition without violating the equal protection guarantee of the Kansas Constitution.

Retained Rights

Section 20 of the Kansas Bill of Rights provides: "This enumeration of rights shall not be construed to impair or deny others retained by the people; and all powers not herein delegated remain with the people."[60] In any challenge to an abortion prohibition, abortion advocates are likely to rely upon the first clause of §20, arguing that abortion is a "retained right." Such an argument probably would not prevail.

Section 20 has seldom been cited by the Kansas Supreme Court and never in support of a unenumerated retained right, which is at least some indication that it is not a source of any substantive rights under the Kansas Consti-

---

55. *Michael M. v. Superior Court*, 450 U.S. 464, 469 (1981).

56. *Jane L. v. Bangerter*, 794 F. Supp. 1537, 1549 (D. Utah 1992).

57. *Geduldig v. Aiello*, 417 U.S. 484, 496 n. 20 (1974) ("[n]ormal pregnancy is an objectively, identifiable physical condition with unique characteristics").

58. *Id.*

59. *Christopher v. State ex rel. Kansas Juvenile Justice Authority*, 143 P.3d at 692 (citation and internal quotation marks omitted).

60. KAN. BILL OF RIGHTS §20 (1998).

tution.[61] An entirely plausible reading of the first clause of § 20 is that the enumeration of certain rights in the state constitution should not be construed to "impair" or "deny" other rights retained by the people under the common law or statutes.[62] But even if § 20 is understood to retain unspecified *constitutional* rights (as opposed to *common law* or *statutory* rights), abortion could not plausibly be considered to be among such rights because, at the time the Kansas Constitution was adopted in 1859, abortion was a crime except to save the life of the pregnant woman. The argument that § 20 retained as an "unenumerated" right conduct that was criminal when the state constitution was adopted is, at the very least, counterintuitive.

The language of the first clause of § 20 may have been based on the Ninth Amendment.[63] In light of that equivalence, § 20 should be given a parallel interpretation. That, in turn, suggests that if no right to abortion exists under the Ninth Amendment, then none would be recognized under § 20. The Supreme Court, however, has rooted the "abortion liberty" in the liberty language of the Due Process Clause of the Fourteenth Amendment, not in the unenumerated rights language of the Ninth Amendment.[64] Because abortion has not

---

61. *See, e.g.*, *State v. Durein*, 80 P. 987, 994–95 (Kan. 1904) (§ 20 does not confer a right to sell intoxicating liquor in violation of state law).

62. This reading is supported, at least indirectly, by the Kansas Supreme Court's recognition in *Lemons v. Noller*, 63 P.2d 177, 182–83 (Kan. 1936), that constitutional restrictions on legislative power are not to be lightly inferred, and that, although an abridgment of power may be express or implied, where implied the implication must be plain and must arise from an express provision with respect to some exact subject matter. Section 20, of course, does not impose any express limitations on legislative power and, therefore, no implied limitation may be derived therefrom. Moreover, the court has held that the powers retained by the people under the second clause of § 20 ("all powers not herein delegated remain with the people") include "the exercise of the police power, or the power to pass legislation for the general welfare of the people," *Manning v. Davis*, 201 P.2d 113, 115 (Kan. 1948), which, in the absence of some other constitutional limitation, would include the power to prohibit abortion.

63. "The enumeration in the Constitution of certain rights, shall not be construed to deny or disparage others retained by the people." U.S. CONST. AMEND. IX (West 2006). *See Johnson v. Board of County Comm'rs of Reno County*, 75 P.2d 849, 857–58 (Kan. 1938) (citing § 20 together with the Ninth Amendment).

64. *See Roe*, 410 U.S. at 153; *Casey*, 505 U.S. at 846. In any event, the Ninth Amendment, standing alone, is not a source of substantive rights. *Gibson v. Matthews*, 926 F.2d 532, 537 (6th Cir. 1991). Although "[s]ome unenumerated rights may be of [c]onstitutional magnitude," that is only "by virtue of other amendments, such as the Fifth or Fourteenth Amendment. A person cannot claim a right that exists solely under the Ninth Amendment." *United States v. Vital Health Products, Ltd.*, 786 F. Supp. 761, 777 (E.D. Wis. 1992), *aff'd mem.*

been recognized as a "retained right" under the Ninth Amendment, it should not be recognized as one under § 20, either.

Conclusion

Based on the foregoing analysis, an argument that the Kansas Constitution protects a right to abortion that is separate from, and independent of, the right to abortion recognized in *Roe v. Wade* would not likely succeed. That, in turn, suggests that if *Roe*, as modified by *Casey*, is ultimately overruled, the State of Kansas could enact and enforce a statute *prohibiting* abortion. Moreover, nothing in the Kansas Constitution precludes Kansas from *regulating* abortion within federal constitutional limits in the meantime.

---

op., sub nom. United States v. LeBeau, 985 F.2d 563 (7th Cir. 1993). *See also Charles v. Brown*, 495 F. Supp. 862, 863 (N.D. Ala. 1980) (same).

CHAPTER 20

KENTUCKY

Summary

The Kentucky Supreme Court has not yet decided whether the Kentucky Constitution protects a right to abortion separate from, and independent of, the right to abortion recognized under the United States Constitution.[1] A careful examination of the state constitution, in light of its history and interpretation, as well as other relevant legal sources, however, suggests that the state supreme court probably would not recognize a state constitutional right to abortion. Thus, if *Roe v. Wade*,[2] as modified by *Planned Parenthood of Southeastern Pennsylvania v. Casey*,[3] were overruled, Kentucky could prohibit abortion. Moreover, nothing in the state constitution, properly understood, precludes the Commonwealth from enacting and enforcing reasonable measures regulating abortion within current federal constitutional limits.

Analysis

The principal pre-*Roe* abortion statute prohibited performance of an abortion upon a pregnant woman unless the procedure was "necessary to preserve her life."[4] Pursuant to *Roe*, § 436.020 was declared unconstitutional (on federal, not state, grounds) by the Kentucky Court of Appeals (the name of Ken-

---

1. The Kentucky Supreme Court has referred to the right to abortion solely as a matter of *federal*, not *state*, constitutional law. *See Grubbs v. Barbourville Health Center, P.S.C.*, 120 S.W.3d 682, 689 & n. 21 (Ky. 2003) ("a woman has a constitutional right to make an informed decision regarding her procreative options") (citing *Roe v. Wade*).

2. 410 U.S. 113 (1973).

3. 505 U.S. 833 (1992).

4. KY. REV. STAT. ANN. § 436.020 (Michie 1962). Another statute punished the offense as a homicide if the woman died as a result thereof. *Id.* § 435.040.

tucky's highest court before 1976) in *Sasaki v. Commonwealth*,[5] and was later repealed.[6]

Based upon arguments that have been raised in Kentucky and other States with similar constitutional provisions,[7] possible sources for an asserted abortion right could include provisions of the Bill of Rights guaranteeing the right of all persons to enjoy and defend their lives and liberties (§ 1(1)), the right of seeking and pursuing their safety and happiness (§ 1(3)), due process of law (§§ 2, 11), equal protection (§§ 1, 2, 3), religious freedom (§§ 1(2), 5) and a remedy by due course of law (§ 14); denying absolute and arbitrary power (§ 2); recognizing inherent and inalienable rights (§ 1) and inherent power in the people (§ 4); and declaring that the rights set forth in the Bill of Rights shall remain inviolate (§ 26).[8] The analysis that follows addresses each of these provisions.

Due Process of Law

Section 2 of the Kentucky Constitution provides: "Absolute and arbitrary power over the lives, liberty and property of freemen exists nowhere in a republic, not even in the largest majority."[9] The Kentucky Supreme Court has held that § 2 is "broad enough to embrace the traditional concepts of both due

---

5. 497 S.W.2d 713 (Ky. 1973). The original opinion in *Sasaki*, in which the court of appeals upheld the statute, 485 S.W.2d 897 Ky. (1972), *vacated and remanded*, 410 U.S. 951 (1973), is discussed later in this analysis, *infra*. Prior to *Roe*, a three-judge federal district court also upheld the statute against a federal constitutional challenge. *Crossen v. Attorney General*, 344 F. Supp. 587 (E.D. Ky. 1972), *vacated and remanded*, 410 U.S. 950 (1973).

6. 1974 Ky. Acts 484, 487, ch. 255, § 19; 1974 Ky. Acts 831, 889, ch. 406, § 336. Kentucky has enacted a statute stating that "[i]f ... the United States Constitution is amended or relevant judicial decisions are reversed or modified, the declared policy of this Commonwealth to recognize and to protect the lives of all human beings regardless of their degree of biological development shall be fully restored." Ky. Rev. Stat. Ann. § 311.710(5) (Michie 2007). In the absence of new legislation criminalizing abortion (the pre-*Roe* statutes having been repealed), this expression of legislative policy would not, by its own terms, make abortion illegal. It contains no operative provisions and authorizes no punishment. Conduct is not criminal in Kentucky unless a statute defines the particular conduct as criminal. *See* Ky. Rev. Stat. Ann. § 500.020(1) (Michie 1996).

7. *See Doe v. Childers*, No. 94 CI02183, Order, Aug. 3, 1995 (Jefferson Circuit Court, Commonwealth of Kentucky) (rejecting state constitutional challenge to statute restricting public funding of abortion).

8. Four other more unlikely sources of an abortion right under the Kentucky Constitution-§§ 1(4), 8 (guaranteeing freedom of speech), § 10 (prohibiting unreasonable searches and seizures) and § 25 (prohibiting involuntary servitude)-are discussed generally in Chapter 3, *supra*.

9. Ky. Const. § 2 (Michie 2002).

process of law and equal protection of the law."[10] And § 11 provides, in relevant part, that an accused cannot "be deprived of his life, liberty or property, unless by the judgment of his peers or the law of the land."[11] On occasion, these provisions have been interpreted to have a substantive component, but statutes generally comply with due process of law if they satisfy the rational basis test,[12] which an abortion statute clearly would. A challenge to an abortion statute more likely would be based on the right of privacy that has been derived from the liberty language of §§ 1and 2, which is discussed in the next section.

Inalienable and Inherent Rights, Absolute and Arbitrary Power

Section 1(1) of the Kentucky Constitution provides: "All men ... have certain inherent and inalienable rights, among which may be reckoned.... [t]he right of enjoying and defending their lives and liberties."[13] Section 1(3) recognizes, as another inherent and inalienable right, "[t]he right of seeking and pursuing ... safety and happiness."[14] Section 2, as noted, denies "[a]bsolute and arbitrary power over the lives, liberty and property of freeman...." Taken together, these provisions have been interpreted as conferring certain privacy rights upon Kentuckians. The lead case in this area is *Commonwealth v. Wasson.*[15]

In *Wasson*, a sharply divided Kentucky Supreme Court held that a criminal statute proscribing consensual homosexual sodomy violated both privacy and equal protection guarantees of the state constitution.[16] In defending the statute against defendant's privacy challenge, the Commonwealth argued that "the majority, speaking through the General Assembly, has the right to criminalize

---

10. *Kentucky Milk Marketing & Antimonopoly Comm'n v. Kroger Co.*, 691 S.W.2d 893, 899 (Ky. 1985).

11. Ky. Const. § 11 (Michie 2002). The phrase, "the law of the land," is a recognized alternative formulation for "due process of law."

12. *See Buford v. Commonwealth*, 942 S.W.2d 909, 912 (Ky. 1997) (statute proscribing trafficking in simulated controlled substances is a rational and legitimate exercise of the Legislature's police power, and does not violate due process).

13. Ky. Const. § 1(1) (Michie 2002).

14. *Id.* § 1(3).

15. 842 S.W.2d 487 (Ky. 1993).

16. For the reasons set forth in the next section of this analysis, the court's equal protection holding, *id.* at 499–502, based upon the unequal treatment of sexual conduct outside of marriage, would have no bearing on an abortion statute's constitutionality.

sexual activity it deems immoral, without regard to whether the activity is conducted in private between consenting adults and is not, in and of itself, harmful to the participants or to others."[17] The Commonwealth argued further that "if not in all instances, at least where there is a Biblical and historical tradition supporting it, there are no limitations in the Kentucky Constitution on the power of the General Assembly to criminalize sexual activity these elected representatives deem immoral."[18] A majority of the court rejected both arguments.

With respect to the latter argument, which rested on the proposition "that homosexual sodomy was punished as an offense at common law [and] that it has been punished by statute in Kentucky since 1860, predating our Kentucky Constitution,"[19] the court noted that "oral copulation," the offense with which the defendant had been charged with soliciting from an undercover police officer, was not a crime at common law or under the sodomy statute in effect at the time the state constitution was adopted.[20] That statute, reflecting the common law, was "limited to *anal* intercourse between *men*," and "punished *neither oral copulation nor any form of deviate sexual conduct between women*."[21] As a consequence, "the statute in question here punishes conduct which has been historically and traditionally viewed as immoral, but much of which [including the conduct which the defendant solicited] has never been punished as criminal."[22]

With respect to the former argument regarding the General Assembly's authority "to criminalize sexual activity it deems immoral," the court held that the liberties protected by §§ 1(1), 1(3) and 2 of the Kentucky Constitution include a right of privacy, even though privacy, as such, is not mentioned in the text itself.[23] The court placed particular emphasis on an early decision of the court of appeals (now the supreme court) striking down an ordinance that criminalized the possession of intoxicating liquor, even for "private use."[24] In *Campbell*, the court held that "[i]t is not within the competency of government to

---

17. *Wasson*, 842 S.W.2d at 490.

18. *Id.* In developing this argument, the Commonwealth stated that "homosexual intercourse is immoral, and that what is beyond the pale of majoritarian morality is beyond the limits of constitutional protection." *Id.*

19. *Id.*

20. *Id.* at 491.

21. *Id.* (emphasis in original).

22. *Id.*

23. *Id.* at 492–99.

24. *Id.* at 492–98 (citing and discussing *Commonwealth v. Campbell*, 117 S.W. 383 (Ky. 1909)).

invade the privacy of a citizen's life and to regulate conduct in which he alone is concerned, or to prohibit him any liberty the exercise of which will not directly injure society."[25] And, in a case decided only six years after *Campbell*, the court of appeals declared unconstitutional a statute that had led to the defendant being arrested for drinking beer in the backroom of an office.[26] The court stated:

> The power of the state to regulate and control the conduct of a private individual is confined to those cases where his conduct injuriously affects others. With his faults or weaknesses, which he keeps to himself, and which do not operate to the detriment of others, the state as such has no concern.[27]

Smith held that "the police power may be called into play [only] when it is reasonably necessary to protect the public health, or public morals, or public safety."[28] "The clear implication is that immorality in private which does 'not operate to the detriment of others,' is placed beyond the reach of state action by the guarantees of liberty in the Kentucky Constitution."[29]

Both *Campbell* and *Wasson* relied heavily on the libertarian philosophy of the nineteenth century English philosopher, John Stuart Mill.[30] In his classic work, *On Liberty*, first published in 1859, Mill expressed a narrow and limited view of the authority of the State's authority to legislate personal conduct:

> The only part of the conduct of anyone, for which he is amenable to society, is that which concerns others. In the part which merely concerns himself, his independence is, of right, absolute.... [T]he principle requires liberty of taste and pursuits; of framing the plan of our life to suit our own character; of doing as we like, subject to such consequences as may follow; without impediment from our fellow crea-

---

25. *Campbell*, 117 S.W. at 385.

26. *Commonwealth v. Smith*, 173 S.W. 340 (Ky. 1915).

27. *Id.* at 343.

28. *Id.*

29. *Wasson*, 842 S.W.2d at 496 (quoting *Smith*, 173 S.W. at 343). *Wasson* also relied upon a decision in which the court of appeals struck down an ordinance "which purported to regulate cigarette smoking in such broad terms that it could be applied to persons who smoked in the privacy of their own home." *Id.* (citing *Hershberg v. City of Barbourville*, 133 S.W. 985 (Ky. 1911)). The ordinance "unreasonably interfer[ed] with the right of the citizen to determine for himself such personal matters." *Hershberg*, 133 S.W. at 986.

30. *Campbell*, 117 S.W. at 386; *Wasson*, 842 S.W.2d at 496–98.

tures, *so long as what we do does not harm them,* even though they should think our conduct foolish, perverse, or wrong.[31]

"Mill's premise," according to *Wasson,* "is that 'physical force in the form of legal penalties,' i.e., criminal sanctions, should not be used as a means to improve the citizen."[32] Thus, "[t]he majority has no moral right to dictate how everyone else should live. Public indignation, while given due weight, should be subject to the overriding test of rational and critical analysis, drawing the line at harmful consequences to others."[33] *Wasson* noted that modern legal philosophers who follow Mill temper this test with an "enlightened paternalism," according to which the law is permitted "to intervene to stop self-inflicted harm such as the result of drug taking, or failure to sue seat belts or crash helmets, not to enforce majoritarian or conventional morality, but because the victim of such self-inflicted harm becomes a burden on society."[34] The majority held that the sodomy statute impermissibly interfered with the privacy rights of homosexuals.[35]

In light of *Wasson,* it is apparent that "the privacy rights guaranteed by the Kentucky Constitution exceed those granted by the United States Constitution."[36] Nevertheless, *Wasson* should not have any effect on the authority of

---

31. John Stuart Mill, *On Liberty and other Essays* 14, 17 (emphasis added) (Oxford University Press 1991). One might think that engaging in sexual conduct that places another person at risk of contracting a deadly disease (AIDS) would qualify as conduct that could "harm" another. The Commonwealth, however, presented no evidence to contradict the defendant's expert witness testimony that the sodomy statute "interferes with efforts to provide therapy to those who may need it," "offers no benefit in preventing the spread of [AIDS], and can be a barrier to getting accurate medical histories, thus having an adverse effect on public health efforts." *Wasson,* 842 S.W.2d at 489–90.

32. *Wasson,* 842 S.W.2d at 496.

33. *Id.*

34. *Id.* at 496–97.

35. *Id.* at 491. In so ruling, the court declined to follow *Bowers v. Hardwick,* 478 U.S. 186 (1986), *overruled, Lawrence v. Texas,* 539 U.S. 558, 578 (2003). *Wasson,* 842 S.W.2d at 489–90, 493, 497–99.

36. *Yeoman v. Commonwealth of Kentucky, Health Policy Board,* 983 S.W.2d 459, 474 (Ky. 1998) (citing *Wasson*). Section 1(1) of the Kentucky Constitution has been interpreted to protect the right of a competent person to refuse unwanted medical treatment, *Woods v. Commonwealth,* 142 S.W.3d 24, 32 (Ky. 2004), but not to suicide or assistance in committing suicide, *id.* at 31 n. 9. It should be noted here that the Supreme Court, departing from its rationale in *Roe,* 410 U.S. at 153 ("[t]his right of privacy ... is broad enough to encompass a woman's decision whether or not to terminate her pregnancy"), no longer analyzes substantive due process claims under the rubric of "privacy," either in the area of abortion, *see Casey,* 505 U.S. at 846–53 (reaffirming *Roe* on the basis of the liberty language of the Due Process Clause without once mentioning privacy), or any other area. *See Cruzan v. Di-*

the Commonwealth (under the state constitution) to prohibit abortion. Unlike the state sodomy statute struck down in *Wasson*, abortion *was* a criminal offense long before the present Kentucky Constitution was adopted in 1891. More importantly, abortion has "harmful consequences to others." "An abortion ends the life of a developing unborn child."[37] Laws enacted for the direct protection of society do not violate the right of privacy.[38]

Abortion has always been treated as a criminal offense in Kentucky. In *Mitchell v. Commonwealth*,[39] decided twelve years before the present Kentucky Constitution was adopted, the Kentucky Court of Appeals noted that abortion after "quickening" was a crime at common law.[40] The court reversed the defendant's conviction for abortion because the indictment failed to allege that the woman was "quick with child."[41] The court concluded that "it never was a punishable offense at common law to produce, with the consent of the mother, an abortion prior to the time when the mother became quick with child."[42] Although compelled to reverse the defendant's conviction, the court expressed its strong view that the Legislature should prohibit all abortions:

> [T]he law should punish abortions and miscarriages, wilfully produced, at any time during the period of gestation. That the child shall be considered in existence from the moment of conception for the

---

rector, Missouri Dep't of Health, 497 U.S. 261, 279 n. 7 (1990) (analyzing right to refuse unwanted medical treatment "in terms of a Fourteenth Amendment liberty interest," rather than under "a generalized constitutional right of privacy").

37. *Cabinet for Human Resources v. Women's Health Services, Inc.*, 878 S.W.2d 806, 809 (Ky. Ct. App. 1994) (McDonald, J., concurring). *See also Commonwealth v. Morris*, 142 S.W.3d 654, 669 (Ky. 2004) (Wintersheimer, J., concurring) ("the true beginning of individual human life ... is conception").

38. *Hyatt v. Commonwealth*, 72 S.W.3d 566, 579 (Ky. 2002) (upholding sex offender registry statute). *See also Lynch v. Commonwealth*, 902 S.W.2d 813, 815–16 (Ky. 1995) (because of the potential danger to others, there is no privacy right to operate a motor vehicle on private property while intoxicated); *Commonwealth v. Harrelson*, 14 S.W.3d 541, 547 (Ky. 2000) (there is no privacy right to possess or cultivate marijuana).

39. 78 Ky. 204 (1879).

40. *Id.* at 206–09. "Quickening" is that stage of pregnancy, usually sixteen to eighteen weeks gestation, when the woman first detects fetal movement.

41. *Id.* at 210.

42. *Id.* If, however, the mother died, the person who caused her death could be charged with either murder or manslaughter, regardless of the stage of pregnancy when the abortion was performed. *Peoples v. Commonwealth*, 9 S.W. 509, 509–11 (Ky. 1888) (affirming conviction of manslaughter for causing the death of a woman in a pre-quickening abortion).

protection of its rights of property, and yet not in existence, until four or five months after the inception of its being, to the extent that it is a crime to destroy it, presents an anomaly in the law that ought to be provided against by the law-making department of the government.[43]

The Legislature ultimately followed this advice by making abortion at any stage of pregnancy a crime, and raising the penalty from a misdemeanor to a felony.[44] The statute remained on the books until after *Roe* was decided.[45]

Prior to the Supreme Court's decision in *Roe v. Wade*, the Kentucky Court of Appeals regularly affirmed convictions for abortion without any hint that either the prosecutions or convictions violated the Kentucky Constitution.[46] Less than four months before *Roe*, the court affirmed a licensed physician's conviction for performing an illegal abortion, rejecting both federal privacy and vagueness challenges to the law.[47] Adopting the opinion of a three-judge federal district court that had upheld the statute, the court of appeals held that Kentucky had "'a compelling interest in the preservation of potential human life.'"[48] When, following *Roe*, the court struck down the state abortion statute, it did so strictly on the basis of the Supremacy Clause and not on any independent state ground.[49]

It is "the declared policy of this Commonwealth to recognize and protect the lives of all human beings regardless of their degree of biological development."[50] Consistent with that policy, Kentucky has enacted a comprehensive scheme of abortion regulations.[51]

---

43. *Mitchell*, 78 Ky. at 209–10.

44. Act of March 22, 1910, Ky. Acts. ch. 58, §§ 1-4 (1910).

45. *Id.*, *codified at* KY STAT. § 1219a (1915), *recodified at* KY. REV. STAT. § 436.020 (1942), *carried forward as* KY REV. STAT. ANN. § 436.020 (1962), *repealed by* 1974 Ky. Acts 484, 487, ch. 255, § 19; 1974 Ky. Acts 831, 889, ch. 406, § 336.

46. *Commonwealth v. Allen*, 231 S.W. 41 (Ky. 1921); *Bain v. Commonwealth*, 330 S.W.2d 400 (Ky. 1959); *Dalzell v. Commonwealth*, 312 S.W.2d 354 (Ky. 1958); *Brown v. Commonwealth*, 440 S.W.2d 520 (Ky. 1969).

47. *Sasaki v. Commonwealth*, 485 S.W.2d 897 (Ky. 1972), *vacated and remanded*, 410 U.S. 951 (1973).

48. *Id.* at 902 (quoting *Crossen v. Attorney General*, 344 F. Supp. at 591).

49. *Sasaki v. Commonwealth*, 497 S.W.2d 713 (Ky. 1973).

50. KY. REV. STAT. ANN. § 311.710(5) (Michie 2007). *See also* §§ 311.720(5) (definition of "fetus"), 311.720(6) (definition of "human being").

51. *Id.* §§ 311.760, 311.780 (adopting trimester framework); § 311.725 (mandating informed consent and a twenty-four hour waiting period); § 311.732 (requiring parental consent); §§ 311.800(3) through 311.800(5) (recognizing individual and institutional rights of conscience and prohibiting discrimination); § 311.715 (restricting public funding of abor-

Kentucky has recognized the rights of unborn children in a variety of contexts outside of abortion, including criminal law, tort law, health care law and property law. Under the criminal code, the killing of an unborn child, other than in an abortion, may be prosecuted as a homicide.[52] And a woman convicted of a capital offense may not be executed while she is pregnant.[53]

In tort law, a statutory cause of action for wrongful death may be brought on behalf of an unborn child who was viable (capable of sustained survival outside the mother's womb, with or without medical assistance) at the time of its death.[54] A common law action for (nonlethal) prenatal injuries may be brought without regard to the stage of pregnancy when the injuries were inflicted.[55] And the Kentucky Supreme Court has refused to recognize wrongful conception, wrongful birth and wrongful life causes of action.[56] "Wrongful life," the court has said, "is a contradiction in terms. It is contrary to the public policy of this State as expressed by the legislature and interpreted by the

---

tion for indigent women); §§311.800(1), 311.800(2) (restricting use of public hospitals and health care facilities for abortion).

52. *Id.* §507A.010 *et seq.* (Michie Supp. 2006). In a case decided under prior law, the Kentucky Supreme Court judicially abrogated the common law "born alive" rule with respect to the killing of a viable unborn child. *Commonwealth v. Morris*, 142 S.W.3d 654 (Ky. 2004) (overruling *Hollis v. Commonwealth*, 652 S.W.2d 61 (Ky. 1983)).

53. Ky. Rev. Stat. Ann. §431.240(2) (Michie 1999).

54. *Mitchell v. Couch*, 285 S.W.2d 901, 906 (Ky. 1955), interpreting Ky. Rev. Stat. Ann. §411.130 (Michie 2005). *See also City of Louisville v. Stuckenborg*, 438 S.W.2d 94, 95 (Ky. 1968) (applying *Mitchell*); *Rice v. Rizk*, 453 S.W.2d 732 (Ky. 1970) (same).

55. *Mitchell*, 285 S.W.2d at 906 (by implication).

56. *Schork v. Huber*, 648 S.W.2d 861 (Ky. 1983) (wrongful conception); *Grubbs v. Barbourville Family Health Center, P.S.C.*, 120 S.W.3d 682 (Ky. 2003) (wrongful life, wrongful birth). A "wrongful conception" cause of action alleges that as the result of a physician's negligence (*e.g.*, an improperly performed sterilization), a woman conceived who had not intended to conceive. A "wrongful life" cause of action is a claim brought on behalf of a child who is born with a physical or mental disability or disease that could have been discovered before the child's birth by genetic testing, amniocentesis or other medical screening. The gravamen of the action is that, as a result of a physician's failure to inform the child's parents of the child's disability or disease (or at least of the availability of tests to determine the presence of the disability or disease), they were deprived of the opportunity to abort the child, thus resulting in the birth of a child suffering permanent physical or mental impairment. A "wrongful birth" cause of action, on the other hand, is a claim, based on the same facts, brought by the parents of the impaired child on their own behalf. For the reasons set forth in the text, very few courts recognize "wrongful life" causes of action because an assessment of damages requires the courts to compare the value of life, albeit with some degree of physical or mental impairment, to nonexistence. Unlike the Kentucky Supreme Court, however, most courts that have considered "wrongful birth" causes of action have recognized them.

courts."[57] "To permit a claim for wrongful life or wrongful birth would undermine the proposition that all human persons, no matter their race, religion, or ability, are precious and worthy of respect."[58]

Under Kentucky's health care statutes, a living will may not direct the withholding or withdrawal of life-sustaining treatment or artificially administered nutrition and hydration from a pregnant woman "unless, to a reasonable degree of medical certainty, ... the procedures will not maintain the woman in a way to permit the continuing development and live birth of the unborn child, will be physically harmful to the woman or prolong severe pain which cannot be alleviated."[59] Durable powers of attorney for health care are subject to the same limitation.[60]

In property law, posthumous children (children conceived before but born after the death of a person who dies without a will) may inherit from a decedent.[61] For the purpose of inheriting remainder interests, posthumous children are treated as if living at the death of their parent(s).[62] Subject to certain exceptions, a child who is born after a parent executes a will, and who is not otherwise provided for in the will, may receive that share he or she would have received if the parent had died without a will.[63]

A right to abortion cannot be found in the text or structure of the Kentucky Constitution. There is no evidence that the framers or ratifiers of the state constitution intended to limit the Legislature's authority to prohibit abortion.[64] Such an intent would have been remarkable in light of the prohibition of abortion except to save the life of the pregnant woman. Moreover, recognition of an abortion right would be manifestly inconsistent with the history and traditions of the Commonwealth, as well as with the precedents of the Kentucky Supreme Court. Taken together, these factors militate against recognition of a right to abortion under the liberty guarantees of the Kentucky Constitution.[65]

---

57. *Schork*, 648 S.W.2d at 863.

58. *Grubbs*, 120 S.W.3d at 693 (Wintersheimer, J., concurring).

59. Ky. Rev. Stat. Ann. §311.629(4) (2007). *See also* §311.625 (form of living will directive).

60. *Id.* §311.629(4).

61. *Id.* §§391.070, 394.460 (Michie 2002).

62. *Id.* §381.140.

63. *Id.* §394.382.

64. *See* 1 Official Report of the Proceedings and Debates in the 1890 Constitution 433-1041 (debate on Bill of Rights in Committee of the Whole); 1041–1245 (debate on Bill of Rights in Convention).

65. *See Williams v. Wilson*, 972 S.W.2d 260, 268–69 (Ky. 1998) (articulating factors to be considered in "a proper methodology for constitutional analysis").

Equal Protection

The Kentucky Supreme Court has identified three provisions of the Bill of Rights, along with two provisions restricting the Legislature's power, as guaranteeing equal protection of the law.[66] Section 1 provides, in relevant part, that "[a]ll men are, by nature, free and equal, and have certain inherent and inalienable rights...."[67] Section 2, as previously noted, prohibits "[a]bsolute and arbitrary power."[68] Section 3 provides, in pertinent part, that "[a]ll men, when they form a social compact, are equal; and no grant of exclusive, separate public emoluments or privileges shall be made to any man or set of men, except in consideration of public service...."[69] And §§ 59 and 60 prohibit local and special legislation.[70] Because of this "additional protection," referring to §§ 59 and 60, the Kentucky Supreme Court has "elected at times to apply a guarantee of individual rights in equal protection cases that is higher than the minimum guaranteed by the Federal Constitution."[71] "Instead of requiring a 'rational basis,' we have construed our Constitution as requiring a 'reasonable basis' or a 'substantial and justifiable reason' for discriminatory legislation in the areas of social and economic policy."[72] "Cases applying the heightened standard," however, "are limited to the particular facts of those cases,"[73] which suggests that the court has not yet developed a methodology for determining when the "heightened standard" will be applied.

For the reasons set forth in the previous section of this analysis, an abortion prohibition would satisfy any applicable standard of review.[74] Nevertheless, rational basis review would appear to be the appropriate standard under the provisions of Kentucky's Constitution that have been interpreted to guaran-

---

66. *Elk Horn Coal Corp. v. Cheyenne Resources, Inc.*, 163 S.W.3d 408, 418 (Ky. 2005); *Kentucky Harlan Coal Co. v. Holmes*, 872 S.W.2d 446, 455 (Ky. 1994) ("Sections 1, 2 and 3 of the Kentucky Constitution ... provide that the legislature does not have arbitrary power and shall treat all persons equally").

67. Ky. Const. § 1 (Michie 2002).

68. *Id.* § 2.

69. *Id.* § 3.

70. *Id.* §§ 59, 60.

71. *Elk Horn Coal Corp.*, 163 S.W.3d at 418.

72. *Id.* at 418–19. The court did not explain how a "reasonable basis" differs from a "rational basis."

73. *Id.* at 419.

74. Under *Sasaki*, the Commonwealth has a "compelling interest" in protecting the life of an unborn child, and a prohibition of abortion is narrowly tailored to promote that interest.

tee equal protection of the law. Neither §59 nor §60, prohibiting local and special legislation, would be implicated by a prohibition of abortion. Legislation does not violate §59 (or, by extension, §60) if it applies equally to all members of a class and if the classification itself is supported by distinctive and natural reasons.[75] A law prohibiting abortion except to save the life of the pregnant woman would apply equally to all members of the class (pregnant women seeking abortions). Moreover, the classification itself (between those women who could obtain abortions and those who could not) is supported by "distinctive and natural reasons," allowing abortion when the life of the woman is endangered, but forbidding them otherwise. An abortion prohibition would be a statewide law of general application. It would not constitute "special" or "local" legislation in violation of §§59 and 60.

Apart from §§59 and 60, equal protection analysis under the Equal Protection Clause of the Fourteenth Amendment and the Kentucky Constitution is "identical."[76] For purposes of both state and federal equal protection analysis, "there are three levels of review: rational basis, strict scrutiny, and the seldom used intermediate scrutiny, which falls somewhere between the other two."[77] "Strict scrutiny applies whenever a statute makes a classification on the basis of a 'suspect class,' such as race, ... or when a statute significantly interferes with the exercise of a fundamental right."[78] Under this standard of review, "the challenged statute can survive only if it is suitably tailored to serve a 'compelling state interest.'"[79] If, on the other hand, "the statute merely affects social or economic policy, it is subject only to a 'rational basis' analysis."[80] Under this standard of review, "legislative distinctions between persons ... must bear a rational relationship to a legitimate state end."[81] Between these two standards of review, there is an intermediate standard of review that applies to "groups, like women, who are not 'suspect classes,' but who have been historically victimized by intense and irrational discrimination."[82] Under this standard of review ("heightened scrutiny"), "discriminatory laws survive equal

---

75. *Schoo v. Rose*, 270 S.W.2d 940, 941 (Ky. 1954). *See also Waggoner v. Waggoner*, 846 S.W.2d 704, 707 (Ky. 1992) (applying *Schoo*).

76. *Yeoman v. Commonwealth of Kentucky*, 983 S.W.2d at 469.

77. *D.F. v. Codell*, 127 S.W.3d 571, 575 (Ky. 2003). Another term for "intermediate scrutiny" is "heightened scrutiny." The terms are used interchangeably in this section of the analysis.

78. *Id.* (citations omitted).

79. *Id.* (citation omitted).

80. *Id.* (citation and internal quotation marks omitted).

81. *Id.* (citation and internal quotation marks omitted).

82. *Id.* (citations and internal quotation marks omitted).

protection analysis only to the extent that they are *substantially related* to a legitimate state interest."[83]

For purposes of state constitutional law, a prohibition of abortion should be reviewed under the rational basis standard. Strict scrutiny would not apply because, for the reasons set forth in the previous section, there is no "fundamental right" to an abortion under the Kentucky Constitution. Moreover, no "suspect class" is involved. Abortion advocates may argue in the alternative that a statute prohibiting abortion discriminates against women and is subject to intermediate scrutiny because only women are capable of becoming pregnant. An abortion prohibition would appear to satisfy this level of scrutiny because the prohibition would be "substantially related" to the "legitimate state interest" in protecting unborn human life. Nevertheless, the standard applicable to sex-based discrimination should not apply to an abortion prohibition. Abortion laws do not discriminate on the basis of sex.

First, the United States Supreme Court has reviewed restrictions on abortion funding under a rational basis standard of review, *not* under the heightened scrutiny required of gender-based classifications.[84] Indeed, the Court has held that "the disfavoring of abortion … is not *ipso facto* sex discrimination," and, citing its decisions in *Harris* and other cases addressing abortion funding, stated that "the constitutional test applicable to government abortion-funding restrictions is not the heightened-scrutiny standard that our cases demand for sex discrimination, … but the ordinary rationality standard."[85]

---

83. *Id.* at 575–76 (citation and internal quotation marks omitted) (emphasis in original). More precisely, the discrimination must be substantially related to an *important* (not just legitimate) state interest. *See Craig v. Boren*, 429 U.S. 190, 197 (1976). The Kentucky Supreme Court has struck down gender based statutes without clearly applying the intermediate standard of review. *See Hummeldorf v. Hummeldorf*, 616 S.W.2d 794, 797 (Ky. 1981) (divorce venue statue, which fixed venue in a divorce action in the county in which the wife resided, was "arbitrary and therefore unconstitutional under [§ 2] of the Kentucky Constitution"); *Commonwealth of Kentucky, Alcoholic Beverage Control Board v. Burke*, 481 S.W.2d 52, 53 (Ky. 1972) (statute that discriminated against women in serving and consuming alcoholic beverages was irrational and unconstitutional).

84. *Harris v. McRae*, 448 U.S. 297, 321–26 (1980).

85. *Bray v. Alexandria Women's Health Clinic*, 506 U.S. 263, 273 (1993). Several state supreme courts and individual state supreme court justices have recognized that abortion regulations and restrictions on abortion funding are not "directed at women as a class" so much as "abortion as a medical treatment, which, because it involves a potential life, has no parallel as a treatment method." *Bell v. Low Income Women of Texas*, 95 S.W.3d 253, 258 (Tex. 2002) (upholding funding restrictions) (citing *Harris*, 448 U.S. at 325). *See also Fischer v. Dep't of Public Welfare*, 502 A.2d 114, 125 (Pa. 1985) ("the basis for the distinction here is not sex, but abortion") (upholding funding restrictions); *Moe v. Secretary of Ad-*

Second, even assuming that an abortion prohibition differentiates between men and women on the basis of sex, and would otherwise be subject to a higher standard of review, the Supreme Court has held that biological differences between men and women may justify different treatment based on those differences. In upholding a statutory rape statute that applied only to males, the Supreme Court noted, "this Court has consistently upheld statutes where the gender classification is not invidious, but rather realistically reflects the fact that the sexes are not similarly situated in certain circumstances."[86] As one federal district court observed: "Abortion statutes are examples of cases in which the sexes are not biologically similarly situated" because only women are capable of becoming pregnant and having abortions.[87]

A statute prohibiting abortion quite obviously can affect only women because only women are capable of becoming pregnant.[88] Unlike laws that use women's ability to become pregnant (or pregnancy itself) to discriminate against them in *other* areas (*e.g.*, employment opportunities), abortion prohibitions cannot fairly be said to involve a distinction between men and women that is a "mere pretext[] designed to erect an invidious discrimination against [women]."[89]

A prohibition of abortion would not interfere with the exercise of a fundamental state constitutional right, nor would it classify upon the basis of a suspect or quasi-suspect characteristic. Accordingly, it would be subject to rational basis review. A law prohibiting abortion would be rationally related to the State's legitimate interest in protecting unborn human life.

---

ministration & Finance, 417 N.E.2d 387, 407 (Mass. 1981) (Hennessey, C.J., dissenting) (funding restrictions were "directed at abortion as a medical procedure, not women as a class"); *Right to Choose v. Byrne*, 450 A.2d 925, 950 (N.J. 1982) (O'Hern, J., dissenting) ("[t]he subject of the legislation is not the person of the recipient, but the nature of the claimed medical service"). Both *Moe* and *Right to Choose* were decided on other grounds. The dissenting justices were addressing alternative arguments raised by the plaintiffs, but not reached by the majority opinions.

86. *Michael M. v. Superior Court*, 450 U.S. 464, 469 (1981). The Kentucky Supreme Court has cited *Michael M.* with approval. *See Payne v. Commonwealth*, 623 S.W.2d 867, 874–75 (Ky. 1981).

87. *Jane L. v. Bangerter*, 794 F. Supp. 1537, 1549 (D. Utah 1992).

88. *Geduldig v. Aiello*, 417 U.S. 484, 496 n. 20 (1974) ("[n]ormal pregnancy is an objectively, identifiable physical condition with unique characteristics").

89. *Id.*

Religious Freedom

Section 1(2) of the Kentucky Constitution provides: "All men ... have certain inherent and inalienable rights, among which may be reckoned.... [t]he right of worshiping Almighty God according to the dictates of their consciences."[90] Section 5 provides:

> No preference shall ever be given by law to any religious sect, society or denomination; nor to any particular creed, mode of worship or system of ecclesiastical polity; nor shall any person be compelled to attend any place of worship, to contribute to the erection or maintenance of any such place, or to the salary or support of any minister of religion; nor shall any man be compelled to send his child to any school to which he may be conscientiously opposed; and the civil rights, privileges or capacities of no person shall be taken away, or in anywise diminished or enlarged, on account of his belief or disbelief of any religious tenet, dogma or teaching. No human authority shall, in any case whatever, control or interfere with the rights of conscience.[91]

In any challenge to a statute prohibiting abortion, abortion advocates may raise either or both of two arguments under §§1(2) and 5. First, relying upon the first clause of the first sentence of §5, they may argue that an abortion prohibition gives a "preference" to a "religious sect, society or denomination" because it reflects sectarian beliefs regarding when human life begins and the sinfulness of abortion. Second, relying upon §1(2) and the last sentence of §5, they may argue in addition (or in the alternative) that an abortion prohibition interferes with a woman's "rights of conscience" by forbidding her from obtaining an abortion that would be allowed by her religion. Neither argument would likely succeed.

In *Triplett v. Livingston County Board of Education*,[92] the Kentucky Court of Appeals held that "[t]he Establishment Clause of the United States Constitution and its counterpart [in] the Kentucky Constitution guarantee that government may nor coerce anyone to support or participate in religion or its exercise, or otherwise act in a way which established state religious faith or tends to do so."[93] The court held further that "[t]he Free Exercise Clause of both constitutions prevents the government from regulating one's religious beliefs."[94]

---

90. Ky. Const. §1(2) (Michie 2002).
91. *Id.* §5.
92. 967 S.W.2d 25 (Ky. Ct. App. 1997).
93. *Id.* at 31 (citations omitted).
94. *Id.* (citations omitted).

Citing *Triplett* and other decisions, a federal district court has noted that "Kentucky courts have looked to the United States Supreme Court for guidance in interpreting provisions of the Kentucky Constitution that deal with religious freedom."[95] This reliance upon federal precedent suggests that a challenge to an abortion statute that would not succeed under the Religion Clauses of the First Amendment would not succeed under §§ 1(2) and 5, either.[96] For the reasons set forth in Chapter 2, *supra*, an abortion statute could not be successfully challenged on First Amendment grounds. Accordingly, a similar challenge under §§ 1(2) and 5 would not likely be successful.[97]

---

95. *Hyman v. City of Louisville*, 132 F. Supp.2d 528, 539 (W.D. Ky. 2001) (citations omitted).

96. The Kentucky Supreme Court has stated that § 5 and § 189, which prohibits public educational funds from being "appropriated to, or used by, or in aid of, any church, sectarian or denominational school," Ky. CONST. § 189 (Michie 2002), "appear to restrict direct aid from state or local government to sectarian schools much more specifically and significantly than the only counterpart provision in the Federal Constitution, which is the 'establishment of religion' clause in the First Amendment." *Fiscal Court of Jefferson County, Kentucky v. Brady*, 885 S.W.2d 681, 686 (Ky. 1994). Section 189, of course, would have no bearing on the constitutionality of an abortion prohibition. In *Kentucky State Board of Education for Elementary & Secondary Education v. Rudasill*, 589 S.W.2d 877 (Ky. 1979), the Kentucky Supreme Court, citing language in § 5 ("nor shall any man be compelled to send his child to any school to which he may be conscientiously opposed"), said that "it is obvious that Section 5 ... is more restrictive of the power of the state to regulate private and parochial schools than is the first amendment ... as it has been applied to the states"). *Id.* at 879 n. 3. Obviously, this restriction would have no effect on the Legislature's authority to prohibit abortion, either.

97. Entirely apart from the Kentucky Supreme Court's reliance on federal precedent in interpreting §§ 1(2) and 5, an argument challenging an abortion prohibition on the basis that it gives a "preference" to a "religious ... denomination," by embodying sectarian views regarding the sinfulness of abortion, would appear to be foreclosed by decisions of the Kentucky Court of Appeals (now the Kentucky Supreme Court) rejecting challenges to Sunday closing laws. *See Commonwealth v. Arlen's Dep't Store of Louisville*, 357 S.W.2d 708, 710 (Ky. 1962) (upholding statute), *appeal dismissed for want of a substantial federal question sub nom. Arlen's Dep't Store of Louisville v. Kentucky*, 371 U.S. 218 (1962); *Gibson Products Co. of Bowling Green, Kentucky v. Lowe*, 440 S.W.2d 793, 795 (Ky. 1969) (following *Arlen* and upholding statute); *Strand Amusement Co. v. Commonwealth*, 43 S.W.2d 321, 322–23 (Ky. 1931) (upholding statute); *Capital Theater v. Commonwealth*, 199 S.W. 1076, 1078 (Ky. 1918) (same). If a law enforcing a "day of rest" does not violate the religion clauses of the Kentucky Constitution, even though it may coincide with sectarian beliefs regarding the Christian Sabbath, then neither would a law prohibiting abortion, regardless of whether the law coincides with religious views regarding the sinfulness of abortion.

Inherent Power

Section 4 of the Kentucky Constitution provides:

> All power is inherent in the people, and all free governments are founded on their authority and instituted for their peace, safety, happiness and the protection of property. For the advancement of these ends, they have at all times an inalienable and indefeasible right to alter, reform or abolish their government in such manner as they may deem proper.[98]

In a challenge to any statute prohibiting abortion that Kentucky may enact, abortion advocates might argue that the statute interferes with the "inherent" power of the people because it does not promote their "peace, safety [and] happiness." Given the purpose of §4, however, this argument would not likely prevail.

Section 4 "declares that for the advancement of the principle of the inherent power of the people to govern themselves, the people 'have at all times an inalienable and indefeasible right to alter, reform or abolish their government in such manner as they may deem proper.'"[99] The purpose of §4, as this passage reveals, is to secure to the people themselves, through the amendment process, the right to decide whether, how and to what extent the organic instrument of government should be changed. Section 4, thus, is not a source of substantive rights. Rather, it recognizes the people as the ultimate source of authority in a republican form of government.[100] As such, it could not serve as a basis for asserting a right to abortion. Whether a given law promotes the "peace, safety [and] happiness" of the people, within the meaning of §4 is a political question for the legislature to decide, not a constitutional question for the judiciary.

Remedy by Due Course of Law

Section 14 of the Kentucky Constitution provides: "All courts shall be open, and every person for an injury done him in his lands, goods, person or reputation, shall have remedy by due course of law, and right and justice administered without sale, denial or delay."[101] Abortion advocates might argue that

---

98. KY. CONST. §4 (Michie 2002).

99. *Funk v. Fielder*, 243 S.W.2d 474, 475 (Ky. 1951).

100. *See Ward v. Harding*, 860 S.W.3d 280, 281 (Ky. 1993) ("[t]hat the Constitution may be so amended [referring to §19(2)] is an indisputable proposition") (citing §26).

101. KY. CONST. §14 (Michie 2002).

a statute prohibiting abortion interferes with a woman's control over her own body, and that such interference constitutes an "injury" to her "person," as those terms are used in § 14, for which there must be a "remedy by due course of law." That "remedy," in turn, would be invalidation of the statute. This argument assumes that § 14 confers substantive rights. The case law is clear, however, that it does not.

As is apparent from its text and structure, § 14 is concerned with *remedies* for tortiously inflicted injuries-it does not purport to establish what *constitutes* an injury to anyone's "lands, goods, person or reputation." Along with § 54 of the Kentucky Constitution, which preserves wrongful death actions,[102] § 14 "prohibit[s] the abolition or diminution of legal remedies for wrongful death, personal injuries, property damage or defamation."[103] Those remedies, however, are derived from other sources of law (the common law and, in the case of wrongful death, statutory law), not § 14. Moreover, the remedies themselves redress injuries recognized by common law or statutory law, not constitutional "injuries." Section 14, in other words, does not *create* any causes of action—it merely *preserves* pre-existing causes of action.[104]

Section 14 is concerned with the availability of private civil causes of action and reasonable access to the courts. It places no limitation on the Commonwealth's authority to define and punish crimes and has never been so interpreted.

Inviolate Rights

Section 26 of the Kentucky Constitution provides: "To guard against transgressions of the high powers which we have delegated, We Declare that everything in this Bill of Rights is excepted out of the general powers of government, and shall forever remain inviolate; and all laws contrary thereto, or contrary to this Constitution."[105] The Kentucky Supreme Court has explained that § 26 "simply provides that everything contained in the Bill of Rights is excepted out of the general powers of government and that all laws contrary to the Bill of Rights, or contrary to the Constitution, shall be

---

102. *Id.* § 54.

103. *Carney v. Moody*, 646 S.W.2d 40, 40 (Ky. 1983), *overruled on other grounds, Perkins v. Northeastern Log Homes*, 808 S.W.2d 809, 817 (Ky. 1991).

104. *Nygaard v. Goodin Bros., Inc.*, 107 S.W.3d 190, 192 (Ky. 2003) ("the legislature may not abolish or diminish the legal remedies for common-law causes of action for personal injuries or death that existed prior to the adoption of the 1891 Kentucky Constitution").

105. KY. CONST. § 26 (2002).

void."[106] "The converse is, of course, that if a legislative enactment does not violate some other section, it is not unconstitutional by reason of anything contained in this section."[107] Accordingly, it could not serve as a source of a right to abortion under the Kentucky Constitution.

Conclusion

Based on the foregoing, an argument that the Kentucky Constitution protects a right to abortion that is separate from, and independent of, the right to abortion recognized in *Roe v. Wade* would not likely succeed. That, in turn, suggests that if *Roe*, as modified by *Casey*, is ultimately overruled, the Commonwealth of Kentucky could enact and enforce a statute *prohibiting* abortion. Moreover, nothing in the Kentucky Constitution precludes Kentucky from *regulating* abortion within federal constitutional limits in the meantime.

---

106. *Nichols v. Henry*, 191 S.W.2d 930, 932 (Ky. 1946). *See also Stephenson v. Commonwealth*, 982 S.W.2d 200, 201 (Ky. 1998) ("Section 26 provides that any law, rule or action contrary to the Constitution or Bill of Rights is void"); *Fletcher v. Cooper*, 163 S.W.3d 852, 872 (Ky. 2005) (same).

107. *Nichols*, 191 S.W.2d at 932.

CHAPTER 21

LOUISIANA

Summary

The Louisiana Supreme Court has not yet decided whether the Louisiana Constitution protects a right to abortion separate from, and independent of, the right to abortion recognized under the United States Constitution.[1] A careful examination of the state constitution, in light of its history and interpretation, as well as other relevant legal sources, however, suggests that the state supreme court probably would not recognize a state constitutional right to abortion. Thus, if *Roe v. Wade*,[2] as modified by *Planned Parenthood of Southeastern Pennsylvania v. Casey*,[3] were overruled, Louisiana could enforce its "trigger" statute, which would prohibit abortion, except when the procedure was "necessary in reasonable medical judgment to prevent the death or substantial risk of death due to a physical condition, or to prevent the serious, permanent impairment of a life-sustaining organ of a pregnant woman."[4] The prohibition becomes effective upon, and to the extent permitted, by a decision of the Supreme Court overruling, "in whole or in part," *Roe v. Wade*, thereby "restoring to the state of Louisiana the authority to prohibit abortion," or upon adoption of a federal

---

1. *See Women's Health Clinic v. State*, 804 So.2d 625 (La. 2001) (holding that the constitutionality of a statute imposing tort liability upon abortion providers in favor of the mother of the unborn child for any injury caused by the abortion was not ripe for determination at a hearing on a motion for summary judgment). *See also State v. Aguillard*, 567 So.2d 674, 677 (La. Ct. App. 1990) ("while the Louisiana legislature may have the intent and desire to afford individuals due process rights from the moment of conception, such legislative intent is specifically curtailed by the basic holding[] of the United States Supreme Court in *Roe* [*v. Wade*], ... that a woman's right to obtain an abortion is constitutionally protected") (rejecting justification-of-others defense in abortion protest prosecutions).
2. 410 U.S. 113 (1973).
3. 505 U.S. 833 (1992).
4. LA. REV. STAT. ANN. §40:1299.30(F) (Supp. 2008). The prohibition itself is set forth in §40:1299.30(C). Section 40:1299.30(D) provides that any violation of §40:1299.30(C) shall be prosecuted pursuant to LA. REV. STAT. ANN. §14:87 (2004).

constitutional amendment which, "in whole or in part, restores to the state of Louisiana the authority to prohibit abortion."[5] Moreover, nothing in the state constitution, properly understood, precludes the State from enacting and enforcing reasonable measures regulating abortion within current federal constitutional limits.

Analysis

The principal pre-*Roe* abortion statute prohibited all abortions.[6] Although § 14:87 did not on its face permit any exceptions, given the requirement of a specific criminal intent,[7] an abortion performed to save the life of the pregnant woman probably would have been lawful. This construction, moreover, would have been consistent with another statute that barred disciplinary action against a physician who performed an abortion for that reason.[8] Pursuant to *Roe*, both § 14:87 and § 37:1285(6) were declared unconstitutional in a pair of three-judge federal district court decisions.[9] After several unsuccessful efforts to revive the pre-*Roe* statute or enact a new statute prohibiting abortion, Louisiana enacted the "trigger" statute described in the previous paragraph.

Based upon arguments that have been raised in other States with similar constitutional provisions, possible sources for an asserted abortion right could include provisions of the Declaration of Rights guaranteeing due process of law (art. I, §2), equal protection (§3), privacy (§5), free exercise of religion (§8) and a remedy by due process of law (§22); prohibiting the establishment of religion (§8); and recognizing retained rights (§24).[10] The analysis that follows addresses each of these provisions.

---

5. *Id.* §40:1299.30(A).

6. La. Rev. Stat. Ann. § 14:87 (1964).

7. *See State v. Sharp*, 182 So.2d 517, 518 (La. 1966).

8. La. Rev. Stat. Ann. §37:1285(6) (1964) (empowering the state board of medical examiners to revoke the license of a physician who performed an abortion "unless [the procedure was] done for the relief of a woman whose life appears in peril after due consultation with another licensed physician"). In *Rosen v. Louisiana Board of Medical Examiners*, 318 F. Supp. 1217 (E.D. La. 1970), *vacated and remanded*, 412 U.S. 902 (1973), the court construed §§14:87 and 37:1285(6) *in pari materia* and upheld their constitutionality. 318 F. Supp. at 1225.

9. *Rosen v. Louisiana Board of Medical Examiners*, 380 F. Supp. 875 (E.D. La. 1974), *summarily aff'd*, 419 U.S. 1098 (1975); *Weeks v. Connick*, Civ. Action No. 73-469 (E.D. La. 1976), *summarily aff'd sub nom. Guste v. Weeks*, 429 U.S. 1056 (1977).

10. Two other more unlikely sources of an abortion right under the Louisiana Constitution-art. I, §3 (last sentence) (prohibiting involuntary servitude) and §7 (guaranteeing freedom of speech)-are discussed generally in Chapter 3, *supra*.

Due Process of Law

Article I, §2, of the Louisiana Constitution provides: "No person shall be deprived of life, liberty, or property except by due process of law."[11] In any state constitutional challenge to Louisiana's "trigger" statute, abortion advocates are likely to rely upon art. I, §2, arguing that the statute interferes with a pregnant woman's substantive due process "liberty" interest in obtaining an abortion.[12] That argument probably would not succeed.

The Louisiana Supreme Court has held that the due process guarantee of art. I, §2, "does not vary from the Due Process Clause of the Fourteenth Amendment to the United States Constitution."[13] That equivalency of interpretation suggests that the Louisiana Supreme Court would not recognize a state due process right to abortion if the United States Supreme Court overrules *Roe*, as modified by *Casey*. And, of course, the Pelican State's abortion prohibition would not take effect unless and until that happened. Even in the absence of an overruling decision, however, it is doubtful that the state supreme court would interpret the state due process clause as securing a right to abortion. The court has stated: "In essence, the crux of due process is protection from arbitrary and unreasonable action and when the ordinance or statute does not affect fundamental rights, but rather is merely economic or social regulation, it need only have a rational relationship to a legitimate governmental interest."[14] Although in *Roe*, the Supreme Court characterized the right to abortion as "fundamental,"[15] it tacitly abandoned that characterization in *Casey*.[16] Thus, even under current federal constitutional doctrine, abortion is not a "funda-

---

11. LA. CONST. art. I, §2 (2006).

12. Article I, §2, has a substantive, as well as a procedural, component. *Bazley v. Tortorich*, 397 So.2d 475, 483 (La. 1981); *West Central Louisiana Entertainment, Inc. v. City of Leesville*, 594 So.2d 973, 975 (La. Ct. App. 1992).

13. *Progressive Security Ins. Co. v. Foster*, 711 So.2d 675, 688 (La. 1998). *See also Smith v. State*, 614 So. 778, 780 (La. Ct. App. 1993) (because state and federal due process clauses "are nearly identical in language," they are "coextensive and … provide the same due process protection"). This was also the intention of the framers. *See* VI RECORDS OF THE LOUISIANA CONSTITUTIONAL CONVENTION OF 1973 (hereinafter RECORDS) 1001 (Louisiana Constitutional Convention Records Commission 1977) (it was "unequivocally" not the intention of the drafters to "go beyond the United States Constitution due process of law clause, as interpreted by the Supreme Court of the United States") (remarks of Delegate Vick).

14. *Progressive Security Ins. Co.*, 711 So.2d at 688 (citation and internal quotation marks omitted). *See also Bazley*, 397 So.2d at 483 (same).

15. 410 U.S. at 152–53.

16. Nowhere in the Joint Opinion in *Casey* does the Court describe the right to abortion as "fundamental." 505 U.S. at 843–901. That the authors of the Joint Opinion intended

mental" right and, therefore, would not be recognized as one under state substantive due process analysis.

In determining whether an asserted liberty interest (or right) should be regarded as "fundamental," the United States Supreme Court applies a two-prong test. First, there must be a "careful description" of the asserted fundamental liberty interest.[17] Second, the interest, so described, must be firmly rooted in "the Nation's history, legal traditions, and practices."[18] Louisiana employs the same test in evaluating state substantive due process claims under art. I, §2.[19] A right to abortion cannot be regarded as "fundamental" under art. I, §2, however, because such a "right" is not firmly rooted in Louisiana's "history, legal traditions, and practices."

Louisiana enacted its first abortion statute in 1856, almost one hundred twenty years before the present state constitution was adopted in 1974. The statute prohibited an abortion at any stage of pregnancy unless the procedure was "necessary for the preservation of the mother's life," and punished the offense as a felony, "if done with intent to destroy [the] child," or as a misdemeanor, "if done with intent to procure the miscarriage of [the] woman."[20] Amended from time to time (including an amendment that raised the grade of the offense to a felony for any abortion), the statute has been amended, but not repealed.[21]

Prior to *Roe*, the Louisiana Supreme Court repeatedly rejected federal constitutional challenges to §14:87, affirming convictions for abortion.[22] In its pre-*Roe* decision rejecting a federal constitutional challenge to §§14:87 (the

---

to recharacterize the nature of the liberty interest at stake in abortion is apparent from their replacement of the "strict scrutiny" standard of review employed in *Roe* and its progeny with the more relaxed "undue burden" standard, allowing for a broader measure of abortion regulation. *Id.* at 869–79.

17. *Washington v. Glucksberg*, 521 U.S. 702, 721 (1997) (citation and internal quotation marks omitted).

18. *Id.* at 710.

19. *Johansen v. Louisiana High School Athletic Ass'n*, 916 So.2d 1081, 1088 n. 3 (La. Ct. App. 2005).

20. LA. REV. STAT. §24, at 138 (1856).

21. *Id, recodified at* LA. REV. STAT. §807 (1870), *recodified* (as amended) *at* LA. CODE CRIM. PROCEDURE & CRIM. STATUTES art. 1281 (1932), *recodified at* LA. CODE CRIM. LAW & PROCEDURE art. 740–87 (1943), *recodified at* LA. REV. STAT. ANN. §14:87 (West 1951), *carried forward as* LA. REV. STAT. ANN. §14:87 (West 1974), *as amended*, LA. REV. STAT. ANN. §14:87 (2004). *See also* nn. 4–5 and accompanying text, *supra*.

22. *State v. Campbell*, 270 So.2d 506 (La. 1972); *State v. Scott*, 255 So.2d 736 (1971); *State v. Shirley*, 237 So.2d 676 (La. 1970); *State v. Pesson*, 235 So.2d 568 (La. 1970). *See also State v. Mauvezin*, 67 So. 816 (La. 1915) (affirming conviction for abortion).

criminal statute) and 37:1285(6) (the provision of the physician disciplinary statute dealing with abortion), the three-judge federal district court found that the statutes had been enacted to protect unborn human life.[23] Subsequent to *Roe*, the Louisiana State Legislature expressed its intention "to regulate abortion to the extent permitted by the decisions of the United States Supreme Court,"[24] and enacted a comprehensive scheme of abortion regulation.[25]

Louisiana has recognized the rights of unborn children in a variety of contexts outside of abortion, including criminal law, tort law and property law. Under the criminal code, the killing of an unborn child, other than in an abortion, may be prosecuted as a homicide.[26] So, too, nonlethal injuries inflicted upon an unborn child may be prosecuted as a battery.[27] And a woman convicted of a capital offense may not be executed while she is pregnant.[28]

In tort law, a statutory cause of action for wrongful death may be brought on behalf of an unborn child without regard to the stage of pregnancy when the injuries causing death were inflicted.[29] And a common law action for (nonlethal) prenatal injuries may be brought without regard to the stage of pregnancy when the injuries were inflicted.[30]

---

23. *Rosen v. Louisiana State Board of Medical Examiners*, 318 F. Supp. at 1224–28. Based upon its reading of the applicable statutes, the court concluded: "[I]t is plain that the State has attempted to provide embryonic and fetal organisms with protection against destruction by other than natural causes in at least the second and succeeding weeks of prenatal development, without regard to whether the organism is capable of sustaining its life outside the womb." *Id.* at 1225.

24. LA. REV. STAT. ANN. §40:1299.35.0 (2001).

25. *Id.* §40:1299.35.6 (Supp. 2008) (mandating informed consent and a twenty-four waiting period); §40:1299.35.5 (2001) (requiring parental consent); §§40:1299.31, 40:1299.32 and 40:1299.33 (recognizing individual and institutional rights of conscience and prohibiting discrimination on account of opposition to abortion); §§40:1299.34.5, 40:1299.35.7 (Supp. 2008) (restricting public funding of abortion); §§14:32.10, 14:32.11, 40:1299.35.16, 40:1299.35.17 (providing criminal penalties and civil remedies for performing partial-birth abortions); §9.2800.12 (subjecting abortion providers to civil liability for any damage occasioned by an abortion).

26. *Id.* §14:32.5 *et seq.* (2007) (feticide); §14:2(A)(11) (definition of "unborn child").

27. *Id.* §§14:33 (definition of battery), 14-34 (aggravated battery), 14:34.1 (second degree battery), 14:34.7 (aggravated second degree battery), and 14:35 (simple battery), considered in conjunction with §14:2(A)(1) (definition of "another"), and §14:2(A)(7) (definition of "person").

28. *Id.* §15:567(D) (2005).

29. *Danos v. St. Pierre*, 402 So.2d 633, 637–39 (La. 1981), interpreting LA. CIV. CODE ANN. art. 2315.2 (Supp. 2008).

30. *Id.* at 638 ("[a] tortfeasor would have to pay damages if his fault causes a child to be born disabled"). *See also Wartelle v. Women's and Children's Hospital, Inc.*, 704 So.2d 778,

In property law, a posthumous child (a child conceived before but born after the death of a decedent) may inherit from a person who dies intestate (without a will).[31] The same rule applies to an afterborn child (a child conceived before the death of a parent but born after the parent executes a will) of a person who dies testate (with a will).[32] An unborn child may be the beneficiary of a trust,[33] as well as a usufruct (a right to possess or control property for a limited period of time),[34] and has standing to assert its property rights.[35] More generally, and subject to the requirement of a subsequent live birth, "[a]n unborn child shall be considered as a natural person for whatever relates to its interest from the moment of conception."[36]

In 1981, only seven years after the present Louisiana Constitution was adopted, the Louisiana State Legislature "solemnly declare[d] and f[ound] in reaffirmation of the longstanding policy of this State, that the unborn child is a human being from the time of conception and is, therefore, a legal person for purposes of the unborn child's right to life and is entitled to the right to life from conception under the laws and Constitution of this State."[37] Given the history of Louisiana's recognition of the rights of unborn children generally, and the prohibition of abortion in particular, dating back to 1856, it is implausible to conclude that the drafters and ratifiers of the 1974 state constitution intended to incorporate a right to abortion in the due process guarantee (art. I, §2) or any other provision of the Declaration of Rights.[38]

Privacy

Art. I, §5, of the Louisiana Constitution provides, in part: "Every person shall be secure in his person, property, communications, houses, papers, and

---

781 (La. 1997) (with respect to prenatal injuries that do not result in death, the unborn child "acquire[s] a cause of action in utero contemporaneous with its tortious injury").

31. LA. CIV. CODE ANN. art. 940 (2000).

32. *Id.* art. 1474. This statute applies to both *inter vivos* gifts (gifts made during a person's lifetime), and gifts *causa mortis* (gifts made at death).

33. LA. REV. STAT. ANN. §9:1801 (2005).

34. LA. CIV. CODE ANN. art. 548 (1980).

35. *Malek v. Yekani-Fard*, 422 So.2d 1151 (La. 1982).

36. LA. CIV. CODE ANN. art. 26 (1999).

37. LA. REV. STAT. ANN. §1299.35.0 (2001). This section was added by 1981 La. Acts, No. 774, §1, eff. July 23, 1981.

38. And there is no evidence that the drafters had such an intent. *See* I OFFICIAL JOURNAL OF THE PROCEEDINGS OF THE CONSTITUTIONAL CONVENTION OF THE STATE OF LOUISIANA 393, 395–99, 405–17, 420–24, 429–31, 437–61, 464–67, 470–84 (Baton Rouge, La. 1974).

effects against unreasonable searches, seizures, or invasions of privacy."[39] In any challenge to Louisiana's "trigger" statute, abortion advocates are most likely to rely upon art. I, §5, arguing that the statute constitutes an "unreasonable ... invasion[]" of a pregnant woman's "privacy." That argument probably would not succeed, however.

The Louisiana Supreme Court's principal authority interpreting the privacy language of art. I, §5 (apart from search and seizure cases) is *State v. Smith*.[40] In *Smith*, the state supreme court held that the state right of privacy does not entitle persons to engage in private, consensual oral or anal sex.[41] A court that is unwilling to recognize a privacy right of consenting adults to engage in non-commercial anal or oral sex in private is not likely to recognize a state privacy right to abortion. That is confirmed by an examination of the *Smith* opinion.

In *Smith*, the state supreme court held that "[a] constitutional right to privacy obviously cannot include the right to engage in private acts which were condemned as criminal, either by statute or case law interpretation thereof, at the very time the Louisiana Constitution was ratified."[42] Although, as a result of the Supreme Court's decision in *Roe* on January 22, 1973, Louisiana could not *enforce* its abortion prohibition at the time the present Louisiana Constitution was ratified on April 24, 1974, abortion remained an act that was "condemned as criminal" by statute (specifically, §14:87).[43]

In *Smith*, the court also determined that to recognize a state constitutional right of privacy to engage in oral or anal sex would violate the separation of powers principle.[44] "Because of the longstanding prohibition against oral and anal sex, the judicial discovery of a constitutional right to engage in oral and anal sex, not withstanding this legislative ban, would be based upon a serious misinterpretation of the Louisiana Constitution and is completely contrary to the constitutional principle of separation of powers."[45] So, too, in light of the

---

39. La. Const. art. I, §5 (2006).

40. 766 So.2d 501 (La. 2000).

41. *Id.* at 505–10. *See also Louisiana Electorate of Gays and Lesbians, Inc. v. State*, 812 So.2d 626 (La. 2002) (same). Although, in interpreting the Due Process Clause of the Fourteenth Amendment to the United States Constitution, the United States Supreme Court has held otherwise, *see Lawrence v. Texas*, 539 U.S. 558 (2003), the Louisiana Supreme Court remains the final authority in interpreting the provisions of the Declaration of Rights of the Louisiana Constitution.

42. 766 So.2d at 508.

43. Louisiana's first abortion statute, enacted in 1856, also antedated the state constitutions of 1868, 1879, 1898, 1913 and 1921.

44. 766 So.2d at 510–12.

45. *Id.* at 512. *See* La. Const. art. II, 2 (2006) (separation of powers). The Louisiana

"longstanding prohibition" of abortion, dating back to 1856, the judicial discovery of a constitutional right to obtain an abortion would also be based upon a "serious misinterpretation" of the state constitution and would be "completely contrary to the constitutional principle of separation of powers." There is no evidence that the framers or ratifiers of the Louisiana Constitution intended the right of privacy (or any other provision of the Declaration of Rights) to limit the Legislature's authority to prohibit abortion.[46]

Equal Protection

Article I, § 3, of the Louisiana Constitution provides, in part:

> No person shall be denied the equal protection of the laws. No law shall discriminate against a person because of race or religious ideas,

---

Supreme Court has recognized a fundamental state constitutional right of privacy in refusing unwanted medical treatment, *see State v. Perry*, 610 So.2d 746, 755 (La. 1992) (insane prisoner could not be compelled to take anti-psychotic drugs against his will "as a necessary and integral antecedent to his execution"); *Hondroulis v. Schumacher*, 553 So.2d 398, 415 (La. 1988) (person has a "fundamental" right "to decide whether to obtain or reject medical treatment"), but that right has a distinguished pedigree in the law. *See Cruzan v. Director, Missouri Dep't of Health*, 497 U.S. 261, 278–79 & n. 7 (1990) (recognizing right of competent patient to refuse unwanted medical treatment); *Washington v. Glucksberg*, 521 U.S. 702, 719–26 & n. 17 (1997) (same). Although *Hondroulis*, an informed consent case, referred to a right to "obtain" or "reject" medical treatment, it is clear that the right to *reject* unwanted treatment cannot be transformed by some strange legal alchemy into a right to *obtain* a particular type of treatment. *See Carniolan v. United States*, 616 F.2d 1120, 1122 (9th Cir. 1980) (constitutional rights of privacy and personal liberty did not afford plaintiff the right "to obtain laetrile [for cancer treatment] free of the lawful exercise of government police power"); *Rutherford v. United States*, 616 F.2d 455, 457 (10th Cir. 1980) (same); *Raich v. Ashcroft*, 248 F. Supp.2d 918, 928 (N.D. Cal. 2003) (same with respect to marijuana), *reversed and remanded*, 352 F.3d 1222 (9th Cir. 2003), *vacated and remanded*, 545 U.S. 1 (2005), *on remand*, 500 F.3d 850, 866 (9th Cir. 2007) ("federal law does not recognize a fundamental [constitutional] right to use medical marijuana prescribed by a licensed physician to alleviate excruciating pain and human suffering"); *United States v. Oakland Cannabis Buyers' Cooperative*, 532 U.S. 483, 489–95 (2001) (there is no "medical necessity" exception to the Controlled Substances Act's prohibitions on manufacturing and distributing marijuana).

46. *See* VI Records at 989–1067, 1072–1148, VII Records at 1149–1269 (debates on Declaration of Rights in Convention). Given the tenor of the debate on § 5, it is questionable whether § 5 has *any* application to privacy of conduct, as opposed to informational privacy or search and seizure law. *Id.* at 1072 (§ 5 is "very, very similar to the Fourth Amendment, prohibition against searches and seizures in the United States Constitution") (remarks of Delegate Vick).

beliefs, or affiliations. No law shall arbitrarily, capriciously or unreasonably discriminate against a person because of birth, age, sex, culture, physical condition or political ideas or affiliations.[47]

In any challenge to Louisiana's "trigger" statute, abortion advocates may argue that the statute discriminates against women on the basis of sex in violation of art. I, §3, because only women are capable of becoming pregnant. Such an argument would not likely prevail.

In *Sibley v. Board of Supervisors of Louisiana State University*,[48] the Louisiana Supreme Court set forth the standards applicable to equal protection challenges under the state constitution:

> Article I, Section 3 commands the courts to decline enforcement of a legislative classification of individuals in three different situations: (1) [w]hen the law classifies individuals by race or religious beliefs, it shall be repudiated completely; (2) [w]hen the statute classifies persons on the basis of birth, age, sex, culture, physical condition, or political ideas or affiliations, its enforcement shall be refused unless the state or other advocate of the classification shows that the classification has a reasonable basis; (3) [w]hen the law classifies on any other basis, it shall be rejected whenever a member of a disadvantaged class shows that it does not suitably further any appropriate state interest.[49]

Assuming that a statute prohibiting abortion may be said to "classify" persons on the basis of "sex,"[50] the State would need to show only that the "classification" has a reasonable basis. The basis for the classification is that only

---

47. LA. CONST. art. I, §3 (2006).

48. 477 So.2d 1094 (La. 1985).

49. *Id.* at 1107–08.

50. That assumption is questionable. Several state supreme courts and individual state supreme court justices have recognized that abortion regulations and restrictions on abortion funding are not "directed at women as a class" so much as "abortion as a medical treatment, which, because it involves a potential life, has no parallel as a treatment method." *Bell v. Low Income Women of Texas*, 95 S.W.3d 253, 258 (Tex. 2002) (upholding funding restrictions) (citing *Harris v. McRae*, 448 U.S. 297, 325 (1980)). *See also Fischer v. Dep't of Public Welfare*, 502 A.2d 114, 125 (Pa. 1985) ("the basis for the distinction here is not sex, but abortion") (upholding funding restrictions); *Moe v. Secretary of Administration & Finance*, 417 N.E.2d 387, 407 (Mass. 1981) (Hennessey, C.J., dissenting) (funding restrictions were "directed at abortion as a medical procedure, not women as a class); *Right to Choose v. Byrne*, 450 A.2d 925, 950 (N.J. 1982) (O'Hern, J., dissenting) ("[t]he subject of the legislation is not the person of the recipient, but the nature of the claimed medical service"). Both *Moe* and *Right to Choose* were decided on other grounds. The dissenting justices

some women and no men are capable of becoming pregnant. Criminal statutes that punish conduct that may be committed only by or against members of one sex do not deny either sex the equal protection of the laws.[51] Accordingly, a statute prohibiting abortion would not violate art. I, §3, of the Louisiana Constitution.

Free Exercise of Religion, Establishment of Religion

Article I, §8, of the Louisiana Constitution provides: "No law shall be enacted respecting an establishment of religion or prohibiting the free exercise thereof."[52] In any state constitutional challenge to Louisiana's "trigger" statute, abortion advocates may raise either or both of two arguments under art. I, §8. First, they may argue that the statute interferes with the "free exercise" of a woman's religious beliefs by forbidding her from obtaining an abortion that would be allowed by her religion. Second, they may argue in the alternative (or in addition) that the statute constitutes an "establishment of religion" because it reflects sectarian beliefs regarding when human life begins and the sinfulness of abortion. Neither argument would likely prevail.

Section 8 is a "paraphrase" of the Religion Clauses of the First Amendment to the United States Constitution and was intended to "adopt ... the ... federal standard...."[53] This intention is confirmed by the relevant case law,[54] as well as the relevant constitutional history.[55] Given the intention to "adopt" the fed-

---

were addressing alternative arguments raised by the plaintiffs, but not reached by the majority opinions.

51. *State v. Fletcher*, 341 So.2d 340, 348 (La. 1976) (upholding rape statute); *State v. Bell*, 377 So.2d 303 (La. 1979) (upholding statutory rape statute).

52. LA. CONST. art. I, §8 (2006).

53. Lee Hargrave, THE LOUISIANA STATE CONSTITUTION[:] A REFERENCE GUIDE 33 (Westport, Conn. 1991).

54. *Seeger v. Parker*, 241 So.2d 213, 216 (La. 1970) (predecessor section to art. I, §8, "embodies ... in full" the "establishment and free exercise clauses of the First Amendment"). *See also* Op. Att'y Gen., No. 75-1731, Jan. 9, 1976 (because the language of art. I, §8, is virtually identical to the parallel provision in the federal constitution, the two constitutional provisions should be interpreted in a like manner, and decisions of the United States Supreme Court construing the Religion Clauses of the First Amendment are applicable in determining the limitations §8 imposes on the state legislature).

55. *See* VI RECORDS at 1126 (what is now §8 is a "reiteration of the first two lines of the Bill of Rights of the Federal Constitution and is a streamlining of the old Louisiana Constitution") (remarks of Delegate Weiss). The framers intended that interpreting §8, the Louisiana Supreme Court would follow federal jurisprudence in interpreting the Religion Clauses of the First Amendment. *Id.* at 1126–27 (remarks of Delegate Weiss).

eral standard, it would appear that a challenge to an abortion statute that would not succeed under the Free Exercise and Establishment Clauses of the First Amendment would not succeed under art. I, §8, of the Louisiana Constitution, either. For the reasons set forth in Chapter 2, *supra*, an abortion statute could not be successfully challenged on First Amendment grounds. Accordingly, a similar challenge under art. I, §8, would not likely be successful.

Remedy by Due Process of Law

Article I, §22, of the Louisiana Constitution provides: "All courts shall be open, and every person shall have an adequate remedy by due process of law and justice, administered without denial, partiality, or unreasonable delay, for injury to him in his person, property, or other rights."[56] In any challenge to Louisiana's "trigger" statute, abortion advocates may argue that the statute interferes with a woman's control over her own body, and that such interference constitutes an "injury" to her "person ... or other rights," as those terms are used in §22, for which there must be a "remedy by due course of law." That "remedy," in turn, would be invalidation of the statute. This argument assumes that art. I, §22, confers substantive rights. The case law is clear, however, that it does not.

The Louisiana Supreme Court has held that art. I, §22, "does not warrant a remedy for every single injury; it applies only to those injuries that constitute violations of established law which the courts can properly recognize."[57] Of course, if "established law," *i.e.*, the statutes enacted by the state legislature, prohibited abortion, then the denial of an abortion would not be a cognizable "injury" for purposes of §22. Even assuming, however, that §22 mandates a "remedy by due course of law" for violation of *constitutional* rights, not just for injuries that are actionable under statutes or the common law, those rights are derived from other sources.

"Where access to the judicial process is not essential to the exercise of a fundamental right, the legislature is free to restrict access to the judicial machinery if there is a rational basis for that restriction."[58] If a fundamental right is at stake, however, "then the State must be prepared to demonstrate a compelling interest before [access to the courts] can be regulated."[59] But whether

---

56. La. Const. art. I, §22 (2006).

57. *Crier v. Whitecloud*, 496 So.2d 305, 310 (La. 1986).

58. *Safety Net for Abused Persons v. Segura*, 692 So.2d 1038, 1042 (La. 1997).

59. *State In the Interest of A.C.*, 643 So.2d 719, 728 (La. 1994) (citation and internal quotation marks omitted), *on rehearing*, 643 So.2d 743 (La. 1994). *See also League of Women Voters of New Orleans v. City of New Orleans*, 381 So.2d 441, 448 (La. 1980) (section 22

a fundamental right *is* at stake depends upon other constitutional provisions (*e.g.*, due process), not §22.[60] Because §22 is not an independent source of substantive constitutional rights, it could not serve as a source of a right to abortion under the Louisiana Constitution.

Retained Rights

Art. I, §24, of the Louisiana Constitution provides: "The enumeration in this constitution of certain rights shall not deny or disparage other rights retained by the individual citizens of the state."[61] In any challenge to Louisiana's "trigger" statute, abortion advocates may argue that the statute interferes with a "retained" right to abortion under §24. Such an argument would not likely prevail.

The Louisiana Supreme Court has never recognized an unenumerated right under art. I, §24, which has been cited in few decisions. In an early case, the state supreme court described the predecessor to §24 in the 1913 Louisiana Constitution (art. 15) as "meaningless,"[62] which hardly suggests that it could serve as the source of unenumerated constitutional rights. Almost sixty years later, the court held that art. I, §§1 and 15, of the 1921 Louisiana Constitution (now art. I, §§1 and 24, respectively[63]) "provide guiding principles upon which our legal system is founded. They do not, however, abrogate other specific provisions of our constitution."[64] In particular, neither provision abro-

---

"guarantees access to the courts but affords greater protection to fundamental interests than to those not of basic constitutional importance").

60. *In the Interest of A.C.*, 643 So.2d at 724–25 ("a parent's interest in a meaningful relationship with his or her children is manifestly a liberty interest protected by the Fourteenth Amendment's due process guarantee") (citation and internal quotation marks omitted); *Society to Oppose Pornography, Inc. v. Thevis*, 255 So.2d 876, 881 (La. Ct. App. 1971) (availability of speedy court review of statute restricting free expression was required by the free speech guarantee of the state constitution).

61. La. Const. art. I, §24 (2006).

62. *State v. McCarroll*, 70 So. 448, 448 (La. 1915) ("the people of this state retain all rights the exercise of which is not prohibited by the Constitution of the State or of the United States").

63. Art. I, §1, provides: "All government, of right, originates with the people, is founded on their will alone, and is instituted to protect the rights of the individual and for the good of the whole. Its only legitimate ends are to secure justice for all, preserve peace, protect the rights, and promote the happiness and general welfare of the people. The rights enumerated in this Article are inalienable by the state and shall be preserved inviolable by the state." La. Const. art. I, §1 (2006).

64. *Bates v. Edwards*, 294 So.2d 532, 535 (La. 1974), *appeal dismissed*, 419 U.S. 811 (1974).

gates art. III, § 1, which vests the legislative power of the State "in a Legislature, which shall consist of a Senate and a House of Representatives."[65] "The 'legislative power' referred to in this article," the supreme court explained, "empower[s] the legislature to enact any laws it sees fit, limited only by the positive provisions of the state and federal constitutions."[66] "The legislature," the court concluded, "has all the power of legislation not specifically denied it by the constitution."[67] In the absence of some other provision of the Declaration of Rights limiting the power of the Legislature to regulate or prohibit abortion, no such limitation may be found in § 24.

Entirely apart from the foregoing, an entirely plausible reading of § 24 is that the enumeration of certain rights in the state constitution should not be construed to "deny or disparage" other rights retained by the people under the common law or statutes. But even if § 24 is understood to retain unspecified *constitutional* rights (as opposed to *common law* or *statutory* rights), abortion could not plausibly be considered to be among such rights because, at the time the 1974 Louisiana Constitution was adopted, abortion was a statutory crime (although not one that could be enforced because of *Roe v. Wade*). The argument that § 24 (or its predecessor section) "retained" as an unenumerated "right" conduct that was criminal (and had been criminal since 1856) when the state constitution was adopted is, at the very least counterintuitive.

The language of § 24 appears to be "derived from the Ninth Amendment,"[68] which provides: "The enumeration in the Constitution of certain rights, shall not be construed to deny or disparage others retained by the people."[69] In light of that equivalence, § 24 should be given a parallel interpretation. That, in turn, suggests that if no right to abortion exists under the Ninth Amendment, then none would be recognized under art. I, § 24. The Supreme Court, however, has rooted the "abortion liberty" in the liberty language of the Due Process Clause of the Fourteenth Amendment, not in the unenumerated rights language of the Ninth Amendment.[70] Because abortion has not been recognized

---

65. La. Const. art. III, § 1 (2006).

66. *Bates*, 294 So.2d at 535.

67. *Id.*

68. Hargrave, The Louisiana State Constitution at 42. That is confirmed by an examination of the convention debates. *See* VII Records at 1224–25 (what is now § 24 "basically comes from the United States Constitution, Amendment No. 9") (remarks of Delegate Roy).

69. U.S. Const. amend. IX (West 2006).

70. *See Roe*, 410 U.S. at 153; *Casey*, 505 U.S. at 846. In any event, the Ninth Amendment, standing alone, is not a source of substantive rights. *Gibson v. Matthews*, 926 F.2d 532, 537 (6th Cir. 1991). Although "[s]ome unenumerated rights may be of [c]onstitutional

as a "retained right" under the Ninth Amendment, it should not be recognized as one under § 24, either.

Conclusion

Based on the foregoing analysis, an argument that the Louisiana Constitution protects a right to abortion that is separate from, and independent of, the right to abortion recognized in *Roe v. Wade* would not likely succeed. That, in turn, suggests that if *Roe*, as modified by *Casey*, is ultimately overruled, the State of Louisiana could enforce its "trigger" statute *prohibiting* abortion. Moreover, nothing in the Louisiana Constitution precludes from *regulating* abortion within federal constitutional limits in the meantime.

---

magnitude," that is only "by virtue of other amendments, such as the Fifth or Fourteenth Amendment. A person cannot claim a right that exists solely under the Ninth Amendment." *United States v. Vital Health Products, Ltd.*, 786 F. Supp. 761, 777 (E.D. Wis. 1992), *aff'd mem. op., sub nom. United States v. LeBeau*, 985 F.2d 563 (7th Cir. 1993). *See also Charles v. Brown*, 495 F. Supp. 862, 863 (N.D. Ala. 1980) (same).

CHAPTER 22

MAINE

Summary

The Maine Supreme Judicial Court has not yet decided whether the Maine Constitution protects a right to abortion separate from, and independent of, the right to abortion recognized under the United States Constitution.[1] A careful examination of the state constitution, in light of its history and interpretation, as well as other relevant legal sources, however, suggests that the state supreme judicial court probably would not recognize a state constitutional right to abortion if *Roe v. Wade*,[2] as modified by *Planned Parenthood of Southeastern Pennsylvania v. Casey*,[3] were overruled. Thus, Maine could prohibit abortion. Moreover, nothing in the state constitution, properly understood, precludes the State from enacting and enforcing reasonable measures regulating abortion within current federal constitutional limits.

Analysis

The principal pre-*Roe* abortion statute prohibited performance of an abortion unless the procedure was "necessary for the preservation of the mother's life."[4] The statute was repealed in 1979.[5]

Based upon arguments that have been raised in other States with similar constitutional provisions, possible sources for an asserted abortion right could

---

1. The Maine Supreme Court has referred to the right to abortion solely as a matter of *federal*, not *state*, constitutional law. *See Macomber v. Dillman*, 505 A.2d 810, 816 n. 3 (Me. 1986) ("[t]he choice not to procreate, as part of a person's right to privacy, is constitutionally guaranteed") (citing *Roe v. Wade*).

2. 410 U.S. 113 (1973).

3. 505 U.S. 833 (1992).

4. ME. REV. STAT. ANN. tit 17, §51 (West 1964).

5. 1979 Me. Laws 513, ch. 405, §1 (1st Sess.).

include provisions of the Declaration of Rights recognizing inherent and unalienable rights (art. I, §1) and inherent power in the people (§2); guaranteeing religious freedom (§3), due process of law and equal protection (§6-A) and a remedy by due course of law (§19); and retaining rights (§24).[6] The analysis that follows addresses each of these provisions.

Inherent and Unalienable Rights

Article I, §1, of the Maine Constitution provides: "All people are born equally free and independent, and have certain natural, inherent and unalienable rights, among which are those of enjoying and defending life and liberty, acquiring, possessing and protecting property, and pursuing and obtaining safety and happiness."[7] In any challenge to a Maine statute prohibiting (or regulating) abortion, abortion advocates would probably argue that the "liberty" interest protected by art. I, §1, includes a right to abortion. Such an argument would not likely prevail, however.

Most of the cases interpreting art. I, §1, have involved either property rights claims or equal protection claims (based upon the "equally free" language of §1). Very few cases have addressed liberty claims (other than liberty of contract) and those have usually been rejected. The Maine Supreme Judicial Court has held that there is no privacy right to engage in sodomy,[8] that art. I, §1, does not create a fundamental right to travel,[9] that there is "no inherent or constitutional right to drive a dangerous automobile on the highway,"[10] or to possess or sell intoxicating liquors.[11] Apart from equal protection claims, claims brought under art. I, §1, have been evaluated under the rational basis standard of review, *i.e.*, whether the law in question has a "reasonable connection with the welfare of the public."[12] An abortion prohibition would readily satisfy this relaxed standard of review.

---

6. Two other more unlikely sources of an abortion right under the Maine Constitution-§4 (guaranteeing freedom of speech) and §5 (prohibiting unreasonable searches and seizures)-are discussed generally in Chapter 3, *supra*.

7. Me. Const. art. I, §1 (West Supp. 2006).

8. *State v. White*, 217 A.2d 212, 214 (Me. 1966).

9. *Brown v. Dep't of Fisheries & Wildlife*, 577 A.2d 1184, 1185, n. 3 (Me. 1990).

10. *State v. Demerritt*, 103 A.2d 106, 108 (Me. 1954). *See also State v. Mayo*, 75 A. 295, 298 (Me. 1909) (same).

11. *State v. Frederickon*, 63 A. 535, 538 (Me. 1905).

12. *State v. Old Tavern Farm*, 180 A. 473, 475 (Me. 1935) (citation and internal quotation marks omitted).

More generally, the Maine Supreme Judicial Court has said that rational basis review applies to the exercise of the State's police power unless the State invades a "fundamental interest."[13] "To rise to the level of a 'fundamental interest' a right must be explicitly or implicitly guaranteed by the Constitution."[14] A right to abortion is not explicitly guaranteed by art. I, § 1. Nor is such a right implicitly guaranteed by art. I, § 1.[15]

At the time Maine became a State in 1820, abortion (after quickening) was a common law offense.[16] In 1840, only twenty years after Maine was admitted to the Union, Maine enacted its first abortion statute, which prohibited performance of an abortion upon a pregnant woman by any means at any stage of pregnancy (before or after quickening) unless the procedure was "necessary to preserve her life."[17] This statute, renumbered from time to time,[18] remained on the books until after *Roe v. Wade* was decided.[19]

In its first opinion interpreting the 1840 statute, the Maine Supreme Judicial Court stated: "It is now equally criminal to produce abortion before and after quickening. And the unsuccessful attempt to cause the destruction of an unborn child is a crime, whether the child be quick or not."[20] In a later opinion, the court explained that the statute was "intended ... to be an express and absolute prohibition" of "the destruction of unborn life for reasons, whatever they may be, other than necessity to save the mother's life...."[21] Prior to the

---

13. *National Hearing Aid Centers, Inc. v. Smith*, 376 A.2d 456, 460 & n. 2 (Me. 1977)

14. *Id.*

15. In interpreting the due process and equal protection guarantee of the Maine Constitution, art. I, § 6-A (which is discussed later in this analysis), the Maine Supreme Judicial Court has identified fundamental rights and liberties as those "which are, objectively, deeply rooted in this Nation's history and tradition." *In re Richard G.*, 770 A.2d 625, 627 (Me. 2001) (quoting *Washington v. Glucksberg*, 521 U.S. 702, 720–21 (1997)). The absence of a state "history and tradition" recognizing a right to abortion (prior to *Roe*) suggests that abortion is not a "fundamental interest" under the liberty language of art. I, § 1, either.

16. *See Smith v. State*, 33 Me. 48, 55 (1851). "Quickening" is that stage of pregnancy, usually sixteen to eighteen weeks gestation, when the woman first detects fetal movement.

17. ME. REV. STAT. ch. 160, § 13 (1840).

18. *Id.*, *recodified at* ME. REV. STAT. ch. 124, § 8 (1857), *recodified at* ME. REV. STAT. ch. 126, § 8, *recodified at* ME. REV. STAT. ch. 126, § 9 (1916), *recodified at* ME. REV. STAT. ch. 135, § 9 (1930), *recodified at* ME. REV. STAT. ch. 121, § 9 (1944), *recodified at* ME. REV. STAT. ANN. ch. 134, § 9 (1954), *recodified at* ME. REV. STAT. ANN. tit. 17, § 51 (West 1964).

19. ME. REV. STAT. ANN. tit. 17, § 51 (West 1964), *repealed by* 1979 Me. Laws 513, ch. 405, § 1 (1st Sess.).

20. *Smith*, 33 Me. at 57.

21. *State v. Rudman*, 136 A. 817, 819 (Me. 1927).

Supreme Court's decision in *Roe v. Wade*, the Maine Supreme Court affirmed convictions for abortion and attempted abortion without any hint that either the prosecutions or convictions violated the Maine Constitution.[22]

A right to abortion cannot be found in the text or structure of the Maine Constitution. There is no evidence that the framers or ratifiers of the state constitution intended to limit the Legislature's authority to prohibit abortion.[23] Such an intent would have been remarkable in light of the common law prohibition of abortion. Since the adoption of an express due process and equal protection guarantee in 1963 (art. I, §6-A), however, a challenge to an abortion statute is more likely to be brought under that provision of the Declaration of Rights, which is considered later in this analysis.

Inherent Power

Article I, §2, of the Maine Constitution provides: "All power is inherent in the people; all free governments are founded in their authority and instituted for their benefit; they have therefore an unalienable and indefeasible right to institute government, and to alter, reform, or totally change the same, when their safety and happiness require it."[24] In a challenge to a statute prohibiting abortion, abortion advocates might argue that the statute interferes with the "power" of the people because it does not promote their "benefit." This argument would not likely succeed.

There is very little case law interpreting art. I, §2. Apart from reserving to the people the right "to alter, reform, or totally change" the organic instrument of government, §2 "reflects the contract theory of government," "under which consent is the only legitimate basis for the exercise of the government's coercive power."[25] "According to that theory, discretionary power is, in effect, political power which must be limited to the politically responsible organs of government."[26] The "delegation doctrine," which derives from the contract theory of government, "has been developed largely in relation to state and federal exercises of the police power to regulate private personal and property rights."[27]

---

22. *Rudman*; *State v. Alquist*, 34 A.2d 21 (Me. 1943).

23. *See* Debates & Proceedings of the Constitutional Convention of 1819, 69–93, 246 (Portland, Maine 1820).

24. Me. Const. art. I, §2 (West Supp. 2006).

25. *Cape Elizabeth School Board v. Cape Elizabeth Teachers Ass'n*, 459 A.2d 166, 171–72 & n. 12 (Me. 1983).

26. *Id.* at 172 (citations omitted).

27. *Id.* at 171–72.

The delegation doctrine places limits on what discretionary authority the State (or its political subdivisions) may repose in agencies and boards that are not directly responsible to the electorate.[28] As such, it would have no bearing on the authority of the State to criminalize certain conduct.

Apart from the foregoing, whether a given law promotes the "benefit" of the people, within the meaning of art. I, §2, presents a political question for the legislature to decide, not a constitutional question for the judiciary.

Religious Freedom

Article I, §3, of the Maine Constitution provides:

> All individuals have a natural and unalienable right to worship Almighty God according to the dictates of their own consciences, and no person shall be hurt, molested or restrained in that person's liberty or estate for worshiping God in the manner and season most agreeable to the dictates of that person's own conscience, nor for that person's religious professions or sentiments, provided that that person does not disturb the public peace, nor obstruct others in their religious worship; — and all persons demeaning themselves peaceably, as good members of the State, shall be equally under the protection of the laws, and no subordination nor preference of any one sect or denomination to another shall ever be established by law, nor shall any religious test be required as a qualification for any office or trust, under this State; and all religious societies in this State, whether incorporate or unincorporate, shall at all times have the exclusive right of electing their public teachers, and contracting with them for their support and maintenance.[29]

In any challenge to a statute prohibiting abortion, abortion advocates may raise either or both of two argument under art. 1, §3. First, they may argue that an abortion prohibition interferes with the rights of conscience secured by §3 by forbidding a woman from obtaining an abortion that would be allowed by her religion. Second, they may argue in the alternative (or in addition) that an abortion prohibition gives a "preference" to "one sect or denomination" because it reflects sectarian beliefs regarding when human life begins and the sinfulness of abortion. Neither argument would likely succeed.

---

28. *See generally Opinion of the Justices*, 261 A.2d 58, 76 (Me. 1970) (discussing Legislature's power to delegate decision making authority to administrative agencies).

29. ME. CONST. art. I, §3 (West Supp. 2006).

With respect to the latter argument, the Maine Supreme Judicial Court has held that analysis under the Establishment Clause and under art. I, §3, of the Maine Constitution are the same.[30] Accordingly, for the reasons set forth in Chapter 2, *supra*, an abortion prohibition would not violate art. I, §3.

With respect to the former argument, the Maine Supreme Judicial Court has developed its own test for evaluating "free exercise" claims. Under that test, "a person challenging a government regulation as a violation of the Free Exercise Clause of the Maine Constitution has the burden of showing ... that the activity burdened by the regulation is motivated by a sincerely held religious belief; and that the challenged regulation restricts the free exercise of that belief."[31] "If the challenger makes those showings, the burden shifts and the State can prevail only by proving both ... that the challenged regulation is motivated by a compelling public interest, and that no less restrictive means can adequately achieve that compelling interest."[32]

It is doubtful that a successful challenge to an abortion prohibition could be mounted under this four-part test. As an initial matter, it is not at all apparent that a statute prohibiting abortion "restricts the free exercise" of activity (abortion) that is "motivated by a sincerely held religious belief." Although a particular religious doctrine may *permit* abortion under certain circumstances, no doctrine in any religion *requires* a woman to undergo an abortion, at least when her life is not in danger (an exception that would be included in any abortion statute the Legislature might enact). If a religious doctrine does not compel certain conduct, a prohibition of that conduct (in a law that does not single out religious practice for regulation) cannot be said to "restrict" free exercise.[33]

Even assuming that the first two parts of the *Rupert* standard were satisfied, a challenge to an abortion prohibition would fail the last two parts. The State has a compelling interest in protecting and preserving the life of the unborn child and there is "no less restrictive means" available to the State, short of outright prohibition, that would "adequately achieve that ... interest." An example, not involving abortion, that illustrates this principle is the line of cases

---

30. *Bagley v. Raymond School Dep't*, 728 A.2d 127, 132 (Me. 1999). *See also Squires v. Inhabitants of City of Augusta*, 153 A.2d 80, 87–88 (Me. 1959) (state and federal separation of church and state principles are the same).

31. *Rupert v. City of Portland*, 605 A.2d 63, 65–66 (Me. 1992) (citation and internal quotation marks omitted).

32. *Id.* at 66 (citation and internal quotation marks omitted). In *Rupert*, the court held that there is no state free exercise right to smoke marijuana.

33. To have standing to raise a free exercise claim against a law prohibiting or regulating abortion, one must allege that one seeks an abortion "under compulsion of religious belief." *Harris v. McRae*, 448 U.S. at 320.

authorizing compulsory blood transfusions on pregnant women (typically, Jehovah's Witnesses) to save the lives of their unborn children,[34] a line of cases, it must be noted, that the Maine Supreme Judicial Court has expressly endorsed.[35]

The prohibition of abortion, for the same end, stands on even firmer ground because it does not implicate the state and federal constitutional right to refuse unwanted medical treatment.[36] Moreover, unlike an order authorizing a blood transfusion of a pregnant woman, which is intended to *save* the life of the unborn child (and very possibly the mother's life as well), the intent in an abortion is to *destroy* the unborn child's life. A statute prohibiting abortion would not violate art. I, § 3.

Due Process of Law, Equal Protection

Article I, § 6-A of the Maine Constitution provides: "No person shall be deprived of life, liberty or property, without due process of law, nor be denied the equal protection of the laws, nor be denied the enjoyment of that person's civil rights or be discriminated against in the exercise thereof."[37] The Maine Supreme Judicial Court has repeatedly held that the due process and equal protection guarantees of the state constitution are no broader in scope than the Due Process and Equal Protection Clauses of the Fourteenth Amendment.[38]

---

34. *See Fosmire v. Nicoleau*, 536 N.Y.S.2d 492, 496 (App. Div. 1989) (dictum) (when "a pregnant adult woman refuses medical treatment and, as a result of that refusal, places the life of her unborn baby in jeopardy," "the State's interest, as *parens patriae*, in protecting the health and welfare of the child is determined to be paramount") (citing *In the Matter of Application of Jamaica Hospital*, 491 N.Y.S.2d 898 (Sup. Ct. 1985) (blood transfusion) (18 weeks gestation); and *Crouse Irving Memorial Hospital, Inc. v. Paddock*, 485 N.Y.S.2d 443 (Sup. Ct. 1985) (blood transfusion) (premature delivery)). *See also Raleigh Fitkin-Paul Morgan Memorial Hospital v. Anderson*, 201 A.2d 537 (N.J. 1964) (same with respect to blood transfusion at 32 weeks gestation); *but see In re Brown*, 689 N.E.2d 397 (Ill. App. Ct. 1997) (*contra*) (blood transfusion).

35. *Osier v. Osier*, 410 A.2d 1027, 1030 n. 4 (Me. 1980) (citing, among other cases, *Raleigh Fitkin-Paul Morgan Memorial Hospital v. Anderson*).

36. *See, e.g., Cruzan v. Director, Missouri Dep't of Health*, 497 U.S. 261, 278–79 & n. 7 (1990); *Washington v. Glucksberg*, 521 U.S. 702, 719–26 & n. 17 (1997); *In re Guardianship of K-M*, 866 A.2d 106, 113 (Me. 2005); *Green v. Comm'r of the Dep't of Mental Health, Mental Retardation & Substance Abuse Services*, 776 A.2d 612, 616 (Me. 2001) ("there is a liberty interest in refusing treatment") (dictum).

37. ME. CONST. art. I, § 6-A (West Supp. 2006).

38. *Carroll F. Look Construction Co., Inc. v. Town of Beals*, 802 A.2d 994, 999 (Me. 2002) (state and federal due process rights are coextensive); *State v. Cote*, 737 A.2d 262, 265 n. 6

For example, consistent with Supreme Court precedent recognizing a liberty interest in refusing unwanted medical treatment,[39] the Maine Supreme Judicial Court has held that a respondent in a guardianship proceeding alleging incapacitation has a liberty interest in refusing to undergo a psychological examination.[40] And the state supreme court has stated that the state and federal constitutions protect "a fundamental and important right to raise one's children."[41] This equivalence of interpretation suggests that the state supreme court probably would *not* recognize a right to abortion under the liberty language of art. I, §6-A, if *Roe*, as modified by *Casey*, were overruled.[42]

In a similar manner, the Maine Supreme Court closely hews to Supreme Court equal protection precedent in deciding equal protection claims under art. I, §6-A. Thus, sex-based classifications are subject to an intermediate standard of review ("heightened scrutiny") under which the classifications must be " 'substantially related' " to the achievement of " 'important governmental objectives.' "[43] An abortion prohibition would appear to satisfy this level of

---

(Me. 1999) ("[d]ue process concepts embodied in the Maine Constitution provide no greater protection to individuals than do those concepts contained within the United States Constitution"); *Botting v. Dep't of Behavioral & Developmental Services*, 838 A.2d 1168, 1176 (Me. 2003) (state and federal equal protection rights are coextensive) (citing *Central Maine Power Co. v. Public Utilities Comm'n*, 734 A.2d 1120, 1130 n. 12 (Me. 1999)).

39. *Cruzan*, 497 U.S. at 278–79 & n. 7.

40. *In re Guardianship of K-M*, 866 A.2d at 113.

41. *In re Heather C.*, 751 A.2d 448, 454 (Me. 2000) (citations omitted). *See also Danforth v. State Dep't of Health & Welfare*, 303 A.2d 794, 800 (Me. 1973) ("[the] Constitution of Maine recognizes [the] right of the parent to custody of his child"). To the extent that the Maine Supreme Court considers federal precedent in determining whether an asserted liberty interest (or right) is "fundamental" under the state due process guarantee, abortion would not qualify as a "fundamental" right. Although the Supreme Court characterized the right to choose abortion as "fundamental" in *Roe*, 410 U.S. at 152–53, it tacitly abandoned that characterization in *Casey*, 505 U.S. at 869–79 (Joint Op. of O'Connor, Kennedy and Souter, JJ., replacing *Roe's* "strict scrutiny" standard of review with the more relaxed "undue burden" standard, allowing for a broader measure of abortion regulation).

42. Whether the court would recognize a state liberty interest in abortion under art. I, §6-A while *Roe* (as modified) remains the law of the land is uncertain. The Maine Legislature has enacted very little legislation purporting to regulate abortion, and such legislation as it has enacted is unlikely to be challenged. *See, e.g.*, MaineCare Benefits Manual, ch. II, §90.05-2(A) (limiting public funding of abortion for indigent women to those circumstances for which federal reimbursement is available, currently life-of-the mother, rape and incest).

43. *State v. Rundlett*, 391 A.2d 815, 818 (Me. 1978) (quoting *Craig v. Boren*, 429 U.S. 190, 197 (1976)). In *Rundlett*, the court upheld the constitutionality of the former statutory rape statute under which only males could be convicted as principals. The classification was jus-

scrutiny because the prohibition would be "substantially related" to the "important governmental objective[]" in protecting unborn children. Nevertheless, the standard applicable to sex-based discrimination would not apply to an abortion prohibition. Abortion laws do not discriminate on the basis of sex.

First, the United States Supreme Court has reviewed restrictions on abortion funding under a rational basis standard of review, *not* under the intermediate (heightened) scrutiny required of gender-based classifications.[44] Indeed, the Court has held that "the disfavoring of abortion ... is not *ipso facto* sex discrimination," and, citing its decisions in *Harris* and other cases addressing abortion funding, stated that "the constitutional test applicable to government abortion-funding restrictions is not the heightened-scrutiny standard that our cases demand for sex discrimination, ... but the ordinary rationality standard."[45]

Second, even assuming that an abortion prohibition differentiates between men and women on the basis of sex, and would otherwise be subject to a higher standard of review, the United States Supreme Court has held that biological differences between men and women may justify different treatment based on those differences. In upholding a statutory rape statute that applied only to males, the Supreme Court noted, "this Court has consistently upheld statutes where the gender classification is not invidious, but rather realistically reflects

---

tified, in the court's view, by the risk of physical injury to young female victims and the threat of pregnancy. *Id.* at 818–22. *See also Beal v. Beal*, 388 A.2d 72 (Me. 1978) (former alimony statute that allowed alimony to be awarded only to women and not to men impermissibly discriminated on the basis of sex). Under current Supreme Court doctrine, the heightened scrutiny applicable to sex-based classifications does *not* apply to the regulation of abortion. *See Bray v. Alexandria Women's Health Clinic*, 505 U.S. 263, 273 (1993).

44. *Harris v. McRae*, 448 U.S. 297, 321–26 (1980).

45. *Bray v. Alexandria Women's Health Clinic*, 506 U.S. 263, 273 (1993). Several state supreme courts and individual state supreme court justices have recognized that abortion regulations and restrictions on abortion funding are not "directed at women as a class" so much as "abortion as a medical treatment, which, because it involves a potential life, has no parallel as a treatment method." *Bell v. Low Income Women of Texas*, 95 S.W.3d 253, 258 (Tex. 2002) (upholding funding restrictions) (citing *Harris*, 448 U.S. at 325). *See also Fischer v. Dep't of Public Welfare*, 502 A.2d 114, 125 (Pa. 1985) ("the basis for the distinction here is not sex, but abortion") (upholding funding restrictions); *Moe v. Secretary of Administration & Finance*, 417 N.E.2d 387, 407 (Mass. 1981) (Hennessey, C.J., dissenting) (funding restrictions were "directed at abortion as a medical procedure, not women as a class"); *Right to Choose v. Byrne*, 450 A.2d 925, 950 (N.J. 1982) (O'Hern, J., dissenting) ("[t]he subject of the legislation is not the person of the recipient, but the nature of the claimed medical service"). Both *Moe* and *Right to Choose* were decided on other grounds. The dissenting justices were addressing alternative arguments raised by the plaintiffs, but not reached by the majority opinions.

the fact that the sexes are not similarly situated in certain circumstances."[46] "Abortion statutes are examples of cases in which the sexes are not biologically similarly situated" because only women are capable of becoming pregnant and having abortions.[47]

A statute prohibiting abortion quite obviously can affect only women because only women are capable of becoming pregnant.[48] Unlike laws that use women's ability to become pregnant (or pregnancy itself) to discriminate against them in *other* areas (*e.g.*, employment opportunities), abortion prohibitions cannot fairly be said to involve a distinction between men and women that is a "mere pretext[] designed to erect an invidious discrimination against [women]."[49]

A prohibition of abortion would not interfere with the exercise of a fundamental state constitutional right, nor would it classify upon the basis of a suspect or quasi-suspect personal characteristic. Accordingly, it would be subject to rational basis review. Under that standard of review, the statute need only be "rationally related to a legitimate state interest."[50] A law prohibiting abortion would be "rationally related" to the "legitimate state interest" in protecting the lives of unborn children.

Remedy by Due Course of Law

Article I, § 19, of the Maine Constitution provides: "Every person, for an injury inflicted on the person or the person's reputation, property or immunities, shall have remedy by due course of law; and right and justice shall be administered freely and without sale, completely and without denial, promptly and without delay."[51] Abortion advocates might argue that a statute prohibiting abortion interferes with a woman's control over her own body, and that such interference constitutes an "injury" to her "person," as those terms are used in § 19, for which there must be a "remedy by due course of law." That "remedy," in turn, would be invalidation of the statute. This argument proceeds on the assumption that art. I, § 19, confers substantive rights. The case law is clear, however, that it does not.

---

46. *Michael M. v. Superior Court*, 450 U.S. 464, 469 (1981).

47. *Jane L. v. Bangerter*, 794 F. Supp. 1537, 1549 (D. Utah 1992).

48. *Geduldig v. Aiello*, 417 U.S. 484, 496 n. 20 (1974) ("[n]ormal pregnancy is an objectively, identifiable physical condition with unique characteristics").

49. *Id.*

50. *City of Cleburne, Texas v. Cleburne Living Center*, 473 U.S. 432, 440 (1985).

51. ME. CONST. art. I, § 19 (West Supp. 2006).

As is apparent from its text and structure, § 19 is concerned with *remedies* for tortiously inflicted injuries—it does not establish what *constitutes* an injury to anyone's "person[,] reputation, property or immunities." Those remedies, however, are derived from the common law and, in certain instances, statutes enacted by the Legislature, not § 19. Moreover, the remedies themselves redress injuries recognized by the common law and statutory law, not constitutional "injuries." Section 19, in other words, does not *create* any new causes of action, but merely *preserves* existing causes of action. Maine case law confirms this understanding.

"The open courts provision," the Maine Supreme Judicial Court has explained, "means [that] the courts must be accessible to all persons alike without discrimination, at times and places designated for their sitting, and afford a speedy remedy for every wrong *recognized by law* as remediable in a court."[52] Section 19 "has never been held to create ... a fundamental right" of plaintiffs "to litigate their claims."[53] Rather, it stands for the more modest proposition "that there should be no wrong without a remedy."[54] Moreover, the "wrong" must be one that is recognized by statute or the common law. If there is no "wrong recognized by law as remediable in a court," then § 19 has no application. "We have never viewed this constitutional provision as granting an action where one did not otherwise exist either under existing statutory or cognizable common law."[55]

Taken as a whole, § 19 is concerned with the availability of private civil causes of action and reasonable access to the courts. It places no limitation on the State's authority to define and punish crimes and has never been so interpreted. Section 19 could not serve as a source of a state constitutional right to abortion.

---

52. *Maine Medical Center v. Cote*, 577 A.2d 1173, 1176 (Me. 1990) (emphasis added). *See also Geary v. Dep't of Behavioral & Developmental Services*, 838 A.2d 1162, 1167 (Me. 2003) (art. I, § 19, provides "a right to a due process or judicial remedy for any *actionable* wrong") (emphasis added); *Gibson v. Nat'l Ben Franklin Ins. Co.*, 387 A.2d 220, 223 (Me. 1978) ("legislation should not be deemed to preclude an injured person from having a remedy of his own for a *recognized* wrong in the absence of a clear manifestation of intent to that effect") (emphasis added).

53. *Langevin v. City of Biddeford*, 481 A.2d 495, 497 n. 2 (Me. 1984).

54. *Black v. Solmitz*, 409 A.2d 634, 635 (Me. 1979).

55. *Nadeau v. State*, 395 A.2d 107, 117 n. 6 (Me. 1978). Even where a statutory or common law right exists, a plaintiff does not have "a right to an unlimited remedy under ... § 19." *Peters v. Saft*, 597 A.2d 50, 54 (Me. 1991) (upholding cap on damages for drams shop actions). *See also Choroszy v. Tso*, 647 A.2d 803, 806–07 Me. 1994) (upholding constitutionality of three-year statute of repose for medical malpractice claims even though statute might cut off a cause of action before it could be discovered).

Retained Rights

Article I, § 24, of the Maine Constitution provides: "The enumeration of certain rights shall not impair nor deny others retained by the people."[56] Abortion advocates may be expected to cite § 24 in support of an asserted right to abortion under the state constitution. A proper interpretation of § 24, however, would not support a right to abortion as a "retained right."

Article I, § 24 has been cited in only one case,[57] and has never been interpreted by the Maine Supreme Judicial Court. That § 24 has been cited only once and has never been interpreted suggests that it would be an unlikely source of a right to abortion (or any other substantive right). An entirely plausible reading of § 24 is that the enumeration of certain rights in the state constitution should not be construed to "impair or deny" other rights retained by the people under the common law or statutes. But even if § 24 is understood to retain unspecified *constitutional* rights (as opposed to *common law* or *statutory* rights), abortion could not plausibly be considered to be among such rights because, at the time the Maine Constitution was adopted in 1819, abortion was a common law crime. The argument that § 24 "retained" as an "unenumerated right" conduct that was criminal when the state constitution was adopted is counterintuitive and contrary to the intent of the framers.[58]

The language of § 24 appears to be based on the Ninth Amendment, which provides: "The enumeration in the Constitution of certain rights, shall not be construed to deny or disparage others retained by the people."[59] In light of that equivalence, § 24 should be given a parallel interpretation. That, in turn, suggests that if no right to abortion exists under the Ninth Amendment, then none would be recognized under art. 1, § 24. The Supreme Court, however, has rooted the "abortion liberty" in the liberty language of the Due Process Clause of the Fourteenth Amendment, not in the unenumerated rights language of the Ninth Amendment.[60] Because abortion has not been recognized as a "retained

---

56. ME. CONST. art. I, § 24 (West Supp. 2006).

57. *State v. McDonough*, 468 A.2d 977, 979 (Me. 1983).

58. Marshall J. Tinkle, THE MAINE CONSTITUTION[:] A REFERENCE GUIDE 54 (Westport, Conn. 1992) (§ 23 "makes clear that the declaration [of rights] does not limit otherwise *existing* rights") (emphasis added).

59. U.S. CONST. AMEND. IX (West 2006). "In all likelihood, the framers based it on the Ninth Amendment to the U.S. Constitution." Tinkle, THE MAINE CONSTITUTION at 54.

60. *See Roe*, 410 U.S. at 153; *Casey*, 505 U.S. at 846. In any event, the Ninth Amendment, standing alone, is not a source of substantive rights. *Gibson v. Matthews*, 926 F.2d 532, 537 (6th Cir. 1991). Although "[s]ome unenumerated rights may be of [c]onstitutional magnitude," that is only "by virtue of other amendments, such as the Fifth or Fourteenth

right" under the Ninth Amendment, it should not be recognized as one under § 24, either.

Conclusion

Based on the foregoing analysis, an argument that the Maine Constitution protects a right to abortion that is separate from, and independent of, the right to abortion recognized in *Roe v. Wade* would not likely succeed. That, in turn, suggests that if *Roe*, as modified by *Casey*, is ultimately overruled, the State of Maine could enact and enforce a statute *prohibiting* abortion. Moreover, nothing in the Maine Constitution precludes Maine from *regulating* abortion within federal constitutional limits in the meantime.

Amendment. A person cannot claim a right that exists solely under the Ninth Amendment." *United States v. Vital Health Products, Ltd.*, 786 F. Supp. 761, 777 (E.D. Wis. 1992), *aff'd mem. op., sub nom. United States v. LeBeau*, 985 F.2d 563 (7th Cir. 1993). *See also Charles v. Brown*, 495 F. Supp. 862, 863 (N.D. Ala. 1980) (same).

CHAPTER 23

MARYLAND

Summary

The Maryland Court of Appeals (Maryland's highest state court) has not yet decided whether the Maryland Constitution protects a right to abortion separate from, and independent of, the right to abortion recognized under the United States Constitution.[1] A careful examination of the state constitution, in light of its history and interpretation, as well as other relevant legal sources, however, suggests that the state court of appeals probably would not recognize a state constitutional right to abortion. Thus, if *Roe v. Wade*,[2] as modified by *Planned Parenthood of Southeastern Pennsylvania v. Casey*,[3] were overruled, Maryland could prohibit abortion. Moreover, nothing in the state constitution, properly understood, precludes the State from enacting and enforcing reasonable measures regulating abortion within current federal constitutional limits.

---

1. In 1989, the Maryland Attorney General observed that "the Court of Appeals has not yet identified any right of privacy protected by the Maryland Constitution." 74 Op. Att'y Gen. 19, 30 (1989). That observation remains true today. *See Doe v. Maryland Board of Social Workers*, 862 A.2d 996, 1008 (Md. 2004) (citing *Montgomery County v. Walsh*, 336 A.2d 97, 104 (Md. 1975) ("the right of privacy is protected by the federal constitution"), *appeal dismissed*, 424 U.S. 901 (1976)). Nor has the court of appeals recognized a subsidiary right to abortion. "No reported decision has concluded that the Maryland Constitution itself grants a right of abortion in addition to that granted by the federal Constitution. To the contrary, every reported Maryland case that has considered the constitutional right has addressed it solely as a matter of federal constitutional law." 74 Op. Att'y Gen. at 29 (citing *Bayne v. Secretary of State*, 392 A.2d 67, 75 n. 7 (Md. 1978); *Coleman v. Coleman*, 471 A.2d 1115 (Md. Ct. Spec. App. 1984); and *State v. Ingel*, 308 A.2d 223 (Md. Ct. Spec. App. 1973)).

2. 410 U.S. 113 (1973).

3. 505 U.S. 833 (1992).

Analysis

The principal pre-*Roe* Maryland abortion statute was based on § 230.3 of the Model Penal Code.[4] An abortion could be performed at any stage of pregnancy when "[c]ontinuation of the pregnancy [was] likely to result in the death of the mother."[5] The statute allowed an abortion to be performed within the first twenty-six weeks of gestation when (1) there was "substantial risk that continuation of the pregnancy would gravely impair the physical or mental health of the mother," (2) there was "substantial risk of the birth of [a] child with grave and permanent physical deformity or mental retardation," or (3) the pregnancy resulted from forcible rape.[6] Pursuant to *Roe*, the limitations on the circumstances under which abortions may be performed and the requirement that all abortions be performed in hospitals were declared unconstitutional (on federal, not state, grounds) by the Maryland Court of Special Appeals (an intermediate state reviewing court) in *State v. Engel*,[7] and *Coleman v. Coleman*,[8] and by the United States Court of Appeals for the Fourth Circuit in *Vuitch v. Hardy*.[9] With the exception of the conscience provisions, all of the provisions of the pre-*Roe* statute, recodified in 1987,[10] were repealed in 1991.[11]

---

4. *See* MD. CODE ANN. art. 43, § 137 (1971). The complete text of § 230.3 of the Model Penal Code is set out in Appendix B to the Supreme Court's decision in *Doe v. Bolton*, 410 U.S. 179, 205–07 (1973).

5. *Id.* § 137(a)(1).

6. *Id.* §§ 137(a)(2)-(4), -(b)(1). In the case of forcible rape, the State's Attorney had to confirm that there was probable cause to believe that the rape had in fact occurred. *Id.* § 137(a)(4). The law imposed other conditions. Abortions could be performed only by licensed physicians in licensed hospitals accredited by the Joint Committee on Accreditation of Hospitals. *Id.* § 137(a). The procedure had to be approved by a hospital review authority, which was required to keep detailed written records of all requests for authorization and its action thereon. *Id.* §§ 137(b)(2), -(c).

7. 308 A.2d 223 (Md. Ct. Sp. App. 1973).

8. 471 A.2d 1115 (Md. Ct. Sp. App. 1984).

9. 473 F.2d 1370 (4th Cir. 1973).

10. MD. CODE ANN., HEALTH-GEN. §§ 20-103, 20-207, 20-208, 20-210, 20-214 (1990).

11. 1991 Md. Laws 1, ch. 1, § 1. In repealing its pre-*Roe* statute, Maryland enacted a new statute providing, among other things, that "the State may not interfere with the decision of a woman to terminate a pregnancy: (1) before the fetus is viable; or (2) at any time during the woman's pregnancy, if (I) the termination procedure is necessary to protect the life or health of the woman; or (ii) the fetus is affected by genetic defect or serious deformity or abnormality." *Id.*, now codified as MD. CODE ANN., HEALTH-GEN. II, § 20-209(b) (2000). Maryland, however, has not restricted post-viability abortions.

Based upon arguments that have been raised in other States with similar constitutional provisions, possible sources for an asserted abortion right could include provisions of the Maryland Declaration of Rights guaranteeing religious freedom (art. 36), a remedy by course of the law of the land (§ 19), due process and equal protection (§ 24) and equality of rights (§ 46); recognizing the right of the people to alter, reform or abolish the form of government (arts. 1, 6); and retaining rights (§ 45).[12] The analysis that follows addresses each of these provisions.

Religious Freedom

Article 36 of the Maryland Declaration of Rights provides, in part:

> That as it is the duty of every man to worship God in such manner as he thinks most acceptable to Him, all persons are equally entitled to protection in their religious liberty; wherefore, no person ought by any law to be molested in his person or estate, on account of his religious persuasion, or profession, or for his religious practice, unless, under the color of religion, he shall disturb the good order, peace or safety of the State, or shall infringe the laws of morality, or injure others in their natural, civil or religious rights; nor ought any person to be compelled to frequent, or maintain, or contribute, unless on contract, to maintain, any place of worship, or any ministry.... [13]

In any challenge to a statute prohibiting abortion, abortion advocates may raise either or both of two arguments under art. 36. First, they may argue that an abortion prohibition interferes with a woman's "religious liberty," guaranteed by the first clause of the article, by forbidding her from obtaining an abortion that would be allowed by her religion. Second, they may argue in the alternative (or in addition) that an abortion prohibition violates the third clause of the article, prohibiting compelled support of religious institutions, because it reflects sectarian beliefs regarding when human life begins and the sinfulness of abortion. Neither argument would likely prevail.

The Maryland Court of Appeals has generally interpreted art. 36 consistently with Supreme Court precedent interpreting the Free Exercise and Es-

---

12. Two other more unlikely sources of an abortion right under the Maryland Declaration of Rights-art. 26 (prohibiting unreasonable searches and seizures) and § 40 (guaranteeing freedom of speech)-are discussed generally in Chapter 3, *supra*.

13. MD. DECL. OF RIGHTS art. 36 (2003).

tablishment Clauses of the First Amendment.[14] In light of the foregoing, it would appear that a challenge to an abortion statute that would not succeed under the Religion Clauses of the First Amendment would not succeed under art. 36, either. For the reasons set forth in Chapter 2, *supra*, an abortion statute could not be successfully challenged on First Amendment grounds. Accordingly, a similar challenge under art. 36 would not likely be successful

Remedy by the Course of the Law of the Land

Article 19 of the Maryland Declaration of Rights provides:

> That every man, for any injury done to him in his person or property, ought to have remedy by the course of the Law of the land, and ought to have justice and right, freely without sale, fully and without any denial, and speedily without delay, according to the Law of the land.[15]

Abortion advocates might argue that any statute prohibiting abortion interferes with a woman's control over her own body, and that such interference causes an "injury" to her "person," as those terms are used in art. 19, for which there must be a "remedy by the course of the Law of the land." That "remedy," in turn, would be invalidation of the statute. This argument assumes that art. 19 confers substantive rights. The case law is clear, however, that it does not.[16]

As is apparent from its text and structure, art. 19 is concerned with *remedies* for tortiously inflicted injuries-it does not establish what *constitutes* an injury to anyone's "person or property." Those remedies, however, are derived from the common law and statues enacted by the Legislature, not art. 19.

---

14. *See Archdiocese of Washington v. Moersen*, 925 A.2d 659, 660–61 (Md. 2007) (free exercise); *Montrose Christian School Corp. v. Walsh*, 770 A.2d 111, 123 (Md. 2001) (same); *Supermarkets General Corp. v. State*, 409 A.2d 250, 257–58 (Md. 1979) (establishment), *appeal dismissed*, 449 U.S. 801 (1980). To the extent that there is any difference, the anti-compulsion language of art. 36 may be *less* rigorous than the Establishment Clause. *See Horace Mann League of the United States of America v. Board of Public Works*, 220 A.3d 51 (Md. 1966) (holding that statutes providing outright matching grants for the construction of buildings at two sectarian colleges violated the Establishment Clause of the First Amendment, but not art. 36).

15. MD. DECL. OF RIGHTS art. 19 (2003).

16. To the extent that art. 19 has been construed as a due process guarantee, *see Attorney General v. Johnson*, 383 A.2d 57, 71 (Md. 1978), *appeal dismissed*, 439 U.S. 805 (1978), *overruled on other grounds*, *Newell v. Richards*, 594 A.2d 1152, 1161 (Md. 1991), it is considered in the next section of this analysis, *infra*.

Moreover, the remedies themselves redress injuries recognized by the common law and statutory law, not constitutional "injuries." Article 19, in other words, does not *create* any new causes of actions, but merely *preserves* existing causes of action.

"Article 19 provides no additional substantive rights but guarantees the availability of other preexisting rights by access to the courts that enforce them."[17] Because art. 19 is not a source of substantive rights, it could not provide a basis for invalidating an otherwise constitutional statute of the State.[18]

Due Process of Law

Article 24 of the Maryland Declaration of Rights provides: "That no man ought to be taken or imprisoned or disseized of his freehold, liberties or privileges, or outlawed, or exiled, or, in any manner, destroyed, or deprived of his life, liberty or property, but by the judgment of his peers, or by the Law of the land."[19] The Maryland Court of Appeals has interpreted art. 24 as a guarantee of due process.[20]

In any challenge to an abortion prohibition, abortion advocates are most likely to rely upon art. 24, arguing that a pregnant woman has a substantive due process liberty interest in obtaining an abortion. That argument, however, probably would not succeed.

The Maryland Court of Appeals has recognized that art. 24 has a substantive, as well as a procedural, component.[21] In interpreting art. 24, the Maryland reviewing courts have applied the Supreme Court's substantive due process analysis.[22] In determining whether an asserted liberty interest (or right) should be regarded as "fundamental," the Supreme Court applies a two-prong test. First, there must be a "careful description" of the asserted fundamental liberty interest.[23] Second, the interest, so described, must be firmly rooted in "the Na-

---

17. Dan Friedman, THE MARYLAND STATE CONSTITUTION[:] A REFERENCE GUIDE 27 (Westport, Conn. 2006) (citing *Doe v. Doe*, 747 A.2d 617, 624–25 (Md. 2000)).

18. It should not be surprising to note, therefore, that no criminal statute has ever been struck down on the authority of the "remedy by course of the Law of the land" language of art. 19.

19. MD. DECL. OF RIGHTS art. 24.

20. *Crawford v. State*, 404 A.2d 244, 254 n. 3 (Md. 1979) (citing *Horace Mann League of the United States of America*, 220 A.3d at 73).

21. *Conaway v. Deane*, 932 A.2d 571, 616–17 (Md. 2007).

22. *Id.* at 616–29 (citing, among other cases, *Washington v. Glucksberg*, 521 U.S. 702 (1997); *Samuels v. Tschechtelin*, 763 A.2d 209, 238 (Md. Ct. Spec. App. 2000) (same)).

23. *Glucksberg*, 521 U.S. at 721 (citation and internal quotation marks omitted).

tion's history, legal traditions, and practices."[24] A right to abortion cannot be regarded as "fundamental" under art. 24, however, because such a "right" is not firmly rooted in Maryland's "history, legal traditions, and practices."[25]

Abortion was a crime at common law in Maryland without regard to the stage of pregnancy when the procedure was performed.[26] Indeed, one scholar has identified at least three colonial prosecutions for abortion in Maryland that arose before 1665, two of which were based on causing abortions before "quickening."[27] In two of the three cases (*Lambrozo* and *Brooks*), "the defendants escaped conviction because, before trial, they married (and thereby disqualified) the principal witnesses against them."[28]

Maryland enacted its first abortion statute in 1867, several months before the present constitution was adopted. The statute prohibited the performance of an abortion upon a pregnant woman at any stage of pregnancy, unless a

---

24. *Id.* at 710. To the extent that the Maryland Court of Appeals recognizes the same fundamental rights under the *state* due course of law guarantee as the Supreme Court does under the *federal* due process guarantee, *see Beeman v. Dep't of Health and Mental Hygiene*, 666 A.2d 1314, 1323 (Md. Ct. Spec. App. 1995) ("the due process clauses of Article 24 of the Maryland Declaration of Rights and the Fourteenth Amendment of the United States Constitution have the same meaning"), abortion would not qualify as a "fundamental" right. Although the Supreme Court characterized the right to choose abortion as "fundamental" in *Roe*, 410 U.S. at 152–53, it tacitly abandoned that characterization in *Casey*, 505 U.S. at 869–79 (Joint Op. of O'Connor, Kennedy and Souter, JJ., replacing *Roe's* "strict scrutiny" standard of review with the more relaxed "undue burden" standard, allowing for a broader measure of abortion regulation).

25. *Compare In re Adoption/Guardianship No. TPR 97011*, 712 A.2d 597, 602 (Md. Ct. Spec. App. 1998) (acknowledging that "the fundamental right of a parent to raise his or her child is in the nature of a liberty interest that is protected under" art. 24 and the Due Process Clause of the Fourteenth Amendment), *with Deane v. Conaway*, 932 A.2d at 616–29 (refusing to recognize same-sex marriage as a fundamental right under art. 24).

26. In a case arising under an abortion statute, the Maryland Court of Appeals noted that "it has been frequently held by courts of high character that abortion is a crime at common law *without regard to the stage of gestation.*" *Lamb v. State*, 10 A. 208, 208 (Md. 1887) (emphasis added).

27. Joseph W. Dellapenna, Dispelling the Myths of Abortion History (Carolina Academic Press, Durham, North Carolina 2006) 215–220 (citing and discussing *Commonwealth v. Lambrozo* (the defendant's name is variously spelled "Lumbrozo" and "Lumbroso"), 53 Md. Archives 387–91 (1663), *Commonwealth v. Brooks* (variously spelled "Brookes" and "Brooke"), 10 Md. Archives 464–65, 488 (1656), and *Commonwealth v. Mitchell*, 10 Md. Archives 171–86 (1652; published 1891)). "Quickening" is that stage of pregnancy, usually sixteen to eighteen weeks gestation, when the woman first detects fetal movement.

28. *Id.* at 215.

"regular practitioner" of medicine, after consultation with two other practitioners, "deemed [the procedure] necessary for the safety of the mother...."[29] This statute was repealed and replaced with a new statute one year later, which raised the class of the offense from a misdemeanor to a felony and narrowed somewhat the scope of the exception for the mother's "safety."[30] Under the new statute, a "regular practitioner of medicine" could perform an abortion when, "after consulting with one or more respectable physicians, he shall be satisfied that the foetus is dead, or that no other method will secure the safety of the mother."[31] This statute remained on the books until 1968, when the Model Penal Code provision was adopted.[32] During that one hundred year period, the Maryland Court of Appeals regularly affirmed convictions for abortion (and manslaughter convictions based upon the death of the woman resulting from an illegal abortion) without any hint that the prosecutions or convictions violated the Maryland Declaration of Rights.[33]

More than one hundred years ago, the Maryland Court of Appeals explained that abortion statutes, both in Maryland and elsewhere, had been strengthened and the penalties for their violation increased precisely because the medical procedures for inducing abortions had become safer:

> It is common knowledge that death is not now the usual, nor, indeed, the always probable, consequence of an abortion. The death of the mother ... more frequently resulted in the days of rude surgery, when the character and properties of powerful drugs were but little known, and the control over their application more limited. But, in these days of advanced surgery and marvelous medical science and skill, operations are performed and powerful drugs administered by skillful and careful men without danger to the life of the patient. Indeed, it is this comparative immunity from danger to the woman which has doubtless led to the great increase of the crime, to the establishment of a class of educated professional abortionists, and to the enactment of the

---

29. Act of March 20, 1867, §11, 1867 Md. Laws, ch. 185, pp. 342–43.

30. Act of March 28, 1868, 1868 Md. Laws, ch. 179, pp. 314–16.

31. *Id.* §2.

32. MD. CODE art. XXX, §1 (Supp. 1868), *recodified at* MD. CODE. art. XXVII, §3 (1888), *recodified at* MD. CODE ANN. art. 27, §3 (1957), *repealed by* Act of May 7, 1968, 1968 Md. Laws, ch. 470, §1.

33. *Jones v. State*, 17 A. 89 (Md. 1889); *Worthington v. State*, 48 A. 355 (Md. 1901); *Wilson v. State*, 26 A.2d 770 (Md. 1942); *Adams v. State*, 88 A.2d 556 (Md. 1952); *Hutson v. State*, 96 A.2d 593 (Md. 1953); *Basoff v. State*, 119 A.2d 917 (Md. 1956); *Roeder v. State*, 244 A.2d 895 (Md. 1968); *Vios v. State*, 246 A.2d 313 (Md. 1968).

severe statutes almost everywhere found to prevent and punish this offense.[34]

The court characterized abortion as an "abhorrent crime," which "can only be efficiently dealt with by severity in the enactment and administration of the law punishing the attempt upon the life of the unborn child."[35]

Maryland has recognized the rights of unborn children in a variety of contexts outside of abortion, including criminal law, tort law and property law. Under the criminal code, the killing of a viable unborn child, other than in an abortion, may be prosecuted as a homicide.[36] And a woman convicted of a capital offense may not be executed while she is pregnant.[37]

In tort law, a statutory cause of action for wrongful death may be brought on behalf of an unborn child who was viable (capable of sustained survival outside the mother's womb, with or without medical assistance) at the time of its death (if the child was stillborn).[38] If the child was born alive before it died as a result of injuries inflicted before birth, the wrongful death action may be brought without regard to viability.[39] A common law action for (nonlethal) prenatal injuries may be brought without regard to the stage of pregnancy when the injuries were inflicted.[40] And the Maryland Court of Appeals has refused to recognize wrongful life causes of action.[41] The court explained that,

---

34. *Worthington v. State*, 48 A. at 356–57.

35. *Id.* at 357.

36. MD. CODE ANN., CRIM. LAW §2-103 (Supp. 2007).

37. *Id.* CORR. SERV. §3-902(e).

38. *State v. Sherman*, 198 A.2d 71, 73 (Md. 1964), interpreting what is now codified at MD. CODE ANN., CTS & JUD. PROC. §3-901 *et seq.* (2006).

39. *Group Health Ass'n v. Blumenthal*, 453 A.2d 1198, 1207 (Md. 1983). In the absence of legislative reform, however, the court has declined to extend the wrongful death act to *non*viable unborn children who were stillborn. *Kandel v. White*, 663 A.2d 1264, 1266–70 (Md. 1995). *See also Smith v. Borello*, 804 A.2d 1151, 1156 (Md. 2002) (following *Kandel*).

40. *Damasiewicz v. Gorsuch*, 79 A.2d 550, 561 (Md. 1951).

41. *Kassama v. Magat*, 792 A.2d 1102, 1114–24 (Md. 2002). A "wrongful life" cause of action is a claim brought on behalf of a child who is born with a physical or mental disability or disease that could have been discovered before the child's birth by genetic testing, amniocentesis or other medical screening. The gravamen of the action is that, as a result of a physician's failure to inform the child's parents of the child's disability or disease (or at least of the availability of tests to determine the presence of the disability or disease), they were deprived of the opportunity to abort the child, thus resulting in the birth of a child suffering permanent physical or mental impairment. Very few courts recognize "wrongful life" causes of action because an assessment of damages requires the courts to compare the value of life, albeit with some degree of physical or mental impairment, to nonexistence. The court of appeals has recognized wrongful birth actions, however. *Reed v. Campagnolo*, 630 A.2d

"for purposes of tort law, an impaired life is *not* worse than non-life, and, for that reason, life is not, and cannot be, an injury."[42]

In property law, a posthumous child (a child conceived before but born after the death of a parent) "shall inherit as if he had been born in the lifetime of the decedent."[43] Subject to certain exceptions, an afterborn child (a child conceived before the death of a parent but born after the parent executes a will) receives that share of the estate he would have received if the decedent had died intestate, or, if there are other children, an equal share.[44]

In light of the history of abortion regulation in Maryland before 1968, the Maryland Court of Appeals' recognition in *Worthington* that the abortion statutes were intended to protect unborn children and the rights extended to unborn children outside the area of abortion, it cannot plausibly be said that art. 24 of the Maryland Constitution confers a right to abortion. More generally, a right to abortion cannot be found in the text or structure of the Maryland Constitution. There is no evidence that the framers of the Maryland Constitution of 1867 intended the Declaration of Rights to limit the Legislature's authority to prohibit abortion.[45] Such an intent would have been remarkable in light of the contemporaneous statutory and longstanding common law prohibition of abortion throughout pregnancy except to save the life of the pregnant woman.[46]

Equal Protection

Except for art. 46, the state equal rights amendment (which is discussed in the next section of this analysis), the Maryland Declaration of Rights does not

---

1145, 1147–52 (Md. 1993). A "wrongful birth" cause of action is a claim, based on the same facts, brought by the parents of an impaired child on their own behalf.

42. *Kassama*, 792 A.2d at 1123 (emphasis in original).

43. MD. CODE ANN., EST. & TRUSTS § 3-107 (2001).

44. *Id.* § 3-301 *et seq.*

45. *See* Philip B. Perlman, DEBATES OF THE MARYLAND CONSTITUTIONAL CONVENTION OF 1867 (as reprinted from articles reported in the *Baltimore Sun*) (Baltimore 1926) 76–83, 89–90, 92–93 (presentation of majority and minority reports on proposed Declaration of Rights); 96–101, 104–08, 119–33, 141–44, 148–64, 171–75 (second reading of Declaration of Rights); 381–83 (third reading and passage of Declaration of Rights).

46. In an early case decided under the Maryland Constitution, the court of appeals held that the object of what is now art. 21 (delineating rights of the accused) and what is now art. 24 (guaranteeing due process) of the Declaration of Rights "was to declare and secure the pre-existing rights of the people as those rights had been established by usage and the settled course of the law." *Lanasa v. State*, 71 A. 1058, 1061 (Md. 1909). Of course, as shown above, there was no "pre-existing right[] of the people" to obtain an abortion at the time the present constitution was adopted in 1867.

expressly guarantee equal protection of the law. The Maryland Court of Appeals, however, has held art. 24 "embodies the same equal protection concepts found in the [Equal Protection Clause] of the Fourteenth Amendment to the U.S. Constitution."[47] Although the federal Equal Protection Clause and "the concept of equal treatment embodied in Art. 24" are "independent of each other so that a violation of one is not necessarily a violation of the other," they are "*in pari materia* and generally apply in like manner and to the same extent...."[48]

The Maryland Court of Appeals generally applies one of three standards of review in determining "whether the equal protection or equal treatment guarantees of the fourteenth amendment or Article 24 have been violated by a challenge enactment."[49] "'Strict scrutiny' is required of a legislative classification when it creates a distinction based upon 'suspect' criteria or when it deprives, infringes upon, or interferes with personal rights or interests deemed to be 'fundamental.'"[50] Laws reviewed under this "rigorous standard" will not pass constitutional muster "unless the State can demonstrate that the statute is necessary to promote a compelling governmental interest."[51]

An intermediate standard of review ("heightened scrutiny") applies when "a statute impacts upon 'sensitive,' although not necessarily suspect criteria of classification (*i.e.*, gender discrimination), or where a statute affects 'important' personal rights or works a 'significant' interference with liberty or a denial of a benefit vital to the individual."[52] To withstand heightened scrutiny analysis, "[a] legislative classification ... must be reasonable, not arbitrary, and must rest upon some ground of difference having a fair and substantial relation to the object of the legislation, so that all persons similarly situated and circumstanced will be treated alike."[53] "This level of review," the court explained, 'does not tolerate random speculation concerning possible justification for a challenged enactment; rather, it pursues the actual purpose of a statute and seriously examines the means chosen to effectuate that purpose.'"[54]

"Where neither a suspect class nor a fundamental right or interest is involved or impaired, or rights or classes which would trigger heightened review are implicated, the least demanding standard of review is applied. Under this

---

47. *Verzi v. Baltimore County*, 635 A.2d 967, 970 (Md. 1994) (citing cases).
48. *Hornbeck v. Somerset County Board of Education*, 458 A.2d 758, 780–81 (Md. 1983).
49. *Id.* at 781.
50. *Id.* (citation omitted).
51. *Id.* (citation omitted).
52. *Id.* at 781–82 (citation omitted).
53. *Id.* at 782.
54. *Id.* (citation omitted).

standard," which is variously referred to as the "reasonable" or "rational" basis test, "a statutory classification will be invalidated only if the means chosen by the legislature are wholly irrelevant to the achievement of the State's objective."[55] The challenged statute will be upheld "when any state of facts reasonably may be conceived to sustain it."[56]

For the reasons set forth in the previous section of this analysis, a prohibition of abortion would not "infringe[] upon, or interfere[] with" a personal right or interest deemed to be "fundamental." Nor would an abortion prohibition classify on the basis of a suspect personal characteristic (*e.g.*, race). Abortion advocates may argue in the alternative that a statute prohibiting abortion discriminates against women and is subject to "heightened scrutiny" because only women are capable of becoming pregnant. An abortion prohibition would appear to satisfy this level of scrutiny because the prohibition would be have "a fair and substantial relation to the object" of protecting unborn human life. Nevertheless, the standard applicable to sex-based discrimination should not apply to an abortion prohibition. Abortion laws do not discriminate on the basis of sex.

First, the United States Supreme Court has reviewed restrictions on abortion funding under a rational basis standard of review, *not* under the heightened scrutiny required of gender-based classifications.[57] Indeed, the Court has held that "the disfavoring of abortion ... is not *ipso facto* sex discrimination," and, citing its decisions in *Harris* and other cases addressing abortion funding, stated that "the constitutional test applicable to government abortion-funding restrictions is not the heightened-scrutiny standard that our cases demand for sex discrimination, ... but the ordinary rationality standard."[58]

---

55. *Id.* (citation omitted).

56. *Id.* (citations omitted).

57. *Harris v. McRae*, 448 U.S. 297, 321–26 (1980).

58. *Bray v. Alexandria Women's Health Clinic*, 506 U.S. 263, 273 (1993). Several state supreme courts and individual state supreme court justices have recognized that abortion regulations and restrictions on abortion funding are not "directed at women as a class" so much as "abortion as a medical treatment, which, because it involves a potential life, has no parallel as a treatment method." *Bell v. Low Income Women of Texas*, 95 S.W.3d 253, 258 (Tex. 2002) (upholding funding restrictions) (citing *Harris*, 448 U.S. at 325). *See also Fischer v. Dep't of Public Welfare*, 502 A.2d 114, 125 (Pa. 1985) ("the basis for the distinction here is not sex, but abortion") (upholding funding restrictions); *Moe v. Secretary of Administration & Finance*, 417 N.E.2d 387, 407 (Mass. 1981) (Hennessey, C.J., dissenting) (funding restrictions were "directed at abortion as a medical procedure, not women as a class"); *Right to Choose v. Byrne*, 450 A.2d 925, 950 (N.J. 1982) (O'Hern, J., dissenting) ("[t]he subject of the legislation is not the person of the recipient, but the nature of the claimed medical service"). Both *Moe* and *Right to Choose* were decided on other grounds.

Second, even assuming that an abortion prohibition differentiates between men and women on the basis of sex, and would otherwise be subject to a higher standard of review, the Supreme Court has held that biological differences between men and women may justify different treatment based on those differences. In upholding a statutory rape statute that applied only to males, the Supreme Court noted, "this Court has consistently upheld statutes where the gender classification is not invidious, but rather realistically reflects the fact that the sexes are not similarly situated in certain circumstances."[59] As one federal district court observed: "Abortion statutes are examples of cases in which the sexes are not biologically similarly situated" because only women are capable of becoming pregnant and having abortions.[60]

A statute prohibiting abortion quite obviously can affect only women because only women are capable of becoming pregnant.[61] Unlike laws that use women's ability to become pregnant (or pregnancy itself) to discriminate against them in *other* areas (*e.g.*, employment opportunities), abortion prohibitions cannot fairly be said to involve a distinction between men and women that is a "mere pretext[] designed to erect an invidious discrimination against [women]."[62]

Because a prohibition of abortion would not infringe upon a fundamental state constitutional right and would not impermissibly classify on the basis of a suspect or quasi-suspect class, it would need to satisfy only the rational basis test. Under that test, the classification will be struck down "only if the means chosen by the legislature are wholly irrelevant to the achievement of the State's objective."[63] A prohibition of abortion would clearly be "relevant" to the State's legitimate objective in protecting unborn human life. Accordingly, Maryland could enact an abortion prohibition without violating the equal protection guarantee of the Maryland Constitution.

Equality of Rights

Article 46 of the Maryland Declaration of Rights provides: "Equality of rights under the law shall not be abridged or denied because of sex."[64] In any

---

The dissenting justices were addressing alternative arguments raised by the plaintiffs, but not reached by the majority opinions.

59. *Michael M. v. Superior Court*, 450 U.S. 464, 469 (1981).

60. *Jane L. v. Bangerter*, 794 F. Supp. 1537, 1549 (D. Utah 1992).

61. *Geduldig v. Aiello*, 417 U.S. 484, 496 n. 20 (1974) ("[n]ormal pregnancy is an objectively, identifiable physical condition with unique characteristics").

62. *Id.*

63. *Hornbeck*, 458 A.2d at 782.

64. MD. DECL. OF RIGHTS art. 46 (2003).

challenge to a statute prohibiting abortion, abortion advocates are likely to argue that because the statute directly affects only women, it violates the "[e]quality of rights" guaranteed by art. 46. Such an argument probably would not prevail.

The Maryland Court of Appeals has held that, under art. 46, "classifications based on gender are suspect and subject to strict scrutiny."[65] The court, however, has recognized that "[d]isparate treatment on account of physical characteristics unique to one sex is generally regarded as beyond the reach of equal rights amendments."[66] This is consistent with the interpretations reviewing courts in other States have given their equal rights provisions.[67] Because only women are capable of becoming pregnant, a law prohibiting abortion would not fall within the scope of art. 46.[68]

---

65. *Murphy v. Edmonds*, 601 A.2d 102, 109 n. 7 (Md. 1992).

66. *Burning Tree Club, Inc. v. Bainum*, 501 A.2d 817, 822 n. 3 (Md. 1985) (Op. of Murphy, C.J.) (citing *Brooks v. State*, 330 A.2d 670 (Md. Ct. Spec. App. 1975)). In *Brooks*, the court of special appeals held that the statute punishing only men for rape as principals in the first degree does not violate the equal rights amendment because only men can commit that crime. 330 A.2d at 673. The court remarked that "[t]he equality of the sexes expresses a societal goal, not a physical metamorphosis." *Id.*

67. The cases have upheld rape statutes, *State v. Rivera*, 612 P.2d 526, 530–31 (Haw. 1980), *State v. Fletcher*, 341 So.2d 340, 348 (La. 1976), *State v. Craig*, 545 P.2d 649 (Mont. 1976), *Finley v. State*, 527 S.W.2d 553, 555–57 (Tex. Crim. App. 1975); statutory rape statutes, *People v. Salinas*, 551 P.2d 703, 705–06 (Colo. 1976), *State v. Bell*, 377 So.2d 303 (La. 1979); an aggravated incest statute, *People v. Boyer*, 349 N.E.2d 50 (Ill. 1976); statutes governing the means of establishing maternity and paternity, *People v. Morrison*, 584 N.E.2d 509 (Ill. App. Ct. 1991), *A v. X, Y & Z*, 641 P.2d 1222, 1224–25 (Wyo. 1982); statutes and rules barring female nudity in bars, *Dydyn v. Dep't of Liquor Control*, 531 A.2d 170, 175 (Conn. App. Ct. 1987); *Messina v. State*, 904 S.W.2d 178, 181 (Tex. App.-Dallas 1995, *no pet.*); an ordinance prohibiting public exposure of female breasts, *City of Seattle v. Buchanan*, 584 P.2d 918, 919–21 (Wash. 1978); and limitations on public funding of abortion, *Fischer v. Dep't of Public Welfare*, 502 A.2d 114, 124–26 (Pa. 1985), *Bell v. Low Income Women of Texas*, 95 S.W.3d 253, 257–64 (Tex. 2002). The one exception is *New Mexico Right to Choose/NARAL v. Johnson*, 975 P.2d 841 (N.M. 1998), in which the New Mexico Supreme Court struck down a state regulation restricting public funding of abortion. In applying "heightened scrutiny," the court failed to recognize that the funding regulation did not use "the unique ability of women to become pregnant and bear children" as a pretext to discriminate against them in *other* respects, *e.g.*, "imposing restrictions on [their] ability to work and participate in public life." *Id.* at 855.

68. The Maryland Attorney General has reached the same conclusion. 74 Op. Att'y Gen. 19, 30–32 (1989). The state equal rights amendment "does not reach distinctions based on immutable, inarguable physical characteristics never found in one sex." *Id.* at 32.

Right to Alter, Reform or Abolish the Form of Government

Article 1 of the Maryland Declaration of Rights provides: "That all Government of right originates from the People, is founded in compact only, and instituted solely for the good of the whole; and they have, at all times, the inalienable right to alter, reform or abolish their Form of Government in such manner as they may deem expedient."[69] And art. 6 provides, in a similar vein:

> That all persons invested with the Legislative or Executive powers of Government are the Trustees of the Public, and, as such, accountable for their conduct: Wherefore, whenever the ends of Government are perverted, and public liberty manifestly endangered, and all other means of redress are ineffectual, the People may, and of right ought, to reform the old, or establish a new Government; the doctrine of non-resistance against arbitrary power and oppression is absurd, slavish and destructive of the good and happiness of mankind.[70]

In any challenge to a statute prohibiting abortion, abortion advocates may argue that the statute does not serve "the good of the whole" People under art. 1, and that it "endanger[s]" the "liberty" of the People under art. 6. Neither argument is likely to prevail.

Article 1, as one commentator has explained, "contains (1) recognition of a compact theory of government; (2) the 'good of the whole' provision; and (3) the reservation to the People of the right to change their form of government."[71] "The Court of Appeals of Maryland," Friedman notes, "has never applied any of the three parts of the provision to provide substantive rights."[72] Article 1 simply "preserves to the people the right to alter, reform, or abolish their form of government in such manner as they may deem expedient."[73] It does not provide a basis for challenging legislation on the ground that the legislation does not promote the "good of the whole."

Much the same may be said of art. 6, which provides "three related, primarily aspirational parts: (1) governmental accountability; (2) the right to reform or replace the government; and (3) the repudiation of the doctrine of

---

69. MD. DECL. OF RIGHTS art. 1 (2003).

70. *Id.* art. 6.

71. Friedman, THE MARYLAND STATE CONSTITUTION at 14.

72. *Id.*

73. *Braverman v. Bar Ass'n of Baltimore City*, 121 A.2d 473, 482 (Md. 1956). *See also Board of Supervisors of Elections for Anne Arundel County*, 229 A.2d 388, 400 (Md. 1967) (under art. 1, the People "retain the sovereign power to rewrite their constitution").

non-resistance."[74] Article 6, Friedman notes, has been "uniformly treated by the courts as exhortatory and not justiciable."[75] The court of appeals has held that "the language of Article 6 [is] merely advisory...."[76] Because art. 6 does not confer judicially enforceable rights, it could not serve as a source of a right to abortion under the Maryland Declaration of Rights.

Retained Rights

Article 45 of the Maryland Declaration of Rights provides: "This enumeration of Rights shall not be construed to impair or deny others retained by the People."[77] In any challenge to a statute prohibiting abortion, abortion advocates may be expected to argue that abortion is a "retained right" under art. 45. That argument would not likely succeed, however.

Article 45 has been cited in very few Maryland decisions and has never been authoritatively construed by either the Maryland Court of Appeals or the Maryland Court of Special Appeals. An entirely plausible reading of art. 45 is that the enumeration of certain rights in the state constitution should not be construed to "impair or deny" other rights retained by the people under the common law or statutes. But even if § 45 is understood to retain unspecified *constitutional* rights (as opposed to *common law* or *statutory* rights), abortion could not plausibly be considered to be among such rights because, at the time the Maryland Constitution was adopted in 1867, abortion was a crime. The argument that the first clause of § 45 "retained" as an "unenumerated" right conduct that was criminal when the state constitution was adopted is, at the very least, counterintuitive.

The language of art. 45 appears to be based on the Ninth Amendment, which provides: "The enumeration in the Constitution of certain rights, shall not be construed to deny or disparage others retained by the people."[78] In light of that equivalence, art. 45 should be given a parallel interpretation. That, in turn, suggests that if no right to abortion exists under the Ninth Amendment,

---

74. Friedman, The Maryland State Constitution at 17.

75. *Id.* at 18 (citing *Bernstein v. Board of Education of Prince George's County*, 226 A.2d 243, 248 (Md. 1967)).

76. *South Easton Neighborhood Ass'n, Inc. v. Town of Easton, Maryland*, 876 A.2d 58, 69 (Md. 2005) (citing *Kerpelman v. Board of Public Works of Maryland*, 276 A.2d 56, 61 (Md. 1971)). *See also Mandel v. O'Hara*, 576 A.2d 766, 780 (Md. 1990) (referring to the "generalized and essentially precatory provisions" of art. 6).

77. Md. Decl. of Rights art. 45 (2003).

78. U.S. Const. amend. IX (West 2006). Friedman, The Maryland State Constitution at 48 (art. 45 is "very similar to the 9th Amendment to the United States Constitution").

then none would be recognized under art. §45. The Supreme Court, however, has rooted the "abortion liberty" in the liberty language of the Due Process Clause of the Fourteenth Amendment, not in the unenumerated rights language of the Ninth Amendment.[79] Because abortion has not been recognized as a "retained right" under the Ninth Amendment, it should not be recognized as one under §45, either.

Conclusion

Based on the foregoing analysis, an argument that the Maryland Constitution protects a right to abortion that is separate from, and independent of, the right to abortion recognized in *Roe v. Wade* would not likely succeed. That, in turn, suggests that if *Roe*, as modified by *Casey*, is ultimately overruled, the State of Maryland could prohibit abortion. Moreover, nothing in the Maryland Constitution precludes Maryland from *regulating* abortion within federal constitutional limits in the meantime.

---

79. *See Roe*, 410 U.S. at 153; *Casey*, 505 U.S. at, 846. In any event, the Ninth Amendment, standing alone, is not a source of substantive rights. *Gibson v. Matthews*, 926 F.2d 532, 537 (6th Cir. 1991). Although "[s]ome unenumerated rights may be of [c]onstitutional magnitude," that is only "by virtue of other amendments, such as the Fifth or Fourteenth Amendment. A person cannot claim a right that exists solely under the Ninth Amendment." *United States v. Vital Health Products, Ltd.*, 786 F. Supp. 761, 777 (E.D. Wis. 1992), *aff'd mem. op., sub nom. United States v. LeBeau*, 985 F.2d 563 (7th Cir. 1993). *See also Charles v. Brown*, 495 F. Supp. 862, 863 (N.D. Ala. 1980) (same).

CHAPTER 24

MASSACHUSETTS

Summary

As the result of a decision of the Massachusetts Supreme Judicial Court interpreting the Massachusetts Constitution, the Commonwealth of Massachusetts could not prohibit any abortion before viability, or any abortion after viability that would be necessary to preserve the pregnant woman's life or health, even if *Roe v. Wade*,[1] as modified by *Planned Parenthood of Southeastern Pennsylvania*,[2] were overruled, unless the state constitution is amended to overturn that decision (or that decision is overruled). The Commonwealth's authority under the state constitution to regulate abortion within current federal constitutional limits is mixed.

Analysis

Massachusetts has not expressly repealed its principal pre-*Roe* abortion statute, which prohibits "unlawful" abortions.[3] The Massachusetts Supreme Judicial Court's opinion in *Moe v. Secretary of Administration & Finance*,[4] how-

---

1. 410 U.S. 113 (1973).

2. 505 U.S. 833 (1992).

3. MASS. GEN. STAT. ANN. ch. 272, § 19 (2000). In a series of pre-*Roe* decisions, the statute was interpreted to allow an abortion if, in the good faith judgment of the physician, the procedure was necessary to preserve the pregnant woman's life or her physical or mental health. *See Kudish v. Board of Registration in Medicine*, 248 N.E.2d 264, 265 (Mass. 1969); *Commonwealth v. Brunelle*, 171 N.E.2d 850, 851–52 (Mass. 1961); *Commonwealth v. Wheeler*, 53 N.E.2d 4, 5 (1944). Whether a statute that, by its express terms or as interpreted, allows abortions for reasons of "mental health" actually prevents any abortions may be questioned, given the pre-*Roe* experience with the California Therapeutic Abortion Act of 1967, CAL. HEALTH & SAFETY CODE § 25950 *et seq.* (West Supp. 1971). *See People v. Barksdale*, 503 P.2d 257, 265 (Cal. 1972) (discussing numbers of abortions performed for alleged reasons of "mental health").

4. 417 N.E.2d 387 (Mass. 1981).

ever, would preclude the Commonwealth from enforcing § 19 or any other statute prohibiting abortion, at least before viability, even if *Roe*, as modified by *Casey*, were overruled.[5]

In *Moe*, the Supreme Judicial Court held that statutory restrictions on public funding of medically necessary abortions violated the guarantee of due process implicit in Article X of the Massachusetts Declaration of Rights, which provides, in pertinent part: "Each individual of the society has a right to be protected by it in the enjoyment of his life, liberty and property, according to standing laws."[6] The statutes in question restricted reimbursement of abortions under the state Medicaid program to circumstances in which the procedure was necessary to prevent a woman's death.[7]

The court declared that it had accepted the formulation of rights announced in *Roe v. Wade* as "an integral part of our jurisprudence."[8] The state guarantee of due process secures the fundamental right of privacy, the court noted, and "affords a greater degree of protection to the right asserted here [abortion] than does the Federal Constitution."[9] Turning to the funding issue, the court recognized that "the State retains wide latitude to decide the manner in which it will allocate benefits."[10] Nevertheless, the State "may not use criteria which discriminatorily burden the exercise of a *fundamental* right."[11] The court agreed with Justice Brennan's dissent in *Harris v. McRae*,[12] that "by ... injecting coercive financial incentives favoring childbirth into a decision that is constitutionally guaranteed to be free from governmental intrusion, [this restriction] deprives the indigent woman of her freedom to choose abortion over maternity, thereby impinging on the due process liberty interest right recognized in *Roe v. Wade*."[13]

---

5. A separate statute purports to restrict abortions during or after the twenty-fourth week of pregnancy to those necessary save the life of the pregnant woman or when continuation of the pregnancy would impose on her a substantial risk of grave impairment of her physical or mental health. *See* MASS. GEN. LAWS ANN. ch. 112, § 12M (West 2003). The allowance of abortion for asserted reasons of "mental health" probably renders this restriction meaningless and unenforceable, as the pre-*Roe* experience with the California Therapeutic Abortion Act demonstrated. *See People v. Barksdale*, 503 P.2d at 265 (reviewing abuse of mental health exception).

6. MASS. CONST, Part 1, art. X (1997).

7. The challenged statutes included MASS. GEN. LAWS ANN. ch. 29, § 20B (1992), and various appropriations riders.

8. *Moe*, 417 N.E.2d at 398.

9. *Id.* at 397–400.

10. *Id.* at 401.

11. *Id.* (emphasis added).

12. 448 U.S. 297 (1980).

13. *Id.* at 333 (Brennan, J., dissenting), quoted in 417 N.E.2d at 402.

Applying a balancing test, the court in *Moe* held that "the interest of the pregnant woman in choosing a medically necessary abortion" clearly outweighed the State's interest "in the preservation of life, albeit potential life."[14] The case was remanded to the trial court with directions to enter a judgment declaring that Medicaid-eligible pregnant women were entitled to nondiscriminatory funding of lawful, medically necessary abortion services, and enjoining the funding restrictions to the extent that they prevented reimbursement to Medicaid providers for such services.[15] Because of its disposition of the due process claim, the court did not reach plaintiffs' equal protection and equal rights arguments.[16]

What are the implications of the *Moe* opinion with respect to laws prohibiting abortion? Although declining to decide whether there is "an absolute right to have abortions or an equivalent right to have … abortions subsidized by the State,"[17] the *Moe* court stated that it had accepted the formulation of rights announced in *Roe v. Wade* as an "integral part of our jurisprudence,"[18] and referred to abortion as a "fundamental" right.[19] Under that formulation, however, the States may not prohibit any pre-viability abortion, or any post-viability abortion that is necessary to preserve the life or health of the pregnant woman.[20]

---

14. *Moe*, 417 N.E.2d at 404.

15. *Id.* at 404–05.

16. *Id.* at 397.

17. *Id.* at 400.

18. *Id.* at 398. In *Doe v. Doe*, 314 N.E.2d 128 (Mass. 1974), for example, the court held that a pregnant woman's husband had no right to prevent her from obtaining an abortion. In *Doe*, the court recognized that the line of cases culminating in *Roe v. Wade* "all … involved a shield for the private citizen against government action, not a sword of government assistance to enable him to overturn the private decisions of his fellow citizens." *Id.* at 130. And in *Framingham Clinic, Inc. v. Selectmen of Southborough*, 367 N.E.2d 606 (Mass. 1977), the court held invalid a zoning by law designed to exclude abortion clinics from the town. The court stated that the "negative constitutional principle" underlying *Roe v. Wade* "forbids the State to interpose material obstacles to the effectuation of a woman's counselled decision to terminate her pregnancy during the first trimester." *Id.* at 612.

19. *Moe*, 417 N.E.2d at 401.

20. The Supreme Court has not yet decided whether a statute prohibiting post-viability abortions must make exceptions for mental, as well as physical, health. *See Voinovich v. Women's Medical Professional Corporation*, 523 U.S. 1036, 1039 (1998) (Thomas, J., dissenting from denial of *certiorari*) (noting that this issue was not addressed in *Doe v. Bolton*, 410 U.S. 179 (1973), the companion case to *Roe v. Wade*). As a result, it is not known whether, as a matter of *state* constitutional law, the Massachusetts Supreme Judicial Court would require a post-viability statute to contain a mental health exception. Under current state law, an abortion may not be performed after the twenty-fourth week of gestation unless the procedure is necessary "to save the life of the mother, or if a continuation of her preg-

The Massachusetts Supreme Judicial Courts's acceptance of *Roe* on state constitutional grounds, combined with the court's repeated acknowledgment of a generalized right of privacy,[21] suggests that any statute attempting to prohibit abortion would not be enforceable before viability, and would be enforceable after viability only if it allowed abortion for reasons relating to the life or health of the pregnant woman. This conclusion is reinforced, at least indirectly, by the court's decision in *Planned Parenthood League of Massachusetts v. Attorney General.*[22]

In *Planned Parenthood League*, the Massachusetts Supreme Judicial Court considered a state due process and equal protection challenge to the Commonwealth's parental consent statute, which requires a minor to obtain the consent of both parents to her having an abortion or else seek court authorization in a judicial bypass hearing.[23] The supreme court unanimously rejected the challenge to the requirement that a minor obtain parental consent or judicial approval, but a majority held that the statute's requirement "that more than one parent give consent to the performance of an unmarried minor's abortion violates the due process provisions of the [Massachusetts] Constitution."[24] Significantly, the court held, as a matter of *state* constitutional interpretation, that the Commonwealth could *not* require parental consent without also providing the minor with the alternative of seeking judicial approval.[25]

In evaluating the constitutionality of requiring either parental consent or judicial approval, the court stated:

> In the case before us we must engage in the same balancing of interests that we used in deciding the *Moe* case. The constitutional right is the same as it was in the *Moe* case, but the burden on that consti-

---

nancy will impose on her a substantial risk of grave impairment of her physical or mental health. MASS. GEN. LAWS ANN. ch 112, § 12M (West 2003).

21. The Massachusetts Supreme Judicial Court has applied state and federal privacy principles in various contexts, including parents' rights to custody of their children, *Dep't of Public Welfare v. J.K.B.*, 393 N.E.2d 406, 407–08 (Mass. 1979); *Custody of a Minor*, 389 N.E.2d 68, 73 (Mass. 1979); choice with regard to medical treatment, *Matter of Spring*, 405 N.E.2d 115, 119 (Mass. 1980); *Comm'r of Correction v. Myers*, 399 N.E.2d 452, 455–56 (Mass. 1979); *Superintendent of Belchertown State School v. Saikewicz*, 370 N.E.2d 417, 424 (Mass. 1977); sexual conduct, *Commonwealth v. Balthazar*, 318 N.E.2d 478, 480 (Mass. 1974); and drug use, *Marcoux v. Attorney General*, 375 N.E.2d 688, 690 (Mass. 1978).

22. 677 N.E.2d 101 (Mass. 1997).

23. MASS. GEN. LAWS ANN. ch. 112, § 12S (West 2003).

24. *Planned Parenthood League*, 677 N.E.2d at 109.

25. *Id.* at 105 ("parental consent … may not constitutionally be made an absolute precondition of the performance of an abortion").

tutional right and the State's interest in the regulation of the exercise of that right are different. Here, the asserted burden on the constitutional right is the requirement of either (a) parental consent or (b) judicial approval. It is, of course, crucial in justification of these alternative requirements that the person seeking to have an abortion is a minor. The State has an obvious interest in the welfare of minors and in the promotion of the interests of parents in the care and upbringing of their children. The question is whether those interests counterbalance the unquestioned limitation that § 12S imposes on a woman's constitutional right of choice.[26]

The clear implication of the foregoing is that if Massachusetts attempted to prohibit either adult *or* minor females from obtaining an abortion (an obvious and insurmountable "limitation" on "a woman's constitutional right of choice"), such a prohibition would not pass muster under the "balancing of interests" test used in *Moe* and *Planned Parenthood League*. This is confirmed by the court's statement in the latter opinion that "[t]he State's interests in support of § 12S [the parental consent statute] have a stronger basis in legally and constitutionally grounded principles than the State's interest (preservation of expected life) implicated in the *Moe* decision [which struck down limitations on public funding of abortion]."[27] In other words, the State's interest in the "preservation of expected life" would not be strong enough to outweigh a woman's "constitutional right of choice" in obtaining an abortion, at least before viability.

Conclusion

Because of the Massachusetts Supreme Judicial Court's decision in *Moe v. Secretary of Administration & Finance*, the Commonwealth of Massachusetts would not be able to prohibit abortions, at least before viability, even if *Roe*, as modified by *Casey*, were overruled, unless the state constitution is amended to overturn the holding in *Moe* (or the latter is overruled). The Commonwealth's authority to regulate abortion within current federal constitutional limits is mixed.

---

26. *Id*. at 104.
27. *Id*. at 106.

CHAPTER 25

MICHIGAN

Summary

The Michigan Supreme Court has not yet decided whether the Michigan Constitution protects a right to abortion separate from, and independent of, the right to abortion recognized under the United States Constitution.[1] A careful examination of the state constitution, in light of its history and interpretation, as well as other relevant legal sources, however, suggests that the state supreme court probably would not recognize a state constitutional right to abortion. Thus, if *Roe v. Wade*,[2] as modified by *Planned Parenthood of Southeastern Pennsylvania v. Casey*,[3] were overruled, Michigan could enforce its pre-*Roe* abortion statutes. Moreover, nothing in the state constitution, properly understood, precludes the State from enacting and enforcing reasonable measures regulating abortion within current federal constitutional limits.

Analysis

The principal pre-*Roe* abortion statute prohibited performance of an abortion upon a pregnant woman "unless the same shall have been necessary to preserve the life of such woman."[4] Section 750.14 has not been ex-

---

1. *See Doe v. Dep't of Social Services*, 487 N.W.2d 166, 173–74 (Mich. 1992) (not deciding issue).

2. 410 U.S. 113 (1973).

3. 505 U.S. 833 (1992).

4. MICH. COMP. LAWS ANN. §750.14 (West 1968). Another statute provided:

"Any person who shall administer to any woman pregnant with a quick child any medicine, drug or substance, whatever, or shall use or employ any instrument or other means, with intent thereby to destroy such child, unless the same shall have been necessary to preserve the life of such mother, shall, in case the death of such child or of such mother be thereby produced, be guilty of manslaughter." *Id*. §750.323. "Quickening" is that stage of

pressly repealed,[5] and the Michigan Court of Appeals has held that it has not been repealed by implication with the enactment of post-*Roe* legislation regulating abortion.[6]

In *Mahaffey v. Attorney General*,[7] the Michigan Court of Appeals held that the Michigan Constitution does not secure a right to abortion that is separate from, and independent of, the right to an abortion recognized in *Roe*, as modified by *Casey*. That decision, which is discussed later in this analysis, would not be binding upon the Michigan Supreme Court, which, to date, has declined to address the issue.[8] If *Roe* were overruled, however, abortion advocates may be expected to mount yet another challenge to §750.14 on state constitutional grounds. Based upon arguments that have been raised in Michigan and other States with similar constitutional provisions, possible sources for an asserted abortion right could include provisions of the Declaration of Rights guaranteeing equal protection (art. I, §§1, 2), freedom of religious belief (§4) and due process of law (§17); and retaining rights (§23).[9] The analysis that follows considers each of these provisions.

Freedom of Religious Belief

Article I, §4, of the Michigan Constitution provides:

Every person shall be at liberty to worship God according to the dictates of his own conscience. No person shall be compelled to attend, or against his consent, to contribute to the erection or support of any place of religious worship, or to pay tithes, taxes or other rates for the support of any minister of the gospel or teacher of religion. No money shall be appropriated or drawn from the treasury for the benefit of any religious sect or society, theological or religious seminary; nor shall property belonging to the state be appropriated for any such purpose. The civil and political rights, privileges and capacities of no per-

---

pregnancy, usually sixteen to eighteen weeks gestation, when the woman first detects fetal movement.

5. *See* MICH. COMP. LAWS ANN. §750.14 (West 2004).

6. *People v. Higuera*, 625 N.W.2d 444, 448–49 (Mich. Ct. App. 2001).

7. 564 N.W.2d 104 (Mich. Ct. App. 1997).

8. *See* n. 1, *supra*.

9. Three other more unlikely sources of an abortion right under the Michigan Constitution-art. I, §5 (guaranteeing freedom of speech), §9 (prohibiting involuntary servitude) and §11 (prohibiting unreasonable searches and seizures)-are discussed generally in Chapter 3, *supra*.

son shall be diminished or enlarged on account of his religious belief.[10]

"Taken together," the Michigan Supreme Court has explained, "these sentences are an expanded and more explicit statement of the establishment and free exercise clauses of the First Amendment to the United States Constitution, the first and fourth sentences constituting the free exercise clause, and the second and third sentences constituting the establishment clause."[11] "They are," accordingly, "subject to similar interpretation."[12]

Given the Michigan Supreme Court's gloss on art. I, §4, abortion advocates may raise either or both of two arguments under §4 against Michigan pre-*Roe* abortion statute (or any other statute prohibiting abortion the State may hereafter enact). First, they may argue that an abortion prohibition interferes with the free exercise of a woman's religion by forbidding her from obtaining an abortion that would be allowed by her religion. Second, they may argue in the alternative (or in addition) that an abortion prohibition constitutes an establishment of religion because it reflects sectarian beliefs regarding when human life begins and the sinfulness of abortion. Neither argument would likely prevail.

With respect to the latter argument (establishment of religion), there is no indication in Michigan case law that the Michigan Supreme Court would not follow Supreme Court precedent interpreting the Establishment Clause in interpreting the second and third sentences of art. I, §4. For the reasons set forth in Chapter 2, *supra*, an abortion statute could not be successfully challenged on the basis of the Establishment Clause. Accordingly, a similar challenge under art. I, §4, would not likely be successful.

With respect to the former argument (free exercise), however, the Michigan Supreme Court does not follow Supreme Court precedent interpreting the Free Exercise Clause in interpreting the first and fourth sentences of art. I, §4. The test to evaluate religious freedom claims under §4, has five elements:

> (1) whether a defendant's belief, or conduct motivated by belief, is sincerely held; (2) whether a defendant's belief, or conduct motivated by belief, is religious in nature; (3) whether a state regulation imposes a burden on the exercise of such belief or conduct; (4) whether a com-

---

10. MICH. CONST. art. I, §4 (West 2003).

11. *Advisory Opinion re: Constitutionality of PA 1970, No. 100*, 180 N.W.2d 265, 274 (Mich. 1970).

12. *Id.*

pelling state interest justifies the burden imposed upon a defendant's belief or conduct; and (5) whether there is a less obtrusive form of regulation available to the state.[13]

A claim that a woman is entitled to an abortion as a matter of religious freedom would most likely fail under the third, fourth and fifth elements of this test. In determining whether a state regulation burdens the exercise of a person's belief or conduct, the Michigan Supreme Court has said:

> A burden may be shown if the "affected individuals [would] be coerced by the Government's action into violating their religious beliefs [or whether] governmental action [would] penalize religious activity by denying any person an equal share of the rights, benefits, and privileges enjoyed by other citizens." Hence, "[a] claimed burden on religious beliefs may be deemed constitutionally in*significant, but only (1) if the claimant's beliefs do not create an irreconcilable conflict between the mandates of law and religious duty, or (2) if the legal requirement does not directly coerce the claimant to act contrary to religious belief....*"[14]

A prohibition of abortion except to save the life of the pregnant woman would not create "an irreconcilable conflict between the mandates of law and religious duty" because there is no doctrine in any religion that *requires* (as opposed to *permits*) a woman to undergo an abortion in circumstances when her life is not in danger.[15] Nor, for the same reason, would an abortion prohibition "directly coerce" a woman "to act contrary to [her] religious belief." In fact, the prohibition would not "coerce" the woman to do anything. If the conduct prohibited by a statute or policy is not fundamental to the practice of one's religion, then the statute or policy is not subject to strict scrutiny review and may be upheld if it is reasonably related to a legitimate state interest.[16] An abortion prohibition is reasonably related to the State's legitimate interest in protecting unborn human life.

---

13. *McCready v. Hoffius*, 586 N.W.2d 723, 729 (Mich. 1998), *vacated in part*, 593 N.W.2d 545 (Mich. 1999).

14. *People v. DeJonge*, 501 N.W.2d 127, 136 (Mich. 1993) (internal citations omitted) (emphasis in original).

15. Whether a particular religious doctrine *permits* abortion under certain circumstances does not present a justiciable free exercise issue because, to have the standing necessary to raise such an issue (with respect to a law that does not single out religious practices for regulation), one must allege that one seeks an abortion "under compulsion of religious belief." *Harris v. McRae*, 448 U.S. at 320.

16. *See Abdur-Ra'oof v. Dep't of Corrections*, 562 N.W.2d 251 (Mich. Ct. App. 1997) (attending Muslim prayer services on Friday is not a fundamental tenet of Islam); *Reid v.*

Even assuming, however, that a pregnant woman could satisfy the first three elements of the *McCready* test, it would seem that she could not satisfy the last two elements. The State has a compelling interest in protecting and preserving the life of the unborn child and there is no "less obtrusive form of regulation available to the state," short of an outright prohibition, that would adequately promote and safeguard that interest. An example, not involving abortion, that illustrates this principle is the line of cases authorizing compulsory blood transfusions on pregnant women (typically, Jehovah's Witnesses) to save the lives of their unborn children.[17] The prohibition of abortion, for the same end, stands on even firmer ground, however, because it does not implicate the federal constitutional right to refuse unwanted medical treatment.[18] Moreover, unlike an order authorizing a blood transfusion of a pregnant woman, which is intended to *save* the life of the unborn child (and very possibly the mother's life as well), the intent in an abortion is to *destroy* the unborn child's life. The prohibition of abortion would not violate art. I, § 4, of the Michigan Constitution.

Due Process of Law

Article I, § 17, provides, in pertinent part, that "[n]o person shall ... be deprived of life, liberty or property, without due process of law...."[19] The Michigan Court of Appeals has repeatedly held that "Michigan's due process guarantee provides no greater protection than does the federal due process guarantee."[20]

Kenowa Hills Public Schools, 680 N.W.2d 62 (Mich. Ct. App. 2004) (participating in extracurricular interscholastic athletic events is not a fundamental tenet of Christianity).

17. *See Fosmire v. Nicoleau*, 536 N.Y.S.2d 492, 496 (App. Div. 1989) (dictum) (when "a pregnant adult woman refuses medical treatment and, as a result of that refusal, places the life of her unborn baby in jeopardy," "the State's interest, as *parens patriae*, in protecting the health and welfare of the child is determined to be paramount") (citing *In the Matter of Application of Jamaica Hospital*, 491 N.Y.S.2d 898 (Sup. Ct. 1985) (blood transfusion) (18 weeks gestation); and *Crouse Irving Memorial Hospital, Inc. v. Paddock*, 485 N.Y.S.2d 443 (Sup. Ct. 1985) (blood transfusion) (premature delivery)). *See also Raleigh Fitkin-Paul Morgan Memorial Hospital v. Anderson*, 201 A.2d 537 (N.J. 1964) (same with respect to blood transfusion at 32 weeks gestation); *but see In re Brown*, 689 N.E.2d 397 (Ill. App. Ct. 1997) (*contra*) (blood transfusion).

18. *See, e.g., Cruzan v. Director, Missouri Dep't of Health*, 497 U.S. 261, 278–79 & n. 7 (1990); *Washington v. Glucksberg*, 521 U.S. 702, 719–26 & n. 17 (1997).

19. MICH. CONST. art. I, § 17 (West 2003).

20. *People v. Conat*, 605 N.W.2d 49, 61 (Mich. Ct. App. 1999) (procedural due process). *See also Syntex Laboratories v. Dep't of Treasury*, 590 N.W.2d 612, 616 (Mich. Ct. App. 1998) (procedural due process); *Gazette v. Pontiac*, 536 N.W.2d 854, 859 (Mich. Ct. App. 1995) (substantive due process); *Gora v. City of Ferndale*, 551 N.W.2d 454, 458 (Mich. Ct. App.

Under this line of authority, if the Supreme Court determines that there is no right to an abortion under the liberty language of the Due Process Clause of the Fourteenth Amendment, then there would be no corresponding state right to an abortion, either.[21]

Apart from the foregoing, the court of appeals has already determined, as has been noted,[22] that there is no independent right to abortion under the Michigan Constitution. The plaintiffs in *Mahaffey* argued that the informed consent statute violated "a woman's right to privacy and due process."[23] In rejecting this argument, the court of appeals made a number of key rulings.

First, and most importantly, the court held that a right to abortion need not be recognized under the state constitution merely because one has been recognized, in *Roe v. Wade,* under the federal constitution.[24] Whether a right to abortion exists under the Michigan Constitution must be decided without reference to whether there is such a right under the United States Constitution. As the Michigan Supreme Court has said:

> Where a right is given to a citizen under federal law, it does not follow that the organic instrument of state government must be interpreted as conferring the identical right. Nor does it follow that where a right given by the federal constitution is not given by a state constitution, the state constitution offends the federal constitution. It is only where the organic instrument of [state] government purports to deprive a citizen of a right granted by the federal constitution that the instrument can be said to violate the [federal] constitution.[25]

1996) (substantive due process), *rev'd on other grounds,* 576 N.W.2d 458 (Mich. 1998); *Saxon v. Dep't of Social Services,* 479 N.W.2d 361, 366 (Mich. Ct. App. 1991) (procedural due process).

21. To the extent that the Michigan Supreme Court considers federal precedent in determining whether an asserted liberty interest (or right) is "fundamental" under the state due process guarantee, abortion would not qualify as a "fundamental" right. Although the Supreme Court characterized the right to choose abortion as "fundamental" in *Roe,* 410 U.S. at 152–53, it tacitly abandoned that characterization in *Casey,* 505 U.S. at 869–79 (Joint Op. of O'Connor, Kennedy and Souter, JJ., replacing *Roe's* "strict scrutiny" standard of review with the more relaxed "undue burden" standard, allowing for a broader measure of abortion regulation).

22. *See* n. 7, *supra,* and accompanying text.

23. *Mahaffey,* 564 N.W.2d at 108.

24. *Id.* at 109.

25. *Sitz v. Dep't of State Police,* 506 N.W.2d 209, 216–17 (Mich. 1993). *See also, id.,* at 217 ("[a]s a matter of simple logic, because the texts were written at different times by different people, the protections afforded may be greater, lesser, or the same").

Second, at the time the 1963 Michigan Constitution was adopted, abortion was a criminal offense and had been a statutory offense for more than 100 years,[26] yet there was no mention of abortion in the proceedings of the 1961 constitutional convention. That indicated that the drafters of the constitution had no intention of altering the existing law on abortion.[27]

Third, less than ten years after the present state constitution was adopted, "essentially the same electorate that approved the constitution rejected a proposal brought by proponents of abortion reform to amend the Michigan abortion statute."[28] That, in turn, meant that the People who adopted the 1963 Constitution did not intend to establish a state constitutional right to abortion.[29]

Fourth, in limiting the application of the state abortion laws following *Roe v. Wade*, the Michigan Supreme Court made it clear that it was doing so only under the compulsion of the Supreme Court's decision in *Roe* and noted that "the public policy of the state [is] to proscribe abortion."[30] Taken together, *Bricker* and *Larkin* "suggest that in Michigan a woman's right to abortion is derived solely from the federal constitution."[31]

Finally, in *Mahaffey*, the court of appeals attributed no significance to the pre-*Roe* decision in *People v. Nixon*.[32] In *Nixon*, the court of appeals affirmed a non-physician's conviction of abortion. In dictum, however, a majority of the court gratuitously stated that the state abortion statutes had not been enacted to protect the life of the unborn child, but only to protect the pregnant woman from dangerous surgical procedures,[33] a statement which is demonstrably false.[34] Because advances in medicine had dramatically reduced the danger of abortion,

---

26. In 1846, Michigan enacted comprehensive statutes prohibiting abortion at any stage of pregnancy except those necessary to save the life of the pregnant woman. *See* Mich. Rev. Stat., ch. 153, §§ 32, 33, 34, p. 662 (1846), which now appear at Mich. Comp. Laws Ann. §§ 750.322, 750.323 and 750.14 (West 2004). Collectively, these statutes, which have never been repealed, "cover[ed] the whole ground." *People v. Olmstead*, 30 Mich. 431, 433 (1874), by making abortion at any stage of pregnancy a crime.

27. *Mahaffey*, 564 N.W.2d at 109–10.

28. *Id.* at 110.

29. *Id.*

30. *People v. Bricker*, 208 N.W.2d 172, 175 (Mich. 1973). *See also Larkin v. Cahalan*, 208 N.W.2d 176, 180 (Mich. 1973).

31. *Mahaffey*, 564 N.W.2d at 111.

32. 201 N.W.2d 635 (Mich. Ct. App. 1972).

33. *Id.* at 639–41.

34. *See People v. Sessions*, 26 N.W. 291, 293 (Mich. 1886): "At common law life is not only sacred, but it is inalienable. To attempt to produce an abortion or miscarriage, except when necessary to save the life of the mother, under advice of medical men, is an unlawful act, and has always been regarded as fatal to the child and dangerous to the mother."

the majority in *Nixon* opined that the blanket denial of a woman's right to obtain an abortion was no longer justified and, for that reason, the statute making abortion a felony no longer existed as it applied to licensed physicians in a proper medical setting.[35] In *Nixon*, the court of appeals never indicated whether its decision was based on state or federal constitutional law, although it would appear that it was based on federal, not state, constitutional law.

In addition to the analysis set forth in *Mahaffey*, the State of Michigan recognizes the rights of unborn children in a variety of contexts outside of abortion, including criminal law, tort law, health care law and property law.

Under the criminal code, the killing or injury of an unborn child, other than in an abortion, may be prosecuted as a homicide or an assault, respectively.[36] In tort law, a statutory cause of action for wrongful death may be brought on behalf of an unborn child without regard to the stage of pregnancy when the injuries causing death were inflicted.[37] A common law action for (nonlethal) prenatal injuries may be brought without regard to the stage of pregnancy when the injuries were inflicted.[38] And Michigan does not recognize either wrongful birth or wrongful life causes of action.[39]

In health care law, a living will may not direct the withholding or withdrawal of life-sustaining treatment from a pregnant patient if that would result in her death.[40] A durable power of attorney for health care is subject to the same limitation.[41]

---

35. *Nixon*, 201 N.W.2d at 639.

36. Mich. Comp. Laws Ann. §750.90a *et seq.* (West 2004).

37. *Id.* §600.2922a (West Supp. 2007).

38. *Id.* (by implication).

39. *Id.* §600.2971 (West Supp. 2007); *Taylor v. Kurapati*, 600 N.W.2d 670, 691 (Mich. Ct. App. 1999) (rejecting line of cases recognizing wrongful birth cause of action), *id.* at 687 (holding that "Michigan law provides for no right to an abortion and, in fact, makes a value judgment favoring childbirth"); *Proffit v. Bartolo*, 412 N.W.2d 232 (Mich. Ct. App. 1987) (rejecting wrongful life cause of action). A "wrongful life" cause of action is a claim brought on behalf of child who is born with a physical or mental disability or disease that could have been discovered before the child's birth by genetic testing, amniocentesis or other medical screening. The gravamen of the action is that, as a result of a physician's failure to inform the child's parents of the child's disability or disease (or at least of the availability of tests to determine the presence of the disability or disease), they were deprived of the opportunity to abort the child, thus resulting in the birth of a child suffering permanent physical or mental impairment. A "wrongful birth" cause of action, on the other hand, is a claim, based upon the same facts, brought by the parents of the impaired child on their own behalf.

40. Mich. Comp. Laws Ann. §700.5509(1)(d) (West 2002).

41. *Id.* §700.5512.

In property law, for purposes of inheriting from a person who dies intestate (without a will), "[a]n individual in gestation at a particular time is treated as living at that time if the individual lives 120 hours [five days] or more after birth."[42] Subject to certain exceptions, an afterborn child (a child conceived before the death of a parent but born after the parent executes a will) receives that share of the estate he would have received if the decedent had died intestate, or, if there are other children, an equal share.[43] The variety of ways in which Michigan recognizes and protects the lives of unborn children outside of abortion reinforces the *Mahaffey* court's conclusion that the Michigan Constitution does not support a right to abortion.

Equal Protection

Article I, §1, of the Michigan Constitution provides: "All political power is inherent in the people. Government is instituted for their equal benefit, security and protection."[44] And art. I, §2, provides: "No person shall be denied the equal protection of the laws;...."[45] The Michigan Supreme Court has held that the equal protection guarantees of the state constitution are no broader in scope than the Equal Protection Clause of the Fourteenth Amendment.[46] This equivalency of interpretation suggests that if the Supreme Court of the United States does not construe the Equal Protection Clause of the Fourteenth Amendment to place limits on the State's authority to prohibit abortion (and it has not done so to date), then the Michigan Supreme Court will not so construe art. I, §§1 and 2, either.

A state equal protection challenge to §750.14 is most likely to be advanced on a theory that abortion prohibitions—indeed, abortion regulations generally— affect only women and, therefore, are gender based and subject to a higher standard of judicial review under both the state and federal constitutions.[47] An abortion prohibition would appear to satisfy this standard because the prohibition would be "substantially related" to the "important governmental interest" in protecting unborn human life. Nevertheless, the standard applicable

---

42. *Id.* §700.2108.

43. *Id.* §700.2302.

44. MICH. CONST. art. I, §1 (West 2003).

45. *Id.* art. I, §2.

46. *Doe v. Dep't of Social Services*, 487 N.W.2d at 175; *Gora v. City of Ferndale*, 576 N.W.2d 141, 145 (Mich. 1998).

47. *Craig v. Boren*, 429 U.S. 190, 197 (1976) (articulating federal standard for gender-based classifications).

to sex-based discrimination should not apply to an abortion prohibition. Abortion laws do not discriminate on the basis of sex.

First, both the Michigan Supreme Court and the United States Supreme Court have reviewed restrictions on abortion funding under a rational basis standard of review, *not* under the intermediate standard ("heightened scrutiny") required of gender based classifications.[48] Indeed, the Supreme Court has held that "the disfavoring of abortion ... is not *ipso facto* sex discrimination," and, citing its decisions in *Harris* and other cases addressing abortion funding, stated that "the constitutional test applicable to government abortion-funding restrictions is not the heightened-scrutiny standard that our cases demand for sex discrimination, ... but the ordinary rationality standard."[49]

Second, even assuming that abortion prohibitions and regulations differentiate between men and women on the basis of sex, and therefore, are subject to a heightened standard of judicial review (intermediate scrutiny), both the Michigan Supreme Court and the United States Supreme Court have held that biological differences between men and women may justify different treatment based on those differences. For example, in *People v. McDonald*,[50] the Michigan Supreme Court rejected a constitutional challenge to a statute under which only men could be prosecuted and convicted of first-degree murder committed in the perpetration or attempted perpetration of a rape.[51] The supreme court observed that "if the classification as drawn in the first-degree murder statute violates equal protection, then most rape laws violate equal protection."[52] That conclusion, however, has been rejected by both state and federal courts.[53] The court added that, even under the proposed federal Equal Rights Amendment,[54] which would have made classifications based on sex suspect and subject to the highest standard of judicial review (strict scrutiny), "statutes proscribing rape by males would remain defensible because they are based on a biological fact unique to males. [Citation omitted]. The classes drawn are physiologically different and equal treatment is thus

---

48. *Doe*, 487 N.W.2d at 179; *Harris v. McRae*, 448 U.S. 297, 321–26 (1980).

49. *Bray v. Alexandria Women's Health Clinic*, 506 U.S. 263, 273 (1993).

50. 293 N.W.2d 588 (Mich. 1980).

51. *Id.* at 592–93.

52. *Id.* at 593.

53. *Id.* (citations omitted).

54. Section 2 of the proposed (but never ratified) federal Equal Rights Amendment provided: "Equality of rights under the law shall not be denied or abridged by the United States or any state on account of sex." S.J. Res. 8, 92nd Cong. (1971); H.J.R. 208, 92nd Cong. (1971).

not constitutionally required."[55] In a case upholding different treatment of mothers and fathers of children born out of wedlock, the Michigan Court of Appeals said, "Gender-based classifications will be upheld when men and women are not actually similarly situated in the area covered by the legislation in question and the statutory classification is realistically based on the differences in their situation."[56] So, too, in upholding a statutory rape statute that applied only to males, the Supreme Court noted, "this Court has consistently upheld statutes where the gender classification is not invidious, but rather realistically reflects the fact that the sexes are not similarly situated in certain circumstances."[57] As one federal district court observed: "Abortion statutes are examples of cases in which the sexes are not biologically similarly situated" because only women are capable of becoming pregnant and having abortions.[58]

A statute prohibiting abortion quite obviously can affect only women because only women are capable of becoming pregnant.[59] Unlike laws that use women's ability to become pregnant (or pregnancy itself) to discriminate against them in *other* areas (*e.g.*, employment opportunities), abortion prohibitions cannot fairly be said to involve a distinction between men and women that is a "mere pretext[] designed to erect an invidious discrimination against [women]."[60]

Retained Rights

Article I, §23, provides: "The enumeration in this constitution of certain rights shall not be construed to deny or disparage others retained by the People."[61] It is questionable whether art. I, §23, by itself, could provide a basis for invalidating §750.14. In *American Motorcycle Ass'n v. Dep't of State of Police*,[62] the court of appeals cited art. I, §23, together with several other state and federal constitutional provisions, in striking down the state motorcycle helmet law.[63] Other

---

55. *McDonald*, 293 N.W.2d at 592–93.

56. *In re RFF*, 617 N.W.2d 745, 756 (Mich. Ct. App. 2000).

57. *Michael M. v. Superior Court*, 450 U.S. 464, 469 (1981).

58. *Jane L. v. Bangerter*, 794 F. Supp. 1537, 1549 (D. Utah 1992).

59. *Geduldig v. Aiello*, 417 U.S. 484, 496 n. 20 (1974) ("[n]ormal pregnancy is an objectively, identifiable physical condition with unique characteristics").

60. *Id.*

61. MICH. CONST. art. I, §23 (West 2003).

62. 158 N.W.2d 72 (Mich. Ct. App. 1968).

63. *Id.* at 73 & n. 3.

than that one decision, which was later overruled,[64] § 23 has never been cited in any opinion invalidating any statute of the State of Michigan.[65]

The court of appeals has noted that art. I, § 23, is the "counterpart" to the Ninth Amendment,[66] which would normally call for a similar construction. That is consistent with the official comment to § 23: "This is a new section taken from the 9th amendment to the U.S. Constitution."[67] If so, § 23 is an unlikely source of an abortion right. The Supreme Court has rooted the "abortion liberty" in the liberty language of the Due Process Clause of the Fourteenth Amendment, not in the unenumerated rights language of the Ninth Amendment.[68] That art. I, § 23, cannot reasonably be interpreted to provide a source for a state right to abortion is evident also from a review of the proceedings of the Constitutional Convention. Delegate Stevens advised the Convention that art. I, § 23, had been proposed because "we cannot anticipate in any declaration of bill of rights all of the things which perhaps should be said."[69] "[W]e do not intend," he explained, "that the statements that we have made here as to the rights of our people shall be limited by the fact that we did not state something *which has always been considered such a right*."[70] In light of Michigan's historical treatment of abortion as a serious criminal offense (dating back 160 years), it cannot plausibly be argued that abortion is a "retained right" under art. I, § 23.

---

64. *See People v. Poucher*, 240 N.W.2d 298 (Mich. Ct. App. 1976), *aff'd*, 247 N.W.2d 798 (Mich. 1976).

65. In *People v. Kevorkian*, 639 N.W.2d 291 (Mich. Ct. App. 2001), the Michigan Court of Appeals affirmed Dr. Kevorkian's conviction for murder. The court declined to consider the defendant's argument that § 23 protects a right to euthanasia because the argument was not developed and cited no supporting authorities. *Id.* at 303.

66. *Id.* at 382–83, 388. The Ninth Amendment provides: "The enumeration in the Constitution of certain rights, shall not be construed to deny or disparage others retained by the people." U.S. Const. amend. IX (West 2006).

67. "Address to the People, What the Proposed New State Constitution Means to You," II Official Record at 3365. *See also* I Official Record at 470 (Committee on Declaration of Rights, Suffrage and Elections): "This language is taken from the ninth amendment to the Constitution of the United States."

68. *See Roe*, 410 U.S. at 153; *Casey*, 505 U.S. at 846. In any event, the Ninth Amendment, standing alone, is not a source of substantive rights. *Gibson v. Matthews*, 926 F.2d 532, 537 (6th Cir. 1991). Although "[s]ome unenumerated rights may be of [c]onstitutional magnitude," that is only "by virtue of other amendments, such as the Fifth or Fourteenth Amendment. A person cannot claim a right that exists solely under the Ninth Amendment." *United States v. Vital Health Products, Ltd.*, 786 F. Supp. 761, 777 (E.D. Wis. 1992), *aff'd mem. op., sub nom. United States v. LeBeau*, 985 F.2d 563 (7th Cir. 1993). *See also Charles v. Brown*, 495 F. Supp. 862, 863 (N.D. Ala. 1980) (same).

69. II Official Record at 569.

70. *Id.* (emphasis added).

Conclusion

Based on the foregoing analysis, an argument that the Michigan Constitution protects a right to abortion that is separate from, and independent of, the right to abortion recognized in *Roe v. Wade* would not likely succeed. That, in turn, suggests that if *Roe*, as modified by *Casey*, were ultimately overruled, the State of Michigan could enforce its pre-*Roe* statute *prohibiting* abortion (or enact and enforce a new statute prohibiting prohibition). Moreover, nothing in the Michigan Constitution precludes the State of Michigan from *regulating* abortion within federal constitutional limitations in the meantime.

CHAPTER 26

MINNESOTA

Summary

As the result of a decision by the Minnesota Supreme Court interpreting the Minnesota Constitution, the State of Minnesota could not prohibit any abortion before viability, or any abortion after viability that would be necessary to preserve the pregnant woman's life or health, even if *Roe v. Wade*,[1] as modified by *Planned Parenthood of Southeastern Pennsylvania v. Casey*,[2] were overruled, unless the state constitution is amended to overturn that decision (or that decision is overruled). Moreover, by virtue of that same decision, Minnesota may not restrict public funding of abortion. Whether the State may regulate abortion within current federal constitutional limits has not been determined.

Analysis

The principal pre-*Roe* abortion statute prohibited performance of an abortion on a pregnant woman unless the procedure was "necessary to preserve her life, or that of the child with which she [was] pregnant."[3] Another statute prohibited a woman from soliciting an abortion or allowing an abortion to be performed upon her (subject to the same exception).[4] Pursuant to *Roe v. Wade*,[5] §617.18 was declared unconstitutional (on federal, not state, grounds) in a pair of decisions by the Minnesota Supreme Court.[6] Sections 617.18 and 617.19 were later repealed.[7] Although it is not known at this time whether the Min-

---

1. 410 U.S. 113 (1973).
2. 505 U.S. 833 (1992).
3. MINN. STAT. ANN. §617.18 (West 1971).
4. *Id.* §617.19. No prosecutions were reported under this statute.
5. 410 U.S. 113 (1973).
6. *State v. Hultgren*, 204 N.W.2d 197 (Minn. 1973); *State v. Hodgson*, 204 N.W.2d 199 (Minn. 1971).
7. 1974 Minn. Laws 265, 268, ch. 177, §7

nesota Legislature would consider legislation prohibiting abortion if *Roe*, as modified by *Casey*, were overruled, the Minnesota Supreme Court probably would declare unconstitutional any prohibition of pre-viability abortions, or a prohibition of post-viability abortions that did not contain exceptions for the pregnant woman's life or health. That is apparent from a review of the state supreme court's decision striking down, on state constitutional grounds, restrictions on public funding of abortion.

In *Women of the State of Minnesota v. Gomez*,[8] the Minnesota Supreme Court considered a challenge to state statutes and administrative regulations that limited public funding of abortion to those for which federal reimbursement was available under federal law (life-of-the-mother, rape and incest).[9] A majority of the court held that the statutes and rules violated an implied right of privacy guaranteed by the state constitution.[10] The right of privacy was derived from art. I, §§ 2, 7 and 10 of the state constitution.[11] Section 2 provides, in part: "No member of this state shall be disfranchised or deprived of any of the rights or privileges secured to any citizen thereof, unless by the law of the land or the judgment of his peers."[12] Section 7 provides, in relevant part: "No person shall be held to answer for a criminal offense without due process of law ... nor be deprived of life, liberty or property without due process of law."[13] And § 10 provides, in pertinent part: "The right of the people to be secure in their persons, homes, papers and effects, against unreasonable searches and seizures shall not be violated.... [14]

The Minnesota Supreme Court first recognized a right of privacy under the Minnesota Constitution in *State v. Gray*.[15] Although the state supreme court did not specify in *Gray* which provisions of the state Bill of Rights secured the right, in a later case the court rooted the right of privacy in art. I, §§ 1, 2 and 10.[16] In *Jarvis*, the court announced that the right of privacy "begins with pro-

---

8. 542 N.W.2d 17 (Minn. 1995).

9. MINN. STAT. ANN. §§ 256B.0625, subd. 16, 256B.40, 261.28, 393.07, subd. 11 (West 1994); Minn. Rules 9505.0220(q), 9505.0235, subpart 2 (1993).

10. *Women of the State of Minnesota*, 542 N.W.2d at 32.

11. *Id.* at 19.

12. MINN. CONST. art. I, § 2 (1976).

13. *Id.* § 7.

14. *Id.* § 10.

15. 413 N.W.2d 107, 111 (Minn. 1987) ("it is our opinion that there does exist a right of privacy guaranteed under and protected by the Minnesota Bill of Rights").

16. *Jarvis v. Levine*, 418 N.W.2d 139, 148 (Minn. 1988). Section 1 provides: "Government is instituted for the security, benefit and protection of the people...." MINN. CONST. art. I, § 1 (1976).

tecting the integrity of one's own body and includes the right not to have it altered or invaded without consent."[17] In *Women of the State of Minnesota*, the court noted that "the right of privacy protects only fundamental rights, and therefore 'a law must impermissibly infringe upon a fundamental right before it will be declared unconstitutional as violative of the right of privacy.'"[18] "Fundamental rights," in turn, "are those 'which have their origin in the express terms of the Constitution or which are necessarily to be implied from those terms.'"[19]

In the funding case, the plaintiffs alleged and the State conceded that the state constitution protects a woman's right to choose to have an abortion.[20] The court supreme agreed with this concession, stating that "[t]he right of procreation without state interference has long been recognized as 'one of the basic civil rights of man ... fundamental to the very existence and survival of the race.'"[21] The court then elaborated on the importance of this right:

> We can think of few decisions more intimate, personal, and profound that a woman's decision between childbirth and abortion. Indeed, this decision is of such great import that it governs whether the woman will undergo extreme physical and psychological changes and whether she will create lifelong attachments and responsibilities.[22]

The court determined that "the right of privacy under the Minnesota Constitution encompasses a woman's right to decide to terminate her pregnancy."[23] Moreover, "any legislation infringing on the decision-making process ... violates this fundamental right."[24]

The court considered the impact of the funding restrictions on poor women and concluded that they infringe on their right of privacy:

> In the present case, the infringement is the state's offer of money to women for health care services necessary to carry the pregnancy to term, and the state's ban on health care funding for women who choose therapeutic abortions. Faced with these two options, financially independent women might not feel particularly compelled to choose either childbirth or abortion based on the monetary incentive alone.

---

17. *Jarvis*, 418 N.W.2d at 148.
18. 542 N.W.2d at 27 (quoting *Gray*, 413 N.W.2d at 111).
19. *Id.* (quoting *Gray*, 413 N.W.2d at 111).
20. *Id.*
21. *Id.* (quoting *Skinner v. Oklahoma ex rel. Williamson*, 316 U.S. 535, 541 (1942)).
22. *Id.*
23. *Id.*
24. *Id.* at 31.

Indigent women, on the other hand, are precisely the ones who would be most affected by an offer of monetary assistance, and it is these women who are targeted by the statutory funding ban. We simply cannot say that an indigent woman's decision whether to terminate her pregnancy is not significantly impacted by the state's offer of comprehensive medical services if the woman carries the pregnancy to term. We conclude, therefore, that these statutes constitute an infringement on the fundamental right of privacy.[25]

Because the funding restrictions "infringe on the fundamental right of privacy, we subject them to strict scrutiny."[26] Based on Minnesota's public policy of favoring childbirth over abortion,[27] the State argued that the funding restrictions were justified by its interest in "the preservation of potential human life and the encouragement and support of childbirth."[28] The supreme court, however, found that this interest was not compelling until viability:

[A] woman's right of privacy encompasses her decision whether to choose health care services necessary to terminate or to continue a pregnancy without interference from the state, "at least until such time as the state's important interest in protecting the potentiality of human life predominates over the right of privacy, which is usually at viability."[29]

Because the challenged provisions "apply at all stages of pregnancy, including prior to viability," the court concluded that "they do not withstand strict scrutiny, and thus must be invalidated."[30] "The statutory scheme, as it exists,

---

25. *Id.* In so concluding, the court answered the question it posed earlier in the opinion, to wit, "whether, having elected to participate in a medical assistance program, the state may selectively exclude from such benefits otherwise eligible persons solely because they make constitutionally protected health care decisions with which the state disagrees." *Id.* at 28.

26. *Id.* at 31 (citing *Skeen v. State*, 505 N.W.2d 299, 312 (Minn. 1993) ("if the challenged statute ... impinges upon a fundamental right explicitly or implicitly protected by the Constitution.... strict scrutiny will apply, and the state will have to prove that the statute is necessary to a compelling government interest")).

27. "Between normal childbirth and abortion it is the policy of the state of Minnesota that normal childbirth is to be given preference, encouragement and support by law and by state action, it being in the best interests of the well being and common good of Minnesota citizens." MINN. STAT. ANN. § 256B.011 (West 1994).

28. *Women of the State of Minnesota*, 542 N.W.2d at 31.

29. *Id.* (quoting *State v. Merrill*, 450 N.W.2d 318, 322 (Minn. 1990)).

30. *Id.* at 32.

takes the decision from the hands of [Medicaid-eligible] women in a manner that, in light of the protections afforded by our own constitution, we simply cannot condone."[31]

The Minnesota Supreme Court's decision in *Women of the State of Minnesota* leaves little doubt that the Minnesota Legislature could not prohibit any abortion before viability, or any abortion after viability that would be necessary to preserve the life or health of the pregnant woman, even if *Roe*, as modified by *Casey*, were overruled unless the state constitution is amended. The court's recognition of a woman's right to choose abortion as a fundamental state constitutional right would override the State's interest in protecting unborn human life, at least until viability, because that interest, in the court's view, does not become compelling until viability.[32] The state supreme court's adoption of the "strict scrutiny" standard of judicial review for abortion regulations would seem to place other state regulations of abortion in jeopardy.[33] Nevertheless, no state constitutional challenges have been brought to date to state laws regulating abortion.

Conclusion

Because of the Minnesota Supreme Court's decision in *Women of the State of Minnesota v. Gomez*, the State of Minnesota could not prohibit abortions, at least before viability, even if *Roe*, as modified by *Casey*, were overruled, unless the state constitution is amended to overturn the holding in *Women of the State of Minnesota* (or the latter is overruled). Moreover, Minnesota may not restrict public funding of abortion. Whether the State may otherwise regulate abortion within current federal constitutional limits has not been determined, but is questionable in light of the decision in *Women of the State of Minnesota*.

---

31. *Id.*

32. The Supreme Court has not decided whether a statute prohibiting post-viability abortions must make exceptions for mental, as well as physical, health reasons. *See Voinovich v. Women's Medical Professional Corporation*, 523 U.S. 1036, 1039 (1998) (Thomas, J., dissenting from denial of *certiorari*) (noting that this issue was not addressed in *Doe v. Bolton*, 410 U.S. 179 (1973), the companion case to *Roe v. Wade*). As a result, it is not known whether, as a matter of *state* constitutional law, the Minnesota Supreme Court would require a post-viability statute to contain a mental health exception. Under current state law, a post-viability abortion may be performed if the procedure is necessary to preserve the life or health of the pregnant woman. MINN. STAT. ANN. § 145.412 subd. 3 (West 2005). The statute does not define the scope of the health exception.

33. *See, e.g.*, MINN. STAT. ANN. § 145.4241 *et seq.* (West 2005) (requiring informed consent); § 144.343, subd. 2-subd. 7 (West 2005) (requiring parental notice).

CHAPTER 27

MISSISSIPPI

Summary

As the result of a decision of the Mississippi Supreme Court interpreting the Mississippi Constitution, the State of Mississippi could not prohibit any abortion before viability, or any abortion after viability that would be necessary to preserve the pregnant woman's life or health, even if *Roe v. Wade*,[1] as modified by *Planned Parenthood of Southeastern Pennsylvania v. Casey*,[2] were overruled, unless the state constitution is amended to overturn that decision (or that decision is overruled). The State, however, may regulate abortion within current federal constitutional limits.

Analysis

Mississippi has not expressly repealed its pre-*Roe* abortion statute, which prohibits performance of an abortion on a woman unless the procedure is "necessary to preserve her life," or when the pregnancy is caused by rape.[3] More recently, the Mississippi Legislature re-enacted the pre-*Roe* abortion prohibition, but converted the prohibition into a "trigger" law that would take effect when *Roe v. Wade* is overruled.[4] Nevertheless, in light of the Mississippi Supreme Court's decision in *Pro-Choice Mississippi v. Fordice*,[5] § 97-3-3 (and the "trigger" law) could not be enforced even if *Roe*, as modified by *Casey*, were overruled, unless the state constitution is amended (or *Pro-Choice Mississippi* is overruled).

Pro-Choice Mississippi was a declaratory judgment action challenging the constitutionality of the Mississippi statutes mandating informed consent (as well

---

1. 410 U.S. 113 (1973).
2. 505 U.S. 833 (1992).
3. MISS. CODE ANN. § 97-3-3 (2005).
4. S.B. 2391, §§ 2, 4, 2007 Leg. Sess. (Miss. 2007).
5. 716 So.2d 645 (Miss. 1998).

as a short waiting period)[6] and parental consent.[7] In *Pro-Choice Mississippi*, a bare majority of the Mississippi Supreme Court held that the unenumerated rights provision of the state constitution protects a right of privacy which, in turn, includes an implied right to obtain an abortion.[8] Article 3, §32 provides: "The enumeration of rights in this constitution shall not be construed to deny and impair other rights retained by, and inherent in, the people."[9]

In *Pro-Choice Mississippi*, the State argued that a right to abortion could not be derived from the Mississippi Constitution because abortion was illegal at the time the constitution was adopted and because the constitution itself was silent on the issue of abortion.[10] The majority opinion rejected both arguments.

With respect to the former argument (illegality of abortion), the court noted that at the time the state constitution was adopted in 1890, abortion was illegal only after "quickening," that stage of pregnancy when the pregnant woman first detects fetal movement.[11] "Thus, at the time the Mississippi Constitution was adopted, abortion was legal until quickening, some four to five months into pregnancy."[12] Accordingly, the court rejected the State's argument that "the framers intended to preclude protection of abortion...."[13]

With respect to the latter argument (silence of the constitution on the issue of abortion), the court acknowledged that "[t]he Mississippi Constitution does not explicitly deny or grant the right to an abortion."[14] Nevertheless, the state constitution has been interpreted to "provid[e] for a right to privacy and the right to one's choices concerning one's body, despite the Constitution's silence on that issue."[15] This right, "whether founded in common law or natural law, is constitutionally guaranteed under Article 3, §32 of the Mississippi Constitution."[16] The right of privacy protects "autonomous bodily integrity," which,

---

6. Miss. Code Ann. §41-41-33 (2007), as amended by S.B. 2391, §3 (requiring woman seeking an abortion to be given the opportunity to view an ultrasound image of the unborn child and hear the child's heartbeat if the heartbeat is audible).

7. *Id.* §41-41-51 *et seq.*, as amended by S.B. 2391, §1 (requiring "clear and convincing evidence" of maturity or best interests in a judicial bypass hearing).

8. *Pro-Choice Mississippi*, 716 So.2d at 650–54 (citing Miss. Const. art. 3, §32 (2005)).

9. Miss. Const. art. 3, §32 (2005).

10. *Pro-Choice Mississippi*, 716 So.2d at 650, 651–52.

11. *Id.* at 650–5 (citing Miss. Code §2884 (1880)). Fetal movement is usually detected between sixteen and eighteen weeks gestation.

12. *Id.* at 651.

13. *Id.*

14. *Id.* at 652.

15. *Id.* (citing *In re Brown*, 478 So.2d 1033 (Miss. 1985)).

16. *Id.* at 653 (citations omitted).

the court held, includes "an implicit right to have an abortion."[17] "Just as the United States Supreme Court has recognized that the federal constitutional right to privacy protects a woman's right to terminate her pregnancy, we find that the state constitutional right to privacy includes an implied right to choose whether or not to have an abortion."[18]

Having determined that the state constitution includes an implied right to have an abortion, the court had to decide what standard of judicial review applies to abortion regulations under the state constitution. Although the Mississippi Supreme Court has applied the "strict scrutiny" standard in other privacy cases,[19] the court determined that such a standard would be inappropriate in the context of abortion and, instead, chose the "undue burden" standard articulated in *Casey*.[20] The court explained:

> The abortion issue is much more complex than most cases involving privacy rights. We are placed in the precarious position of both protecting a woman's right to terminate her pregnancy before viability and protecting unborn life. In an attempt to create a workable framework out of these diametrically opposed positions, we adopt the well reasoned decision in *Casey*, applying the undue burden standard to analyze laws restricting abortion.[21]

Applying the "undue burden" standard, the court upheld both the informed consent and parental consent statutes.[22]

The Mississippi Supreme Court's adoption of the "undue burden" standard of judicial review as a matter of state constitutional analysis would clearly preclude the State of Mississippi from enforcing §97-3-3 (as amended by the "trigger" law) if *Roe*, as modified by *Casey*, is overruled, unless the state constitution is amended to overturn the holding in *Pro-Choice Mississippi*.[23] The State, however, may regulate abortion to the extent permitted by *Casey*.

---

17. *Id.*

18. *Id.* at 654.

19. *Id.* (citing *In re Brown* and *Mississippi Employment Security Comm'n v. McGlothin*, 556 So.2d 324 (Miss. 1990)).

20. *Id.* at 654–55.

21. *Id.* at 655.

22. *Id.* at 655–60.

23. The Supreme Court has not yet decided whether a statute prohibiting post-viability abortions must make exceptions for mental, as well as physical, health. *See Voinovich v. Women's Medical Professional Corporation*, 523 U.S. 1036, 1039 (1998) (Thomas, J., dis-

Conclusion

Because of the Mississippi Supreme Court's decision in *Pro-Choice Mississippi v. Fordice*, the State of Mississippi could not enforce § 97-3-3 (or the "trigger" law), even if *Roe*, as modified by *Casey*, were overruled, unless the state constitution is amended to overturn the holding in *Pro-Choice Mississippi* (or the latter is overruled). The State may, however, regulate abortion within federal constitutional limits in the meantime.

---

senting from denial of *certiorari*) (noting that this issue was not addressed in *Doe v. Bolton*, 410 U.S. 179 (1973), the companion case to *Roe v. Wade*). As a result, it is not known whether, as a matter of *state* constitutional law, the Mississippi Supreme Court would require a post-viability statute to contain a mental health exception. Mississippi does not presently have a post-viability statute.

CHAPTER 28

MISSOURI

Summary

The Missouri Supreme Court has not yet decided whether the Missouri Constitution protects a right to abortion separate from, and independent of, the right to abortion recognized under the United States Constitution.[1] A careful examination of the state constitution, in light of its history and interpretation, as well as other relevant legal sources, however, suggests that the state supreme court probably would not recognize a state constitutional right to abortion. Thus, if *Roe v. Wade*,[2] as modified by *Planned Parenthood of Southeastern Pennsylvania v. Casey*,[3] were overruled, Missouri could enact a statute prohibiting abortion. Moreover, nothing in the state constitution, properly understood, precludes the State from enacting and enforcing reasonable measures regulating abortion within current federal constitutional limits.

Analysis

The principal pre-*Roe* Missouri abortion statute prohibited performance of an abortion upon a pregnant woman unless the procedure was "necessary to preserve her life or that of an unborn child."[4] Pursuant to *Roe*, § 599.100 was

---

1. The state supreme court has held, however, that neither the natural rights provision of the state constitution (art. I, § 2), nor the state due process guarantee (art. I, § 10) should be construed any more broadly, with respect to abortion, than the Due Process Clause of the Fourteenth Amendment. *Reproductive Health Services of Planned Parenthood of the St. Louis Region, Inc. v. Nixon*, 185 S.W.3d 685, 692 (Mo. 2006) (statute mandating twenty-four hour waiting period for abortion does not violate the due process clause of the state constitution or state constitutional rights to liberty and privacy).

2. 410 U.S. 113 (1973).

3. 505 U.S. 833 (1992).

4. Mo. ANN. STAT. § 599.100 (Vernon 1969). If the abortion resulted in the death of either the pregnant woman or a "quick child," the offense was classified as manslaughter, oth-

declared unconstitutional (on federal, not state, grounds) and its enforcement permanently enjoined in an unreported decision of a three-judge federal court.[5] The statute was later repealed.[6]

Based upon arguments that have been raised in Missouri and other States with similar constitutional provisions, possible sources for an asserted abortion right could include provisions of the Bill of Rights guaranteeing religious freedom (art. I, §5), a certain remedy (§14), due process of law (§10) and equal rights (§2); recognizing natural rights (§2), political power in the people (§1) and the right of the people to alter or abolish the form of government (§3); and prohibiting religious "preferences" (§7).[7] The analysis that follows addresses each of these provisions.

Religious Freedom, Prohibiting Religious "Preferences"

Article I, §5, of the Missouri Constitution provides, in part, that "all men have a natural and indefeasible right to worship Almighty God according to the dictates of their own consciences," and that "no human authority can control or interfere with the rights of conscience...."[8] Article I, §7, provides, in part, that "no preferences shall be given to ... any church, sect or creed of religion...."[9]

In any challenge to a statute prohibiting abortion, abortion advocates may raise either or both of two arguments under art. I, §§5 and 7. First, they may argue that an abortion prohibition interferes with a woman's "rights of conscience" under art. I, §5, by forbidding her from obtaining an abortion that would be

---

erwise it was treated as "the felony of abortion." *Id.* A "quick" child, under Missouri law, meant a child who had "quickened." "Quickening" is that stage of pregnancy, usually sixteen to eighteen weeks gestation, when the pregnant woman first detects fetal movement. A separate statute prohibited the "willful killing of an unborn quick child (by any injury to the mother of such child) which would be murder if resulted in the death of such mother," and punished the offense as manslaughter. *Id.* §599.090.

5. *Rodgers v. Danforth*, Civ. No. 18360-2 (W.D. Mo. May 18, 1973), *aff'd*, 414 U.S. 1035 (1973). In its original decision, decided before *Roe*, the same three-judge court dismissed the challenge to the law on abstention grounds. *Rodgers v. Danforth*, Civ. No. 18360-2 (W.D. Mo. Sep. 10, 1970), *vacated and remanded*, 410 U.S. 949 (1973).

6. 1977 Mo. Laws 658, 662–63.

7. Two other more unlikely sources of an abortion right under the Missouri Constitution-art. I, §8 (guaranteeing freedom of speech) and §15 (prohibiting unreasonable searches and seizures)-are discussed generally in Chapter 3, *supra.*

8. Mo. CONST. art. I, §5 (West 2003).

9. *Id.* art. I, §7.

allowed by her religion. Second, they may argue in the alternative (or in addition) that an abortion prohibition constitutes a "preference" in favor of a "church, sect or creed of religion" within the meaning of art. I, §7, because it reflects sectarian beliefs regarding when human life begins and the sinfulness of abortion. Neither argument is likely to prevail.

Apart from school aid issues,[10] which are not implicated in an abortion prohibition, the religion clauses of the Missouri Constitution have generally been construed in a manner similar to that of the Free Exercise and Establishment Clauses of the First Amendment.[11] The similarity of construction suggests that a challenge to an abortion statute that would not succeed under the Religion Clauses of the First Amendment would not succeed under art. I, §5, or art. I, §7, either. For the reasons set forth in Chapter 2, *supra*, an abortion statute could not be successfully challenged on First Amendment grounds. Accordingly, a similar challenge under art. I, §5, or art. I, §7, would not likely be successful.[12]

---

10. *See Paster v. Tussey*, 512 S.W.2d 97, 101–02 (Mo. 1974) (noting, with reference to school aid issues, that "the provisions of the Missouri Constitution declaring that there shall be a separation of church and state are not only more explicit but more restrictive than the Establishment Clause [of the First Amendment] of the United States Constitution"). *See also Oliver v. State Tax Comm'n of Missouri*, 37 S.W.3d 243, 251 (Mo. Ct. App. 2001) (identifying "the focus on prohibiting state resources to the promotion of religion [in the first clause of art. I, §7]" as "[o]ne point of difference in particularity with the United States Constitution").

11. *See Boone v. State*, 147 S.W.3d 801, 805–06 (Mo. Ct. App. 2004) (upholding state sexual offender registration program); *Oliver v. State Tax Comm'n*, 37 S.W.3d at 247–52 (upholding requirement that state tax returns be signed under oath or affirmation) *See also Clayton by Clayton v. Place*, 884 F.2d 376, 381 (8th Cir. 1989) (construing Establishment Clause and art. I, §7, together).

12. Entirely apart from the Missouri courts' reliance on federal precedent in interpreting art. I, §5, and art. I, §7, an argument challenging an abortion prohibition on the basis that it gives a "preference" to religion by embodying sectarian views regarding the sinfulness of abortion would appear to be foreclosed by decisions of the Missouri Supreme Court rejecting challenges to a Sunday closing laws. *See Komen v. City of St. Louis*, 289 S.W. 838, 842 (Mo. 1926); *State v. Chicago, B. & Q. Railroad Co.*, 143 S.W. 785, 786 (Mo. 1912). In the former case, the state supreme court held that St. Louis could adopt an ordinance requiring nonessential businesses to close one day a week, even if "the one selected be regarded by a great majority of the people as one of particular sanctity." 289 S.W. at 842. If mandating a day of rest on Sunday does not violate the "rights of conscience" protected by art. I, §5, or the anti-preference language of art. I, §7, even though it may coincide with sectarian beliefs regarding the Christian Sabbath, then neither would a law prohibiting abortion, regardless of whether the law coincides with religious views regarding the sinfulness of abortion.

Certain Remedy

Article I, § 14, of the Missouri Constitution provides, in part, that "the courts of justice shall be open to every person, and certain remedy afforded for every injury to person, property or character…."[13] Abortion advocates might argue that a statute prohibiting abortion interferes with a woman's control over her own body, and that such interference constitutes an "injury" to her "person," as those terms are used in § 14, for which there must be a "certain remedy." That "remedy," in turn, would be invalidation of the statute. This argument assumes that art. I, § 14, confers substantive rights. The case law is clear, however, that it does not.

Section 14, the Missouri Court of Appeals has explained, "was never intended to create rights but to protect citizens in enforcing rights recognized by law."[14] More than one hundred twenty-five years ago, the Missouri Supreme Court held that the "certain remedy" provision "means only that for such wrongs as are recognized by the law of the land, the courts shall be open and afford a remedy."[15] If the Legislature determines that certain conduct (*e.g.*, abortion) shall be illegal, then, of course, there is there is no "legally cognizable" right to engage in such conduct and, therefore, no "injury" for which § 14 mandates a remedy. Because art. I, § 14, is not a source of substantive rights, it could not provide a basis for invalidating an otherwise constitutional statute of the State.[16]

Due Process of Law, Natural Rights

Article I, § 10, of the Missouri Constitution provides that "no person shall be deprived of life, liberty or property without due process of law."[17] Article I, § 2, provides, in part, that "all persons have a natural right to life, liberty, the pursuit of happiness and the enjoyment of the gains of their own industry…."[18]

---

13. Mo. Const. art. I, § 14 (West 2003).

14. *Horner v. David Distributing Co.*, 599 S.W.2d 100, 102 (Mo. Ct. App. 1980) (citing, among other cases, *Schulte v. Missionaries of La Salette Corp. of Missouri*, 352 S.W.2d 636, 641 (Mo. 1961) ("Section 14 … was never intended to create rights, but merely to protect citizens in enforcing rights recognized by the law, without discrimination")).

15. *Landis v. Campbell*, 79 Mo. 433, 439 (1883) (construing predecessor section to § 14).

16. It should not be surprising to note, therefore, that no criminal statute has ever been struck down on the authority of the "certain remedy" language of art. I, § 14.

17. Mo. Const. art. I, § 10 (West 2003).

18. *Id.* art. I, § 2.

In any challenge to an abortion prohibition that Missouri may enact, abortion advocates are most likely to rely upon art. I, §1, and art. I, §19, arguing that the prohibition interferes with a pregnant woman's "liberty" interest in obtaining an abortion. Such an argument probably would not succeed, however.

The Missouri Supreme Court, as previously noted, has held that neither the natural rights provision of the state constitution (art. I, §2), nor the state due process guarantee (art. I, §10) should be construed any more broadly, with respect to abortion, than the Due Process Clause of the Fourteenth Amendment.[19] This holding suggests that the court would not recognize a right to abortion if the Supreme Court overrules *Roe*, as modified by *Casey*. Even in the absence of an overruling decision, however, it is unlikely that the Missouri Supreme Court would recognize a right to abortion that is separate from, and independent of, the right to abortion recognized in *Roe*.

In determining whether an asserted liberty interest (or right) should be regarded as "fundamental" for purposes of substantive due process analysis under the Fourteenth Amendment (infringement of which would call for strict scrutiny review), the Supreme Court applies a two-part test. First, there must be a "careful description" of the asserted fundamental liberty interest.[20] Second, the interest, so described, must be firmly rooted in "the Nation's history, legal traditions, and practices."[21] *Id.* at 710. The Missouri Supreme Court applies the same test in determining whether an asserted liberty interest (or right) should be regarded as "fundamental" under the state constitution.[22]

---

19. *See* n. 1, *supra*.

20. *Washington v. Glucksberg*, 521 U.S. 702, 721 (1997) (citation and internal quotation marks omitted).

21. *Id.* at 710. To the extent that the Missouri Supreme Court considers federal precedent in determining whether an asserted liberty interest (or right) is "fundamental" under the state due process guarantee, abortion would not qualify as a "fundamental" right. Although the Supreme Court characterized the right to choose abortion as "fundamental" in *Roe*, 410 U.S. at 152–53, it tacitly abandoned that characterization in *Casey*, 505 U.S. at 869–79 (Joint Op. of O'Connor, Kennedy and Souter, JJ., replacing *Roe's* "strict scrutiny" standard of review with the more relaxed "undue burden" standard, allowing for a broader measure of abortion regulation).

22. *Doe v. Phillips*, 194 S.W.3d 833, 842–43 (Mo. 2006) (citing *Glucksberg* in support of decision upholding statute requiring registration of sex offenders); *State ex rel. Nixon v. Powell*, 167 S.W.3d 702, 705 (Mo. 2005) (applying same standard in upholding statute requiring reimbursement of the costs of inmate's care during incarceration); *In re Marriage of Woodson*, 92 S.W.3d 780, 783 (Mo. 2003) (following *Glucksberg*). Apart from the "liberty" language set forth in art. I, §§2 and 10, which is discussed in the text, it is not likely that the state supreme court would rely on a state constitutional right of privacy to invalidate an abortion prohibition. In *Barber v. Time, Inc.*, 159 S.W.2d 291 (Mo. 1942), the Missouri

A right to abortion is not "firmly rooted" in the State's "history, legal traditions, and practices." Missouri enacted its first abortion statute in 1825, only four years after being admitted to the Union. The statute prohibited anyone from "wilfully and maliciously" administering or causing to be administered "any poison, or other noxious, poisonous or destructive substance or liquid, with an intention ... to cause or procure the miscarriage of any woman then being with child...."[23] This statute was replaced with the enactment of a new criminal code in 1835 that contained three provisions relating to abortion and the killing of an unborn child. The first provision prohibited "[t]he wilful killing of any unborn quick child, by any injury to the mother of such child, which would be murder if it resulted in the death of said mother," and punished the offense as "manslaughter in the first degree."[24] The second provision prohibited anyone from administering "to any woman pregnant with a quick child, any medicine drug or substance whatever," or using or employing "any instrument or other means, with intent thereby to destroy such child, unless the same shall have been necessary to preserve the life of such mother, or shall have been advised by a physician to be necessary for that purpose...."[25] This was deemed "manslaughter in the second degree.[26] The third provision prohibited a physician or any other person from "wilfully" administering "to any pregnant woman, any medicine, drug, substance or thing whatever," or using or employing "any instrument of means whatsoever, with intent thereby to procure abortion, or the miscarriage of any such woman, unless the same shall have been necessary to preserve the life of such woman, or shall have been advised by a physician to be necessary for that purpose...."[27] This offense was punishable

---

Supreme Court stated that a right of privacy may grow out of a state constitutional right to liberty and the pursuit of happiness. *Id.* at 294. *Barber* recognized a common law cause of action for invasion of privacy based upon the unauthorized publication of personal medical information in a weekly news magazine. *Barber* involved *informational* privacy, and the state supreme court has refused to extend its reach to embrace *conduct*. *See Cruzan by Cruzan v. Harmon*, 760 S.W.2d 408, 417 n. 13 (Mo. 1988) (noting that *Barber* "provides protection against the publication of private facts and springs from the well-known tort of invasion of privacy," but holding that the decision is "inapplicable in cases involving decisions of personal autonomy"), *aff'd sub nom. Cruzan v. Director, Missouri Dep't of Health*, 497 U.S. 261 (1990). *See also State v. Walsh*, 713 S.W.2d 508, 513 (Mo. 1986) (declining to recognize an unfettered right of privacy).

23. Act of Jan. 14, 1825, §12, DIGEST OF LAWS OF MISSOURI, Vol. 1, p. 283 (1825).
24. Act of March 20, 1835, art. II, §9.
25. *Id.* art, II, §10.
26. *Id.*
27. *Id.* art. II, §36.

"by imprisonment in a county jail not exceeding one year, or by a fine not exceeding five hundred dollars, or by both such fine and imprisonment."[28] These three provisions, variously amended, remained on the books until 1907,[29] when pre-quickening abortion was reclassified as a felony.[30] The separate abortion offenses were combined into one offense and, along with the offense for the willful killing of an unborn child (by an injury to the mother), remained on the books until after *Roe v. Wade* was decided.[31]

Prior to *Roe v. Wade*, the Missouri reviewing courts regularly affirmed abortion convictions (and manslaughter convictions based upon the death of the woman resulting from an illegal abortion) without any hint that either the prosecutions or convictions violated the state constitution.[32] On October 3, 1972, only a few months before *Roe* was decided, the Missouri Supreme Court rejected a federal constitutional challenge to § 599.100. In *Rodgers v. Danforth*,[33] the state supreme court held that the statute was not unconstitutionally vague, that it did not violate the rights of privacy of pregnant women or deny them equal protection of the laws or due process of law and that the statute did not

---

28. *Id.*

29. Act of March 20, 1835, art. II, §§ 9, 10, 36, Mo. Rev. Stat., pp. 168–69, 172 (1835); Act of March 27, 1845, art. II, §§ 9, 10, 39, Mo. Rev. Stat., pp. 180, 183 (1845); Act of Dec. 8, 1855, art. II, §§ 9, 10, 40, Mo. Rev. Stat., pp. 560–61, 567–68 (1855), *recodified at* Mo. Gen. Stat. ch. 200, §§ 9, 10, 34 (1866), *recodified at* Mo. Rev. Stat. §§ 1240, 1241, 1268 (1879), *recodified at* Mo. Rev. Stat. §§ 3467, 3468, 3495 (1889), *recodified at* Mo. Rev. Stat. §§ 1824, 1825, 1853 (1899).

30. Act of March 20, 1907, 1907 Mo. Laws, p. 230, *codified as* Mo. Rev. Stat. §§ 4457, 4458, 4459 (1909). The Act restated § 1824, expressly repealed § 1825 and replaced it with a new section, and repealed by implication § 1853 and replaced it with a new section. *See State ex rel Gaston v. Shields*, 130 S.W. 298, 299–300 (Mo. 1910) (explaining changes effected by the Act of March 20, 1907).

31. Mo. Rev. Stat. §§ 3238, 3239 (1919), *recodified at* Mo. Rev. Stat. § 3990, 3991 (1929), *recodified at* Mo. Rev. Stat. § 4384, 4385 (1942), *recodified at* Mo. Stat. Ann. § 559.090, 550.100 (Vernon 1969), *repealed by* 1977 Mo. Laws 658, 662–63.

32. *State v. Edmonson*, 33 S.W. 17 (Mo. 1895); *State v. McLeod*, 37 S.W. 298 (Mo. 1896); *State v. Dean*, 85 Mo. App. 473 (1900); *State v. Hogan*, 100 S.W. 528 (Mo. Ct. App. 1907); *State v. Aitken*, 144 S.W. 499 (Mo. 1912); *State v. Hawkins*, 210 S.W. 4 (Mo. 1919); *State v. Steele*, 217 S.W. 80 (Mo. 1919); *State v. Johnson*, 246 S.W. 894 (Mo. 1922); *State v. Harmon*, 278 S.W. 733 (Mo. 1925); *State v. Futrell*, 46 S.W.2d 588 (Mo. 1931); *State v. Gunther*, 169 S.W.2d 404 (Mo. 1943); *State v. Fitzgerald*, 174 S.W.2d 211 (Mo. 1943); *State v. Seddon*, 208 S.W.2d 212 (Mo. 1948); *State v. Miller*, 261 S.W.2d 103 (Mo. 1953); *State v. Hacker*, 291 S.W.2d 155 (Mo. 1956); *State v. Stillman*, 301 S.W.2d 830 (Mo. 1957); *State v. Scown*, 312 S.W.2d 782 (Mo. 1958); *State v. Siekermann*, 367 S.W.2d 643 (Mo. 1963); *State v. Steele*, 445 S.W.2d 636 (Mo. 1969); *State v. Robinson*, 420 S.W.2d 272 (Mo. 1967).

33. 486 S.W.2d 258 (Mo. 1972).

constitute "an establishment of religion."[34] In *Rodgers*, the parties stipulated that "unborn children have all the qualities and attributes of adult human persons, differing only in age or maturity," and that, "[m]edically, human life is a continuum from conception to death."[35] Based upon this stipulation and the Supreme Court's then recent decision in *Furman v. Georgia*,[36] striking down the death penalty, as applied, the Missouri Supreme Court said that it "anticipate[d] at least equal solicitude for the lives of innocents," and upheld the statute.[37] The state supreme court's decision in *Rodgers* rejecting a multi-faceted *federal* constitutional challenge to § 599.100 suggest, at a minimum, that the court would not likely accept a *state* constitutional challenge to an abortion prohibition.

Subsequent to *Roe*, the State of Missouri adopted a strong public policy in favor of childbirth over abortion:

> It is the intention of the general assembly of the state of Missouri to grant the right to life to all humans, born and unborn, and to regulate abortion to the full extent permitted by the Constitution of the United States, decisions of the United States Supreme Court, and federal statutes.[38]

Consistent with that policy, Missouri has enacted a comprehensive scheme of abortion regulation.[39]

---

34. *Id.* at 259.

35. *Id.*

36. 408 U.S. 238 (1972).

37. *Rodgers*, 486 S.W.2d at 259.

38. Mo. Stat. Ann. § 188.010 (West 2004).

39. *Id.* §§ 188.027, 188.039 (West 2004) (mandating informed consent and a twenty-four hour waiting period); § 188.028 (requiring parental consent and a twenty-four hour waiting period); § 188.250 (West Supp. 2007) (prohibiting persons from aiding or assisting minors in obtaining an abortion without the parental consent required by law); § 197.032 (West 2004) (recognizing individual and institutional rights of conscience); §§ 188.100 through 188.120 (prohibiting discrimination against persons who object to abortion); §§ 188.205, 188.210, 188.215 (restricting public funding of abortion for indigent women, performance of abortions by public employees in their official capacity and the use of public facilities for the performance of abortions); § 188.043 (mandating minimum levels of medical malpractice insurance for physicians performing abortions); § 188.030 (West Supp. 2007) (requiring physicians performing abortions to have surgical privileges at a nearby hospital that offers obstetrical or gynecological care); § 376.805 (West 2002) (no health insurance policy may provide coverage for elective abortions except by an optional rider for which an additional premium must be paid).

Apart from the State's policy of regulating abortion to the fullest extent permitted by federal law, the Missouri General Assembly has found that "[t]he life of each human being begins at conception[;]" that [u]nborn children have protectable interests in life, health, and well being[;]" and that "[t]he natural parents of unborn children have protectable interests in the life, health, and well-being of their unborn children."[40] Based upon these findings, the General Assembly has declared that, effective January 1, 1988,

> the laws of this state shall be interpreted and construed to acknowledge on behalf of the unborn child at every stage of development, all the rights, privileges, and immunities available to other persons, citizens, and residents of this state, subject only to the Constitution of the United States, and decisional interpretations thereof by the United States Supreme Court and specific provisions to the contrary in the statutes and constitution of this state.[41]

Given this rule of construction, Missouri reviewing courts have held that the unborn child is a "person," as that word is used in the criminal statutes prohibiting first-degree murder,[42] second-degree murder[43] and manslaughter.[44] And a woman convicted of a capital offense may not be executed while she is pregnant.[45]

In tort law, a statutory cause of action for wrongful death may be brought on behalf of an unborn child without regard to the stage of pregnancy when the injuries causing death were inflicted.[46] A common law action for (non-lethal) prenatal injuries may be brought without regard to the stage of pregnancy when the injuries were inflicted.[47] And Missouri has banned wrongful life and wrongful birth causes of action.[48]

---

40. *Id.* § 1.205.1(1)-(3).

41. *Id.* § 1.205.2. For purposes of § 1.205, the term "unborn children" or "unborn child" includes "all unborn child or children or the offspring of human beings from the moment of conception until birth at every stage of biological development." *Id.* § 1.205.3.

42. *State v. Holcomb*, 956 S.W.2d 286, 289–90 (Mo. Ct. App. 1997).

43. *State v. Bailey*, 191 S.W.2d 52, 55 (Mo. Ct. App. 2005); *State v. Rollen*, 133 S.W.3d 57, 61–64 (Mo. Ct. App. 2003).

44. *State v. Knapp*, 843 S.W.2d 345, 347–49 (Mo. 1992).

45. Mo. STAT. ANN. § 546.800 *et seq.* (West 2002).

46. *Connor v. Monkem Co., Inc.*, 898 S.W.2d 89, 90–93 (Mo.1995), interpreting Mo. STAT. ANN. § 537.080 (West 2000).

47. *O'Grady v. Brown*, 654 S.W.2d 904, 910–11 (Mo. 1983) (by implication in wrongful death case).

48. Mo. STAT. ANN. § 188.130 (West 2004). A "wrongful life" cause of action is a claim brought on behalf of a child who is born with a physical or mental disability or disease that could have been discovered before the child's birth by genetic testing, amniocentesis or

In health care law, "The declaration [under a living will] to withdraw or withhold treatment by a patient diagnosed as pregnant by the attending physician shall have no effect during the course of the declarant's pregnancy."[49] Finally, in property law, a posthumous child or descendant of a person who dies intestate (without a will) "shall inherit in like manner, as if born in the lifetime of the intestate...."[50] And, subject to certain exceptions, a child born after a person executes a will receives the same share of the testator's estate that he would have received if he had been born before the will was executed.[51]

A right to abortion is not "firmly rooted" in the "history, legal traditions, and practices" of the State of Missouri. Nor can such a right be derived from the text, structure or history of the Missouri Constitution.[52] There is no indication that either the framers or ratifiers of the state constitution intended to recognize a right to abortion.[53] Such an intent would have been remarkable in light

---

other medical screening. The gravamen of the action is that, as a result of a physician's failure to inform the child's parents of the child's disability or disease (or at least of the availability of tests to determine the presence of the disability or disease), they were deprived of the opportunity to abort the child, thus resulting in the birth of a child suffering permanent physical or mental impairment. A "wrongful birth" cause of action, on the other hand, is a claim, based upon the same facts, brought by the parents of the impaired child on their own behalf. Even before the effective date of § 188.130, the Missouri Supreme Court had refused to recognize either cause of action. *See Wilson v. Kuenzi*, 751 S.W.2d 741, 743–46 (Mo. 1988).

49. Mo. Stat. Ann. § 459.025 (West 2007).

50. *Id.* § 474.050 (West 1992). A "posthumous" child or descendant is a child or descendant who was conceived before but born after the death of the intestate.

51. *Id.* § 474.240.

52. In interpreting the intent of the framers of the Missouri Constitution of 1945, the Missouri Supreme Court looks to the language of the constitution and the history of its adoption. *Doe v. Phillips*, 194 S.W.3d at 841. *See also Cruzan by Cruzan v. Harmon*, 760 S.W.2d at 417 ("Missouri's Constitution must be interpreted according to its plain language and in a manner consistent with the understanding of the people who adopted it").

53. *See* Debates of the Missouri Constitutional Convention of 1943–44, 1013–31, 1051, 1073–1168, 1177–1490, 1655–82, 1931–74 (second reading on the Bill of Rights); 5567–84 (Report of Committee on Phraseology, Arrangement and Engrossment); 5717–33, 5971–96 (third and final reading on Bill of Rights). The convention debates are available on microfilm at the State Historical Society of Missouri based on a certified verbatim stenotype transcription. It should be noted that there is no basis for considering abortion as a reserved right under the Missouri Constitution. In drafting the present constitution, the Committee on the Preamble and Bill of Rights deleted a reserved rights provision that had been in the 1875 Missouri Constitution. Speaking on behalf of the Committee, Delegate Marr explained that "it was the unanimous opinion of the Committee that if there were specific rights that should be protected, it would be preferable to list them in separate sections rather than in the general statement [referring to reserved rights], so we eliminated that section...."

of the contemporaneous and longstanding prohibition of abortion except to save the life of the mother, a prohibition that antedated the adoption of the present constitution by more than one hundred twenty five years.

Equal Rights

Article I, §2, of the Missouri Constitution provides, in part, that "all persons are created equal and are entitled to equal rights and opportunity under the law...."[54] The Missouri Supreme Court has held that the equal rights guarantee of art. I, §2, of the Missouri Constitution is "coextensive" with the Equal Protection Clause of the Fourteenth Amendment,[55] and "provides the same protection...."[56]

For purposes of both state and federal equal protection analysis, a statute that infringes upon a fundamental right or classifies upon the basis of a suspect personal characteristic is subject to the strict scrutiny standard of judicial review. Under that standard, the statute is presumed to be unconstitutional and will not be upheld unless "it is necessary to accomplish a compelling state interest."[57] Strict scrutiny would not apply to review of an abortion prohibition because, for the reasons set forth in the preceding section of this analysis, neither the recognition of natural rights (art. I, §2), nor the guarantee of due process (art. I, §10), confers a "fundamental right" to abortion. Nor would the prohibition of abortion classify persons on the basis of a "suspect" personal characteristic (*e.g.*, race).

Abortion advocates may argue in the alternative, however, that a statute prohibiting abortion discriminates against women and is subject to intermediate scrutiny under art. I, §2, because only women are capable of becoming pregnant. For purposes of both state and federal equal protection analysis, "classifications by gender must serve important governmental objectives and must be substantially related to achievement of those objectives."[58] An abortion prohibition would appear to satisfy this level of scrutiny because the prohibition would be "substantially related" to the "important governmental objec-

---

Id. at 1012. An effort to restore a reserved rights provision on the floor of the Convention was thereafter defeated. *Id.* at 1484–86.

54. Mo. Const. art. I, §2 (West 2003).

55. *Bernat v. State*, 192 S.W.3d 863, 867 (Mo. 2006).

56. *In re Care & Treatment of Coffman*, 225 S.W.3d 439, 445 (Mo. 2007).

57. *Bernat*, 192 S.W.3d at 867 (citation and internal quotation marks omitted).

58. *Wengler v. Druggists Mutual Ins. Co.*, 583 S.W.2d 162, 164 (Mo. 1979), *rev'd on other grounds*, 446 U.S. 142 (1980).

tive" of protecting unborn human life. Nevertheless, the standard applicable to sex-based discrimination should not apply to an abortion prohibition. Abortion laws do not discriminate on the basis of sex.

First, the United States Supreme Court has reviewed restrictions on abortion funding under a rational basis standard of review, *not* under the intermediate (heightened) scrutiny required of gender-based classifications.[59] Indeed, the Court has held that "the disfavoring of abortion ... is not *ipso facto* sex discrimination," and, citing its decisions in *Harris* and other cases addressing abortion funding, stated that "the constitutional test applicable to government abortion-funding restrictions is not the heightened-scrutiny standard that our cases demand for sex discrimination, ... but the ordinary rationality standard."[60]

Second, even assuming that an abortion prohibition differentiates between men and women on the basis of sex, and would otherwise be subject to a higher standard of review, the Supreme Court has held that biological differences between men and women may justify different treatment based on those differences. In upholding a statutory rape statute that applied only to males, the Supreme Court noted, "this Court has consistently upheld statutes where the gender classification is not invidious, but rather realistically reflects the fact that the sexes are not similarly situated in certain circumstances."[61] As one federal district court observed: "Abortion statutes are examples of cases in which

---

59. *Harris v. McRae*, 448 U.S. 297, 321–26 (1980).

60. *Bray v. Alexandria Women's Health Clinic*, 506 U.S. 263, 273 (1993). Several state supreme courts and individual state supreme court justices have recognized that abortion regulations and restrictions on abortion funding are not "directed at women as a class" so much as "abortion as a medical treatment, which, because it involves a potential life, has no parallel as a treatment method." *Bell v. Low Income Women of Texas*, 95 S.W.3d 253, 258 (Tex. 2002) (upholding funding restrictions) (citing *Harris*, 448 U.S. at 325). *See also Fischer v. Dep't of Public Welfare*, 502 A.2d 114, 125 (Pa. 1985) ("the basis for the distinction here is not sex, but abortion") (upholding funding restrictions); *Moe v. Secretary of Administration & Finance*, 417 N.E.2d 387, 407 (Mass. 1981) (Hennessey, C.J., dissenting) (funding restrictions were "directed at abortion as a medical procedure, not women as a class"); *Right to Choose v. Byrne*, 450 A.2d 925, 950 (N.J. 1982) (O'Hern, J., dissenting) ("[t]he subject of the legislation is not the person of the recipient, but the nature of the claimed medical service"). Both *Moe* and *Right to Choose* were decided on other grounds. The dissenting justices were addressing alternative arguments raised by the plaintiffs, but not reached by the majority opinions.

61. *Michael M. v. Superior Court*, 450 U.S. 464, 469 (1981). *See State v. Stokely*, 842 S.W.2d 77, 79–80 (Mo. 1992) (citing *Michael M.* with approval); *State v. Taylor*, 726 S.W.2d 335, 337 (Mo. 1987) (following *Michael M.*); *State v. Lorenze*, 592 S.W.2d 523, 526 (Mo. Ct. App. 1979) (rejecting equal protection challenge to forcible rape statute which applied only to males committing crime against females).

the sexes are not biologically similarly situated" because only women are capable of becoming pregnant and having abortions.[62]

A statute prohibiting abortion quite obviously can affect only women because only women are capable of becoming pregnant.[63] Unlike laws that use women's ability to become pregnant (or pregnancy itself) to discriminate against them in *other* areas (*e.g.*, employment opportunities), abortion prohibitions cannot fairly be said to involve a distinction between men and women that is a "mere pretext[] designed to erect an invidious discrimination against [women]."[64]

A prohibition of abortion would not interfere with the exercise of a fundamental state constitutional right, nor would it classify upon the basis of a suspect or quasi-suspect characteristic. Accordingly, it would be subject to rational basis review. A law prohibiting abortion would be rationally related to the State's legitimate interest in protecting unborn human life.

Political Power

Article I, § 1, of the Missouri Constitution provides that "all political power is vested in and derived from the people," and "all government of right originates from the people, is founded upon their will only, and is instituted solely for the good of the whole."[65] In a challenge to a statute prohibiting abortion, abortion advocates might argue that the statute interferes with the "political power" of the people because it does not serve "the good of the whole." Given the purpose of § 1, however, this argument would not likely prevail.

Article I, § 1, itself, imposes no restraints, express or implied, on the legislature's power. Such restraints as do exist are found in other provisions of the state constitution (principally, other sections of the Bill of Rights).[66] Accordingly, § 1, which simply recognizes that political power rests in the people,[67] would

---

62. *Jane L. v. Bangerter*, 794 F. Supp. 1537, 1549 (D. Utah 1992). *See also In re Interest of J.D.G.*, 498 S.W.2d 786, 793 (Mo. 1973) (questioning whether intermediate standard of review for sex-based classifications should be applied "to laws which by their very nature must distinguish between males and females, such as rape statutes).

63. *Geduldig v. Aiello*, 417 U.S. 484, 496 n. 20 (1974) ("[n]ormal pregnancy is an objectively, identifiable physical condition with unique characteristics").

64. *Id.*

65. Mo. CONST. art. I, § 1 (West 2003).

66. *See Three Rivers Junior College District of Poplar Bluff, Missouri v. Statler*, 421 S.W.2d 235, 238 (Mo. 1967) ("the legislature has the power to enact any law not prohibited by the federal or state constitution").

67. Article I, § 1, recognizes "the basic fact that the people themselves are the source of all governmental power. Their will is supreme. They spell out in their constitution what

not prevent the General Assembly from enacting an abortion prohibition. Whether a given law serves "the good of the whole," within the meaning of art. I, §1, presents a political question for the legislature (and, ultimately, the people) to decide, not a constitutional question for the judiciary.

Right to Alter or Abolish the Form of Government

Article I, §3, of the Missouri Constitution provides:

> That the people of this state have the inherent, sole and exclusive right to regulate the internal government and police thereof, and to alter or abolish their constitution and form of government whenever they may deem it be necessary to their safety and happiness, provided such change be not repugnant to the Constitution of the United States.[68]

In any challenge to a statute prohibiting abortion, abortion advocates might argue that the statute interferes with the "inherent, sole and exclusive right" of the people to "regulate the internal government" because it does not promote their "safety and happiness." Given the purpose of §3, this argument would not likely prevail.

The purpose of art. I, §3, is to secure to the people themselves, through the amendment process, the right to decide whether, how and to what extent the organic instrument of government should be changed. Section 3, thus, is not a source of substantive rights (other than the right to "alter or abolish" the state constitution). Rather, it recognizes the people as the ultimate source of authority in a republican form of government.[69] As such, it could not serve as a basis for asserting a right to abortion. Whether a given law promotes the "safety and happiness" of the people, within the meaning of §3, is a political question for the legislature to decide, not a constitutional question for the judiciary.

---

form their government shall take and what powers it shall have." *State of Missouri ex rel. St. Louis Fire Fighters Ass'n Local No. 73, AFL-CIO v. Stemmler*, 479 S.W.2d 456, 458 (Mo. 1972).

68. Mo. Const. art. I, §3 (West 2003).

69. *State of Missouri ex rel. St. Louis Fire Fighters Ass'n Local No. 73, AFL-CIO*, 479 S.W.2d at 458 (recognizing the people as "the source of all governmental power," and noting that "when the people ... write or amend their constitution, they may insert any provision they desire, subject only to the limitation that it must not violate restrictions which the people have imposed on themselves and on the states by provisions which they have written into the federal constitution") (citing art. I, §3).

Conclusion

Based on the foregoing analysis, an argument that the Missouri Constitution protects a right to abortion that is separate from, and independent of, the right to abortion recognized in *Roe v. Wade* would not likely succeed. That, in turn, suggests that if *Roe*, as modified by *Casey*, is ultimately overruled, the State of Missouri could enact and enforce a statute *prohibiting* abortion. Moreover, nothing in the Missouri Constitution precludes Missouri from *regulating* abortion within federal constitutional limits in the meantime.

CHAPTER 29

MONTANA

Summary

As the result of a decision of the Montana Supreme Court, the State of Montana could not prohibit any abortion before viability, or any abortion after viability that would be necessary to preserve the pregnant woman's life or health, even if *Roe v. Wade*,[1] as modified by *Planned Parenthood of Southeastern Pennsylvania v. Casey*,[2] were overruled, unless the state constitution is amended to overturn that decision (or that decision is overruled). Moreover, by virtue of that same decision, Montana has little or no authority to enact and enforce reasonable measures regulating abortion within current federal constitutional limits.

Analysis

The principal pre-*Roe* abortion statute prohibited performance of an abortion unless the procedure was "necessary to preserve the life of the mother."[3] Another statute prohibited a woman from soliciting an abortion or allowing an abortion to be performed upon her (subject to the same exception).[4] Pursuant to *Roe v. Wade*, these statutes were declared unconstitutional (on federal, not state, grounds) by a three-judge federal district court in *Doe v. Woodahl*[5] and were later repealed.[6] Although it is not known at this time whether the

---

1. 410 U.S. 113 (1973).
2. 505 U.S. 833 (1992).
3. MONT. CODE ANN. §94-401 (1969), later renumbered as §94-5-611 by 1973 Mont. Laws ch. 513, §29.
4. *Id.* §94-402 (1969), later renumbered as §94-5-612 by 1973 Mont. Laws ch. 513, §29. No prosecutions were reported under this statute.
5. 360 F.Supp. 20 (D. Mont. 1973).
6. 1977 Mont. Laws 1130, 1171–72, ch. 359, §77.

Montana Legislature would consider legislation prohibiting abortion if *Roe*, as modified by *Casey*, were overruled, it is virtually certain that the Montana Supreme Court would declare unconstitutional any statute prohibiting pre-viability abortions, or any statute prohibiting post-viability abortions that did not allows such abortions to be performed to preserve the life or health of the pregnant woman. That is apparent from a review of the state supreme court's decision striking down, on state constitutional grounds, a law prohibiting non-physicians from performing abortions.

In *Armstrong v. State*,[7] the Montana Supreme Court considered a challenge to two state statutes that prohibited physicians' assistants from performing abortions.[8] The challenge was based on the right of privacy provision of the Montana Constitution. Article II, § 10, of the Montana Constitution provides: "The right of individual privacy is essential to the well-being of a free society and shall not be infringed without the showing of a compelling state interest."[9] Because "the right of privacy is explicit in the Declaration of Rights of Montana's Constitution, it is a fundamental right."[10] As such, "legislation infringing the exercise of the right of privacy must be reviewed under a strict-scrutiny analysis—i.e., the legislation must be justified by a compelling state interest and must be narrowly tailored to effectuate only that compelling interest."[11]

In *Armstrong*, the court held that "the right of each individual to make medical judgments affecting her or his bodily integrity and health in partnership with a chosen health care provider free from the interference of the government" is "protected under the personal autonomy component of the fundamental right of individual privacy set out in Article II, Section 10 of the Montana Constitution."[12] The court held further that "a woman's right to seek and obtain pre-viability abortion services," which implicates her "procreative autonomy," is "a protected form of personal autonomy."[13] "Implicit" in the latter right, the court explained, is "a woman's moral right and moral responsibility to decide, up to the point of fetal viability, what her pregnancy demands of her in the context of her individual values, her beliefs as to the sanctity of life,

---

7. 989 P.2d 364 (Mont. 1999).

8. Mont. Code Ann. §§ 37-20-103, 50-20-109(1)(a) (1995).

9. Mont. Const. art. II, § 10 (2005).

10. *Armstrong*, 989 P.2d at 374 (citing *Gryczan v. State*, 942 P.2d 112, 122 (Mont. 1997) (striking down state sodomy law)).

11. *Id.* (citations omitted).

12. *Id.* at 375.

13. *Id.*

and her personal situation."[14] Equating the choice of abortion with the choice of childbirth, the court said that "the State has no more compelling interest or constitutional justification for interfering with the exercise of this right if the woman chooses to terminate her pre-viability pregnancy than it would if she chose to carry the fetus to term."[15]

With these principles in mind, the court turned to a consideration of the State's authority to regulate the practice of medicine. The court recognized that "[the] right of choice in making personal health care decisions and in exercising autonomy is not without limits."[16] Thus, "[i]n narrowly defined instances the state, by clear and convincing evidence, may demonstrate a compelling interest in and obligation to legislate or regulate to preserve the safety, health and welfare of a particular class of patients or the general public from a medically-acknowledged, *bona fide* health risk."[17] "Subject to this narrow qualification, however, the legislature has neither a legitimate presence nor voice in the patient/health care provider relationship superior to the patient's right of personal autonomy which protects that relationship from infringement by the state."[18] The State, in the court's view, failed to show that the statutes prohibiting physicians' assistants from performing abortions were necessary to protect women from unsafe medical procedures:

> There is simply no evidence in the record of this case that laws requiring pre-viability abortions to be performed only by a physician to the exclusion of a trained, experienced and medically competent physician assistant-certified, working under the supervision of a licenses physician, are necessary to protect the life, health or safety of women in this State. Indeed, there is overwhelming evidence to the contrary and that the 1995 amendments to §37-20-103 ... and §50-20-109 ... were the product of and grounded in nothing other than the divisive and vocal politics of abortion.[19]

Having held the 1995 amendments to §§37-20-103 and 50-20-109 unconstitutional under art. II, §10, the court added a brief coda, suggesting that "the rights of personal and procreative autonomy at issue here also find pro-

---

14. *Id*. at 377.
15. *Id*.
16. *Id*. at 380.
17. *Id*.
18. *Id*.
19. *Id*. at 382.

tection in more than just Article II, Section 10."[20] The majority opinion, how-ever, was based squarely on § 10.[21]

In light of the Montana Supreme Court's decision in *Armstrong*, it is ap-parent that Montana could not prohibit any abortion before viability, or any abortion after viability that would be necessary to preserve the pregnant woman's life or health, even if *Roe*, as modified by *Casey*, were overruled, unless the state constitution is amended to overturn the holding in *Armstrong* (or the lat-ter is overruled).[22] It is equally apparent that the State may not enact many statutes regulating abortion or restricting public funding of abortion, even though such statutes would pass federal constitutional muster.

Conclusion

Because of the Montana Supreme Court's decision in *Armstrong v. State*, the State of Montana could not prohibit abortions, at least before viability, even if *Roe*, as modified by *Casey*, were overruled, unless the state constitution is amended to overturn the holding in *Armstrong* (or the latter is overruled). Moreover, because of that same decision, the State has little or no authority to regulate abortion within current federal constitutional limits.

---

20. *Id.* at 383 (citing, as possible sources, art. II, §§ 3 (inalienable rights), 4 (individual dignity), 5 (freedom of religion), 7 (freedom of speech), 17 (due process)). Two justices, specially concurring, disassociated themselves from the majority's ruminations on these al-ternative theories. *Id.* at 384 (Gray, J., specially concurring, joined by Turnage, C.J.).

21. *Id.* at 384 (summarizing holdings).

22. The Supreme Court has not yet decided whether a statute prohibiting post-viabil-ity abortions must make exceptions for mental, as well as physical, health. *See Voinovich v. Women's Medical Professional Corporation*, 523 U.S. 1036, 1039 (1998) (Thomas, J., dis-senting from denial of *certiorari*) (noting that this issue was not addressed in *Doe v. Bolton*, 410 U.S. 179 (1973), the companion case to *Roe v. Wade*). As a result, it is not known whether, as a matter of *state* constitutional law, the Montana Supreme Court would require a post-viability statute to contain a mental health exception. Under current state law, a post-viability abortion may be performed only to save the life of the pregnant woman or to pre-vent substantial and irreversible impairment of a major bodily function. MONT. CODE ANN. § 50-20-109 (2007). The constitutionality of this statute has not been litigated.

CHAPTER 30

NEBRASKA

Summary

The Nebraska Supreme Court has not yet decided whether the Nebraska Constitution protects a right to abortion separate from, and independent of, the right to abortion recognized under the United States Constitution.[1] A careful examination of the state constitution, in light of its history and interpretation, as well as other relevant legal sources, however, suggests that the state supreme court probably would not recognize a state constitutional right to abortion. Thus, if *Roe v. Wade*,[2] as modified by *Planned Parenthood of Southeastern Pennsylvania v. Casey*,[3] were overruled, Nebraska could enact a statute prohibiting abortion. Moreover, nothing in the state constitution, properly understood, precludes the State from enacting and enforcing reasonable measures regulating abortion within current federal constitutional limits.

Analysis

The pre-*Roe* abortion statutes prohibited performance of an abortion unless the procedure was "necessary to preserve the life of the mother, or shall have been advised by two physicians to be necessary for such purpose."[4] Pursuant to *Roe*, the statutes were declared unconstitutional (on federal, not state,

---

1. The Nebraska Supreme Court has referred to the right to abortion solely as a matter of *federal*, not *state*, constitutional law. *See In re Petition of Anonymous I*, 558 N.W.2d 784, 789 (Neb. 1997) (relying upon "the constitutional right of a woman, in consultation with her physician, to choose to terminate her pregnancy as established by *Roe v. Wade*").

2. 410 U.S. 113 (1973).

3. 505 U.S. 833 (1992).

4. Neb. Rev. Stat. §§ 28-404, 28-405 (1964).

grounds) in an unreported judgment of a three-judge federal district court,[5] and were later repealed.[6]

Based upon arguments that have been raised in other States with similar constitutional provisions, possible sources for an asserted abortion right could include provisions of the Declaration of Rights recognizing inherent and inalienable rights (art. I, §1); guaranteeing due process of law (§3), equal protection (§3), religious freedom (§4) and a remedy by due course of law (§13); and retaining rights (§26).[7] The analysis that follows addresses each of these provisions.

Inalienable Rights, Due Process of Law

Article I, §1, of the Nebraska Constitution provides:

> All persons are by nature free and independent, and have certain inherent and inalienable rights; among these are life, liberty, the pursuit of happiness, and the right to keep and bear arms for security or defense of self, family, home and others, and for lawful common defense, hunting, recreational use, and all other lawful purposes, and such rights shall not be denied or infringed by the state or any subdivision thereof. To secure these rights, and the protection of property, governments are instituted among people, deriving their just powers from the consent of the governed.[8]

Article I, §3, provides, in part: "No person shall be deprived of life, liberty, or property, without due process of law...."[9]

In any challenge to a Nebraska statute prohibiting abortion, abortion advocates are most likely to rely upon the "inherent and inalienable" rights language of art. I, §1, and the due process language of §3, arguing that the statute interferes with a pregnant woman's "liberty" in obtaining an abortion. Such an argument probably would not succeed.[10]

---

5. *Doe v. Exon*, Civil No. 71-L-199 (D. Neb. Feb. 21, 1973).

6. 1973 Neb. Laws 801, 806, L.B. 286, §24.

7. Three other more unlikely sources of an abortion right under the Nebraska Constitution-§2 (prohibiting involuntary servitude), §5 (guaranteeing freedom of speech) and §7 (prohibiting unreasonable searches and seizures)-are discussed generally in Chapter 3, *supra*.

8. NEB. CONST. art. I, §1 (2001).

9. *Id.* art. I, §3.

10. It should be noted that, under the state constitution, "No legislative act shall be held unconstitutional except by the concurrence of five judges." NEB. CONST. art. V, §2 (2001). There are seven judges on the Nebraska Supreme Court. *Id.* The requirement of a "supermajority" to declare a state statute unconstitutional makes the task of those who would

The Nebraska Supreme Court has held that the state constitution does not recognize any broader privacy or substantive due process rights than are recognized under the federal constitution.[11] This holding suggests that the state supreme court would not recognize a state right to abortion if *Roe*, as modified by *Casey*, were overruled. But even in the absence of an overruling decision, it is unlikely that the Nebraska Supreme Court would recognize a right to abortion that is separate from, and independent of, the right to abortion recognized in *Roe v. Wade*.

In determining whether an asserted liberty interest (or right) should be regarded as "fundamental" for purposes of substantive due process analysis under the Fourteenth Amendment, the Supreme Court applies a two-part test. First, there must be a "careful description" of the asserted fundamental liberty interest.[12] Second, the interest, so described, must be firmly rooted in "the Nation's history, legal traditions, and practices."[13] The Nebraska Supreme Court has frequently cited *Glucksberg* in determining whether an asserted liberty interest should be regarded as fundamental for purposes of the state constitu-

---

challenge the constitutionality of any statute that much more difficult.

11. *Hamit v. Hamit*, 715 N.W.2d 512, 524 (Neb. 2006) (citing *State v. Senters*, 699 N.W.2d 810, 814 (Neb. 2005)). *See also Robotham v. State*, 488 N.W.2d 533, 539 (Neb. 1992) (noting that "[n]o Nebraska case recognizes a right to privacy, based on our Constitution, broader than the narrow federal constitutional right"); *In re Adoption of Baby Girl H.*, 635 N.W.2d 256, 264–65 (Neb. 2001) (applying same analysis under state and federal due process clauses to state adoption statutes). It should be noted here that the Supreme Court, departing from its rationale in *Roe*, 410 U.S. at 153 ("[t]his right of privacy ... is broad enough to encompass a woman's decision whether or not to terminate her pregnancy"), no longer analyzes substantive due process claims under the rubric of "privacy," either in the area of abortion, *see Casey*, 505 U.S. at 846–53 (reaffirming *Roe* on the basis of the liberty language of the Due Process Clause without once mentioning privacy), or any other area. *See Cruzan v. Director, Missouri Dep't of Health*, 497 U.S. 261, 279 n. 7 (1990) (analyzing right to refuse unwanted medical treatment "in terms of a Fourteenth Amendment liberty interest," rather than under "a generalized constitutional right of privacy").

12. *Washington v. Glucksberg*, 521 U.S. 702, 721 (1997) (citation and internal quotation marks omitted).

13. *Id.* at 710. To the extent that the Nebraska Supreme Court considers federal precedent in determining whether an asserted liberty interest (or right) is "fundamental" under the state due process guarantee, abortion would not qualify as a "fundamental" right. Although the Supreme Court characterized the right to choose abortion as "fundamental" in *Roe*, 410 U.S. at 152–53, it tacitly abandoned that characterization in *Casey*, 505 U.S. at 869–79 (Joint Op. of O'Connor, Kennedy and Souter, JJ., replacing *Roe's* "strict scrutiny" standard of review with the more relaxed "undue burden" standard, allowing for a broader measure of abortion regulation).

tion.[14] A right to abortion, however, is not firmly rooted in the State's "history, legal traditions, and practices."

Nebraska enacted its first abortion statute in 1866–67, while it was still a territory and nine years before the present constitution was adopted. The statute prohibited performance of an abortion upon "any woman then being with child" without exception, and punished the crime as a misdemeanor.[15] This statute was replaced by a pair of statutes in 1873. The first statute made it a felony to perform an abortion at any stage of gestation *in utero* "with intent thereby to destroy [a] vitalized embryo, or foetus," if the abortion resulted in the death of either the unborn child or the pregnant woman, unless the procedure was "necessary to preserve the life of the [woman], or shall have been advised by two physicians to be necessary for such purpose...."[16] The second statute punished as a misdemeanor an abortion performed "with intent thereby to procure the miscarriage of any [pregnant] woman," subject to the same exception.[17] These statutes remained on the books, essentially unchanged, for one hundred years.[18]

Prior to *Roe v. Wade*, the Nebraska Supreme Court affirmed convictions of both physicians and laypersons for performing abortions, without any hint that the prosecutions or convictions were precluded by the state constitution.[19] In 1946, the state supreme court stated that in using the term "foeticide" to describe the victim of an illegal abortion, "the Legislature ... meant the unlawful destruction of an unborn child, *in* [*sic*] *ventre sa mere*, at any stage of pregnancy."[20]

---

14. *Citizens of Decatur for Equal Education v. Lyons-Decatur School District*, 739 N.W.2d 742, 758 (Neb. 2007) (state constitution does not provide a fundamental right to equal and adequate funding of public schools); *Hamit v. Hamit*, 715 N.W.2d at 520 (state constitution recognizes fundamental right of parents to make decisions concerning the care, custody and control of their children); *In re Adoption of Baby Girl H.*, 635 N.W.2d at 264 (same).

15. Neb. (Terr.) Stat. pt. III, ch. IV, § 42 (1866–67).

16. Neb. Gen. Stat. ch. 58, § 6 (1873).

17. *Id.* ch. 58, § 39.

18. Neb. Gen. Stat. ch. 58, §§ 6, 39 (1873), *recodified at* Neb. Stat. pt. III, ch. II, § 6, ch. IV, § 39 (1887), *recodified at* Neb. Comp. Stat. Ann. §§ 7637, 7674 (1905), *recodified at* Neb. Stat. Ann. §§ 2055, 2095 (1907), *recodified at* Neb. Rev. Stat. §§ 8584, 8585 (1913), *recodified at* Neb. Comp. Stat. Ann. §§ 9547, 9548 (1922), *recodified at* Neb. Comp. Stat. Ann. §§ 28-404, 28-405 (1929), *carried forward as* Neb. Rev. Stat. §§ 28-404, 28-405 (1956), *carried forward as* Neb. Rev. Stat. §§ 28-404, 28-405 (1964), *repealed by* 1973 Neb. Laws 801, 806, L.B. 286, § 24.

19. *Fields v. State*, 185 N.W. 400 (Neb. 1921); *Rice v. State*, 234 N.W. 566 (Neb. 1931).

20. *Hans v. State*, 22 N.W.2d 385, 389 (Neb. 1946). The phrase, "*en ventre sa mere*," is Law French for "in its mother's womb." Black's Law Dictionary 534 (6th ed. 1990).

The public policy of the State of Nebraska is "to provide protection for the life of the unborn child whenever possible...."[21] Consistent with that policy, Nebraska has enacted a comprehensive scheme of abortion regulation.[22]

Nebraska has recognized the rights of unborn children in a variety of contexts outside of abortion, including criminal law, tort law, health care law and property law. Under the criminal code, the killing of an unborn child, other than in an abortion, may be prosecuted as a homicide.[23] So, too, non-lethal injuries inflicted upon an unborn child may be prosecuted as an assault.[24] And a woman convicted of a capital offense may not be executed while she is pregnant.[25]

In tort law, a statutory cause of action for wrongful death may be brought on behalf of an unborn child without regard to the gestational age of the child at the time of its death.[26] A common law action for (nonlethal) prenatal injuries may be brought without regard to the stage of pregnancy when the injuries were inflicted.[27]

Under Nebraska's health care statutes, life-sustaining treatment may not be withheld or withdrawn under a living will from a woman who is known to be pregnant "so long as it is probable that the fetus will develop to the point live birth with continued application of life-sustaining treatment."[28] Durable powers of attorney for health care are subject to the same limitation.[29]

In property law, heirs conceived before but born after the death of a person who dies without a will "inherit as if they had been born in the lifetime of the decedent."[30] And, subject to certain exceptions, "[i]f a testator [a person who

---

21. NEB. REV. STAT. §28-325 (2003).

22. *Id.* §28-327 *et seq.* (2003) (mandating informed consent and a twenty-four hour waiting period); §71-6901 *et seq.* (2001 & Supp. 2006) (requiring parental notice and a forty-eight hour waiting period); §§28-337 *et seq.* (2003) (recognizing individual and institutional rights of conscience); 417 NEB. ADMIN. CODE §10-005.09 (2003) (restricting public funding of abortion for indigent women).

23. *Id.* §28-388 *et seq.* (2003 & Supp. 2006).

24. *Id.* §28-395 *et seq.* (Supp. 2006).

25. *Id.* §§29-2540, 29-2541 (2003).

26. *Id.* §30-809 (Supp. 2006).

27. This conclusion necessarily follows from the statutory recognition of a cause of action for wrongful death for the death of an unborn child at any stage of gestation. *See also Miles v. Box Butte County*, 489 N.W.2d 829 (Neb. 1992) (affirming award of damages for prenatal injuries sustained near full term delivery).

28. NEB. REV. STAT. §20-408(3) (1999).

29. *Id.* §30-3417(1)(b) (2001).

30. *Id.* §30-2308 (2001). The right of an afterborn relative to inherit is subject to a requirement that the relative survive the decedent by 120 hours (five days). *Id.* §30-2304.

has executed a will] fails to provide in his will for any of his children born or adopted after the execution of his will, the omitted child receives a share in the estate equal in value to that which he would have received if the testator had died intestate [without a will]...."[31]

In light of Nebraska's longstanding tradition of prohibiting abortion, which goes back more than one hundred years before *Roe v. Wade* was decided and antedates the 1875 Nebraska Constitution, the absence of any indication that the framers intended to recognize a right to abortion,[32] and the State's continuing interest in protecting the rights of unborn children, it cannot plausibly be said that either the inalienable rights provision or the due process guarantee of the Nebraska Constitution secures a "liberty" interest in obtaining an abortion.

Equal Protection

Article I, §3, of the Nebraska Constitution provides, in part: "No person shall ... be denied equal protection of the laws."[33] The Nebraska Supreme Court has held that the state and federal constitutions have "identical requirements for equal protection challenges."[34] Accordingly, the state supreme court "do[es] not distinguish between the two constitutions" in its analysis of such challenges.[35] Consistent with federal equal protection analysis, the Nebraska Supreme Court,

---

31. *Id.* §30-2321(a).

32. The minutes of the 1875 Nebraska Constitutional Convention have been lost. The proceedings were reconstructed from the journal of the convention, the memories of members of the convention and contemporaneous newspaper accounts and letters. *See* III NEBRASKA CONSTITUTIONAL CONVENTIONS (hereinafter CONVENTIONS) 538–41 (first and second readings of the Declaration of Rights), 575–77 (debate in Convention of the Whole) (York, Neb. 1913). The 1871 constitution, which was rejected by the voters, was "the real model upon whose lines the present constitution [was] based. The record of 1871 is, therefore, the most valuable existing commentary on [the] present [constitution]." I CONVENTIONS at 10 (York, Neb. 1906). There is no indication in the proceedings of the 1871 constitutional convention that the drafters intended to recognize a right to abortion. *Id.* at 506–23 (second reading); 204–46, 339–51, 356–95, 482, 484 (debate in Committee of the Whole); II CONVENTIONS at 93–96 (third reading) (York, Neb. 1907). It is their intention that controls. *See First Trust Co. of Lincoln v. Smith*, 277 N.W. 762, 777 (Neb. 1938) ("[t]he meaning of a Constitution is fixed when it is adopted, and it is not different at any subsequent time when a court has occasion to pass on it").

33. NEB. CONST. art. I, §3 (2001).

34. *In re Phoenix L.*, 708 N.W.2d 786, 795 (Neb. 2006).

35. *Id.*

in interpreting the equal protection guarantee of art. I, §3, has held that "[i]f a legislative classification involves either a suspect class or a fundamental right, courts will analyze the statute with strict scrutiny."[36] "Under this test," the court explained, "strict accordance must exist between the classification and the statute's purpose. The result the Legislature seeks to carry out must be a compelling state interest, and the means employed in the statute must be such that no less restrictive alternative exists."[37] "On the other hand," the court continued, "if a statute involves economic or social legislation not implicating a fundamental right or suspect class, courts will ask only whether a rational relationship exists between a legitimate state interest and the statutory means selected by the Legislature to accomplish that end. Upon a showing that such a rational relationship exists, courts will uphold the legislation."[38] Finally, "[s]ome legislative classifications, such as those based on gender, are reviewed under an intermediate level of scrutiny."[39] Under that level of scrutiny, the legislation must be "substantially related" to the achievement of "important governmental objectives."[40]

For the reasons set forth in the preceding section of this analysis, the Nebraska Constitution does not confer a "fundamental right" to abortion. And an abortion prohibition does not discriminate on the basis of race or any other suspect personal characteristic. Abortion advocates may argue in the alternative that a statute prohibiting abortion discriminates against women and is subject to intermediate scrutiny because only women are capable of becoming pregnant. An abortion prohibition would appear to satisfy this level of scrutiny because the prohibition would be substantially related to the important governmental objective in protecting unborn human life. Nevertheless, the standard applicable to sex-based discrimination should not apply to an abortion prohibition. Abortion laws do not discriminate on the basis of sex.

First, the United States Supreme Court has reviewed restrictions on abortion funding under a rational basis standard of review, *not* under the heightened scrutiny required of gender-based classifications.[41] Indeed, the Court has held that "the disfavoring of abortion ... is not *ipso facto* sex discrimination," and, citing its decisions in *Harris v. McRae* and other cases addressing abortion funding, stated that "the constitutional test applicable to government

---

36. *Gourley ex rel. Gourley v. Methodist Health System*, 663 N.W.2d 43, 70 (Neb. 2003).
37. *Id.*
38. *Id.* (citation omitted).
39. *Id.* (citation omitted).
40. *Craig v. Boren*, 429 U.S. 190, 197 (1976).
41. *Harris v. McRae*, 448 U.S. 297, 321–26 (1980).

abortion-funding restrictions is not the heightened-scrutiny standard that our cases demand for sex discrimination, ... but the ordinary rationality standard."[42]

Second, even assuming that an abortion prohibition differentiates between men and women on the basis of sex, and would otherwise be subject to a higher standard of review, the Supreme Court has held that biological differences between men and women may justify different treatment based on those differences. In upholding a statutory rape statute that applied only to males, the Supreme Court noted, "this Court has consistently upheld statutes where the gender classification is not invidious, but rather realistically reflects the fact that the sexes are not similarly situated in certain circumstances."[43] As one federal district court observed: "Abortion statutes are examples of cases in which the sexes are not biologically similarly situated" because only women are capable of becoming pregnant and having abortions.[44]

A statute prohibiting abortion quite obviously can affect only women because only women are capable of becoming pregnant.[45] Unlike laws that use women's ability to become pregnant (or pregnancy itself) to discriminate against them in *other* areas (*e.g.*, employment opportunities), abortion prohibitions cannot fairly be said to involve a distinction between men and women that is a "mere pretext[] designed to erect an invidious discrimination against [women]."[46]

---

42. *Bray v. Alexandria Women's Health Clinic*, 506 U.S. 263, 273 (1993). Several state supreme courts and individual state supreme court justices have recognized that abortion regulations and restrictions on abortion funding are not "directed at women as a class" so much as "abortion as a medical treatment, which, because it involves a potential life, has no parallel as a treatment method." *Bell v. Low Income Women of Texas*, 95 S.W.3d 253, 258 (Tex. 2002) (upholding funding restrictions) (citing *Harris*, 448 U.S. at 325). *See also Fischer v. Dep't of Public Welfare*, 502 A.2d 114, 125 (Pa. 1985) ("the basis for the distinction here is not sex, but abortion") (upholding funding restrictions); *Moe v. Secretary of Administration & Finance*, 417 N.E.2d 387, 407 (Mass. 1981) (Hennessey, C.J., dissenting) (funding restrictions were "directed at abortion as a medical procedure, not women as a class"); *Right to Choose v. Byrne*, 450 A.2d 925, 950 (N.J. 1982) (O'Hern, J., dissenting) ("[t]he subject of the legislation is not the person of the recipient, but the nature of the claimed medical service"). Both *Moe* and *Right to Choose* were decided on other grounds. The dissenting justices were addressing alternative arguments raised by the plaintiffs, but not reached by the majority opinions.

43. *Michael M. v. Superior Court*, 450 U.S. 464, 469 (1981).

44. *Jane L. v. Bangerter*, 794 F. Supp. 1537, 1549 (D. Utah 1992).

45. *Geduldig v. Aiello*, 417 U.S. 484, 496 n. 20 (1974) ("[n]ormal pregnancy is an objectively, identifiable physical condition with unique characteristics").

46. *Id.*

Because a prohibition of abortion would not infringe upon a fundamental state constitutional right and would not impermissibly classify on the basis of a suspect or quasi-suspect class, it would need to satisfy only the rational basis test. Under that test, "courts will ask only whether a rational relationship exists between a legitimate state interest and the statutory means selected by the Legislature to accomplish that end."[47] A prohibition of abortion would have a "rational relationship" to the "legitimate state interest" in protecting unborn human life. Accordingly, Nebraska could enact an abortion prohibition without violating the equal protection guarantee of the Nebraska Constitution.

Religious Freedom

Article I, §4, of the Nebraska Constitution provides, in part: "All persons have a natural and indefeasible right to worship Almighty God according to the dictates of their own consciences.... [N]o preference shall be given by law to any religious society, nor shall any interference with the rights of conscience be permitted."[48]

In any challenge to a statute prohibiting abortion, abortion advocates may raise either or both of two arguments under art. I, §4. First, they may argue that an abortion prohibition interferes with a woman's "right of conscience" by forbidding her from obtaining an abortion that would be allowed by her religion. Second, they may argue in the alternative (or in addition) that an abortion prohibition gives a "preference" to a "religious society" because it reflects sectarian beliefs regarding when human life begins and the sinfulness of abortion. Neither argument would likely prevail.

The Nebraska Supreme Court has not determined whether analysis under the Free Exercise and Establishment Clauses of the First Amendment and under art. I, §4, of the Nebraska Constitution are the same. Nevertheless, the state supreme court has frequently construed the state and federal provisions together, giving them the same interpretation.[49] In light of the similarity of in-

---

47. *Gourley*, 663 N.W.2d at 70.

48. NEB. CONST. art. I, §4 (2001).

49. *See, e.g., State v. Bjorklund*, 604 N.W.2d 169, 221–22 (Neb. 2000); *Palmer v. Palmer*, 545 N.W.2d 751, 754–56 (Neb. 1996). Without referring to art. I, §4, the court has held that "[a]n individual's religious beliefs do not excuse the individual from compliance with an otherwise valid law regarding conduct that the State is free to regulate." *Medlock v. Medlock*, 642 N.W.2d 113, 129 (Neb. 2002) (citing *Employment Division, Dep't of Human Resources of Oregon v. Smith*, 494 U.S. 872 (1990)). *See also Douglas County v. Anaya*, 694 N.W.2d 601, 604–08 (Neb. 2005) (same). That holding would preclude a challenge to an abortion statute under art. I, §4, assuming that §4 and the Free Exercise Clause are con-

terpretation, a challenge to an abortion statute that would not succeed under the Religion Clauses of the First Amendment probably would not succeed under art. I, §4, either. For the reasons set forth in Chapter 2, *supra*, an abortion statute could not be successfully challenged on First Amendment grounds. Accordingly, a similar challenge under art. I, §4, would not likely be successful.

Remedy by Due Course of Law

Article I, §13, of the Nebraska Constitution provides, in part: "All courts shall be open, and every person, for any injury done him or her in his or her lands, goods, person, or reputation, shall have a remedy by due course of law and justice administered without denial or delay...."[50] Abortion advocates might argue that a statute prohibiting abortion interferes with a woman's control over her own body, and that such interference constitutes an "injury" to her "person," as those terms are used in §13. The "remedy" for such interference, in turn, would be invalidation of the statute. This argument erroneously assumes that art. I, §13, confers substantive rights.

As is apparent from its text and structure, §13 is concerned with *remedies* for tortiously inflicted injuries-it does not establish what *constitutes* an injury to anyone's "lands, goods, person, or reputation." Those remedies, however, are derived from the common law and statues enacted by the Legislature, not §13. Moreover, the remedies themselves redress injuries recognized by the common law and statutory law, not constitutional "injuries." Section 13, in other words, does not *create* any new causes of actions, but merely *preserves* existing causes of action. Nebraska case law confirms this understanding.

Article I, §13, the Nebraska Supreme Court has explained,

> does not create any new rights but is merely a declaration of a general fundamental principle. It is a primary duty of the courts to safeguard this declaration of right and remedy but, where no right of action is

---

strued in the same manner. In an earlier decision, the court supreme court held that it would violate the "preference" language of art. I, §4, "to require the state superintendent of public instruction to apportion part of the interest and income from the state common school trust funds to a school in part sectarian." *State ex rel. Public School District No. 6, Cedar County v. Taylor*, 240 N.W. 573, 574 (Neb. 1932). Without citing the First Amendment, the court's decision in *Taylor* is clearly consistent with Establishment Clause jurisprudence.

50. NEB. CONST. art. I, §13 (2001).

given or remedy exists under either the common law or some statute, this constitutional provision creates none.[51]

Even with respect to existing causes of action, "plaintiffs ... are not assured that a cause of action will remain immune from legislative or judicial limitation or elimination."[52] In sum, art. I, § 13, is not a source of substantive rights and could not provide a basis for challenging an otherwise constitutional statute of the State.[53]

Retained Rights

Article I, § 26, of the Nebraska Constitution provides: "This enumeration of rights shall not be construed to impair or deny others, retained by the people, all powers not herein delegated, remain with the people."[54] Abortion advocates may be expected to cite § 26 in support of an asserted right to abortion under the state constitution. A proper interpretation of § 26, however, would not support a right to abortion as a "retained right."

Article I, § 26, has been cited in very few Nebraska decisions and authoritatively interpreted in none. An entirely plausible reading of § 26 is that the enumeration of certain rights in the state constitution should not be construed to "impair or deny" other rights retained by the people under the common law or statutes. But even if § 26 is understood to retain unspecified *constitutional* rights (as opposed to *common law* or *statutory* rights), abortion could not plausibly be considered to be among such rights because, at the time the Nebraska Constitution was adopted in 1875, abortion was a crime. The argument that § 26 "retained" as an "unenumerated right" conduct that was criminal when the state constitution was adopted is, at the very least, counterintuitive.

The language of § 26 appears to be based on the Ninth Amendment.[55] In light of that equivalence, § 26 should be given a parallel interpretation. That, in turn, suggests that if no right to abortion exists under the Ninth Amendment,

---

51. *Muller v. Nebraska Methodist Hospital*, 70 N.W.2d 86, 91 (Neb. 1955), *overruled on other grounds*, *Myers v. Drozda*, 141 N.W.2d 852, 853–54 (Neb. 1966). *See also Pullen ex rel. Voboril v. Novak*, 99 N.W.2d 16, 21 (Neb. 1959) (same); *State v. Lotter*, 586 N.W.2d 591, 614 (Neb. 1998) (same).

52. *Gourley ex rel. Gourley v. Nebraska Methodist Hospital*, 663 N.W.2d at 74.

53. It should not be surprising to note, therefore, that no criminal statute has ever been struck down on the authority of the "remedy by due course of law" language of art. I, § 13.

54. NEB. CONST. art. I, § 26 (2001).

55. "The enumeration in the Constitution of certain rights, shall not be construed to deny or disparage others retained by the people." U.S. CONST. AMEND. IX (West 2006).

then none would be recognized under art. I, § 26. The Supreme Court, however, has rooted the "abortion liberty" in the liberty language of the Due Process Clause of the Fourteenth Amendment, not in the unenumerated rights language of the Ninth Amendment.[56] Because abortion has not been recognized as a "retained right" under the Ninth Amendment, it should not be recognized as one under § 26, either.

Conclusion

Based on the foregoing analysis, an argument that the Nebraska Constitution protects a right to abortion that is separate from, and independent of, the right to abortion recognized in *Roe v. Wade* would not likely succeed. That, in turn, suggests that if *Roe*, as modified by *Casey*, is ultimately overruled, the State of Nebraska could enact and enforce a statute *prohibiting* abortion. Moreover, nothing in the Nebraska Constitution precludes Nebraska from *regulating* abortion within federal constitutional limits in the meantime.

---

56. *See Roe*, 410 U.S. at 153; *Casey*, 505 U.S. at 846. In any event, the Ninth Amendment, standing alone, is not a source of substantive rights. *Gibson v. Matthews*, 926 F.2d 532, 537 (6th Cir. 1991). Although "[s]ome unenumerated rights may be of [c]onstitutional magnitude," that is only "by virtue of other amendments, such as the Fifth or Fourteenth Amendment. A person cannot claim a right that exists solely under the Ninth Amendment." *United States v. Vital Health Products, Ltd.*, 786 F. Supp. 761, 777 (E.D. Wis. 1992), *aff'd mem. op., sub nom. United States v. LeBeau*, 985 F.2d 563 (7th Cir. 1993). *See also Charles v. Brown*, 495 F. Supp. 862, 863 (N.D. Ala. 1980) (same).

CHAPTER 31

NEVADA

Summary

The Nevada Supreme Court has not yet decided whether the Nevada Constitution protects a right to abortion separate from, and independent of, the right to abortion recognized under the United States Constitution.[1] A careful examination of the state constitution, in light of its history and interpretation, as well as other relevant legal sources, however, suggests that the state supreme court probably would not recognize a state constitutional right to abortion if *Roe v. Wade*,[2] as modified by *Planned Parenthood of Southeastern Pennsylvania v. Casey*,[3] were overruled. Thus, Nevada could prohibit abortion. Moreover, nothing in the state constitution, properly understood, precludes the State from enacting and enforcing reasonable measures regulating abortion within current federal constitutional limits.

Analysis

The principal pre-*Roe* abortion statute prohibited performance of an abortion upon a pregnant woman unless the procedure was "necessary to preserve her life or that of the [unborn] child."[4] Another statute prohibited a woman from soliciting an abortion or allowing an abortion to be performed upon

---

1. The Nevada Supreme Court has referred to the right to abortion solely as a matter of *federal*, not *state*, constitutional law. *See Greco v. United States*, 893 P.2d 345, 349 (Nev. 1995) ("[t]hose who do not wish to undertake the many burdens associated with the birth and continued care of [a disabled] child have the legal right ... to terminate their pregnancies") (citing *Roe v. Wade* and a state statute codifying *Roe*).

2. 410 U.S. 113 (1973).

3. 505 U.S. 833 (1992).

4. NEV. REV. STAT. § 201.120 (1967).

her after "quickening" (subject to the same exception).[5] The substantive provisions of the pre-*Roe* statutes, which were never declared unconstitutional, were repealed in 1973.[6] Under a ballot initiative approved in 1990, abortions may be performed through the twenty-fourth week of gestation for any reason, and after the twenty-fourth week to prevent grave impairment of the pregnant woman's physical or mental health.[7] Because the statute was adopted by an initiative, it may be repealed or amended only by another vote of the people.[8]

Based upon arguments that have been raised in other States with similar constitutional provisions, possible sources for an asserted abortion right could include provisions of the Declaration of Rights recognizing inalienable rights (art. 1, §1), and political power in the people (§2); guaranteeing liberty of conscience (§3), and due process of law (§8(5)); and retaining rights (§20), as well as art. 4, §21 (equal protection).[9] The analysis that follows addresses each of these provisions.

Inalienable Rights

Article 1, §1, of the Nevada Constitution provides, in relevant part: "All men are by Nature free and equal and have certain inalienable rights among which are those of enjoying and defending life and liberty...."[10] In any challenge to a Nevada statute prohibiting (or regulating) abortion, abortion advocates would probably argue that the "liberty" interest protected by art. 1, §1, includes a right to abortion. Such an argument would not likely prevail, however.

There is very little case law interpreting §1, and the Nevada Supreme Court has never declared a statute or ordinance unconstitutional on the basis that it violated §1.[11] The state supreme court *has* rejected various privacy based claims

---

5. *Id.* §200.220. "Quickening" is that stage of pregnancy, usually sixteen to eighteen weeks gestation, when the woman first detects fetal movement. No prosecutions were reported under this statute.

6. 1973 Nev. Stat. 1637, 1639–40, ch. 766, §§7, 8.

7. Nev. Rev. Stat. Ann. §442.250 (Michie 2000).

8. *Choose Life Campaign '90' v. Del Papa*, 801 P.2d 1384, 1385 (Nev. 1990) (citing Nev. Const. art. 19, §1(3) (2008)).

9. Two other more unlikely sources of an abortion right under the Nevada Constitution-§9 (guaranteeing freedom of speech) and §18 (prohibiting unreasonable searches and seizures)-are discussed generally in Chapter 3, *supra*.

10. Nev. Const. art. 1, §1 (2008).

11. In *State ex rel. Roman Catholic Bishop v. Hill*, 90 P.2d 217 (Nev. 1939), the court determined that certain provisions of a local zoning ordinance could not be applied to a

brought under this section,[12] and it is doubtful that the court would recognize abortion as a fundamental "liberty" interest under § 1, either.

The Nevada Supreme Court has held that "[a] liberty interest is deemed fundamental ... if it is 'deeply rooted in this Nation's history and tradition.'"[13] A "liberty interest" in abortion is *not* "deeply rooted" in the State's history and tradition and cannot be deemed to be "fundamental" under the state constitution.

Nevada enacted its first abortion statute in 1861, three years before it was admitted to the Union. The statute prohibited performance of an abortion upon a pregnant woman by any means at any stage of pregnancy unless a physician determined that the procedure was "necessary ... in order to save her life."[14] This statute remained on the books until it was superseded by a 1911 statute which restated the prohibition.[15] That statute permitted an abortion to be performed upon a pregnant woman only if it was necessary "to preserve her life or that of the child whereof she [was] pregnant."[16]

Prior to the Supreme Court's decision in *Roe v. Wade*, the Nevada Supreme Court affirmed convictions for abortion and attempted abortion without any

---

church. Although the plaintiff cited art. 1, §§ 1, 4 and 8 in support of his argument, the ordinance was struck down (as applied) on due process grounds only. *Id.* at 223.

12. *See, e.g., Atteberry v. State*, 438 P.2d 789, 791 (Nev. 1968) (act requiring registration of persons convicted of felonies does not violate their privacy rights under art. 1, § 1); *Norman v. City of Las Vegas*, 177 P.2d 442, 446 (Nev. 1947) (ordinance requiring prospective employees of certain business establishments selling alcoholic beverages at retail for consumption on the premises to be fingerprinted and photographed did not violate employees' right of privacy).

13. *Kirkpatrick v. Eighth Judicial District Court*, 43 P.3d 998, 1005 (Nev. 2002) (quoting *Moore v. City of East Cleveland, Ohio*, 431 U.S. 494, 503 (1977)). *See also In re Guardianship of L.S. & H.S.*, 87 P.3d 521, 527 (Nev. 2004) (same). It is apparent from an examination of the opinions in *Kirkpatrick* and *In re Guardianship of L.S. & H.S.* that the court was articulating a standard applicable to both federal *and* state liberty claims. A similar mode of analysis was employed in *Worthington v. Second Judicial District Court*, 142 P. 230 (Nev. 1914), in which the state supreme court held that there is no federal or state constitutional right to a divorce. The court stated that "divorce is not among the inalienable rights of man or the ones granted by Magna Carta, the federal or state [c]onstitution, or the common law, and, except at the will and subject to any restrictions imposed by the Legislature, has never been recognized as one of the guaranteed privileges of the citizen...." *Id.* at 241.

14. NEV. (TERR.) LAWS, ch. XXVIII, § 42 (1861), *recodified at* NEV. COMP. LAWS, Vol. I, § 2348, ch. LV, § 42 (1873), *recodified at* NEV. GEN. STAT. § 4605, ch. XXII, § 42 (1885).

15. CRIMES & PUNISHMENTS § 182 (1911), *codified at* NEV. REV. LAWS § 6447 (1912), *recodified at* NEV. COMP. LAWS § 10129 (1929), *recodified at* NEV. REV. STAT. § 201.120 (1959), *repealed by* 1973 Nev. Stat. 1637, 1639–40, ch. 766, §§ 7, 8.

16. *Id.*

hint that either the prosecutions or convictions violated the Nevada Constitution.[17] That in itself is an indication that the (now repealed) abortion prohibition was constitutional.[18] Subsequent to *Roe*, the Nevada Legislature enacted a variety of statutes regulating abortion, including statutes mandating informed consent and requiring parental notice.[19] And in a ballot initiative, the people of Nevada prohibited abortions after the twenty-fourth week of gestation, except to preserve the pregnant woman's life or health.[20]

Nevada has recognized the rights of unborn children in a variety of contexts outside of abortion, including criminal law, tort law, health care law and property law. Under the criminal code, the willful killing of an unborn quick child by any injury committed upon the mother of the child is manslaughter.[21] And a woman convicted of a capital offense may not be executed while she is pregnant.[22]

In tort law, a statutory cause of action for wrongful death may be brought on behalf of an unborn child who was viable (capable of sustained survival outside the mother's womb, with or without medical assistance) at the time of its death.[23] A common law action for (nonlethal) prenatal injuries may be brought without regard to the stage of pregnancy when the injuries were inflicted.[24] And the Nevada Supreme Court has refused to recognize wrongful pregnancy and wrongful life causes of action.[25]

---

17. *State v. Cushing*, 120 P.2d 208 (Nev. 1941); *State v. Elges*, 251 P.2d 590 (Nev. 1952); *Wyatt v. State*, 367 P.2d 104 (Nev. 1961); *Adams v. State*, 407 P.2d 169 (Nev. 1965).

18. "Where an act of the Legislature has for a long period of years been enforced by the courts of a state, without its constitutionality being challenged, that fact may be considered a virtual recognition of its constitutionality." *Worthington*, 142 P. at 233. The Nevada abortion laws went unchallenged for more than one hundred years.

19. Nev. Rev. Stat. Ann. §442.253 (2005) (informed consent); §§442.255, 442.2555 (2005) (parental notice). The parental notice statute is currently unenforceable. *See Glick v. McKay*, 937 F.2d 434 (9th Cir. 1991). *See also* Nevada Medicaid Services Manual, Attachments G, H (limiting public funding of abortion for indigent women to those circumstances in which federal reimbursement is available, currently life-of-the-mother, rape and incest).

20. Nev. Rev. Stat. Ann. §442.250 (2005).

21. *Id.* §200.210 (2006).

22. *Id.* §176.465 *et seq.* (2006).

23. *White v. Yup*, 458 P.2d 617, 621–24 (Nev. 1969), interpreting what is now codified at Nev. Rev. Stat. Ann. §41.085 (2006).

24. *Id.* at 620–21.

25. *Szekeres by Szekeres v. Robinson*, 715 P.2d 1076, 1078 (Nev. 1986) (refusing to recognize cause of action for the birth of a normal child as the result of a failed surgical sterilization procedure); *Greco v. United States*, 893 P.2d at 347–48 (denying wrongful life cause of action). A "wrongful life" cause of action is a claim brought on behalf of a child who is

Under Nevada's health care statutes, a declaration under the Uniform Act on the Rights of the Terminally Ill may not direct the withholding or withdrawal of life-sustaining treatment from a qualified patient who is known to be pregnant "so long as it is probable that the fetus will develop to the point of live birth with continued application of life-sustaining treatment."[26] And the attorney in fact under a durable power of attorney for health care may not consent to an abortion on behalf of the principal.[27]

In property law, children conceived before but born after the death of their parents are treated as if living at the death of their parent(s) for the purpose of inheriting remainder interests.[28] And, subject to certain exceptions, a child who is born after a parent executes a will, and who is not otherwise provided for in the will, may receive that share he or she would have received if the parent had died without a will.[29]

A right to abortion cannot be found in the text or structure of the Nevada Constitution. There is no evidence that the framers or ratifiers of the state constitution intended to limit the Legislature's authority to prohibit abortion.[30] Such an intent would have been remarkable in light of the contemporaneous prohibition of abortion except to save the life of the pregnant woman. Moreover, recognition of an abortion right would be manifestly inconsistent with the history and traditions of the State, as well as with the precedents of the Nevada Supreme Court. Taken together, these factors militate against recognition of a right to abortion under the inalienable rights guarantee of the Nevada Constitution.

---

born with a physical or mental disability or disease that could have been discovered before the child's birth by genetic testing, amniocentesis or other medical screening. The gravamen of the cause of action is that, as a result of a physician's failure to inform the child's parents of the child's disability or disease (or at least of the availability of tests to determine the presence of the disability or disease), they were deprived of the opportunity to abort the child, thus resulting in the birth of a child suffering permanent physical or mental impairment. The state supreme court has recognized wrongful birth actions, however. *Greco*, 893 P.2d at 348–49. A "wrongful birth" cause of action is a claim based upon the same facts, brought by the parents of the impaired child on their own behalf.

26. NEV. REV. STAT. ANN. §449.624(4) (2005).

27. *Id.* §449.850(1)(e) (2005).

28. *Id.* §111.085 (2004). *See also* §111.080.

29. *Id.* §133.160 (2003).

30. *See* OFFICIAL REPORT OF THE DEBATES AND PROCEEDINGS DEBATES IN THE CONSTITUTIONAL CONVENTION OF THE STATE OF NEVADA 41–50, 51–73 (debate on Declaration of Rights in Committee of the Whole); 194–202, 777–78, 780–85 (debate on Declaration of Rights in Convention) (1864).

Inherent Political Power

Article 1, §2, of the Nevada Constitution provides, in part: "All political power is inherent in the people[.] Government is instituted for the protection, security and benefit of the people; and they have the right to alter or reform the same whenever the public good may require it."[31] In a challenge to a statute prohibiting abortion, abortion advocates might argue that the statute interferes with the "political power" of the people because it does not promote their "protection, security and benefit...." Given the purpose of §2, this argument would not likely succeed.

The Nevada Supreme Court has held that §2 "expressly gives the Legislature the full power and authority to alter or reform the law whenever in their judgment the public good may require it," and, "as to the power, wisdom, or expediency of the law, these matters are entirely within the province of the legislative department."[32] Accordingly, the constitutionality of statutes enacted by the Legislature is not subject to challenge under §2.[33]

Liberty of Conscience

Article 1, §4, of the Nevada Constitution provides, in pertinent part: "The free exercise and enjoyment of religious profession and worship without discrimination or preference shall forever be allowed in this State...."[34] In any challenge to a statute prohibiting abortion, abortion advocates may raise either or both of two arguments under art. I, §4. First, they may argue that an abortion prohibition interferes with the "free exercise and enjoyment" of a woman's "religious profession" by forbidding her from obtaining an abortion that would be allowed by her religion. Second, they may argue in the alternative (or in addition) that an abortion prohibition gives a "preference" to religion because it reflects sectarian beliefs regarding when human life begins and the sinfulness of abortion. Neither argument would likely succeed.

---

31. Nev. Const. art. 1, §2 (2008).

32. *Riter v. Douglass*, 109 P. 444, 447 (Nev. 1910). The Legislature, of course, may not amend the state constitution without a vote of the people

33. Ordinances adopted by municipalities, however, may be challenged under §2. *See Lothrop v. Seaborn*, 23 P.2d 1109, 1111 (Nev. 1933) (in the absence of a statute granting a preference to a county over the claims of general depositors, a county does not have a right of preference over other depositors of a bank on the basis of sovereignty, because only the State inherited the prerogative of sovereignty from the common law).

34. Nev. Const. art. 1, §4 (2008).

There is very little case law interpreting art. 1, §4, and none suggesting that the Nevada Supreme Court would interpret §4 in a manner that would be inconsistent with the Supreme Court's interpretation of the Free Exercise and Establishment Clauses of the First Amendment. Assuming that in interpreting §4, the state supreme court would follow Supreme Court precedent interpreting the Religion Clauses, the court would not invalidate an abortion prohibition on the basis of art. 1, §4 (see Chapter 2, *supra*).

Due Process of Law

Article 1, §8(5) of the Nevada Constitution provides: "No person shall be deprived of life, liberty, or property, without due process of law."[35] The Nevada Supreme Court has not recognized a state constitutional right of privacy, as such.[36] Nevertheless, the state supreme court *has* held that the state due process guarantee has a substantive, as well as a procedural, component which essentially corresponds to the substantive component of the federal Due Process Clause.[37] Because of this congruence of interpretation, should the United States Supreme Court ultimately determine that the liberty language of the Due Process Clause of the Fourteenth Amendment does not confer a right to abortion, then the Nevada Supreme Court would not hold that art. 1, §8(5) does, either.[38]

---

35. NEV. CONST. art. 1, §8(5) (2008).

36. *See McKay v. Bergstedt*, 801 P.2d 617, 622 (Nev. 1990) (declining to root right to refuse unwanted medical treatment in a state right of privacy). *See also State v. Eighth Judicial District Court*, 668 P.2d 282 (Nev. 1983) (holding that the federal right of privacy does not extend to commercial sexual activities); *Techtow v. City Council of North Las Vegas*, 775 P.2d 227 (Nev. 1989) (reviewing provisions of massage parlor ordinance under the federal constitution only).

37. *McKay v. Bergstedt*, 801 P.2d at 622 n. 5 (art 1, §8(5) "tracks the Fourteenth Amendment of the United States Constitution in protecting its citizens against deprivation of their right to liberty without due process of law") (in addition to the common law right to refuse unwanted medical treatment, patient had state and federal liberty interest in refusing such treatment). *See also In re Guardianship of L.S. & H.S.*, 87 P.3d at 527 & n. 25 (citing both state and federal due process clauses in support of holding that a "parent has a fundamental liberty interest in the care, custody, and management of his child") (citation and internal quotation marks omitted).

38. Whether the court would recognize a state liberty interest in abortion under art. 1, §8(5) while *Roe* (as modified) remains the law of the land is uncertain. None of the Nevada statutes regulating abortion has been challenged on state grounds to date. It should be noted that to the extent that the Nevada Supreme Court recognizes the same fundamental rights under the *state* due process guarantee as the Supreme Court does under the *federal* due process guarantee, abortion would not qualify as a "fundamental" right. Although the

Equal Protection

Article 4, §21, of the Nevada Constitution provides: "In all cases enumerated in the preceding section, and in all other cases where a general law can be made applicable, all laws shall be general and of uniform operation throughout the State."[39] Although §21 does not include express equal protection language, the Nevada Supreme Court has described §21, as the "equal protection clause" of the Nevada Constitution,[40] and has held that the standard for testing the validity of legislation under art. 4, §21, is the same as the federal standard under the Equal Protection Clause.[41] Under that standard,

> The threshold question ... is whether a statute effectuates dissimilar treatment of similarly situated persons. In analyzing alleged equal protection violations, the level of scrutiny that applies varies according to the type of classification created. Where a case presents no judicially recognized suspect class or fundamental right that would warrant intervention under a standard of strict scrutiny or where it presents no quasi-suspect class such as sex, illegitimates or the poor that would warrant application of intermediate level scrutiny, we analyze the challenged law under the rational basis test. A statute meets rational basis review so long as it is reasonably related to a legitimate government interest.[42]

Strict scrutiny would not apply because, for the reasons set forth in the previous section, there is no "fundamental right" to an abortion under the Nevada Constitution. Moreover, no "suspect class" is involved. Abortion advocates may argue in the alternative, however, that a statute prohibiting abortion dis-

---

Supreme Court characterized the right to choose abortion as "fundamental" in *Roe*, 410 U.S. at 152–53, it tacitly abandoned that characterization in *Casey*, 505 U.S. at 869–79 (Joint Op. of O'Connor, Kennedy and Souter, JJ., replacing *Roe's* "strict scrutiny" standard of review with the more relaxed "undue burden" standard, allowing for a broader measure of abortion regulation).

39. NEV. CONST. art. 4, §21 (2008). The "preceding section" enumerates classes of prohibited "local" or "special" legislation, including laws "[f]or the punishment of crimes and misdemeanors." *Id.* art. 4, §20.

40. *Salaiscooper v. Eighth Judicial District Court*, 34 P.2d 509, 516 & n. 23 (Nev. 2001).

41. *State Farm Fire & Casualty Co. v. All Electric, Inc.*, 660 P.2d 995, 997 (Nev. 1983) (citation omitted).

42. *Rico v. Rodriguez*, 120 P.3d 812, 817 (Nev. 2005). Another term for "intermediate scrutiny" is "heightened scrutiny." The terms are used interchangeably in this section of the analysis.

criminates against women and is subject to intermediate scrutiny because only women are capable of becoming pregnant. An abortion prohibition would appear to satisfy this level of scrutiny because the prohibition would be substantially related to the important governmental objective of protecting unborn human life. Nevertheless, the standard applicable to sex-based discrimination should not apply to an abortion prohibition. Abortion laws do not discriminate on the basis of sex.

First, the United States Supreme Court has reviewed restrictions on abortion funding under a rational basis standard of review, *not* under the intermediate standard ("heightened scrutiny") required of gender-based classifications.[43] Indeed, the Court has held that "the disfavoring of abortion ... is not *ipso facto* sex discrimination," and, citing its decisions in *Harris* and other cases addressing abortion funding, stated that "the constitutional test applicable to government abortion-funding restrictions is not the heightened-scrutiny standard that our cases demand for sex discrimination, ... but the ordinary rationality standard."[44]

Second, even assuming that an abortion prohibition differentiates between men and women on the basis of sex, and would otherwise be subject to a higher standard of review, the Supreme Court has held that biological differences between men and women may justify different treatment based on those differences. In upholding a statutory rape statute that applied only to males, the Supreme Court noted, "this Court has consistently upheld statutes where the gender classification is not invidious, but rather realistically reflects the fact that the sexes are not similarly situated in certain circumstances."[45] As one fed-

---

43. *Harris v. McRae*, 448 U.S. 297, 321–26 (1980).

44. *Bray v. Alexandria Women's Health Clinic*, 506 U.S. 263, 273 (1993). Several state supreme courts and individual state supreme court justices have recognized that abortion regulations and restrictions on abortion funding are not "directed at women as a class" so much as "abortion as a medical treatment, which, because it involves a potential life, has no parallel as a treatment method." *Bell v. Low Income Women of Texas*, 95 S.W.3d 253, 258 (Tex. 2002) (upholding funding restrictions) (citing *Harris*, 448 U.S. at 325). *See also Fischer v. Dep't of Public Welfare*, 502 A.2d 114, 125 (Pa. 1985) ("the basis for the distinction here is not sex, but abortion") (upholding funding restrictions); *Moe v. Secretary of Administration & Finance*, 417 N.E.2d 387, 407 (Mass. 1981) (Hennessey, C.J., dissenting) (funding restrictions were "directed at abortion as a medical procedure, not women as a class); *Right to Choose v. Byrne*, 450 A.2d 925, 950 (N.J. 1982) (O'Hern, J., dissenting) ("[t]he subject of the legislation is not the person of the recipient, but the nature of the claimed medical service"). Both *Moe* and *Right to Choose* were decided on other grounds. The dissenting justices were addressing alternative arguments raised by the plaintiffs, but not reached by the majority opinions.

45. *Michael M. v. Superior Court*, 450 U.S. 464, 469 (1981). The Nevada Supreme Court has cited *Michael M.* with approval. *See Constancio v. State*, 639 P.2d 547, 548–49 (Nev.

eral district court observed: "Abortion statutes are examples of cases in which the sexes are not biologically similarly situated" because only women are capable of becoming pregnant and having abortions.[46]

A statute prohibiting abortion quite obviously can affect only women because only women are capable of becoming pregnant.[47] Unlike laws that use women's ability to become pregnant (or pregnancy itself) to discriminate against them in *other* areas (*e.g.*, employment opportunities), abortion prohibitions cannot fairly be said to involve a distinction between men and women that is a "mere pretext[] designed to erect an invidious discrimination against [women]."[48]

A prohibition of abortion would not interfere with the exercise of a fundamental state constitutional right, nor would it classify upon the basis of a suspect or quasi-suspect characteristic. Accordingly, it would be subject to rational basis review.[49] A law prohibiting abortion would be rationally related to the State's legitimate interest in protecting unborn human life.

Retained Rights

Article 1, § 20, of the Nevada Constitution provides: "This enumeration of rights shall not be construed to impair or deny others retained by the people."[50] Abortion advocates may be expected to cite § 20 in support of an asserted right to abortion under the state constitution. A proper interpretation of § 20, however, would not appear to support a right to abortion as a "retained right."

Section 20 has been cited in only a handful of cases decided by the Nevada Supreme Court, and never as the sole basis on which a statute has been declared unconstitutional.[51] The state supreme court has held that § 20 is the

---

1982) (upholding former forcible rape statute that applied only to males because only female victims could become pregnant from rape). *See also Olson v. State*, 588 P.2d 1018, 1019 (Nev. 1979) (same with respect to statutory rape statute that applied only to males).

46. *Jane L. v. Bangerter*, 794 F. Supp. 1537, 1549 (D. Utah 1992).

47. *Geduldig v. Aiello*, 417 U.S. 484, 496 n. 20 (1974) ("[n]ormal pregnancy is an objectively, identifiable physical condition with unique characteristics").

48. *Id.*

49. Apart from the equal protection analysis that is set forth in the text, *supra*, it would not appear that a law prohibiting abortion would violate art. 4, §§ 20 and 21. An abortion prohibition would be a statewide law of general application.

50. NEVADA CONST. art. 1, § 20 (2008).

51. In *Zale-Las Vegas, Inc. v. Bulova Watch Co.*, 396 P.2d 683 (Nev. 1964), the court cited art. 1, § 20, along with §§ 1 and 8, and art. 4, § 1, in an opinion striking down the Fair Trade Act. The basis of the decision, however, was that the statute was an unreasonable exercise of the police power. In *Marymount v. Nevada State Bank*, 111 P. 295 (Nev. 1910), the court cited art. 1, § 20, along with §§ 1 and 8, in an opinion striking down a statute that pro-

"equivalent" of the Ninth Amendment.[52] In light of that equivalence, § 20 should be given a parallel interpretation. That, in turn, suggests that if no right to abortion exists under the Ninth Amendment, then none would be recognized under art. 1, § 20. The Supreme Court, however, has rooted the "abortion liberty" in the liberty language of the Due Process Clause of the Fourteenth Amendment, not in the unenumerated rights language of the Ninth Amendment.[53] Because abortion has not been recognized as a "retained right" under the Ninth Amendment, it should not be recognized as one under § 20, either.

The Nevada Supreme Court has implied that art. 1, § 20, retains only those rights that were enjoyed at the time the state constitution was adopted (1864).[54] Abortion, however, was a crime at the time the constitution was adopted (see discussion in the first section of this analysis, *supra*). Accordingly, abortion may not be regarded as a "retained right," that is, a right that existed at the time the state constitution was adopted in 1864.

Conclusion

Based on the foregoing analysis, an argument that the Nevada Constitution protects a right to abortion that is separate from, and independent of, the right to abortion recognized in *Roe v. Wade* would not likely succeed. That, in turn, suggests that if *Roe*, as modified by *Casey*, is ultimately overruled, the State of

---

hibited individuals (as opposed to corporations) from engaging in the banking business. In its opinion, the court noted that "[a]t common law the business of banking was regarded as one of the lawful occupations in which citizens might engage," and added that the banking business "is one of the ancient and ordinary occupations...." *Id.* at 296, 297 (citation and internal quotation marks omitted).

52. *State v. Eighth Judicial District Court*, 708 P.2d 1022, 1024 (Nev. 1985) (statute requiring motorcyclists to wear protective helmets while operating their motorcycles does not violate any "right to privacy" under art. 1, § 20). The Ninth Amendment provides: "The enumeration in the Constitution of certain rights, shall not be construed to deny or disparage others retained by the people." U.S. Const. amend. IX (West 2006).

53. *See Roe*, 410 U.S. at 153; *Casey*, 505 U.S. at 846. In any event, the Ninth Amendment, standing alone, is not a source of substantive rights. *Gibson v. Matthews*, 926 F.2d 532, 537 (6th Cir. 1991). Although "[s]ome unenumerated rights may be of [c]onstitutional magnitude," that is only "by virtue of other amendments, such as the Fifth or Fourteenth Amendment. A person cannot claim a right that exists solely under the Ninth Amendment." *United States v. Vital Health Products, Ltd.*, 786 F. Supp. 761, 777 (E.D. Wis. 1992), *aff'd mem. op., sub nom. United States v. LeBeau*, 985 F.2d 563 (7th Cir. 1993). *See also Charles v. Brown*, 495 F. Supp. 862, 863 (N.D. Ala. 1980) (same).

54. *Riter v. Douglass*, 109 P. at 451.

Nevada could enact and enforce a statute *prohibiting* abortion. Moreover, nothing in the Nevada Constitution precludes Nevada from *regulating* abortion within federal constitutional limits in the meantime.

CHAPTER 32

NEW HAMPSHIRE

Summary

The New Hampshire Supreme Court has not yet decided whether the New Hampshire Constitution protects a right to abortion separate from, and independent of, the right to abortion recognized under the United States Constitution.[1] A careful examination of the state constitution, in light of its history and interpretation, as well as other relevant legal sources, however, suggests that the state supreme court probably would not recognize a state constitutional right to abortion. Thus, if *Roe v. Wade*,[2] as modified by *Planned Parenthood of Southeastern Pennsylvania v. Casey*,[3] were overruled, New Hampshire could prohibit abortion. Moreover, nothing in the state constitution, properly understood, precludes the State from enacting and enforcing reasonable measures regulating abortion within current federal constitutional limits.

Analysis

The principal pre-*Roe* abortion statute prohibited performance of an abortion upon a pregnant woman before "quickening" for any reason,[4] and after quickening unless, "by reason of some malformation or of difficult or protracted labor, it shall have been necessary to preserve the life of the woman or shall

---

1. The New Hampshire Supreme Court has referred to the right to abortion solely as a matter of *federal*, not *state*, constitutional law. *See Smith v. Cote*, 513 A.2d 341, 343–44 (N.H. 1986) ("the United States Supreme Court has held that a woman has a constitutionally secured right to terminate a pregnancy") (citing *Roe v. Wade*).

2. 410 U.S. 113 (1973).

3. 505 U.S. 833 (1992).

4. N.H. REV. STAT. ANN. §585.12 (1955) (a misdemeanor).

have been advised by two physicians to be necessary for that purpose."[5] These statutes, which were never declared unconstitutional, were repealed in 1997.[6]

Based upon arguments that have been raised in other States with similar constitutional provisions, possible sources for an asserted abortion right could include provisions of the New Hampshire Bill of Rights guaranteeing due process of law (art. 15), equal protection (arts. 1, 2, 12), rights of conscience (art. 3), religious freedom (art. 4) and a certain remedy (art. 14); recognizing inherent rights (art. 2); prohibiting religious favoritism (art. 6); and urging frequent recurrence to fundamental principles (art. 38).[7] The analysis that follows addresses each of these provisions.

Inherent Rights, Due Process of Law

Article 2 of the New Hampshire Bill of Rights provides, in pertinent part: "All men have certain natural, essential, and inherent rights-among which are, the enjoying and defending life and liberty; acquiring, possessing, and protecting, property; and, in a word, of seeking and obtaining happiness."[8] Article 15 provides, in part: "No subject shall be ... deprived of his life, liberty, or estate, but by the judgment of his peers, or the law of the land...."[9] "Law of the land" has been consistently construed to mean "due process of law."[10]

In any challenge to an abortion prohibition, abortion advocates are likely to rely upon articles 2 (inherent rights) and 15 (due process) of the Bill of Rights in support of a right to abortion. That reliance would be misplaced, however.

The New Hampshire Supreme Court has not developed a methodology for determining whether an asserted right (or liberty interest) is protected by the inherent rights language of art. 2 or the due process guarantee of art. 15.[11] The

---

5. *Id.* §585.13 (a felony). "Quickening" is that stage of pregnancy, usually sixteen to eighteen weeks gestation, when a woman first detects fetal movement. Under a third statute, if the woman died as a result of the performance of an illegal abortion, the offense was raised to second degree murder. *Id.* §585.14.

6. 1997 N.H. Laws 81, ch. 99, §1.

7. Two other more unlikely sources of an abortion right under the New Hampshire Constitution Bill of Rights-art. 19 (prohibiting unreasonable searches and seizures) and art. 22 (guaranteeing freedom of speech)-are discussed generally in Chapter 3, *supra*.

8. N.H. Const. Part I, art. 2 (2001).

9. *Id.* Part I, art. 15.

10. *Appeal of Portsmouth Trust*, 423 A.2d 603, 605 (N.H. 1980).

11. The court has repeatedly stated that art. 15 "is at least as protective of individual liberties as the fourteenth amendment," *In re Tracy M.*, 624 A.2d 963, 965 (N.H. 1993), but, with two exceptions noted in the text, all of the cases in which such statements appear

court has recognized, however, that certain liberty interests are "fundamental" under art. 2 or art. 15, including "[t]he right of parents to raise and care for their children,"[12] and the right of persons to refuse unwanted medical treatment.[13] Each of these rights has a long and distinguished pedigree in the law.[14]

The court, on the other hand, has held that "nothing in the history of Anglo-American jurisprudence" supports a "fundamental right" to parole,[15] that an adult has no privacy right to engage in sexual intercourse with a minor,[16] and that an otherwise healthy prison inmate does not have the right to starve himself to death.[17] Taken together, these cases suggest that the presence (or absence) of a history and tradition of extending legal protection to an asserted

---

concerned *procedural* due process, not *substantive* due process. *Id.* (standard of proof required in abuse and neglect proceedings); *State v. Gregoire*, 384 A.2d 132, 133 (N.H. 1978) (standard of proof required in criminal recommitment hearings); *In re Shelby R.*, 804 A.2d 435, 437 (N.H. 2002) (recognizing right to court-appointed counsel in abuse and neglect proceedings); *In re Eduardo L.*, 621 A.2d 923, 928 (N.H. 1993) (no right to cross- examine witnesses in a juvenile certification hearing); *Chandler v. Bishop*, 702 A.2d 813, 816 (N.H. 1997) (procedural due process required in child custody disputes).

12. *In re R.A.*, 891 A.2d 564, 572 (N.H. 2005) (citing *In re Nelson*, 825 A.2d 501, 502 (N.H. 2003)). *See also In re Berg*, 886 A.2d 980, 983–84 (N.H. 2005) (same); *In re Shelby R.*, 804 A.2d 435, 437 (N.H. 2002) (same); *Petition of Kerry D.*, 737 A.2d 662, 665 (N.H. 1999) (same); *State v. Robert H.*, 393 A.2d 1387, 1389 (N.H. 1978) (same), *disavowed on other grounds*, *In re Tricia H.*, 493 A.2d 1146, 1151 (N.H. 1985); *Provencal v. Provencal*, 451 A.2d 374, 377 (N.H. 1982) ("a parent's interest in decisions regarding the custody and rearing of his children is a fundamental right which is protected by the due process provisions of the State and Federal Constitutions").

13. *Opinion of the Justices*, 465 A.2d 484, 488 (N.H. 1983) (due process guarantee of art. 15 provides persons with certain fundamental liberty interests, including the right of mentally ill persons "to be free from unjustified intrusion upon their personal security"), *id.* at 489 ("the right of mentally ill persons to refuse medical treatment is a liberty interest which is protected by our State Constitution"); *State v. Hayes*, 389 A.2d 1379, 1381 (N.H. 1978) (criminal defendant has a fundamental right to be free from compulsory medication which could control or alter his normal thought process).

14. "[T]he constitutional right of parents to assume the primary role in decisions concerning the rearing of their children," the state supreme court has observed, "reflects a 'strong tradition' founded on the history and culture of Western civilization, and because the parental rule is 'now established beyond debate as an enduring American tradition.'" *State v. Robert H.*, 393 A.2d at 1388 (quoting *Wisconsin v. Yoder*, 406 U.S. 205, 232 (1972)). *Cruzan v. Director, Missouri Dep't of Health*, 497 U.S. 261, 278–79 & n. 7 (1990) (recognizing right of competent patient to refuse unwanted medical treatment); *Washington v. Glucksberg*, 521 U.S. 702, 719–26 & n. 17 (1997) (same).

15. *State v. Farrow*, 386 A.2d 808, 811 (N.H. 1978).

16. *Goodrow v. Perrin*, 403 A.2d 864, 866 (N.H. 1979).

17. *In re Caulk*, 480 A.2d 93, 95–97 (N.H. 1984).

liberty interest (or right) is of critical importance in determining whether that interest (or right) will be recognized as "fundamental" under art. 2 or art. 15 of the Bill of Rights.[18] There is no history and tradition of extending legal protection to abortion, however.

New Hampshire enacted its first abortion statute in 1848.[19] Under § 1, it was a misdemeanor to attempt to perform an abortion upon a pregnant woman "unless the same shall have been necessary to preserve the life of such woman, or shall have been advised by two physicians to be necessary for that purpose...."[20] Under § 2, it was a felony to attempt to perform an abortion upon a pregnant woman "quick with child," subject to the same exception.[21] Under § 3, if the woman upon whom an abortion was performed or attempted in violation of § 1 or § 2 died, the offense was raised to second degree murder.[22] Section 4 made it a misdemeanor for a woman voluntarily to submit to an illegal abortion.[23] These statutes remained on the books until 1997.[24] In 1873, one hundred years before *Roe v. Wade* was decided, the New Hampshire Supreme Court upheld a murder conviction based upon the performance of an illegal abortion that resulted in the death of the pregnant woman.[25] And on December 29, 1972, barely three weeks before *Roe* was decided, the New Hampshire Supreme Court held that a physician who caused the death of a pregnant woman in the course of performing an illegal abortion could be indicted and

---

18. To the extent that the New Hampshire Supreme Court may consider federal precedent in determining whether an asserted liberty interest (or right) is "fundamental" under the state due process guarantee, abortion would not qualify as a "fundamental" right. Although the Supreme Court characterized the right to choose abortion as "fundamental" in *Roe*, 410 U.S. at 152–53, it tacitly abandoned that characterization in *Casey*, 505 U.S. at 869–79 (Joint Op. of O'Connor, Kennedy and Souter, JJ., replacing *Roe's* "strict scrutiny" standard of review with the more relaxed "undue burden" standard, allowing for a broader measure of abortion regulation).

19. N.H. Laws, ch. 743, § 1 *et seq.* (1848), *codified at* N.H. Compiled Stat. § 227.11 *et seq.* (1853).

20. Ch. 743, § 1, *codified at* N.H. Compiled Stat. § 227.11 (1853).

21. *Id.* § 2, *codified at* N.H. Compiled Stat. § 227.12 (1853).

22. *Id.* § 3, *codified at* N.H. Compiled Stat. § 227.13 (1853).

23. *Id.* § 4, *codified at* N.H. Compiled Stat. § 227.14 (1853). No prosecutions were reported under this section, which was later deleted.

24. N.H. Compiled Stat. § 227.11 *et seq.* (1853), *recodified at* N.H. Gen. Stat. ch. 264, § 11 *et seq.* (1867), *recodified at* N.H. Gen. Laws § 282:11 *et seq.* (1878), *recodified at* N.H. Pub. Stat. § 278:11 *et seq.* (1900), *recodified at* N.H. Pub. Laws § 392:12 *et seq.* (1926), *recodified at* N.H. Rev. Laws § 455.12 *et seq.* (1942), *recodified at* N.H. Rev. Stat. Ann. § 585:12 *et seq.* (1955), *repealed by* 1997 N.H. Laws 81, ch. 99, § 1.

25. *State v. Wood*, 53 N.H. 484 (1873).

prosecuted for manslaughter or, depending upon the circumstances, second degree murder.[26] During the one hundred years between *Wood* and *Millette*, the constitutionality of the state abortion statutes was never challenged. Even before the enactment of the first abortion statute in 1848, abortion was a common law crime, as the state supreme court recognized in a prosecution for homicide of the mother based upon the performance of an illegal abortion.[27]

New Hampshire has recognized the rights of unborn children in a variety of contexts outside of abortion, including tort law, health care law and property law. In tort law, a statutory cause of action for wrongful death may be brought on behalf of an unborn viable child who was viable (capable of sustained survival outside the mother's womb, with or without medical assistance) at the time of its death.[28] A common law action for (nonlethal) prenatal injuries may be brought without regard to the stage of pregnancy when the injuries were inflicted.[29] And the New Hampshire Supreme Court has refused to recognize wrongful life causes of action.[30]

Under New Hampshire's health care statutes, living wills may not direct the withholding or withdrawal of life-sustaining procedures from a pregnant woman,[31] and an agent under a durable power of attorney for health care is similarly limited (subject to narrow exceptions).[32] In property law, subject to certain exceptions, an afterborn child (a child conceived before the death of a

---

26. *State v. Millette*, 299 A.2d 150 (N.H. 1972).

27. *State v. McNab*, 20 N.H. 160, 160–61 (N.H. 1849). *See also Poliquin v. MacDonald*, 135 A.2d 249, 251 (N.H. 1957) ("[t]he common law has always been most solicitous for the welfare of the fetus in connection with its inheritance rights as well as protecting it under the criminal law").

28. *Poliquin*, 135 A.2d at 251, interpreting N.H. Rev. Stat. Ann. § 556.12 (2006). In the absence of legislative reform, however, the court has declined to extend the wrongful death act to *non*viable children who were stillborn. *Wallace v. Wallace*, 421 A.2d 134 (N.H. 1980).

29. *Bennett v. Hymers*, 147 A.2d 108, 110 (N.H. 1958).

30. *Smith v. Cote*, 513 A.2d at 351–55. A "wrongful life" cause of action is a claim brought on behalf of a child who is born with a physical or mental disability or disease that could have been discovered before the child's birth by genetic testing, amniocentesis or other medical screening. The gravamen of the cause of action is that, as a result of a physician's failure to inform the child's parents of the child's disability or disease (or at least of the availability of tests to determine the presence of the disability or disease), they were deprived of the opportunity to abort the child, thus resulting in the birth of a child suffering permanent physical or mental impairment. The state supreme court has recognized wrongful birth actions, however. *Smith*, 513 A.2d at 344–48. A "wrongful birth" cause of action is a claim, based upon the same facts, brought by the parents of the impaired child on their own behalf.

31. N.H. Rev. Stat. Ann. § 137-H:14 (2006).

32. Id. § 137-J:2(V)(c).

parent but born after the parent executes a will) inherits that portion of the decedent's estate that he would have received if the decedent had died intestate (without a will).[33]

A right to abortion cannot be found in the text, structure or history of the New Hampshire Constitution. There is no evidence that the framers of the New Hampshire Constitution intended to limit the Legislature's authority to prohibit abortion. Such an intent would have been remarkable in light of the common law (and later statutory) prohibition of abortion except to save the life of the pregnant woman.

Equal Protection

Three provisions of the New Hampshire Bill of Rights guarantee (or have been interpreted to guarantee) equal protection of the law. Article 1 provides, in pertinent part: "All men are born equally free and independent...."[34] The second sentence of art. 2 provides: "Equality of rights under the law shall not be denied or abridged by this state on account of face, creed, color, sex or national origin."[35] And art. 12 provides, in part: "Every member of the community has a right to be protected by it, in the enjoyment of his life, liberty, and property; he is therefore bound to contribute his share in the expense of such protection, and to yield his personal service when necessary."[36]

For purposes of state equal protection analysis, the New Hampshire Supreme Court applies one of three standards of review. If the classification involves a suspect class or affects a fundamental right, then the strict scrutiny standard applies. Under that standard, the government must show that the classification is necessary to promote "a compelling State interest."[37] If the classification involves an important substantive right, then the court applies the "fair and substantial relationship" test. Under that standard, "the classification 'must be reasonable, not arbitrary, and must rest upon some ground of difference having a fair and substantial relation to the object of the legislation.'"[38] Finally, if the classification does not involve a suspect class, a fundamental right or an important substantive right, then the court applies rational basis review. Under that standard, the classification will be upheld if it is "rationally related to a legitimate state purpose."[39]

---

33. *Id.* § 551:10.
34. N.H. Const. Part I, art. 1 (2001).
35. *Id.* Part I, art. 2 (second sentence).
36. *Id.* Part I, art. 12 (first sentence).
37. *LeClair v. LeClair*, 624 A.2d 1350, 1355 (N.H. 1993).
38. *Id.* at 1356 (citation and internal quotation marks omitted).
39. *Id.* (citation and internal quotation marks omitted).

For the reasons set forth in the previous section of this analysis, a prohibition of abortion would not infringe upon "a fundamental right," nor would it
implicate "an important substantive right."[40] The New Hampshire Supreme
Court has held that sex-based classifications are "suspect,"[41] but it is doubtful
that a prohibition of abortion would be subjected to strict scrutiny review
under the state constitution. Reviewing courts in other States with equal rights
provisions have consistently held that laws that differentiate between the sexes
are permissible and do not violate the state guarantee of gender equality if they
are based upon the unique physical characteristics of a particular sex.[42] As one

---

40. Only two "important substantive rights" have been recognized under the state constitution, the right to a tort recovery, *Brannigan v. Usitalo*, 587 A.2d 1280, 1284 (N.H. 1990),
and the right to use and enjoy private real property subject to zoning regulations, *Asselin
v. Town of Conway*, 607 A.2d 132, 133 (N.H. 1992). Even if abortion were considered an "important substantive right," a prohibition of abortion would arguably satisfy this intermediate standard of judicial review because the prohibition would have a "fair and substantial
relation" to the "object of the legislation," *i.e.*, to preserve unborn human life.

41. *State v. LaPorte*, 587 A.2d 1237, 1239 (N.H. 1991). For example, in *Cheshire Medical Center v. Holbrook*, 663 A.2d 1344 (N.H. 1995), the court held that the common law doctrine of "necessaries," under which a husband was liable for necessaries supplied to his wife,
but no corresponding obligation was imposed on a wife for necessaries furnished to her
husband, was predicated on anachronistic assumptions about marital relations and female
dependence, and violated the equal protection guarantee of the state constitution. *Id.* at
1346–47. "[A] common law rule that distributes benefits or burdens on the basis of gender must be necessary to serve a compelling State interest." *Id.* at 1347. *See also Buckner v.
Buckner*, 415 A.2d 871 (N.H. 1980) (to construe alimony statute to treat husbands less favorably than wives, allowing wives to receive alimony, but not husbands, would violate art.
2 of the New Hampshire Bill of Rights).

42. The cases have upheld rape statutes, *State v. Rivera*, 612 P.2d 526, 530–31 (Haw.
1980), *State v. Fletcher*, 341 So.2d 340, 348 (La. 1976), *Brooks v. State*, 330 A.2d 670, 672–73
(Md. Ct. Sp. App. 1975), *State v. Craig*, 545 P.2d 649 (Mont. 1976), *Finley v. State*, 527
S.W.2d 553, 555–57 (Tex. Crim. App. 1975); statutory rape statutes, *People v. Salinas*, 551
P.2d 703, 705–06 (Colo. 1976), *State v. Bell*, 377 So.2d 303 (La. 1979); an aggravated incest statute, *People v. Boyer*, 349 N.E.2d 50 (Ill. 1976); statutes governing the means of es-
tablishing maternity and paternity, *People v. Morrison*, 584 N.E.2d 509 (Ill. App. Ct. 1991),
A v. X, Y & Z, 641 P.2d 1222, 1224–25 (Wyo. 1982); statutes and rules barring female nudity in bars, *Dydyn v. Dep't of Liquor Control*, 531 A.2d 170, 175 (Conn. App. Ct. 1987);
Messina v. State, 904 S.W.2d 178, 181 (Tex. App.-Dallas 1995, *no pet.*); an ordinance prohibiting public exposure of female breasts, *City of Seattle v. Buchanan*, 584 P.2d 918, 919–21
(Wash. 1978); and limitations on public funding of abortion, *Fischer v. Dep't of Public Welfare*, 502 A.2d 114, 124–26 (Pa. 1985), *Bell v. Low Income Women of Texas*, 95 S.W.3d 253,
257–64 (Tex. 2002). The one exception is *New Mexico Right to Choose/NARAL v. Johnson*,
975 P.2d 841 (N.M. 1998), in which the New Mexico Supreme Court struck down a state
regulation restricting public funding of abortion. In applying "heightened scrutiny," the
court failed to recognize that the funding regulation did not use "the unique ability of

federal district court observed: "Abortion statutes are examples of cases in which the sexes are not biologically similarly situated" because only women are capable of becoming pregnant and having abortions.[43]

A statute prohibiting abortion quite obviously can affect only women because only women are capable of becoming pregnant.[44] Unlike laws that use women's ability to become pregnant (or pregnancy itself) to discriminate against them in *other* areas (*e.g.*, employment opportunities), abortion prohibitions cannot fairly be said to involve a distinction between men and women that is a "mere pretext[] designed to erect an invidious discrimination against [women]."[45]

An abortion prohibition would not classify on the basis of a suspect personal characteristic, nor would it infringe upon fundamental or important substantive rights. Accordingly, it would be subject to rational basis review. Under that standard of review, legislation must be "rationally related to a legitimate governmental interest."[46] A prohibition of abortion would be "rationally related" to the "legitimate governmental interest" in protecting unborn human life. Accordingly, a statute prohibiting abortion would not violate the equal protection guarantees of the New Hampshire Constitution.

Rights of Conscience and Religious Freedom

Article 4 of the New Hampshire Bill of Rights provides: "Among the natural rights, some are, in their very nature unalienable, because no equivalent can be given or received for them. Of this kind are the Rights of Conscience."[47] And art. 5 provides, in part:

> Every individual has a natural and unalienable right to worship God according to the dictates of his own conscience, and reason; and no subject shall be hurt, molested, or restrained, in his person, liberty, or estate, for worshiping God in the manner and season most agree-

---

women to become pregnant and bear children" as a pretext to discriminate against them in *other* respects, *e.g.*, "imposing restrictions on [their] ability to work and participate in public life." *Id.* at 855.

43. *Jane L. v. Bangerter*, 794 F. Supp. 1537, 1549 (D. Utah 1992).

44. *Geduldig v. Aiello*, 417 U.S. 484, 496 n. 20 (1974) ("[n]ormal pregnancy is an objectively, identifiable physical condition with unique characteristics").

45. *Id.*

46. *Boulders v. Town of Strafford*, 903 A.2d 1021, 1029 (N.H. 2006).

47. N.H. Const. Part I, art. 4 (2001).

able to the dictates of his own conscience; or for his religious profession, sentiments, or persuasion....[48]

In any challenge to a statute prohibiting abortion, abortion advocates may argue that the statute interferes with a woman's "Rights of Conscience" under art. 4, and "restrain[s]" her "liberty" to follow her "religious profession" under art. 5, by forbidding her from obtaining an abortion that would be allowed by her religion. There is relatively little case law under either art. 4 or art. 5, but what case law there is suggests that a challenge to an abortion statute based on either provision would not likely succeed.

More than sixty-five years ago, the New Hampshire Supreme Court held that "[a] religious doctrine that divine law should be obeyed rather than man's law when the two conflict may be entitled to statement but not to observance."[49] The state supreme court has continued to adhere to this holding.[50] These decisions offer little support to a religiously (or conscience) based challenge to a statute prohibiting abortion. Entirely apart from the foregoing, the court has expressed the view that "it is necessary in a free exercise case for one to show the coercive effect of the enactment as it operates against him in the practice of his religion."[51] A statute prohibiting abortion would not "coerce" any woman in the practice of her religion, however, because no doctrine in any religion *requires*, as opposed to *permits*, a woman to obtain an abortion unless it is necessary to save her life, an exception which would be included in any abortion statute. A challenge to an abortion prohibition would not likely succeed under either art. 4 or art. 5 of the New Hampshire Bill of Rights.

---

48. *Id.* Part I, art. 5.

49. *State v. Cox*, 16 A.2d 508, 515 (N.H. 1940), *aff'd*, 312 U.S. 569 (1941).

50. *See Petition of Smith*, 652 A.2d 154, 160 (N.H. 1994) (article 5 "prohibits the State from revoking the petitioner's license [to practice psychology] for his religious views but does not prohibit revocation for acts that otherwise constitute unprofessional conduct, regardless of their religious character"); *Appeal of Trotzer*, 719 A.2d 584, 589 (N.H. 1998) (same). Three years before *Cox* was decided, the court upheld a mandatory vaccination statute, holding that the refusal of a father, on religious grounds to have his school age son vaccinated did not "involve any question of religious liberty." *State v. Drew*, 192 A. 629, 631 (N.H. 1937).

51. *Opinion of the Justices*, 228 A.2d 161, 163 (N.H. 1967). Of course, a law that singles out religious practices for regulation would present an entirely different question. *See Church of the Lukumi Babalu Aye, Inc. v. City of Hialeah*, 508 U.S. 520 (1993) (a law that is aimed at specific religious practices must satisfy the "strict scrutiny" standard of judicial review).

Prohibiting Religious Favoritism

Article 6 of the New Hampshire Bill of Rights provides, in part: "[E]very person, denomination or sect shall be equally under the protection of the law; and no subordination of any one sect, denomination or persuasion to another shall ever be established."[52] In any challenge to a statute prohibiting abortion, abortion advocates may argue that the statute does not treat religious denominations and sects "equally" because it "subordinat[es]" the views of those denominations and sects that allow abortion to the views of those who do not.

The New Hampshire Supreme Court has not had occasion to interpret this language from art. 6 of the Bill of Rights. Without expressly holding that art. 5 (guaranteeing religious freedom) and art. 6 (prohibiting religious favoritism) are the state equivalents of the Free Exercise and Establishment Clauses of the First Amendment, the state supreme court has interpreted the state and federal provisions in a consistent manner.[53] That consistency of interpretation suggests that a challenge to an abortion statute that would not succeed under the Religion Clauses of the First Amendment would not succeed under art. 5 or art. 6 of the New Hampshire Bill of Rights, either. For the reasons set forth in Chapter 2, *supra*, an abortion statute could not be successfully challenged on First Amendment grounds. Accordingly, a similar challenge under art. 5 or art. 6 of the New Hampshire Constitution would not likely be successful.

Certain Remedy

Article 14 of the New Hampshire Bill of Rights provides, in part: "Every subject of this state is entitled to a certain remedy, by having recourse to the laws, for all injuries he may receive in his person, property, or character...."[54] In any challenge to a statute prohibiting abortion, abortion advocates may argue that the statute interferes with a woman's control over her own body, and that such interference constitutes an "injury" to her "person," as those terms are used in art. 14, for which the law must provide a "certain remedy." That "remedy," in turn, would be invalidation of the statute. This argument erroneously assumes that art. 14 is, in itself, a source of legal rights, as opposed to a guarantee that there will be a remedy for wrongs defined by *other* sources of law.

---

52. N.H. CONST. Part I, art. 5 (2001).
53. *See Opinion of the Justices*, 228 A.2d 161, 162–65 (N.H. 1967).
54. N.H. CONST. Part I, art. 14 (2001).

As is apparent from its text and structure, art. 14 is concerned with *remedies* for tortiously inflicted injuries-it does not establish what *constitutes* an injury to anyone's "person, property, or character." Those remedies, however, are derived from the common law and, in certain instances, statues enacted by the Legislature, not art. 14. Moreover, the remedies themselves redress injuries recognized by the common law and statutory law, not constitutional "injuries." Article 14, in other words, does not *create* any new causes of actions, but merely *preserves* existing causes of action. New Hampshire case law confirms this understanding.

Article 14 "provides that all citizens have a right to the redress of *actionable* injuries."[55] Whether an injury is "actionable," however, depends on "the statutory and common law rights applicable at the time of the injury."[56] If no statutory or common law rights have been affected (which would be the case if the State prohibited abortion), then there is no "injury" for which the law requires a "certain remedy." Article 14 is concerned with the availability of private civil causes of action and reasonable access to the courts. It places no limitation on the State's power to define and punish crimes and has never been so interpreted.

Fundamental Principles

Article 38 of the New Hampshire Bill of Rights provides:

> A frequent recurrence to the fundamental principles of the constitution, and a constant adherence to justice, moderation, temperance, industry, frugality, and all the social virtues, are indispensably necessary to preserve the blessings of liberty and good government; the people ought, therefore, to have a particular regard to all those principles in the choice of their officers and representatives, and they have a right to require of their law-givers and magistrates, an exact and constant observance of them, in the formation and execution of the laws necessary for the good administration of government.[57]

Abortion advocates might argue that a right to abortion must be regarded as a "fundamental principle" under art. 8. Such an argument is not likely to gain much traction, however. Article 38 urges "frequent recurrence to the fundamental principles of the constitution...." By its own terms, however,

---

55. *Gonya v. Comm'r, New Hampshire Insurance Dep't*, 899 A.2d 278, 281 (N.H. 2006) (emphasis added).

56. *Trovato v. DeVeau*, 736 A.2d 1212, 1214 (N.H. 1999).

57. N.H. Const. Part I, §38 (2001).

art. 38 does not create or establish any "fundamental principles." The New Hampshire Supreme Court has said in passing that art. 38 does not impose any specific requirements, but "merely advises or admonishes."[58] Article 38, therefore, would not be a plausible source of an abortion right under the New Hampshire Constitution.

Conclusion

Based on the foregoing analysis, an argument that the New Hampshire Constitution protects a right to abortion that is separate from, and independent of, the right to abortion recognized in *Roe v. Wade* would not likely succeed. That, in turn, suggests that if *Roe*, as modified by *Casey*, is ultimately overruled, the State of New Hampshire could enact and enforce a statute *prohibiting* abortion. Moreover, nothing in the New Hampshire Constitution precludes New Hampshire from *regulating* abortion within federal constitutional limits in the meantime.

---

58. *State v. Elbert*, 480 A.2d 854, 862 (N.H. 1984).

CHAPTER 33

NEW JERSEY

Summary

As the result of decisions by the New Jersey Supreme Court interpreting the New Jersey Constitution, the State of New Jersey could not prohibit any abortion before viability, or any abortion after viability that would be necessary to preserve the pregnant woman's life or health, even *Roe v. Wade*,[1] as modified by *Planned Parenthood of Southeastern Pennsylvania v. Casey*,[2] were overruled, unless the state constitution is amended to overturn those decisions (or those decisions are overruled). Moreover, by virtue of those same decisions, New Jersey has little or no authority to enact and enforce reasonable regulations of abortion even within current federal constitutional limits.

Analysis

The pre-*Roe* abortion statute prohibited performance of an abortion on a pregnant woman "maliciously or without lawful justification."[3] This statute was declared unconstitutional (on federal, not state, grounds) by a three-judge federal district court in 1972,[4] and was repealed in 1978.[5] Although it is unlikely that the New Jersey Legislature would consider legislation prohibiting abortion if *Roe*, as modified by *Casey*, were overruled, it is virtually certain that the New Jersey Supreme Court would declare unconstitutional any statute pro-

---

1. 410 U.S. 113 (1973).

2. 505 U.S. 833 (1992).

3. N.J. Stat. Ann. § 21:87-1 (West 1969). There was little case law interpreting this language although, at a minimum, it appears that the statute would have allowed an abortion necessary to save the life of the woman. *See State v. Moretti*, 244 A.2d 499, 504 (N.J. 1968).

4. *Y.W.C.A. of Princeton, N.J. v. Kugler*, 342 F.Supp. 1048 (D. N.J. 1972), *vacated and remanded*, 475 F.2d 1398 (3d Cir. 1973), *judgment reinstated*, Civil No. 264–70 (D. N.J. July 24, 1973), *aff'd mem. op.*, 493 F.2d 1402 (3d Cir. 1974).

5. 1978 N.J. Laws 482, 687–88, ch. 95, § 2C:98-2.

hibiting abortion before viability or any statute prohibiting abortion after viability that did not contain exceptions for the life and health of the pregnant woman. That is apparent from a review of the state supreme court's decisions striking down, on state constitutional grounds, laws restricting public funding of abortion and requiring minors to notify their parents of their intention to obtain an abortion (or seek waiver of the notice requirement in a judicial bypass hearing).

In Right to Choose v. Byrne,[6] the New Jersey Supreme Court reviewed the constitutionality of a state statute that prohibited public funding of abortion unless the pregnant woman's life was endangered.[7] A majority of the court held that § 30:4D-6.1 violated the equal protection of the laws guaranteed by the New Jersey Constitution.[8] The opinion was based on art. I, ¶ 1, of the state constitution, which provides:

> All persons are by nature free and independent, and have certain natural and unalienable rights, among which are those of enjoying and defending life and liberty, of acquiring possessing, and protecting property, and of pursuing and obtaining safety and happiness.[9]

By implication, the language of this provision protects the right of privacy and guarantees equal protection of the laws.[10] In *Right to Choose*, the court first considered the character of the right that was implicated by the funding statute. Although the New Jersey Constitution does not guarantee a fundamental right to health or to funding for an abortion, "[t]he right to choose whether to have an abortion ... is a *fundamental right* of all pregnant women, including those entitled to Medicaid reimbursement for necessary medical treatment."[11] "As to that group of women," the court continued, "the challenged statute discriminates between those for whom medical care is necessary for childbirth and those for whom an abortion is medically necessary."[12]

> Under [§] 30:4D-6.1, those needing abortions receive funds only when their lives are at stake. By granting funds when life is at risk, but with-

---

6. 450 A.2d 925 (N.J. 1982).

7. N.J. Stat. Ann. § 30:4D-6.1 (1981).

8. *Right to Choose*, 450 A.2d at 941.

9. N.J. Const. art. I, ¶ 1 (1997).

10. *Right to Choose*, 450 A.2d at 933–34.

11. *Id.* at 934 (emphasis added).

12. *Id.*

holding them when health is endangered, the statute denies equal protection to those women entitled to necessary medical services under Medicaid.

Thus, *the statute impinges upon the fundamental right of a woman to control her body and destiny. That right encompasses one of the most intimate decisions in human experience, the choice to terminate a pregnancy or bear a child. This intensely personal decision is one that should be made by a woman in consultation with trusted advisers, such as her doctor, but without undue government interference.* In this case, however, the State admittedly seeks to influence the decision between abortion and childbirth. Indeed, it concedes that, for a woman who cannot afford either medical procedure, the statute skews the decision in favor of childbirth at the expense of the mother's health.[13]

The statute could not be justified by the State's asserted interest in the protection of "potential life." Conceding the legitimacy of that interest, the court determined that "at no point during pregnancy may it outweigh the superior interest in the life and health of the mother."[14] "Yet the funding restriction gives priority to potential life at the expense of maternal health."[15]

The legislature is under no obligation to pay for any of the costs of medically necessary procedures relating to pregnancy. Nevertheless,

[o]nce it undertakes to fund medically necessary care attendant upon pregnancy, … government must proceed in a neutral manner.… [I]t is not neutral to fund services medically necessary for childbirth while refusing to fund medically necessary abortions. Nor is it neutral to provide one woman with the means to protect her life at the expense of a fetus and to force another woman to sacrifice her health to protect a potential life.[16]

Even under a deferential standard of equal protection review, §30:4D-6.1 failed to pass constitutional muster:

This distinction between life and health is not rationally related to any legitimate state interest. Thus, the statute would fail even the minimum rationality test. *Although the State has a legitimate interest in*

---

13. *Id.* at 934–35 (emphasis added).
14. *Id.* at 935 (citation omitted).
15. *Id.*
16. *Id.*

*protecting potential life, that interest ceases to be legitimate when the re-
sult is to deprive a woman of her right to choose to protect her life and
health.*[17]

In *Right to Choose*, the supreme court held that although the state constitution does not require funding of elective, nontherapeutic abortions, "[a]
woman's right to choose to protect her health by terminating her pregnancy outweighs the State's asserted interest in protecting a potential life at the expense
of her health."[18] Accordingly, the restriction of public funding of abortion violated the New Jersey Constitution.[19]

To save the statute, the court deleted the constitutional defect and construed
§ 30:4D06.1 to limit public funding of abortion to those "medically necessary"
to preserve the life or health of the woman.[20] The determination of "medical
necessity" was left up to the discretion of the woman's physician, guided by
regulations adopted by the Department of Human Services.[21]

The New Jersey Supreme Court's decision in *Right to Choose* leaves little
doubt that the New Jersey Legislature could not prohibit any abortion before
viability for any reason, or after abortion viability that would be necessary to
preserve the life or health of the pregnant woman, even if *Roe*, as modified by
Casey, were overruled. The court held that "[t]he right to choose whether to
have an abortion ... is a *fundamental right* of all pregnant women."[22] Perhaps
the key passage from the opinion is the court's statement that "*at no point during pregnancy* may [the State's interest in "potential life"] outweigh the superior interest in the life and health of the mother."[23]

---

17. *Id.* at 935 n. 6 (emphasis added).

18. *Id.* at 937.

19. *Id.*

20. *Id.* at 937–38.

21. *Id.* at 938. Those guidelines, promulgated pursuant to the lower court's decision in
Right to Choose, state that in determining whether an abortion is "medically necessary," a
physician may consider "[p]hysical, emotional, and psychological factors," as well as "[f]amily
reasons," and "age." N.J. ADMIN. CODE tit. 108, § 10:53-1.14(b).

22. *Right to Choose*, 450 A.2d at 934 (emphasis added).

23. *Id.* at 935 (emphasis added). *See also, id.,* at 937 ("[a] woman's right to choose to
protect her health by terminating her pregnancy outweighs the State's asserted interest in
protecting a potential life at the expense of her health"). The Supreme Court has not yet decided whether a statute prohibiting post-viability abortions must make exceptions for mental, as well as physical, health. *See Voinovich v. Women's Medical Professional Corporation,*
523 U.S. 1036, 1039 (1998) (Thomas, J., dissenting from denial of *certiorari*) (noting that
this issue was not addressed in *Doe v. Bolton,* 410 U.S. 179 (1973), the companion case to
Roe v. Wade). As a result, it is not known whether, as a matter of *state* constitutional law,

In *Planned Parenthood of Central New Jersey v. Farmer*,[24] a majority of the New Jersey Supreme Court struck down the State's parental notice statute.[25] The supreme court held that "the classification created by the Legislature [between minors seeking abortion and those carrying to term] burdens the 'fundamental right of a woman to control her body and destiny.' "[26] Acknowledging that "the State has a substantial interest in preserving the family and protecting the rights of parents," the court determined that "the insubstantial connection between the notification requirement and the interests expressed by the State is not sufficient to sustain the statute" "[w]hen weighed against the right of a young woman to make the most personal and intimate decision whether to carry a child to term...."[27] The court characterized "a minor's right to control her reproductive decisions" as "among the most fundamental of the rights she possesses...."[28]

Relying upon *Right to Choose*, the supreme court held that the state constitution "affords greater protection of a woman's right of privacy than does its federal counterpart."[29] Specifically, the language of art. I, §1, of the New Jersey Constitution "is 'more expansive ... than that of the United States Constitution' [and] incorporates within its terms the right of privacy and its concomitant rights, including a woman's right to make certain fundamental choices."[30] "[A] woman's right to control her body and her future [is] fundamental to individual liberty."[31]

In balancing the minor's liberty interest against the State's interests, the court determined that the parental notification statute subjected minors who choose abortion to burdens not imposed on minors who choose childbirth, including having to comply with the mechanics and inherent delay of the statute and the judicial bypass procedure provided thereunder (for minors who choose not to notify their parents).[32] To justify this difference in treatment, the State asserted its interests in "protect[ing] minors from their own immaturity, fos-

---

the New Jersey Supreme Court would require a post-viability statute to contain a mental health exception. Presently, New Jersey does not have a post-viability statute.

    24. 762 A.2d 620 (N.J. 2000).

    25. N.J. STAT. ANN. §9:17A1-1 *et seq.* (2002).

    26. *Planned Parenthood of Central New Jersey*, 762 A.2d at 621 (quoting *Right to Choose v. Byrne*, 450 A.2d at 934).

    27. *Id.* at 622.

    28. *Id.*

    29. *Id.* at 626; *see also, id.*, at 631–32.

    30. *Id.* at 631 (quoting *Right to Choose*, 450 A.2d at 933).

    31. *Id.* at 632.

    32. Id. at 633–36.

ter[ing] and preserv[ing] the family structure, and protect[ing] parents' rights to raise their children in a manner they deem appropriate."[33] The court found that none of these interests withstood scrutiny.

With respect to the State's first interest, protecting minors from their own immaturity, the court observed that "the State has recognized a minor's maturity in matters relating to her sexuality, reproductive decisions, substance-abuse treatment, and placing her children for adoption."[34] Moreover, according to evidence presented by the plaintiff abortion providers, "minors are quite capable of making informed, thoughtful decisions about the risks of and the reasons for both abortion and childbirth."[35]

With respect to the State's second interest, fostering and preserving the family structure, the court noted the "reality" that the parental notification act "applies to many young women who are justified in not notifying a parent about their abortion decisions" because of "abusive home environments and parental inadequacy...."[36] According to the court, "a law mandating parental notification prior to an abortion can neither mend nor create lines of communication between parent and child"[37] "Indeed," the court continued, "it is the parties' pre-existing relationship that determines whether a young woman involves a parent in the difficult decision whether to seek an abortion."[38] The court observed that "the younger the minor, the more likely it is that she will notify and seek guidance from an adult in her life."[39]

With respect to the State's third interest, the court recognized "the right of parents to raise their children with limited government interference," but added that their right "to direct the care and custody of their children" was subordinate to the desire of their minor children "to exercise a fundamental right independent of parental involvement."[40] The court concluded that "the proffered statutory reasons for requiring parental notification are not furthered by the statute."[41]

In the final section of the majority opinion, the court held that art. I, ¶ 1, of the New Jersey Constitution "does not permit the State to impose disparate

---

33. *Id.* at 636.
34. *Id.*
35. *Id.*
36. *Id.* at 637.
37. *Id.*
38. *Id.*
39. *Id.* at 638 (citing evidence that "ninety percent of minors under age fifteen notify at least one parent about their intent to obtain an abortion").
40. *Id.*
41. *Id.*

and unjustifiable burdens on different classes of young women when fundamental constitutional rights hang in the balance."[42]

> The State has failed to demonstrate a substantial need for the Parental Notification for Abortion Act, even that the asserted need is capable of realization through enforcement of the Act's provisions. Nor does the State offer adequate justification for distinguishing between minors seeking an abortion and minors seeking medical and surgical care relating to their pregnancies. To the contrary, plaintiffs present compelling evidence that neither the interests of parents nor the interests of minors are advanced by the Notification Act, and further that there is no principled basis for imposing special burdens only on that class of minors seeking an abortion.[43]

The court held that "the State's interest in enforcing the statutory classification fails to override the substantial intrusions it imposes on a young woman's fundamental right to an abortion and is unconstitutional under the equal protection principles set forth in our State Constitution."[44]

In *Right to Choose* and *Planned Parenthood of Central New Jersey*, the New Jersey Supreme Court struck down restrictions on public funding of abortion and a requirement that minors notify their parents of their intention to obtain an abortion (or seek a waiver of notice in a judicial bypass hearing). Both cases were based on state equal protection principles and both essentially held that the State may not distinguish between abortion and childbirth. Given these decisions, it is apparent that, in the absence of a state constitutional amendment, New Jersey could not prohibit any pre-viability abortions, or any post-viability abortions that would be necessary to preserve the life or health of the pregnant woman, unless *Roe*, as modified by *Casey*, were overruled. And, as *Right to Choose* and *Planned Parenthood of Central New Jersey* themselves demonstrate, the State has little or no authority to regulate abortion or restrict public funding of abortion even within current federal constitutional limits.

Entirely apart from *Right to Choose*, the New Jersey Supreme Court has shown itself to be friendly to abortion rights claims and hostile to rights asserted on behalf of the unborn. The court, for example, has recognized wrongful birth and wrongful life causes of action,[45] has denied recovery for the wrongful death of

---

42. *Id.*

43. *Id.*

44. *Id.* at 638–39.

45. *Berman v. Allen*, 404 A.2d 8 (N.J. 1979) (wrongful birth); *Schroeder v. Perkel*, 432 A.2d 834 (N.J. 1981) (*same*); *Procanik v. Cillo*, 478 A.2d 755 (N.J. 1984) (wrongful life). A

an unborn child,[46] and, in disregard of express statutory language,[47] has held that private, nonprofit, non-sectarian hospitals, which are quasi-public institutions, may not refuse to perform elective abortions.[48] Moreover, in a decision that is not easily reconciled with the "neutrality" principles enunciated in *Right to Choose*, the state supreme court held that a New Jersey welfare program that denied a family receiving public assistance an increase in their cash benefit upon the birth of an additional child did not unduly influence or coerce poor women "to avoid having children or to abort their pregnancies...."[49]

Conclusion

Because of the New Jersey Supreme Court's decisions in *Right to Choose v. Byrne* and *Planned Parenthood of Central New Jersey v. Farmer*, the State of New Jersey could not prohibit abortions, at least before viability, even if *Roe*, as modified by *Casey*, were overruled, unless the state constitution is amended to overturn the holdings in those decisions (or the decisions themselves are overruled). Moreover, because of those same decisions, the State has little or no authority to regulate abortion within current federal constitutional limits.

"wrongful birth" cause of action is a claim brought on behalf of the parents of a child who is born with a physical or mental disability or disease that could have been discovered before the child's birth by genetic testing, amniocentesis or other medical screening. The gravamen of the action is that, as a result of a physician's failure to inform the child's parents of the child's disability or disease (or at least of the availability of tests to determine the presence of the disability or disease), they were deprived of the opportunity to abort the child, thus resulting in the birth of a child suffering permanent physical or mental impairment. A "wrongful life" cause of action, on the other hand, is a claim, based on the same facts, brought on behalf of the child.

46. *Graf v. Taggert*, 204 A.2d 140 (1964).

47. N.J. Stat. Ann. § 2A:65A-1 *et seq.* (2000).

48. *Doe v. Bridgeton Hospital Ass'n*, 366 A.2d 641 (N.J. 1976).

49. *Sojourner A. v. New Jersey Dep't of Human Services*, 828 A.2d 306, 315 (N.J. 2003).

CHAPTER 34

NEW MEXICO

Summary

As the result of a decision by the New Mexico Supreme Court interpreting the New Mexico Constitution, the State of New Mexico could not prohibit any abortion before viability, or any abortion after viability that would be necessary to preserve the pregnant woman's life or health, even if *Roe v. Wade*,[1] as modified by *Planned Parenthood of Southeastern Pennsylvania v. Casey*,[2] were overruled, unless the state constitution is amended to overturn that decision (or that decision is overruled). Moreover, by virtue of that same decision, New Mexico may not restrict public funding of abortion. Whether the State may regulate abortion within current federal constitutional limits has not been determined, but is doubtful.

Analysis

The pre-*Roe* New Mexico abortion statute was based on §230.3 of the Model Penal Code.[3] An abortion could be performed at any stage of pregnancy when (1) continuation of the pregnancy was likely to result in the death of the woman or "grave impairment" of her physical or mental health, (2) the child probably will have a "grave physical or mental defect," or (3) the pregnancy resulted from reported rape or incest.[4] Pursuant to the Supreme Court's abortion decisions, the limitations on the circumstances under which an abortion could be performed and the requirement that all abortions be performed in hospitals were declared unconstitutional (on federal, not state, grounds) by the New Mexico

---

1. 410 U.S. 113 (1973).

2. 505 U.S. 833 (1992).

3. N.M. STAT. ANN. §40A-5-1 *et seq.* (Michie 1972). The complete text of §230.3 of the Model Penal Code is set out in Appendix B to the Supreme Court's decision in *Doe v. Bolton*, 410 U.S. 179, 205–07 (1973).

4. *Id.* §40A-5-1. The statute also imposed other conditions.

Court of Appeals in *State v. Strance*.[5] The pre-*Roe* statute has not been repealed,[6] but would not be enforceable, even if *Roe*, as modified by *Casey*, were overruled, because of a decision of the New Mexico Supreme Court striking down, on state constitutional grounds, restrictions on public funding of abortion.

In *New Mexico Right to Choose/NARAL v. Johnson*,[7] the New Mexico Supreme Court considered a challenge to a state administrative regulation that limited public funding of abortion to those for which federal reimbursement was available under federal law (life-of-the-mother, rape and incest).[8] The court held that the regulation violated the equal rights amendment of the state constitution,[9] which provides: "Equality of rights under law shall not be denied on account of the sex of any person."[10]

The court first had to determine whether the state equal rights amendment "afford[s] Medicaid-eligible women greater protection against gender discrimination than they receive under federal law."[11] After a review of the text and history of the state constitution, the court concluded that "New Mexico's Equal Rights Amendment is a specific prohibition that provides a legal remedy for the invidious consequences of the gender-based discrimination that prevailed under the common law and civil law tradition that preceded it."[12] "As such," the court continued, "the Equal Rights Amendment requires a searching judicial inquiry concerning state laws that employ gender-based discriminations," an inquiry that "must begin from the premise that such classifications are presumptively unconstitutional, and it is the State's burden to rebut this presumption."[13] It is apparent from the court's opinion that "searching judicial inquiry" is simply another phrase for strict scrutiny.[14] To require anything less than strict

---

5. 506 P.2d 1217 (N.M. Ct. App. 1971).

6. The statute has been renumbered and now appears at N.M. STAT. ANN. § 30-5-1 *et seq.* (Michie 2004).

7. 975 P.2d 841 (N.M. 1998).

8. Pregnancy Termination Procedures, N.M. Dept. of Human Services, Medical Assistance Division Regulation, 6 N.M. Reg. 684 (April 29, 1995), *codified at* 8 N.M. Admin. Code, 4 M.A.D. 766 (May 1, 1995). The regulation is generally referred to as Rule 766.

9. *Right to Choose*, 975 P.2d at 850–57.

10. N.M. CONST. art. II, § 18 (Michie 1992). The equal rights language was added to § 18 in 1972, and was effective as of January 1, 1973.

11. *Right to Choose*, 975 P.2d at 851.

12. *Id.* at 853.

13. *Id.*

14. *Id.* This is evident from the court's statements later in its opinion that "a gender-based classification that operates to the disadvantage of women" is "presumptively unconstitutional," and can survive "heightened scrutiny" only if the State shows that the classification is "the least restrictive means" of advancing "a compelling justification." *Id.* at 856, 857.

scrutiny (*e.g.*, the "intermediate scrutiny" standard employed by the United States Supreme Court in evaluating gender-based discrimination) would undermine the purpose of the equal rights amendment and the intention of the people who adopted it.[15]

The court next had to decide whether heightened scrutiny was required where the classification in question (Rule 766) was "based on a 'physical condition' with respect to which men and women are not similarly situated."[16] The court acknowledged that "not all classifications based on physical characteristics unique to one sex are instances of invidious discrimination."[17] Nevertheless, such classifications are presumptively unconstitutional.[18] "[T]o determine whether a classification based on a physical characteristic unique to one sex results in the denial of 'equality of rights under law' within the meaning of New Mexico's Equal Rights Amendment, we must ascertain whether the classification operates to the disadvantage of persons so classified."[19] The court determined that the abortion funding regulation "[did] not apply the same standard of medical necessity to both men and women," and, therefore, operated to the disadvantage of women.[20] As a consequence, the State was required to show that Rule 766 was supported by "a compelling justification."[21]

The court rejected both of the State's purported justifications of the rule-that it was a legitimate cost-saving measure, and that it also protected the "potential life of the unborn."[22] With respect to the former justification, the court determined that any reduction in the costs to the State by not paying for "medically necessary" abortions would be more than offset by having to pay for the costs associated with pre-natal care and childbirth of poor women who would not be able to obtain an abortion with private funds.[23]

With respect to the latter justification, the court, citing *Roe* and *Casey*, noted that "the State's interest in the potential life of the unborn is never compelling enough to outweigh the interest in the life and health of the mother."[24] Even

---

15. *Id.* at 853 (citing *Opinion of the Justices to the House of Representatives*, 371 N.E.2d 426, 428 (Mass. 1977) (interpreting Massachusetts equal rights amendment)).

16. *Id.* at 854.

17. *Id.*

18. *Id.*

19. *Id.* (citation and internal quotation marks omitted).

20. *Id.* at 844, 855–56.

21. *Id.* at 856.

22. *Id.*

23. *Id.*

24. *Id.* at 857. The New Mexico Supreme Court's invocation of *Roe* and *Casey*, in the context of a public funding issue, is curious. The Supreme Court's decisions in *Harris v.*

assuming that at some stage of a woman's pregnancy the State's interest becomes sufficiently compelling to support the denial of public funding, "Rule 766 is not the least restrictive means of advancing this interest because it prohibits state funding for most medically necessary abortions at all stages of a woman's pregnancy and without regard to her health except in life-threatening situations."[25]

The New Mexico Supreme Court's decision in *New Mexico Right to Choose/NARAL v. Johnson* leaves little doubt that, in the absence of a state constitutional amendment, New Mexico could not enforce the pre-*Roe* abortion statute or enact a statute prohibiting any abortion before viability, or prohibiting any abortion after viability that would be necessary to preserve the life or health of the pregnant woman, even if *Roe*, as modified by *Casey*, were overruled.[26] Admittedly, the court declined to address the plaintiffs' alternative argument that the "a woman's right to reproductive choice is among the inherent rights guaranteed by Article II, Section 4 of the New Mexico Constitution,"[27] and that Rule 766 "unlawfully infringes upon this right because it favors childbirth over abortion."[28] Nevertheless, the court's equal rights analysis suggests that the court would apply the strict scrutiny standard of judicial review to the pre-*Roe* abortion statute or any other statute that attempted to prohibit abortion. Under that standard, the State could not prohibit any abortion before viability (because its interest in "potential life" does not become compelling until viability) or after viability, if the abortion were necessary to preserve the pregnant woman's life or health.

McRae, 448 U.S. 297 (1980), and *Williams v. Zbaraz*, 448 U.S. 358 (1980), make it clear that, regardless of the weight of the relative interests at stake in the abortion decision, neither the federal government nor the State must fund "medically necessary" abortions.

25. *Right to Choose*, 975 P.2d at 857.

26. The Supreme Court has not yet decided whether a statute prohibiting post-viability abortions must make exceptions for mental, as well as physical, health. *See Voinovich v. Women's Medical Professional Corporation*, 523 U.S. 1036, 1039 (1998) (Thomas, J., dissenting from denial of *certiorari*) (noting that this issue was not addressed in *Doe v. Bolton*, 410 U.S. 179 (1973), the companion case to *Roe v. Wade*). As a result, it is not known whether, as a matter of *state* constitutional law, the New Mexico Supreme Court would require a post-viability statute to contain a mental health exception. Presently, New Mexico does not have a post-viability statute.

27. Article II, §4, provides: "All persons are born equally free, and have certain natural, inherent and inalienable rights, among which are the rights of enjoying and defending life and liberty, of acquiring, possessing and protecting property, and seeking and obtaining safety and happiness." N.M. CONST. art. II, §4 (Michie 1992).

28. *Right to Choose*, 975 P.2d at 844.

Conclusion

Because of the New Mexico Supreme Court's decision in *New Mexico Right to Choose/NARAL v. Johnson*, the State of New Mexico could not prohibit abortions, at least before viability, even if *Roe*, as modified by *Casey*, were overruled, unless the state constitution is amended to overturn the holding in *Right to Choose* (or the latter is overruled). Moreover, New Mexico may not restrict public funding of abortion. Whether the State may otherwise regulate abortion within current federal constitutional limits has not been determined, but is doubtful in light of *Right to Choose*.

CHAPTER 35

NEW YORK

Summary

As the result of a decision of the New York Court of Appeals (New York's highest state court) interpreting the New York Constitution, the State of New York could not prohibit any abortion before viability, or any abortion after viability that would be necessary to preserve the pregnant woman's life or health, even if *Roe v. Wade*,[1] as modified by *Planned Parenthood of Southeastern Pennsylvania v. Casey*,[2] were overruled, unless the state constitution is amended (or the language in that decision is repudiated in a subsequent decision of the court of appeals). The State's authority under the state constitution to regulate abortion within current federal constitutional limits is unknown because no such regulations have been enacted to date.

Analysis

In 1970, New York adopted an "abortion-on-demand" statute which allows a woman to have an abortion for any reason through the twenty-fourth week of pregnancy, after which time an abortion may be performed only to save her life.[3] Although it is unlikely that the New York Legislature would consider leg-

---

1. 410 U.S. 113 (1973).
2. 505 U.S. 833 (1992).
3. N.Y. PENAL LAW § 125.00 *et seq.* (McKinney 2004). In a pre-*Roe* decision, the New York Court of Appeals rejected a federal constitutional challenge to the law brought by a guardian *ad litem* on behalf of a class of unborn children. *Byrn v. New York City Health & Hospitals Corp.*, 286 N.E.2d 887 (N.Y. 1972), *appeal dismissed for want of a substantial federal question*, 410 U.S. 949 (1973). Under *Roe*, the restriction of post-24 week abortions to life-of-the-mother situations is unconstitutional to the extent that it prohibits an abortion determined to be necessary for the pregnant woman's health. The Supreme Court has not yet decided whether a statute prohibiting post-viability abortions must make exceptions for mental, as well as physical, health. *See Voinovich v. Women's Medical Professional Corporation*, 523 U.S.

islation prohibiting pre-viability abortions if *Roe*, as modified by *Casey*, were overruled, it is even more unlikely that the New York Court of Appeals would uphold a prohibition of abortion, at least before viability, in the absence of a state constitutional amendment authorizing such legislation.

In *Hope v. Perales*,[4] the court of appeals considered a challenge to the Prenatal Care Assistance Program (PCAP), which pays for prenatal care and related services (but not abortion) for women slightly above the poverty line.[5] In the course of its opinion (which upheld the constitutionality of the program), the court noted that "it is undisputed by defendants that the fundamental right of reproductive choice, inherent in the due process liberty right guaranteed by our State Constitution [referring to art. I, § 6 (last sentence)], is at least as extensive as the Federal constitutional right [recognized in *Roe*]."[6] This language leaves little room for doubt that the court of appeals would strike down any law attempting to prohibit abortion. Moreover, although New York has not enacted any laws regulating abortion since *Roe* was decided, the court's repeated reference to the right to choose abortion as "fundamental,"[7] suggests that the court would view with hostility efforts to regulate abortion. That suggestion is supported by the court's comment that PCAP did not impose "any *direct* burden" on women seeking abortions.[8]

Conclusion

Because of the language in the New York Court of Appeals' decision in *Hope v. Perales*, the State of New York could not prohibit abortions, at least before

---

1036, 1039 (1998) (Thomas, J., dissenting from denial of *certiorari*) (noting that this issue was not addressed in *Doe v. Bolton*, 410 U.S. 179 (1973), the companion case to *Roe v. Wade*). As a result, it is not known whether, as a matter of *state* constitutional law, the New York Court of Appeals would require a post-viability statute to contain a mental health exception.

4. 634 N.E.2d 183 (N.Y. 1994).

5. As a matter of state policy, New York pays for all "medically necessary" abortions of women below the poverty line.

6. *Hope*, 634 N.E.2d at 186 (citing, among other cases, *Rivers v. Katz*, 495 N.E.2d 337 (N.Y. 1986), in which the court of appeals stated: "In our system of government, where notions of individual autonomy and free choice are cherished, it is the individual who must have the final say in respect to decisions regarding his medical treatment in order to insure that the greatest possible protection is accorded his autonomy and freedom from unwanted interference with the furtherance of his own desires." *Id.* at 341 (citations omitted)).

7. *Id.* at 186, 187, 188.

8. *Id.* at 186 (emphasis added).

viability, even if *Roe*, as modified by *Casey*, were overruled, unless the state constitution is amended (or the Court of Appeals repudiates the language in *Hope* regarding abortion right under the New York Constitution). Whether the State may regulate abortion within current federal constitutional limits is doubtful, but has not yet been determined.

CHAPTER 36

NORTH CAROLINA

Summary

The North Carolina Supreme Court has not yet decided whether the North Carolina Constitution protects a right to abortion separate from, and independent of, the right to abortion recognized under the United States Constitution.[1] A careful examination of the state constitution, in light of its history and interpretation, as well as other relevant legal sources, however, suggests that the state supreme court probably would not recognize a state constitutional right to abortion. Thus, if *Roe v. Wade*,[2] as modified by *Planned Parenthood of Southeastern Pennsylvania v. Casey*,[3] were overruled, North Carolina could enact a statute prohibiting abortion. Moreover, nothing in the state constitution, properly understood, precludes the State from enacting and enforcing reasonable measures regulating abortion within current federal constitutional limits.

---

1. The North Carolina Supreme Court has referred to the right to abortion solely as a matter of *federal*, not *state*, constitutional law. *See, e.g., Azzolino v. Dingfelder*, 337 S.E.2d 528, 535 (N.C. 1985) ("pregnant women have been recognized as having an absolute constitutional right, at least until a certain point in their pregnancy, to have an abortion performed for any reason at all or for no reason") (citing *Roe v. Wade*); *State ex rel. Utilities Comm'n v. Carolina Utility Customers Ass'n, Inc.*, 446 S.E.2d 332, 346 n. 6 (N.C. 1994) (same). *See also Stam v. State*, 267 S.E.2d 335, 341 (N.C. Ct. App. 1980) ("a woman has a substantive due process right to choose whether to have an abortion in the first trimester of pregnancy without any state interference") (referring to *Roe*), *aff'd*, 275 S.E.2d 439 (N.C. 1981).

2. 410 U.S. 113 (1973).

3. 505 U.S. 833 (1992).

Analysis

The pre-*Roe* North Carolina abortion statutes were based on § 230.3 of the Model Penal Code.[4] Sections 14-44 and 14-45 prohibited all abortions.[5] Section 14-45.1 excepted from the scope of §§ 14-44 and 14-45 abortions performed by licensed physicians in licensed hospitals when (1) there was "substantial risk that continuance of the pregnancy would threaten the life or gravely impair the health of [the pregnant woman]," (2) there was "substantial risk [that] the child would be born with grave physical or mental defect," or (3) the pregnancy resulted from incest or promptly reported rape.[6] The statutes did not place any express limitation on the stage of pregnancy at which an authorized abortion could be performed.[7] In May 1973, § 14-45.1 was substantially amended to conform to the Supreme Court's abortion decisions.[8]

Based upon arguments that have been raised in North Carolina and other States with similar constitutional provisions, possible sources for an asserted abortion right could include provisions of the Declaration of Rights guaranteeing religious liberty (art. I, § 13), a remedy by due course of law (§ 18), due process of law (§ 19), equality (§ 1) and equal protection (§ 19); recognizing political power in the people (§ 2), the right of the people to alter or abolish the form of government (§ 3) and inalienable rights (§ 1); emphasizing the importance of frequent recurrence to fundamental principles (§ 35); and retaining rights (§ 36).[9] The analysis that follows addresses each of these provisions.

---

4. N.C. GEN. STAT. § 14-44 *et seq.* (1969). The complete text of § 230.3 of the Model Penal Code is set out in Appendix B to the Supreme Court's decision in *Doe v. Bolton*, 410 U.S. 179, 205–07 (1973).

5. *Id.* §§ 14-44, 14-45.

6. *Id.* § 14-45.1. This statute imposed other conditions. Except in emergencies, no abortion could be performed unless the attending physician and two other physicians examined the woman and certified in writing the circumstances which they believed justified an abortion. *Id.* If the woman seeking the abortion was a minor, the written consent of her parents or her guardian was required, or her husband, if the minor was married. *Id.* There was also a residency requirement. *Id.*

7. In a pre-*Roe* decision, a three-judge federal district court rejected a federal constitutional challenge to the statutes. *Corkey v. Edwards*, 322 F. Supp. 1248 (W.D. N.C. 1971), *vacated and remanded*, 412 U.S. 902 (1973).

8. 1973 N.C. Sess. Laws 1057–58, ch. 711, §§ 1, 2.

9. Three other more unlikely sources of an abortion right under the North Carolina Constitution-art. I, § 14 (guaranteeing freedom of speech), § 17 (prohibiting involuntary servitude) and § 20 (prohibiting unreasonable searches and seizures)-are discussed generally in Chapter 3, *supra*.

Religious Liberty

Article I, §13, of the North Carolina Constitution provides: "All persons have a natural and inalienable right to worship Almighty God according to the dictates of their own consciences, and no human authority shall, in any case whatever, control or interfere with the rights of conscience."[10] Article I, §19, prohibits "discrimination by the State because of ... religion...."[11] Although §13 does not contain express language prohibiting the establishment of a religion, it has been construed, along with the anti-discrimination language of §19, to include such a prohibition, similar to the Establishment Clause of the First Amendment.[12]

In any challenge to a statute prohibiting abortion, abortion advocates may raise either or both of two arguments under art. I, §13. First, they may argue that an abortion prohibition interferes with a woman's "rights of conscience" by forbidding her from obtaining an abortion that would be allowed by her religion. Second, they may argue in the alternative (or in addition) that an abortion prohibition constitutes an "establishment of religion" because it reflects sectarian beliefs regarding when human life begins and the sinfulness of abortion. Neither argument would likely prevail.

The North Carolina Supreme Court has held that the freedom protected by the "rights of conscience" language of art. I, §13, "is no more extensive than the freedom to exercise one's religion, which is protected by the First Amendment to the Constitution of the United States."[13] More generally, the state supreme court has stated that, "[t]aken together, these provisions [referring to art. I, §13, the anti-discrimination language of art. I, §19, and the Free Exercise and Establishment Clauses of the First Amendment] may be said to coalesce into a singular guarantee of freedom of religious profession and worship, as well as an equally firmly established principle of separation of church and state."[14] The North Carolina Supreme Court's identification of the protections afforded by art. I, §13, and the anti-discrimination language of art. I, §19, with those afforded by the Free Exercise and Establishment Clauses suggests that a challenge to an abor-

---

10. N.C. Const. art. I, §13 (2003).

11. *Id.* art. I, §19.

12. *Heritage Village Church & Missionary Fellowship, Inc. v. State*, 263 S.E.2d 726, 730 (N.C. 1980).

13. *In re Williams*, 152 S.E.2d 317, 325 (1967).

14. *Heritage Village Church*, 263 S.E.2d at 730 (citation and internal quotation marks omitted). *See also Harris v. Matthews*, 643 S.E.2d 566, 569 (N.C. 2007) (referring to state and federal provisions as "comparable").

tion statute that would not succeed under the Religion Clauses of the First Amendment would not succeed under art. I, §13, or art. I, §19, either. For the reasons set forth in Chapter 2, *supra*, an abortion statute could not be successfully challenged on First Amendment grounds. Accordingly, a similar challenge under art. I, §13, or art. I, §19, would not likely be successful.[15]

Remedy by Due Course of Law

Article I, §18, of the North Carolina Constitution provides, in part, that "every person for an injury done him in his lands, goods, person, or reputation shall have remedy by due course of law...."[16] Abortion advocates might argue that a statute prohibiting abortion interferes with a woman's control over her own body, and that such interference constitutes an "injury" to her "person," as those terms are used in §18, for which there must be a "remedy by due course of law." That "remedy," in turn, would be invalidation of the statute. This argument assumes that art. I, §18, confers substantive rights. The case law is clear, however, that it does not.

The North Carolina Supreme Court has noted that the "remedy" guaranteed by art. I, §18, "for an injury done" is qualified by the words "by due course of law."[17] "This means," the court explained, "that the remedy constitutionally guaranteed must be one that is *legally cognizable*. The legislature has the power to define the circumstances under which a remedy is legally cognizable and those under which it is not."[18] If the Legislature determines that certain con-

---

15. Entirely apart from the North Carolina Supreme Court's reliance on federal precedent in interpreting art. I, §13, and the anti-discrimination language of art. I, §19, an argument challenging an abortion prohibition on the basis that it "establishes" a religion by embodying sectarian views regarding the sinfulness of abortion would appear to be foreclosed by a decision of the court rejecting a challenge to a Sunday closing law. In *Raleigh Mobile Home Sales, Inc. v. Tomlinson*, 174 S.E.2d 542, 546 (N.C. 1970), the state supreme court held that "a law requiring the observance of Sunday as a day of rest and relaxation" did not constitute "a law establishing a religion" merely because "it is in harmony with the religious beliefs of most Christian denominations"). If mandating a "day of rest" on Sunday does not violate art. I, §13, or the anti-discrimination language of art. I, §19, even though it may be "in harmony with the religious beliefs of most Christian denominations," then neither would a law prohibiting abortion, regardless of whether the law "harmon[izes]" with religious views regarding the sinfulness of abortion.

16. N.C. Const. art. I, §18 (2003).

17. *Lamb v. Wedgwood South Corp.*, 302 S.E.2d 868, 882 (N.C. 1983).

18. *Id.* (emphasis added). *See also Pinkham v. Unborn Children of Jather Pinkham*, 40 S.E.2d 690, 694 (N.C. 1946) ("no person has a vested right in a continuance of the common or statute law").

duct (*e.g.*, abortion) shall be illegal, then, of course, there is there is no "legally cognizable" right to engage in such conduct and, therefore, no "injury" for which § 18 mandates a remedy. Because art. I, § 18, is not a source of substantive rights, it could not provide a basis for invalidating an otherwise constitutional statute of the State.[19]

Due Process of Law, Inalienable Rights

Article I, § 19, of the North Carolina Constitution provides, in part: "No person shall be ... deprived of his life, liberty or property, but by the law of the land."[20] Article I, § 1, provides, in part, that "all persons ... are endowed by their Creator with certain inalienable rights; that among these are life, liberty, the enjoyment of the fruits of their own labor, and the pursuit of happiness."[21] The North Carolina Supreme Court has held that "the Law of the Land Clause ... is synonymous with due process of law as found in the Fourteenth Amendment to the Federal Constitution."[22] The same standard of judicial review applies to statutes challenged under art. I, § 1, and the "law of the land" clause of art. I, § 19.[23]

In any challenge to an abortion prohibition that North Carolina may enact, abortion advocates are most likely to rely upon art. I, § 1, and the "law of the land" clause of art. I, § 19, arguing that the prohibition interferes with a pregnant woman's "liberty" interest in obtaining an abortion. Such an argument probably would not succeed, however.

The North Carolina Supreme Court has recognized that the "law of the land" clause of art. I, § 19, like the federal Due Process Clause, has a substan-

---

19. It should not be surprising to note, therefore, that no criminal statute has ever been struck down on the authority of the "remedy by due course of law" language of art. I, § 18.

20. N.C. Const. art. I, § 19 (2003).

21. *Id.* art. I, § 1.

22. *State v. Bryant*, 614 S.E.2d 479, 485 (N.C. 2005). In interpreting the "law of the land" clause, however, the North Carolina Supreme Court is *not* bound by the Supreme Court's interpretation of the Due Process Clause of the Fourteenth Amendment. *McNeill v. Harnett County*, 398 S.E.2d 475, 481 (N.C. 1990).

23. *Treants Enterprises v. Onslow County*, 360 S.E.2d 783, 785 (N.C. 1987). As one commentator has observed, however, "[t]he rights to life, liberty, and the pursuit of happiness have not given rise to much litigation, presumably because of more detailed provisions elsewhere in the constitution...." John V. Orth, The North Carolina State Constitution[:] A Reference Guide 38 (Westport, Conn. 1993). Accordingly, the analysis that follows will focus on the "law of the land" clause of art. I, § 19.

tive, as well as a procedural, component.[24] "Not every deprivation of liberty or property," the court explained, "constitutes a violation of substantive due process granted under article I, section 19."[25] "Generally, any such deprivation is only unconstitutional where the challenged law bears no rational relation to a valid state objective."[26] "If," however, "the right is ... fundamental, then the court must apply a strict scrutiny analysis wherein the party seeking to apply the law must demonstrate that it serves a compelling state interest."[27] A "fundamental right," in turn, is "a right explicitly or implicitly guaranteed to individuals by the United States Constitution or a state constitution."[28]

The North Carolina Constitution does not explicitly guarantee a right to obtain an abortion. Nor, in light of the history, legal traditions and practices of the State, can it be said that it implicitly guarantees such a right, either.[29]

In a case decided in 1880, the North Carolina Supreme Court recognized that abortion was a common law crime at any stage of pregnancy. In *State v. Slagle*,[30] the court held that the offense of abortion "may be committed at any stage of pregnancy,"[31] not just after "quickening" (that stage of pregnancy, usually sixteen to eighteen weeks gestation, when the woman first detects fetal movement). The following year, North Carolina enacted its first abortion statute.[32]

---

24. *See Affordable Care, Inc. v. North Carolina State Board of Dental Examiners*, 571 So.2d 52, 59 (N.C. 2002).

25. *Id.*

26. *Id.*

27. *Id.*

28. *Comer v. Ammons*, 522 S.E.2d 77, 82 (N.C. App. 1999). To the extent that the North Carolina Supreme Court recognizes the same fundamental rights under the *state* "law of the land" guarantee as the Supreme Court does under the *federal* due process guarantee, abortion would not qualify as a "fundamental" right. Although the Supreme Court characterized the right to choose abortion as "fundamental" in *Roe*, 410 U.S. at 152–53, it tacitly abandoned that characterization in *Casey*, 505 U.S. at 869–79 (Joint Op. of O'Connor, Kennedy and Souter, JJ., replacing *Roe's* "strict scrutiny" standard of review with the more relaxed "undue burden" standard, allowing for a broader measure of abortion regulation).

29. Indeed, it is not at all apparent that the North Carolina Supreme Court has ever recognized a fundamental right under the "law of the land" clause of art. I, § 19. The court, for example, has held that there is no protected privacy right to practice unorthodox medical treatment. *In re Guess*, 393 S.E.2d 833, 839–40 (N.C. 1990) (homeopathic medicine). *See also Majebe v. Board of Medical Examiners*, 416 S.E.2d 404, 407 (N.C. Ct. App. 1992) (same with respect to practice of acupuncture).

30. 83 N.C. 631 (1880).

31. *Id.* at 632.

32. 1881 N.C. Laws 584, ch. 351.

Section 1 made it a felony to perform an abortion upon "any woman either pregnant or quick with child ... intent thereby to destroy said child, unless the same shall have been necessary to preserve the life of such mother...."[33] Section 2 made it a misdemeanor to perform an abortion upon "any pregnant woman ... with intent thereby to procure the miscarriage of any such woman...."[34] These sections remained on the books, substantially unchanged, until 1967,[35] when North Carolina enacted a statute based on the Model Penal Code.[36] In 1947, the North Carolina Supreme Court held that § 1 of the 1881 Act "was designed to protect the life of a child *in* [*sic*] *ventre sa mere*...."[37]

Prior to *Roe*, the North Carolina Supreme Court regularly affirmed abortion convictions without any hint or suggestion that the prosecutions or convictions were barred by the state constitution.[38] Subsequent to *Roe*, the North Carolina Legislature enacted a range of legislation regulating the practice of abortion.[39]

From the time when North Carolina was admitted to the Union, when abortion was a common law crime, until 1967, when the Model Penal Code provision was enacted, the State of North Carolina prohibited abortion except to save the life of the pregnant woman. That history, along with the state supreme court's acknowledgment that the very first abortion statute had been designed to protect unborn human life, strongly suggests that there is no fundamental

---

33. *Id.* § 1.

34. *Id.* § 2.

35. N.C. Code §§ 975, 976 (1883), *recodified at* N.C. Rev. Stat. §§ 3618, 3619 (1908), *recodified at* N.C. Cons. Stat. §§ 4226, 4227 (1919), *recodified at* N.C. Gen. Stat. §§ 14-44, 14-45 (1953).

36. *See* nn. 4-6 and accompanying text, *supra.*

37. *State v. Jordon*, 227 N.C. 579, 580 (N.C. 1947). The phrase, "*en ventre sa mere*," is Law French for "in its mother's womb." Black's Law Dictionary 534 (6th ed. 1990). *See also State v. Powell*, 106 S.E.133, 133 (N.C. 1921) (the criminal intent proscribed by § 1 was "the purpose to destroy the child").

38. *State v. Crews*, 38 S.E. 293 (N.C. 1901); *State v. Shaft*, 81 S.E. 932 (N.C. 1914); *State v. Brady*, 99 S.E. 7 (N.C. 1919); *State v. Martin*, 109 S.E. 74 (N.C. 1921); *State v. Evans*, 190 S.E. 724 (N.C. 1937); *State v. Baker*, 193 S.E. 22 (N.C. 1937); *State v. Thompson*, 4 S.E.2d 615 (N.C. 1939); *State v. Diliard*, 27 S.E.2d 85 (N.C. 1943); *State v. Furley*, 95 S.E.2d 448 (N.C. 1956); *State v. Lee*, 103 S.E.2d 295 (N.C. 1958); *State v. Perry*, 108 S.E.2d 447 (N.C. 1959); *State v. Hoover*, 113 S.E.2d 281 (N.C. 1960); *State v. Brooks*, 148 S.E.2d 263 (N.C. 1966). *See also State v. Slagle*, 83 N.C. 631 (1880) (decided under common law).

39. N.C. Gen. Stat. § 90-21-6 *et seq.* (2005) (mandating parental consent); §§ 108A-25(b), 108A- 54, 108A-56 (2005), 10A N.C. Admin. Code 220.0117 (restricting public funding of abortion for indigent women); N.C. Gen. Stat. § 14-45.1(a) (2005) (authorizing clinic regulations), 10A N.C. Admin. Code 14E.0101 *et seq.* (clinic regulations); N.C. Gen. Stat. § 14-45.1(e), (f) (recognizing individual and institutional rights of conscience).

interest in obtaining an abortion under the liberty clauses of art. I, §§ 1 and 19 of the North Carolina Constitution. That suggestion, in turn, is supported by other sources of law. North Carolina has recognized the rights of unborn children in a variety of contexts outside of abortion, including criminal law, tort law, health care law, property law and guardianship law.[40]

In criminal law, causing the stillbirth of an unborn child is a crime, without regard to the state of pregnancy when stillbirth is caused.[41] In tort law, a statutory cause of action for wrongful death may be brought on behalf of an unborn child who was viable (capable of sustained survival outside the mother's womb, with or without medical assistance) at the time of its death.[42] A common law cause of action for (nonlethal) prenatal injuries may be brought without regard to the stage of pregnancy when the injuries were inflicted.[43] And the North Carolina Supreme Court has refused to recognize either wrongful life or wrongful birth causes of action.[44]

In property law, the "[l]ineal descendants and other relatives of an intestate [a person who dies without a will] born within 10 lunar months [280 days] after the death of the intestate, shall inherit as if they had been born in the lifetime of the intestate and had survived him."[45] Under another statute, an

---

40. The North Carolina Supreme Court, however, has held that the unborn child is not a "person," as that term is used in art. I, §§ 1 and 19, of the North Carolina Constitution. *State v. Stam*, 275 S.E.2d 439, 441 (N.C. 1981).

41. N.C. GEN. STAT. § 14-18.2 (2005).

42. *DiDonato v. Workman*, 358 S.E.2d 489, 491–93 (N.C. 1987), interpreting N.C. GEN. STAT. § 28A-18-2 (2007).

43. *Stetson* v. Easterling, 161 S.E.2d 531, 534 (N.C. 1968).

44. *Azzolino v. Dingfelder*, 337 S.E.2d at 532–33 (wrongful life), *id.* at 533–37 (wrongful birth). With respect to the latter cause of action, the court rejected the view that "the existence of a human life can constitute an injury cognizable at law." *Id.* at 534. A "wrongful life" cause of action is a claim brought on behalf of a child who is born with a physical or mental disability or disease that could have been discovered before the child's birth by genetic testing, amniocentesis or other medical screening. The gravamen of the action is that, as a result of a physician's failure to inform the child's parents of the child's disability or disease (or at least of the availability of tests to determine the presence of the disability or disease), they were deprived of the opportunity to abort the child, thus resulting in the birth of a child suffering permanent physical or mental impairment. For the reasons set forth in the text, very few courts recognize "wrongful life" causes of action because an assessment of damages requires the courts to compare the value of life, albeit with some degree of physical or mental impairment, to nonexistence. A "wrongful birth" cause of action, on the other hand, is a claim, based on the same facts, brought on behalf of the parents of the impaired child. Unlike the North Carolina Supreme Court, most courts that have considered "wrongful birth" causes of action have recognized them.

45. N.C. GEN. STAT. § 29-9 (2005).

unborn child "shall be deemed a person capable of taking by deed or other writing any estate whatever in the same manner as if he were born."[46] And, subject to certain exceptions, an afterborn child (a child conceived before the death of a parent but born after the parent executes a will) receives the same share of the decedent's estate that he would have received if the decedent had died intestate.[47] Finally, a court may appoint a guardian *ad litem* to protect the interests of an unborn child.[48]

In light of the history of abortion regulation in North Carolina, the North Carolina Supreme Court's recognition that the first abortion statute was intended to protect unborn children, the enactment of legislation regulating abortion and its funding, and the rights extended to unborn children outside the area of abortion, it cannot plausibly be said that the liberty clauses of the North Carolina Constitution confer a right to abortion. More generally, a right to abortion cannot be found in the text or structure of the North Carolina Constitution. There is no evidence that either the framers or ratifiers of either the 1868 or 1971 North Carolina Constitution intended the Declaration of Rights to limit the Legislature's authority to prohibit abortion.[49]

Equality, Equal Protection

Article I, § 1, of the North Carolina Constitution provides, in part, that "all persons are created equal...."[50] Article I, § 19, provides, in part: "No person shall be denied the equal protection of the laws...."[51] The North Carolina Supreme Court has held that the equal protection clause of art. I, § 19, "is functionally equivalent to the Equal Protection Clause of the Fourteenth Amendment to the Constitution of the United States."[52] Accordingly, "[w]hen resolving challenged classifications under the equal protection clause of the State Constitution, this Court applies the same test used by federal courts under the

---

46. *Id.* § 41-5.

47. *Id.* § 31-5.5.

48. Rule 17(b)(4) of the North Carolina Rules of Civil Procedure.

49. *See* JOURNAL OF THE CONSTITUTIONAL CONVENTION OF THE STATE OF NORTH CAROLINA AT ITS SESSION 1868 165-71, 209–16 (first and second readings of the Declaration of Rights); 226–32 (third reading of the Declaration of Rights)(Raleigh 1868); REPORT OF THE NORTH CAROLINA STATE CONSTITUTION STUDY COMMISSION TO THE NORTH CAROLINA STATE BAR AND THE NORTH CAROLINA BAR ASSOCIATION 73–75 (discussing proposed revisions to the Declaration of Rights) (Raleigh 1968).

50. N.C. CONST. art. I, § 1 (2003).

51. *Id.* art. I, § 19.

52. *White v. Pate*, 304 S.E.2d 199, 203 (N.C. 1983).

parallel clause in the United States Constitution."[53] Under that test, "[i]f the statute does not impact upon a suspect class or a fundamental right, it is necessary to show only that the classification created by the statute bears a rational relationship to some legitimate state interest."[54]

Strict scrutiny would not apply to review of an abortion prohibition because, for the reasons set forth in the preceding section of this analysis, neither the recognition of inalienable rights (art. I, §1), nor the guarantee of due process (art. I, §19), confers a "fundamental right" to abortion. Nor would the prohibition of abortion classify persons on the basis of a "suspect" personal characteristic (*e.g.*, race).

Abortion advocates may argue in the alternative, however, that a statute prohibiting abortion discriminates against women and is subject to intermediate scrutiny under both art. I, §1, and art. I, §19, because only women are capable of becoming pregnant. For purposes of both state and federal equal protection analysis, "[g]ender-based distinctions in the law must 'serve important governmental objectives and must be substantially related to achievement of those objectives'...."[55] An abortion prohibition would appear to satisfy this level of scrutiny because the prohibition would be "substantially related" to the "important governmental objective" of protecting unborn human life. Nevertheless, the standard applicable to sex-based discrimination should not apply to an abortion prohibition. Abortion laws do not discriminate on the basis of sex.

First, the United States Supreme Court has reviewed restrictions on abortion funding under a rational basis standard of review, *not* under the intermediate (heightened) scrutiny required of gender-based classifications.[56] Indeed, the Court has held that "the disfavoring of abortion ... is not *ipso facto* sex discrimination," and, citing its decisions in *Harris* and other cases addressing abortion funding, stated that "the constitutional test applicable to government abortion-funding restrictions is not the heightened-scrutiny standard that our cases demand for sex discrimination, ... but the ordinary rationality standard."[57]

---

53. *Bacon v. Lee*, 549 S.E.2d 840, 856 n. 11 (N.C. 2001).

54. *Richardson v. North Carolina Dep't of Corrections*, 478 S.E.2d 501, 505 (N.C. 1996).

55. *Dunn v. Pate*, 431 S.E.2d 178, 182 (N.C. 1993) (quoting *Craig v. Boren*, 429 U.S. 190, 197 (1976)). *See also Morrison-Tiffin v. Hampton*, 451 S.E.2d 650, 655 (N.C. Ct. App. 1995) (same).

56. *Harris v. McRae*, 448 U.S. 297, 321–26 (1980).

57. *Bray v. Alexandria Women's Health Clinic*, 506 U.S. 263, 273 (1993). Several state supreme courts and individual state supreme court justices have recognized that abortion regulations and restrictions on abortion funding are not "directed at women as a class" so much as "abortion as a medical treatment, which, because it involves a potential life, has no parallel as a treatment method." *Bell v. Low Income Women of Texas*, 95 S.W.3d 253, 258 (Tex. 2002) (upholding funding restrictions) (citing *Harris*, 448 U.S. at 325). *See also Fis-*

Second, even assuming that an abortion prohibition differentiates between men and women on the basis of sex, and would otherwise be subject to a higher standard of review, the Supreme Court has held that biological differences between men and women may justify different treatment based on those differences. In upholding a statutory rape statute that applied only to males, the Supreme Court noted, "this Court has consistently upheld statutes where the gender classification is not invidious, but rather realistically reflects the fact that the sexes are not similarly situated in certain circumstances."[58] As one federal district court observed: "Abortion statutes are examples of cases in which the sexes are not biologically similarly situated" because only women are capable of becoming pregnant and having abortions.[59]

A statute prohibiting abortion quite obviously can affect only women because only women are capable of becoming pregnant.[60] Unlike laws that use women's ability to become pregnant (or pregnancy itself) to discriminate against them in *other* areas (*e.g.*, employment opportunities), abortion prohibitions cannot fairly be said to involve a distinction between men and women that is a "mere pretext[] designed to erect an invidious discrimination against [women]."[61]

A prohibition of abortion would not interfere with the exercise of a fundamental state constitutional right, nor would it classify upon the basis of a suspect or quasi-suspect characteristic. Accordingly, it would be subject to rational basis review. A law prohibiting abortion would be rationally related to the State's legitimate interest in protecting unborn human life.[62]

---

cher v. Dep't of Public Welfare, 502 A.2d 114, 125 (Pa. 1985) ("the basis for the distinction here is not sex, but abortion") (upholding funding restrictions); *Moe v. Secretary of Administration & Finance*, 417 N.E.2d 387, 407 (Mass. 1981) (Hennessey, C.J., dissenting) (funding restrictions were "directed at abortion as a medical procedure, not women as a class"); *Right to Choose v. Byrne*, 450 A.2d 925, 950 (N.J. 1982) (O'Hern, J., dissenting) ("[t]he subject of the legislation is not the person of the recipient, but the nature of the claimed medical service"). Both *Moe* and *Right to Choose* were decided on other grounds. The dissenting justices were addressing alternative arguments raised by the plaintiffs, but not reached by the majority opinions.

58. *Michael M. v. Superior Court*, 450 U.S. 464, 469 (1981). The North Carolina Supreme Court reached the same result in a decision two years earlier. *See State v. Wilson*, 250 S.E.2d 621, 629–30 (N.C. 1979) (upholding statutory rape statute that applied only to males).

59. *Jane L. v. Bangerter*, 794 F. Supp. 1537, 1549 (D. Utah 1992).

60. *Geduldig v. Aiello*, 417 U.S. 484, 496 n. 20 (1974) ("[n]ormal pregnancy is an objectively, identifiable physical condition with unique characteristics").

61. *Id.*

62. *See Rosie J. v. Dep't of Human Resources*, 491 S.E.2d 535, 537 (N.C. 1997) ("[t]he encouragement of childbirth is a legitimate governmental objective") (upholding restrictions on public funding of abortion).

Political Power

Article I, §2, of the North Carolina Constitution provides: "All political power is vested in and derived from the people; all government of right originates from the people, is founded upon their will only, and is instituted solely for the good of the whole."[63] In a challenge to a statute prohibiting abortion, abortion advocates might argue that the statute interferes with the "political power" of the people because it does not serve "the good of the whole." Given the purpose of §2, however, this argument would not likely prevail.

Article I, §2, itself, imposes no restraints, express or implied, on the legislature's power. Such restraints as do exist are found in other provisions of the state constitution (principally, other sections of the Declaration of Rights).[64] Accordingly, §2, which simply recognizes that political power rests in the people,[65] would not prevent the General Assembly from enacting an abortion prohibition. Whether a given law serves "the good of the whole," within the meaning of art. I, §2, presents a political question for the legislature (and, ultimately, the people) to decide, not a constitutional question for the judiciary.

Right to Alter or Abolish the Form of Government

Article I, §3, of the North Carolina Constitution provides:

> The people of this State have the inherent, sole and exclusive right of regulating the internal government and police thereof, and of altering or abolishing their Constitution and form of government whenever it may be necessary to their safety and happiness; but every such right shall be exercised in pursuance of law and consistently with the Constitution of the United States.[66]

In any challenge to a statute prohibiting abortion, abortion advocates might argue that the statute interferes with the "inherent, sole and exclusive right"

---

63. N.C. Const. art. I, §2 (2003).

64. "All power which is not expressly limited by the people in our State Constitution remains with the people, and an act of the people through their representatives in the legislature is valid unless prohibited by that Constitution." *State ex rel. Martin v. Preston*, 385 S.E.2d 473, 479 (N.C. 1989). *See also Painter v. Wake County Board of Education*, 217 S.E.2d 650, 659 (N.C. 1975) ("[a]n Act of our General Assembly is legal when the Constitution contains no prohibition against it") (discussing art. I, §2).

65. *See Martin v. Thornburg*, 359 S.E.2d 472, 479 (N.C. 1987) ("the sovereign power … is vested in and derived from the people").

66. N.C. Const. art. I, §3 (2003).

of the people to "regulat[e] the internal government" because it does not promote their "safety and happiness." Given the purpose of § 3, this argument
would not likely prevail.

The purpose of art. I, § 3, is to secure to the people themselves, through
the amendment process, the right to decide whether, how and to what extent the organic instrument of government should be changed. Section 3,
thus, is not a source of substantive rights (other than the right to "alter or
abolish" the state constitution). Rather, it recognizes the people as the ultimate source of authority in a republican form of government. As such, it
could not serve as a basis for asserting a right to abortion. Whether a given
law promotes the "safety and happiness" of the people, within the meaning
of § 3, is a political question for the legislature to decide, not a constitutional
question for the judiciary.

One commentator has observed that §§ 2 and 3 of the North Carolina Declaration of Rights "contain both a general and a specific assertion of democratic
theory."[67] Because North Carolina's first constitution lacked a preamble, "these
sections originally served to declare the revolutionary faith in popular sovereignty."[68] "Displaced in 1868, when a conventional preamble was added, they
now serve as a fuller theoretical statement of that principle."[69] Nevertheless,
"[b]ecause of their abstractness, they do not give rise to justiciable rights; the
details of democracy ... are reserved for later articles of the constitution," while
"[t]he mechanics of constitutional amendment are set out in Article XIII."[70]

Fundamental Principles

Article I, § 35, of the North Carolina Constitution provides: "A frequent recurrence to fundamental principles is absolutely necessary to preserve the blessings of liberty."[71]

Abortion advocates might argue that a right to abortion must be regarded
as a "fundamental principle" under art. I, § 35. Such an argument is not likely
to gain much traction, however. Section 35 urges "frequent recurrence to fundamental principles," but does not, by its own terms, create or establish any "fundamental principles." Art. I, § 35, therefore, would not be a plausible source of
an abortion right under the North Carolina Constitution

---

67. Orth, The North Carolina State Constitution at 39.
68. *Id.* at 40.
69. *Id.*
70. *Id.*
71. N.C. Const. art. I, § 35 (2003).

Section 35 is not a source of substantive rights,[72] but simply a "salutary reminder" to "[a]ll generations ... to return *ad fontes* (to the sources) and rethink for themselves the implications of the fundamental principles of self-government that animated the revolutionary generation."[73]

Retained Rights

Article I, §36, of the North Carolina Constitution provides: "The enumeration of rights in this Article shall not be construed to impair or deny others retained by the people."[74] In any challenge to a statute prohibiting abortion, abortion advocates may be expected to argue that abortion is a "retained right" under §36. Such an argument would not likely prevail.

Article I, §36, has been cited in relatively few North Carolina decisions and authoritatively interpreted in none. The North Carolina Supreme Court has never recognized an unenumerated right under §36. An entirely plausible reading of §36 is that the enumeration of certain rights in the state constitution should not be construed to "impair or deny" other rights retained by the people under the common law or statutes. But even if §36 is understood to retain unspecified *constitutional* rights (as opposed to *common law* or *statutory* rights), abortion could not plausibly be considered to be among such rights because, at the time the 1868 North Carolina Constitution was adopted, abortion was a common law crime.[75] The argument that §36 "retained" as an unenumerated "right" conduct that was criminal when the state constitution was adopted is, at the very least counterintuitive.

The language of §36 appears to be based on the Ninth Amendment, which provides: "The enumeration in the Constitution of certain rights, shall not be construed to deny or disparage others retained by the people."[76] In light of that equivalence, §36 should be given a parallel interpretation. That, in turn, suggests that if no right to abortion exists under the Ninth Amendment, then none would be recognized under art. I, §36. The Supreme Court, however, has rooted the "abortion liberty" in the liberty language of the Due Process Clause of the Fourteenth Amendment, not in the unenumerated rights lan-

---

72. *Auger v. Auger*, 573 S.E.2d 125, 131 (N.C. 2002).

73. Orth, THE NORTH CAROLINA STATE CONSTITUTION at 76.

74. N.C. CONST. art. I, §36 (2003).

75. It was also a statutory crime, subject to the exceptions previously noted, when the 1971 North Carolina Constitution was adopted.

76. U.S. CONST. AMEND. IX (West 2006). Orth, THE NORTH CAROLINA STATE CONSTITUTION at 77 (Section 36 was "modeled on the Ninth Amendment").

guage of the Ninth Amendment.[77] Because abortion has not been recognized as a "retained right" under the Ninth Amendment, it should not be recognized as one under § 36, either.

Conclusion

Based on the foregoing analysis, an argument that the North Carolina Constitution protects a right to abortion that is separate from, and independent of, the right to abortion recognized in *Roe v. Wade* would not likely succeed. That, in turn, suggests that if *Roe*, as modified by *Casey*, is ultimately overruled, the State of North Carolina could enact and enforce a statute *prohibiting* abortion. Moreover, nothing in the North Carolina Constitution precludes North Carolina from *regulating* abortion within federal constitutional limits in the meantime.

---

77. *See Roe*, 410 U.S. at 153; *Casey*, 505 U.S. at 846. In any event, the Ninth Amendment, standing alone, is not a source of substantive rights. *Gibson v. Matthews*, 926 F.2d 532, 537 (6th Cir. 1991). Although "[s]ome unenumerated rights may be of [c]onstitutional magnitude," that is only "by virtue of other amendments, such as the Fifth or Fourteenth Amendment. A person cannot claim a right that exists solely under the Ninth Amendment." *United States v. Vital Health Products, Ltd.*, 786 F. Supp. 761, 777 (E.D. Wis. 1992), *aff'd mem. op., sub nom. United States v. LeBeau*, 985 F.2d 563 (7th Cir. 1993). *See also Charles v. Brown*, 495 F. Supp. 862, 863 (N.D. Ala. 1980) (same).

CHAPTER 37

NORTH DAKOTA

Summary

The North Dakota Supreme Court has not yet decided whether the North Dakota Constitution protects a right to abortion separate from, and independent of, the right to abortion recognized under the United States Constitution.[1] A careful examination of the state constitution, in light of its history and interpretation, as well as other relevant legal sources, however, suggests that the state supreme court probably would not recognize a state constitutional right to abortion. Thus, if *Roe v. Wade*,[2] as modified by *Planned Parenthood of Southeastern Pennsylvania v. Casey*,[3] were overruled, North Dakota could enforce its "trigger" statute, which would prohibit abortion, except "to prevent the death of the pregnant female," and in cases where the pregnancy resulted from "gross sexual imposition, sexual imposition, sexual abuse of a ward, or incest."[4] The law takes effect "on the date the legislative council approves by motion the recommendation of the attorney general to the legislative council that it is reasonably probable that Section 1 would be upheld as constitutional."[5] Moreover, nothing in the state constitution, properly understood, precludes the State from enacting and enforcing reasonable measures regulating abortion within current federal constitutional limits.

---

1. The North Dakota Supreme Court has referred to the right to abortion solely as a matter of federal, not state, constitutional law. *See State v. Sahr*, 470 N.W.2d 185, 191 (N.D. 1991) ("constitutional limits [on the State's ability to protect unborn human life and maternal health] are set by the United States Supreme Court") (citing *Roe v. Wade*).

2. 410 U.S. 113 (1973).

3. 505 U.S. 833 (1992).

4. H.B. 1466, §1, 2007 Leg. Sess. (N.D. 2007).

5. *Id.* §2.

Analysis

The principal pre-*Roe* abortion statute prohibited performance of an abortion upon a pregnant woman unless the procedure was "necessary to preserve her life."[6] Another statute prohibited a woman from soliciting an abortion or allowing an abortion to be performed upon her (subject to the same exception).[7] Pursuant to *Roe*, these statutes were declared unconstitutional (on federal, not state, grounds) by a three-judge federal district court in *Leigh v. Olson*,[8] and were repealed.[9]

Based upon arguments that have been raised in other States with similar constitutional provisions, possible sources for an asserted abortion right could include provisions of the Declaration of Rights guaranteeing equal protection (art. I, §§ 1, 21, 22) and due process of law (§ 12), freedom of religion (§ 3) and a remedy by due process of law (§ 9); recognizing inalienable rights (§ 1) and inherent political power in the people (§ 2); and declaring that the rights set forth in art. I shall remain inviolate (§ 20).[10] The analysis that follows addresses each of these provisions.

Inalienable Rights, Due Process of Law

Article I, § 1, of the North Dakota Constitution provides, in pertinent part, that "[a]ll individuals are by nature equally free and independent and have certain inalienable rights, among which are those of enjoying and defending life and liberty; acquiring, possessing and protecting property and reputation; [and] pursuing and obtaining safety and happiness...."[11] And § 12 provides, in part, that "[n]o person shall ... be deprived of life, liberty or property without due process of law."[12] The North Dakota Supreme Court has held that "the due process clause protects and insures the use and enjoyment of the rights

---

6. N.D. Cent. Code § 12-25-01 (1970). When an abortion was performed upon a woman "pregnant with a quick child," and the death of either the woman or the child resulted, the offense was manslaughter. *Id.* § 12-25-02.

7. *Id.* § 12-25-04. No prosecutions were reported under this statute.

8. 385 F. Supp. 255 (D. N.D. 1974).

9. 1973 N.D. Laws 215, 300, ch. 116, § 41.

10. Three other more unlikely sources of an abortion right under the North Dakota Constitution-art. I, § 4 (guaranteeing freedom of speech), § 6 (prohibiting involuntary servitude) and § 8 (prohibiting unreasonable searches and seizures)-are discussed generally in Chapter 3, *supra*.

11. N.D. Const. art. I, § 1 (1998).

12. *Id.* art. I, § 12.

declared by section 1 of the Constitution," and that "there cannot be a violation of section 1 unless there be also a violation of section 13 [now § 12]."[13]

The North Dakota Supreme Court has not developed a methodology for determining whether an asserted liberty interest is protected by the inalienable rights language of art. I, § 1, as secured by the due process guarantee of § 12.[14] The court has held that, taken together, art. I, § 1, and the due process guarantee of art. I, § 12, protect the right to enjoy the domestic relations and the privileges of the family and the home, as well as the fundamental, natural right of parents to the custody and companionship of their children and to make decisions regarding their upbringing.[15] These rights have long been recognized. "The history and culture of Western civilization reflects a strong tradition of parental concern for the nurture and upbringing of their children. This primary role of the parents in the upbringing of their children is now established beyond debate as an enduring American tradition."[16]

The North Dakota Supreme Court's reliance in *Hoff* upon a "strong tradition" recognizing the rights of parents in raising their children suggests that the presence (or absence) of such a tradition is of critical importance in determining whether an asserted liberty interest (or right) will be recognized under art. I, §§ 1 and 12 of the North Dakota Constitution.[17] That sugges-

---

13. *State v. Cromwell*, 9 N.W.2d 914, 918, 919 (N.D. 1943). The actual holding in *Cromwell*, that the State could not require the licensing of photographers, was called into question in *Johnson v. Elkin*, 263 N.W.2d 123, 128–30 (N.D. 1978). In *Johnson*, the court criticized *Cromwell* and held that "there is no general constitutional prohibition against legislation limiting entry into occupations or professions. Any occupation or profession may be subject to the police power." *Id.* at 130. Notwithstanding this critique, the North Dakota Supreme Court has refused to abandon completely substantive due process as a state constitutional standard. *See Arneson v. Olson*, 270 N.W.2d 125, 132 (N.D. 1978).

14. To the extent that the North Dakota Supreme Court may consider federal precedent in determining whether an asserted liberty interest (or right) is "fundamental" under the state due process guarantee, abortion would not qualify as a "fundamental" right. Although the Supreme Court characterized the right to choose abortion as "fundamental" in *Roe*, 410 U.S. at 152–53, it tacitly abandoned that characterization in *Casey*, 505 U.S. at 869–79 (Joint Op. of O'Connor, Kennedy and Souter, JJ., replacing *Roe's* "strict scrutiny" standard of review with the more relaxed "undue burden" standard, allowing for a broader measure of abortion regulation).

15. *Hoff v. Berg*, 595 N.W.2d 285, 289 (N.D. 1999); *Matter of the Adoption of K.A.S.*, 499 N.W.2d 558, 564–65 (N.D. 1993); *In re J.Z.*, 190 N.W.2d 27, 29 (N.D. 1971); *State v. Cromwell*, 9 N.W.2d 914, 919 (N.D. 1943).

16. *Wisconsin v. Yoder*, 406 U.S. 205, 232–33 (1972), quoted in *Hoff*, 595 N.W.2d at 288.

17. The court, for example, has held that the law requiring the operator of or passenger on a motorcycle to wear a crash helmet does not violate art. I, § 1, or § 12 (formerly § 13). *State v. Odegaard*, 165 N.W.2d 677, 678–80 (N.D. 1969).

tion is confirmed by the court's statement that, "[i]n construing a constitutional provision we must undertake to ascribe to the words used that meaning which the people understood them to have when the constitutional provision was adopted."[18] "In so doing," the court explained, "it is appropriate to consider contemporaneous and long-standing practical interpretations of the provision by the Legislature where there has been acquiescence by the people in such interpretations."[19] Unlike the right of parents to control the upbringing of their children, there is no "strong tradition" of permitting abortion in North Dakota law. The law, in fact, has consistently prohibited abortion since territorial days.

North Dakota enacted its first abortion statutes in 1877, twelve years *before* the 1889 Constitution was adopted and North Dakota was admitted as a State.[20] One provision prohibited abortion upon a pregnant woman at any stage of her pregnancy except when the procedure was necessary "to preserve her life...."[21] Another provision prohibited a woman from soliciting an abortion or allowing an abortion to be performed upon her (subject to the same exception).[22] These statutes remained on the books until after *Roe v. Wade* was decided.[23] Both physicians and non-physicians were prosecuted and convicted for performing illegal abortions and for murder based on the death of the pregnant woman resulting from an illegal abortion.[24] On November 7, 1972, less than three months before *Roe*, the people of North Dakota, by a three-to-one margin, rejected a ballot initiative that would have "liberalized" the State's abortion law.[25]

---

18. *Kadrmas v. Dickinson Public Schools*, 402 N.W.2d 897, 899 (N.D. 1987) (citation omitted), *aff'd*, 487 U.S. 450 (1988).

19. *Id.* (citations omitted).

20. Act of Feb. 17, 1877, §337, *codified at* DAKOTA (TERR.) PENAL CODE §337 (1877).

21. *Id.* Another provision of the Penal Code raised the penalty to manslaughter in the first degree if the procedure resulted in the death of either the woman or a "quick child" with which she was pregnant. *Id.* §252.

22. *Id.* §338. No prosecutions were reported under this statute.

23. DAKOTA (TERR.) COMPILED LAWS §§6538, 6539 (1887), *recodified at* N.D. REV. CODES §§7177, 7178 (1895), *recodified at* N.D. REV. CODES §§8912, 8913 (1905), *recodified at* N.D. COMPILED LAWS §§9604, 9605 (1913), *recodified at* N.D. REV. CODE §§12-2501, 12-2504 (1943), *recodified at* N.D. CENT. CODE §§12-25-01, 12-25-04 (1970), *repealed by* 1973 N.D. Laws 215, 300, ch. 116, §41.

24. *See, e.g., State v. Dimmick*, 296 N.W. 146 (N.D. 1941) (affirming conviction for performing an illegal abortion); *State v. Shortridge*, 211 N.W. 336 (N.D. 1926) (affirming physician's conviction of murder based upon performing an illegal abortion).

25. *Official Abstract of Votes Cast at the General Election Held November 7, 1972*; Office of the Secretary of State of North Dakota, Nov. 21, 1972 (Measure No. 1: Yes: 62,604; No: 204,852).

The North Dakota Legislature has stated that "[b]etween normal childbirth and abortion, it is the policy of the state of North Dakota that normal childbirth is to be given preference, encouragement, and support by law and by state action, it being in the best interests of the well-being and common good of North Dakota citizens."[26] Consistent with that policy, North Dakota has enacted a comprehensive scheme of abortion regulation.[27]

North Dakota has recognized the rights of unborn children in a variety of contexts outside of abortion, including criminal law, tort law, health care law and property law. Under the criminal code, the killing of an unborn child, other than in an abortion, may be prosecuted as a homicide.[28] So, too, nonlethal injuries inflicted upon an unborn child may be prosecuted as an assault.[29]

In tort law, a statutory cause of action for wrongful death may be brought on behalf of an unborn child who was viable (capable of sustained survival outside the mother's womb, with or without medical assistance) at the time of its death.[30] A common law action for (nonlethal) prenatal injuries may be brought without regard to the stage of pregnancy when the injuries were inflicted.[31] And North Dakota has banned wrongful life causes of action.[32]

Under North Dakota's health care statutes, health care directives (formerly living wills and durable powers of attorney for health care) may not direct the withholding or withdrawal of life-sustaining treatment or artificially administered nutrition and hydration from a pregnant woman "unless, to a reason-

---

26. N.D. Cent. Code § 14-02.3-01 (2004).

27. Id. § 14-02.1-04 (2004) (adopting trimester framework of Roe v. Wade); §§ 14-02.1-02(5), 14-02.1-03(1) (mandating informed consent and a twenty-four hour waiting period); § 14-02.1-03.1 (requiring parental notice and a twenty-four hour waiting period); § 23-16-14 (2002) (recognizing individual and institutional rights of conscience); §§ 14-02.3-01, 14-02.3-04 (restricting public funding of abortion for indigent women and the use of public facilities for the performance of abortions).

28. Id. § 12.1-17.1-01 through 12.1-17.1-04 (1997).

29. Id. §§ 12.1-17.1-05, 12.1-17.1-06.

30. Hopkins v. McBane, 359 N.W.2d 862, 864 (N.D. 1984), interpreting N.D. Cent. Code § 32-21-01 (1996).

31. Id. at 864.

32. N.D. Cent. Code § 32-03-43 (1996). A "wrongful life" cause of action is a claim brought on behalf of a child who is born with a physical or mental disability or disease that could have been discovered before the child's birth by genetic testing, amniocentesis or other medical screening. The gravamen of the cause of action is that, as a result of a physician's failure to inform the child's parents of the child's disability or disease (or at least of the availability of tests to determine the presence of the disability or disease), they were deprived of the opportunity to abort the child, thus resulting in the birth of a child suffering permanent physical or mental impairment.

able degree of medical certainty…, such health care will not maintain [her] in such a way as to permit the continuing development and live birth of the unborn child or will be physically harmful or unreasonably painful to the [woman] or will prolong severe pain that cannot be alleviated by medication."[33] In property law, afterborn heirs (heirs conceived before a decedent's death but born after the decedent executes a will) may inherit from a decedent if they live 120 or more hours (five days) after birth.[34] For the purpose of inheriting future interests, posthumous children (children conceived before but born after the death of a person who dies without a will) are treated as if living at the death of their parent(s).[35] Finally, "[a] child conceived by not yet born is to be deemed an existing person so far as may be necessary for its interests in the event of its subsequent birth."[36]

A right to abortion cannot be found in the text, structure or history of the North Dakota Constitution. There is no evidence that the framers or ratifiers of the North Dakota Constitution intended to limit the Legislature's authority to prohibit abortion.[37] Such an intent would have been remarkable in light of the contemporaneous and longstanding prohibition of abortion except to save the life of the mother.

Equal Protection

Three provisions of the North Dakota Constitution guarantee equal protection of the law. Article I, § 1, states, in pertinent part, that "[a]ll individuals are by nature equally free and independent…."[38] Section 21 provides: "No special privileges or immunities shall ever be granted which may not be altered, revoked or repealed by the legislative assembly; nor shall any citizen or class of citizens be granted privileges or immunities which upon the same terms shall not be granted to all citizens."[39] And § 22 provides that "[a]ll laws of a general nature shall have a uniform operation."[40] Sections 21 and 22 have long

---

33. *Id.* § 23-06.5-09(5) (Supp. 2005). *See also id.* § 23-07-5.03(6) (prohibiting health care agent from authorizing an abortion).

34. *Id.* § 30.1-04-08 (1996).

35. *Id.* § 47-02-19 (1999). *See also id.* § 47-02-29.

36. *Id.* § 14-10-15 (2004).

37. *See* Proceedings & Debates of the First Constitutional Convention of North Dakota 357–71 (debate on Declaration of Rights in Committee of the Whole); 531–37 (debate on Declaration of Rights in Convention) (Bismarck, N.D. 1889).

38. N.D. Const. art. I, § 1 (1998).

39. *Id.* art. I, § 21.

40. *Id.* art. I, § 22.

been viewed "as our state constitutional guarantee of equal protection,"[41] and "the methods of analysis for resolving challenges to legislative classifications under these ... provisions [referring the Equal Protection Clause of the Fourteenth Amendment and §§ 21 and 22 of the North Dakota Constitution] are essentially the same."[42]

> When a statute is challenged on equal protection grounds, we first locate the appropriate standard of review. We apply strict scrutiny to an inherently suspect classification or infringement of a fundamental right and strike down the challenged statutory classification unless it is shown that the statute promotes a compelling governmental interest and that the distinctions drawn by the law are necessary to further its purpose. When an important substantive right is involved, we apply an intermediate standard of review which requires a close correspondence between statutory classification and legislative goals. When no suspect class, fundamental right, or important substantive right is involved, we apply a rational basis standard and sustain the legislative classification unless it is patently arbitrary and bears no rational relationship to a legitimate governmental purpose.[43]

For the reasons set forth in the first section of this analysis, a prohibition of abortion would not infringe upon "a fundamental right," nor would it implicate "an important substantive right."[44] The North Dakota Supreme Court has held that sex-based classifications are "inherently suspect,"[45] but it is doubtful that a

---

41. *Bismarck Public School District No. 1 v. State*, 511 N.W.2d 247, 255 (N.D. 1994).

42. *Gange v. Clerk of the Burleigh County District Court*, 429 N.W.2d 429, 432 (N.D. 1988). Although art. I, § 1, also contains "equal protection" language, § 1 is seldom cited in cases presenting equal protection issues.

43. *Id.* at 433 (citations and internal quotation marks omitted). Another term for "intermediate scrutiny" is "heightened scrutiny." The terms are used interchangeably in this section of the analysis.

44. The North Dakota Supreme Court has identified "the right to recover for personal injuries [as] an important substantive right." *Hanson v. Williams County*, 389 N.W.2d 319, 325 (N.D. 1986).

45. *State ex rel. Olson v. Maxwell*, 259 N.W.2d 621, 627, 631 (N.D. 1977). In a decision handed down one year earlier, the court, applying rational basis review, expressed the opinion that the failure to recognize a wife's right to recover damages for loss of consortium of her husband under the Dram Shop Act would violate art. I, § 21 (formerly § 20) when the husband had a right to recover damages for loss of consortium of his wife. *Hastings v. James River Aerie No. 2337-Fraternal Order of Eagles*, 246 N.W.2d 747, 751 (N.D. 1976). *Maxwell* has seldom been cited in later decisions and, along with the earlier North Dakota cases it cited, appears to have misstated the Supreme Court's standard for evaluating sex-based clas-

prohibition of abortion would be subjected to strict scrutiny review under the state constitution or even intermediate review under the federal constitution.

First, the United States Supreme Court has reviewed restrictions on abortion funding under a rational basis standard of review, *not* under the intermediate standard ("heightened scrutiny") required of gender-based classifications.[46] Indeed, the Court has held that "the disfavoring of abortion ... is not *ipso facto* sex discrimination," and, citing its decisions in *Harris* and other cases addressing abortion funding, stated that "the constitutional test applicable to government abortion-funding restrictions is not the heightened-scrutiny standard that our cases demand for sex discrimination, ... but the ordinary rationality standard."[47]

Second, even assuming that an abortion prohibition differentiates between men and women on the basis of sex, and would otherwise be subject to a higher standard of review, the Supreme Court has held that biological differences between men and women may justify different treatment based on those differences. In upholding a statutory rape statute that applied only to males, the Supreme Court noted, "this Court has consistently upheld statutes where the gender classification is not invidious, but rather realistically reflects the fact that the sexes are not similarly situated in certain circumstances."[48] As one federal district court observed: "Abortion statutes are examples of cases in which

---

sifications, which is intermediate, not strict, scrutiny. *Craig v. Boren*, 429 U.S. 190, 197 (1976). In any event, for the reasons set forth in the text, a prohibition of abortion would not be subject to either standard of review.

46. *Harris v. McRae*, 448 U.S. 297, 321–26 (1980).

47. *Bray v. Alexandria Women's Health Clinic*, 506 U.S. 263, 273 (1993). Several state supreme courts and individual state supreme court justices have recognized that abortion regulations and restrictions on abortion funding are not "directed at women as a class" so much as "abortion as a medical treatment, which, because it involves a potential life, has no parallel as a treatment method." *Bell v. Low Income Women of Texas*, 95 S.W.3d 253, 258 (Tex. 2002) (upholding funding restrictions) (citing *Harris*, 448 U.S. at 325). *See also Fischer v. Dep't of Public Welfare*, 502 A.2d 114, 125 (Pa. 1985) ("the basis for the distinction here is not sex, but abortion") (upholding funding restrictions); *Moe v. Secretary of Administration & Finance*, 417 N.E.2d 387, 407 (Mass. 1981) (Hennessey, C.J., dissenting) (funding restrictions were "directed at abortion as a medical procedure, not women as a class"); *Right to Choose v. Byrne*, 450 A.2d 925, 950 (N.J. 1982) (O'Hern, J., dissenting) ("[t]he subject of the legislation is not the person of the recipient, but the nature of the claimed medical service"). Both *Moe* and *Right to Choose* were decided on other grounds. The dissenting justices were addressing alternative arguments raised by the plaintiffs, but not reached by the majority opinions.

48. *Michael M. v. Superior Court*, 450 U.S. 464, 469 (1981). The North Dakota Supreme Court has acknowledged this principle in upholding the different treatment accorded men and women under the State's parentage statutes. *See B.H. v. K.D.*, 506 N.W.2d 368, 376 (N.D. 1993)

the sexes are not biologically similarly situated" because only women are capable of becoming pregnant and having abortions.[49]

A statute prohibiting abortion quite obviously can affect only women because only women are capable of becoming pregnant.[50] Unlike laws that use women's ability to become pregnant (or pregnancy itself) to discriminate against them in *other* areas (*e.g.*, employment opportunities), abortion prohibitions cannot fairly be said to involve a distinction between men and women that is a "mere pretext[] designed to erect an invidious discrimination against [women]."[51]

Because a prohibition of abortion "is neither inherently suspect, nor does it infringe upon fundamental or important substantive rights, in order to pass constitutional muster all that is required is that it pass the rational basis test."[52] Under that test, the classification must be "rationally related to [a] legitimate legislative goal."[53] A prohibition of abortion would be "rationally related" to the "legitimate legislative goal" of protecting unborn human life. Accordingly, the North Dakota "trigger" statute would not violate the equal protection guarantees of the North Dakota Constitution.

Freedom of Religion

Article I, § 3, of the North Dakota Constitution provides, in relevant part: "The free exercise and enjoyment of religious profession and worship, without discrimination or preference[,] shall be forever guaranteed in this state...."[54]

In any challenge to a statute prohibiting abortion, abortion advocates may raise either or both of two arguments under art. I, § 3. First, they may argue that an abortion prohibition interferes with the "free exercise and enjoyment" of a woman's "religious profession" by forbidding her from obtaining an abortion that would be allowed by her religion. Second, they may argue in the alternative (or in addition) that an abortion prohibition gives a "preference" to religion because it reflects sectarian views regarding when human life begins and sinfulness of abortion. Neither argument would likely succeed.

---

49. *Jane L. v. Bangerter*, 794 F. Supp. 1537, 1549 (D. Utah 1992).

50. *Geduldig v. Aiello*, 417 U.S. 484, 496 n. 20 (1974) ("[n]ormal pregnancy is an objectively, identifiable physical condition with unique characteristics").

51. *Id.*

52. *B.H. v. K.D.*, 506 N.W.2d at 376.

53. *Id.*

54. N.D. Const. art. I, § 3 (1998).

The North Dakota Supreme Court has held that the Free Exercise and Establishment Clauses of the First Amendment are "[t]o the same effect" as art. I, §3 (formerly art. I, §4).[55] This equivalency of interpretation suggest that a challenge to the State's "trigger" statute (or any other abortion prohibition North Dakota may enact) that would not succeed under the Religion Clauses of the First Amendment would not succeed under art. I, §3, either. For the reasons set forth in Chapter 2, *supra*, an abortion statute could not be successfully challenged on First Amendment grounds. Accordingly, a similar challenge under art. I, §3, would not likely be successful.[56]

Remedy by Due Process of Law

Article I, §9, of the North Dakota Constitution provides, in part: "All courts shall be open, and every man for an injury done him in his lands, goods, person or reputation shall have remedy by due process of law, and right and justice administered without sale, denial or delay."[57] Abortion advocates might argue that a statute prohibiting abortion (either the "trigger" law or another law enacted by the legislature) interferes with a woman's control over her own body, and that such interference constitutes an "injury" to her "person," as those terms are used in §9, for which there must be "remedy by due process of law." That "remedy," in turn, would be invalidation of the statute. This argument erroneously assumes that art. I, §9, is, in itself, a source of legal rights, as opposed to a guarantee that there will be a remedy for wrongs defined by *other* sources of law.

---

55. *Bendewald v. Ley*, 168 N.W. 693, 696 (N.D. 1917). *See also State ex rel. Heitkamp v. Family Life Services, Inc.*, 616 N.W.2d 826, 838–41 (N.D. 2000) (applying the same standards); *State v. Burckard*, 579 N.W.2d 194, 196 (N.D. 1998) (same); *State v. Rivinius*, 328 N.W.2d 220 (N.D. 1982) (construing Free Exercise Clause and art. I, §3, *in pari materia*); *Martian v. Martian*, 328 N.W.2d 844 (N.D. 1983) (same).

56. Apart from the foregoing, an argument that an abortion prohibition gives a "preference" to religion, by embodying sectarian views of the morality of abortion, would appear to be foreclosed by decisions of the North Dakota Supreme Court rejecting challenges to Sunday closing laws *See State ex rel. Temple v. Barnes*, 132 N.W. 215 (N.D. 1911) (upholding statute); *City of Bismarck v. Materi*, 177 N.W.2d 530, 545–46 (N.D. 1970) (upholding ordinance). If a law enforcing a "day of rest" does not violate art. I, §3, of the North Dakota Constitution, even though it may coincide with sectarian beliefs regarding the Christian Sabbath, then neither would a law prohibiting abortion, regardless of whether the law coincides with religious views regarding the sinfulness of abortion.

57. N.D. CONST. art. I, §9 (1998).

As is apparent from its text and structure, §9 is concerned with *remedies* for tortiously inflicted injuries-it does not establish what *constitutes* an injury to anyone's "lands, goods, person or reputation." Those remedies, however, are derived from the common law and, in certain instances, statues enacted by the Legislature, not §9. Moreover, the remedies themselves redress injuries recognized by the common law and statutory law, not constitutional "injuries." Section 9, in other words, does not *create* any new causes of actions, but merely *preserves* existing causes of action. North Dakota case law confirms this understanding.

Article I, §9, "does not require a remedy for every alleged wrong," but "it does guarantee an important substantive right-the right of access to courts for the redress of wrongs."[58] That "right of access," however, is concerned exclusively with "redress of wrongs," and does not purport to define the "wrongs" for which redress is available. The "wrongs" are defined by other sources of law (statutory or common law).

Taken as a whole, §9 is concerned with the availability of private civil causes of action and reasonable access to the courts. It places no limitation on the State's power to define and punish crimes and has never been so interpreted.

Inherent Political Power

Article I, §2, of the North Dakota Constitution provides: "All political power is inherent in the people. Government is instituted for the protection, security and benefit of the people, and they have a right to alter or reform the same whenever the public good may require."[59] In a challenge to North Dakota's "trigger" statute (or any other abortion prohibition), abortion advocates might argue that the statute interferes with the "inherent" political power of the people because it does not promote their "protection, security and benefit...." Given the purpose of §2, this argument would not likely prevail.

Section 2 secures to the people themselves, through the amendment process, the right to decide whether, how and to what extent the organic instrument of government should be changed.[60] For that reason, §2 cannot be regarded as a

---

58. *Bulman v. Hulstrand Construction Co., Inc.*, 521 N.W.2d 632, 65 (N.D. 1994).

59. N.D. CONST. art. I, §2 (1998).

60. *Larkin v. Gronna*, 285 N.W. 59, 62 (N.D. 1939) ("[t]he people of this state are the sole authority in determining whether [a] proposed change [to the constitution] is such as is required by the public good). The people, not the Legislature, have "plenary power by constitutional amendment, to provide such method of government for the state or any portion thereof as they please, so long as there is no violation of the federal relations." *Id.*

source of substantive rights.[61] Rather, it is "a limit on state intervention in the right of the people to have a republican form of government."[62] As such, it could not serve as a basis for asserting a right to abortion. Whether a given law promotes "the protection, security and benefit of the people," within the meaning of art. II, §2, presents a political question for the legislature (and, ultimately, the people) to decide, not a constitutional question for the judiciary.

Inviolate Rights

Article I, §20, of the North Dakota Constitution provides: "To guard against transgressions of the high powers which we have delegated, we declare that everything in this article is excepted out of the general powers of government and shall forever remain inviolate."[63] Section 20 does not confer any rights, but merely limits the ability of the Legislature to enact legislation that restricts the rights otherwise protected under art. I.[64]

Conclusion

Based on the foregoing analysis, an argument that the North Dakota Constitution protects a right to abortion that is separate from, and independent of, the right to abortion recognized in *Roe v. Wade* would not likely succeed. That, in turn, suggests that if *Roe*, as modified by *Casey*, is ultimately overruled, the State of North Dakota could enforce its "trigger" statute *prohibiting* abortion. Moreover, nothing in the North Dakota Constitution precludes North Dakota from *regulating* abortion within federal constitutional limits in the meantime.

---

61. *Riemers v. Super Target of Grand Forks, Target Corp.*, 363 F. Supp.2d 1182, 1185 (D. N.D. 2005).

62. *Id.* (citations omitted).

63. N.D. CONST. art. I, §20 (1998).

64. *Larkin v. Gronna*, 285 N.W. at 62–63.

CHAPTER 38

Ohio

Summary

The Ohio Supreme Court has not yet decided whether the Ohio Constitution protects a right to abortion separate from, and independent of, the right to abortion recognized under the United States Constitution.[1] A careful examination of the state constitution, in light of its history and interpretation, as well as other relevant legal sources, however, suggests that the state supreme court probably would not recognize a state constitutional right to abortion if *Roe v. Wade*,[2] as modified by *Planned Parenthood of Southeastern Pennsylvania v. Casey*,[3] were overruled. Thus, Ohio could prohibit abortion. Moreover, nothing in the state constitution, properly understood, precludes the State from enacting and enforcing reasonable measures regulating abortion within current federal constitutional limits.

Analysis

The pre-*Roe* abortion statute prohibited performance of an abortion upon a pregnant woman unless the procedure was "necessary to preserve her life, or [it was] advised by two physicians to be necessary for that purpose."[4] Pursuant to *Roe*, §2901.16 was declared unconstitutional (on federal, not state, grounds) by the Ohio Supreme Court in *State v. Kruze*.[5] While Kruze's petition for *cer-*

---

1. See *Preterm Cleveland v. Voinovich*, 627 N.E.2d 570 (Ohio Ct. App. 1993) (recognizing right to abortion under art. I, §1, of the Ohio Constitution), *cert. denied*, 624 N.E.2d 194 (Ohio 1993). The court of appeals' decision in *Preterm Cleveland* is discussed in the first section of this analysis, *infra*.

2. 410 U.S. 113 (1973).

3. 505 U.S. 833 (1992).

4. Ohio Rev. Code Ann. §2901.16 (Baldwin 1953).

5. 295 N.E.2d 916 (Ohio 1973). Prior to *Roe*, the Ohio Supreme Court, in a pair of unreported orders, dismissed defendant's appeal in *Kruze* for want of a substantial constitu-

tiorari was pending, the statute was repealed,[6] and its substantive provisions reenacted.[7] That statute, in turn, was repealed in 1974.[8]

Based upon arguments that have been raised in Ohio and other States with similar constitutional provisions, possible sources for an asserted abortion right could include provisions of the Bill of Rights recognizing inalienable rights (art. I, § 1); guaranteeing due course of law and a remedy by due course of law (§ 16), equal protection (§ 2) and rights of conscience (§ 7); and retaining rights (§ 20).[9] The analysis that follows addresses each of these provisions.

Inalienable Rights

Article I, § 1, of the Ohio Constitution provides: "All men are, by nature, free and independent, and have certain inalienable rights, among which are those of enjoying and defending life and liberty, acquiring, possessing and protecting property, and seeking and obtaining happiness and safety."[10]

In *Preterm Cleveland v. Voinovich*,[11] the Ohio Court of Appeals held that the "liberty" language of art. I, § 1, guarantees "the choice of a woman whether to bear a child," which choice "necessarily includes the right of a woman to have an abortion so long as there is no valid and constitutional statute restricting or limiting that right."[12] The court held further, however, that such guarantee is not broader than the corollary right conferred by the Due Process Clause of the Fourteenth Amendment, as interpreted by *Roe* and modified by *Casey*.[13] Accordingly, the court upheld an informed consent statute similar to the one that passed federal constitutional scrutiny in *Casey*.[14]

As previously noted, the Ohio Supreme Court denied review of the decision in *Preterm Cleveland*.[15] Nevertheless, in a case of first impression decided seven

---

tional question and overruled his motion for leave to appeal. *State v. Kruze*, No. 72-11 (Ohio Mar. 10, 1972), *vacated and remanded*, 410 U.S. 951 (1973).

6. 134 Ohio Laws 1868 (1971–72).

7. *Id.* at 1943–44.

8. 135 Ohio Laws 988 (1974).

9. Three other more unlikely sources of an abortion right under the Ohio Constitution-§ 6 (prohibiting involuntary servitude), § 11(guaranteeing freedom of speech) and § 14 (prohibiting unreasonable searches and seizures)-are discussed generally in Chapter 3, *supra*.

10. OHIO CONST. art. I, § 1 (LexisNexis 2004).

11. 627 N.E.2d 570 (Ohio Ct. App. 1993).

12. *Id.* at 575.

13. *Id.* at 577.

14. *Id.* at 577–78.

15. *See* n. 1, *supra*.

years later, the state supreme court effectively undermined the jurisprudential basis of the court of appeals' opinion. In *State v. Williams*,[16] the Ohio Supreme Court held that the language of art. I, § 1, "is not an independent source of [judicially enforceable] self-executing protections. Rather, it is a statement of fundamental ideals upon which a limited government is created."[17] As such, art. I, § 1, "requires other provisions of the Ohio Constitution or legislative definition to give it practical effect. That is so because its language lacks the completeness required to offer meaningful guidance for judicial enforcement."[18] Article I, § 1, by its own terms, provides no "standards for judicial enforcement" of the rights set forth therein and, therefore, those rights are not self-executing.[19] Although *Williams* did not discuss abortion or cite *Preterm Cleveland*, it follows from the holding in *Williams* that no judicially enforceable right to abortion can be derived solely from art. I, § 1, of the Ohio Constitution. Accordingly, an abortion prohibition could not be successfully challenged under art. I, § 1.

Due Course of Law and Remedy by Due Course of Law

Article I, § 16, of the Ohio Constitution provides: "All courts shall be open, and every person, for an injury done him in his lands, goods, person, or reputation, shall have remedy by due course of law, and shall have justice administered without denial or delay."[20]

The Ohio Supreme Court has interpreted art. I, § 16, to provide two distinctive guarantees: "(1) that legislative enactments may abridge individual rights only by due course of law, ... a guarantee which is equivalent to the Due Process Clause of the Fourteenth Amendment," and "(2) that all courts shall be open to every person with a right to a remedy for injury to his person, property or reputation, with the opportunity for such remedy being granted at a meaningful time and in a meaningful manner."[21] In any challenge to a statute prohibiting abortion, abortion advocates are likely to rely on both of these guarantees. That reliance would be misplaced, however.

---

16. 728 N.E.2d 342 (Ohio 2000).

17. *Id.* at 354.

18. *Id.*

19. *Id.*

20. OHIO CONST. art. I, § 16 (LexisNexis 2004).

21. *Sedar v. Knowlton Construction Co.*, 551 N.E.2d 938, 944 (Ohio 1990), *overruled on other grounds*, *Brenneman v. R.M.I. Co.*, 639 N.E.2d 425, 530 (Ohio 1994).

The due course of law guarantee of art. I, § 16, "provides substantially the same safeguards as does [the Due Process Clause of] the Fourteenth Amendment."[22] Accordingly, Ohio courts "look to federal case law to delineate the right[s] [of parties] under both the state and federal provisions."[23] This reliance on federal case law suggests that the Ohio Supreme Court would not recognize a right to abortion under the "due course of law" language of art. I, § 16, if *Roe*, as modified by *Casey*, were overruled. Moreover, for the reasons that follow, the Ohio Supreme Court is not likely to recognize a right to an abortion under the "due course of law" language of art. I, § 16, even in the absence of a Supreme Court decision overruling *Roe*.

In interpreting the state "due course of law" guarantee, Ohio courts have applied the Supreme Court's substantive due process analysis.[24] In determining whether an asserted liberty interest (or right) should be regarded as "fundamental," the Supreme Court applies a two-prong test. First, there must be a "careful description" of the asserted fundamental liberty interest.[25] Second, the interest, so described, must be firmly rooted in "the Nation's history, legal traditions, and practices."[26] A right to abortion cannot be regarded as "fundamental" under art. I, § 16, however, because such a "right" is not firmly rooted in Ohio's "history, legal traditions, and practices."[27]

Ohio enacted its first abortion statute on February 27, 1834, seventeen years before the current constitution was adopted in 1851.[28] Section 1 of the statute made it a misdemeanor, punishable by imprisonment in the county jail not to exceed one year or by a fine not exceeding $500.00, or both, to attempt to per-

---

22. *Steele v. Hamilton County Community Mental Health Board*, 736 N.E.2d 10, 16 (Ohio 2000)

23. *State ex rel. Heller v. Miller*, 399 N.E.2d 66, 67 (Ohio 1980).

24. *State v. Small*, 833 N.E.2d 736, 740–41 (Ohio Ct. App. 2005) (citing *Washington v. Glucksberg*, 521 U.S. 702 (1997)).

25. *Glucksberg*, 521 U.S. at 721 (citation and internal quotation marks omitted).

26. *Id.* at 710.

27. To the extent that the Ohio Supreme Court recognizes the same fundamental rights under the *state* due course of law guarantee as the Supreme Court does under the *federal* due process guarantee, abortion would not qualify as a "fundamental" right. Although the Supreme Court characterized the right to choose abortion as "fundamental" in *Roe*, 410 U.S. at 152–53, it tacitly abandoned that characterization in *Casey*, 505 U.S. at 869–79 (Joint Op. of O'Connor, Kennedy and Souter, JJ., replacing *Roe's* "strict scrutiny" standard of review with the more relaxed "undue burden" standard, allowing for a broader measure of abortion regulation).

28. Act of Feb. 27, 1834, 1834 Ohio Laws 20, 21, *codified at* OHIO GEN. STAT. ch. 35, §§ 111(1), 112(2), at 252 (1841), *recodified at* OHIO STAT. ch. 33, §§ 162, 163, at 296–97 (1854).

form an abortion on any pregnant woman at any stage of pregnancy unless the procedure "shall have been necessary to preserve [her] life…, or shall have been advised by two physicians to be necessary for that purpose …"[29] Subject to the same exception, §2 of the statute made it a "high misdemeanor," punishable by imprisonment in the penitentiary for not less than one nor more than seven years, to attempt to perform an abortion after "quickening," "with intent thereby to destroy such child," if either the child or the mother died "in consequence thereof."[30]

Section 2 of the Act of February 27, 1834, was amended by an Act of April 13, 1867, which eliminated the requirement of quickening as a condition of imposing the greater punishment for the death of the unborn child or the mother.[31] Sections 1 and 2 of the 1834 statute, as amended by the Act of April 13, 1867, were later combined into a single section which remained on the books until shortly before *Roe v. Wade* was decided, when the law was repealed and replaced with the same substantive provisions.[32] Almost one hundred years ago, the Ohio Supreme Court explained that the "reason and policy" of the abortion statute was "to protect women and unborn babes from dangerous criminal practice…."[33]

Prior to *Roe*, the Ohio reviewing courts regularly affirmed the convictions of persons (including licensed physicians) for performing abortions, without any hint that the prosecutions or convictions violated the Ohio Constitution.[34] Subsequent to *Roe*, the principal abortion statute was declared unconstitutional solely on the authority of *Roe v. Wade* and not on any independent state grounds.[35]

"It is the public policy of the state of Ohio to prefer childbirth over abortion to the extent that it is constitutionally permissible."[36] Consistent with that

---

29. Act of Feb. 27, 1834, §1. *See Wilson v. State*, 2 Ohio St. 319, 321 (1853) (holding "the offence to be complete, if the medicine, drug, substance, or thing to be administered, or instrument used, with the intent prescribed, at any time during the period of gestation").

30. Act of Feb. 27, 1834, §2. "Quickening" is that stage of pregnancy, usually sixteen to eighteen weeks gestation, when the woman first detects fetal movement.

31. Act of Apr. 13, 1867, §1, 1867 Ohio Laws 135–36.

32. OHIO CRIM. CODE ch. III, §8 (1878), *recodified at* OHIO REV. STAT. §6815 (1890), *recodified at* OHIO GEN. CODE §12412 (1910), *recodified at* OHIO REV. CODE ANN. §2901.16 (Baldwin 1953). *See* nn. 6–8 and accompanying text, *supra*.

33. *State v. Tippie*, 105 N.E. 75, 77 (Ohio 1913).

34. *State v. McCoy*, 39 N.E. 316 (Ohio 1894), *State v. Lehr*, 119 N.E. 730 (Ohio 1918); *State v. Jones*, 70 N.E.2d 913 (Ohio Ct. Ap. 1946); *State v. Coran*, 94 N.E.2d 562 (Ohio Ct. App. 1948); *State v. Brown*, 137 N.E.2d 609 (Ohio Ct. App. 1955); *State v. Roche*, 135 N.E.2d 789 (Ohio Ct. App. 1956); *State v. Allgood*, 171 N.E. 186 (Ohio Ct. App. 1959).

35. *State v. Kruze*, 295 N.E.2d 916 (Ohio 1973).

36. OHIO REV. CODE ANN. §9.041 (Baldwin Supp. 2007).

policy, Ohio has enacted a comprehensive scheme of abortion regulation.[37] Moreover, Ohio has recognized the rights of unborn children in a variety of contexts outside of abortion, including criminal law, tort law, health care law and property law.

Under the criminal code, the killing or injury of an unborn child, other than in an abortion, may be prosecuted as a homicide or an assault, respectively.[38] And a woman convicted of a capital offense may not be executed while she is pregnant.[39]

In tort law, a statutory cause of action for wrongful death may be brought on behalf of an unborn child who was viable (capable of sustained survival outside the mother's womb, with or without medical assistance) at the time of its death.[40] A common law action for (nonlethal) prenatal injuries may be brought on behalf of an unborn child who was viable at the time the injuries were inflicted.[41] And Ohio has banned both wrongful birth and wrongful life causes of action.[42]

---

37. OHIO REV. CODE ANN. § 2317.56 (LexisNexis 2005) (mandating informed consent and a twenty-four hour waiting period); § 2919.12.1 (LexisNexis 2006) (requiring parental notice); § 4731.01 (LexisNexis 2006) (recognizing individual and institutional rights of conscience and prohibiting discrimination against persons who object to abortion); § 5105.55(B) (LexisNexis Supp. 2007) (refusal to submit to an abortion or to give consent therefor shall not result in the loss of public assistance benefits or any other rights or privileges); § 5101.56 (LexisNexis 2007) (restricting public funding of abortion for indigent women); § 3701.34.1 (LexisNexis Supp. 2007) (licensing and regulating abortion facilities); §§ 2919.16, 2919.17 (LexisNexis 2006) (prohibiting post-viability abortions); § 2919.15.1 (LexisNexis 2006) (prohibiting partial-birth abortions). The post-viability prohibition was declared unconstitutional and its enforcement enjoined on federal constitutional grounds in *Women's Medical Professional Corp. v. Voinovich*, 911 F. Supp. 1051, 1078–81 (S.D. Ohio), *aff'd* 130 F.3d 187, 203–10 (6th Cir. 1995), *cert denied*, 523 U.S. 1036 (1999).

38. OHIO REV. CODE ANN. § 2903.01 (aggravated murder); § 2903.02 (murder); § 2903.03 (voluntary manslaughter); § 2903.04 (involuntary manslaughter); § 2903.04.1 (reckless homicide); § 2903.05 (negligent homicide); § 2903.06 (aggravated vehicular homicide, vehicular homicide and vehicular manslaughter); § 2903.08 (aggravated vehicular assault), vehicular assault); § 2903.11 (felonious assault); § 2903.12 (aggravated assault); § 2903.13 (assault); § 2903.14 (negligent assault); § 2903.21 (aggravated menacing); § 2903.21.1 (menacing by stalking) (LexisNexis 2006). *See also* OHIO REV. CODE ANN. § 2903.09 (exceptions for legal abortions and conduct of the pregnant woman herself).

39. *Id.* § 2949.31.

40. *Werling v. Sandy*, 476 N.E.2d 1053 (Ohio 1985), interpreting OHIO REV. CODE ANN. § 2125.01 *et seq.* (LexisNexis 2002). The state court of appeals, however, has refused to allow wrongful death actions to be brought on behalf of *non*viable children who were stillborn. *Griffiths v. Doctors Hospital*, 780 N.E.2d 603, 606 (Ohio Ct. App. 2002).

41. *Williams v. Marion Rapid Transit*, 87 N.E.2d 334 (Ohio 1949).

42. OHIO REV. CODE ANN. § 2305.11.6 (LexisNexis Supp. 2007). A "wrongful birth" cause of action is a claim brought by the parents of a child who is born with a physical or

Under the State's health care statutes, a living will may not direct the withholding or withdrawal of life-sustaining treatment from a pregnant patient.[43] And an agent acting under a under a durable power of attorney for health care may not refuse or withdraw health care from a pregnant patient "if the refusal or withdrawal of the health care would terminate the pregnancy, unless the pregnancy or the health care would pose a substantial risk to [her] life … or unless [her] attending physician and at least one other physician who has examined [her] determine, to a reasonable degree of medical certainty and in accordance with reasonable medical standards, that the fetus would not be born alive."[44]

In property law, a posthumous child (a child conceived before but born after the death of a person who dies without a will) may inherit from an intestate (a person who dies without a will).[45] Subject to certain exceptions, afterborn heirs (heirs conceived before a decedent's death but born after the decedent executes a will) of a person who dies testate (with a will) receive that share of the estate that they would have received if the decedent had died intestate.[46] And a court may appoint a trustee to represent the future interests of an unborn child.[47]

A right to abortion cannot be found in the text or structure of the Ohio Constitution. There is no evidence that either the framers or ratifiers of the Ohio Constitution intended the Bill of Rights to limit the Legislature's authority to prohibit abortion.[48] Such an intent would have been remarkable in light of the contemporaneous and longstanding prohibition of abortion except to save the life of the mother. A right to abortion, therefore, is not firmly rooted in Ohio's history, legal traditions and practices, and, for this reason, cannot be derived from the "due course of law" language of art. I, § 16.

---

mental disability or disease that could have been discovered before the child's birth by genetic testing, amniocentesis or other medical screening. The gravamen of the action is that, as a result of a physician's failure to inform the parents of the child's disability or disease (or at least of the availability of tests to determine the presence of the disability or disease), they were deprived of the opportunity to abort the child, thus resulting in the birth of a child suffering permanent physical or mental impairment. A "wrongful life" cause of action, on the other hand, is a claim, based on the same facts, brought on behalf of the impaired child.

43. *Id.* § 2133.06(B) (LexisNexis 2002).
44. *Id.* § 1337.13(D) (LexisNexis 2006).
45. *Id.* § 2105.14 (LexisNexis 2007).
46. *Id.* § 2107.34.
47. *Id.* § 2307.13.1 (LexisNexis 2005).
48. *See* 2 Report of the Debates & Proceedings of the Convention for the Revision of the Constitution of the State of Ohio (1850–51), 326–31, 33–37 (debate on Bill of Rights in Committee of the Whole); 462–82, 498–550, 559, 651, 688–93 (debate on Bill of Rights in Convention) (Columbus, Ohio 1851).

Nor can such a right be derived from the "right to a remedy" language of § 16, upon which abortion advocates may also rely.[49] The "right to a remedy" guarantee of § 16 "refers to wrongs that are recognized by law."[50] Section 16, in other words, "guarantees a remedy for every *legally cognizable* injury to person, property, or reputation," but it is "ultimately up to the legislature to define what injuries are legally cognizable."[51] For example, in upholding a statute abolishing the common law causes of action for breach of promise to marry, alienation of affections, criminal conversation and seduction, the Ohio Supreme Court held that "the legislative branch of state government, unless prohibited by constitutional limitations [*e.g.*, art. I, § 19a[52]], may modify or entirely abolish common-law actions."[53] If the Ohio General Assembly made abortion illegal, then the denial of an abortion (by virtue of state law) could not be regarded as a "legally cognizable injury." Indeed, there is no decision of any Ohio court declaring a criminal statute unconstitutional under the "right to a remedy" guarantee of art. I, § 16.

In sum, neither the "due course of law" guarantee nor the "right to a remedy" guarantee of art. I, § 16, supports a right to abortion.

Equal Protection

Article I, § 2, of the Ohio Constitution provides:

> All political power is inherent in the people. Government is instituted for their equal protection and benefit, and they have the right to alter, reform, or abolish the same, whenever they may deem it necessary; and no special privileges or immunities shall ever be granted, that may not be altered, revoked, or repealed by the General Assembly.[54]

---

49. Briefly, the argument would be that a statute prohibiting abortion interferes with a woman's control over her own body, and that such interference constitutes an "injury" to her "person," as those terms are used in § 16, for which there must be a "remedy by due course of law." That "remedy," in turn, would be invalidation of the statute. This argument assumes that the "right to a remedy" language of art. I, § 16, confers substantive rights. As the case law in the text makes clear, however, it does not.

50. *Haskins v. Bias*, 441 N.E.2d 842, 844 (Ohio Ct. App. 1981). *See also Slusher v. Oeder*, 476 N.E.2d 714, 716 (Ohio Ct. App. 1984) (same).

51. *Vrabel v. Vrabel*, 459 N.E.2d 1298, 1305 (Ohio Ct. App. 1983) (emphasis in original).

52. Article I, § 19a, prohibits the General Assembly from abolishing wrongful death causes of action. Ohio Const. art. I, § 19a (LexisNexis 2004).

53. *Strock v. Pressnell*, 527 N.E.2d 1235, 1240–41 (Ohio 1988).

54. Ohio Const. art. I, § 2 (LexisNexis 2004).

The Ohio Supreme Court has stated that the phrase in art. I, § 2, that "[g]overnment is instituted for [the people's] equal protection and benefit" is "essentially identical" to the Equal Protection Clause of the Fourteenth Amendment.[55] Accordingly, "[t]he limitations placed upon government action by the federal and state Equal Protection Clauses are essentially the same."[56] For purposes of both state and federal equal protection analysis, "all statutes are subject to at least rational-basis review, which requires that a statutory classification be rationally related to a legitimate government purpose."[57] "When a discriminatory classification based on sex or illegitimacy is at issue," the courts "employ heightened or intermediate scrutiny and require that the classification be substantially related to an important governmental objective."[58] Finally, "when classifications affect a fundamental constitutional right, or when they are based on race or national origin," the courts "conduct a strict-scrutiny analysis."[59]

For the reasons set forth in the preceding section of this analysis, the Ohio Constitution does not confer a "fundamental constitutional right" to abortion. Nor would an abortion prohibition discriminate on the basis of race or any other suspect personal characteristic. Abortion advocates may argue in the alternative that a statute prohibiting abortion discriminates against women and is subject to intermediate scrutiny because only women are capable of becoming pregnant. An abortion prohibition would appear to satisfy this level of scrutiny because the prohibition would be "substantially related" to the "important governmental objective" of protecting unborn human life. Nevertheless, the standard applicable to sex-based discrimination should not apply to an abortion prohibition. Abortion laws do not discriminate on the basis of sex.

First, the United States Supreme Court has reviewed restrictions on abortion funding under a rational basis standard of review, *not* under the heightened scrutiny required of gender-based classifications.[60] Indeed, the Court

---

55. *State ex rel. Heller v. Miller*, 399 N.E.2d 66, 67 (Ohio 1980). The language in art. I, § 2, giving the people the right to "alter, reform, or abolish" government, like the first sentence declaring that "[a]ll political power is inherent in the people," is simply "a statement of political principle derived from the Declaration of Independence. In practical terms, the people's right to reform or abolish government is accomplished through the electoral process and through amendment to the constitution as outlined in Article XVI." Steven H. Steinglass & Gino J. Scarselli, THE OHIO STATE CONSTITUTION[:] A REFERENCE GUIDE 81 (Westport, Conn. 2004).

56. *McCrone v. Bank One Corp.*, 839 N.E.2d 1, 4 (Ohio 2005).

57. *State v. Thompson*, 767 N.E.2d 251, 255 (Ohio 2002) (citation omitted).

58. *Id.* (citation omitted).

59. *Id.* (citation omitted).

60. *Harris v. McRae*, 448 U.S. 297, 321–26 (1980).

has held that "the disfavoring of abortion ... is not *ipso facto* sex discrimination," and, citing its decisions in *Harris* and other cases addressing abortion funding, stated that "the constitutional test applicable to government abortion-funding restrictions is not the heightened-scrutiny standard that our cases demand for sex discrimination, ... but the ordinary rationality standard."[61]

Second, even assuming that an abortion prohibition differentiates between men and women on the basis of sex, and would otherwise be subject to a higher standard of review, the Supreme Court has held that biological differences between men and women may justify different treatment based on those differences. In upholding a statutory rape statute that applied only to males, the Supreme Court noted, "this Court has consistently upheld statutes where the gender classification is not invidious, but rather realistically reflects the fact that the sexes are not similarly situated in certain circumstances."[62] As one federal district court observed: "Abortion statutes are examples of cases in which the sexes are not biologically similarly situated" because only women are capable of becoming pregnant and having abortions.[63]

A statute prohibiting abortion quite obviously can affect only women because only women are capable of becoming pregnant.[64] Unlike laws that use women's ability to become pregnant (or pregnancy itself) to discriminate

---

61. *Bray v. Alexandria Women's Health Clinic*, 506 U.S. 263, 273 (1993). Several state supreme courts and individual state supreme court justices have recognized that abortion regulations and restrictions on abortion funding are not "directed at women as a class" so much as "abortion as a medical treatment, which, because it involves a potential life, has no parallel as a treatment method." *Bell v. Low Income Women of Texas*, 95 S.W.3d 253, 258 (Tex. 2002) (upholding funding restrictions) (citing *Harris*, 448 U.S. at 325). *See also Fischer v. Dep't of Public Welfare*, 502 A.2d 114, 125 (Pa. 1985) ("the basis for the distinction here is not sex, but abortion") (upholding funding restrictions); *Moe v. Secretary of Administration & Finance*, 417 N.E.2d 387, 407 (Mass. 1981) (Hennessey, C.J., dissenting) (funding restrictions were "directed at abortion as a medical procedure, not women as a class"); *Right to Choose v. Byrne*, 450 A.2d 925, 950 (N.J. 1982) (O'Hern, J., dissenting) ("[t]he subject of the legislation is not the person of the recipient, but the nature of the claimed medical service"). Both *Moe* and *Right to Choose* were decided on other grounds. The dissenting justices were addressing alternative arguments raised by the plaintiffs, but not reached by the majority opinions.

62. *Michael M. v. Superior Court*, 450 U.S. 464, 469 (1981). In *Preterm Cleveland v. Voinovich*, discussed in the first section of this analysis, the Ohio Court of Appeals cited *Michael M.* with approval. *See Preterm Cleveland*, 627 N.E.2d at 582.

63. *Jane L. v. Bangerter*, 794 F. Supp. 1537, 1549 (D. Utah 1992).

64. *Geduldig v. Aiello*, 417 U.S. 484, 496 n. 20 (1974) ("[n]ormal pregnancy is an objectively, identifiable physical condition with unique characteristics").

against them in *other* areas (*e.g.*, employment opportunities), abortion prohibitions cannot fairly be said to involve a distinction between men and women that is a "mere pretext[] designed to erect an invidious discrimination against [women]."[65]

Because a prohibition of abortion would not infringe upon a fundamental state constitutional right and would not impermissibly classify on the basis of a suspect or quasi-suspect class, it would need to satisfy only the rational basis test. Under that test, the classification must bear "a rational relationship to a legitimate governmental interest."[66] A prohibition of abortion would have a "rational relationship" to the "legitimate governmental interest" in protecting unborn human life. Accordingly, Ohio could enact an abortion prohibition without violating the equal protection guarantee of the Ohio Constitution.

Rights of Conscience

Article I, §7, of the Ohio Constitution provides, in relevant part:

> All men have a natural and indefeasible right to worship Almighty God according to the dictates of their own conscience.... and no preference shall be given, by law, to any religious society; nor shall any interference with the rights of conscience be permitted.[67]

In any challenge to a statute prohibiting abortion, abortion advocates may raise either or both of two arguments under art. I, §7. First, they may argue that an abortion prohibition interferes with a woman's "rights of conscience" by forbidding her from obtaining an abortion that would be allowed by her religion. Second, they may argue in the alternative (or in addition) that an abortion prohibition gives a "preference" to a "religious society" because it reflects sectarian views regarding when human life begins and the sinfulness of abortion. Neither argument would likely succeed.

With respect to the latter, argument, the Ohio Supreme Court has held that Establishment Clause analysis and analysis under art. I, §7, of the Ohio Constitution are the same.[68] Accordingly, an abortion prohibition that would not

---

65. *Id.*

66. *Menefee v. Queen City Metro*, 550 N.E.2d 181, 182 (Ohio 1990).

67. OHIO CONST. art. I, §7 (LexisNexis 2004).

68. *Simmons-Harris. v. Goff*, 711 N.E.2d 203, 211–12 (Ohio 1999). Under that test, "a statute does not violate the Establishment Clause when (1) it has a secular legislative purpose, (2) its primary effect neither advances nor inhibits religion, and (3) it does not ex-

violate the Establishment Clause would not violate art. I, §7, either.[69] For the reasons set forth in Chapter 2, a statute prohibiting abortion would not violate the Establishment Clause. Accordingly, it would not violate art. I, §7.

With respect the former argument, the Ohio Supreme Court has developed its own test for evaluating state "free exercise" claims:

> We hold that under Section 7, Article I of the Ohio Constitution, the standard for reviewing a generally applicable, religion-neutral state regulation that allegedly violates a person's right to free exercise of religion is whether the regulation serves a compelling state interest and is the least restrictive means of furthering that interest.[70]

"To state a prima facie free exercise claim [under art. I, §7], the plaintiff must show that his religious beliefs are truly held and that the governmental enactment has a coercive affect [sic] against him in the practice of his religion."[71]

It is doubtful that a successful challenge to an abortion prohibition could be mounted under this standard. As an initial matter, it is not at all apparent that a statute prohibiting abortion would have a "coercive [e]ffect" upon a pregnant woman in the practice of her religion. Although a particular religious doctrine may *permit* abortion under certain circumstances, no doctrine in any religion *requires* a woman to undergo an abortion, at least when her life is not

---

pressly entangle government with religion." *Simmons*, 711 N.E.2d at 208 (citing *Lemon v. Kurtzman*, 403 U.S. 602, 612–13 (1971)).

69. In *Preterm Cleveland*, the court of appeals rejected plaintiffs' argument that the Ohio informed consent statute violated art. I, §7. It was "neither the purpose nor effect" of the statute, the court concluded, "'to force women to adhere to a particular religious viewpoint'" regarding the morality of abortion. *Preterm Cleveland*, 627 N.E.2d at 579 (quoting plaintiffs' brief).

70. *Humphrey v. Lane*, 728 N.E.2d 1039, 1043 (Ohio 2000).

71. *Id.* at 1045 (emphasis added). A *prima facie* case is not made out unless there is a clear conflict between the requirements of law and the requirements of one's religion. For example, in *State v. Bontrager*, 683 N.E.2d 126 (Ohio Ct. App. 1996), the Ohio Court of Appeals upheld the conviction of a member of the Old Order Amish faith for failure to wear "hunter orange" apparel while hunting during deer gun-hunting season as required by state law. Although the Old Order Amish faith prohibits the wearing of bright colors (which would include hunter orange), the religion does not require its members to engage in the hunting of deer. *Id.* at 129–30. The court determined that "hunting is not an aspect central to the Amish religion in which one must engage to practice the religion properly." *Id.* at 130. *See also State v. Swartzentruber*, 556 N.E.2d 531, 534 (Ohio Mun. Ct. 1989) ("nothing in the defendant's religion compels him to hunt deer in order to follow the dictates of his church").

in danger (an exception that would likely be included in any abortion statute the Legislature might enact). If a religious doctrine does not *require* certain conduct, a prohibition of that conduct, even if otherwise permitted by a person's religious beliefs, cannot be said to "coerce" a person in the free exercise of her religious beliefs.[72]

Even assuming that a pregnant woman could make out a *prima facie* case under *Humphrey* (that her sincere religious beliefs *required* her to obtain an abortion that was prohibited by law), a challenge to the prohibition on state "free exercise" grounds would most likely fail. The State has a compelling interest in protecting and preserving the life of the unborn child and an outright prohibition is "the least restrictive means of furthering that interest." An example, not involving abortion, that illustrates this principle is the line of cases authorizing compulsory blood transfusions on pregnant women (typically, Jehovah's Witnesses) to save the lives of their unborn children,[73] a line of cases, it must be noted, that the Ohio Supreme Court has tacitly recognized.[74] The prohibition of abortion, for the same end, stands on even firmer ground because it does not implicate the federal and state constitutional right to refuse unwanted medical treatment.[75] Moreover, unlike an order authorizing a blood transfusion of a pregnant woman, which is intended to *save* the life of the unborn child (and very possibly the mother's life as well), the intent in an abor-

---

72. To have standing to raise a free exercise claim against a law prohibiting or regulating abortion, one must allege that one seeks an abortion "under compulsion of religious belief." *Harris v. McRae*, 448 U.S. at 320. Of course, a law that singles out religious practices for regulation would present an entirely different question. *See Church of the Lukumi Babalu Aye, Inc. v. City of Hialeah*, 508 U.S. 520 (1993) (a law that is aimed at specific religious practices must satisfy the "strict scrutiny" standard of judicial review).

73. *See Fosmire v. Nicoleau*, 536 N.Y.S.2d 492, 496 (App. Div. 1989) (dictum) (when "a pregnant adult woman refuses medical treatment and, as a result of that refusal, places the life of her unborn baby in jeopardy," "the State's interest, as *parens patriae*, in protecting the health and welfare of the child is determined to be paramount") (citing *In the Matter of Application of Jamaica Hospital*, 491 N.Y.S.2d 898 (Sup. Ct. 1985) (blood transfusion) (18 weeks gestation); and *Crouse Irving Memorial Hospital, Inc. v. Paddock*, 485 N.Y.S.2d 443 (Sup. Ct. 1985) (blood transfusion) (premature delivery)). *See also Raleigh Fitkin-Paul Morgan Memorial Hospital v. Anderson*, 201 A.2d 537 (N.J. 1964) (same with respect to blood transfusion at 32 weeks gestation); *but see In re Brown*, 689 N.E.2d 397 (Ill. App. Ct. 1997) (*contra*) (blood transfusion).

74. *In re Milton*, 505 N.E.2d 255, 259 (Ohio 1987) (by implication) (citing *Raleigh Fitkin-Paul Morgan Memorial Hospital*).

75. *See, e.g., Cruzan v. Director, Missouri Dep't of Health*, 497 U.S. 261, 278–79 & n. 7 (1990); *Washington v. Glucksberg*, 521 U.S. 702, 719–26 & n. 17 (1997); *Steele v. Hamilton County Community Mental Health Board*, 736 N.E.2d 10, 15–16 (Ohio 2000) (recognizing right of an adult to refuse unwanted medical treatment).

tion is to *destroy* the unborn child's life. A statute prohibiting abortion would not violate art. I, § 7.

Retained Rights

Article I, § 20, of the Ohio Constitution provides: "The enumeration of rights shall not be construed to impair or deny other retained by the people; and all powers, not herein delegated, remain with the people."[76] Abortion advocates may be expected to cite § 20 in support of an asserted right to abortion under the state constitution. A proper interpretation of § 20, however, would not support a right to abortion as a "retained right."

Article I, § 20, has been cited in few cases and interpreted in almost none, which suggests that it would be an unlikely source of a right to abortion (or any other substantive right). In *State ex rel. Attorney General v. Covington*,[77] the Ohio Supreme Court held that § 20 imposes no limitations on the Legislature's power.[78] But even if the holding in *Covington* were disregarded, § 20 would not support a right to abortion.

The retention of rights language of § 20 appears to be "modeled" on the Ninth Amendment, which provides: "The enumeration in the Constitution of certain rights, shall not be construed to deny or disparage others retained by the people."[79] In light of the source from which § 20 was drawn, it should be given a parallel interpretation. That, in turn, suggests that if no right to abortion exists under the Ninth Amendment, then none would be recognized under § 20. The Supreme Court, however, has rooted the "abortion liberty" in the liberty language of the Due Process Clause of the Fourteenth Amendment, not in the unenumerated rights language of the Ninth Amendment.[80] Because abor-

---

76. OHIO CONST. art. I, § 20 (LexisNexis 2004).

77. 29 Ohio St. Rep. 102 (1876).

78. *Id.* at 112. This holding is consistent with the view that the enumeration of certain *constitutional* rights should not be construed to "impair or deny" *common law* or *statutory* rights retained by the people.

79. U.S. CONST. AMEND. IX (West 2006). Steinglass and Scarselli, THE OHIO STATE CONSTITUTION at 114.

80. *See Roe*, 410 U.S. at 153; *Casey*, 505 U.S. at 846. In any event, the Ninth Amendment, standing alone, is not a source of substantive rights. *Gibson v. Matthews*, 926 F.2d 532, 537 (6th Cir. 1991). Although "[s]ome unenumerated rights may be of [c]onstitutional magnitude," that is only "by virtue of other amendments, such as the Fifth or Fourteenth Amendment. A person cannot claim a right that exists solely under the Ninth Amendment." *United States v. Vital Health Products, Ltd.*, 786 F. Supp. 761, 777 (E.D. Wis. 1992), *aff'd mem. op., sub nom. United States v. LeBeau*, 985 F.2d 563 (7th Cir. 1993). *See also Charles v. Brown*, 495 F. Supp. 862, 863 (N.D. Ala. 1980) (same).

tion has not been recognized as a "retained right" under the Ninth Amendment, it should not be recognized as one under § 20, either.

Finally, assuming that § 20 retains rights that are judicially enforceable, it would be reasonable to limit those rights to those that were enjoyed at the time the state constitution was adopted.[81] Abortion, however, was a crime when the present Ohio Constitution was adopted in 1851. Accordingly, abortion may not be regarded as a "retained" right.

Conclusion

Based on the foregoing analysis, an argument that the Ohio Constitution protects a right to abortion that is separate from, and independent of, the right to abortion recognized in *Roe v. Wade* would not likely succeed. That, in turn, suggests that if *Roe*, as modified by *Casey*, is ultimately overruled, the State of Ohio could enact and enforce a statute *prohibiting* abortion. Moreover, nothing in the Ohio Constitution precludes Ohio from *regulating* abortion within federal constitutional limits in the meantime.

---

81. In *State v. Boone*, 95 N.E. 924 (Ohio 1911), the Ohio Supreme Court held that the rights reserved by § 20 would have included, for example, trial by jury, even if that right had not been expressly guaranteed by the state constitution. *Id.* at 926. A right to a trial by jury, of course, long antedated adoption of the Ohio Constitution.

CHAPTER 39

OKLAHOMA

Summary

The Oklahoma Supreme Court has not yet decided whether the Oklahoma Constitution protects a right to abortion separate from, and independent of, the right to abortion recognized under the United States Constitution.[1] A careful examination of the state constitution, in light of its history and interpretation, as well as other relevant legal sources, however, suggests that the state supreme court probably would not recognize a state constitutional right to abortion. Thus, if *Roe v. Wade*,[2] as modified by *Planned Parenthood of Southeastern Pennsylvania v. Casey*,[3] were overruled, Oklahoma could enforce its pre-*Roe* abortion statutes (or enact new statutes prohibiting abortion). Moreover, nothing in the state constitution, properly understood, precludes the State from enacting and enforcing reasonable measures regulating abortion within current federal constitutional limits.

Analysis

The principal pre-*Roe* statute prohibited performance of an abortion upon a pregnant woman unless the procedure was "necessary to preserve her life."[4] Another statute prohibited a woman from soliciting an abortion or allowing an abortion to be performed upon her (subject to the same exception).[5] Pur-

---

1. *See In re Initiative Petition No. 349*, 838 P.2d 1, 12 n. 29 (Okla. 1992) (striking abortion initiative from the ballot because, if adopted, it would violate the federal constitution).
2. 410 U.S. 113 (1973).
3. 505 U.S. 833 (1992).
4. Okla. State. Ann. tit. 21, §861 (West 1971).
5. *Id.* tit. 21, §862. No prosecutions were reported under this statute. When an abortion was performed upon a woman "pregnant with a quick child," and the death of either the woman or the child resulted, the offense was manslaughter. *Id.* §714.

suant to *Roe*, these statutes were declared unconstitutional (on federal, not state, grounds) by the Oklahoma Court of Criminal Appeals in *Jobe v. State*,[6] and by a three-judge federal district court in *Henrie v. Derryberry*.[7] The statutes have not been repealed.[8]

Based upon arguments that have been raised in other States with similar constitutional provisions, possible sources for an asserted abortion right could include provisions of the state constitution guaranteeing religious liberty (art. I, §2), a speedy and certain remedy (art. II, §6) and due process of law and equal protection (art. II, §7); recognizing inherent political power in the people (art. II, §1) and inherent rights (art. II, §2); and retaining rights (art. II, §33).[9] The analysis that follows addresses each of these provisions.

Religious Liberty

Article I, §2, of the Oklahoma Constitution provides, in part: "Perfect toleration of religious sentiment shall be secured, and no inhabitant of the State shall ever be molested in person or property on account of his or her mode of religious worship; and no religious test shall be required for the exercise of civil or political rights."[10]

In any state constitutional challenge to a statute prohibiting abortion, abortion advocates may argue that an abortion prohibition interferes with the "[p]erfect toleration of religious sentiment" mandated by art. I, §2, by for-

---

6. 509 P.2d 481 (Okla. 1973).

7. 358 F. Supp. 719 (N.D. Okla. 1973).

8. OKLA. STAT. ANN. tit. 21, §§861, 862 (West 2002).

9. Two other more unlikely sources of an abortion right under the Oklahoma Constitution-art. II, §22 (guaranteeing freedom of speech) and §30 (prohibiting unreasonable searches and seizures)-are discussed generally in Chapter 3, *supra*.

10. OKLA. CONST. art. I, §2 (West 2005). The Oklahoma Supreme Court has interpreted art. II, §5, of the Oklahoma Constitution, to place greater restrictions on the use of public money or property for sectarian purposes than are required by the Establishment Clause. *Compare Gurney v. Ferguson*, 122 P.2d 1002 (Okla. 1941) (school buses operated at public expense may not transport children attending parochial schools), and *Board of Education for Independent School District No. 52 v. Antone*, 384 P.2d 911 (Okla. 1963) (same), *with Everson v. Board of Education*, 330 U.S. 1 (1947) (*contra*). Section 5, however, is limited by its terms to the use of public money or property for such purposes and, therefore, would have no bearing on the constitutionality of an abortion prohibition. Without reference to the state constitution, the state supreme court has recognized that the federal Establishment Clause "does not bar state or federal regulation of conduct which happens to coincide with religious belief." *Tulsa Area Hospital Council v. Oral Roberts University*, 626 P.2d 316, 321 (Okla. 1981).

bidding a woman from obtaining an abortion that would be allowed by her religion. This argument would not likely succeed.

Oklahoma courts have not explicitly equated art. I, §2, with the Free Exercise Clause of the First Amendment, but their decisions reflect a close congruence between First Amendment analysis and analysis under art. I, §2.[11] That congruence suggests that a challenge to a statute that would not succeed under the Free Exercise Clause would not succeed under art. I, §2, either. For the reasons set forth in Chapter 2, *supra*, an abortion statute could not be successfully challenged under the Free Exercise Clause. Accordingly, it would not be subject to a successful challenge under art. I, §2.

Speedy and Certain Remedy

Article II, §6, of the Oklahoma Constitution provides: "The courts of justice of the State shall be open to every person, and speedy and certain remedy afforded for every wrong and for every injury to person, property, or reputation; and right and justice shall be administered without sale, denial, delay, or prejudice."[12] Abortion advocates might argue that a statute prohibiting abortion interferes with a woman's control over her own body, and that such interference challenge an "injury" to her "person," as those terms are used in §6, for which there must be a "certain remedy." That "remedy," in turn, would be invalidation of the statute. This argument assumes that art. II, §6, confers substantive rights. The case law is clear, however, that it does not.

The "right to a remedy" guarantee of art. II, §6, "does not impose any substantive limitation on the legislature."[13] The guarantee "is a mandate to the judiciary and is not intended to be a limitation on the authority of the legislature. [Citation omitted]. The constitutional guarantee mandates that the courts should be open and affords a remedy for those wrongs that are recognized by

---

11. See *Lewellyn v. State*, 592 P.2d 538, 539–40 & nn. 2, 3 (Okla. Crim. App. 1979) (no free exercise right to distribute a controlled substance); *Wahid v. State*, 716 P.2d 678, 680 (Okla. Crim. App. 1986) (same); *State ex rel. Roberts v. McDonald*, 787 P.2d 466, 468–69 (Okla. Civ. App. 1989) (statute requiring licensing of all child care facilities did not violate free exercise rights of church operating "boys ranch"); *Emch v. City of Guymon*, 127 P.2d 855, 859 (Okla. Crim. App. 1942) (municipal ordinance prohibiting distribution of newspapers, handbills, tracts or books within the city limits without first securing a permit from the city clerk could not be applied to the distribution of religious literature by Jehovah's Witnesses) (following *Cantwell v. Connecticut*, 310 U.S. 296 (1940)).

12. Okla. Const. art. II, §6 (West 2005).

13. *Rivas v. Parkland Manor*, 12 P.3d 452, 457 (Okla. 2000) (citation omitted).

the laws of the land."[14] Article II, §6, was not "intended to preserve a particular remedy for given causes of action in any certain court of the state, nor was it intended to deprive the Legislature of the power to abolish remedies for future accruing causes of action…, or to create new remedies for other wrongs as in its wisdom it might determine."[15] If the Oklahoma Legislature retains its pre-*Roe* statutes prohibiting abortion (or enacts new ones), then the denial of an abortion (by virtue of state law) could not be regarded as a wrong "recognized by the laws of the land." There is no decision of any Oklahoma court declaring a criminal statute unconstitutional under the "right to a remedy" guarantee of art. II, §6. Article II, §6, is not a source of substantive rights enforceable against the Legislature.

Due Process of Law, Inherent Rights

Article II, §7, of the Oklahoma Constitution provides: "No person shall be deprived of life, liberty, or property without due process of law."[16] Article II, §2, provides: "All persons have the inherent right to life, liberty, the pursuit of happiness, and the enjoyment of the gains of their own industry."[17]

In any state challenge to a statute prohibiting abortion (either the pre-*Roe* statutes, if *Roe* is overruled, or any other statutes prohibiting abortion Oklahoma may enact), abortion advocates are most likely to rely upon these two provisions to argue that the statutes interfere with a pregnant woman's "liberty" interest in obtaining an abortion.[18] That reliance would probably be misplaced.

Due process of law under art. II, §7, has both a procedural and a substantive component. "The fundamental requisites of procedural due process are

---

14. *Id.* at 457–58. *See also St. Paul Fire & Marine Ins. Co. v. Getty Oil Co.*, 782 P.2d 915, 919 (Okla. 1989) (§6 "requires that a complainant must be given access to a court **if he has suffered a wrong which is recognized in the law**") (bold in original); *Nash v. Baker*, 522 P.2d 1335, 1337–38 (Okla. Civ. App. 1974) (same).

15. *Adams v. Iten Biscuit Co.*, 162 P. 938, 942 (Okla. 1917). *See, e.g., Wilson v. Still*, 819 P.2d 714 (Okla. 1991) (upholding statute abolishing common law causes of action for seduction and alienation of affections).

16. Okla. Const. art. II, §7 (West 2005).

17. *Id.* art. II, §2.

18. The Oklahoma Supreme Court has declined to speculate on whether the "scope of individual liberty" guaranteed by art. II, §§2 and 7, secures a state right to abortion. *In re Initiative Petition No. 349*, 838 P.2d at 12 n. 29. The court's citation of art. II, §§2 and 7, however, suggests that these would be the most likely claimed sources of an abortion right under the Oklahoma Constitution. In light of that suggestion, and in view of the parallel construction the provisions have been given, they are considered together in this section of the analysis.

notice, the right to be heard before a fair and impartial tribunal having jurisdiction of the subject matter, and the right to confront witnesses."[19] "Substantive due process," on the other hand, "requires that a law shall not be unreasonable, arbitrary or capricious and that the means selected shall have a reasonable and substantial relation to the objective being sought."[20] A prohibition of abortion would satisfy this standard because it would be reasonably and substantially related to the State's objective to protect unborn human life. Abortion advocates, however, would likely argue that a right to an abortion is a *fundamental* liberty interest under art. II, §7. That argument probably would not prevail.

The Oklahoma Constitution "contains independent sources of rights and liberties, which may, under some circumstances, offer more protection than the federal constitution."[21] Although "States are free to interpret their own due process clauses to afford protection beyond that granted by the federal constitution, even when the state and federal constitutions are similarly or identically phrased,"[22] the Oklahoma Supreme Court has held that the "[d]ue process protections encompassed within the two constitutions are coextensive."[23]

The Oklahoma Supreme Court has held that in evaluating substantive due process claims, courts must consider "our history, legal traditions and practices."[24] The court's reliance on such sources has been reflected in its decisions.

---

19. *Williams v. State ex rel. Dep't of Public Safety*, 791 P.2d 120, 124 (Okla. Civ. App. 1990).

20. *Id. See also Jack Lincoln Shops, Inc. v. State Dry Cleaners' Board*, 135 P.2d 332, 333 (Okla. 1943) (a statute restricting the exercise of a liberty or property interest will not be annulled as a violation of substantive due process "unless it is clearly irrelevant to the policy the Legislature may adopt or is arbitrary, unreasonable or discriminatory"), *appeal dismissed*, 320 U.S. 208 (1943).

21. *Turner v. City of Lawton*, 733 P.2d 375, 379 (Okla. 1986) (applying exclusionary rule to civil administrative proceedings) (interpreting art. II, §30).

22. *Messenger v. Messenger*, 827 P.2d 865, 872 n. 42 (Okla. 1992). *See also County Comm'rs of Muskogee County v. Lowery*, 136 P.3d 639, 647–52 (Okla. 2006) (declining to follow the Supreme Court's decision in *Kelo v. City of New London*, 545 U.S. 469 (2005), in interpreting the eminent domain provisions of the state constitution).

23. *Barzellone v. Presley*, 126 P.3d 588, 593 n. 26 (Okla. 2005). *See also Henry v. Schmidt*, 91 P.3d 651, 656 n. 36 (Okla. 2004) (same); *DuLaney v. Oklahoma State Dep't of Health*, 868 P.2d 676, 685 n. 33 (Okla. 1993) (state due process clause "has a definitional sweep that is coextensive with its federal counterpart"). In an earlier case, the state supreme court held that "[d]ue process of law under our State Constitution … is the same thing as due process of law under the Federal Constitution…." *McKeever Drilling Co. v. Egbert*, 40 P.2d 32, 35 (Okla. 1934).

24. *In re Baby Girl L*, 51 P.3d 544, 551 (Okla. 2002) (citing *Washington v. Glucksberg*, 521 U.S. 702, 710 (1997), and *Michael H. v. Gerald D.*, 491 U.S. 110, 127 n. 6 (1989)).

The Oklahoma Supreme Court has "repeatedly recognized that the right of a parent to the care, custody, companionship and management of his or her child is a fundamental right protected by the federal and state constitutions."[25] This right, of course, is firmly rooted in the history and traditions of the American people and, ultimately, English common law.[26] As the Supreme Court has observed, "The history and culture of Western civilization reflect a strong tradition of parental concern for the nurture and upbringing of their children. This primary role of the parents in the upbringing of their children is now established beyond debate as an enduring American tradition."[27] In a similar vein, the state supreme court has recognized a right to "corporal [bodily] integrity,"[28] which also has deep roots in English and American common law.[29]

A right to abortion, however, has no roots in the law of Oklahoma. The first territorial legislature enacted a prohibition of abortion in 1890, seventeen years before Oklahoma adopted a state constitution and was admitted to the Union. One statute prohibited the performance of an abortion upon a pregnant woman for any reason at any stage of pregnancy, "unless the same [was] necessary to preserve her life...."[30] Another statute prohibited a woman from soliciting an abortion or allowing an abortion to be performed upon her (subject to the same exception).[31] These statutes have never been repealed.[32]

---

25. *Matter of Adoption of Darren Todd H.*, 615 P.2d 287, 290 (Okla. 1980) (citing cases). *See also In re Herbst*, 971 P.2d 395, 397–98 (Okla. 1998) (same); *Delk v. Markel American Insurance Co.*, 81 P.3d 629, 639 n. 45 (Okla. 2003) (same). "The liberty interest ... of parents in the care, custody, and control of their children ... is perhaps the oldest of the fundamental liberty interests recognized by this Court." *Troxel v. Granville*, 530 U.S. 57, 65 (2000) (citing, among other cases, *Meyer v. Nebraska*, 262 U.S. 390 (1923)).

26. "The parental interest in the custody of a child rests on the common law." *Davis. v. Davis*, 708 P.2d 1102, 1109 n. 33 (Okla. 1985).

27. *Wisconsin v. Yoder*, 406 U.S. 205, 232 (1972).

28. *Blocker v. Martin*, 868 P.2d 1316, 1316 (Okla. 1994).

29. "No right is held more sacred, or is more carefully guaranteed by the common law, than the right of every individual to the possession and control of his own person, free from all restraint or interference of others, unless by clear and unquestioned authority of law." *Union Pacific Railway Co. v. Botsford*, 141 U.S. 250, 251 (1891).

30. Okla. (Terr.) Stat. §2187 (1890).

31. *Id.* §2188. No prosecutions were reported under this statute.

32. Okla. (Terr.) Stat. §§2187, 2188 (1890), *recodified at* Okla. (Terr.) Stat. §§2177, 2178 (1893), *recodified at* Okla. (Terr.) Stat. §§2268, 2269 (1903), *recodified at* Okla. Comp. Laws §§2370, 2371 (1909), *recodified at* Okla. Rev. Laws §§2436, 2437 (1910), *recodified at* Okla. Comp. Stat. Ann. §§1859, 1860 (1921), *recodified at* Okla. Rev. Stat. §§1834, 1835 (1931), *recodified at* Okla. Stat. Ann. tit. 21, §§861, 862 (West 1937).

Before *Roe v. Wade* was decided, the Oklahoma Court of Criminal Appeals affirmed convictions for abortion (and manslaughter convictions based upon the death of the woman resulting from an illegal abortion) without any hint that the prosecutions or convictions were barred by the state constitution.[33] And in *Bowlan v. Lunsford*,[34] the Oklahoma Supreme Court explained that the state abortion statutes "were enacted and designed for the protection of the unborn child and, through it, society."[35] After *Roe* was decided, the court of criminal appeals declared the state abortion statutes unconstitutional on federal grounds only.[36]

The Oklahoma Legislature has enacted a comprehensive scheme of abortion regulation.[37] And the Oklahoma Supreme Court has repeatedly rejected constitutional challenges to those statutes.[38]

Oklahoma has recognized the rights of unborn children in a variety of contexts outside of abortion. In criminal law, Oklahoma has defined "human being," as used to describe the subject of a homicide, to include an unborn child at every stage of gestation.[39] And a woman convicted of a capital offense may not be executed while she is pregnant.[40]

---

33. *Greenwood v. State*, 105 P. 371 (Okla. Crim. App. 1909); *Copus v. State*, 224 P. 364 (Okla. Crim. App. 1924); *Wilson v. State*, 252 P. 1106 (Okla. Crim. App. 1927).

34. 54 P.2d 666 (Okla. 1936).

35. *Id.* at 668.

36. *Jobe v. State*, 509 P.2d at 482.

37. OKLA. REV. STAT. ANN. tit. 63, §1-738.1 *et seq.* (West Supp. 2007) (mandating informed consent and a twenty-four-hour waiting period); *id.*, §1-740.1 *et seq.* (West Supp. 2007) (requiring parental notice and consent and a forty-eight-hour waiting period); id., §1-741 (West 2004) (restricting post-viability abortions); *id.*, §1-731(B) (West 2004) (requiring abortions after the first trimester to be performed in general hospitals); id., §1-738.6 *et seq.* (West Supp. 2007) (mandating that information regarding fetal pain be made available to women seeking abortions after the twentieth week of pregnancy); *id.*, §1-741 (West 2004) (protecting individual and institutional rights of conscience). *See also* OKLA. ADMIN. CODE §§317:30-5-2(a)(2)(Q), 317:30-5-2(b)(7)(J), 317:30-5-6, 317:30- 5-50, 317:30-59(8), 317:30-5-610 (restricting public funding of abortion for indigent women).

38. *Spencer by and through Spencer v. Seikel*, 742 P.2d 1126, 1130 (Okla. 1987) (upholding prohibition of abortion after viability except to prevent the death of or impairment to the health of the pregnant woman); *Davis v. Fieker*, 952 P.2d 505, 514–16 (Okla. 1997) (upholding statute requiring all abortions after the end of the first trimester to be performed in general hospitals).

39. OKLA. REV. STAT. ANN. tit. 21, §691(B) (West Supp. 2007). Before the statutory definition of homicide was amended to include unborn children at any stage of gestation, the Oklahoma Court of Criminal Appeals had rejected the common law "born-alive" rule and held that a viable unborn child is a human being who may be the victim of a homicide. *Hughes v. State*, 868 P.2d 730, 736 (Okla. Crim. App. 1994). In that case, which involved a full term pregnancy, the court said that "[a] viable human fetus is nothing less than a human life." *Id.* at 734.

40. OKLA. REV. STAT. ANN. tit. 22, §§1010, 1011 (West 2003).

In tort law, a statutory cause of action for wrongful death may be brought on behalf of an unborn child regardless of when the injuries causing death were inflicted.[41] In a medical malpractice case based upon a failure to disclose treatment alternatives, the Oklahoma Supreme Court held that where a fetus was viable when a physician discovered that it was suffering from hydrocephalus, the physician had no duty to disclose to the mother information about abortion as an alternative treatment because abortion after viability is prohibited in Oklahoma unless the mother's life or health is endangered.[42]

Under Oklahoma's health care laws, in the absence of specific authorization from the patient, life-sustaining treatment and/or artificially administered nutrition and/or hydration may not be withheld or withdrawn from a pregnant patient pursuant to an advance directive.[43] A guardian may not consent to an abortion on behalf of a pregnant ward without specific court authorization, except in a medical emergency where the procedure is necessary to preserve the ward's life.[44]

In property law, posthumous children (children conceived before but born after the death of a parent) "are considered as living at the death of their parents" for purposes of inheritance.[45] And, subject to certain exceptions, afterborn children (children conceived before the death of a parent but born after the parent executes a will) receive the same share of the testate's estate that they would have received if the testate had died intestate (without a will).[46] A court may appoint a guardian or a guardian *ad litem* to represent the interests of "persons not in being" in proceedings to determine future interests in real estate.[47] More generally, "[a] child conceived, but not born, is to be deemed an existing person so far as may be necessary for its interest in the event of it subsequent birth."[48]

In light of Oklahoma's unbroken tradition, dating back to territorial days, of prohibiting abortion except to preserve the life of the pregnant woman, as well as the State's solicitude for the rights of the unborn child in other areas of law, it cannot reasonably be said that the liberty guaranteed by art. II, § 7, encompasses a right to abortion-fundamental or otherwise.[49]

---

41. *Id.* tit. 12, § 1053(F) (West Supp. 2007).

42. *Spencer by and through Spencer v. Seikel*, 742 P.2d at 1130.

43. OKLA. REV. STAT. ANN. tit. 63, §§ 3101.4 (Advance Directive for Health Care Form, § V(a)); 3101.8(C) (West Supp. 2007).

44. *Id.* tit. 30, § 3-119 (West Supp. 2007).

45. *Id.* tit. 84, § 228 (West 1990).

46. *Id.* tit. 84, § 131.

47. *Id.* tit. 12, § 1147.1 (West 2000).

48. *Id.* tit. 15, § 15 (West 1996).

49. To the extent that the Oklahoma Supreme Court considers federal precedent in determining whether an asserted liberty interest (or right) is "fundamental" under the state due

Nor can it be said that the "inherent right to ... liberty" guaranteed by art. II, §2, encompasses a right to abortion.[50] The Oklahoma Supreme Court has held, in reference to art. II, §2, that "[legislative] acts, which to some extent interfere with an individual's constitutionally guaranteed privilege of certain inherent rights may be sustained as being within the police power, *or in the interest of the general welfare*."[51] "And this is true," the Court added, "whether the act in question interferes with the right to enjoyment of the gains of a person's own industry, to freedom of contract, *or the exercise of natural rights reserved to all*."[52] Apart from the State's authority to legislate "in the interest of the general welfare," which would appear to support a prohibition of abortion, there is no reasonable basis on which one could conclude that there is a "natural" or "inherent" right to obtain an abortion under art. II, §2.

The Oklahoma Supreme Court has equated the substantive rights protected by art. II, §2, with those protected by the state and federal due process clauses.[53] That equivalence of interpretation suggests that if a right to abortion is not protected by the due process guarantee of the state constitution (art. II, §7), then it would not be protected by the inherent rights provision (art. II, §2), either. Moreover, in evaluating "inherent rights" claims under art. II, §2, the Oklahoma Supreme Court applies the same historically-based analysis of asserted liberty and property interests that it does with respect to such interests under art. II, §7.[54]

A right to abortion cannot be found in the text or structure of the Oklahoma Constitution. There is no evidence that either the framers or ratifiers of

---

process guarantee, abortion would not qualify as a "fundamental" right. Although the Supreme Court characterized the right to choose abortion as "fundamental" in *Roe*, 410 U.S. at 152–53, it tacitly abandoned that characterization in *Casey*, 505 U.S. at 869–79 (Joint Op. of O'Connor, Kennedy and Souter, JJ., replacing *Roe's* "strict scrutiny" standard of review with the more relaxed "undue burden" standard, allowing for a broader measure of abortion regulation).

50. Because neither the pre-*Roe* statutes nor any that are likely to be enacted hereafter forbid or would forbid an abortion to preserve the life of the pregnant woman, there would be no conflict between such statutes and the "inherent right to life" protected by art. II, §2.

51. *One Chicago Coin's Play Boy Marble Board v. State ex rel. Adams*, 212 P.2d 129, 132 (Okla. 1949) (emphasis in original).

52. *Id.* (emphasis added). *See also Jack Lincoln Shops, Inc.*, 135 P.2d at 333 (same).

53. *Eastern Oklahoma Building & Construction Trades Council v. Pitts*, 82 P.3d 1008, 1011–12 (Okla. 2003); *Edmondson v. Pearce*, 91 P.3d 605, 623–24 (Okla. 2004).

54. *Edmondson*, 91 P.3d at 624 (in holding that the people, acting through the initiative process, could outlaw cockfighting, the court noted that "criminal statutes prohibiting cruelty to animals or instigating fights between animals have been part of Oklahoma law since at least the early 20th Century").

the Oklahoma Constitution intended the state constitution to limit the Legislature's authority to prohibit abortion.[55] Such an intent would have been remarkable in light of the contemporaneous prohibition of abortion except to save the life of the pregnant woman.

Equal Protection

Although the Oklahoma Constitution does not contain express equal protection language, both the Oklahoma Supreme Court and the Oklahoma Court of Criminal Appeals have determined that "[t]he same equal protection component found in the [Equal Protection Clause of the] fourteenth amendment ... is present in the [state] due process clause ..."[56] "The right to equal protection guaranteed under Oklahoma's Constitution has consistently been interpreted as coextensive with the right to equal protection guaranteed under the federal constitution."[57]

"When analyzing a case on equal-protection grounds, a court will apply one of three standards of review, depending upon (a) the basis of the classification, (b) the nature of the interests impaired by the classification, and (c) the character of state interests offered in support of the classification."[58] These standards of review are strict scrutiny, heightened scrutiny and rational basis scrutiny.[59] Strict scrutiny, under which a classification will not be upheld unless it is necessary to promote a compelling state interest, applies "[w]henever

---

55. *See* PROCEEDINGS & DEBATES OF THE CONSTITUTIONAL CONVENTION OF OKLAHOMA, Dec. 19, 1906, to March 11, 1907 (1907), Dec. 19, 1906 (afternoon session), Jan. 3, 1907 (morning and afternoon sessions), Jan. 4, 1907 (afternoon session), Jan. 7, 1907 (morning session), Jan. 8, 1907 (morning session); Jan. 9, 1907 (morning session), Jan. 10, 1907 (morning session), Jan. 11, 1907 (morning session), Jan. 14, 1907 (morning and afternoon sessions); Jan. 15, 1907 (morning session) (debate on Bill of Rights in Committee of the Whole). The Committee of the Whole's final report on the Bill of Rights was approved by the Convention on March 6, 1907, without further debate (although the final draft of the entire constitution was opened for a handful of amendments before it was given its final approval).

56. *Presley v. Board of County Comm'rs of Ottachie County*, 981 P.2d 309, 312 (Okla. 1999); *Gladstone v. Bartlesville Independent School District No. 30*, 66 P.3d 442, 446 n. 15 (Okla. 2003) (identifying "a functional equivalent of [the Equal Protection Clause] in the anti-discrimination component of [the] state constitution's due process section"); *Trice v. State*, 853 P.2d 203, 215 n. 4 (Okla. Crim. App. 1993).

57. *Sawatzky v. City of Oklahoma City*, 906 P.2d 785, 786 (Okla. Crim. App. 1995), (citing *Callaway v. City of Edmond*, 791 P.2d 104, 106 n.1 (Okla Crim. App. 1990)).

58. *Black v. Ball Janitorial Service, Inc.*, 730 P.2d 510, 513 n. 8 (Okla. 1986).

59. *Id.*

a challenged classification is directed at a suspect class or the classification burdens the exercise of a fundamental right...."[60] Heightened scrutiny applies to "[l]egislative classifications based on gender or illegitimacy...."[61] Under this standard, "a law must be substantially related to an important governmental interest."[62] The Oklahoma reviewing courts have struck down a variety of statutes that discriminated on account of sex.[63] Rational basis review applies to all other classifications. Under this standard, a classification will be upheld if there is a "rational relationship" between the classification and a legitimate state interest.[64]

Strict scrutiny review would not apply to an abortion prohibition because, for the reasons set forth in the preceding section of this analysis, neither the due process guarantee (art. II, §7), nor the inherent rights provision (art. II, §1), of the state constitution confers a "fundamental right" to abortion. Nor would the prohibition of abortion classify persons on the basis of a "suspect" personal characteristic.

Abortion advocates may argue in the alternative, however, that a statute prohibiting abortion discriminates against women and is subject to heightened scrutiny because only women are capable of becoming pregnant. An abortion prohibition would appear to satisfy this level of scrutiny because the prohibition would be "substantially related" to the "important governmental interest" in protecting unborn human life. Nevertheless, the standard applicable to sex-based discrimination (heightened scrutiny) would not apply to an abortion prohibition. Abortion laws do not discriminate on the basis of sex.

---

60. *Id.*

61. *Id.*

62. *Id.* In a similar vein, the Oklahoma Court of Criminal Appeals has held that "to withstand equal protection challenge gender-based classifications must serve important governmental objectives and be substantially related to achievement of those objectives." *Matter of D.H.W.*, 614 P.2d 81, 82 (Okla. Crim. App. 1980) (citing *Craig v. Boren*, 429 U.S. 190, 197 (1976)).

63. *See, e.g., Edwards v. State*, 591 P.2d 313, 316–17 (Okla. Crim. App. 1979) (statute providing different ages at which males and females could be prosecuted as adults); *State v. Beverage License No. BEV-75-45 of Wm. Gene Morris*, 561 P.2d 509 (Okla. 1977) (statute providing different ages at which males and females could purchase beer); *Bassett v. Bassett*, 521 P.2d 434 (Okla. Civ. App. 1974) (statute providing different ages at which males and females attain their majority) (intrafamily tort immunity): *Account Specialists & Credit Collections, Inc. v. Jackman*, 970 P.2d 202, 204–05 (Okla. Civ. App. 1998) (statute making husband liable for necessaries provided to wife by third parties, but not making wife liable for necessaries provided to husband).

64. *Black*, 730 P.2d at 513 n. 8.

First, the United States Supreme Court has reviewed restrictions on abortion funding under a rational basis standard of review, *not* under the heightened scrutiny required of gender-based classifications.[65] Indeed, the Court has held that "the disfavoring of abortion ... is not *ipso facto* sex discrimination," and, citing its decisions in *Harris* and other cases addressing abortion funding, stated that "the constitutional test applicable to government abortion-funding restrictions is not the heightened-scrutiny standard that our cases demand for sex discrimination, ... but the ordinary rationality standard."[66]

Second, even assuming that an abortion prohibition differentiates between men and women on the basis of sex, and would otherwise be subject to a higher standard of review, the Supreme Court has held that biological differences between men and women may justify different treatment based on those differences. In upholding a statutory rape statute that applied only to males, the Supreme Court noted, "this Court has consistently upheld statutes where the gender classification is not invidious, but rather realistically reflects the fact that the sexes are not similarly situated in certain circumstances."[67] As one federal district court observed: "Abortion statutes are examples of cases in which

---

65. *Harris v. McRae*, 448 U.S. 297, 321–26 (1980).

66. *Bray v. Alexandria Women's Health Clinic*, 506 U.S. 263, 273 (1993). Several state supreme courts and individual state supreme court justices have recognized that abortion regulations and restrictions on abortion funding are not "directed at women as a class" so much as "abortion as a medical treatment, which, because it involves a potential life, has no parallel as a treatment method." *Bell v. Low Income Women of Texas*, 95 S.W.3d 253, 258 (Tex. 2002) (upholding funding restrictions) (citing *Harris*, 448 U.S. at 325). *See also Fischer v. Dep't of Public Welfare*, 502 A.2d 114, 125 (Pa. 1985) ("the basis for the distinction here is not sex, but abortion") (upholding funding restrictions); *Moe v. Secretary of Administration & Finance*, 417 N.E.2d 387, 407 (Mass. 1981) (Hennessey, C.J., dissenting) (funding restrictions were "directed at abortion as a medical procedure, not women as a class"); *Right to Choose v. Byrne*, 450 A.2d 925, 950 (N.J. 1982) (O'Hern, J., dissenting) ("[t]he subject of the legislation is not the person of the recipient, but the nature of the claimed medical service"). Both *Moe* and *Right to Choose* were decided on other grounds. The dissenting justices were addressing alternative arguments raised by the plaintiffs, but not reached by the majority opinions.

67. *Michael M. v. Superior Court*, 450 U.S. 464, 469 (1981). The Oklahoma Court of Criminal Appeals has repeatedly cited *Michael M.* with approval in cases rejecting equal protection challenges to criminal statutes that applied to men, but not women. *Eberhardt v. State*, 727 P.2d 1374, 1376–77 (Okla. Crim. Ap. 1986) (upholding forcible rape statute that applied only to males); *Mahoney v. State*, 664 P.2d 1042, 1045 (Okla. Crim. App. 1983) (same); *Tubbs v. State*, 631 P.2d 758, 759 (Okla. Crim. App. 1981) (upholding statutory rape statute). *See also State v. Johnson*, 765 P.2d 1226, 1228 (Okla. Crim. App. 1988) (upholding statute imposing criminal penalties on an unwed mother for concealing stillbirth or the death of her child).

the sexes are not biologically similarly situated" because only women are capable of becoming pregnant and having abortions.[68]

A statute prohibiting abortion quite obviously can affect only women because only women are capable of becoming pregnant.[69] Unlike laws that use women's ability to become pregnant (or pregnancy itself) to discriminate against them in *other* areas (*e.g.*, employment opportunities), abortion prohibitions cannot fairly be said to involve a distinction between men and women that is a "mere pretext[] designed to erect an invidious discrimination against [women]."[70]

A prohibition of abortion would not interfere with the exercise of a fundamental state constitutional right, nor would it classify upon the basis of a suspect or quasi-suspect characteristic. Accordingly, it would be subject to rational basis review. A law prohibiting abortion would be rationally related to the State's legitimate interest in protecting unborn human life.

Inherent Political Power

Article II, § 1, of the Oklahoma Constitution provides:

> All political power is inherent in the people; and government is instituted for their protection, security, and benefit, and to promote their general welfare; and they have the right to alter or reform the same whenever the public good may require it: Provided, such change be not repugnant to the Constitution of the United States.[71]

In any challenge to the pre-*Roe* Oklahoma's abortion statutes (or any other statutes prohibiting abortion the State may enact), abortion advocates might argue that the statute interferes with the "inherent" political power of the people because it does not promote their "general welfare." Given the purpose of § 1, this argument would not likely prevail.

In *Cofield v. Farrell*,[72] the Oklahoma Supreme Court held that "the people of this state, by section 1 of article 2 of the Constitution, have specifically re-

---

68. *Jane L. v. Bangerter*, 794 F. Supp. 1537, 1549 (D. Utah 1992). The Oklahoma Court of Criminal Appeals has recognized that "the Equal Protection Clause does not require that both genders be treated equally if they are not similarly situated." *State v. Johnson*, 765 P.2d at 1228.

69. *Geduldig v. Aiello*, 417 U.S. 484, 496 n. 20 (1974) ("[n]ormal pregnancy is an objectively, identifiable physical condition with unique characteristics").

70. *Id.*

71. OKLA. CONST. art. II, § 1 (West 2005).

72. 134 P. 407 (Okla. 1913).

served the right to alter or reform said Constitution, conditioned that such change be not repugnant to the Constitution of the United States."[73] The right of the people to "alter or reform" the state constitution extended to repealing a provision of the Enabling Act that prohibited transfer of the state capital from Guthrie prior to 1913.[74] As the foregoing cases make clear, the purpose of art. II, §1, is to secure to the people themselves, through the amendment process, the right to decide whether, how and to what extent the organic instrument of government should be changed. Section 1, thus, is not a source of substantive rights (other than the right to "alter or reform" the state constitution). Rather, it recognizes the people as the ultimate source of authority in a republican form of government.[75] As such, it could not serve as a basis for asserting a right to abortion. Whether a given law promotes the "general welfare" of the people, as that term in used in art. II, §1, presents a political question for the legislature (and, ultimately, the people) to decide, not a constitutional question for the judiciary.

Retained Rights

Article II, §33, of the Oklahoma Constitution provides: "The enumeration in this Constitution of certain rights shall not be construed to deny, impair or disparage others retained by the people."[76] In any challenge to the pre-*Roe* statutes prohibiting abortion (or any new statutes prohibiting abortion), abortion advocates may be expected to argue that abortion is a "retained right" under art. II, §33.

Article II, §33, has been cited in very few Oklahoma decisions and authoritatively interpreted in none. An entirely plausible reading of §33 is that the enumeration of certain rights in the state constitution should not be construed to "deny, impair or disparage" other rights retained by the people under the common law or statutes. But even if §33 is understood to retain unspecified

---

73. *Id.* at 420–21.

74. *Smith v. State*, 113 P. 932, 936 (Okla. 1910).

75. In *Cooper v. Cartright*, 195 P.2d 290 (Okla. 1948), the Oklahoma Supreme Court cited art. II, §1, along with art. II, §4 (prohibiting interference with the right of suffrage), and art. III, §7 (now art. III, §5) (declaring elections to be free and equal and prohibiting interference with the free exercise of the right of suffrage), in support of its holding that the right to reorganize an old or to organize a new political party is a right inherent in the electors of the State and is a necessary accompaniment of popular government under a constitution resting all political power inherently in the people and preventing interference with the free exercise of the right of suffrage. *Id.* at 293.

76. OKLA. CONST. art. II, §33 (West 2005).

constitutional rights (as opposed to *common law* or *statutory* rights), abortion could not plausibly be considered to be among such rights because, at the time the Oklahoma Constitution was adopted in 1907, abortion was a crime. The argument that § 33 "retained" as an "unenumerated right" conduct that was criminal when the state constitution was adopted is, at the very least, counterintuitive.

The language of § 33 appears to be based on the Ninth Amendment, which provides: "The enumeration in the Constitution of certain rights, shall not be construed to deny or disparage others retained by the people."[77] In light of that equivalence, § 33 should be given a parallel interpretation. That, in turn, suggests that if no right to abortion exists under the Ninth Amendment, then none would be recognized under art. II, § 33. The Supreme Court, however, has rooted the "abortion liberty" in the liberty language of the Due Process Clause of the Fourteenth Amendment, not in the unenumerated rights language of the Ninth Amendment.[78] Because abortion has not been recognized as a "retained right" under the Ninth Amendment, it should not be recognized as one under § 33, either.

Conclusion

Based on the foregoing analysis, an argument that the Oklahoma Constitution protects a right to abortion that is separate from, and independent of, the right to abortion recognized in *Roe v. Wade* would not likely succeed. That, in turn, suggests that if *Roe*, as modified by *Casey*, is ultimately overruled, the State of Oklahoma could enforce its pre-*Roe* statutes *prohibiting* abortion (or enact new statutes prohibiting abortion). Moreover, nothing in the Oklahoma Constitution precludes Oklahoma from *regulating* abortion within federal constitutional limits in the meantime.

---

77. U.S. CONST. AMEND. IX (West 2006).

78. *See Roe*, 410 U.S. at 153; *Casey*, 505 U.S. at 846. In any event, the Ninth Amendment, standing alone, is not a source of substantive rights. *Gibson v. Matthews*, 926 F.2d 532, 537 (6th Cir. 1991). Although "[s]ome unenumerated rights may be of [c]onstitutional magnitude," that is only "by virtue of other amendments, such as the Fifth or Fourteenth Amendment. A person cannot claim a right that exists solely under the Ninth Amendment." *United States v. Vital Health Products, Ltd.*, 786 F. Supp. 761, 777 (E.D. Wis. 1992), *aff'd mem. op., sub nom. United States v. LeBeau*, 985 F.2d 563 (7th Cir. 1993). *See also Charles v. Brown*, 495 F. Supp. 862, 863 (N.D. Ala. 1980) (same).

CHAPTER 40

OREGON

Summary

The Oregon Supreme Court has not yet decided whether the Oregon Constitution protects a right to abortion separate from, and independent of, the right to abortion recognized under the United States Constitution.[1] A careful examination of the state constitution, in light of its history and interpretation, as well as other relevant legal sources, however, suggests that the state supreme court probably would not recognize a state constitutional right to abortion. Thus, if *Roe v. Wade*,[2] as modified by *Planned Parenthood of Southeastern Pennsylvania v. Casey*,[3] were overruled, Oregon could prohibit abortion. Moreover, nothing in the state constitution, properly understood, precludes the State from enacting and enforcing reasonable measures regulating abortion within current federal constitutional limits.

---

1. In *Planned Parenthood Ass'n, Inc. v. Dep't of Human Resources of the State of Oregon*, 663 P.2d 1247 (Or. Ct. App. 1983), the Oregon Court of Appeals held that an administrative rule of the Department of Human Resources restricting public funding of abortions for indigent women violated the privileges and immunities provision of the state constitution. *Id.* at 1257–60 (citing art. I, §20). In light of its disposition of the case, the court deemed it "unnecessary" to decide whether the Oregon Constitution protects "an independent right of procreation choice." *Id.* at 1256–57. On appeal, the Oregon Supreme Court affirmed the judgment of the court of appeals, but on alternative grounds (that the rule was invalid because it exceeded the agency's authority under the enabling statutes). *Planned Parenthood Ass'n, Inc. v. Dep't of Human Resources of the State of Oregon*, 687 P.2d 785, 787–93 (Or. 1984). Significantly, the state supreme court held that the court of appeals ruling on the constitutional question and the constitutional challenge itself were "premature." *Id.* at 787. No decision of the Oregon Supreme Court recognizes a state right to abortion.

2. 410 U.S. 113 (1973).

3. 505 U.S. 833 (1992).

Analysis

The principal pre-*Roe* Oregon abortion statutes were based on § 230.3 of the Model Penal Code.[4] The statutes allowed an abortion to be performed upon a pregnant woman before the one hundred fiftieth day of pregnancy when (1) there was "substantial risk that continuance of the pregnancy [would] greatly impair the physical or mental health of the mother," (2) "[t[he child would be born with serious physical or mental defect," or (3) "[t]he pregnancy resulted from felonious intercourse."[5] After the one hundred fiftieth day, abortion was permitted only if "the life of the pregnant woman [was] in imminent danger."[6] Pursuant to *Roe*, most of these statutes were declared unconstitutional (on federal, not state, grounds) in an unreported decision of a three-judge federal district court,[7] and were later repealed.[8]

Based upon arguments that have been raised in Oregon and other States with similar constitutional provisions, possible sources for an asserted abortion right could include provisions of the Bill of Rights guaranteeing freedom of worship and freedom of religious opinion (art. I, § 2, 3), a remedy by due course of law (§ 10) and equality of privileges and immunities (§ 20); recognizing natural rights (§ 1); and retaining rights (§ 33).[9] The analysis that follows addresses each of these provisions.

---

4. OR. REV. STAT. § 435.405 *et seq.* (1969). The complete text of § 230.3 of the Model Penal Code is set out in Appendix B to the Supreme Court's decision in *Doe v. Bolton*, 410 U.S. 179, 205–07 (1973).

5. *Id.* §§ 435.415(1)(a)-(c).

6. *Id.* §§ 435.425(1), 445(1). The law imposed other conditions. Abortions could be performed only by licensed physicians in licensed hospitals. *Id.* §§ 435.405(2) 435.405(3), 435.415(3). Except in emergency cases, two other physicians had to certify in writing the circumstances justifying an abortion. *Id.* §§ 435.425(1), 435.445(1). If the person seeking an abortion was a minor, the written consent of her parents was required; and, if she was married and living with her husband, his written consent. *Id.* § 435.435.

7. *Benson v. Johnson*, No. 70-226 (D. Or. Feb. 1973).

8. 1983 Or. Laws 868, ch. 470, § 1.

9. Three other more unlikely sources of an abortion right under the Oregon Constitution-art. I, § 8 (guaranteeing freedom of speech), § 9 (prohibiting unreasonable searches and seizures) and § 34 (prohibiting involuntary servitude)-are discussed generally in Chapter 3, *supra*.

Freedom of Worship, Freedom of Religious Opinion

Article I, §2, of the Oregon Constitution provides: "All men shall be secure in the Natural right, to worship Almighty God according to the dictates of their own consciences."[10] Article I, §3, provides: "No law shall in any case whatever control the free exercise, and enjoyment of religeous (*sic*) opinions, or interfere with the rights of conscience."[11]

In any state constitutional challenge to a statute prohibiting abortion, abortion advocates may argue that an abortion prohibition interferes with a woman's "rights of conscience" and the "free exercise" of her religious opinions by forbidding her from obtaining an abortion that would be allowed by her religion. Such an argument would not likely prevail.

In interpreting art. I, §§2 and 3, the Oregon Supreme Court has held:

> A law that is neutral toward religion or nonreligion as such, that is neutral among religions, and that is part of a general regulatory scheme having no purpose to control or interfere with rights of conscience or with religious opinions does not violate the guarantees of religious freedom in Article I, sections 2 and 3.[12]

A statute prohibiting abortion cannot be said to adopt a "religious" view of the sinfulness of abortion, as the Supreme Court recognized in *Harris v. McRae*.[13] At issue in *Harris* was the constitutionality of the Hyde Amendment, which restricts federal funding of abortion. The Hyde Amendment was challenged on multiple grounds, including the Establishment Clause of the First Amendment. The Court held that the Establishment Clause is not violated merely because "a statute 'happens to coincide or harmonize with the tenets of some or all religions.'"[14] Noting that the Hyde Amendment "is as much a reflection of 'traditionalist' values toward abortion, as it is an embodiment of the views of any particular religion," the Court held that "the fact that the funding restrictions in the Hyde Amendment may coincide with the religious tenets of the Roman Catholic Church does not, without more, contravene the Establishment Clause."[15] For the same reason, the fact that an abortion prohibition may "coincide with" the

---

10. OR. CONST. art. I, §2 (2007).

11. *Id.* art. I, §3.

12. *Meltebeke v. Bureau of Labor and Industries*, 903 P.2d 351, 361 (Or. 1994).

13. 448 U.S. 297 (1980).

14. *Id.* at 319.

15. *Id.* at 319–20.

"religious tenets" of the Catholic Church (or any other church) does not, by itself, violate art. I, §§2 and 3 of the Oregon Constitution.

Nor would a prohibition of abortion "control or interfere with rights of conscience or with religious opinions" because there is no doctrine in any religion that *requires* (as opposed to *permits*) a woman to undergo an abortion in circumstances when her life is not in danger. Whether a particular religious doctrine *permits* abortion for reasons which are not recognized by law does not present a justiciable claim under art. I, §§2 and 3 of the Oregon Constitution.[16]

Natural Rights, Retained Rights

Article I, §1, of the Oregon Constitution provides:

> We declare that all men, when they form a social compact are equal in right; that all power is inherent in the people; and all free governments are founded on their authority, and instituted for their peace, safety and happiness; and they have at all times a right to alter, reform or abolish the government in such manner as they may think proper.[17]

Article I, §33, provides: "This enumeration of rights and privileges shall not be construed to impair or deny others retained by the people."[18] In any challenge to an abortion prohibition, abortion advocates are likely to rely upon art. I, §§1 and 33, arguing that the prohibition of abortion interferes with both the "safety and happiness" of the people under §1, and a "retained right" to abortion under §33. It is not likely that either argument would prevail.

Article I, §1, enunciates general principles of republican political theory (that government derives its authority from the people and exists to promote their "peace, safety and happiness"). By its own terms, §1 does not create any judicially enforceable rights and has not been so interpreted. The Oregon Supreme Court has observed that "the framers of the Oregon Constitution did not include any express announcement of the 'inalienable' natural rights of man in their constitution. They were content to announce that 'all men, when they form a social compact, are equal in right,' and that 'all power is inherent

---

16. To have standing to challenge an abortion law that does not single out a particular religion for regulation, one must allege that one seeks an abortion "under compulsion of religious belief." *Harris*, 448 U.S. at 320.

17. OR. CONST. art. I, §1 (2007).

18. *Id.* art. I, §33.

in the people.'"[19] Article I, §1, therefore, would not appear to be a source of substantive rights, as Professor (later Justice) Linde observed almost forty years ago.[20]

Article I, §33, recognizes that the enumeration of rights and privileges in the Bill of Rights should not be understood "to impair or deny others retained by the people," but does not indicate whether such unenumerated "rights" and "privileges" are of *constitutional* (as opposed to *common law* or *statutory*) origin or how they might be identified. An argument that an abortion prohibition would violate either art. I, §1, or art. I, §33, is likely to based upon privacy theory. The Oregon Court of Appeals, however, has held that "[t]hese provisions, taken separately or together, have never been construed as providing a general right of privacy under the Oregon Constitution."[21] Accordingly, they would not likely serve as a source of a subsidiary right to abortion.

Even assuming that either art. I, §1, or art. I, §33, confers substantive constitutional rights, including a right to privacy, abortion could not plausibly be considered to be one of them. Oregon enacted its first abortion statute in 1853, six years before Oregon became a State and joined the Union. The statute prohibited performance of an abortion upon a woman "pregnant with a quick child ... with intent thereby to destroy such child, unless the same shall have been necessary to preserve the life of [the] mother," and punished the offense as manslaughter if the procedure resulted in the death of either the pregnant woman or the (quick) child.[22] The territorial statute was replaced by a later statute, enacted in 1864, eliminating the quickening distinction and prohibit-

---

19. *State v. Ciancanelli*, 121 P.3d 613, 628 (Or. 2005) (citing art. I, §1). This was not an oversight by the framers. "The absence of any declaration of 'inalienable' natural rights was noted and decried by some Oregonians at the time" the state constitution was being considered, "but probably did not affect the ultimate decision to adopt the constitution." *Id.*

20. " ... Section 1, which the draftsman began with 'we declare' means just that; it is a declaration of the ideological premises of the 'social compact,' which might possibly be drawn upon in giving historic meaning to other provisions of the constitution, *but which does not furnish an independent source for judicial invalidation of legislative authority.*" Hans Linde, *Without Due Process*, 49 OR. L. REV. 125, 144 (1970) (emphasis added).

21. *Does 1, 2, 3, 4, 5, 6 & 7 v. State*, 903 P.2d 822, 834 (Or. Ct. App. 1999). *See also V.L.Y. v. Board of Parole and Post-Prison Supervision*, 72 P.3d 993, 1004, n. 20 (Or. Ct. App. 2003) (not deciding whether there is a state constitutional right of privacy), *rev'd on other grounds*, 106 P.3d 145 (Or. 2005). The Oregon Supreme Court has noted the "problematic character" of privacy claims under the Oregon Constitution. *Planned Parenthood Ass'n, Inc.*, 687 P.2d at 787 n. 1 (citing *Sterling v. Cupp*, 625 P.2d 123, 126–29 (Or. 1981)).

22. OR. (TERR.) STAT., ch. III, §13, at 187 (1853–54). A "quick" child, within the meaning of this statute, refers to "quickening." "Quickening" is that stage of pregnancy, usually sixteen to eighteen weeks gestation, when the woman first detects fetal movement.

ing an abortion at any stage of pregnancy (subject to the same exception).[23] This statute remained on the books until Oregon adopted §230.3 of the Model Penal Code in 1969.[24]

Prior to 1937, the Oregon Medical Practice Act defined the terms "unprofessional" or "dishonorable conduct," for which a physician's license to practice medicine could be denied, suspended or revoked, as including "the procuring or aiding or abetting in procuring a criminal abortion...."[25] In 1937, the Act was amended to provide that a physician was subject to professional discipline for "procuring or aiding or abetting in procuring an abortion unless such is done for the relief of a woman whose health appears in peril after due consultation with another licensed medical physician and surgeon."[26] Two years later, the Act was amended again to define abortion as

> ... the expulsion of the foetus at a period of uterogestation so early that it has not acquired the power of sustaining life; provided it shall be conclusively presumed for the purpose of this statute that the foetus has not acquired such power earlier than one hundred fifty (150) days after gestation, and a disputable presumption of lack of such power shall arise if the expulsion takes place earlier than two hundred forty (240) days after gestation.[27]

As a result of these two amendments, a physician licensed to practice medicine in Oregon was not subject to discipline under the Medical Practice Act for performing an abortion upon a woman within the first one-hundred fifty days of gestation (and possibly up through the two-hundred and fortieth day) if the abortion was performed "for the relief of a woman whose health appear[ed] in peril" after consultation with another licensed physician. In *State v. Buck*,[28] the Oregon Supreme Court held that the provisions of Criminal Abortion Act, which allowed abortion only to save the life of the pregnant woman, had to be construed *in pari materia* (together) with those of the Med-

---

23. Act of Oct. 19, 1864, OR. GEN. LAWS, CRIM. CODE, ch. 43, §509, at 528 (1845–1864).

24. OR. GEN. LAWS, CRIM. CODE, ch. 43, §509 (1845–1864), *recodified at* HILL'S OR. LAWS §1721 (1887), *recodified at* BELLINGER & COTTON'S OR. CODES AND STATUTES §1748 (1901), *recodified at* LORD'S OR. LAWS §1900 (1920), *recodified at* OR. CODE ANN. §14-208 (1930), *recodified at* OR. COMP. LAWS ANN. §23-408 (1940), *recodified at* OR. REV. STAT. §163.060 (1953), *repealed by* 1969 Or. Laws ch. 684, §17.

25. OR. CODE ANN. §68-2106 (1930).

26. 1937 Or. Laws ch. 277, §1, p. 408, *codified at* OR. COMP. LAWS ANN. §54-931(b) (1940).

27. 1939 Or. Laws ch. 153, §3, p. 320, *codified at* OR. COMP. LAWS ANN. §54-901 (1940).

28. 262 P.2d 495 (Or. 1953).

ical Practice Act, which allowed abortion for health reasons, as well.[29] As a result of the interplay of the different statutes, the court concluded that "a medical doctor has the legal right to perform an abortion, as defined in the Medical Practice Act, provided he acts for the relief of a woman whose health appears in peril because of her pregnant condition after consultation with another medical doctor...."[30] Thus, from the amendment in the Medical Practice Act in 1937 until the Criminal Abortion Act was repealed in 1969, a physician could perform an abortion (within the gestational time frame indicated) for reasons of the pregnant woman's health, as well as to save her life.

Before *Roe v. Wade* was decided, the Oregon Supreme Court affirmed convictions for abortion (and manslaughter convictions based upon the death of the woman resulting from an illegal abortion) without any hint that the prosecutions or convictions were barred by the state constitution.[31] The state supreme court described illegal abortions as "*mala in se* [evil in themselves],"[32] and held that the purpose of the statutes prohibiting abortion was to prevent "acts done intentionally to cause the death of the unborn child."[33] Long after *Roe* was decided, the Oregon Court of Appeals noted that at the time the Oregon Constitution was adopted, "Oregon's criminal law seemingly recognized the separate existence of a fetus from its mother."[34]

Oregon has recognized the rights of unborn children in several contexts outside of abortion, including tort law, health care law and property law. In tort law, for example, a statutory cause of action for wrongful death may be brought on behalf of an unborn child who was viable (capable of sustained survival outside the mother's womb, with or without medical assistance) at the time of its death.[35] And a common law action for (nonlethal) prenatal injuries may be brought on behalf of an unborn child who was viable at the time

---

29. *Id.* at 501–02.

30. *Id.* at 502.

31. *State v. Jeannet*, 192 P.2d 983 (Or. 1948); *State v. Bennett*, 437 P.2d 821 (Or. 1968); *State v. Marsh*, 485 P.2d 1252 (Or. 1971).

32. *State v. Elliott*, 277 P.2d 754, 758 (Or. 1954).

33. *State v. Elliott*, 383 P.2d 382, 385 (Or. 1963).

34. *Christiansen v. Provident Health System of Oregon Corp.*, 150 P.3d 50, 56 n. 14 (Or. Ct. App. 2006). *See also Mallison v. Pomeroy*, 291 P.2d 225, 228 (Or. 1955) ("[i]n Oregon, we have recognized by statute the separate entity of an unborn child by protecting him in his property rights and against criminal conduct").

35. *Libbee v. Permanente Clinic*, 518 P.2d 636 (Or. 1974), interpreting OR. REV. STAT. § 30.020 (2007). The state court of appeals, however, has refused to allow wrongful death actions to be brought on behalf of *non*viable children who were stillborn. *LaDu v. Oregon Clinic, P.C.*, 998 P.2d 733 (Or. Ct. App. 2000).

the injuries were inflicted.[36] Both *Libbee* and *Mallison* held that a viable un-born child is a "person," as that term is used in the "right to a remedy" guar-antee of the Oregon Constitution (art. I, §10).[37] In health care law, an agent acting under a durable power of attorney for health care may not consent to an abortion on behalf of his or her principal.[38]

In property law, "persons conceived before the death of the decedent and born alive thereafter inherit as though they were alive at the time of the death of the decedent."[39] And, subject to certain exceptions, a child who is born after a parent executes a will, and who is not otherwise provided for in the will, may receive that share he or she would have received if the parent had died without a will (or a share equal to that provided to other children in the will).[40]

In light of the history of abortion regulation in Oregon prior to 1969, the Oregon Supreme Court's recognition in *State v. Elliott* that the abortion statutes were intended to protect unborn children and the rights extended to unborn children outside the area of abortion, it cannot plausibly be said that either art. I, §1, or art. I, §33, of the Oregon Constitution confers a right to abor-tion. More generally, a right to abortion cannot be found in the text or struc-ture of the Oregon Constitution.[41] There is no evidence that the framers of the Oregon Constitution of 1859 intended the Bill of Rights to limit the Legisla-ture's authority to prohibit abortion.[42] Such an intent would have been re-

---

36. *Mallison v. Pomeroy*, 291 P.2d at 228.

37. *Libbee*, 518 P.2d at 640; *Mallison*, 291 P.2d at 228. In *Libbee*, the court noted the extensive criticism to which *Roe v. Wade* has been subjected. 518 P.2d at 640 n. 14.

38. Or. Rev. Stat. §127.540(5).

39. *Id.* §112.075 (2007).

40. *Id.* §112.405.

41. This conclusion is supported, at least indirectly, by the Oregon Supreme Court's decision in *State v. Clowes*, 801 P.2d 789 (Or. 1990). In *Clowes*, which affirmed the convic-tions of abortion protestors for criminal trespass at an abortion clinic, the state supreme court stated that even if Oregon law prohibited abortions, "*Roe* and its progeny would be relevant to the extent that they would render such a law invalid." *Id.* at 795 n. 24. Significantly, the court did *not* say that such a prohibition would violate the *state* constitution.

42. *See* Charles Henry Carey, The Oregon Constitution and Proceedings and De-bates of the Constitutional Convention of 1857, 117 (first reading), 179 (second read-ing), 296–306, 309–18, 321 (debate on Bill of Rights in Committee of the Whole); 327–31 (amendments), 342–43 (third reading and final passage on floor of Convention) (Salem, Oregon 1926). It is the framers' understanding at the time the constitution was drafted in 1857 that is of particular relevance in interpreting what rights they intended to protect. *Smothers v. Gresham Transfer, Inc.*, 23 P.3d 333, 350–51 (Or. 2001). *See also Priest v. Pearce*, 840 P.2d 65, 67 (Or. 1992) (in interpreting a provision of the Oregon Constitution, the

markable in light of the contemporaneous and longstanding prohibition of abortion except to save the life of the pregnant woman.

Remedy by Due Course of Law

Article I, § 10, of the Oregon Constitution provides: "No court shall be secret, but justice shall be administered, openly and without purchase, completely and without delay, and every man shall have remedy by due course of law for injury done him in his person, property, or reputation."[43]

Abortion advocates might argue that a statute prohibiting abortion interferes with a woman's control over her own body, and that such interference constitutes an "injury" to her "person," as those terms are used in § 10, for which there must be a "remedy by due course of law." That "remedy," in turn, would be invalidation of the statute. This argument assumes that art. I, § 10, confers substantive rights. The case law is clear, however, that it does not.[44]

As is apparent from its text and structure, § 10 is concerned with *remedies* for injuries-it does not establish what *constitutes* an injury to anyone's "person, property, or reputation." Those remedies, however, are derived from the common law, not § 10. Moreover, the remedies themselves redress injuries recognized by the common law, not constitutional "injuries."

The mandate of art. I, § 10, that "every man shall have remedy by due course of law for injury done to him in his person, property, or reputation," "expresses a limitation on the exercise of legislative power" with respect to "wrongs or harms to rights that are recognized by the common law, that is, for which common-law causes of action existed."[45] "[I]f the common law [at the time the Oregon Constitution was drafted in 1857] provided a cause of action for an injury to one of the rights that the remedy clause protects [rights respecting person, property or reputation]," then the legislature may not abolish that cause

---

Oregon Supreme Court considers "[i]ts specific wording, the case law surrounding it, and the historical circumstances that led to its creation").

43. OR. CONST. art. I, § 10 (2007).

44. It should be noted that the Oregon Supreme Court has clarified that the remedy by due course of law guarantee of art. I, § 10, "is neither in text nor in historical function the equivalent of a due process clause," *Cole v. State by and through the Oregon Dep't of Revenue*, 655 P.2d 171, 173 (Or. 1982), and, in particular, "is not equivalent to the guarantee of due process of law of the Fourteenth Amendment." *Smothers*, 23 P.3d at 355. Rather, "the remedy clause guarantees remedy by due course of law for injuries to person, property, or reputation that already have occurred." *Id.*

45. *Smothers*, 23 P.3d at 355.

of action unless it provides a statutory remedy "for the same wrongs or harms...."[46] There was no "right" to abortion at common law, however. Abortion was a common law crime (at least after quickening) at the time the Oregon Constitution was drafted in 1857. Because there was no right to abortion at that time (either under the common law or under the statutes of the Oregon Territory), a woman who has been denied an abortion (by a statute prohibiting abortion) could not be said to have suffered an "injury" for which art. I, § 10, requires a "remedy. Section 10 is concerned with the availability of civil causes of action to redress private injuries to rights recognized at common law. It places no limitation on the State's power to define and punish crimes and has never been so interpreted.

Privileges and Immunities

Article I, § 20, of the Oregon Constitution provides: "No law shall be passed granting to any citizen or class of citizens, privileges, or immunities, which, upon the same terms shall not equally belong to all citizens."[47] To challenge a statute under art. I, § 20, a plaintiff must show, first, "that another group has been granted a 'privilege' or immunity' which [plaintiff's] group as not been granted," second, that the statute "discriminates against a 'true class' on the basis of characteristics which [the class has] apart from that statute," and, third, "that the distinction between the classes is either impermissibly based on persons' immutable characteristics, which reflect 'invidious' social or political premises, or has no rational foundation in light of the state's purpose."[48] As the Oregon Supreme Court has explained, "classifications based on immutable traits are suspect," while "distinctions ... based on personal [or social] characteristics that are not immutable" are reviewed to determine "whether the legislature had a rational basis for making the distinction."[49]

---

46. *Id.* at 356.

47. Or. Const. art. I, § 20 (2007).

48. *Withers v. State of Oregon*, 987 P.2d 1247, 1251 (Or. Ct. App. 1999) (citation and internal quotation marks omitted). A "true class," for purposes of art. I, § 20, is one that exists independently of the classification created by the challenged legislation. *Id.* Such a class "consists of persons who, regardless of laws that may treat them as a group, share some trait or characteristic that is widely regarded as forming the basis for meaningful social or ethnic categories such as race, legitimacy, gender, or geographical residence." *Jury Service Resource Center v. Carson*, 110 P.3d 594, 600 (Or. Ct. App. 2005), *rev'd on other grounds*, 134 P.3d 948 (Or. 2006).

49. *In re Marriage of Crocker*, 22 P.3d 759, 766 (Or. 2000). In *Crocker*, the court held that marital status is not an immutable characteristic. *Id. See also Seto v. Tri-County Metro. Trans-*

In any challenge to a statute prohibiting abortion that Oregon may enact, abortion advocates are likely to argue that the prohibition discriminates against women in violation of art. I, § 20, because only women are capable of becoming pregnant. Such an argument probably would not prevail.

The Oregon Supreme Court has recognized that "when classifications are made on the basis of gender, they are ... inherently suspect," and thus subject to a more rigorous standard of review.[50] "The suspicion may be overcome," however, "if the reason for the classification reflects specific biological differences between men and women."[51] A prohibition of abortion, of course, *does* reflect "specific biological differences between men and women" because only women are capable of becoming pregnant.[52] Unlike laws that use women's ability to become pregnant (or pregnancy itself) to discriminate against them in *other* areas (*e.g.*, employment opportunities), abortion prohibitions cannot fairly be said to involve a distinction between men and women that is a "mere pretext[] designed to erect an invidious discrimination against [women]."[53] Accordingly, they would not be subject to the strict scrutiny standard of review under art. I, § 20, of the Oregon Constitution.

Abortion advocates may also argue that any distinction in an abortion statute between those women for whom an abortion would be allowed (*e.g.*, to preserve their life or health) and those for whom an abortion would be prohibited grants a "privilege" to the former class that would not be available to the latter class, in violation of art. I, § 20. To the extent that such a distinction could be said to create differing classes of women, the distinction is clearly not one based on an "immutable trait[]," and, therefore, would be subject to rational basis review.[54] The legislature would have a rational basis for making a distinction between, for example, life and health threatening pregnancies on the one hand, and pregnancies that posed no such risks, allowing abortions in

---

portation District, 814 P.2d 1060 (Or. 1991) (same with respect to geographic classification).

50. *Hewitt v. State Accident Insurance Fund Corp.*, 653 P.2d 870, 977–78 (Or. 1982).

51. *Id.* at 978.

52. *Jane L. v. Bangerter*, 794 F. Supp. 1537, 1549 (D. Utah 1992) ("[a]bortion statutes are examples of cases in which the sexes are not biologically similarly situated").

53. *Geduldig v. Aiello*, 417 U.S. 484, 496 n. 20 (1974) ("[n]ormal pregnancy is an objectively, identifiable physical condition with unique characteristics").

54. *Jane L. v. Bangerter*, 794 F. Supp. at 1534 ("[p]rohibiting elective abortions except in certain circumstances determined by the legislature to embody the public policy of the State is a rational way of promoting [the State's] interest in potential human life while balancing the interest of the pregnant woman").

the former case, but not the latter. In sum, a prohibition of abortion would not violate the privileges and immunities provision of the Oregon Constitution.

Conclusion

Based on the foregoing analysis, an argument that the Oregon Constitution protects a right to abortion that is separate from, and independent of, the right to abortion recognized in *Roe v. Wade* would not likely succeed. That, in turn, suggests that if *Roe*, as modified by *Casey*, is ultimately overruled, the State of Oregon could enact and enforce a statute *prohibiting* abortion. Moreover, nothing in the Oregon Constitution precludes Oregon from *regulating* abortion within federal constitutional limits in the meantime.

CHAPTER 41

PENNSYLVANIA

Summary

The Pennsylvania Supreme Court has not yet decided whether the Pennsylvania Constitution protects a right to abortion separate from, and independent of, the right to abortion recognized under the United States Constitution.[1] A careful examination of the state constitution, in light of its history and interpretation, as well as other relevant legal sources, however, suggests that the state supreme court probably would not recognize a state constitutional right to abortion. Thus, if *Roe v. Wade*,[2] as modified by *Planned Parenthood of Southeastern Pennsylvania v. Casey*,[3] were overruled, Pennsylvania could prohibit abortion. Moreover, nothing in the state constitution, properly understood, precludes the Commonwealth from enacting and enforcing reasonable measures regulating abortion within current federal constitutional limits.

Analysis

The principal pre-*Roe* statutes prohibited "unlawful abortions."[4] The statues themselves did not define what an "unlawful" abortion was, nor was the word authoritatively interpreted by the Pennsylvania Supreme Court. Pursuant to *Roe*, the statutes were declared unconstitutional (on federal, not state,

---

1. The Pennsylvania Supreme Court has referred to the right to abortion solely as a matter of *federal*, not *state*, constitutional law. See *Nixon v. Commonwealth*, 839 A.2d 277, 287 (Pa. 2003) ("women's right to terminate pregnancy is a fundamental interest protected under the right of privacy") (citing *Roe v. Wade*); *Fischer v. Dep't of Public Welfare*, 502 A.2d 114, 116 (Pa. 1985) (noting that *Roe v. Wade* had effect of "sweeping aside previous prohibitions [of abortion]").

2. 410 U.S. 113 (1973).

3. 505 U.S. 833 (1992).

4. PA. STAT. ANN. tit. 18, §§ 4718, 4719 (West 1963).

grounds) by the Pennsylvania Supreme Court in a pair of decisions,[5] and were later repealed.[6]

Based upon arguments that have been raised in Pennsylvania and other States with similar constitutional provisions, possible sources for an asserted abortion right could include provisions of the state constitution guaranteeing equal protection (art. I, §§ 1, 26, and art. III, § 32), religious freedom (art. I, § 3), a remedy by due course of law (§ 11) and equality of rights (§ 28); recognizing inherent rights (§ 1) and inherent power in the people (§ 2); prohibiting anyone from being deprived of life, liberty or property, "unless by the judgment of his peers or the law of the land" (§ 9); reserving powers in the people (§ 25); and prohibiting discrimination in civil rights (§ 26).[7] The analysis that follows addresses each of these provisions.

Religious Freedom

Article I, § 3, of the Pennsylvania Constitution provides:

> All men have a natural and indefeasible right to worship Almighty God according to the dictates of their own consciences; no man can of right be compelled to attend, erect or support any place of worship, or to maintain any ministry against his consent; no human authority can, in any case whatever, control or interfere with the rights of conscience, and no preference shall ever be given by law to any religious establishment or modes of worship.[8]

In any challenge to a statute prohibiting abortion, abortion advocates may raise either or both of two arguments under art. I, § 3. First, they may argue that an abortion prohibition interferes with a woman's "rights of conscience" by forbidding her from obtaining an abortion that would be allowed by her religion. Second, they may argue in the alternative (or in addition) that an abortion prohibition constitutes a "preference" in favor of a "religious establishment" because it reflects sectarian beliefs regarding when human life begins and the sinfulness of abortion. Neither argument is likely to prevail.

---

5. *Commonwealth v. Page*, 303 A.2d 215 (Pa. 1973); *Commonwealth v. Jackson*, 312 A.2d 13 (Pa. 1973).

6. 1974 Pa. Laws 639, Acts No. 209, § 10.

7. Two other more unlikely sources of an abortion right under the Pennsylvania Constitution-art. I, § 7 (guaranteeing freedom of speech) and § 8 (prohibiting unreasonable searches and seizures)-are discussed generally in Chapter 3, *supra*.

8. Pa. Const. art. I, § 3 (2007)

Article I, §3, has generally been construed in a manner similar to that of the Free Exercise and Establishment Clauses of the First Amendment.[9] The similarity of construction suggests that a challenge to an abortion statute that would not succeed under the Religion Clauses of the First Amendment would not succeed under art. I, §3, either. For the reasons set forth in Chapter 2, *supra*, an abortion statute could not be successfully challenged on First Amendment grounds. Accordingly, a similar challenge under art. I, §3, would not likely be successful.[10]

Remedy by Due Course of Law

Article I, §11, of the Pennsylvania Constitution provides, in part, that "every man for an injury done him in his lands, goods, person or reputation shall have remedy by due course of law...."[11] Abortion advocates might argue that a statute prohibiting abortion interferes with a woman's control over her own body, and that such interference constitutes an "injury" to her "person," as those terms are used in §11, for which there must be a "remedy by due course of law." That "remedy," in turn, would be invalidation of the statute. This argument assumes that art. I, §11, confers substantive rights. The case law is clear, however, that it does not.

Article I, §11, "can be invoked only with respect to a legal injury."[12] "A legal injury is one for which the law recognizes a remedy or a cause of action."[13] Accordingly, nothing in art. I, §11, "can be construed as requiring that this Court create a legally recognized injury were none had previously been recognized."[14] If the Legislature determines that certain conduct (*e.g.*, abortion) shall be illegal, then, of course, there is there is no right to engage in such conduct and, therefore, no "legally recognized injury" for which §11 mandates a remedy.

---

9. See *Christian School Ass'n v. Commonwealth of Pennsylvania, Dep't of Labor and Industry*, 423 A.2d 1340, 1343–47 & n. 3 (Pa. Commw. Ct. 1980) (construing art. I, §3, and the Free Exercise Clause together); *Bishop Leonard Regional Catholic School*, 593 A.2d 28, 32–34 (Pa. Commw. Ct. 1991) (construing art. I, §3, and the Establishment Clause together).

10. That conclusion is reinforced by an old decision of the Pennsylvania Supreme Court. In *Commonwealth v. Herr*, 78 A. 68 (Pa. 1910), the state supreme court held that "the religious freedom and the rights of conscience guaranteed by the [state] [c]onstitution do not necessarily stand in the way of the enforcement of laws commanding or prohibiting the commission of acts even by those who conscientiously believe it to be their religious or moral duty to do or refrain from doing them." *Id.* at 72.

11. Pa. Const. art. I, §11 (2007).

12. *Singer v. Sheppard*, 346 A.2d 897, 903 (Pa. 1975) (plurality).

13. *Wapner v. Somers*, 630 A.2d 885, 887 (Pa. Super. Ct. 1993).

14. *Id.*

Because art. I, §11, is not a source of substantive rights, it could not provide a basis for invalidating an otherwise constitutional statute of the State.[15]

Law of the Land (Due Process of Law)

Article I, §9, of the Pennsylvania Constitution provides, in part, that no person "can be deprived of his life, liberty or property, unless by the judgment of his peers or the law of the land."[16] "The terms 'law of the land' and 'due process of law' are legal equivalents."[17]

In any challenge to a statute Pennsylvania may enact prohibiting abortion, abortion advocates would probably rely upon art. I, §9, arguing that the statute interferes with a woman's "liberty" interest in obtaining an abortion. Such an argument is not likely to succeed. The Pennsylvania Supreme Court has held that "the due process provision of the Pennsylvania Constitution [referring to art. I, §9] does not provide greater protections than its federal counterpart [the Due Process Clause of the Fourteenth Amendment]."[18] Because art. I, §9, does not provide any greater protection than the federal Due Process Clause, the Pennsylvania Supreme Court would not recognize a *state* due process liberty interest in abortion if the United States Supreme Court no longer recognized a *federal* due process liberty interest in abortion. Any state constitutional challenge to an abortion prohibition would more likely be based on the "inherent rights" language of art. I, §1, which is discussed in the following section.

Inherent Rights

Article I, §1, of the Pennsylvania Constitution provides: "All men are born equally free and independent, and have certain inherent and indefeasible rights, among which are those of enjoying and defending life and liberty, of acquiring, possessing and protecting property and reputation, and of pursuing their own happiness." [19] The Pennsylvania Supreme Court has recognized that art. I, §1, protects a right of privacy.[20]

---

15. It should not be surprising to note, therefore, that no criminal statute has ever been struck down on the authority of the "remedy" language of art. I, §11.

16. PA. CONST. art. I, §9 (2007).

17. *Eiffert v. Pennsylvania Central Brewing Co.*, 15 A.2d 723, 726 (Pa. Super. Ct. 1940).

18. *Commonwealth v. Louden*, 803 A.2d 1181, 1184 (Pa. 2002) (citing *Commonwealth v. Snyder*, 713 A.2d 596, 602 (Pa. 1998)).

19. PA. CONST. art. I, §1 (2007).

20. *McKusker v. Workmen's Compensation Appeal Board*, 639 A.2d 776, 778 (Pa. 1994) (citing *Stenger v. Lehigh Valley Hospital Center*, 609 A.2d 796, 800 (Pa. 1992) (informational

The Pennsylvania reviewing courts have not developed a methodology for determining whether given conduct is protected by the state right of privacy. Nevertheless, their decisions strongly suggest that, regardless of its source in the Declaration of Rights, the state right of privacy embraces only that conduct which traditionally has enjoyed the protection of the law.[21] There is no tradition of protecting a right to abortion in Pennsylvania law, however.

In at least two cases decided before the Commonwealth enacted its first abortion statutes in 1860, the Pennsylvania Supreme Court recognized that abortion was a common law crime without regard to whether the pregnant woman had experienced "quickening," which is that stage of pregnancy (usually sixteen to eighteen weeks gestation) when the woman first detects fetal movement.[22] The 1860 statutes prohibited and punished as a felony an abortion performed at any stage of pregnancy (providing a more severe sentence when the death of the pregnant woman or a "quick" child resulted).[23] Amended from time to time, those statutes remained on the books until after *Roe v. Wade* was decided.[24]

Prior to *Roe*, the Pennsylvania Superior Court (an intermediate court of review for criminal cases) regularly affirmed convictions for abortions without

---

privacy), and *In re B.*, 394 A.2d 419, 425 (Pa. 1978) (same)). Whether the right of privacy derives from other provisions of the Declaration of Rights as well as § 1 is unclear. *Compare Commonwealth v. Nixon*, 761 A.2d 1151, 1156 (Pa. 2000) ("both constitutions do offer protections of personal privacy, which results from the 'penumbra' of articulated rights"), and *In re B.*, 394 A.2d at 425 (plurality) (citing multiple provisions of the Declaration of Rights), *with In re June 1979 Allegheny County Investigating Grand Jury*, 415 A.2d 73, 77–78 (Pa. 1980) (rooting the state right of privacy in art. I, § 1).

21. *Compare Coleman v. Workers' Compensation Appeal Board*, 842 A.2d 349, 354 (Pa. 2004) ("people have a privacy interest in preserving their bodily integrity, which may be afforded constitutional protections") (upholding mandated physical examination of Workers' Compensation claimant), and *In re Duran*, 769 A.2d 497, 503–05 (Pa. Super. Ct. 2001) (recognizing that the right to refuse unwanted medical treatment has been given constitutional status, but deciding case on common law grounds), *with Commonwealth v. Arnold*, 514 A.2d 890, 893 (Pa. Super. Ct. 1986) (no fundamental right to engage in incest), and *Commonwealth v. Dodge*, 429 A.2d 1143, 1147–49 (Pa. Super. Ct. 1981) (no right to engage in prostitution).

22. *Mills v. Commonwealth*, 13 Pa. 630, 632 (1850) ("[t]he moment the womb is instinct with embryo life, and gestation has begun, the crime may be perpetrated"); *Commonwealth v. Demain*, 6 Penn. Law Jour. 29, 31 (Brightly's N.P. Reports 441, 444 *) (1846) (noting that it is not necessary, in an indictment for abortion, "to aver quickness on the part of the mother; it is sufficient to set forth that she was big and pregnant").

23. Pa. Laws No. 374, §§ 87, 88 (1860).

24. *Id., carried forward as* PA. STAT. ANN. tit. 18, §§ 2071, 2072 (1930), *recodified at* PA. STAT. ANN. tit. 18, §§ 4718, 4719 (West 1945), *repealed by* 1974 Pa. Laws 639, Acts No. 209, § 10.

any hint that the prosecutions or convictions violated the Pennsylvania Constitution.[25] In an early case, the Pennsylvania Supreme Court recognized, on the basis of its wording, that the abortion statute had been enacted with an intent to protect unborn human life.[26] Subsequent to *Roe*, the General Assembly enacted the Abortion Control Act which expresses the Legislature's intention "to protect ... the life and health of the woman subject to abortion and to protect the life and health of the child subject to abortion."[27] The Act also mandates a rule of construction:

> In every relevant civil or criminal proceeding in which it is possible to do so without violating the Federal Constitution, the common and statutory law of Pennsylvania shall be construed so as to extent to the unborn the equal protection of the laws and to further the public policy of this commonwealth encouraging childbirth over abortion.[28]

Consistent with the Commonwealth's policy of "encouraging childbirth over abortion," Pennsylvania has enacted a comprehensive scheme of abortion regulation.[29]

Pennsylvania has recognized the rights of unborn children in a variety of contexts outside of abortion, including criminal law, tort law, health care law and property law. Under the "Crimes Against the Unborn Child Act," the killing

---

25. *Commonwealth v. Rosenberry*, 3 Pa. Super 408 (1897); *Commonwealth v. Mitchell*, 6 Pa. Super 369 (1898); *Commonwealth v. Keene*, 7 Pa. Super 293 (1898); *Commonwealth v. Kline*, 66 Pa. Super. 285 (1917); *Commonwealth v. Longwell*, 79 Pa. Super 68 (1922); *Commonwealth v. Heffelfinger*, 82 Pa. Super. 351 (1923); *Commonwealth v. Kelsea*, 157 A. 42 (Pa. Super. Ct. 1931); *Commonwealth v. Trombetta*, 200 A. 107 (Pa. Super. 1938); *Commonwealth v. Myers*, 22 A.2d 81 (Pa. Super Ct. 1941); *Commonwealth v. Kazmierowski*, 24 A.2d 653 (Pa. Super. Ct. 1942); *Commonwealth v. Spanos*, 34 A.2d 902 (Pa. Super Ct. 1944); *Commonwealth v. Thomas*, 49 A.2d 412 (Pa. Super. Ct. 1946); *Commonwealth v. Fisher*, 203 A.2d 364 (Pa. Super. Ct. 1964).

26. *Railing v. Commonwealth*, 1 A. 314, 315 (Pa. 1885).

27. PA. CONST. STAT. ANN. tit. 18, §3202(a) (West 2000).

28. *Id.* tit. 18, §3202(d).

29. *Id.* tit. 18, §3205 (West 2000) (mandating informed consent and a twenty-four hour waiting period); tit. 18, §3206 (West Sup. 2008) (requiring parental consent); tit. 18, §§3202(d), 3213(d), -(f) (West 2000) (recognizing individual and institutional rights of conscience); tit. 18, §3215 (West 2000), tit. 62, §453 (West 1996) (restricting public funding of abortion for indigent women, and the use of public facilities for the performance of abortions); tit. 18, §3207 (West 2000) (mandating clinic regulations); tit. 18, §3211 (prohibiting abortions after the twenty-fourth week of pregnancy).

or injury of an unborn child, other than in an abortion, may be prosecuted as a homicide or as aggravated assault.[30]

In tort law, a statutory cause of action for wrongful death may be brought on behalf of an unborn child who was viable (capable of sustained survival outside the mother's womb, with or without medical assistance) at the time of its death.[31] A common law cause of action for (nonlethal) prenatal injuries may be brought without regard to the stage of pregnancy when the injuries were inflicted.[32] And Pennsylvania has banned wrongful life and wrongful birth causes of actions.[33] In a decision rejecting a federal constitutional challenge to the statute, the Pennsylvania Superior Court stated that the statute "reflect[s] the state's view that a handicapped child should not be deemed better off dead and of less value than a 'normal' child."[34]

In health care law, except in very limited circumstances, life-sustaining treatment, nutrition and hydration may not be withheld or withdrawn from a pregnant patient under a living will or a health care directive.[35] In property law, persons conceived before the death of a decedent who died intestate (without a will) but born thereafter, "shall take as if they had been born in his lifetime."[36]

---

30. *Id.* tit. 26, §2601 *et seq.* (West 1998). The constitutionality of the Act was upheld in *Commonwealth v. Bullock,* 913 A.2d 207 (Pa. 2006).

31. *Amadio v. Levin,* 501 A.2d 1085 (Pa. 1985), interpreting Pa. Cons. Stat. Ann. tit. 42, §8301 (West 2007). In the absence of legislative reform, however, the court has declined to extend the wrongful death act to *non*viable children who are stillborn. *See Coveleski v. Bubnis,* 634 A.2d 608 (Pa. 1993). If, however, the child is born alive, then dies as the result of prenatal injuries, an action for wrongful death will lie without regard to the stage of pregnancy when the fatal injuries were inflicted. *Hudak v. Georgy,* 634 A.2d 600 (Pa. 1993).

32. *Sinkler v. Kneale,* 164 A.2d 93 (Pa. 1960).

33. Pa. Cons. Stat Ann. tit. 42, §8305(a) (West 2007). A "wrongful life" cause of action is a claim brought on behalf of a child who is born with a physical or mental disability or disease that could have been discovered before the child's birth by genetic testing, amniocentesis or other medical screening. The gravamen of the action is that, as a result of a physician's failure to inform the child's parents of the child's disability or disease (or at least of the availability of tests to determine the presence of the disability or disease), they were deprived of the opportunity to abort the child, thus resulting in the birth of a child suffering permanent physical or mental impairment. A "wrongful birth" cause of action, on the other hand, is a claim, based upon the same facts, brought by the parents of the impaired child on their own behalf.

34. *Dansby v. Thomas Jefferson University Hospital,* 623 A.2d 816, 820 (Pa. Super. Ct. 1993). The court added that "[t]he protection of fetal life has been recognized to be an important state interest." *Id.* at 821. *See also Edmunds v. Western Pennsylvania Hospital Radiology Associates,* 607 A.2d 1083 (Pa. Commw. Ct. 1992) (upholding statute).

35. Pa. Cons. Stat. Ann. tit. 20, §5429 (West Supp. 2008).

36. *Id.* tit. 20, §2104(4) (West 2005).

A similar rule applies to the beneficiaries under the will of a person who died testate (with a will).[37]

In light of Pennsylvania's longstanding tradition of prohibiting abortion, both at common law and under statute, which antedates the 1874 Pennsylvania Constitution, the absence of any indication that the framers intended to recognize a right to abortion,[38] and the State's continuing interest in protecting the rights of unborn children, it cannot plausibly be said that the state right of privacy secures a right to obtain an abortion that is separate from, and independent of, the right to an abortion recognized in *Roe v. Wade*.

Equal Protection

Three provisions of the Pennsylvania Constitution guarantee (or have been construed to guarantee) equal protection of the laws. Article I, §1, of the Pennsylvania Constitution provides, in part, "All men are born equally free and independent...."[39] Article I, §26, prohibits the Commonwealth (and any of its political subdivisions) from denying to any person "the enjoyment of any civil right," or discriminating against any person "in the exercise of any civil right."[40] And art. III, §32, provides, in part: "The General Assembly shall pass no local or special law in any case which has been or can be provided for by general law.... Nor shall the General Assembly indirectly enact any special or local law by the partial repeal of a general law...."[41] State and federal equal protection claims are analyzed under the same standards.[42]

---

37. *Id.* tit. 20, §2514(4).

38. *See* Debates of the Convention to Amend the Constitution of Pennsylvania (Harrisburg, Pennsylvania 1873), Vol. III, 195–96 (majority report of the Committee on Declaration of Rights), 219–23 (minority report); Vol. IV, 645–93, 711–40, 747–73 (debate on Declaration Rights in Committee of the Whole); Vol. V, 561–89, 591–634 (second reading); Vol VII, 249–67, 282–87, 295–300 (third reading). It should be noted that the Pennsylvania Constitutional Convention of 1967–68 was prohibited from revising the Declaration of Rights of the 1874 Constitution. *See Commonwealth v. Schaeffer*, 536 A.2d 354, 358 n. 14 (Pa. Super. Ct. 1987) (Kelly, J., concurring and dissenting) (setting forth the relevant constitutional history).

39. Pa. Const. art. I, §1 (2007).

40. *Id.* art. I, §26.

41. *Id.* art. III, §32.

42. *Commonwealth v. Albert*, 758 A.2d 1149, 1151 (Pa. 2000) (citing art. I, §26); *Love v. Borough of Stroudsburg*, 597 A.2d 1137, 1139 (Pa. 1991) (citing art. I, §§1, 26); *Fischer*, 502 A.2d at 120–23 (citing art. I, §1, and art. III, §32). Art. I, §26, is discussed separately in the following section of this analysis, *infra*.

For purpose of both state and federal equal protection analysis, there are three standards of judicial review. Under the first standard, which is known as rational basis scrutiny, legislation "is presumed to be valid and will be sustained if the classification drawn by the statute is rationally related to a legitimate state interest."[43] Under the second standard, intermediate (or heightened) scrutiny, which applies to sex-based classifications, the classification must be "substantially related to a sufficiently important governmental interest."[44] Under the third standard, strict scrutiny, which applies to statutes that classify "by race, alienage, or national origin" or "impinge" on the exercise of fundamental "personal rights protected by the Constitution," the classification "will be sustained only if [it is] suitably tailored to serve a compelling state interest."[45]

Strict scrutiny review would not apply to an abortion prohibition because, for the reasons set forth in the preceding two sections of this analysis, a prohibition of abortion would not "impinge" upon the exercise of a fundamental personal right (either due process or privacy). Nor would the prohibition of abortion classify persons on the basis of a "suspect" personal characteristic (race, alienage or national origin). Abortion advocates may argue in the alternative, however, that a statute prohibiting abortion discriminates against women and should be subject to intermediate scrutiny because only women are capable of becoming pregnant. An abortion prohibition would appear to satisfy this level of scrutiny because the prohibition would be "substantially related" to the "important governmental interest" in protecting unborn children. Nevertheless, the standard applicable to sex-based discrimination (intermediate scrutiny) would not apply to an abortion prohibition. Abortion laws do not discriminate on the basis of sex.

First, the United States Supreme Court has reviewed restrictions on abortion funding under a rational basis standard of review, *not* under the intermediate (heightened) scrutiny required of gender-based classifications.[46] Indeed, the Court has held that "the disfavoring of abortion ... is not *ipso facto* sex discrimination," and, citing its decisions in *Harris* and other cases addressing abortion funding, stated that "the constitutional test applicable to government abortion-funding restrictions is not the heightened-scrutiny standard that our cases demand for sex discrimination, ... but the ordinary rationality standard."[47]

---

43. *City of Cleburne, Texas v. Cleburne Living Center*, 473 U.S. 432, 440 (1985).

44. *Id.* at 441. A similar standard applies to classifications based on illegitimacy. *See Mills v. Habluetzel*, 456 U.S. 91, 99 (1982) (classification must be "substantially related to a legitimate state interest").

45. *City of Cleburne, Texas v. Cleburne Living Center*, 473 U.S. 432, 440 (1985).

46. *Harris v. McRae*, 448 U.S. 297, 321–26 (1980).

47. *Bray v. Alexandria Women's Health Clinic*, 506 U.S. 263, 273 (1993).

Second, even assuming that an abortion prohibition differentiates between men and women on the basis of sex, and would otherwise be subject to a higher standard of review, the United States Supreme Court has held that biological differences between men and women may justify different treatment based on those differences. In upholding a statutory rape statute that applied only to males, the Supreme Court noted, "this Court has consistently upheld statutes where the gender classification is not invidious, but rather realistically reflects the fact that the sexes are not similarly situated in certain circumstances."[48] "Abortion statutes are examples of cases in which the sexes are not biologically similarly situated" because only women are capable of becoming pregnant and having abortions.[49]

A statute prohibiting abortion quite obviously can affect only women because only women are capable of becoming pregnant.[50] Unlike laws that use women's ability to become pregnant (or pregnancy itself) to discriminate against them in *other* areas (*e.g.*, employment opportunities), abortion prohibitions cannot fairly be said to involve a distinction between men and women that is a "mere pretext[] designed to erect an invidious discrimination against [women]."[51]

A prohibition of abortion would not interfere with the exercise of a fundamental state constitutional right, nor would it classify upon the basis of a suspect or quasi-suspect characteristic. Accordingly, it would be subject to rational basis review. Under that standard of review, the statute need only be "rationally related to a legitimate state interest."[52] A law prohibiting abortion would be "rationally related" to the "legitimate state interest" in protecting the lives of unborn children.

In rejecting an equal protection challenge to a statute restricting public funding of abortion, the Pennsylvania Supreme Court held that the classification drawn by the statute-between those abortions which are necessary to preserve the life of the pregnant woman and all other abortions-was "specifically related to the ends sought [the preservation of life], in that it accomplishes the preservation of the maximum amount of lives: i.e., those unaborted new babies, and those mothers who will survive though their fetus be aborted."[53] This

---

48. *Michael M. v. Superior Court*, 450 U.S. 464, 469 (1981).

49. *Jane L. v. Bangerter*, 794 F. Supp. 1537, 1549 (D. Utah 1992).

50. *Geduldig v. Aiello*, 417 U.S. 484, 496 n. 20 (1974) ("[n]ormal pregnancy is an objectively, identifiable physical condition with unique characteristics").

51. *Id.*

52. *Cleburne*, 473 U.S. at 440.

53. *Fischer*, 502 A.2d at 122–23.

analysis would have obvious implications in any challenge to a "life-of-the-mother" abortion statute the Commonwealth may enact.[54]

Equality of Rights

Article I, § 28, of the Pennsylvania Constitution provides: "Equality of rights under the law shall not be denied or abridged in the Commonwealth of Pennsylvania because of the sex of the individual."[55] In any challenge to a statute prohibiting abortion Pennsylvania may enact, abortion advocates would probably rely upon art. I, § 28, arguing that the statute denies women "equality of rights" because it affects only women. Such an argument would not likely succeed.

In *Henderson v. Henderson*,[56] the Pennsylvania Supreme Court held that "[t]he thrust of the Equal Rights Amendment [art. I, § 28] is to ensure equality of rights under the law and to eliminate sex as a basis for distinction."[57] As a consequence, "[t]he sex of citizens of this Commonwealth is no longer a permissible factor in the determination of their legal rights and responsibilities. The law will not impose different benefits or different burdens upon the members of a society based on the fact that they may be man or woman."[58] Notwithstanding this "absolutist" standard, the state supreme court recognizes that biological differences between the sexes may justify a disparity in treatment.

In *Fischer v. Dep't of Public Welfare*, the Pennsylvania Supreme Court rejected an equal rights challenge to a statute restricting public funding of abortions for indigent women. Plaintiffs argued that "because only a woman can have an abortion then the statute necessarily utilizes 'sex as a basis for distinction.'"[59] The state supreme court called this argument "simplistic," explaining

---

54. Significantly, in *Fischer*, the court held that the classification satisfied the "intermediate scrutiny test," and might even satisfy the strict scrutiny test, if that test had applied. *Id.* at 122 & n. 12 (recognizing that the State's interest "in promoting live births" might be compelling). *See also, id.*, at 122 ("to say that the Commonwealth's interest in attempting to preserve a potential life is not important, is to fly in the face of our own existence").

55. Pa. Const. art. I, § 28 (2007).

56. 327 A.2d 60 (Pa. 1974).

57. *Id.* at 62.

58. *Id.* In *Henderson*, the state supreme court declared unconstitutional a former statute that allowed the payment of temporary alimony, attorney fees and expenses to the wife in a divorce action, but not to the husband. *See also Commonwealth v. Butler*, 328 A.2d 851, 855 (Pa. 1974) ("sex may no longer be accepted as an exclusive classifying tool") (striking down discriminatory parole eligibility rules).

59. 502 A.2d at 125 (quoting *Henderson*, 327 A.2d at 62).

that "the basis for the distinction here is not sex, but abortion, and the statute does not accord varying benefits to men and women because of their sex, but accords varying benefits to one class of women, as distinct from another, based on a voluntary choice made by the women."[60]

> The mere fact that only women are affected by this statute does not necessarily mean that women are being discriminated against on the basis of sex. In this world there are certain immutable facts of life which no amount of legislation may change. As a consequence there are certain laws which necessarily will only affect one sex. Although we have not previously addressed this situation, other ERA jurisdictions have; and the prevailing view amongst our sister state jurisdictions is that the E.R.A. "does not prohibit differential treatment among the sexes when, as here, that treatment is reasonably and genuinely based on physical characteristics unique to one sex."[61]

"[T]he decision whether or not to carry a fetus to term is so unique as to have no concomitance in the male of the species."[62] The statute restricting public funding of abortion, "which is solely direct to that unique facet[,] is in no way analogous to those situations where the distinctions were 'based exclusively on the circumstances of sex, social stereotypes connected with gender, [or] culturally induced dissimilarities.' "[63] The court concluded that, in the context of the challenge to the abortion funding statute, "the Pennsylvania Equal Rights Amendment affords appellant no basis for relief."[64]

In light of the Pennsylvania Supreme Court's decision in *Fischer*, it is apparent that a challenge to an abortion prohibition based on the state Equal Rights Amendment (art. I, §28) would not succeed.

Prohibiting Discrimination in Civil Rights

Article I, §26, of the Pennsylvania Constitution provides: "Neither the Commonwealth nor any political subdivision thereof shall deny to any person the enjoyment of any civil right, nor discriminate against any person in the exercise of any civil right."[65] In a challenge to a statute prohibiting abortion, abor-

---

60. *Id.* at 125.

61. *Id.* (quoting *People v. Salinas*, 551 P.2d 703, 703 (Colo. 1976)).

62. *Id.* at 126.

63. *Id.* (quoting *Salinas*, 551 P.2d at 706).

64. *Id.*

65. Pa. Const. art. I, §26 (2007).

tion advocates might argue that the statute violates the "civil right[s]" protected by art. I, §26. Such an argument would not likely succeed.

Article I, §26, "does not in itself define a new substantive civil right."[66] It merely "make[s] more explicit the citizenry's constitutional safeguards not to be harassed or punished for the exercise of their constitutional rights."[67] Section 26, thus, has no relevance except to an equal protection claim "that focuses on the assertion that a person has been penalized for the exercise of a constitutional freedom."[68] Such freedoms, however, are derived from *other* sources of law (the constitution and statutes of the Commonwealth), not from §26. Accordingly, art. I, §26 would not provide a basis for challenging an abortion prohibition.

Inherent Power in the People

Article I, §2, of the Pennsylvania Constitution provides:

> All power is inherent in the people, and all free governments are founded on their authority and instituted for their peace, safety and happiness. For the advancement of these ends they have at all times an inalienable and indefeasible right to alter, reform, or abolish their government in such manner as they may think proper.[69]

In any challenge to a statute prohibiting abortion Pennsylvania may enact, abortion advocates might argue that the statute interferes with the "inherent" power of the people because it does not promote their "peace, safety and happiness." Given the purpose of §2, this argument would not likely prevail.

Section 2 has seldom been cited by the Pennsylvania reviewing courts, and never in support of striking down a state statute. The first sentence of §2 is simply a statement of a republican theory of government, to wit, that all political power is ultimately derived from the people and is to be exercised for their "peace, safety and happiness." The second sentence of §2, which recognizes the right of the people to "alter, reform, or abolish their form of government in such manner as they may think proper," secures to the people themselves, acting through the amendment process, the right to decide whether, how and to what extent the organic instrument of government should be

---

66. *McIlvaine v. Pennsylvania State Police*, 296 A.2d 630, 633 (Pa. Commw. Ct. 1972), *op. adopted*, 309 A.2d 801, 803 (Pa. 1973).

67. *Fischer*, 502 A.2d at 121.

68. *Probst v. Commonwealth of Pennsylvania, Dep't of Transportation, Bureau of Driver Licensing*, 840 A.2d 1135, 1143 n. 14 (Pa. 2004) (citing *Fischer*).

69. Pa. Const. art. I, §2 (2007).

changed.[70] Section 2, thus, is not a source of substantive rights (other than the right to change the state constitution). Whether a given law promotes the "peace, safety and happiness" of the people, as those terms are used in art. I, § 2, presents a political question for the legislature (and, ultimately, the people) to decide, not a constitutional question for the judiciary.

Reserving Powers in the People

Article I, § 25, of the Pennsylvania Constitution provides: "To guard against transgressions of the high powers which we have delegated, we declare that everything in this article is excepted out of the general powers of government and shall forever remain inviolate."[71] Abortion advocates might argue that a statute prohibiting abortion "transgress[es]" against the powers delegated to the legislature by the constitution. Such an argument is not likely to succeed.

Article I, § 25, articulates "[t]he concept of the sanctity of those rights set forth under Article I," and deems them to be "inviolable."[72] Section 25 is not an independent source of substantive rights, but simply secures rights guaranteed by other provisions of the Declaration of Rights from being violated by legislative enactment, an executive regulation or a judicial decision.[73] As a federal district court in Pennsylvania stated, § 25 "lacks any practical importance, 'except to add emphasis to the prohibitions laid upon legislative power.'"[74] Accordingly, it could not provide a basis for asserting a right to abortion under the state constitution.

Conclusion

Based on the foregoing analysis, an argument that the Pennsylvania Constitution protects a right to abortion that is separate from, and independent of,

---

70. *See Stander v. Kelley*, 90 Dauph. 205, 210 (Dauphin County Court 1968), *aff'd*, 250 A.2d 474 (Pa. 1969) (recognizing that, under § 2, the people can give their consent to an alteration of the existing frame of government by the mode provided in the existing constitution, by passing a law to call a convention or by resolution).

71. PA. CONST. art. I, § 25 (2007).

72. *Gondelman v. Commonwealth*, 554 A.2d 896, 904 (Pa. 1989) (citing *Spayd v. Ringing Rock Lodge No. 665, Brotherhood of Railroad Trainmen of Pottstown*, 113 A. 70, 72 (Pa. 1921)).

73. *Bergdoll v. Commonwealth*, 858 A.2d 185, 201 (Pa. Commw. Ct. 2004), *aff'd per curiam*, 874 A.2d. 1148 (Pa. 2005); *Commonwealth v. Hashem*, 584 A.2d 1378, 1382 (Pa. 1991).

74. *Nicolette v. Caruso*, 315 F. Supp.2d 710, 727 (W.D. Pa. 2003) (quoting Thomas R. White, COMMENTARIES ON THE CONSTITUTION OF PENNSYLVANIA 171 (1907)).

the right to abortion recognized in *Roe v. Wade* would not likely succeed. That, in turn, suggests that if *Roe*, as modified by *Casey*, is ultimately overruled, the Commonwealth of Pennsylvania could enact and enforce a statute *prohibiting* abortion. Moreover, nothing in the Pennsylvania Constitution precludes Pennsylvania from *regulating* abortion within federal constitutional limits in the meantime.

CHAPTER 42

RHODE ISLAND

Summary

As the result of express language in the Rhode Island Constitution, a right to abortion may not be derived from the due process and equal protection guarantee of the Declaration of Rights. The Rhode Island Supreme Court has not yet decided whether any other provision of the Rhode Island Constitution protects a right to abortion separate from, and independent of, the right to abortion recognized under the United States Constitution. A careful examination of the state constitution, in light of its history and interpretation, however, suggests that the state supreme court probably would not recognize a state right to abortion. Thus, if *Roe v. Wade*,[1] as modified by *Planned Parenthood of Southeastern Pennsylvania v. Casey*,[2] were overruled, Rhode Island could enforce its post-*Roe* statute prohibiting abortion (or enact a new statute prohibiting abortion). Moreover, nothing in the state constitution, properly understood, precludes the State from enacting and enforcing reasonable measures regulating abortion within current federal constitutional limits.

Analysis

The principal pre-*Roe* abortion statute prohibited the performance of an abortion upon a woman unless the procedure was "necessary to preserve her life."[3] Pursuant to *Roe v. Wade*,[4] this statute was declared unconstitutional (on federal, not state, grounds) in a pair of unreported decisions by a three-judge

---

1. 410 U.S. 113 (1973).
2. 505 U.S. 833 (1992).
3. R.I. GEN. LAWS § 11-3-1 (1956).
4. 410 U.S. 113 (1973).

federal district court,[5] and was repealed in 1973.[6] In response, Rhode Island reenacted the statute, adding a "conclusive presumption" that "human life commences at the instant of conception," that said human life "is a person within the language and meaning of the fourteenth amendment of the Constitution of the United States."[7] This statute was also declared unconstitutional (again, on federal, not state, grounds) by the federal district court,[8] but its enforcement was not enjoined. Although the statute is not enforceable under current federal constitutional doctrine, it has not been repealed,[9] and would be enforceable if *Roe*, as modified by *Casey*, were overruled. Nothing in the Rhode Island Constitution would preclude enforcement of §11-3-1 or a comparable abortion prohibition.

Due Process and Equal Protection

Article I, §2, of the Rhode Island Declaration of Rights provides:

> All free governments are instituted for the protection, safety, and happiness of the people. All laws, therefore, should be made for the good of the whole; and the burdens of the state ought to be fairly distributed among its citizens. No person shall be deprived of life, liberty or property without due process of law, nor shall any person be denied equal protection of the laws. No otherwise qualified person shall, solely by reason of race, gender or handicap be subject to discrimination by the state, its agents or any person or entity doing business with the state. *Nothing in this section shall be construed to grant or secure any right relating to abortion or the funding thereof.*[10]

Given the last sentence, it is apparent that no right to abortion (or abortion funding) could be based on any of the constitutional guarantees secured by §2. Thus, abortion advocates could not rely on the due process, equal protection, anti-discrimination or any other language of §2 as a source of abor-

---

5. *Women of Rhode Island v. Israel*, No. 4605 (D. R.I. Feb. 7, 1973); *Rhode Island Abortion Counseling Service v. Israel*, No. 4586 (D. R.I. Feb. 7, 1973).

6. 1973 R.I. Pub. Laws 67, 68, ch. 15, §1.

7. *Id.* 68–70, ch. 15, §2.

8. *Doe v. Israel*, 358 F. Supp. 1193 (D. R.I. 1973), *aff'd*, 482 F.2d 156 (1st Cir. 1973) (dissolving stay and denying stay).

9. R.I. GEN. LAWS §11-3-1 (2002).

10. R.I. CONST. art. I, §2 (2004) (emphasis added).

tion rights.[11] But what about other provisions of the Declaration of Rights? Based upon arguments that have been raised elsewhere, other possible sources for an asserted abortion right would include provisions guaranteeing freedom of religion (art. I, §3) and the right to a remedy (§5); and retaining rights (§24).[12] The analysis that follows shall consider each of these provisions.

Freedom of Religion

Art. I, §3, of the Rhode Island Constitution provides, in part:

> … we … declare that no person shall be compelled to frequent or to support any religious worship, place or ministry, whatever, except in fulfillment of such person's voluntary contract; nor enforced, restrained, molested, or burdened in body or goods; nor disqualified from holding any office; nor otherwise suffer on account of such person's religious belief; and that every person shall be free to worship God according to the dictates of each person's conscience, and to profess and by argument to maintain such person's opinion in matters of religion; and that the same shall in no wise diminish, enlarge, or affect the civil capacity of any person.[13]

In any challenge to a statute prohibiting abortion, abortion advocates may argue that the statute interferes with a woman's right to "worship God according to the dictates of [her] conscience," and "to profess and … maintain [her] opinion in matters of religion" by forbidding her from obtaining an abortion that would be allowed by her religion. As a consequence of this interference, it might be argued, the statute would cause the woman to "suffer on account of [her] religious belief" in violation of art. I, §3.[14] This argument would not likely prevail.

----

11. Referring to art. I, §2, two commentators have expressed the view that "the final sentence of the 1986 revision specifically disavows that any such right to abortion is conferred under state law." Patrick T. Conley and Robert G. Flanders, Jr., THE RHODE ISLAND CONSTITUTION[:] A REFERENCE GUIDE 54 (Westport, Conn. 2007).

12. Two other more unlikely sources of an abortion right under the Rhode Island Constitution-art. I, §21 (guaranteeing freedom of speech) and §6 (prohibiting unreasonable searches and seizures)-are discussed generally in Chapter 3, *supra*.

13. R.I. CONST. art. I, §3 (2001).

14. An argument based on the first clause of art. I, §3, which forbids anyone from being "compelled to frequent or to support any religious worship, place or ministry," would not appear to be available in a challenge to an abortion prohibition. In context, the quoted language is clearly aimed at compelled attendance at or financial support of churches or other

The Rhode Island Supreme Court has held that art. I, § 3, of the Rhode Island Constitution "is no more restrictive as to religious freedoms than the language of the Federal Constitution."[15] Given this equivalency of interpretation, a statute prohibiting or regulating abortion would not violate art. I, § 3, of the Rhode Island Constitution unless it also violated the Free Exercise Clause of the First Amendment. For the reasons set forth in Chapter 2, an abortion statute could not be successfully challenged under the Free Exercise Clause. Accordingly, a similar challenge under I, § 3, would not likely be successful.

Right to a Remedy

Article I, § 5, of the Rhode Island Constitution provides:

> Every person within this state ought to find a certain remedy, by having recourse to the laws, for all injuries or wrongs which may be received in one's person, property, or character. Every person ought to obtain right and justice freely; and without purchase, completely and without denial; promptly and without delay; conformably to the laws.[16]

Abortion advocates might argue that a statute prohibiting abortion interferes with a woman's control over her own body, and that such interference constitutes an "injury" to her "person," as those terms are used in the first sentence of § 5, for which there must be a "certain remedy." That "remedy," in turn, would be invalidation of the statute. This argument assumes that art. I, § 5, confers substantive rights. The case law is clear, however, that it does not.

In *Henry v. Cherry & Walsh*,[17] the Rhode Island Supreme Court held that, in the absence of implementing legislation, the language of art. I, § 5, did *not* require the court to recognize a common law cause of action for violation of a right to privacy,[18] a holding that was reaffirmed seventy years later,[19] and

---

religious institutions. A prohibition of abortion, however, would not "compel" anyone "to frequent or to support" any church or religion.

15. *In re Palmer*, 386 A.2d 1112, 1114 n.1 (R.I. 1978) (citing *Bowerman v. O'Connor*, 247 A.2d 82 (R.I. 1968)). *See also In re Philip S.*, 881 A.2d 931, 935 n. 9 (R.I. 2005) (noting "[s]imilar protection" under art. I, § 3).

16. R.I. Const. art. I, § 5 (2004).

17. 73 A. 97 (R.I. 1909).

18. *Id.* at 106–07.

19. *See Kalian v. People Acting Through Community Effort, Inc.*, 408 A.2d 608, 609 (R.I. 1979). In *Kalian*, the Rhode Island Supreme Court held that "the creation of new rights of action in the field of individual privacy is a question for the … Legislature." *Id.*

cited with approval only two years ago.[20] Any lingering doubt that art. I, §5, is not a source of substantive rights should be dispelled by the Rhode Island Supreme Court's decision in *Smiler v. Napolitano*.[21] In *Smiler*, the state supreme court said that "the purely aspirational language of the provision [referring to art. I, §5], indicated by the repeated use of 'ought,' leads substantial support to the conclusion that this constitutional provision is announcing a laudable principle and not a workable rule of law."[22] Section 5 places no limitation on the State's authority to define and punish crimes and has never been so interpreted.

Retained Rights

Finally, art. I, §24, of the Rhode Island Constitution provides:

> The enumeration of the foregoing rights shall not be construed to impair or deny others retained by the people. The rights guaranteed by this Constitution are not dependent on those guaranteed by the Constitution of the United States.[23]

If a right to abortion is not conferred by any of the preceding enumerated rights secured by the Rhode Island Declaration of Rights, it is not likely that it would be recognized as a "retained right" under §24, either.

First, recognition of a right to abortion as an implied retained right under §24 would seem to conflict with the express exclusion of such a right under §2. To be sure, under §24, the enumeration of rights does not preclude recognition of an unenumerated right, at least where the state constitution is silent regarding that right. Nevertheless, it would be a peculiar reading of the state constitution to say that a "right" explicitly withdrawn in one section is implicitly guaranteed in another. Second, to date, the Rhode Island Supreme Court has not recognized a single unenumerated right under §24. Third, the supreme court *has* held that "any rights reserved ... by the Rhode Island constitution are subject to the General Assembly's police power."[24] In the absence

---

20. *See DeSantis v. Prelle*, 891 A.2d 873, 881 (R.I. 2006).

21. 911 A.2d 1035 (R.I. 2006).

22. *Id.* at 1039.

23. R.I. CONST. art. I, §24 (2004). Prior to the adoption of the present Rhode Island Constitution in 1986, the first sentence of what is now §24 was the entirety of art. I, §23.

24. *State v. Ramsdell*, 285 A.2d 399, 403 (R.I. 1971) (legislature's "abolition of the right to resist an unlawful arrest [was] unquestionably a proper exercise of the police power"). *See also State v. Storms*, 308 A.2d 463, 464 (R.I. 1973) (§23 [now §24] "in no sense assures a right of self-defense").

of an express constitutional limitation on the General Assembly's authority to prohibit or regulate abortion, the retention of rights language of § 24 would not provide a basis for challenging the exercise of that authority. Fourth, although the state supreme court has not expressed an opinion on the matter, the statement in § 24 that "[t]he enumeration of the foregoing rights should not be construed to impair or deny others retained by the people" may mean only that the enumeration of specific constitutional rights in the first twenty-three sections of the Declaration of Rights does not "impair or deny" common law or statutory rights, an entirely reasonable reading of § 24.

Conclusion

Based on the foregoing analysis, an argument that the Rhode Island Constitution protects a right to abortion separate from, and independent of, the right to abortion that is recognized in *Roe v. Wade* would not likely succeed. That, in turn, suggests that if *Roe*, as modified by *Casey*, is ultimately overruled, the State of Rhode Island could enforce its post-*Roe* statute *prohibiting* abortion (or enact a new statute prohibiting abortion). Moreover, nothing in the Rhode Island Constitution precludes Rhode Island from *regulating* abortion within federal constitutional limitations in the meantime.

CHAPTER 43

SOUTH CAROLINA

Summary

The South Carolina Supreme Court has not yet decided whether the South Carolina Constitution protects a right to abortion separate from, and independent of, the right to abortion recognized under the United States Constitution.[1] A careful examination of the state constitution, in light of its history and interpretation, as well as other relevant legal sources, however, suggests that the state supreme court probably would not recognize a state constitutional right to abortion. Thus, if *Roe v. Wade*,[2] as modified by *Planned Parenthood of Southeastern Pennsylvania v. Casey*,[3] were overruled, South Carolina could enact a statute prohibiting abortion. Moreover, nothing in the state constitution, properly understood, precludes the State from enacting and enforcing reasonable measures regulating abortion within current federal constitutional limits.

Analysis

The pre-*Roe* South Carolina abortion statutes were based on § 230.3 of the Model Penal Code.[4] Sections 16-82 and 16-83 prohibited performance of an abortion upon a pregnant woman unless the procedure was "necessary to preserve her life or the life of [her] child,"[5] and § 16-84 made a woman's participation

---

1. The South Carolina Supreme Court has referred to the right to abortion solely as a matter of *federal*, not *state*, constitutional law. *See Hendrix v. Taylor*, 579 S.E.2d 320, 323 n. 12 (S.C. 2003) ("[t]he United States Supreme Court has recognized a constitutional right to privacy in various situations") (citing *Roe v. Wade*).

2. 410 U.S. 113 (1973).

3. 505 U.S. 833 (1992).

4. S.C. CODE ANN. § 16-82 *et seq.* (1971). The complete text of § 230.3 of the Model Penal Code is set out in Appendix B to the Supreme Court's decision in *Doe v. Bolton*, 410 U.S. 179, 205–07 (1973).

5. *Id.* §§ 16-82, 16-83.

in her own abortion a criminal offense.[6] Section 16-87 excepted from the scope of these sections abortions performed by licensed physicians in licensed hospitals when (1) there was "substantial risk that continuance of the pregnancy would threaten the life or gravely impair the mental or physical health of the woman," (2) there was "substantial risk that the child would be born with grave physical or mental defect," or (3) the pregnancy resulted from a reported act of incest or rape.[7] The statutes did not place any express limitation on the stage of pregnancy at which an authorized abortion could be performed. Pursuant to *Roe*, the statutes were declared unconstitutional (on federal, not state, grounds) in *State v. Lawrence*,[8] and were repealed in 1974.[9]

Based upon arguments that have been raised in other States with similar constitutional provisions, possible sources for an asserted abortion right could include provisions of the Declaration of Rights guaranteeing religious freedom (art. I, §2), a speedy remedy (§9), due process of law (§3), privacy (§10) and equal protection (§3).[10] The analysis that follows addresses each of these provisions.

Religious Freedom

Article I, §2, of the South Carolina Constitution provides:

> The General Assembly shall make no law respecting an establishment of religion or prohibiting the free exercise thereof, or abridging the freedom of speech or of the press; or the right of the people peaceably to assemble and to petition the government or any department thereof for a redress of grievances.[11]

---

6. *Id.* §16-84. No prosecutions were reported under this statute.

7. *Id.* §16-87. This section, expanding the reasons for which an abortion could be performed, was added in 1970. 1970 S.C. Acts 1892, No. 821. Section 16-87 imposed other conditions. Abortions could be performed only in a licensed hospital, after three physicians had examined the woman and certified in writing to the existence of the circumstances justifying the abortion under the law. *Id.* §16-87. Except in emergencies, the woman had to be a resident of the State for ninety days immediately preceding the operation. *Id.* If the woman seeking the abortion was a minor or an incompetent, the written consent of her parents or guardian was required and, if she was married, the written consent of her husband or guardian. *Id.*

8. 198 S.E.2d 253 (S.C. 1973).

9. 1974 S.C. Acts 2837, 2841, Act. No. 1215, §8.

10. One other more unlikely source of an abortion right under the South Carolina Constitution-art. I, §2 (guaranteeing, among other rights, freedom of speech)-is discussed generally in Chapter 3, *supra*.

11. S.C. Const. art. I, §2 (1997).

In any challenge to a statute prohibiting abortion, abortion advocates may raise either or both of two arguments under art. I, § 2. First, they may argue that an abortion prohibition interferes with the "free exercise" of a woman's religious freedom by forbidding her from obtaining an abortion that would be allowed by her religion. Second, they may argue in the alternative (or in addition) that an abortion prohibition constitutes an "establishment of religion" because it reflects sectarian beliefs regarding when human life begins and the sinfulness of abortion. Neither argument would likely prevail.

The South Carolina Supreme Court has observed that "[t]he language of the first amendment to the Constitution of the United States and the language of Article 1, Section 4 [now § 2], of the Constitution of South Carolina are, for all intents and purposes the same."[12] Thus, the same reasoning "is applicable to both constitutional provisions."[13] Given this equivalence of language and interpretation, a challenge to an abortion statute that would not succeed under the Religion Clauses of the First Amendment would not succeed under art. I, § 2, either. For the reasons set forth in Chapter 2, *supra*, an abortion statute could not be successfully challenged on First Amendment grounds. Accordingly, a similar challenge under art. I, § 2, would not likely be successful.[14]

Speedy Remedy

Article I, § 9, of the South Carolina Constitution provides: "All courts shall be public, and every person shall have speedy remedy therein for wrongs sustained."[15] Abortion advocates might argue that a statute prohibiting abortion

---

12. *Hunt v. McNair*, 187 S.E.2d 645, 648 (S.C. 1972) (interpreting both free exercise and establishment clauses).

13. *Id. See also Pearson v. Church of God*, 458 S.E.2d 68, 70 (S.C. 1995) (construing state and federal free exercise guarantees the same).

14. Entirely apart from the South Carolina Supreme Court's reliance on federal precedent in interpreting art. I, § 2, an argument challenging an abortion prohibition on the basis that it "establishes" a religion by embodying sectarian views regarding the sinfulness of abortion would appear to be foreclosed by a decision of the court rejecting a challenge to a Sunday closing law. In *Carolina Amusement Co. v. Martin*, 115 S.E.2d 273, 282 (S.C. 1960), the state supreme court, referring to Sunday closing laws generally, stated that "[t]hat the day of rest selected by the legislative bodies coincides with the Christian Sabbath is no reason to invalidate the laws" under the state and federal provisions barring establishment of a religion. If mandating a "day of rest" on Sunday does not violate art. I, § 2, even though it may "coincide[]" with Christian beliefs, then neither would a law prohibiting abortion, regardless of whether the law "coincides" with religious views regarding the sinfulness of abortion.

15. S.C. CONST. art. I, § 9 (1997).

interferes with a woman's control over her own body, and that such interference constitutes a "wrong," as that term is used in §9, for which there must be a "speedy remedy." That "remedy," in turn, would be invalidation of the statute. Such an argument would be foreclosed by the South Carolina Supreme Court's decision in *State v. Lagerquist*.[16] In *Lagerquist*, the court held that "[t]he guaranty [in art. I, §9] of a speedy remedy for wrongs sustained has no application to a criminal prosecution."[17] This holding would preclude any reliance upon art. I, §9, in challenging a criminal statute of the State.

Due Process of Law

Article I, §3, of the South Carolina Constitution provides, in part: "nor shall any person shall be deprived of life, liberty or property without due process of law...."[18]

In any challenge to an abortion prohibition that South Carolina may enact, abortion advocates are most likely to rely upon art. I, §3, arguing that the prohibition interferes with a pregnant woman's "liberty" interest in obtaining an abortion. Such an argument probably would not succeed, however

The South Carolina Supreme Court has recognized that there is a substantive, as well as a procedural, component to the due process guarantee of art. I, §3.[19] The court, however, has adopted a single standard for reviewing all state substantive due process challenges to state statutes, to wit, "[w]hether [the statute] bears a reasonable relationship to any legitimate interest of government."[20] This standard, of course, is the rational basis standard,[21] and it applies (to *state* substantive due process challenges) without regard to whether the liberty interest involved is characterized as fundamental or non-fundamental.[22] A statute prohibiting abortion would have a "reasonable relation-

---

16. 176 S.E.2d 141 (S.C. 1970).

17. *Id.* at 143.

18. S.C. CONST. art. I, §3 (1997).

19. *Fraternal Order of Police v. South Carolina Dep't of Revenue*, 574 S.E.2d 717, 724 (S.C. 2002).

20. *R.L. Jordan Co., Inc. v. Boardman Petroleum, Inc.*, 527 S.E.2d 783, 785 (S.C. 2000). *See also Sloan v. South Carolina Board of Physical Therapy Examiners*, 636 S.E.2d 598, 614 (S.C. 2006) (same).

21. *In re Treatment and Care of Luckabaugh*, 568 S.E.2d 338, 347 n. 7 (S.C. 2002) ("when reviewing a challenge to a state statute under the South Carolina Constitution we apply the rational basis test"); *Sunset Cay, LLC v. City of Folly Beach*, 593 S.E.2d 462, 470 (S.C. 2004) (same).

22. In *Luckabaugh*, the court found that a statute infringing upon a fundamental liberty interest (not to be confined against one's will) satisfied the more rigorous strict scrutiny

ship" to the "legitimate interest of government" in protecting unborn human life. Accordingly, the statute would satisfy the rational basis standard applicable to challenges brought under the due process guarantee of art. I, § 3.

Privacy

Article I, § 10, of the South Carolina Constitution provides:

> The right of the people to be secure in their persons, houses, papers and effects against unreasonable searches and seizures and unreasonable invasions of privacy shall not be violated, and no warrants shall issue but upon probable cause, supported by oath or affirmation, and particularly describing the place to be searched, the person or thing to be seized and the information to be obtained.[23]

In any challenge to a statute prohibiting abortion, abortion advocates may be expected to rely upon the language of art. I, § 10, arguing that the statute constitutes an "unreasonable invasion" of the "privacy" of a pregnant woman to obtain an abortion. This argument would not likely prevail, however.

The South Carolina Supreme Court has stated that art. I, § 10, "specifically recognizes a right to privacy."[24] The court, however, has not identified any *state* (as opposed to *federal*) right of privacy as fundamental.[25] Moreover, in context, the prohibition of "unreasonable invasions of privacy" set forth in § 10, would appear to be limited to the *means* by which criminal conduct is discovered, and not whether the *conduct* itself is constitutionally protected.[26] Even assum-

---

standard of review required by the Due Process Clause of the *federal* constitution and, therefore, that the statute also satisfied the rational basis standard applicable under the corollary provision of the *state* constitution (art. I, § 3).

23. S.C. Const. art. I, § 10 (1997).

24. *Hendrix v. Taylor*, 579 S.E.2d at 323 n. 12. *See also Southern Bell Tel. & Tel. Co. v. Hamm*, 409 S.E.2d 775, 779 (S.C. 1991) (same).

25. It should be noted here that the Supreme Court, departing from its rationale in *Roe*, 410 U.S. at 153 ("[t]his right of privacy ... is broad enough to encompass a woman's decision whether or not to terminate her pregnancy"), no longer analyzes substantive due process claims under the rubric of "privacy," either in the area of abortion, *see Casey*, 505 U.S. at 846–53 (reaffirming *Roe* on the basis of the liberty language of the Due Process Clause without once mentioning privacy), or any other area. *See Cruzan v. Director, Missouri Dep't of Health*, 497 U.S. 261, 279 n. 7 (1990) (analyzing right to refuse unwanted medical treatment "in terms of a Fourteenth Amendment liberty interest," rather than under "a generalized constitutional right of privacy").

26. This issue is explored in more detail in Chapter 3, *supra*. The "unreasonable invasions of privacy" language, added in 1970, *see* 1970 S.C. Acts 2684, 2686, No. 1268, § 1,

ing, however, that the privacy language of § 10 extends to certain types of conduct, abortion cannot reasonably be considered to be protected by a right of privacy.

Abortion after "quickening" was a common law offense in South Carolina.[27] In 1883, South Carolina enacted its first abortion statute.[28] Section 1 prohibited performance of an abortion that resulted in the death of either the pregnant woman or of her unborn child "unless the same shall have been necessary to preserve her life or the life of such child...."[29] Section 2 prohibited performance of an abortion that did not result in the death of either the pregnant woman or her unborn child.[30] Section 3 prohibited a pregnant woman from soliciting an abortion or allowing an abortion to be performed upon her (subject to the same exception set forth in § 1).[31] In 1948, the South Carolina Supreme Court held that § 1 of the 1883 applied only to abortions performed after quickening (a felony), while § 2 applied to pre-quickening abortions (a misdemeanor).[32] In the same opinion, the court held that the 1883 Act had been enacted to prevent the "destruction of a child" either before or after quickening.[33] The provisions of the original South Carolina abortion law remained on the books until 1967,[34] when the State broadened the reasons for which abortions could be performed.[35]

"was designed to protect the citizen from improper use of electronic devices, computer data banks, etc." FINAL REPORT OF THE COMMITTEE TO MAKE A STUDY OF THE SOUTH CAROLINA CONSTITUTION OF 1895: REPORT TO THE GENERAL ASSEMBLY OF 1969 15 (Columbia, South Carolina). "Since it is almost impossible to describe all of the devices which exist or which may be perfected in the future, the Committee recommends only a broad statement of policy, leaving the details to be regulated by law and court decision." *Id.* It is apparent from the Committee's Final Report that the amended language was aimed at protecting informational privacy, not privacy of conduct.

27. *State v. Steadman*, 51 S.E.2d 91, 93 (S.C. 1948) (discussing common law offense of abortion). "Quickening" is that stage of pregnancy, usually sixteen to eighteen weeks gestation, when a woman first detects fetal movement.

28. 1883 S.C. Acts 547–48, Act No. 354, §§ 1-3.

29. *Id.* § 1.

30. *Id.* § 2.

31. *Id.* § 3. No prosecutions were reported under this provision.

32. *State v. Steadman*, 51 S.E.2d at 93.

33. *Id.*

34. The provisions of the 1883 act were codified at S.C. REV. STAT., CRIM. L. §§ 122, 137, 138 (1893), *recodified at* S.C. CRIM. CODE §§ 122, 139, 140 (1902), *recodified at* S.C. CRIM. CODE §§ 12, 25, 26 (1922), *recodified at* S.C. CODE §§ 1112, 1113, 1114 (1932), *recodified at* S.C. CODE §§ 16-82, 16-83, 16-84 (1952).

35. *See* nn. 4-7, *supra*, and accompanying text.

Prior to *Roe*, the South Carolina Supreme Court regularly affirmed abortion convictions without any hint or suggestion that the prosecutions or convictions were barred by the state constitution.[36] Pursuant to *Roe*, the South Carolina declared the pre-*Roe* abortion statutes unconstitutional on federal grounds only.[37] Subsequent to *Roe*, the South Carolina Legislature enacted a comprehensive scheme of abortion regulation.[38]

From the time when South Carolina was admitted to the Union, when abortion was a common law crime, until 1967, when the State added to the reasons for which an abortion could be performed, the State of South Carolina strictly limited the circumstances under which an abortion could be performed. That history, along with the state supreme court's acknowledgment that the very first abortion statute had been designed to prevent the "destruction of a child," strongly suggests that there is no fundamental interest in obtaining an abortion under the liberty clauses of art. I, §3, of the South Carolina Constitution. That suggestion is supported by South Carolina's recognition of the rights of unborn children in a variety of contexts outside of abortion, including criminal law, tort law, health care law and property law.

In criminal law, a person who commits a violent crime that causes the death of, or bodily injury to, an unborn child at the time the crime was committed, is guilty of a separate and distinct offense under the State's criminal code.[39] Under this provision, the gestational age of the unborn child at the time of the crime causing its death or injury is irrelevant to criminal liability. A viable fetus (a fetus that is capable of sustained survival outside the mother's womb, with our without medical assistance) is a "child," as that term is used in the child abuse and endangerment statute.[40] A pregnant woman who causes the

---

36. *State v. Morrow*, 18 S.E. 853 (S.C. 1893); *State v. Parsons*, 172 S.E. 424 (S.C. 1934); *State v. Steadman*, 59 S.E.2d 168 (S.C. 1950); *State v. Hutto*, 165 S.E.2d 72 (S.C. 1968).

37. *State v. Lawrence*, 198 S.E.2d 253 (S.C. 1973).

38. S.C. CODE ANN. §44-41-31 through 44-41-37 (2002) (mandating parental consent); §1-1-1035 (2005) (restricting public funding of abortion for indigent women); §§44-41-30, 44-41-310 *et seq.* (2002) (mandating informed consent); §§44-41-70(b), 44-41-75 (2002) (authorizing clinic regulations), S.C. ADMIN. CODE R. 61-12 (Supp. 2007) (clinic regulations); S.C. CODE ANN. §§44-41-40, 44-41-50 (2002) (recognizing individual and institutional rights of conscience).

39. S.C. CODE ANN. §16-3-1083 (Supp. 2007). Prior to the adoption of this statute, the South Carolina Supreme Court had held that the word "person," as used in the homicide statutes, included viable fetuses. *State v. Horne*, 319 S.E.2d 703, 704 (S.C. 1984); *State v. Ard*, 505 S.E.2d 328, 330–31 (S.C. 1998).

40. *Whitner v. State*, 492 S.E.2d 777, 779–84 (S.C. 1997), interpreting S.C. CODE §20-7-50 (Supp. 2007).

death of her viable unborn child by ingesting illegal drugs may be prosecuted for homicide by child abuse.[41] And a woman who is convicted of a capital offense may not be executed while she is pregnant or for at least nine months thereafter.[42]

In tort law, a statutory cause of action for wrongful death may be brought on behalf of an unborn child who was viable (capable of sustained survival outside the mother's womb, with or without medical assistance) at the time of its death.[43] A common law cause of action for (nonlethal) prenatal injuries may be brought for injuries sustained after viability.[44] And the South Carolina Supreme Court has refused to recognize wrongful life causes of action.[45]

In health care law, under the Death with Dignity Act, life-sustaining procedures may not be withheld or withdrawn from a woman who has been diagnosed as pregnant during the course of her pregnancy.[46] The same limitation applies to a health care power of attorney.[47]

In property law, children and other lineal descendants of an intestate (a person who dies without a will) "conceived before his death but born within ten months thereafter inherit as if they had been born in the lifetime of the decedent."[48] And, subject to certain exceptions, an afterborn child (a child

---

41. *State v. McKnight*, 576 S.E.2d 168, 174–75 (S.C. 2003), interpreting S.C. CODE ANN. § 16-3-85 (2003).

42. S.C. CODE ANN. § 16-3-20(A) (2003).

43. *Fowler v. Woodward*, 138 S.E.2d 42, 44–45 (S.C. 1962), interpreting what is now codified at S.C. CODE ANN. § 15-51-10 (2005). In the absence of legislative reform, however, the court has declined to extend the wrongful death act to *non*viable children who were stillborn. *See Crosby v. Glasscock Trucking Co., Inc.*, 532 S.E.2d 856 (S.C. 2000).

44. *Hall v. Murphy*, 113 S.E.2d 790, 793 (S.C. 1960). The court has not had occasion yet to determine whether an action for (nonlethal) prenatal injuries may be brought on behalf of an unborn child who sustained the injuries before viability.

45. *Willis v. Wu*, 607 S.E.2d 63, 71 (S.C. 2004) (concluding that "being born with a naturally occurring defect or impairment does not constitute a legally cognizable injury"). A "wrongful life" cause of action is a claim brought on behalf of a child who is born with a physical or mental disability or disease that could have been discovered before to the child's birth by genetic testing, amniocentesis or other medical screening. The gravamen of the action is that, as a result of a physician's failure to inform the child's parents of the child's disability or disease (or at least of the availability of tests to determine the presence of the disability or disease), they were deprived of the opportunity to abort the child, thus resulting in the birth of a child suffering permanent physical or mental impairment. *Willis* did not involve a "wrongful birth" cause of action which is a claim, based on the same facts, brought on behalf of the parents of the impaired child.

46. S.C. CODE ANN. § 44-77-70 (2002).

47. *Id.* § 62-5-504(G) (Supp. 2007).

48. *Id.* § 62-2-108.

conceived before the death of a parent but after the parent executes a will) receives the same share of the decedent's estate that he would have received if
the decedent had died intestate.[49]

In light of the history of abortion regulation in South Carolina, the South Carolina Supreme Court's recognition that the first abortion statute was intended
to protect unborn children, the enactment of legislation regulating abortion
and its funding, and the rights extended to unborn children outside the area of
abortion, it cannot plausibly be said that the privacy language of art. I, § 10,
confers a right to abortion. More generally, a right to abortion cannot be found
in the text or structure of the South Carolina Constitution. There is no evidence that the framers of the 1895 South Carolina Constitution intended the Declaration of Rights to limit the Legislature's authority to prohibit abortion.[50]

Equal Protection

Article I, § 3, of the South Carolina Constitution provides, in part: "[n]or
shall any person be denied the equal protection of the laws."[51] The South Carolina Supreme Court has held that "[i]f there is no suspect or quasi-suspect
class and no fundamental right involved, a statute should be tested under the
'rational basis' standard."[52] Strict scrutiny would not apply to review of an
abortion prohibition because, for the reasons set forth in the preceding sections
of this analysis, neither the guarantee of due process (art. I, § 3), nor the prohibition of "unreasonable invasions of privacy" (art. I, § 10), confers a "fundamental right" to abortion. Nor would the prohibition of abortion classify
persons on the basis of a "suspect" personal characteristic (*e.g.*, race).

Abortion advocates may argue in the alternative, however, that a statute
prohibiting abortion discriminates against women and is subject to intermediate scrutiny under both art. I, § 3, because only women are capable of becoming
pregnant. For purposes of both state and federal equal protection analysis, a
gender-based classification "must serve an important governmental objective

---

49. *Id.* § 62-2-302.

50. *See* JOURNAL OF THE CONSTITUTIONAL CONVENTION OF THE STATE OF SOUTH CAR-
OLINA 274–77 (Report of Committee on Declaration of Rights), 345–47 (first reading),
652–55 (second reading), 712 (adopted) (Columbia, South Carolina 1895).

51. S.C. CONST. art. I, § 3 (1997).

52. *State v. Thompson*, 563 S.E.2d 325, 329 (S.C. 2002) (citation omitted). *See also City
of Beaufort v. Holcombe*, 632 S.E.2d 894, 897 (S.C. 2006) (same); *Denene, Inc. v. City of
Charleston*, 596 S.E.2d 917, 920 (S.C. 2004) (same); *Sunset Cay, LLC v. City of Folly Beach*,
593 S.E.2d at 469 (same).

and be substantially related to the achievement of that objective."[53] An abortion prohibition would appear to satisfy this level of scrutiny because the prohibition would be "substantially related" to the "important governmental objective" of protecting unborn human life. Nevertheless, the standard applicable to sex-based discrimination should not apply to an abortion prohibition. Abortion laws do not discriminate on the basis of sex.

First, the United States Supreme Court has reviewed restrictions on abortion funding under a rational basis standard of review, *not* under the intermediate (heightened) scrutiny required of gender-based classifications.[54] Indeed, the Court has held that "the disfavoring of abortion ... is not *ipso facto* sex discrimination," and, citing its decisions in *Harris* and other cases addressing abortion funding, stated that "the constitutional test applicable to government abortion-funding restrictions is not the heightened-scrutiny standard that our cases demand for sex discrimination, ... but the ordinary rationality standard."[55]

Second, even assuming that an abortion prohibition differentiates between men and women on the basis of sex, and would otherwise be subject to a higher standard of review, both the United States Supreme Court and the South Carolina Supreme Court have held that biological differences between men and women may justify different treatment based on those differences. In upholding a statutory rape statute that applied only to males, the Supreme Court noted, "this Court has consistently upheld statutes where the gender classification is not invidious, but rather realistically reflects the fact that the sexes

---

53. *State v. Wright*, 563 S.E.2d 311, 312 (S.C. 2002) (citing *Craig v. Boren*, 429 U.S. 190, 197 (1976)).

54. *Harris v. McRae*, 448 U.S. 297, 321–26 (1980).

55. *Bray v. Alexandria Women's Health Clinic*, 506 U.S. 263, 273 (1993). Several state supreme courts and individual state supreme court justices have recognized that abortion regulations and restrictions on abortion funding are not "directed at women as a class" so much as "abortion as a medical treatment, which, because it involves a potential life, has no parallel as a treatment method." *Bell v. Low Income Women of Texas*, 95 S.W.3d 253, 258 (Tex. 2002) (upholding funding restrictions) (citing *Harris*, 448 U.S. at 325). *See also Fischer v. Dep't of Public Welfare*, 502 A.2d 114, 125 (Pa. 1985) ("the basis for the distinction here is not sex, but abortion") (upholding funding restrictions); *Moe v. Secretary of Administration & Finance*, 417 N.E.2d 387, 407 (Mass. 1981) (Hennessey, C.J., dissenting) (funding restrictions were "directed at abortion as a medical procedure, not women as a class"); *Right to Choose v. Byrne*, 450 A.2d 925, 950 (N.J. 1982) (O'Hern, J., dissenting) ("[t]he subject of the legislation is not the person of the recipient, but the nature of the claimed medical service"). Both *Moe* and *Right to Choose* were decided on other grounds. The dissenting justices were addressing alternative arguments raised by the plaintiffs, but not reached by the majority opinions.

are not similarly situated in certain circumstances."[56] The South Carolina Supreme Court has held that "[a] statute will be upheld where the gender classification realistically reflects the fact that the sexes are not similarly situated in certain circumstances."[57] "Abortion statutes are examples of cases in which the sexes are not biologically similarly situated" because only women are capable of becoming pregnant and having abortions.[58]

A statute prohibiting abortion quite obviously can affect only women because only women are capable of becoming pregnant.[59] Unlike laws that use women's ability to become pregnant (or pregnancy itself) to discriminate against them in *other* areas (*e.g.*, employment opportunities), abortion prohibitions cannot fairly be said to involve a distinction between men and women that is a "mere pretext[] designed to erect an invidious discrimination against [women]."[60]

A prohibition of abortion would not interfere with the exercise of a fundamental state constitutional right, nor would it classify upon the basis of a suspect or quasi-suspect characteristic. Accordingly, it would be subject to rational basis review. "Under the rational basis test, the requirements of equal protection are satisfied when: (1) the classification bears a reasonable relation to the legislative purpose sought to be affected; (2) the members of the class are treated alike under similar circumstances and conditions; and (3) the classification rests on some reasonable basis."[61] A law prohibiting abortion would bear a "reasonable relation to the legislative purpose sought to be affected," *i.e.*, to protect the lives of unborn children; it would treat all members of the class (pregnant women seeking abortion) alike under similar circumstances (the prohibition and whatever exceptions it might contain would apply equally to all women); and the classification would rest "on some reasonable basis," *e.g.*, a prohibition that contained an exception for the life of the pregnant woman would not allow an abortion, which results in the death of an unborn child, to be performed unless the life of the pregnant woman were in danger.

---

56. *Michael M. v. Superior Court*, 450 U.S. 464, 469 (1981). The South Carolina Supreme Court has cited *Michael M.* with approval. *See Griffin v. Warden, CCI*, 286 S.E.2d 145, 146–47 (S.C. 1982) (disparity in punishment between sexual offenses committed by adult males against minor females and those committed by adult females against minor males was justified by the possibility of minor female victims becoming pregnant).

57. *In re Interest of Joseph T.*, 430 S.E.2d 523, 524 (S.C. 1993).

58. *Jane L. v. Bangerter*, 794 F. Supp. 1537, 1549 (D. Utah 1992).

59. *Geduldig v. Aiello*, 417 U.S. 484, 496 n. 20 (1974) ("[n]ormal pregnancy is an objectively, identifiable physical condition with unique characteristics").

60. *Id.*

61. *Denene, Inc. v. City of Charleston*, 596 S.E.2d at 920.

Conclusion

Based on the foregoing analysis, an argument that the South Carolina Constitution protects a right to abortion that is separate from, and independent of, the right to abortion recognized in *Roe v. Wade* would not likely succeed. That, in turn, suggests that if *Roe*, as modified by *Casey*, is ultimately overruled, South Carolina could enact and enforce a statute *prohibiting* abortion. Moreover, nothing in the South Carolina Constitution precludes South Carolina from *regulating* abortion within federal constitutional limits in the meantime.

CHAPTER 44

SOUTH DAKOTA

Summary

The South Dakota Supreme Court has not yet decided whether the South Dakota Constitution protects a right to abortion separate from, and independent of, the right to abortion recognized under the United States Constitution.[1] A careful examination of the state constitution, in light of its history and interpretation, as well as other relevant legal sources, however, suggests that the state supreme court probably would not recognize a state constitutional right to abortion. Thus, if *Roe v. Wade*,[2] as modified by *Planned Parenthood of Southeastern Pennsylvania v. Casey*,[3] were overruled, South Dakota could enforce its "trigger" statute, which would prohibit abortion, except "to preserve the life of the pregnant female," and which would take effect "on the date that the states are recognized by the United States Supreme Court to have the authority to prohibit abortion at all stages of pregnancy."[4] Moreover, nothing in the state constitution, properly understood, precludes the State from enacting and enforcing reasonable measures regulating abortion within current federal constitutional limits.

---

1. The South Dakota Supreme Court has referred to the right to abortion solely as a matter of *federal*, not *state*, constitutional law. *See State v. Bowers*, 498 N.W.2d 202, 206 (S.D. 1993) (abortion is a "constitutionally protected right") (citing *Roe v. Wade* in case rejecting necessity defense in abortion protest prosecution); *Wiersma v. Maple Leaf Farms*, 543 N.W.2d 787, 792 n. 5 (S.D. 1996) ("[t]he right to abort protects a mother's 'liberty interest' and 'fundamental right to privacy' in voluntarily choosing to end her pregnancy in the first trimester") (citing *Roe* in wrongful death case).

2. 410 U.S. 113 (1973).

3. 505 U.S. 833 (1992).

4. S.D. CODIFIED LAWS § 22-17-5.1 (2006).

Analysis

The principal pre-*Roe* abortion statute prohibited performance of an abortion upon a pregnant woman unless the procedure was "necessary to preserve her life."[5] Another statute prohibited a woman from soliciting an abortion or allowing an abortion to be performed upon her (subject to the same exception).[6] Pursuant to *Roe*, § 22-17-1 was declared unconstitutional (on federal, not state, grounds) by the South Dakota Supreme Court in *State v. Munson*.[7] Sections 22-17-1 and 22-17-2 were later repealed.[8]

Based upon arguments that have been raised in other States with similar constitutional provisions, possible sources for an asserted abortion right could include provisions of the Bill of Rights guaranteeing due process of law and equal protection (art. VI, §§ 2, 18), freedom of religion (§ 3) and a remedy by due course of law (§ 20); and recognizing inherent rights (§ 1), inherent political power in the people (§ 26) and the importance of frequent recurrence to the fundamental principles of government (§ 27).[9] The analysis that follows addresses each of these provisions.

Inherent Rights, Due Process of Law

Article VI, § 1, of the South Dakota Constitution provides:

> All men are born equally free and independent, and have certain inherent rights, among which are those of enjoying and defending life and liberty, of acquiring and protecting property and the pursuit of happiness. To secure these rights governments are instituted among men, deriving their just powers from the consent of the governed.[10]

---

5. S.D. COMPILED LAWS § 22-17-1 (1967).

6. *Id.* 22-17-2. No prosecutions were reported under this statute.

7. 206 N.W.2d 434 (S.D. 1973). In its original decision, the South Dakota Supreme court upheld the constitutionality of the statute against a federal constitutional challenge. *State v. Munson*, 201 N.W.2d 123 (S.D. 1972), *vacated and remanded*, 410 U.S. 950 (1973).

8. 1973 S.D. Laws 206, 209 ch. 146, § 15; 1976 S.D. Laws 227, 257, ch. 158, § 17-1; 1977 S.D. Laws 258, 282, ch. 189, § 126.

9. Two other more unlikely sources of an abortion right under the South Dakota Constitution-art. VI, § 5 (guaranteeing freedom of speech) and § 11 (prohibiting unreasonable searches and seizures)-are discussed generally in Chapter 3, *supra*.

10. S.D. CONST. art. VI, § 1 (2004).

Article VI, §2, provides, in pertinent part: "No person shall be deprived of life, liberty or property without due process of law."[11]

The South Dakota Supreme Court has not developed a methodology for determining whether an asserted liberty interest is protected by the inherent rights language of art. VI, §1, or the due process guarantee of §2. With respect to the former provision, however, the state supreme court held in an early case that the "personal liberty" secured by §1 "consists of the right of locomotion-to go where one pleases, and when, and to do that which may lead to one's business or pleasure, only so far restrained as the rights of others may make it necessary for the welfare of all other citizens."[12] In *Christnacht*, the court struck down a city ordinance that declared that any male person found to be associating with known or reputed prostitutes within the city limits should be deemed a "pimp," and, upon conviction, fined and imprisoned. The court explained that the ordinance, if upheld, "would prevent personal effort on the part of male citizens to uplift and ameliorate the condition of fallen women. Ministers of the gospel, physicians, nurses, welfare workers-all would be subject to the infamous appellation contained in the ordinance and to the pains and penalties of the ordinance."[13]

In *State v. Nuss*,[14] the state supreme court cited art. VI, §1, along with art. VI, §2, the due process guarantee, in support of its decision striking down a statute that capped the amount of advance tuition that certain institutions could collect.[15] The majority opinion stated that "[e]conomic freedom is one of the inherent rights guaranteed to all men by [art. VI, §1] of the South Dakota Constitution and protected by the [state] due process clause."[16] "The term 'liberty' [as] used in the Constitution means more than freedom from arrest or restraint. It includes freedom of action; freedom to own, control, and use property, and freedom to pursue any lawful trade, business or calling."[17]

Christnacht and *Nuss* are the only decisions to date in which the South Dakota Supreme Court has invalidated a state statute or local ordinance on

---

11. *Id.* art. VI, §2.

12. *City of Watertown v. Christnacht*, 164 N.W. 62, 62 (S.D. 1917) (citation and internal quotation marks omitted).

13. *Id.*

14. 114 N.W.2d 633 (S.D. 1962).

15. *Id.* at 635.

16. *Id.* Notwithstanding its paean of praise to "economic freedom," the South Dakota Supreme Court has held that the legislature may limit the hours of work, *State v. Collins*, 198 N.W. 557 (S.D. 1924), fix prices, *Siefkes v. Clark Title Co.*, 215 N.W.2d 648 (S.D. 1974), and license, *City of Sioux Falls v. Kadinger*, 50 N.W.2d 797 (S.D. 1951), and tax businesses and occupations, *Schmitt v. Nord*, 27 N.W.2d 910 (S.D. 1947), *Mundell v. Graph*, 256 N.W. 121 (S.D. 1934), all as the public interest may require.

17. *Id.*

the ground that it conflicted with the "liberty" secured by art. VI, § 1. The court's marked reluctance to base declarations of unconstitutionality on § 1, as well as its understanding of what the term "liberty" means, suggest that § 1 would be an unlikely source of an abortion right under the South Dakota Constitution.

With respect to the due process guarantee (art. VI, § 2), the supreme court has recognized that § 2 has a substantive, as well as a procedural, component.[18] " 'Due process of law,' when applied to substantive rights, means that the government is without the right to deprive a person of life, liberty or property by an act that has no reasonable relation to any proper governmental purpose by which it is so far beyond the necessity of the case as to be an arbitrary exercise of governmental power."[19] Phrased somewhat differently, "substantive due process of law requires that the exercise of the police power must not be unreasonable or unduly oppressive and that the regulatory means employed by the legislature must have a real and substantial relation to the objects sought to be attained."[20]

A prohibition of abortion would not be "unreasonable" or "unduly oppressive." Moreover, "the means employed by the legislature," criminal penalties, would have a "real and substantial relation to the object[] sought to be attained," which would be the protection of the life of the unborn child. Indeed, in rejecting a challenge to the constitutionality of the principal pre-*Roe* abortion statute, the South Dakota Supreme Court, noting a "fundamental difference between the right to use contraceptives and the right to terminate a pregnancy," held that the State "has a compelling and legitimate interest to determine when, where, and by whom a pregnancy shall be terminated."[21]

The South Dakota Supreme Court acknowledges that where a fundamental liberty interest is at stake, a higher standard of judicial review is required. The court, however, has never recognized a liberty interest as "fundamental" in the absence of Supreme Court precedent.[22] That, in turn, suggests that if

---

18. *See generally Knowles v. United States*, 544 N.W.2d 183, 199 & n. 20 (S.D. 1996) (Op. of Gilbertson, J.). In an earlier case, however, the state supreme court appeared to question the legitimacy of substantive due process analysis. *See Behrns v. Burke*, 229 N.W.2d 86, 88 n. 6 (S.D. 1975).

19. *Crowley v. State*, 268 N.W.2d 616, 619 (S.D. 1978).

20. *Matter of Application of Katz v. South Dakota State Board of Medical & Osteopathic Examiners*, 432 N.W.2d 274, 278 (S.D. 1988). *See also Knowles*, 544 N.W.2d at 199–200 (to satisfy state substantive due process review, statute must have a "real and substantial relation" to its stated purpose, and the means of achieving that purpose must not be "unreasonable, arbitrary or capricious").

21. *State v. Munson*, 201 N.W.2d at 125, 127.

22. *See, e.g., Steintruger v. Miller*, 612 N.W.2d 591, 598 (S.D. 2000) ("persons involuntarily committed have a federal constitutionally protected liberty interest to refuse the ad-

the Supreme Court overruled *Roe*, as modified by *Casey*, then the South Dakota Supreme Court is unlikely to recognize abortion as a fundamental liberty interest under art. VI, §2.[23]

Apart from the foregoing, the historical and contemporary treatment of abortion and the rights of the unborn child outside the context of abortion would militate against recognition of an abortion right under the state constitution. South Dakota enacted its first abortion statutes in 1877, twelve years *before* the 1889 Constitution was adopted and thirteen years before South Dakota was admitted as a State.[24] One statute prohibited abortion upon a pregnant woman at any stage of her pregnancy except when the procedure was necessary "to preserve her life...."[25] This prohibition remained on the books until after *Roe v. Wade* was decided,[26] and, as previously noted, was upheld in a pre-*Roe* decision of the state supreme court.[27] Another statute prohibited a woman from soliciting an abortion or allowing an abortion to be performed upon her

---

ministration of psychotropic drugs"); *People in Interest of P.B.*, 371 N.W.2d 366, 372 (S.D. 1985) ("[p]arents have a fundamental liberty interest in the care, custody, and management of their children"); *Matter of Adoption of Bellows*, 366 N.W.2d 848, 851 (S.D. 1985) (same); *People in Interest of S.L.H.*, 342 N.W.2d 672, 677 (S.D. 1983) (same). None of the foregoing cases cited art. VI, §2, of the South Dakota Constitution, all of which were based on Supreme Court precedent. To the extent that the South Dakota Supreme Court recognizes the same fundamental rights under the *state* due process guarantee as the Supreme Court does under the *federal* due process guarantee, abortion would not qualify as a "fundamental" right. Although the Supreme Court characterized the right to choose abortion as "fundamental" in *Roe*, 410 U.S. at 152–53, it tacitly abandoned that characterization in *Casey*, 505 U.S. at 869–79 (Joint Op. of O'Connor, Kennedy and Souter, JJ., replacing *Roe's* "strict scrutiny" standard of review with the more relaxed "undue burden" standard, allowing for a broader measure of abortion regulation).

23. This conclusion is reinforced by the state supreme court's statement that counsel seeking recognition of a new state constitutional right "must demonstrate that the text, history, or purpose of the South Dakota constitutional provision [in question] supports a different interpretation from the corresponding federal provision." *State v. Kottman*, 707 N.W.2d 114, 120 (S.D. 2005) (citation and internal quotation marks omitted).

24. Act of Feb. 17, 1877, §337, *codified at* DAKOTA (TERR.) PENAL CODE §337 (1877).

25. *Id.* Another provision of the Penal Code raised the penalty to manslaughter in the first degree if the procedure resulted in the death of either the woman or a "quick child" with which she was pregnant. *Id.* §252.

26. DAKOTA (TERR.) PENAL CODE §337 (1877), *recodified at* DAKOTA (TERR.) COMPILED LAWS §6538 (1887), *recodified at* S.D. REV. PENAL CODE §342 (1903), *recodified at* S.D. REV. CODE §4116 (1919), *recodified at* S.D. CODE §13.3101 (1939), *recodified at* S.D. COMPILED LAWS §22-17-1 (1967), *repealed by* 1973 S.D. Laws 206, 209 ch. 146, §15; 1976 S.D. Laws 227, 257, ch. 158, §17-1; 1977 S.D. Laws 258, 282, ch. 189, §126.

27. *See* n. 7, *supra*.

(subject to the same exception), which also remained on the books until after *Roe* was decided.[28]

The South Dakota Legislature has found "that all abortions, whether surgically or chemically induced, terminate the life of a whole, separate, unique, living human being."[29] Consistent with that finding, and the public policy to favor childbirth over abortion, South Dakota has enacted a comprehensive scheme of abortion regulation.[30]

South Dakota has recognized the rights of unborn children in a variety of contexts outside of abortion, including criminal law, tort law, health care law and property law. Under the criminal code, the killing of an unborn child, other than in an abortion, may be prosecuted as a homicide.[31] So, too, non-lethal injuries inflicted upon an unborn child may be prosecuted as assault, aggravated assault or vehicular battery.[32] And a woman convicted of a capital offense may not be executed while she is pregnant.[33]

In tort law, a statutory cause of action for wrongful death may be brought on behalf of an unborn child without regard to the stage of pregnancy when the injuries causing death were inflicted.[34] A common law action for (non-lethal) prenatal injuries may be brought without regard to the stage of pregnancy when the injuries were inflicted.[35] And South Dakota has banned wrongful conception, wrongful birth and wrongful life causes of action.[36]

---

28. DAKOTA (TERR.) PENAL CODE § 338 (1877), *recodified at* DAKOTA (TERR.) COMPILED LAWS § 6539 (1887), *recodified at* S.D. REV. PENAL CODE § 343 (1903), *recodified at* S.D. REV. CODE § 4117 (1919), *recodified at* S.D. CODE § 13.3102 (1939), *recodified at* S.D. COMPILED LAWS § 22-17-2 (1967), *repealed by* 1973 S.D. Laws 206, 209 ch. 146, § 15; 1976 S.D. Laws 227, 257, ch. 158, § 17-1; 1977 S.D. Laws 258, 282, ch. 189, § 126. No prosecutions were reported under this statute.

29. S.D. CODIFIED LAWS § 34-23A-1.2 (Supp. 2006).

30. *Id.* § 34-23A-10.1 (Supp. 2006) (mandating informed consent and a twenty-four hour waiting period); §§ 34-23A-7, 34-23A-7.1 (Supp. 2006) (requiring parental notice and a forty-eight hour waiting period); §§ 34-23A-11 through 34-23A-14 (2004) (recognizing individual and institutional rights of conscience); § 28-6-4.5 (2005) (restricting public funding of abortion for indigent women).

31. *Id.* § 22-16-1 *et seq.* (2006) (homicide); § 22-17-6 (2006) (intentional killing of a human fetus) (2006).

32. *Id.* §§ 22-18-1.2 (simple assault), 22-18-1.3 (aggravated assault), 22-18-36 (vehicular battery (2006).

33. *Id.* §§ 23A-27A-27 through 23A-27A-30 (2004).

34. *Wiersma v. Maple Leaf Farms*, 543 N.W.2d at 789–92, interpreting S.D. CODIFIED LAWS. § 21-5-1 (2004).

35. *Id.* at 792 (by implication).

36. S.D. CODIFIED LAWS § 21-55-1 *et seq.* (2004). A "wrongful conception" cause of action alleges that as the result of a physician's negligence (*e.g.*, an improperly performed sterilization), a woman conceived who had not intended to conceive. A "wrongful birth" cause

Under South Dakota's health care statutes, a living will may not direct the withholding or withdrawal of life-sustaining treatment or artificially administered nutrition and hydration from a pregnant woman "unless, to a reasonable degree of medical certainty, ... such procedures will not maintain the woman in such a way as to permit the continuing development and live birth of the unborn child or will be physically harmful to the woman or prolong severe pain which cannot be alleviated by medication."[37] Durable powers of attorney for health care are subject to the same limitation.[38]

In property law, heirs conceived before but born after the death of a person who has not executed a will may inherit from a decedent if they live 120 or more hours (five days) after birth.[39] Subject to certain exceptions, if a testator (a person who has executed a will) fails to provide in his will for any of his children born or adopted after the execution of his will, the omitted child receives a share in the estate equal in value to that which he would have received if the testator had died intestate (or a share equal to that provided to other children in the will).[40] And, for the purpose of inheriting future interests, posthumous children (children conceived before but born after the death of a person who dies without a will) are treated as if living at the death of their parent(s).[41]

A right to abortion cannot be found in the text, structure or history of the South Dakota Constitution. There is no evidence that the framers or ratifiers of the South Dakota Constitution intended to limit the Legislature's authority to prohibit abortion.[42] Such an intent would have been remarkable in light of the contemporaneous and longstanding prohibition of abortion except to save the life of the mother.

---

of action is a claim brought by the parents of a child who is born with a physical or mental disability or disease that could have been discovered before the child's birth by genetic testing, amniocentesis or other medical screening. The gravamen of the action is that, as a result of a physician's failure to inform the parents of the child's disability or disease (or at least of the availability of tests to determine the presence of the disability or disease), they were deprived of the opportunity to abort the child, thus resulting in the birth of a child suffering permanent physical or mental impairment. A "wrongful life" cause of action, on the other hand, is a claim, based on the same facts, brought on behalf of the impaired child.

37. S.D. CODIFIED LAWS. §34-12D-10 (2004).

38. Id. §59-7-2.8 (2004).

39. Id. §29A-2-108 (2004).

40. Id. §29A-2-302.

41. Id. §43-3-14. See also id. §43-3-16.

42. See 1 (SOUTH) DAKOTA CONSTITUTIONAL CONVENTION (1885 Convention) 131, 280, 290–91, 339; 2 SOUTH DAKOTA CONSTITUTIONAL CONVENTION (1889 Convention) 131–34, 144–45, 281, 340–45, 347–64 (Huron, South Dakota 1907). With the exception of art. VI, §26, there was little or no debate on any of the provisions of the Bill of Rights discussed herein.

Equal Protection

Three provisions of the South Dakota Bill of Rights have been interpreted to guarantee equal protection. Article VI, § 1, provides in part that "All men are born equally free and independent...."[43] Article VI, § 18, provides: "No law shall be passed granting to any citizen, class of citizens or corporation, privileges and immunities which upon the same terms shall not equally belong to all citizens or corporations."[44] And art. VI, § 26, provides, in pertinent part, that "[a]ll political power is inherent in the people, and all free government is founded on their authority, and is instituted for their equal protection and benefit...."[45]

Referring to art. VI, § 18, as an "equal protection clause," the South Dakota Supreme Court has held that both § 18 and the Equal Protection Clause of the Fourteenth Amendment "guarantee equal protection of the laws to all persons."[46] And they are given a similar interpretation:

> In both federal and state equal protection analysis, there are three tests to be applied depending upon the nature of the interest involved. First, the strict scrutiny test applies only to fundamental rights or suspect classes. [Citation omitted]. Second, the intermediate or substantial relation test applies to legitimacy and gender. [Citation omitted]. Third, the rational basis test applies to all other classes. [Citation omitted].[47]

---

43. S.D. CONST. art. VI, § 1 (2004).

44. *Id.* art. VI, § 18.

45. *Id.* art. VI, § 26. A fourth provision that has been interpreted to require equality, but which could have no relevance to the abortion issue, is art. VI, § 19, which provides, in part: "Elections shall be free and equal...." S.D. CONST. art. VI, § 19 (2004). The South Dakota Supreme Court has held that the language in art. VI, § 19, that elections "shall be free and equal," and in art. VI, § 26, that "all free government is founded" on the authority of the people and is "instituted for their equal protection and benefit," "are but details or elaborations of the equal protection clause of our Art. VI, Section 1...." *Bailey v. Jones*, 139 N.W.2d 385, 389 (S.D. 1966). In *Bailey*, the court held that the elections of county commissioners must accord with the "one person, one vote" doctrine. Other than *Bailey* and *County of Tripp v. State*, 264 N.W.2d 213, 216 (S.D. 1978) (upholding statute providing for attachment of unorganized county to organized county for administration of governmental and financial affairs), § 26 has not been cited in any decision addressing equal protection issues. One delegate to the 1889 South Dakota Constitutional Convention described § 26 as a "Fourth of July declaration ... to hand down to our children, and our children's children." SOUTH DAKOTA CONSTITUTIONAL CONVENTION, Vol. 2, at 343 (remarks of Delegate Moody).

46. *State v. Krahwinkel*, 656 N.W.2d 451, 460 (S.D. 2002).

47. *Id.* at 460 n. 9. Another term for "intermediate scrutiny" is "heightened scrutiny." The terms are used interchangeably in this section of the analysis.

The strict scrutiny test would not apply to the review of an abortion prohibition under the South Dakota Constitution because, for the reasons set forth
in the first section of this analysis, there is no "fundamental right" to abortion
under the state constitution. Nor would the prohibition of abortion classify
persons on the basis of a "suspect" personal characteristic.

Abortion advocates may argue in the alternative, however, that a statute
prohibiting abortion discriminates against women and should be subject to
the "intermediate or substantial relation test" because only women are capable of becoming pregnant. Under this standard of review, "classifications by
gender must serve important governmental objectives and must be substantially
related to achievement of those objectives."[48] An abortion prohibition would
appear to satisfy this level of scrutiny because the prohibition of abortion would
be "substantially related" to the "important governmental objective" of protecting unborn human life. Nevertheless, the test applicable to gender-based
discrimination (intermediate review) should not apply to an abortion prohibition. Abortion laws do not discriminate on the basis of gender.

First, the United States Supreme Court has reviewed restrictions on abortion funding under a rational basis standard of review, *not* under the heightened scrutiny required of gender-based classifications.[49] Indeed, the Court has
held that "the disfavoring of abortion ... is not *ipso facto* sex discrimination,"
and, citing its decisions in *Harris* and other cases addressing abortion funding,
stated that "the constitutional test applicable to government abortion-funding
restrictions is not the heightened-scrutiny standard that our cases demand for
sex discrimination, ... but the ordinary rationality standard."[50]

---

48. *Craig v. Boren*, 429 U.S. 190, 197 (1976).

49. *Harris v. McRae*, 448 U.S. 297, 321–26 (1980).

50. *Bray v. Alexandria Women's Health Clinic*, 506 U.S. 263, 273 (1993). Several state
supreme courts and individual state supreme court justices have recognized that abortion
regulations and restrictions on abortion funding are not "directed at women as a class" so
much as "abortion as a medical treatment, which, because it involves a potential life, has
no parallel as a treatment method." *Bell v. Low Income Women of Texas*, 95 S.W.3d 253, 258
(Tex. 2002) (upholding funding restrictions) (citing *Harris*, 448 U.S. at 325). *See also Fischer v. Dep't of Public Welfare*, 502 A.2d 114, 125 (Pa. 1985) ("the basis for the distinction
here is not sex, but abortion") (upholding funding restrictions); *Moe v. Secretary of Administration & Finance*, 417 N.E.2d 387, 407 (Mass. 1981) (Hennessey, C.J., dissenting)
(funding restrictions were "directed at abortion as a medical procedure, not women as a
class"); *Right to Choose v. Byrne*, 450 A.2d 925, 950 (N.J. 1982) (O'Hern, J., dissenting)
("[t]he subject of the legislation is not the person of the recipient, but the nature of the
claimed medical service"). Both *Moe* and *Right to Choose* were decided on other grounds.
The dissenting justices were addressing alternative arguments raised by the plaintiffs, but
not reached by the majority opinions.

Second, even assuming that abortion prohibitions and regulations differentiate between men and women on the basis of sex, and therefore, are subject to a heightened standard of judicial review (intermediate scrutiny), the Supreme Court has held that biological differences between men and women may justify different treatment based on those differences. In upholding a statutory rape statute that applied only to males, the Supreme Court noted, "this Court has consistently upheld statutes where the gender classification is not invidious, but rather realistically reflects the fact that the sexes are not similarly situated in certain circumstances."[51] As one federal district court observed: "Abortion statutes are examples of cases in which the sexes are not biologically similarly situated" because only women are capable of becoming pregnant and having abortions.[52]

A statute prohibiting abortion quite obviously can affect only women because only women are capable of becoming pregnant.[53] Unlike laws that use women's ability to become pregnant (or pregnancy itself) to discriminate against them in *other* areas (*e.g.*, employment opportunities), abortion prohibitions cannot fairly be said to involve a distinction between men and women that is a "mere pretext[] designed to erect an invidious discrimination against [women]."[54]

A prohibition of abortion would be reviewed under the "rational basis" test which, for purposes of state equal protection analysis, consists of two parts: "The first part of the test is whether the statute sets up arbitrary classifications among various persons subject to it. The second part of the test is whether there is a rational relationship between the classification and some legitimate legislative purpose."[55] An abortion prohibition would satisfy both parts of this test

First, it would not set up an "arbitrary classification[] among various persons subject to it," but would apply to all persons in the same manner. Second, as the South Dakota Supreme Court has already acknowledged,[56] there would be a rational relationship between the "classification" and the legitimate legislative purpose of preserving unborn human life.

---

51. *Michael M. v. Superior Court*, 450 U.S. 464, 469 (1981).

52. *Jane L. v. Bangerter*, 794 F. Supp. 1537, 1549 (D. Utah 1992).

53. *Geduldig v. Aiello*, 417 U.S. 484, 496 n. 20 (1974) ("[n]ormal pregnancy is an objectively, identifiable physical condition with unique characteristics").

54. *Id.*

55. *State v. Krahwinkel*, 656 N.W.2d at 460 (citations omitted). *See also In re Davis*, 681 N.W.2d 452, 454 (S.D. 2004) (articulating state equal protection test).

56. *State v. Munson*, 201 N.W.2d at 127.

Freedom of Religion

Article VI, §3, of the South Dakota Constitution provides:

> The right to worship God according to the dictates of conscience shall never be infringed. No person shall be denied any civil or political right, privilege or position on account of his religious opinions; but the liberty of conscience hereby secured shall not be so construed as to excuse licentiousness, the invasion of the rights of others, or justify practices inconsistent with the peace or safety of the state.
>
> No person shall be compelled to attend or support any ministry or place of worship against his consent nor shall any preference given be given by law to any religious establishment or mode of worship. No money or property of the state shall be given or appropriated for the benefit of any sectarian or religious society or institution.[57]

In any challenge to South Dakota's "trigger law" (or any other prohibition that South Dakota may hereafter enact), abortion advocates may raise either or both of two arguments under art. VI, §3. First, they may argue that an abortion prohibition interferes with the "liberty of conscience" mandated by the first paragraph of §3 by forbidding a woman from obtaining an abortion that would be allowed by her religious beliefs. Second, they may argue in the alternative (or in addition) that an abortion prohibition gives a "preference" to a "sectarian or religious society or institution" because it reflects sectarian beliefs regarding when human life begins and the sinfulness of abortion. Neither argument would likely succeed.

Apart from school-aid issues, there is relatively little case law interpreting art. VI, §3. The freedom of religion guarantee of art. VI, §3, has been interpreted consistently with the Free Exercise Clause of the First Amendment.[58] In *Northwestern Lutheran Academy*, the South Dakota Supreme Court held that

---

57. S.D. Const. art. VI, §3 (2004).

58. *See Matter of Northwestern Lutheran Academy*, 290 N.W.2d 845, 849–51 (S.D. 1980) (art. VI, §3, and Free Exercise Clause did not excuse teachers in Lutheran school from obligation to pay unemployment compensation tax), *rev'd on other grounds sub nom. St. Martin Lutheran Church v. South Dakota*, 451 U.S. 772 (1981); *State v. Van Daalan*, 11 N.W.2d 523 (S.D. 1943) (Jehovah's Witnesses who were distributing religious literature which was sold on some occasions and given away free of charge on others could not be compelled to pay retail sales tax on such sales of religious literature, and, therefore, could not be convicted of engaging in business as retailers without a permit by the director of taxation and of failing to make sales tax returns as required by law). For a discussion of free exercise claims, *see* Chapter 2, *supra*.

"to demonstrate that legislation conflicts with the Free Exercise Clause, 'it is necessary ... for one to show the coercive effect of the enactment as it operates against him in the practice of his religion.'"[59] A prohibition of abortion would not "coerce" any woman in the practice of her religion because there is no doctrine in any religion *requiring*, as opposed to *permitting*, a pregnant woman to obtain an abortion except in circumstances where her life is in danger, an exception which the law has always recognized.

Moreover, by its express terms, the "liberty of conscience" secured by the first paragraph of §3 "shall not be so construed as to excuse licentiousness, *the invasion of the rights of others*, or justify practices inconsistent with the peace or safety of the state." Given South Dakota's recognition of the rights of the unborn child in a variety of contexts,[60] an abortion could be viewed as an "invasion of the rights of [an]other[]," *i.e.*, the unborn child, and thus not protected by the "liberty of conscience" language of §3.

With respect to the second paragraph of §3, the South Dakota Supreme Court has held that art. VI, §3, and art. VIII, §16,[61] "are not mere reiterations of the Establishment Clause of the United States Constitution but are more restrictive as prohibiting aid 'in every form.'"[62] That the second paragraph of §3, in conjunction with art. VIII, §16, is more restrictive than the Establishment Clause with respect to financial aid to "any sectarian or religious society or institution" has no bearing on the constitutionality of a prohibition of abortion. A challenge to an abortion prohibition brought under the second paragraph of §3 more likely would be based on the argument that it gives a "preference" to a "religious establishment" by embodying a particular religion's

---

59. 290 N.W.2d at 849 (quoting *School District of Abington v. Schempp*, 374 U.S. 202, 223 (1963)). Of course, a law that singles out religious practices for regulation would present an entirely different question. *See Church of the Lukumi Babalu Aye, Inc. v. City of Hialeah*, 508 U.S. 520 (1993) (a law that is aimed at specific religious practices must satisfy the "strict scrutiny" standard of judicial review).

60. See the discussion in the section addressing inherent rights and due process of law, *supra*.

61. "No appropriation of lands, money or other property or credits to aid any sectarian school shall ever be made by the state, or any county or municipality within the state, nor shall the state or any county or municipality within the state accept any grant, conveyance, gift or bequest of lands, money other property to be used for sectarian purposes, and no sectarian instruction shall be allowed in any school or institution aided or supported by the state." S.D. CONST. art. VIII, §16 (2004).

62. *McDonald v. School Board of Yankton Independent School District No. 1 of Yankton, South Dakota*, 246 N.W.2d 93, 98 (S.D. 1976) (quoting *Synod of Dakota v. State*, 50 N.W. 632, 635 (S.D. 1891)). In *McDonald*, the court struck down a statute authorizing the loaning of textbooks to private, including parochial, schools.

view of the "sinfulness of abortion and the time at which life commences."[63] Such an argument probably would not prevail.

In *Harris v. McRae*, the Supreme Court rejected an Establishment Clause challenge to the constitutionality of the Hyde Amendment, which restricts federal funding of abortion. The Court held that the Establishment Clause is not violated merely because "a statute 'happens to coincide or harmonize with the tenets of some or all religions.' "[64] Noting that the Hyde Amendment "is as much a reflection of 'traditionalist' values toward abortion, as it is an embodiment of the views of any particular religion," the Court held that "the fact that the funding restrictions in the Hyde Amendment may coincide with the religious tenets of the Roman Catholic Church does not, without more, contravene the Establishment Clause."[65] There is no indication in the case law interpreting art. VI, §3, that the South Dakota Supreme Court would give the language prohibiting a "preference" to "any religious establishment" a different reading than the Supreme Court has given to the Establishment Clause. And, it must be noted, the state supreme court has never invalidated a criminal law on this basis.

Remedy by Due Course of Law

Article VI, §20, of the South Dakota Constitution provides: "All courts shall be open, and every man for an injury done him in his property, person or reputation, shall have remedy by due course of law, and right and justice, administered without denial or delay."[66] Abortion advocates might argue that a statute prohibiting abortion interferes with a woman's control over her own body, and that such interference constitutes an "injury" to her "person," as those terms are used in §20, for which there must be a "remedy by due course of law." That "remedy," in turn, would be invalidation of the statute. This argument assumes that art. VI, §20, confers substantive rights. The case law is clear, however, that it does not.

Article VI, §20, was meant to allow

> unhindered access to the courthouse by a person who had a valid cause
> of action based on existing statute or the common law, timely and

---

63. *Harris v. McRae*, 448 U.S. at 319.

64. *Id.* (citation omitted).

65. *Id.* at 319–20. It should be added that no state or federal court has accepted an Establishment Clause argument against an abortion statute, and two courts have rejected such arguments brought under state constitutions. *See Right to Choose v. Byrne*, 450 A.2d 923, 938–39 (N.J. 1982); *Jane L. v. Bangerter*, 794 F. Supp. 1528, 1534–35 (D. Utah 1992) (interpreting Utah law).

66. S.D. Const. art. VI, §20 (2004).

properly brought, who then would be allowed to present their [*sic*] case to a human fact finder. In other words, under those conditions, a litigant was guaranteed its day in court.[67]

"While a litigant is guaranteed his day in court, such is only the case for legally cognizable causes of actions."[68] There is "no basis for a claim that Art. VI, sec. 20 could by itself become a sword to create a cause of action or become a shield to prohibit statutorily recognized barriers to recovery...."[69] Because §20 does not, by its own terms, "create a cause of action," it could not be relied upon as a source of a right to abortion. A litigant "cannot use the 'open courts' provision to override an otherwise valid act of the Legislature."[70]

Fundamental Principles

Article VI, §27, of the South Dakota Constitution provides: "The blessings of a free government an only be maintained by a firm adherence to justice, moderation, temperance, frugality and virtue and by frequent recurrence to fundamental principles."[71] Abortion advocates might argue that a right to abortion must be regarded as a "fundamental principle" under §27. Such an argument is not likely to gain much traction, however. Section 27 urges "frequent recurrence to fundamental principles." By its own terms, however, the provision does not create or establish any "fundamental principles." Section 27 has seldom been cited by the South Dakota Supreme Court,[72] and has never been relied upon as a provision that confers substantive rights. It would not be a plausible source of an abortion right under the South Dakota Constitution.

Conclusion

Based on the foregoing analysis, an argument that the South Dakota Constitution protects a right to abortion that is separate from, and independent of, the right to abortion recognized in *Roe v. Wade* would not likely succeed. That,

---

67. *Wegleitner v. Sattler*, 582 N.W.2d 688, 698 (S.D. 1998).

68. *Hancock v. Western South Dakota Juvenile Services Center*, 647 N.W.2d 722, 725 (S.D. 2002). *See also Behrns v. Burke*, 229 N.W.2d 86, 88 (S.D. 1975) (same).

69. *Wegleitner*, 582 N.W.2d at 698.

70. *Hancock*, 647 N.W.2d at 725.

71. S.D. Const. art. VI, §27 (2004).

72. *See Matter of Clark*, 340 N.W.2d 189, 192 (S.D. 1983); *State ex rel. Mills v. Wilder*, 42 N.W.2d 891, 895 (S.D. 1950).

in turn, suggests that if *Roe*, as modified by *Casey*, is ultimately overruled, the State of South Dakota could enforce its "trigger" statute *prohibiting* abortion. Moreover, nothing in the South Dakota Constitution precludes from *regulating* abortion within federal constitutional limits in the meantime.

CHAPTER 45

TENNESSEE

Summary

As the result of a pair of decisions by the Tennessee Supreme Court interpreting the Tennessee Constitution, the State of Tennessee could not recognize unborn children as "persons" or prohibit any abortion before viability, or any abortion after viability that would be necessary to preserve the pregnant woman's life or health, even if *Roe v. Wade*,[1] as modified by *Planned Parenthood of Southeastern Pennsylvania v. Casey*,[2] were overruled, unless the state constitution is amended to overturn those decisions (or those decisions are overruled). Moreover, by virtue of those same decisions, Tennessee has little or no authority to regulate abortion within current federal constitutional limits.

Analysis

The pre-*Roe* abortion statutes prohibited performance of an abortion unless the procedure was necessary "to preserve the life of the mother."[3] The substantive provisions of these statutes were repealed with the enactment of post-*Roe* legislation.[4] Although it is not known at this time whether the Tennessee Legislature would consider legislation prohibiting abortion if *Roe*, as modified by *Casey*, were overruled, it is virtually certain that the Tennessee Supreme Court would declare unconstitutional any statute prohibiting abortion, at least before viability. That is apparent from review of state supreme court decisions holding that legal personhood is not conferred until birth and recognizing a right to abortion under the state constitution.

---

1. 410 U.S. 113 (1973).
2. 505 U.S. 833 (1992).
3. Tenn. Code Ann. §§ 39-301, 39-302 (1956).
4. 1973 Tenn. Pub. Acts 901 *et seq.*, ch. 235, §§ 1, 3.

In *Davis v. Davis*,[5] the Tennessee Supreme Court considered the novel issue of how cryogenically-preserved "pre-embryos" should be disposed of when the donors of the genetic material divorced and disagreed as to what should done with the pre-embryos. A "pre-embryo," according to the court, is the "currently accepted [medical and scientific] term" to describe a zygote from immediately after cell division begins until fourteen days after fertilization.[6] The supreme court agreed with the court of appeals that, "even after viability, [fetuses] are not given legal status [under state law] equivalent to that of a person already born."[7] Nor do pre-embryos, embryos or fetuses "enjoy protection under federal law."[8] Pre-embryos do not have the legal status of "persons" or any "legally cognizable interests separate from those of their progenitors."[9] The court concluded that pre-embryos are neither "persons," nor "property," but "occupy an interim category that entitles them to special respect because of their potential for human life."[10]

The Davises did not provide by contract or otherwise for the disposition of their pre-embryos in the event of their divorce (or other circumstances in which they would disagree about their disposition). Nor was there any statutory or common law authority to guide state courts in resolving disputes over the proper disposition of pre-embryos.[11] The state supreme court, therefore, turned to a discussion of the parties' respective rights of "procreational autonomy."[12] The court recognized that a right of privacy, grounded in the concept of liberty, exists not only under the federal constitution, but also the state constitution.[13] In support of the latter holding, the court cited §§ 1, 2, 3, 7, 8, 19 and 27 of the Tennessee Declaration of Rights.[14]

Section 1 provides:

---

5. 842 S.W.2d 588 (Tenn. 1992).

6. *Id.* at 593.

7. *Id.* at 594–95 (citing *Hamby v. McDaniel*, 559 S.W.2d 774 (Tenn. 1977) (denying recovery for wrongful death of a viable fetus that is not first born alive), and statutes decriminalizing abortion and incorporating the trimester approach to abortion regulation).

8. *Id.* at 595 (citing *Roe*, 410 U.S. at 162 ("the unborn have never been recognized in the law as persons in the whole sense")).

9. *Id.*

10. *Id.* at 597.

11. *Id.* at 590.

12. *Id.* at 598–603.

13. *Id.* at 598.

14. *Id.* at 599–600. Curiously, the majority overlooked its own decision in *Hawk v. Hawk*, 855 S.W.2d 573 (Tenn. 1993), in which the court held that art. I, §8, is the only constitutional provision in which a right of privacy may be textually grounded. *Id.* at 579.

That all power is inherent in the people, and all free governments are founded on their authority, and instituted for their peace, safety, and happiness; for the advancement of those ends they have at all times, an unalienable and indefeasible right to alter, reform or abolish the government in such manner as they may think proper.[15]

Section 2 provides: "That government being instituted for the common benefit, the doctrine of non-resistance against arbitrary power and oppression is absurd, slavish, and destructive of the good and happiness of mankind."[16]

Section 3 guarantees freedom of worship ("no human authority can, in any case whatever, control or interfere with the rights of conscience").[17] Section 7 prohibits unreasonable searches and seizures ("the people shall be secure in their persons, houses, papers and possessions, from unreasonable searches and seizures").[18] Section 8 provides: "That no man shall be taken or imprisoned, or disseized of his freehold, liberties or privileges, or outlawed, or exiled, or in any manner destroyed or deprived of his life, liberty or property, but by the judgment of his peers or the law of the land."[19] Section 19 guarantees freedom of speech and press (the "free communication of thoughts and opinions, is one of the invaluable rights of man, and every citizen may freely speak, write and print on any subject, being responsible for the abuse of that liberty")[20] And §27 regulates the quartering of soldiers ("no soldier shall, in time of peace, be quartered in any house without the consent of the owner").[21]

The drafters of the Tennessee Constitution of 1796 "foresaw the need to protect individuals from unwarranted governmental intrusion into matters ... involving intimate questions of personal and family concern."[22] Based on the language and development of the state constitution, the *Davis* court concluded that "there is a right of individual privacy guaranteed under and protected by the liberty clauses of the Tennessee Declaration of Rights."[23] Moreover, "the right of procreation is a vital part of an individual's right to privacy."[24] The

---

15. TENN. CONST. art. I, §1 (1995).
16. *Id.* §2.
17. *Id.* §3.
18. *Id.* §7.
19. *Id.* §8.
20. *Id.* §19.
21. *Id.* §27.
22. *Davis*, 842 S.W.2d at 600.
23. *Id.*
24. *Id.*

right of procreational autonomy, which the court held to be "inherent in our most basic concepts of liberty,"[25] "is composed of two rights of equal significance-the right to procreate and the right to avoid procreation."[26] Significantly, the "decisional authority" to exercise these rights "rests in the gamete-providers alone, at least to the extent that their decisions have an impact upon their individual reproductive status."[27] In other words, "no other person or entity has an interest sufficient to permit interference with the gamete-providers' decision to continue or terminate the IVF [*in vitro* fertilization] process, because no one else bears the consequences of these decisions in the way that the gamete-providers do."[28] Finally, "the state's interest in potential human life is insufficient to justify an infringement on the gamete-providers' procreational autonomy."[29]

After balancing the parties' interests, the court determined that the husband's interest in avoiding parenthood outweighed his ex-wife's interest in donating the pre-embryos to another couple.[30] In the last part of its opinion, the court announced the general principles that should apply in resolving disputes regarding the disposition of pre-embryos produced by *in vitro* fertilization:

> [D]isputes involving the disposition of pre-embryos produced by *in vitro* fertilization should be resolved, first by looking to the preference of the progenitors. If their wishes cannot be ascertained, or if there is [a] dispute, then their prior agreement concerning disposition should be carried out. If no prior agreement exists, then the relative interests of the parties in using or not using the pre-embryos must be weighed. Ordinarily, the party wishing to avoid procreation should prevail, assuming that the other party has a reasonable possibility of achieving parenthood by means other than use of the pre-embryos in question. If no other reasonable alternatives exist, then the argument in favor of using the preembryos to achieve pregnancy should be considered. However, if the party seeking control of the preembryos intends merely to donate them to another couple, the objecting party obviously has the greater interest and should prevail.[31]

---

25. *Id.* at 601.
26. *Id.*
27. *Id.* at 602.
28. *Id.*
29. *Id.*
30. *Id.* at 603–04.
31. *Id.* at 604.

The Tennessee Supreme Court's decision in *Davis v. Davis* did not address the issue of abortion, as such. Nevertheless, the court's recognition of a state right of privacy which encompasses "procreational autonomy" was to be of critical significance when the court considered the State's authority to regulate abortion. In *Planned Parenthood of Middle Tennessee v. Sundquist,*[32] the state supreme court entertained a challenge to state statutes requiring second-trimester abortions to be performed in hospitals, mandating informed consent and physician-only counseling, imposing a two-day waiting period and restricting medical emergency abortions to those necessary to save the life of the pregnant woman.[33] A majority of the court held that the statutes violated the implied right of privacy guaranteed by the state constitution.[34]

In *Planned Parenthood of Middle Tennessee*, the court "reaffirm[ed] the holding [in *Davis*] that the right of privacy, including the right of procreational autonomy, arises from specific provisions of the state constitution...."[35] After reviewing various contexts in which state and federal privacy rights have been recognized, the court held that "a woman's right to obtain a legal termination of her pregnancy is sufficiently similar in character to those personal and private decisions and activities identified in state and federal precedent to implicate a cognizable privacy interest."[36] Although not all privacy interests rise to the level of a fundamental right, "[t]he concept of ordered liberty embodied in our constitution requires our finding that a woman's right to legally terminate her pregnancy is fundamental."[37]

> The provisions of the Tennessee Constitution imply protection of an individual's right to make inherently personal decisions, and to act on those decisions, without government interference. A woman's termination of her pregnancy is just such an inherently intimate and per-

---

32. 38 S.W.3d 1 (Tenn. 2000).

33. Tenn. Code. Ann. §§ 39-15-201(c)(2) (hospitalization requirement); 39-15-202(b)(1)-(3), (b)(5)-(c) (requiring attending physician to provide informed consent); 39-15-202 (d)(1) (mandating two-day waiting period); 39-15-202(d)(3), -(g) (medical emergency exception) (2006). The State did not defend the constitutionality of the residency requirement, Tenn. Code Ann. § 39-15-201(d), which was struck down by the trial court, and did not appeal the holdings of the trial court and the court of appeals declaring unconstitutional a provision in the informed consent law requiring physicians to inform their patients that "abortion in a considerable number of cases constitutes a major surgical procedure," *id.* § 39-15-202(b)(4).

34. *Planned Parenthood of Middle Tennessee*, 38 S.W.3d at 18–25.

35. *Id.* at 5, n. 3 (citing Tenn. Const. art I, §§ 1, 2, 3, 7, 8, 19 and 27).

36. *Id.* at 11.

37. *Id.* at 15.

sonal enterprise. This privacy interest is closely aligned with matters of marriage, child rearing, and other procreational interests that have been previously held to be fundamental. To distinguish it as some-how non-fundamental would require this Court to ignore the obvious corollary.[38]

Having decided that "a woman's right to legally terminate her pregnancy is fundamental," the court held that "a state regulation which interferes with that right" cannot be upheld as constitutional unless it withstands "strict scrutiny."[39] Under that standard, "it is the State's burden to show that the regulation is jus-tified by a compelling state interest and narrowly tailored to achieve that interest."[40] The court recognized two compelling interests: First, "the State ... has a com-pelling interest in maternal health from the beginning of pregnancy."[41] Sec-ond, "the State's interest in potential life becomes compelling at viability."[42]

The court struck down the second-trimester hospitalization requirement be-cause it was not "narrowly tailored to further [the compelling] state interest" in maternal health.[43] This holding was based on evidence that "abortions can be performed safely outside the hospital setting through at least the first eighteen weeks of pregnancy."[44] The court also struck down the informed consent re-quirement, the two-day waiting period requirement and the medical emergency exceptions to each of those requirements.[45] With respect to informed consent, the court determined that the requirement that the statutorily mandated coun-seling be provided in person by a physician "is not narrowly tailored to accom-plish" the State's interest in ensuring that a woman contemplating an abortion be informed "in accordance with the recognized standard of acceptable profes-sional practice."[46] "Because it is not necessary that the physician personally im-part the required information to the woman in order for informed consent to occur, the physician-only counseling requirement is not narrowly tailored to further a compelling state interest and will not be upheld."[47]

---

38. *Id.*
39. *Id.*
40. *Id.* at 18.
41. *Id.* at 17.
42. *Id.*
43. *Id.* at 18.
44. *Id.*
45. *Id.* at 21–25.
46. *Id.* at 21 (internal quotation marks omitted).
47. *Id.* at 22. Although the court recognized that some of the provisions of the informed consent statute were narrowly tailored to further the State's compelling interest in mater-

With respect to the waiting period, the court cited evidence purporting to show that most women have seriously reflected upon their decision before making an appointment to have an abortion, that few women have reported any benefit from being required to wait before undergoing an abortion and that "patient mortality rates for abortions increase as the length of pregnancy increases."[48] The court also expressed the view that the mandatory waiting period, by requiring two trips to a physician, may be problematic for women who work, poor women, women who are in abusive relationships and women who have to travel great distances to an abortion clinic.[49] Although arguing that "the waiting period requirement furthers its interest in potential life and ... protects maternal health by ensuring that the woman has adequate time to reflect on her decision after hearing the statutorily prescribed information," the State did not argue that the provision is "narrowly tailored to further a compelling state interest...."[50] Without discussing the State's interest in "potential life," the court concluded that "the State has simply failed to carry its burden to show that the two-day waiting period requirement ... is narrowly tailored to further its compelling interest in maternal health."[51] Accordingly, the requirement was held unconstitutional.[52]

With respect to the medical emergency exceptions, the court found that they were not "narrowly tailored to advance the State's interests in maternal health" and, therefore, were unconstitutional, because "they do not contain adequate provisions that will permit immediate abortions necessary to protect a woman's health."[53]

In the penultimate paragraph of the majority opinion, the court stated:

> [A] woman's right to terminate her pregnancy is a vital part of the right to privacy guaranteed by the Tennessee Constitution. That right is inherent in the concept of ordered liberty embodied in the Tennessee Constitution and is similar to other privacy interests that have previously been held to be fundamental. We therefore conclude that this

---

nal health, it declined to "elide" the unconstitutional provisions because of its conclusion that "the legislature would not have enacted the informed consent provisions in [the] absence of the physician-only counseling requirement...." *Id.* at 22 & n. 11.

48. *Id.* at 23–24.
49. *Id.* at 24.
50. *Id.* at 22.
51. *Id.* at 24.
52. *Id.*
53. *Id.*

specific privacy interest is fundamental. Therefore, the statutory provisions regulating abortion must be subject to strict scrutiny analysis.[54]

Under that analysis, abortion statutes will not be upheld unless they are "narrowly tailored to further compelling state interests."[55]

As Justice Barker observed in his scholarly dissent, "the effect of the Court's holding today is to remove from the people all power, except by constitutional amendment, to enact reasonable regulations of abortion."[56] Although the State has a compelling interest in maternal health throughout pregnancy, that interest may be advanced only by "narrowly tailored" regulations. With the possible exception of "narrowly tailored" clinic regulations, it is questionable whether any regulations could meet this rigorous standard.[57] More significantly, by determining that the State's interest in "potential life" only becomes compelling at viability,[58] the opinion would preclude the State of Tennessee from prohibiting abortion, at least before viability,[59] even if *Roe*, as modified by *Casey*, were overruled. Moreover, the State may not regulate abortion within current federal constitutional limits unless the regulation in question passes the "strict scrutiny" standard of judicial review, which is strict in theory and usually fatal in application.

Conclusion

Because of the Tennessee Supreme Court's decisions in *Davis v. Davis* and *Planned Parenthood of Middle Tennessee v. Sundquist*, the State of Tennessee

---

54. *Id.* at 25.

55. *Id.*

56. *Id.* at 39 (Barker, J., dissenting).

57. *See, e.g.*, TENN. CODE ANN. § 37-10-301 *et seq.* (2005 & Supp. 2006) (mandating parental consent). The Tennessee Supreme Court has not yet ruled on the constitutionality of the parental consent statute.

58. *Id.* at 17.

59. The Supreme Court has not yet decided whether a statute prohibiting post-viability abortions must make exceptions for mental, as well as physical, health. *See Voinovich v. Women's Medical Professional Corporation*, 523 U.S. 1036, 1039 (1998) (Thomas, J., dissenting from denial of *certiorari*) (noting that this issue was not addressed in *Doe v. Bolton*, 410 U.S. 179 (1973), the companion case to *Roe v. Wade*). As a result, it is not known whether, as a matter of *state* constitutional law, the Tennessee Supreme Court would require a post-viability statute to contain a mental health exception. Under current state law, a post-viability abortion may be performed if the procedure is necessary to preserve the pregnant woman's life or health. TENN. CODE ANN. § 39-15-201(c)(3) (2006). The statute does not define the scope of the health exception.

could not prohibit abortion, at least before viability, even if *Roe*, as modified by *Casey*, were overruled. Moreover, the State has little or no authority to regulate abortion within current federal constitutional limits.

CHAPTER 46

TEXAS

Summary

The Texas Supreme Court has not yet decided whether the Texas Constitution protects a right to abortion separate from, and independent of, the right to abortion recognized under the United States Constitution.[1] A careful examination of the state constitution, in light of its history and interpretation, as well as other relevant legal sources, however, suggests that the state supreme court probably would not recognize a state constitutional right to abortion. Thus, if *Roe v. Wade*,[2] as modified by *Planned Parenthood of Southeastern Pennsylvania v. Casey*,[3] were overruled, Texas could enforce its pre-*Roe* abortion statutes (or enact new ones if the pre-*Roe* statues have been repealed by implication). Moreover, nothing in the state constitution, properly understood, precludes the State from enacting and enforcing reasonable measures regulating abortion within current federal constitutional limits.

Analysis

The pre-*Roe* abortion statutes prohibited performance of an abortion upon a pregnant woman unless the procedure was undertaken "for the purpose of saving [her] life."[4] These statutes were declared unconstitutional

---

1. *See Bell v. Low Income Women of Texas*, 95 S.W.3d 253, 265 (Tex. 2002) (upholding restrictions on public funding of abortion for indigent women).

2. 410 U.S. 113 (1973).

3. 505 U.S. 833 (1992).

4. TEX. PENAL CODE ANN. arts. 1191, 1192, 1193, 1194, 1196 (West 1961), *transferred to* TEX. REV. CIV. STAT. ANN. arts. 4512.1, 4512.2, 4512.3, 4512.4, 4512.6 (West 1976). *See* Tex. Acts 1973, ch. 399, §5 & Disp. Table at 996e.

(on federal, not state, grounds) in *Roe v. Wade*,[5] but have not been repealed.[6]

Based upon arguments that have been raised in Texas and other States with similar constitutional provisions, possible sources for an asserted abortion right could include provisions of the Bill of Rights guaranteeing equal rights (art. I, §3), equality under the law (§3a), freedom of worship (§6), a remedy by due course of law (§13) and due course of the law of the land (§19); recognizing inherent political power in the people (§2); and declaring that the rights set forth in art. I shall remain inviolate (§29).[7] The analysis that follows addresses each of these provisions.

Inherent Political Power

Article I, §2, of the Texas Constitution provides:

> All political power is inherent in the people, and all free governments are founded on their authority, and instituted for their benefit. The faith of the people of Texas stands pledged to the preservation of a republican form of government, and, subject to this limitation only, they have at all times the inalienable right to alter, reform or abolish their government in such manner as they may think expedient."[8]

In any state constitutional challenge to the pre-*Roe* Texas abortion statutes (or any other statutes prohibiting abortion Texas may enact), abortion advocates might argue that the statutes interfere with the "inherent" political power

---

5. Prior to *Roe*, the Texas Court of Criminal Appeals rejected a constitutional challenge to the statutes. *Thompson v. State*, 493 S.W.2d 913 (Tex. Crim. App. 1971), *vacated and remanded*, 410 U.S. 950 (1973), *on remand*, 493 S.W.2d 793 (Tex. Crim. App. 1973). The original opinion in *Thompson* is discussed later in this analysis, *intra*.

6. Although the pre-*Roe* statutes have not been reprinted in the current volumes of either the Texas Revised Civil Statutes Annotated or the Texas Penal Code, they have not been expressly repealed. In *McCorvey v. Hill*, 385 F.3d 846 (5th Cir. 2004), however, the Fifth Circuit Court of Appeals held that the statutes were repealed by implication with the enactment of significant post-*Roe* legislation regulating the practice of abortion. That holding, however, is not binding upon a state court. Even assuming that the pre-*Roe* statutes have been repealed, the Texas Legislature may consider enacting new legislation prohibiting abortion, in which case the analysis set forth in the text would still apply.

7. Two other more unlikely sources of an abortion right under the Texas Constitution-art. I, §8 (guaranteeing freedom of speech) and §9 (prohibiting unreasonable searches and seizures)-are discussed generally in Chapter 3, *supra*.

8. TEX. CONST. art. I, §2 (Vernon 2007).

of the people because they do not "benefit" them. Given the purpose of §2, this argument would not likely prevail.

By virtue of §2, the people "expressly ... reserve to themselves the 'inalienable right' and authority to alter, change, or abolish such ordained form of government."[9] As a consequence, "not only was there no power granted to the Legislature to in any measure change the form of government, but it is expressly withheld and retained by the people in themselves exclusively."[10]

The purpose of §2 is to secure to the people themselves, through the amendment process, the right to decide whether, how and to what extent the organic instrument of government should be changed. Section 2, thus, is not a source of substantive rights. Rather, it recognizes the people as the ultimate source of authority in a republican form of government. As such, it could not serve as a basis for asserting a right to abortion. Whether a given law "benefits" the people, within the meaning of art. I, §2, presents a political question for the legislature to decide, not a constitutional question for the judiciary.

Equal Rights

Article I, §3, of the Texas Constitution provides: "All free men, when they form a social compact, have equal rights, and no man, or set of men, is entitled to exclusive public emoluments, or privileges, but in consideration of public services."[11] The Texas Supreme Court has repeatedly held that "the federal analytical approach applies to equal protection challenges under [§3 of] the Texas Constitution."[12] Given this congruity of interpretation, if the United States Supreme Court does not recognize a right to abortion under the Equal Protection Clause, then the Texas Supreme Court would not recognize a corresponding right under §3, either.[13]

---

9. *Ex parte Farnsworth*, 135 S.W. 535, 537 (Tex. Crim. App. 1911). This authority is limited by the guarantee in §2 of "a republican form of government." *Ramsey v. Dunlop*, 205 S.W.2d 979, 983 (Tex. 1947).

10. *Farnsworth*, 135 S.W. at 537.

11. Tex. Const. art. I, §3 (Vernon 2007). Although §3 does not use the words "equal protection," the Texas Supreme Court has "typically referred to the guarantee of equal rights afforded by article I, section 3 by that term." *Bell v. Low Income Women of Texas*, 95 S.W.3d at 257 n. 4 (citing cases).

12. *Bell*, 95 S.W.3d at 266 (citing *Rose v. Doctors Hospital*, 801 S.W.2d 841, 846 (Tex. 1990) ("Texas cases echo federal standards when determining whether a statute violates equal protection"); and *Richards v. League of United Latin American Citizens*, 868 S.W.2d 306, 310–11 (Tex. 1993)).

13. Whether an argument could be raised that an abortion prohibition constitutes sex discrimination is discussed in the following section of this analysis.

Equality under the Law

Article I, §3a of the Texas Constitution provides, in relevant part: "Equality under the law shall not be denied or abridged because of sex, race, color, creed, or national origin."[14] In any challenge to the pre-*Roe* Texas abortion statutes (or any other statutes prohibiting abortion Texas may enact) abortion advocates may argue that the prohibition of abortion discriminates against women in violation of art. I, §3a, because only women can become pregnant. Such an argument would not likely succeed, however.

The Texas Supreme Court follows a three-step process for evaluating claims brought under the state equal rights amendment (art. I, §3a). The court first decides whether equality under the law has been denied. Second, if equality under the law has been denied, then the state equal rights amendment requires the court to determine whether equality has been denied *because* of a person's membership in a class protected by the amendment. Third, if the court concludes that equality has been denied because of a person's membership in a protected class, then the challenged statute, ordinance or policy cannot stand unless it is narrowly tailored to serve a compelling governmental interest.[15]

That an abortion prohibition can directly affect only women does not mean that equality under the law has been denied *because* of a woman's sex. As the Texas Supreme Court observed in rejecting a challenge to the public policy of not paying for any abortions for which federal reimbursement was not available under the Hyde Amendment, "[t]he classification is not so much directed at women as a class as it is abortion as a medical treatment, which, because it involves a potential life, has no parallel as a treatment method."[16] For that reason, the court was unable to say that the classification was, by it own terms, "because of sex."[17]

The court also determined that the funding restrictions could not be characterized as "a pretext designed to prefer males over females in the provision of health care...."[18] " ... we do not believe [that] the discouragement of abortion through funding restrictions can, by itself, be considered purposeful discrimination against women as a class.... The biological truism that abortions can only be performed on women does not necessarily mean that governmental

---

14. Tᴇx. Cᴏɴsт. art. I, §3a (Vernon 2007).

15. *Bell*, 95 S.W.3d at 257.

16. *Id.* at 258 (citing *Harris v. McRae*, 448 U.S. 297, 325 (1980) ("[a]bortion is inherently different from other medical procedures, because no other procedure involves the purposeful termination of a potential life")).

17. *Id.*

18. *Id.*

action restricting abortion funding discriminates on the basis of gender."[19] Rather, "those restrictions implement a legitimate governmental purpose to favor childbirth over abortion."[20]

So, too, a statute prohibiting abortion could not be said to discriminate against women "because of sex" in violation of art. I, §3 a. It would be more appropriate to view the prohibition as one "directed at … abortion as a medical treatment.…" In light of the State's interest in protecting unborn human life, the prohibition of abortion could not be regarded as a pretext to discriminate against women in favor of men. For purposes of the state equal rights amendment, therefore, an abortion prohibition would be subject to rational basis review.[21] The prohibition of abortion is rationally related to the State's "legitimate governmental purpose to favor childbirth over abortion." Accordingly, a statute prohibiting abortion would not violate the state equal rights amendment.

Freedom of Worship

Article I, §6, of the Texas Constitution provides, in pertinent part:

> All men have a natural and indefeasible right to worship Almighty God according to the dictates of their own consciences. No man shall be compelled to attend, erect or support any place of worship, or to maintain any ministry against his consent. No human authority ought, in any case whatever, to control or interfere with the rights of conscience in matters of religion, and no preference shall ever be given by law to any religious society or mode of worship.[22]

In any challenge to the pre-*Roe* statutes prohibiting abortion, abortion advocates may raise either or both of two arguments under art. I, §6. First, they may argue that an abortion prohibition interferes with the "rights of conscience" guaranteed by the first and last sentences of §6 by forbidding a woman from obtaining an abortion that would be allowed by her religion. Second, they may argue in the alternative (or in addition) that, in violation of the last sentence of §6, an abortion prohibition gives a "preference" to a "religious society" because it reflects sectarian beliefs regarding when human life begins and the sinfulness of abortion. Neither argument would likely prevail.

---

19. *Id.* at 263.

20. *Id.*

21. *Id.* at 264 (for purposes of art. I, §3a, rational basis review applies to classifications that do not discriminate "because of" sex).

22. Tex. Const. art. I, §6 (Vernon 2007).

Texas courts have not explicitly equated art. I, §6, with the Free Exercise and Establishment Clauses of the First Amendment, but their decisions reflect a close congruence between First Amendment analysis and analysis under §6.[23] This congruence suggests that a challenge to an abortion statute that would not succeed under the Religion Clauses of the First Amendment would not succeed under art. I, §6, either.[24] For the reasons set forth in Chapter 2, *supra*, an abortion statute could not be successfully challenged on First Amendment grounds. Accordingly, a similar challenge under art. I, §6, would not likely be successful.[25]

---

23. *See Scott v. State*, 80 S.W.3d 184, 191 (Tex. App.-Waco 2002, *pet. ref'd*) (art. I, §6, is "comparable" to the Free Exercise Clause); *State v. Corpus Christi People's Baptist Church, Inc.*, 683 S.W.2d 692 (Tex. 1985) (requiring church operated child care facilities to be licensed and regulated does not violate the religion clauses of either the state or federal constitution); *Matter of Marriage of Knighton*, 723 S.W.2d 274, 278 (Tex. App.-Amarillo 1987, *no writ*) ("the State cannot prefer the religious views of one parent over the other in deciding the best interest of a child" in a child custody dispute) (relying on both state and federal religion clauses); *Watts v. Watts*, 563 S.W.2d 314, 316–17 (Tex. Civ. App.-Dallas, *no writ*) (same); *Salvaggio v. Barnett*, 248 S.W.3d 244 (Tex. Civ. App. 1952-Galveston, *writ ref'd n.r.e.*) (same).

24. For example, state courts have repeatedly cited and relied upon the Supreme Court's decision in *Employment Division, Dep't of Human Resources of Oregon v. Smith*, 494 U.S. 872 (1990), interpreting the Free Exercise Clause of the First Amendment, in rejecting freedom of religion claims brought under art. I, §6, against neutral laws of general application. *See Mauldin v. Texas State Board of Plumbing Examiners*, 94 S.W.3d 867, 872 (Tex. App.-Austin 2002, *no writ*) (state licensing board could require plumbers to provide social security numbers as a condition of licensure); *Ramos v. State*, 934 S.W.2d 358, 367–68 (Tex. Crim. App. 1996) (excusing jurors who are opposed to the death penalty on moral or religious grounds does not violate their religious freedom). In *Ramos*, the court held that "[r]eligious freedoms are not implicated by neutral laws governing activities the government has the right to regulate merely because some religious groups may be disproportionately affected." 934 S.W.2d at 367. *See also Voice of Cornerstone Church Corp. v. Pizza Property Partners*, 160 S.W.3d 657, 672 (Tex. App.-Austin 2005, *no writ*) ("Texas courts have routinely rejected the notion that a facially neutral, otherwise valid restrictive covenant violates constitutional religious freedom protections if applied against a church").

25. Entirely apart from the foregoing, the argument that an abortion prohibition gives a "preference" to religious beliefs would appear to be foreclosed by decisions of the Texas Supreme Court and the Texas Court of Criminal Appeals rejecting challenges to Sunday closing laws *See Gabel v. Houston*, 29 Tex. 335, 345–47 (1867) (upholding ordinance); *Ex parte Brown*, 61 S.W. 396 (Tex. Crim. App. 1901) (upholding statute). If a law enforcing a "day of rest" does not violate the religion clause of the Texas Constitution, even though it may coincide with sectarian beliefs regarding the Christian Sabbath, *Gabel*, 29 Tex. at 346 (ordinance does not "pretend to give any preference to any religion or mode of worship"), then neither would a law prohibiting abortion, regardless of whether the law coincides with religious views regarding the morality of abortion.

Remedy by Due Course of Law

Article I, § 13, of the Texas Constitution provides, in part: "All courts shall be open, and every person for an injury done him, in his lands, goods, person or reputation, shall have remedy by due course of law."[26] Abortion advocates might argue that a statute prohibiting abortion interferes with a woman's control over her own body, and that such interference constitutes an "injury" to her "person," as those terms are used in § 13, for which there must be a "remedy by due course of law." That "remedy," in turn, would be invalidation of the statute. This argument erroneously assumes that art. I, § 13, confers substantive rights. The case law is clear, however, that it does not.

As is apparent from its text and structure, § 13 is concerned with *remedies* for injuries-it does not establish what *constitutes* an injury to anyone's "lands, goods, person or reputation." Those remedies, however, are derived from the common law, not § 13. Moreover, the remedies themselves redress injuries recognized by the common law, not constitutional "injuries." Section 13, in other words, "does not create any new rights, but ensures that the courts shall be open and afford a remedy for causes of action recognized at common law."[27]

Section 13 is concerned with the availability of private civil causes of action and reasonable access to the courts. It places no limitation on the State's power to define and punish crimes and has never been so interpreted.

Due Course of Law

Article I, § 19, of the Texas Constitution provides: "No citizen of this State shall be deprived of life, liberty, property, privileges or immunities, or in any manner disfranchised, except by the due course of the law of the land."[28] Section 19 is the most likely source of an asserted abortion right under the Texas Constitution. Relying principally on § 19, the Texas Supreme Court has recognized a state constitutional right of privacy in the nondisclosure of personal matters.[29] Whether the privacy right extends to conduct, however, is doubtful.[30]

---

26. Tex. Const. art. I, § 13 (Vernon 2007).

27. *Green Int'l, Inc. v. State*, 877 S.W.2d 428, 436 (Tex. App.-Austin 1994, *writ denied*) (citing *In the Interest of B.M.N.*, 570 S.W.2d 493, 498 (Tex. Civ. App.-Texarkana 1978, *no writ*)).

28. Tex. Const. art. I, § 19 (Vernon 2007).

29. *TSEU v. Texas Dep't of Mental Health & Mental Retardation*, 746 S.W.2d 203 (Tex. 1987) (forbidding mandatory polygraph testing of public employees).

30. *See City of Sherman v. Henry*, 928 S.W.2d 464 (Tex. 1996) (state right of privacy does not extend to adultery); *Lawrence v. State*, 41 S.W.3d 349, 360–62 (Tex. App.-Hous-

In evaluating state constitutional claims, the Texas Supreme Court has looked to the text of the constitution itself; the intent of the framers who drafted it and the people who approved it; the historical context in which it was written; the legal traditions of the State; and the judicial precedents interpreting the particular provision in question and similar provisions in the federal constitution.[31]

Article I, § 19, does not expressly confer a right to abortion. Nor can such a right fairly be implied. Abortion has long been a serious criminal offense in Texas. In 1854, less than ten years after being admitted to the Union and more than twenty years before the present constitution was adopted, Texas enacted its first abortion statute. The statute prohibited anyone from "unlawfully and maliciously" using any drug or device "with the intent to procure the miscarriage of any woman being with child."[32] This statute was superseded by an Act of August 28, 1856, as amended by an Act of February 12, 1858.[33] Under these statutes, which punished a completed abortion as a felony and an attempted abortion as a misdemeanor, an abortion could be procured or attempted only "by medical advice for the purpose of saving the life of the mother."[34] The abortion statutes remained essentially unchanged until they were struck down by the Supreme Court in *Roe v. Wade.*

For decades before *Roe* was decided, the Texas Court of Criminal Appeals regularly affirmed convictions for abortion and attempted abortion without any hint that either the prosecutions or convictions violated the Texas Constitution.[35] Less than fifteen months before *Roe*, the court of criminal appeals af-

---

ton [14th Dist] 2001, *pet. ref'd*) (same with respect to homosexual sodomy), *reversed on other grounds*, 539 U.S. 558 (2003). Apart from privacy based claims, the Texas Supreme Court has recognized fundamental "substantive due process" rights under art I, § 19, only on rare occasion, and never in the absence of a longstanding tradition of protecting the right being asserted. *See Eggemeyer v. Eggemeyer*, 554 S.W.2d 137, 140 (Tex. 1977) (right to own property); *Spann v. City of Dallas*, 235 S.W. 513, 515 (Tex. 1921) (right to use property). For the reasons set forth in the text, *infra*, there is no tradition protecting a right to abortion in Texas law.

31. *City of Sherman*, 928 S.W.2d at 472.

32. Tex. Gen. Laws, ch. XLIX, § 1 (1854).

33. *Codified at* Tex. Gen. Stat. Digest, ch. VII, arts. 531–536, p. 524 (Oldham & White 1859), *carried forward as* Tex. Penal Code Ann. arts. 1191–1196 (West 1961).

34. *Id.*

35. *Willingham v. State*, 25 S.W. 424 (Tex. Crim. App. 1894); *Cave v. State*, 26 S.W. 503 (1894); *Moore v. State*, 40 S.W. 287 (Tex. Crim. App. 1897); *Hunter v. State*, 41 S.W. 602 (Tex. Crim. App. 1897); *Fretwell v. State*, 67 S.W. 1021 (Tex. Crim. App. 1902); *Reum v. State*, 90 S.W. 1109 (Tex. Crim. App. 1905); *Link v. State*, 164 S.W. 987 (Tex. Crim. App. 1914); *Shaw v. State*, 165 S.W. 930 (Tex. Crim. App. 1914); *Fondren v. State*, 169 S.W. 411 (Tex. Crim. App. 1914); *Hunter v. State*, 196 S.W. 820 (Tex. Crim. App. 1917); *Hammett v. State*,

firmed a physician's conviction for performing an illegal abortion, rejecting both privacy and vagueness challenges.[36]

Quoting art. I, § 19, the court said that "[t]he State of Texas is committed to preserving the lives of its citizens so that no citizen 'shall be deprived of life, ... except by the due course of the law of the land.'"[37] The court determined that the Texas abortion statutes were "designed to protect fetal life," and held that this purpose "justifies prohibiting termination of the life of the fetus or embryo except for the purpose of saving the life of the mother."[38] In light of the decision in *Thompson*, it is difficult to understand how art. I, § 19, could be construed to confer a "liberty" interest in ending a life that is specifically protected by § 19.

Texas has enacted a comprehensive scheme of abortion regulation.[39] Moreover, Texas has recognized the rights of unborn children in a variety of con-

---

209 S.W. 661 (Tex. Crim. App. 1919); *Earnest v. State*, 224 S.W. 777 (Tex. Crim. App. 1920); *Jordan v. State*, 92 S.W.2d 1024 (Tex. Crim. App. 1936); *Pearson v. State*, 165 S.W.2d 725 (Tex. Crim. App. 1942); *Housman v. State*, 230 S.W.2d 541 (Tex. Crim. App. 1950); *Jarquin v. State*, 232 S.W.2d 736 (Tex. Crim. App. 1950); *Welch v. State*, 264 S.W.2d 100 (Tex. Crim. App. 1953); *Mayberry v. State*, 271 S.W. 635 (Tex. Crim. App. 1954); *Cortez v. State*, 275 S.W.2d 123 (Tex. Crim. App. 1954); *Owens v. State*, 283 S.W.2d 749 (Tex. Crim. App. 1955); *Romero . State*, 308 S.W.2d 49 (Tex. Crim. App. 1957); *Parnell v. State*, 312 S.W.2d 506 (Tex. Crim. App. 1958); *Veevers v. State*, 354 S.W.2d 161 (Tex. Crim. App. 1962); *Fletcher v. State*, 362 S.W.2d 845 (Tex. Crim. App. 1962).

36. *Thompson v. State*, 493 S.W.2d 913 (Tex. Crim. App. 1971), *vacated and remanded*, 410 U.S. 950 (1973), *on remand*, 493 S.W.2d 793 (Tex. Crim. App. 1973).

37. 493 S.W.2d at 918. Although art. I, § 19, secures rights to "citizens," not "persons," the constitutional protections afforded by § 19 have been extended to persons who are not, in a strict sense, "citizens." *See Ismail v. Ismail*, 702 S.W.2d 216, 220 n. 2 (Tex. App.-Houston [1st Dist.] 1985, *writ ref'd n.r.e.*) (due course of law guarantee protects nonresident aliens); *Pintor v. Martinez*, 202 S.W.2d 333, 335 (Tex. Civ. App.-Austin 1947, *writ ref'd, n.r.e.*) (due process guarantee protects resident aliens).

38. *Thompson*, 493 S.W.2d at 918.

39. Tex. Health & Safety Code Ann. § 171.011 *et seq.* (Vernon Supp. 2006) (mandating informed consent and a twenty-four hour waiting period); Tex. Fam. Code Ann. § 33.001 *et seq.* (Vernon 2002) (requiring parental notice and a forty-eight hour waiting period); Tex. Occ. Code Ann. § 164.052(a)(19) (Vernon Supp. 2006) (requiring parental consent); Tex. Occ. Code Ann. § 103.001 *et seq.* (Vernon 2004) (recognizing individual and institutional rights of conscience and prohibiting discrimination against persons who object to abortion); Tex. Hum. Res. Code Ann. § 32.024e (Vernon 2001), 25 Tex. Admin. Code § 29.1121 (2002), Texas Dep't of Health, 2000 *Texas Medicaid Provider Procedures Manual*, § 33.4.1 (restricting public funding of abortion); Tex. Health & Safety Code Ann.§ 245.001 *et seq.* (Vernon 2001 & Supp. 2006) (licensing and regulating abortion facilities); Tex. Occ. Code Ann. § 164.052(a)(18) (Vernon Supp. 2006) (restricting post-viability abortions).

texts outside of abortion, including criminal law, tort law, health care law, property law, family law and guardianship law.

Under the penal code, the killing or injury of an unborn child, other than in an abortion, may be prosecuted as a homicide or an assault.[40] In tort law, a statutory cause of action for wrongful death may be brought on behalf of an unborn child without regard to the stage of pregnancy when the injuries causing death were inflicted.[41] A common law action for (nonlethal) prenatal injuries may be brought without regard to stage of pregnancy when the injuries were inflicted.[42] And Texas does not recognize wrongful life causes of action.[43]

Under the State's health care statutes, an advance directive may not direct the withholding or withdrawal of life-sustaining treatment from a pregnant patient.[44] DNR orders are subject to the same limitation.[45] And a medical power of attorney may not authorize an abortion.[46]

In property law, a child *en ventre sa mere* (in the mother's womb) is included among those children in being at the time of the decedent's death.[47] A posthumous child (a child conceived before but born after the death of a dece-

---

40. TEX. PENAL CODE ANN. § 1.07(26) (defining "individual" to include "an unborn child at every stage of gestation from fertilization until birth") (Vernon Supp. 2006); §§ 19.06 (exceptions to scope of homicide offenses), 22.12 (exceptions to scope of assaultive offenses) (Vernon Supp. 2006).

41. TEX. CIV. PRAC. & REM. CODE ANN. § 71.001(4) (Vernon Supp. 2006).

42. *Yandell v. Delgado*, 471 S.W.2d 569 (Tex. 1971). *See also Brown v. Shwarts*, 968 S.W.2d 331, 334 (Tex. 1998).

43. *Nelson v. Krusen*, 678 S.W.2d 918, 924–25 (Tex. 1984). A "wrongful life" cause of action is a claim brought on behalf of a child who is born with a physical or mental disability or disease that could have been discovered before the child's birth through genetic testing, amniocentesis or other medical screening. The gravamen of the action is that, as a result of a physician's failure to inform the child's parents of the child's disability or disease (or at least of the availability of tests to determine the presence of the disability or disease), they were deprived of the opportunity to abort the child, thus resulting in the birth of a child suffering permanent physical or mental impairment. The Texas Supreme Court does recognize wrongful birth actions, however. *Jacobs v. Theimer*, 519 S.W.2d 846, 848–50 (Tex. 1975). A "wrongful birth" action is a claim, based upon the same facts, brought by the parents of the impaired child on their own behalf.

44. TEX. HEALTH & SAFETY CODE ANN. § 166.049 (Vernon 2001).

45. *Id.* § 166.098.

46. *Id.* § 166.152(f)(4). *See also* § 166.163 (form of disclosure statement).

47. *James v. James*, 164 S.W. 47, 47 (Tex. Civ. App.-San Antonio 1914, *writ dismissed w.o.j.*). *See also* TEX. PROB. CODE ANN. § 67 (Vernon Supp. 2006) (pretermitted child), § 67(c) (defining "pretermitted child" to include a child of a testator "who, during the lifetime of the testator *or after his death*, is born or adopted after the execution of the will of the testator") (emphasis added).

dent) may recover damages for the death of his father.[48] The rule against perpetuities, which limits the time within which an interest in a trust must vest, allows a period of gestation to be added to a "life in being" at the time the interest is created.[49]

In family law, a suit to terminate parental rights may be commenced before birth.[50] And a guardian *ad litem* may be appointed to represent the interest of an unborn child in any proceeding if the court determines that representation of the child's interest otherwise would be inadequate.[51] The same rule applies to probate proceedings.[52]

A right to abortion cannot be found in the text or structure of the Texas Constitution. There is no evidence that either the framers or ratifiers of the Texas Constitution intended the Bill of Rights to limit the Legislature's authority to prohibit abortion.[53] Such an intent would have been remarkable in light of the contemporaneous prohibition of abortion except to save the life of the mother.[54]

To paraphrase what the Texas Supreme Court said in *City of Sherman*, "[w]hile the constitution's framers may have been willing to die for the right of free expression, … there is no indication that they were willing to make any sacrifice for the right to [have an abortion]."[55] Moreover, "the fact that constitutional guarantees continue to evolve over time does not mean that we are allowed to create new guarantees that are not present in either the text or the intent of the constitution."[56] There is no basis for the argument that abortion is protected as a "fundamental right" under the Texas Constitution. Abortion,

---

48. *Nelson v. Galveston, H. & S.A. Ry. Co.*, 14 S.W. 1021 (Tex. 1890).

49. TEX. PROP. CODE ANN. §112.036 (Vernon 2007).

50. TEX. FAM. CODE ANN. §161.102(2) (Vernon 2002).

51. TEX. PROP. CODE ANN. §115.014(1) (Vernon 2007).

52. TEX. PROB. CODE ANN. §34A (Vernon 2003).

53. *See* Seth Shepard McKay, DEBATES IN THE TEXAS CONSTITUTIONAL CONVENTION OF THE STATE OF TEXAS OF 1875, 234–42 (debate on the Bill of Rights in Committee of the Whole), 290–95 (debate on the Bill of Rights in Convention) (1930); JOURNAL OF THE CONSTITUTIONAL CONVENTION OF THE STATE OF TEXAS OF 1875, 337–39, 346–57, 434–36.

54. *See City of Sherman v. Henry*, 928 S.W.2d at 473 (rejecting asserted privacy interest to engage in adultery where adultery was a crime from before the time when the 1876 Constitution was adopted until 1973).

55. *Id.*

56. *Id. See also Jones v. Ross*, 173 S.W.2d 1022, 1024 (Tex. 1943) (noting that it is "the settled law of this State that the provisions of our State Constitution mean what they meant when they were promulgated and adopted, and their meaning is not different at any subsequent time. Constitutional provisions must be construed in light of conditions existing at the time of [their] adoption").

like adultery, is "not a right implicit in the concept of liberty in Texas or deeply rooted in this state's history and tradition."[57]

Apart from fundamental rights, a law is not unconstitutional under the due course of law guarantee of art. I, § 19, unless it is not reasonably related to a legitimate governmental purpose. But the Texas Supreme Court has recognized that the State has a "legitimate governmental purpose to favor childbirth over abortion."[58] The legitimacy of that interest extends to the State's abortion statutes, which were "designed to protect fetal life," a purpose the Texas Court of Criminal Appeals held "justifies prohibiting termination of the life of the fetus or embryo except for the purpose of saving the life of the mother."[59]

Inviolate Rights

Article I, § 29, of the Texas Constitution provides:

> To guard against transgressions of the high powers herein delegated, we declare that everything in this "Bill of Rights" is excepted out of the general powers of government, and shall forever remain inviolate, and all laws contrary thereto, or to the following provisions, shall be void.[60]

This language simply means that "[w]hen the Legislature has clearly and directly done that which our Bill of Rights says shall not be done, then it becomes the duty of the judiciary to declare such enactments null and void."[61] Section 29 is not itself a source of substantive rights, but requires invalidation of acts that are otherwise inconsistent with the Bill of Rights.[62] This is recognized

---

57. *City of Sherman*, 928 S.W.2d at 473. To the extent that the Texas Supreme Court considers federal precedent in determining whether an asserted liberty interest (or right) is "fundamental" under the due course of law guarantee, abortion would not qualify as a "fundamental" right. Although the Supreme Court characterized the right to choose abortion as "fundamental" in *Roe*, 410 U.S. at 152–53, it tacitly abandoned that characterization in *Casey*, 505 U.S. at 869–79 (Joint Op. of O'Connor, Kennedy and Souter, JJ., replacing *Roe's* "strict scrutiny" standard of review with the more relaxed "undue burden" standard, allowing for a broader measure of abortion regulation).

58. *Bell v. Low Income Women of Texas*, 95 S.W.3d at 263.

59. *Thompson v. State*, 493 S.W.2d at 918.

60. TEX. CONST. art. I, § 29 (Vernon 2007).

61. *Murphy v. Phillips*. 63 S.W.2d 404, 408 (Tex. Civ. App. 1933), *appeal dismissed as moot*, 73 S.W.2d 92 (Tex. 1934).

62. *Travelers' Ins. Co. v. Marshall*, 76 S.W.2d 1007, 1009–10, 1025 (Tex. 1934) (impairment of contracts).

by the official commentary: "Article I ... enumerates ... inalienable rights and Section 29 demonstrates that they are not delegated by the people to their government, and, furthermore, any infringement by the government thereof is void."[63] Section 29 could not be a source of an abortion right under the Texas Constitution.

Conclusion

Based on the foregoing analysis, an argument that the Texas Constitution protects a right to abortion that is separate from, and independent of, the right to abortion recognized in *Roe v. Wade* would not likely succeed. That, in turn, suggests that if *Roe*, as modified by *Casey*, is ultimately overruled, the State of Texas could enforce its pre-*Roe* statutes *prohibiting* abortion (or enact and enforce new statutes prohibiting abortion). Moreover, nothing in the Texas Constitution precludes Texas from *regulating* abortion within federal constitutional limits in the meantime.

---

63. TEX. CONST. art. I, § 29, Interpretive Commentary (Vernon 2007).

CHAPTER 47

UTAH

Summary

The Utah Supreme Court has not yet decided whether the Utah Constitution protects a right to abortion separate from, and independent of, the right to abortion recognized under the United States Constitution.[1] A careful examination of the state constitution, in light of its history and interpretation, as well as other relevant legal sources, however, suggests that the state supreme court probably would not recognize a state constitutional right to abortion if *Roe v. Wade*,[2] as modified by *Planned Parenthood v. Casey*,[3] were overruled. Thus, Utah could enforce its post-*Roe* statute prohibiting abortion (or enact a new prohibition).[4] Moreover, nothing in the state constitution, properly un-

---

1. *See Wood v. University of Utah Medical Center*, 67 P.3d 436, 447–48 (Utah 2003) (upholding statute banning wrongful birth and wrongful life causes of action). The implications of the *Wood* opinion with respect to the issue of abortion are discussed in the due process section of the analysis, *infra*. A "wrongful birth" cause of action is a claim brought by the parents of a child who is born with a physical or mental disability or disease that could have been discovered before the child's birth by genetic testing, amniocentesis or other medical screening. The gravamen of the action is that, as a result of a physician's failure to inform the parents of the child's disability or disease (or at least of the availability of tests to determine the presence of the disability or disease), they were deprived of the opportunity to abort the child, thus resulting in the birth of a child suffering permanent physical or mental impairment. A "wrongful life" cause of action, on the other hand, is a claim, based on the same facts, brought on behalf of the impaired child.

2. 410 U.S. 113 (1973).

3. 505 U.S. 833 (1992).

4. Utah Code Ann. §76-7-302 (Supp. 2007). Under the statute, which is not currently enforceable, *see Jane L. v. Bangerter*, 809 F. Supp. 865 (D. Utah 1992), *aff'd in part, rev'd in part*, 61 F.3d 1493 (10th Cir. 1995), *rev'd and remanded sub nom. Leavitt v. Jane L.*, 518 U.S. 137 (1996), *on remand*, 102 F.3d 1112 (10th Cir. 1996), *cert. denied*, 520 U.S. 1274 (1997), an abortion may be performed at any time of pregnancy if the procedure is "necessary to

derstood, precludes the State from enacting and enforcing reasonable measures regulating abortion within current federal constitutional limits.

Analysis

The principal pre-*Roe* abortion statute prohibited performance of an abortion upon a pregnant woman unless the procedure was "necessary to preserve her life."[5] Another statute prohibited a woman from soliciting an abortion or allowing an abortion to be performed upon her (subject to the same exception).[6] Pursuant to *Roe*, §§ 76-2-1 and 76-2-2 were declared unconstitutional (on federal, not state, grounds) in an unreported decision of a three-judge federal district court.[7] The statues were repealed in 1973.[8]

Based upon arguments that have been raised in Utah and other States with similar constitutional provisions, possible sources for an asserted abortion right could include provisions of the Declaration of Rights recognizing inalienable rights (art. I, § 1), inherent political power in the people (§ 2), and the importance of frequent recurrence to the fundamental principles of government (§ 27); guaranteeing religious liberty (§ 4), due process of law (§ 7), equal protection (§§ 2, 24), and a remedy by due course of law (§ 16); and retaining rights (§ 25); as well as a provision in another article of the state constitution guaranteeing equal rights (art. IV, § 1).[9] The analysis that follows addresses each of these provisions.

---

save the pregnant woman's life," "to prevent grave damage to the pregnant woman's medical health," or "to prevent the birth of a child that would be born with grave defects." *Id.* §§ 76-7-302(2)(a), -(d), -(e). An abortion may also be performed during the first twenty weeks of gestation when the pregnancy results from a reported act of rape or incest. *Id.* §§ 76-7-302(2)(b), -(c).

5. UTAH CODE ANN. § 76-2-1 (1953).

6. *Id.* § 76-2-2. No prosecutions were reported under this statute.

7. *Doe v. Rampton*, No. C-234-70 (D. Utah 1973). Prior to *Roe*, the same court upheld the pre-*Roe* statute. *Doe v. Rampton*, No. C-234-70 (D. Utah Sep. 29, 1971), *vacated and remanded* 410 U.S. 950 (1973).

8. 1973 Utah Laws 584, 684, ch. 196, (sub.) ch. 10, pt. 14, § 76-10-1401.

9. Three other more unlikely sources of an abortion right under the Utah Constitution-§ 14 (prohibiting unreasonable searches and seizures), § 15 (guaranteeing freedom of speech)and § 21 (prohibiting involuntary servitude)-are discussed generally in Chapter 3, *supra*.

Inalienable Rights

Article I, § 1, of the Utah Constitution provides:

All men have the inherent and inalienable right to enjoy and defend their lives and liberties; to acquire, possess and protect property; to worship according to the dictates of their consciences; to assembly peaceably, protest against wrongs, and petition for redress of grievances; to communicate freely their thoughts and opinions, being responsible for the abuse of that right.[10]

Only two of the rights identified in art. I, § 1—the right of persons "to enjoy and defend their lives and liberties," and their right "to worship according to the dictates of their consciences"—might be cited in support of an asserted right to abortion. These rights, however, are secured by other, more specific and detailed provisions of the state constitution, specifically, art. I, § 7 (due process of law), with respect to the right to life and liberty, and art. I, § 4 (religious liberty), with respect to the right to worship. Because the right to enjoy and defend one's life and liberty and the right to worship according to the dictates of one's conscience do not appear to be broader in scope than their corollary provisions (§§ 7 and 4, respectively) in the Utah Declaration of Rights, they are considered in the sections of the analysis addressing the due process and religious liberty guarantees, *infra*.

Inherent Political Power

Article I, § 2, of the Utah Constitution provides: "All political power is inherent in the people; and all free governments are founded on their authority for their equal protection and benefit, and they have the right to alter or reform their government as the public welfare may require."[11]

In any challenge to a statute prohibiting abortion, abortion advocates may rely on art. I, § 2, arguing that an abortion prohibition does not promote the "equal protection and benefit" of the people because it discriminates against women, or at least against those women seeking abortions.[12] Reliance on § 2 for such an argument would be misplaced, however. The Utah Supreme Court

---

10. UTAH CONST. art. I, § 1 (1991).

11. *Id.* art. I, § 2.

12. Apart from the "equal protection and benefit" language, § 2 simply recognizes the right of the people to amend ("alter or reform") the organic instrument of state government "as the public welfare may require."

has characterized the "equal protection" language of §2 as "more a statement of a purpose of government than a legal standard than can be used to measure the legality of governmental action."[13] As such, it would not provide a constitutional basis for challenging a statute prohibiting abortion.

Fundamental Principles

Article I, §27, of the Utah Constitution provides: "Frequent recurrence to fundamental principles is essential to the security of individual rights and the perpetuity of free government."[14] Abortion advocates might argue that a right to abortion should be regarded as a "fundamental principle." Such an argument wold not likely succeed, however. Section 27 urges "frequent recurrence to fundamental principles," but does not create or establish any "fundamental principles," which are set forth in other provisions of the Declaration of Rights.

Section 27 has seldom been cited by the Utah Supreme Court, and has never been relied upon as a provision that, by itself, confers substantive rights.[15] A federal district court has expressed the opinion that art. I, §§26 (stating that the provisions of the state constitution are "mandatory and prohibitory") and 27 "appear to be declaratory of general constitutional principles rather than an enumeration of individual constitutional rights as such.[16] That is confirmed by an examination of the proceedings of the 1895 Utah Constitutional Convention.

In opposing a motion to strike §27, Heber Wells, Chairman of the Standing Committee on the Preamble and Declaration of Rights, characterized art. I, §27, as a "patriotic utterance," which "did no harm in the declaration of rights...."[17] Orson Whitney, a member of the same committee, also opposed the motion to strike, describing §27 as a section "which declares a fundamental principle without guaranteeing it."[18] He added, "The declaration of a general principle does not hurt anything," and urged that it be retained in the draft constitution.[19] Finally, Franklin S. Richards, another delegate opposed to strik-

13. *Malan v. Lewis*, 693 P.2d 661, 669 n. 13 (Utah 1984).

14. UTAH CONS. art. I, §27 (1991).

15. In *Rackley v. Fairview Care Centers, Inc.*, 23 P.3d 1022, 1028 (Utah 2001), the Utah Supreme Court stated, in dictum, that art. I, §§1 and 27, "protect the right to acquire, possess, and protect property."

16. *MacArthur v. San Juan County*, 416 F. Supp. 2d 1098, 1179 (D. Utah 2005).

17. 1 OFFICIAL REPORT OF THE PROCEEDINGS AND DEBATES OF THE CONVENTION ASSEMBLED AT SALT LAKE CITY ON THE FOURTH DAY OF MARCH 1895, TO ADOPT A CONSTITUTION FOR THE STATE OF UTAH (1898) (hereinafter PROCEEDINGS) 362.

18. *Id.*

19. *Id.*

ing §27, stated that the "admonition" that there be "frequent recurrence to fundamental principles" was "not enforceable in itself."[20] In light of the foregoing remarks, it would be implausible to regard art. I, §27, as the source of any substantive rights.

Religious Liberty

Article I, §4, of the Utah Constitution provides:

> The rights of conscience shall never be infringed. The State shall make no law respecting an establishment of religion or prohibiting the free exercise thereof; no religious test shall be required as a qualification for any office or public trust or for any vote at any election; nor shall any person be incompetent as a witness or juror on account of religious belief or the absence thereof. There shall be no union of Church and State, nor shall any church dominate the State or interfere with its functions. No public money or property shall be appropriated for or applied to any religious worship, exercise or instruction, or for the support of any ecclesiastical establishment. No property qualification shall be required of any person to vote, or hold office, except as provided in this Constitution.[21]

In any challenge to the State's abortion prohibition (or any other prohibition Utah may enact), abortion advocates may raise either or both of two arguments under art. I, §4. First, they may argue that an abortion prohibition interferes with the "free exercise" of a woman's religious beliefs (as well as her "rights of conscience") by forbidding her from obtaining an abortion that would be allowed by her religion. Second, they may argue in the alternative (or in addition) that an abortion prohibition constitutes an "establishment of religion" because it reflects sectarian beliefs regarding when human life begins and the sinfulness of abortion. Neither argument would likely prevail.[22]

The Utah Supreme Court has not yet determined "whether the free exercise clause of article I, section 4 of the Utah Constitution provides protection

---

20. *Id.*

21. UTAH CONST. art. I, §4 (1991).

22. In *Jane L. v. Bangerter*, 794 F. Supp. 1528 (D. Utah. 1992), the federal district court held that the present abortion prohibition (*see* n. 4, *supra*) does not violate either the state guarantee of "free exercise" or the state prohibition of "an establishment of religion." *Id.* at 1534–35. Although that decision would not be binding upon a state court, it may be regarded as persuasive.

over and above that provided by the First Amendment to the United States Constitution."[23] And, although other provisions of § 4 may be interpreted to place greater restrictions on the State than are imposed by the First Amendment,[24] the state supreme court has not shown any inclination to interpret the "establishment of religion" language of § 4 more rigorously than the Supreme Court has interpreted the Establishment Clause.

The Utah Supreme Court has recognized that "the Establishment and Free Exercise Clauses of the First Amendment of the United States Constitution are repeated almost verbatim in article I, section 4."[25] The equivalency of language suggests an equivalency of interpretation.[26] Accordingly, a challenge to an abortion statute that would not succeed under the Religion Clauses of the First Amendment would probably not succeed under art. I, § 4, either. For the reasons set forth in Chapter 2, *supra*, an abortion statute could not be successfully challenged on First Amendment grounds. Accordingly, a similar challenge under art. I, § 4, would not likely be successful.

Due Process of Law

Article I, § 7, of the Utah Constitution provides: "No person shall be deprived of life, liberty, or property, without due process of law."[27] The most

---

23. *Jeffs v. Stubbs*, 970 P.2d 1234, 1239 (Utah 1998). *See also State v. Holm*, 137 P.3d 726, 738 (Utah 2006) (quoting *Jeffs*). In *Jane L. v. Bangerter*, the federal district court noted that "there is a lack of substantial case law on the issue of Utah's Free Exercise Clause." 794 F. Supp. at 1535. Nevertheless, in one case that discussed the issue, "the Utah Supreme Court adopted the analysis of the United States Supreme Court." *Id.* (citing *In re State in Interest of Black*, 283 P.2d 887, 901–05 (Utah 1955)). For the reasons set forth in the text, that analysis would not require invalidation of a statute prohibiting abortion.

24. *See Society of Separationists v. Whitehead*, 870 P.2d 916, 930–31 & n. 36 (Utah 1993) (whether the Salt Lake City Council's practice of permitting prayers to be said during the portion of city council meetings set aside for opening remarks violated the third and fourth sentences of art. I, § 4, would not be decided on the basis of precedent interpreting the Establishment Clause of the First Amendment).

25. *Id.* at 935 n. 43 (citing Brad C. Smith, Comment, *Be No More Children: An Analysis of Article I, Section 4 of the Utah Constitution*, 1992 UTAH L. REV. 1431, 1457 ("the 1895 Constitution incorporated the religion clauses of the Federal Constitution")).

26. *See Jane L. v. Bangerter*, 794 F. Supp. at 1534–35 (noting that "[t]here is very little Utah law interpreting the 'Establishment Clause' provision of Article I, § 4," and "[w]hat little law there is suggests that the Utah Supreme Court would find federal constitutional analysis persuasive") (citing *Thomas v. Daughters of Utah Pioneers*, 197 P.2d 477, 488–90 (1948), *appeal dismissed*, 336 U.S. 930 (1949)).

27. UTAH CONST. art. I, § 7 (1991). *See also id.*, art. I, § 1 (recognizing the right of all persons "to enjoy and defend their lives and liberties").

likely source of an asserted abortion right under the Utah Constitution would be art. I, §7, the due process guarantee.[28] Abortion advocates would argue that an abortion prohibition interferes with a pregnant woman's liberty interest in obtaining an abortion.[29] Although the Utah Supreme Court has held that the state constitution does not give any more protection to abortion than does the federal constitution,[30] it has not yet decided whether art. I, §7 (or any other provision of the Utah Constitution), protects a right to abortion separate from, and independent of, the right to abortion recognized by the Supreme Court under the United States Constitution. The court's analysis of state substantive due process claims suggests, however, that it probably would *not* recognize a state right to abortion if *Roe*, as modified by *Casey*, is overruled.[31]

In *In re J.P.*,[32] the Utah Supreme Court relied upon art. I, §7 (due process), and §25 (retained rights), in support of its holding that "the Utah Constitution recognizes and protects the inherent and retained right of a parent to maintain parental ties to his or her child...."[33] In its analysis of §7, the state supreme court concluded that the "liberty right" of parents in raising their children "is fundamental to the existence of the institution of the family, which is 'deeply rooted in this Nation's history and tradition,' *Moore v. City of East Cleveland*, 431 U.S. 494, 503 ... (1977) (plurality), and in the 'history and culture of Western civilization.' *Wisconsin v. Yoder*, 406 U.S. 205, 232 ... (1972)."[34] "This rooting in history and the common law," the court explained, "validates and limits the due process protection afforded parental rights, in contrast to substantive

---

28. *See Wood v. University of Utah Medical Center*, 67 P.3d at 449 ("[t]he right to obtain an abortion ... is properly within the realm of substantive due process").

29. Curiously, in their challenge to the current abortion prohibition (which was later struck down on federal constitutional grounds), the plaintiffs in *Jane L. v. Bangerter* did not raise any state substantive due process claims. They cited art. I, §7, only in support of their vagueness challenge to the law. 794 F. Supp. at 1532–33.

30. *Wood v. University of Utah Medical Center*, 67 P.3d at 448.

31. To the extent that the Utah Supreme Court may recognize the same fundamental rights under the *state* due process guarantee as the Supreme Court does under the *federal* due process guarantee, abortion would not qualify as a "fundamental" right. Although the Supreme Court characterized the right to choose abortion as "fundamental" in *Roe*, 410 U.S. at 152–53, it tacitly abandoned that characterization in *Casey*, 505 U.S. at 869–79 (Joint Op. of O'Connor, Kennedy and Souter, JJ., replacing *Roe's* "strict scrutiny" standard of review with the more relaxed "undue burden" standard, allowing for a broader measure of abortion regulation).

32. 648 P.2d 1364 (Utah 1982).

33. *Id.* at 1377. The court's treatment of §25 is discussed in the section of this analysis addressing retained rights, *infra*.

34. *Id.* at 1375.

due process innovations undisciplined by any but abstract formulae."[35] Significantly, the court *distinguished* "substantive due process cases like *Roe v. Wade,* ... which rely on a 'right of privacy' not mentioned in the Constitution, to establish other rights unknown at common law [*i.e.,* abortion]."[36]

The Utah Supreme Court's insistence in *In re J.P.* that state substantive due process liberty interests be rooted "in history and the common law," and its disparagement of *Roe v. Wade,* which "relie[d] on a 'right of privacy' not mentioned in the Constitution to establish other rights unknown at common law," leave little doubt that the court would not recognize a state right to abortion if *Roe,* as modified by *Casey,* is overruled. A right to abortion is not "deeply rooted" in Utah's history and tradition and, therefore, may not be considered a fundamental liberty interest protected by the due process guarantee of the Utah Constitution.

Utah enacted its first abortion statute on March 4, 1876, almost twenty years before the State adopted its constitution and was admitted to the Union. The statute, which prohibited all abortions at any stage of pregnancy except to preserve the life of the pregnant woman, remained essentially unchanged until it was repealed after *Roe v. Wade* was decided.[37] In a case decided more than one hundred years ago, the Utah Supreme Court held that the statute was enacted to prevent "the criminal destruction of the foetus at any time before birth...."[38]

In enacting its (currently unenforceable) abortion prohibition in 1991,[39] the Legislature found that the State has "a compelling interest in the protection of the lives of unborn children.[40] Recognizing that "life founded on inherent and inalienable rights is entitled to protection of law and due process," the Legislature found that "unborn children have inherent and inalienable rights" that are entitled to protection by the State of Utah under art. I, §§1 (inalienable rights) and 7 (due process) of the Utah Constitution.[41]

---

35. *Id.* (citing *Moore v. City of East Cleveland,* 431 U.S. at 503 n. 12).

36. *Id.*

37. UTAH (TERR.) COMP. LAWS tit. XXI (PENAL CODE), §142 (1876), *recodified at* UTAH COMP. LAWS §4507 (1888), *recodified at* UTAH REV. STAT. §4226 (1898), *recodified at* UTAH COMP. LAWS §8118 (1917), *recodified at* UTAH CODE ANN. §103.2-1 (1943), *recodified at* UTAH CODE ANN. §76-2-1 (1953). Another statute, first enacted in 1898, prohibited a woman from soliciting an abortion or allowing an abortion to be performed upon her (subject to the same exception). UTAH REV. STAT. §4227 (1898), *recodified at* UTAH COMP. LAWS §8119 (1917), *recodified at* UTAH CODE ANN. §103.2-2 (1943), *recodified at* UTAH CODE ANN. §76-2-2 (1953). No procecutions were reported under this statute. Both statutes were repealed in 1973. *See* n. 8, *supra.*

38. *State v. Crook,* 51 P. 1091, 1093 (Utah 1898).

39. *See* n. 4, *supra.*

40. UTAH CODE ANN. §76-7-301.1(2) (2003).

41. *Id.* §§76-7-301.1(1), -(3).

In addition to these legislative findings, the State of Utah has adopted a public policy "to encourage all persons to respect the right to life of all other persons, regardless of age, development, condition or dependency, including all persons with a disability and all unborn children."[42] Consistent with that policy (and apart from the abortion prohibition struck down in 1992), Utah has enacted a comprehensive scheme of abortion regulation.[43] Moreover, Utah recognizes the rights of unborn children in a variety of contexts outside of abortion, including criminal law, tort law, health care law and property law.

Under the criminal code, the killing of an unborn child, other than in an abortion, may be prosecuted as a homicide.[44] And a woman convicted of a capital offense may not be executed while she is pregnant.[45] In tort law, although the Utah Supreme Court has not yet decided whether a wrongful death action may be brought on behalf of an unborn child,[46] the State has barred wrongful birth and wrongful life causes of action.[47]

Under the State's health care statutes, a living will may not direct the withholding or withdrawal of life-sustaining treatment from a pregnant patient.[48] And a durable power of attorney for health care is subject to the same limitation.[49]

In property law, heirs of a decedent conceived before but born after the death of a decedent who dies without a will may inherit from an intestate (a person who dies without a will) if they live for at least 120 hours (five days) after birth.[50] And, subject to certain exceptions, afterborn children (children who are conceived before the death of a parent but born after the parent executes a will) receive that share of the estate that they would have received if the decedent had died intestate.[51]

---

42. UTAH CODE ANN. § 78-11-23 (2002).

43. *Id.* § 76- 7-305 (Supp. 2007) (mandating informed consent and a twenty-four hour waiting period); §§ 76-7-304, 76-7-305 (Supp. 2007) (requiring both parental notice and consent; § 76-7-306 (2003) (recognizing individual and institutional rights of conscience); § 76-7-331 (Supp. 2007) (restricting public funding of abortion for indigent women); § 76-7-326 (Supp. 2007) (prohibiting partial-birth abortions).

44. *Id.* § 76-5-201(1) (2003) (all categories of homicide).

45. *Id.* § 77-19-202 (Supp. 2007).

46. *State Farm Mutual Automobile Ins. Co. v. Clyde*, 920 P.2d 1183, 1187 n. 4 (Utah 1996). *See* UTAH CODE ANN. § 78-11-6 (Supp. 2007).

47. UTAH CODE ANN. §§ 78-11-24, 78-11-25 (2002).

48. *Id.* § 75-2-1109 (1993).

49. *Id.* § 75-2a-123.

50. *Id.* § 75-2-108 (Supp. 2006).

51. *Id.* § 75-3-302 (1993).

A right to abortion cannot be found in the text or structure of the Utah Constitution. There is no evidence that either the framers or ratifiers of the Utah Constitution intended art. I, §7, or any other provision of the Declaration of Rights to limit the Legislature's authority to prohibit abortion.[52] Such an intent would have been remarkable in light of the contemporaneous and longstanding prohibition of abortion except to save the life of the pregnant woman. For the foregoing reasons, a right to abortion cannot be regarded as a substantive due process "liberty" interest protected by art. I, §7, of the state constitution.

Equal Protection

Article I, §24, of the Utah Constitution provides: "All laws of a general nature shall have uniform operation."[53] Article I, §2, provides, in relevant part, that "all free governments are founded on their [the people's] authority for their equal protection and benefit...."[54] The Utah Supreme Court has at times referred to either art. I, §24, or art. I, §2, or both, as the constitutional source of state equal protection principles.[55] Nevertheless, the court has since clarified that although §2 "uses the language 'equal protection,'" such language, while relevant to the construction of §24, "is more a statement of a purpose of government than a legal standard that can be used to measure the legality of governmental action."[56] Accordingly, state equal protection analysis is based on art. I, §24.

Section 24 is "generally considered the equivalent of the Equal Protection Clause of the 14th Amendment...."[57] Both provisions "embody the same general prin-

---

52. 1 PROCEEDINGS at 228–42, 244–62, 273–96, 304–15, 319–44, 345–67, 393 (debate on Declaration of Rights in Committee of the Whole); 492–95, 622–51 (debate on Declaration of Rights in Convention).

53. UTAH CONST. art. I, §24 (1991).

54. *Id.* art. I, §2.

55. *See, e.g., Allen v. Intermountain Health Care, Inc.*, 635 P.2d 30, 31 & nn. 5, 10 (Utah 1981); *Redwood Gym v. Salt Lake County Comm'n*, 624 P.2d 1138, 1146 n. 2 (Utah 1981).

56. *Malan v. Lewis*, 693 P. 661, 669 n. 13 (Utah 1984). *See also Wood v. University of Utah Medical Center*, 67 P.3d 436, 448 (Utah 2002) (although plaintiffs presented their state equal protection argument (art. I, §2) and their Uniform Operation of Laws argument (art. I, §24) as two separate arguments, the state supreme court "consider[ed] them as one argument because the Uniform Operation of Laws provision is, in fact, the Utah equal protection guarantee"); *In re Criminal Investigation*, 754 P.2d 633, 657 n. 2 (Utah 1988) (same). *But see Gallivan v. Walker*, 54 P.3d 1069, 1984 n. 8 (Utah 2002) (article I, §2, "articulates a fundamental philosophical, political, and legal principle that underlies and informs our analysis under its companion uniform operation of laws article").

57. *Liedtke v. Schettler*, 649 P.2d 80, 81 n. 1 (Utah 1982).

ciple: persons similarly situated should be treated similarly, and persons in different circumstances should not be treated as if their circumstances were the same."[58] The Utah Supreme Court, however, applies a different standard for *state* equal protection analysis than the Supreme Court applies for *federal* equal protection analysis. Under art. I, §24, a two-part test is employed to ensure the uniform operation of the laws: "First, a law must apply equally to all persons within a class. Second, the statutory classifications and the different treatment given the classes must be based on differences that have a reasonable tendency to further the objectives of the statute."[59]

Abortion advocates are likely to argue that an abortion prohibition violates art. I, §24, because the prohibition affects only women, not men, and thereby discriminates against women in favor of men; because it discriminates between those women who choose to have abortions and those who choose not to have abortions; and because it discriminates between those women seeking abortions for reasons that are allowed by the law and those seeking abortions for reasons not allowed by the law. None of these arguments would likely prevail.

With respect to the first classification, the Utah Supreme Court has held that "[i]n the matter of pregnancy there is no way to find equality between men and women,"[60] a point recognized by the Supreme Court, as well.[61] In *Jane L. v. Bangerter*, the federal district court rejected a state equal protection challenge to the current Utah abortion prohibition, holding that "[m]en and women are not 'similarly situated' with respect to ability to carry a child," because women are "the only sex capable of [becoming pregnant and] having abortions."[62]

With respect to the second classification, the Utah Supreme Court has refused to recognize women "who choose to have an abortion, as opposed to those who choose not to," as a "class" for purposes of art. I, §24.[63] The court explained:

> At the present we see no reason why persons who would make a particular choice-abortion in this case-should, for constitutional pur-

---

58. *Malan*, 693 P.2d at 669.

59. *Id.* at 670 (citations omitted).

60. *Turner v. Dep't of Employment Security*, 531 P.2d 870, 871 (Utah 1975) (rejecting state and federal challenges to unemployment compensation statute that denied benefits to pregnant women during the twelve weeks before and the six weeks after delivery of a baby), *vacated and remanded on other grounds*, 423 U.S. 44 (1978).

61. *See Geduldig v. Aiello*, 417 U.S. 483 (1974) (rejecting an equal protection challenge to a California statute excluding pregnancy from the list of conditions that qualified for disability benefits).

62. 794 F. Supp. at 1534.

63. *Wood v. University of Utah Medical Center*, 67 P.3d at 449.

poses, be recognized as a class and treated any differently from those who would choose otherwise. The right to obtain an abortion, the right asserted by plaintiffs and upon which they claim exercise of should entitle them to additional protection as a class, is properly within the realm of substantive due process, not equal protection.[64]

With respect to the third classification, "[p]rohibiting elective abortions except in certain circumstances determined by the legislature to embody the public policy of the State is a rational way of promoting [the State's] interest in potential human life while balancing the interest of the pregnant woman."[65] None of the "classifications" created in an abortion prohibition (either the current one or any one that is likely to be enacted hereafter) would contravene the principles of art. I, §24.

Equal Rights

Article IV, §1, of the Utah Constitution provides: "The rights of citizens of the State of Utah to vote and hold office shall not be denied or abridged on account of sex. Both male and female citizens of this State shall enjoy equally all civil, political and religious rights and privileges."[66]

In any challenge to a statute prohibiting abortion, abortion advocates are likely to argue that the prohibition discriminates against women in favor of men in violation of the second sentence of IV, §1. Such an argument probably would not prevail, however.

The Utah Supreme Court has not yet determined what standard of review applies to sex-based classifications.[67] The court has indicated, however, that at least heightened scrutiny (the federal standard) would apply.[68] Under that standard, a classification based on sex would have to be "substantially related" to an "important governmental objective[]."[69] Although a prohibition of abor-

---

64. *Id.*

65. *Jane L. v. Bangerter*, 794 F. Supp. at 1534.

66. UTAH CONST. art. IV, §1 (1991).

67. *See Redwood Gym v. Salt Lake County Comm'n*, 624 P.2d 1138, 1147 (Utah 1981) (not deciding whether "a classification based on sex ... is or should be inherently suspect under Utah law).

68. *Pusey v. Pusey*, 728 P.2d 117, 119–20 (Utah 1986) (abolishing "gender-based preferences in child custody cases" as inconsistent with the Equal Protection Clause of the Fourteenth Amendment and art. IV, §1, of the Utah Constitution). *See also In re Estate of Scheller*, 783 P.2d 70, 76 (Utah Ct. App. 1989) (reviewing case law).

69. *Craig v. Boren*, 429 U.S. 190, 197 (1976).

tion would appear to satisfy that standard of review, because the prohibition would be "substantially related" to the "important governmental objective" of protecting unborn human life, it is not at all clear that heightened scrutiny would be the appropriate standard.

A statute prohibiting abortion quite obviously can affect only women because only women are capable of becoming pregnant.[70] Unlike laws that use women's ability to become pregnant (or pregnancy itself) to discriminate against them in *other* areas (*e.g.*, employment opportunities), abortion prohibitions cannot fairly be said to involve a distinction between men and women that is a "mere pretext[] designed to erect an invidious discrimination against [women]."[71] Indeed, the Supreme Court has recognized that "the disfavoring of abortion ... is not *ipso facto* sex discrimination."[72] "[T]he constitutional test applicable to government abortion funding restrictions," the Court explained, "is not the heightened-scrutiny that our cases demand for sex discrimination, but the ordinary rationality standard."[73]

Even assuming that the Utah Supreme Court interprets art. IV, § 1, to require strict, as opposed to intermediate, scrutiny of sex-based classifications, a prohibition of abortion would not run afoul of the state equal rights guarantee. Reviewing courts in other States with equal rights provisions have consistently held that laws that differentiate between the sexes are permissible and do not violate the state guarantee of gender equality if they are based upon the unique physical characteristics of a particular sex.[74]

---

70. *Geduldig v. Aiello*, 417 U.S. at 496 n. 20 ("[n]ormal pregnancy is an objectively, identifiable physical condition with unique characteristics").

71. *Id.*

72. *Bray v. Alexandria Women's Health Clinic*, 506 U.S. 263, 273 (1993).

73. *Id.* (citations omitted).

74. The cases have upheld rape statutes, *State v. Rivera*, 612 P.2d 526, 530–31 (Haw. 1980), *State v. Fletcher*, 341 So.2d 340, 348 (La. 1976), *Brooks v. State*, 330 A.2d 670, 672–73 (Md. Ct. Sp. App. 1975), *State v. Craig*, 545 P.2d 649 (Mont. 1976), *Finley v. State*, 527 S.W.2d 553, 555–57 (Tex. Crim. App. 1975); statutory rape statutes, *People v. Salinas*, 551 P.2d 703, 705–06 (Colo. 1976), *State v. Bell*, 377 So.2d 303 (La. 1979); an aggravated incest statute, *People v. Boyer*, 349 N.E.2d 50 (Ill. 1976); statutes governing the means of establishing maternity and paternity, *People v. Morrison*, 584 N.E.2d 509 (Ill. App. Ct. 1991), *A v. X, Y & Z*, 641 P.2d 1222, 1224–25 (Wyo. 1982); statutes and rules barring female nudity in bars, *Dydyn v. Dep't of Liquor Control*, 531 A.2d 170, 175 (Conn. App. Ct. 1987); *Messina v. State*, 904 S.W.2d 178, 181 (Tex. App.-Dallas 1995, *no pet.*); an ordinance prohibiting public exposure of female breasts, *City of Seattle v. Buchanan*, 584 P.2d 918, 919–21 (Wash. 1978); and limitations on public funding of abortion, *Fischer v. Dep't of Public Welfare*, 502 A.2d 114, 124–26 (Pa. 1985), *Bell v. Low Income Women of Texas*, 95 S.W.3d 253, 257–64 (Tex. 2002). The one exception is *New Mexico Right to Choose/NARAL v. Johnson*,

The Utah Supreme Court has recognized that "[n]ot all legal provisions which take gender into consideration create ... sex-based classifications."[75] Moreover, "[i]n the matter of pregnancy there is no way to find equality between men and women."[76] Only women are capable of become pregnant and bearing children. Because of this unique physical characteristic, a law prohibition abortion could not be said to deny women equal "civil ... rights" under art. I, §4.

Remedy by Due Course of Law

Article I, §11, of the Utah Constitution provides, in part: "All courts shall be open, and every person, for an injury done to him in his person, property or reputation, shall have remedy by due course of law, which shall be administered without denial or unnecessary delay...."[77] Abortion advocates might argue that a statute prohibiting abortion interferes with a woman's control over her own body, and that such interference constitutes an "injury" to her "person," as those words are used in §11, for which there must be a "remedy by due course of law." That "remedy," in turn, would be invalidation of the statute. This argument assumes that art. I, §11, confers substantive rights. The case law is clear, however, that it does not.

As is apparent from its text and structure, §11 is concerned with *remedies* for tortiously inflicted injuries-it does not establish what *constitutes* an injury to anyone's "person, property or reputation."[78] Those remedies, however, are derived from other sources of law, not §11. Moreover, the remedies themselves redress injuries recognized by the common law, not constitutional "injuries." Section 11, in other words, does not *create* any new causes of action,

---

975 P.2d 841 (N.M. 1998), in which the New Mexico Supreme Court struck down a state regulation restricting public funding of abortion. In applying "heightened scrutiny," the court failed to recognize that the funding regulation did not use "the unique ability of women to become pregnant and bear children" as a pretext to discriminate against them in *other* respects, *e.g.*, "imposing restrictions on [their] ability to work and participate in public life." *Id.* at 855.

75. *Redwood Gym v. Salt Lake County Comm'n*, 624 P.2d at 1147.

76. *Turner v. Dep't of Employment Security*, 531 P.2d at 871.

77. UTAH CONST. art. I, §11 (1991).

78. Section 11 is "primarily concerned ... with the availability of legal remedies for vindicating the great interest that individuals in a civilized society have in the integrity of their persons, property, and reputations." *Berry by and through Berry v. Beech Aircraft*, 717 P.2d 670, 677 n. 4 (Utah 1985).

but merely *preserves* existing causes of action.[79] Utah case law confirms this understanding.

The Utah Supreme Court has fashioned a two-part test for determining whether a statute abolishing a remedy or a cause of action violates art. I, § 11: "First, ... the law [must otherwise provide] an injured person an effective and reasonable alternative remedy by 'due course of law' for vindication of his constitutional interest."[80] Second, if there is no substitute or alternative remedy provided, abrogation of the remedy or cause of action may be justified only if there is a clear social or economic evil to be eliminated and the elimination of an existing legal remedy is not an arbitrary or unreasonable means for achieving the objective."[81] This test necessarily presupposes that the challenged statute "abrogated an *existing* remedy or cause of action,"[82] *i.e.*, a remedy or cause of action "that existed at the time of enactment, not whether the statute abolished a legal remedy that existed at the time of statehood."[83]

Utah does not recognize a cause of action based upon interference with a pregnant woman's legal right to obtain an abortion. Thus, the current abortion prohibition (if the federal barrier to its enforcement is removed), or enactment of a new prohibition would not abrogate any *existing* cause of action. Even if the Utah Supreme Court were to recognize a cause of action for interfering with a woman's right to obtain an abortion,[84] recognition of such a cause of action would not preclude Utah from prohibiting abortion.[85] Finally, even assuming that a *criminal* abortion statute had to be justified under the second part of the test set forth in *Berry v. Beech Aircraft* governing the abrogation of *civil* causes of action, it would pass muster as a reasonable means of eliminating a "social ... evil."

---

79. *Brown v. Wightman*, 151 P. 366, 366–67 (Utah 1915) (art. I, § 11, does not "creat[e] new rights, or ... giv[e] new remedies where none otherwise are given, but ... place[s] a limitation upon the Legislature to prevent that branch of state government from closing the doors of the courts against any person who has a legal right which is enforceable in accordance with some known remedy").

80. *Id.* at 680.

81. *Id.* (citations omitted).

82. *Wood v. University of Utah Medical Center*, 67 P.3d at 442 (emphasis added) (citing *Cruz v. Wright*, 765 P.2d 869, 870–71 (Utah 1988)).

83. *Id.* (citing *Day v. State ex rel. Dep't of Public Safety*, 980 P.2d 1171, 1184 (Utah 1999)).

84. Recognition of such a cause of action would appear to be inconsistent with the Legislature's public policy choice to bar wrongful birth and wrongful life causes of actions. UTAH CODE ANN. §§ 78-11-24, 78-11-25 (2002).

85. Section 11 does not purport to limit the authority of the State to define and punish crimes and has never been so construed. *See, e.g., Nelson v. Smith*, 154 P.2d 634, 638 (Utah 1944) (statute making the practice of law without a license a crime does not violate art. I, § 11).

Retained Rights

Article I, § 25, of the Utah Constitution provides: "This enumeration of rights shall not be construed to impair or deny others retained by the people."[86] In any challenge to a prohibition of abortion, abortion advocates are likely to argue that abortion is a "retained right" under art. I, § 25. A proper interpretation of § 25, however, would not support a right to abortion as a retained right.

As noted in a preceding section of this analysis (due process), the Utah Supreme Court cited art. I, § 7 (due process), and § 25 (retained rights), in support of its holding that "the Utah Constitution recognizes and protects the inherent and retained right of a parent to maintain parental ties to his or her child...."[87] In its analysis of § 25, the court concluded that "the right of a parent not to be deprived of parental rights without a showing of unfitness, abandonment, or substantial neglect is so fundamental to our society and so basic to our constitutional order ... that it ranks among those referred to in Article I, § 25 of the Utah Constitution and the Ninth Amendment of the United States Constitution as being retained by the people."[88] The state supreme court has not recognized abortion as a "retained right" under § 25. And, given the methodology employed in *In re J.P.*, no such right is likely to be recognized.[89]

"The rights inherent in family relationships," the court explained, "are the most obvious examples of rights retained by the people. They are 'natural,' 'intrinsic,' or 'prior' in the sense that our Constitutions *presuppose* them, as they presuppose the right to own and dispose of property."[90] Moreover, the right of parents in the upbringing of their children "is rooted not in state or federal statutory or constitutional law, *to which it is logically and chronologically prior*, but in nature and human instinct."[91]

The court's emphasis that parental rights over their children are "natural" and "instinctive," and antedate the adoption of the state and federal constitu-

---

86. UTAH CONST. art. I, § 25 (1991).

87. *In re J.P.*, 648 P.2d at 1377.

88. *Id.* at 1375. The Ninth Amendment provides: "The enumeration in the Constitution of certain rights, shall not be construed to deny or disparage others retained by the people." U.S. CONST. AMEND. IX (West 2006).

89. Apart from parental rights issues, the Utah Supreme Court has not recognized any other "retained right" under § 25. *See MacArthur v. San Juan County*, 416 F. Supp. 2d 1098, 1178–79 (D. Utah 2005) (discussing case law).

90. 648 P.2d at 1373 (emphasis added).

91. *Id.* (emphasis added).

tions (and their retention of rights provisions), strongly suggests that only long established rights qualify as "retained rights" under § 25. That suggestion is confirmed by the court's analysis of the substantive due process right of parents to raise their children, which was based on a review of the State's (and the Nation's) legal history and tradition.[92] For the reasons set forth in the discussion of Utah's due process guarantee (art. I, § 7), however, there is no basis for asserting a right to abortion under the Utah Constitution. Abortion at any stage of pregnancy (except to save the life of the pregnant woman) was a crime from 1876, twenty years before Utah was admitted to the Union, until *Roe v. Wade* was decided almost one hundred years later.

In addition to the foregoing, in *In re J.P.*, the Utah Supreme Court clearly implied that art. I, § 25, of the Utah Constitution was modeled on the Ninth Amendment to the United States Constitution.[93] In light of the source from which § 25 was drawn, it should be given a parallel interpretation. That, in turn, suggests that if no right to abortion exists under the Ninth Amendment, then none would be recognized under § 25. The Supreme Court, however, has rooted the "abortion liberty" in the liberty language of the Due Process Clause of the Fourteenth Amendment, not in the unenumerated rights language of the Ninth Amendment.[94] Because abortion has not been recognized as a "retained right" under the Ninth Amendment, it should not be recognized as one under § 25, either.

Conclusion

Based on the foregoing analysis, an argument that the Utah Constitution protects a right to abortion that is separate from, and independent of, the right to abortion recognized in *Roe v. Wade* would not likely prevail. That, in turn, suggests that if *Roe*, as modified by *Casey*, is ultimately overruled, the State

---

92. *Id.* at 1372–73, 1374–75.

93. *Id.* at 1372–73, 1375, 1377 (discussing art. I, § 25, and the Ninth Amendment in the same context).

94. *See Roe*, 410 U.S. at 153; *Casey*, 505 U.S. at 846. In any event, the Ninth Amendment, standing alone, is not a source of substantive rights. *Gibson v. Matthews*, 926 F.2d 532, 537 (6th Cir. 1991). Although "[s]ome unenumerated rights may be of [c]onstitutional magnitude," that is only "by virtue of other amendments, such as the Fifth or Fourteenth Amendment. A person cannot claim a right that exists solely under the Ninth Amendment." *United States v. Vital Health Products, Ltd.*, 786 F. Supp. 761, 777 (E.D. Wis. 1992), *aff'd mem. op., sub nom. United States v. LeBeau*, 985 F.2d 563 (7th Cir. 1993). *See also Charles v. Brown*, 495 F. Supp. 862, 863 (N.D. Ala. 1980) (same).

Utah could enforce its current statute *prohibiting* abortion (or enact a new statute prohibiting abortion). Moreover, nothing in the Utah Constitution precludes Utah from *regulating* abortion within federal constitutional limits in the meantime.

CHAPTER 48

VERMONT

Summary

As the result of a decision of the Vermont Supreme Court interpreting the Vermont Constitution, the State of Vermont probably could not prohibit any abortion before viability, or any abortion after viability that was necessary to preserve the pregnant woman's life or health, even if *Roe v. Wade*,[1] as modified by *Planned Parenthood of Southeastern Pennsylvania v. Casey*,[2] were overruled, unless the state constitution is amended to overturn that decision (or that decision is overruled). The State's authority under the state constitution to regulate abortion within current federal constitutional limits is unknown because no such regulations have been enacted to date.

Analysis

Vermont has not expressly repealed its pre-*Roe* abortion statute, which prohibits performance of an abortion upon a woman unless the procedure is "necessary to preserve her life."[3] Nevertheless, in light of the Vermont Supreme Court's pre-*Roe* decision in *Beecham v. Leahy*,[4] it is unlikely that § 101 (or any other prohibition) could be enforced, at least before viability, even if *Roe*, as modified by *Casey*, were overruled.

Beecham was a declaratory judgment action challenging the validity of the Vermont abortion statute. In its opinion, the Vermont Supreme Court noted that the "prohibitory provisions" of the statute "specifically do not apply" to the pregnant woman herself, and concluded that "[t]he legislature, by this act,

---

1. 410 U.S. 113 (1973).
2. 505 U.S. 833 (1992).
3. Vt. Stat. Ann. tit. 13, § 101 (1988).
4. 287 A.2d 836 (Vt. 1972).

has not denied her the right to be aborted."[5] "As to her, her personal rights have been left to her, and there is no legislative declaration saying that her own concerns for her personal integrity are in any way criminal or proscribed."[6] With respect to the pregnant woman, therefore, "the law is left as it was at the time of the adoption of our constitution."[7] According to the court, there was general agreement "that such proscriptions as there were against abortion certainly did not come into play until the fetus had 'quickened,' if indeed it was then ever a separate crime from homicide."[8]

The abortion statute's exclusion of the pregnant woman herself from criminal liability constituted an "implicit recognition by the legislature of the [woman's] contended for personal rights...."[9] The court determined that the abortion statute had been enacted to protect pregnant women.[10] In light of that purpose, "the statute is valid and necessary," but only to the extent that it "prevents unskilled and untrained persons from acting in an area properly medical [in nature]."[11] To the extent that the statute denies a pregnant woman the assistance of a trained physician to perform an abortion, however, it is arbitrary:

> The stringent restrictions on the exercise of expert and informed judgment by doctors with reference to their patients stands differently. Indeed, the asserted purpose of protecting the pregnant woman's health rings seriously false. On the one hand the legislation, by specific reference, leaves untouched in the woman herself those rights respecting her own choice to bear children now coming to be recognized in many jurisdictions. [Citation omitted]. Yet, tragically, unless her life itself is at stake, the law leaves her only to the recourse of attempts at self-induced abortion, uncounselled and unassisted by a doctor, in a situation where medical attention is imperative.[12]

---

5. *Beecham*, 287 A.2d at 839, referring to the last sentence of § 101 which provides that "the woman whose miscarriage is caused or attempted shall not be liable to the penalties prescribed by this section."

6. *Id.*

7. *Id.*

8. *Id.* (citations omitted). "Quickening" is that stage of pregnancy, usually sixteen to eighteen weeks gestation, when the woman first detects fetal movement.

9. *Id.*

10. *Id.* (citing *State v. Howard*, 32 Vt. 380, 399 (1859)).

11. *Id.*

12. *Id.*

The court acknowledged that "there is a place for regulation of medical practice for the protection of the health and well-being of citizens in this area."[13] Section 101, however, "is not regulative, but prohibitive."[14] "Although it avoids confrontation with the rights of the [pregnant woman], it unlawfully impinges upon them to a measure beyond the justifications of governmental action."[15] The regulation of abortion is "an appropriate area for legislative action, provided such legislation does not, as the present law does, restrict to the point of unlawful prohibition."[16] However, "as the law now stands, barring, as it does, the medical aid the [pregnant woman] seeks in her present circumstances, it is invalid, and cannot be resorted to by way of a criminal prosecution against the doctor."[17]

Without specifying whether its decision was based on state or federal constitutional grounds, the court held:

> [T]he legislature, having affirmed the right of a woman to abort, cannot simultaneously, by denying medical aid in all but cases where it is necessary to preserve her life, prohibit its safe exercise. This is more than regulation, and an anomaly fatal to the application of this statute to medical practitioners.[18]

In response to a motion for clarification, the court stated on rehearing that if the police power "is invoked through means or methods which are unreasonable, inappropriate, oppressive or discriminatory, constitutional limitations are transgressed, individual rights are invalidated and the action is void."[19]

> Even if a statute purports to have been enacted for the protection of public health, safety or morals, if it has no just relation to such objects, or is a plain and palpable invasion of constitutional rights, the courts have a duty to adjudge and thereby give effect to the Constitution. [Citation omitted].

> [T]he infirmity of the present statute [is] that ... without reason or warrant, [it] deprives a woman of medical aid, even though she may be afflicted in body or mind, or both, short of imminent death, in relation to the exercise of a right recognized and allowed by the very same statute.[20]

---

13. *Id.*
14. *Id.*
15. *Id.* at 839–40.
16. *Id.* at 840 (citation omitted).
17. *Id.*
18. *Id.* (citations omitted).
19. *Id.* at 841 (citation omitted).
20. *Id.*

It is not clear whether the decision in *Beecham* ultimately rests upon state or federal constitutional grounds (or both). Nevertheless, the language of the opinion strongly suggests that the Vermont Supreme Court would not uphold an abortion prohibition, even one that included (as § 101 does not) a declaration that a woman has no *statutory* right to obtain an abortion (except to save her life). This is apparent not only from the court's "rights-based" rhetoric, but, critically, from its statement that the regulation of abortion is "an appropriate area for legislative action, *provided such legislation does not … restrict to the point of unlawful prohibition.*"[21] *Beecham* suggests that, in the absence of a state constitutional amendment authorizing such legislation, the Vermont Supreme Court would invalidate any statute that attempted to prohibit abortion, at least before viability.[22] In the court's own words, a prohibition would constitute "a plain and palpable invasion of constitutional rights."[23] Whether the court would uphold legislation prohibiting post-viability abortions or regulating abortion is unknown because, since *Roe*, Vermont has enacted no such legislation.

Conclusion

Because of the Vermont Supreme Court's decision in *Beecham v. Leahy*, the State of Vermont probably could not enforce tit. 13, § 101 (or any other abortion prohibition), at least before viability, even if *Roe*, as modified by *Casey*, were overruled, unless the state constitution is amended to overturn the holding in *Beecham* (or the latter is overruled). Whether the State may regulate abortion within current federal constitutional limits is unknown and has not been determined.

---

21. *Id.* at 840 (emphasis added). A prohibition is "unlawful," of course, only if it is unconstitutional.

22. The Supreme Court has not yet decided whether a statute prohibiting post-viability abortions must make exceptions for mental, as well as physical, health. *See Voinovich v. Women's Medical Professional Corporation*, 523 U.S. 1036, 1039 (1998) (Thomas, J., dissenting from denial of *certiorari*) (noting that this issue was not addressed in *Doe v. Bolton*, 410 U.S. 179 (1973), the companion case to *Roe v. Wade*). As a result, it is not known whether, as a matter of *state* constitutional law, the Vermont Supreme Court would require a post-viability statute to contain a mental health exception.

23. *Id.* at 841.

CHAPTER 49

VIRGINIA

Summary

The Virginia Supreme Court has not yet decided whether the Virginia Constitution protects a right to abortion separate from, and independent of, the right to abortion recognized under the United States Constitution.[1] A careful examination of the state constitution, in light of its history and interpretation, as well as other relevant legal sources, however, suggests that the state supreme court probably would not recognize a state constitutional right to abortion. Thus, if *Roe v. Wade*,[2] as modified by *Planned Parenthood of Southeastern Pennsylvania v. Casey*,[3] were overruled, Virginia could enact a statute prohibiting abortion. Moreover, nothing in the state constitution, properly understood, precludes the State from enacting and enforcing reasonable measures regulating abortion within current federal constitutional limits.

Analysis

The pre-*Roe* Virginia abortion statutes were based on § 230.3 of the Model Penal Code.[4] An abortion could be performed only by a licensed physician in an accredited hospital when (1) continuation of the pregnancy was likely to result in the death of the woman or "substantially impair" her mental or physical health, (2) there was a "substantial medical likelihood" that "the child

---

1. The Virginia Supreme Court has referred to the right to abortion solely as a mater of *federal*, not *state*, constitutional law. *See Miller v. Johnson*, 343 S.E.2d 301, 304 (Va. 1986) ("[w]ithin specified limits a woman is entitled to have an abortion if she so chooses") (citing *Roe v. Wade*).

2. 410 U.S. 113 (1973).

3. 505 U.S. 833 (1992).

4. VA. CODE ANN. § 18.1-62 *et seq.* (Michie Supp. 1971). The complete text of § 230.3 of the Model Penal Code is set out in Appendix B to the Supreme Court's decision in *Doe v. Bolton*, 410 U.S. 179, 205–07 (1973).

[would] be born with an irremediable and incapacitating mental or physical defect," or (3) the pregnancy resulted from incest or promptly reported rape.[5] The statutes did not place any express limitation on the stage of pregnancy at which an authorized abortion could be performed. The statutes were repealed in 1975.[6]

Based upon arguments that have been raised in other States with similar constitutional provisions, possible sources for an asserted abortion right could include provisions of the state constitution guaranteeing free exercise of religion and prohibiting the establishment of religion (art. I, § 16); guaranteeing due process of law (§ 11); prohibiting discrimination (§ 11); recognizing equality and inherent rights (§ 1); providing that government is instituted for the common benefit (§ 3); urging frequent recurrence to fundamental principles (§ 15); and recognizing unenumerated rights (§ 17).[7] The analysis that follows addresses each of these provisions.

Free Exercise of Religion, Prohibition of the Establishment of Religion

Article I, § 16, of the Virginia Constitution provides:

> That religion or the duty which we owe to our Creator, and the manner of discharging it, can be directed only by reason and conviction, not by force or violence; and, therefore, all men are equally entitled to the free exercise of religion, according to the dictates of conscience; and that it is the mutual duty of all to practice Christian forbearance, love, and charity towards each other. No man shall be compelled to frequent or support any religious worship, place, or ministry whatsoever, nor shall be enforced, restrained, molested, or burthened in his body or goods, nor shall otherwise suffer on account of his religious opinions or belief; but all men shall be free to profess

---

5. § 18.1-62.1(c). The law imposed other conditions. A hospital review board had to give its written consent. *Id.* § 18.1-62.1(d). If the abortion was being sought because of the unborn child's mental or physical defect, the written consent of the woman's husband was necessary. *Id.* § 18.1-62.1(e). In the case of a minor, the written consent of her parent or guardian was necessary, or, if the woman was married, the written consent of her husband. *Id.*

6. 1975 Va. Acts 18, ch. 14, § 1, ch. 15, § 1.

7. Two other more unlikely source of an abortion right under the Virginia Constitution-art. I, § 10 (prohibiting unreasonable searches and seizures) and art. I, § 12 (guaranteeing freedom of speech)-are discussed generally in Chapter 3, *supra.*

and by argument to maintain their opinions in matters of religion, and the same shall in nowise diminish, enlarge, or affect their civil capacities. And the General Assembly shall not prescribe any religious test whatever, or confer any peculiar privileges or advantages on any sect or denomination, or pass any law requiring or authorizing any religious society, or the people of any district within this Commonwealth, to levy on themselves or others, any tax for the erection or repair of any house of public worship, or for the support of any church or ministry; but it shall be left to every person to select his religious instructor, and to make for his support such private contract as he shall please.[8]

In any challenge to a statute prohibiting abortion, abortion advocates may raise either or both of two arguments under art. I, § 16. First, relying upon the second clause of the first sentence of § 16, they may argue that an abortion prohibition interferes with the "free exercise" of a woman's religious freedom by forbidding her from obtaining an abortion that would be allowed by her religion. Second, relying upon the third sentence of § 16, they may argue in the alternative (or in addition) that in prohibiting abortion, the General Assembly has conferred a "peculiar privilege[] or advantage[]" on a religious "sect or denomination" because such prohibition reflects sectarian beliefs regarding when human life begins and the sinfulness of abortion. Neither argument would likely prevail.

The Virginia Supreme Court has not expressly equated the "free exercise" and anti-establishment clauses of art. I, § 16, with the Free Exercise and Establishment Clauses of the First Amendment. Nevertheless, as a leading commentator on the Virginia Constitution has observed, "Virginia's courts, in interpreting § 16, follow the federal approach closely."[9] The case law supports Professor Howard's observation.[10] That consistency of approach suggests that

---

8. VA. CONST. art. I, § 16 (Michie 2005).

9. A.E. Dick Howard, COMMENTARIES ON THE CONSTITUTION OF VIRGINIA (hereinafter COMMENTARIES) 296 (1974).

10. *Cha v. Korean Presbyterian Church of Washington*, 553 S.E.2d 511, 515 (Va. 2001) ("[t]he Free Exercise Clause of the First Amendment to the Constitution of the United States and Article I, § 16 of the Commonwealth of Virginia do not permit a circuit court to substitute its secular judgment for a church's judgment when the church makes decisions regarding the selection or retention of its pastor"); *Habel v. Industrial Development Authority of the City of Lynchburg*, 400 S.E.2d 516, 518 (Va. 1991) (treating the Supreme Court's construction of the Establishment Clause of the First Amendment as "helpful and persuasive ... in construing the analogous state constitutional provision"). *See also Horen v. Commonwealth*, 479 S.E.2d 553, 556–57 (Va. Ct. App. 1997) (construing Free Exercise Clause and art. I,

a challenge to an abortion statute that would not succeed under the First Amendment would not succeed under art. I, §16, either. For the reasons set forth in Chapter 2, *supra*, an abortion statute could not be successfully challenged on First Amendment grounds. Accordingly, a similar challenge under art. I, §16, would not likely be successful.[11]

Due Process of Law

Article I, §11, of the Virginia Constitution provides, in part, that "no person shall be deprived of his life, liberty, or property without due process of law."[12] In any challenge to an abortion prohibition Virginia may enact if *Roe* is overruled, abortion advocates are most likely to rely upon the due process guarantee of art. I, §11, arguing that the prohibition of abortion interferes with a woman's liberty interest in obtaining an abortion. Such an argument probably would not prevail.

The due process guarantee of art. I, §11, has a substantive, as well as a procedural, component, guaranteeing fundamental rights and liberties.[13] In determining whether an asserted liberty interest (or right) should be regarded as "fundamental," the United States Supreme Court applies a two-prong test. First,

---

§16, together). The Commission on Constitutional Revision, which drafted the present state constitution, noted that "in American constitutional law, state and federal, religious freedom has two independent aspects: free exercise of religion, and no establishment of religion." THE CONSTITUTION OF VIRGINIA[:] REPORT OF THE COMMISSION ON CONSTITUTIONAL REVISION (hereinafter CCR REPORT) 101 (1969).

11. Entirely apart from the Virginia Supreme Court's reliance on federal precedent in interpreting art. I, §16, an argument challenging an abortion prohibition on the basis that it "establishes" a religion by embodying sectarian views regarding the sinfulness of abortion would appear to be foreclosed by a decision of the court rejecting a challenge to a Sunday closing law. *See Mandell v. Haddon*, 121 S.E.2d 516, 523–24 (Va. 1961). In *Mandell*, the state supreme court held that "[t]he mere fact that the legislature selected Sunday, which is the traditional day for religious observance, for closing stores does not change the character of the ... Sunday law from a secular to a religious law." Id. at 524. If mandating a "day of rest" on Sunday does not violate art. I, §16, even though it may coincide with Christian beliefs regarding the sanctity of the Christian Sabbath, then neither would a law prohibiting abortion, regardless of whether the law coincides with religious views regarding the sinfulness of abortion.

12. VA. CONST. art. I, §11 (Michie 2005).

13. *Paris v. Commonwealth*, 545 S.E.2d 557, 560 (Va. Ct. App. 2001) ("[t]he United States and Virginia Constitutions provide for substantive due process which protects ... fundamental rights and liberties") (citation and internal quotation marks omitted).

there must be a "careful description" of the asserted fundamental liberty interest.[14] Second, the interest, so described, must be firmly rooted in "the Nation's history, legal traditions, and practices."[15] The Virginia reviewing courts employ the same test in evaluating state substantive due process claims.[16] A right to abortion cannot be regarded as "fundamental" under art. I, § 11, because such a "right" is not firmly rooted in Virginia's "history, legal traditions, and practices."[17]

Virginia enacted its first abortion statute in 1848. The statute made it a crime "to administer to any pregnant woman, any medicine, drug or substance whatever, or use or employ any instrument or other means with intent thereby to destroy the child with which such woman may be pregnant, or to produce abortion or miscarriage, and ... thereby destroy such child, or produce such abortion or miscarriage, unless the same shall have been done to preserve the life of the woman...."[18] If the death of a "quick child" resulted, the offense was punished as a felony; if the death of a child, not quick, resulted, the offense was punished as a misdemeanor.[19] In 1873, the distinction in punishments between causing the death of a "quick child" or a "child, not quick" was eliminated and all abortions were punished as felonies (subject to an exception when the abortion was performed "in good faith, with the intention of saving the life of [the

---

14. *Washington v. Glucksberg*, 521 U.S. 702, 721 (1997) (citation and internal quotation marks omitted).

15. *Id.* at 710.

16. *Paris*, 545 S.E.2d at 560; *McCabe v. Commonwealth*, 650 S.E.2d 508, 510–13 (Va. 2007) (following *Glucksberg* methodology in holding that a felon does not have a "fundamental or specially protected due process right" "to be free from post-incarceration registration" as a sex offender).

17. To the extent that Virginia reviewing courts recognize the same fundamental rights under the *state* due process guarantee as the Supreme Court does under the *federal* due process guarantee, *see McCabe*, 650 S.E.2d at 510–13, *Paris*, 545 S.E.2d at 560, *Willis v. Mallett*, 561 S.E.2d 705, 708 (Va. 2002) (due process guarantees of art. I, § 11, and § 1 of the Fourteenth Amendment "are virtually the same"), abortion would not qualify as a "fundamental" right. Although the Supreme Court characterized the right to choose abortion as "fundamental" in *Roe*, 410 U.S. at 152–53, it tacitly abandoned that characterization in *Casey*, 505 U.S. at 869–79 (Joint Op. of O'Connor, Kennedy and Souter, JJ., replacing *Roe's* "strict scrutiny" standard of review with the more relaxed "undue burden" standard, allowing for a broader measure of abortion regulation).

18. Act of March 14, 1848, ch. 120, tit. II, ch. III, § 9, 1847–48 Va. Acts 96, *codified at* VA. CODE tit. 54, ch. 191, § 8 (1849).

19. *Id.* For purposes of this statute, a "quick child" referred to "quickening," that stage of pregnancy, usually sixteen to eighteen weeks gestation, when the woman first detects fetal movement.

pregnant] woman or [her unborn] child."[20] This statute remained on the books, essentially unchanged, until the Commonwealth enacted a statute based on the Model Penal Code in 1970.[21]

Prior to *Roe v. Wade*, the Virginia Supreme Court regularly affirmed the convictions for abortion without any hint or suggestion that either the prosecutions or the convictions were barred by the Virginia Constitution.[22] In *Anderson v. Commonwealth*, the state supreme court explained that the abortion statute had been enacted "to protect the health and lives of pregnant women and their unborn children from those who intentionally and not in good faith would thwart nature by performing or causing abortion or miscarriage."[23] One year earlier, the court was even more emphatic about the purpose of the statute, which was passed, "not for the protection of the woman, but for the protection of the unborn child and through it society."[24] Subsequent to *Roe*, the Virginia legislature amended its abortion statute to conform to the trimester framework adopted in *Roe* (and later abandoned in *Casey*).[25] The Commonwealth has enacted a comprehensive scheme of abortion regulation.[26]

Virginia has recognized the rights of unborn children in a variety of contexts outside of abortion, including criminal law, property law and health care law. In criminal law, the killing of a fetus is a homicide.[27] In property law, heirs conceived before but born after the death of a decedent who dies without a will "shall inherit as if they had been born during the lifetime of the decedent."[28] And, subject to certain exceptions, children born after a person executes a will take that share of the estate they would have received if

---

20. Va. Code tit. 54, ch. 187, §8 (1873).

21. Va. Code tit. 54, ch. 187, §8 (1873), *recodified at* Va. Code Ann. §3670 (1887), *recodified at* Va. Code Ann. §4401 (1919), *recodified at* Va. Code §18-68 (Michie 1950), *recodified at* Va. Code §18.1-62 (Michie 1960), *amended by* 1970 Va. Acts, ch. 508. *See* nn. 4-5, *supra*, and accompanying text.

22. *Coffman v. Commonwealth*, 50 S.E.2d 431 (Va. 1948); *Anderson v. Commonwealth*, 58 S.E.2d 72 (Va. 1950); *Mendoza v. Commonwealth*, 103 S.E.2d 1 (Va. 1958); *Russo v. Commonwealth*, 148 S.E.2d 820 (Va. 1966).

23. 58 S.E.2d at 75.

24. *Miller v. Bennett*, 56 S.E.2d 217, 221 (Va. 1949).

25. Va. Code §§18.2-73, 18.2-74, 18.2-75 (Michie 2004).

26. *Id.* §18.2-76 (Michie 2004) (mandating informed consent and a twenty-four hour waiting period); §16.1-241(V) (Michie Supp. 2007) (requiring parental consent); §18.2-75 (Michie 2004) (recognizing individual and institutional rights of conscience); §§32.1-92.1, 32.1-92.2 (restricting public funding of abortion for indigent women).

27. *Id.* §18.2-32.2 (Michie 2004).

28. *Id.* §64.1-8.1 (Michie 2007).

the decedent had died intestate (without a will).[29] Finally, in health care law, an advance directive may not authorize the performance of a non-therapeutic abortion.[30]

A right to abortion cannot be found in the text, structure or history of the Virginia Constitution. There is no evidence that the framers or ratifiers of the state constitution intended to limit the Legislature's authority to prohibit abortion.[31] Such an intent would have been remarkable in light of Virginia's history of prohibiting abortion which dates back to 1848, the Virginia Supreme Court's repeated statements that the abortion statute was intended to protect unborn human life and the Commonwealth's recognition of the rights of unborn children outside the context of abortion.

Prohibiting Discrimination

Article I, § 11, of the Virginia Constitution provides, in part, that "the right to be free from any governmental discrimination upon the basis of religious conviction, race, color, sex, or national origin shall not be abridged, except that the mere separation of the sexes shall not be considered discrimination."[32] In any challenge to an abortion prohibition Virginia may enact, abortion advocates may be expected to rely upon art. I, § 11, arguing that the prohibition of abortion discriminates against women because only women can become pregnant. Such an argument would not likely prevail, however.

Although art. I, § 11, does not contain express language guaranteeing equal protection, the Virginia Supreme Court has repeatedly held that the anti-discrimination language of § 11, is the equivalent of the Equal Protection Clause of the Fourteenth Amendment, that § 11 is no broader in scope than the Equal Protection Clause and that it should be given the same interpretation.[33] Given this congruence of interpretation, if an abortion prohibition would not vio-

---

29. *Id.* §§ 64.1-70, 64.1-70-1.

30. *Id.* § 54.1-2986(c) (Michie 2005).

31. *See* CCR Report at 85-101 (explanation of draft of Bill of Rights).

32. Va. Const. art. I, § 11 (Michie 2005).

33. Article I, § 11, "prohibits invidious, arbitrary discrimination upon the basis of sex. It is no broader than the equal protection clause of the Fourteenth Amendment to the United States Constitution." *Archer v. Mays*, 194 S.E.2d 707, 711 (Va. 1973). In *Wilkins v. West*, 571 S.E.2d 100 (Va. 2002), the Virginia Supreme Court reaffirmed *Archer*, stating that anti-discrimination clause of art. I, § 11 is "congruent with the federal equal protection clause...." *Id* at 111. Accordingly, the court would "continue to apply the standards and nomenclature developed under the equal protection clause ... to claims involving claims of discrimination under Article I, § 11 of the state constitution...." *Id.*

late the federal Equal Protection Clause, then it would not violate the anti-discrimination clause of art. I, § 11, either.

For purpose of both state and federal equal protection analysis, there are three standards of judicial review. Under the first standard, which is known as rational basis scrutiny, legislation "is presumed to be valid and will be sustained if the classification drawn by the statute is rationally related to a legitimate state interest."[34] Under the second standard, intermediate (or heightened) scrutiny, which applies to sex-based classifications, the classification must be "substantially related to a sufficiently important governmental interest."[35] Under the third standard, strict scrutiny, which applies to statutes that classify "by race, alienage, or national origin" or "impinge" on the exercise of fundamental "personal rights protected by the Constitution," the classification "will be sustained only if [it is] suitably tailored to serve a compelling state interest."[36]

Strict scrutiny review would not apply to an abortion prohibition because, for the reasons set forth in the preceding section of this analysis (due process of law), a prohibition of abortion would not "impinge" upon the exercise of a fundamental personal right. Nor would the prohibition of abortion classify persons on the basis of a "suspect" personal characteristic (race, alienage or national origin). Abortion advocates may argue in the alternative, however, that a statute prohibiting abortion discriminates against women and is subject to intermediate scrutiny because only women are capable of becoming pregnant. An abortion prohibition would appear to satisfy this level of scrutiny because the prohibition would have be "substantially related" to the "important governmental interest" in protecting unborn human life. Nevertheless, the standard applicable to sex-based discrimination (intermediate scrutiny) would not apply to an abortion prohibition. Abortion laws do not discriminate on the basis of sex.

First, the United States Supreme Court has reviewed restrictions on abortion funding under a rational basis standard of review, *not* under the intermediate (heightened) scrutiny required of gender-based classifications.[37] Indeed, the Court has held that "the disfavoring of abortion ... is not *ipso facto* sex discrimination," and, citing its decisions in *Harris* and other cases addressing abortion funding, stated that "the constitutional test applicable to government

---

34. *City of Cleburne, Texas v. Cleburne Living Center*, 473 U.S. 432, 440 (1985).

35. *Id.* at 441. A similar standard applies to classifications based on illegitimacy. *See Mills v. Habluetzel*, 456 U.S. 91, 99 (1982) (classification must be "substantially related to a legitimate state interest").

36. *City of Cleburne*, 473 U.S. at 440.

37. *Harris v. McRae*, 448 U.S. 297, 321–26 (1980).

abortion-funding restrictions is not the heightened-scrutiny standard that our cases demand for sex discrimination, ... but the ordinary rationality standard."[38]

Second, even assuming that an abortion prohibition differentiates between men and women on the basis of sex, and would otherwise be subject to a higher standard of review, the United States Supreme Court has held that biological differences between men and women may justify different treatment based on those differences. In upholding a statutory rape statute that applied only to males, the Supreme Court noted, "this Court has consistently upheld statutes where the gender classification is not invidious, but rather realistically reflects the fact that the sexes are not similarly situated in certain circumstances."[39] "Abortion statutes are examples of cases in which the sexes are not biologically similarly situated" because only women are capable of becoming pregnant and having abortions.[40]

A statute prohibiting abortion quite obviously can affect only women because only women are capable of becoming pregnant.[41] Unlike laws that use women's ability to become pregnant (or pregnancy itself) to discriminate against them in *other* areas (*e.g.*, employment opportunities), abortion prohibitions cannot fairly be said to involve a distinction between men and women that is a "mere pretext[] designed to erect an invidious discrimination against [women]."[42]

A prohibition of abortion would not interfere with the exercise of a fundamental state constitutional right, nor would it classify upon the basis of a sus-

---

38. *Bray v. Alexandria Women's Health Clinic*, 506 U.S. 263, 273 (1993). Several state supreme courts and individual state supreme court justices have recognized that abortion regulations and restrictions on abortion funding are not "directed at women as a class" so much as "abortion as a medical treatment, which, because it involves a potential life, has no parallel as a treatment method." *Bell v. Low Income Women of Texas*, 95 S.W.3d 253, 258 (Tex. 2002) (upholding funding restrictions) (citing *Harris*, 448 U.S. at 325). *See also Fischer v. Dep't of Public Welfare*, 502 A.2d 114, 125 (Pa. 1985) ("the basis for the distinction here is not sex, but abortion") (upholding funding restrictions); *Moe v. Secretary of Administration & Finance*, 417 N.E.2d 387, 407 (Mass. 1981) (Hennessey, C.J., dissenting) (funding restrictions were "directed at abortion as a medical procedure, not women as a class"); *Right to Choose v. Byrne*, 450 A.2d 925, 950 (N.J. 1982) (O'Hern, J., dissenting) ("[t]he subject of the legislation is not the person of the recipient, but the nature of the claimed medical service"). Both *Moe* and *Right to Choose* were decided on other grounds. The dissenting justices were addressing alternative arguments raised by the plaintiffs, but not reached by the majority opinions.

39. *Michael M. v. Superior Court*, 450 U.S. 464, 469 (1981).

40. *Jane L. v. Bangerter*, 794 F. Supp. 1537, 1549 (D. Utah 1992).

41. *Geduldig v. Aiello*, 417 U.S. 484, 496 n. 20 (1974) ("[n]ormal pregnancy is an objectively, identifiable physical condition with unique characteristics").

42. *Id.*

pect or quasi-suspect characteristic. Accordingly, it would be subject to rational basis review. Under that standard of review, the statute need only be "rationally related to a legitimate state interest."[43] A law prohibiting abortion would be "rationally related" to the "legitimate state interest" in protecting the lives of unborn children.

Equality and Inherent Rights

Article I, § 1, of the Virginia Constitution provides:

> That all men are by nature equally free and independent and have certain inherent rights, of which, when they enter into a state of society, they cannot, by any compact, deprive or divest their posterity; namely, the enjoyment of life and liberty, with the means of acquiring and possessing property, and pursuing and obtaining happiness and safety.[44]

In any challenge to a statute prohibiting abortion, abortion advocates may rely on art. I, § 1, arguing that the prohibition deprives women of their liberty to obtain an abortion, thereby denying them their "happiness and safety." Such an argument would not likely prevail.

The Virginia Court of Appeals has described the language of art. I, § 1, as "ideological … rather than literal,"[45] thereby suggesting that § 1 does not create judicially enforceable constitutional rights.[46] That suggestion is confirmed by the history of its adoption. "George Mason drafted the first four sections of the Bill of Rights as a political philosophy to set Virginia properly on her new course. His words have survived two hundred years with no substantial changes, as a statement of those ideals which the framers felt should guide the future of the Commonwealth."[47] Professor Howard noted that in drafting the 1971 Constitution, "the Commission on Constitutional Revision was aware of proposals that all language not judicially enforceable be eliminated from the Bill of Rights.

---

43. *Cleburne*, 473 U.S. at 440.

44. VA. CONST. art. I, § 1 (Michie 2005).

45. *Paris v. Commonwealth*, 545 S.E.2d at 558 n. 4.

46. Art. I, § 1, has not been cited in support of a decision of the Virginia Supreme Court to strike down a state statute or municipal ordinance since 1942. *See Williams v. City of Richmond*, 14 S.E.2d 287 (Va. 1942) (ordinance imposing a flat $50 tax on all businesses not otherwise taxed violated art. I, § 1, of the Virginia Constitution, and the Due Process and Equal Protection Clauses of the Fourteenth Amendment).

47. Howard, COMMENTARIES at 58.

It recommended, however, that Mason's words be retained as a reminder of the Commonwealth's ideological heritage[:]"[48] "Section 1 has often been discussed in decisions of the Virginia Supreme Court of Appeals [now the Virginia Supreme Court], but its language, strictly speaking, is more exhortatory than enforceable."[49] As such, it is not a source of judicially enforceable substantive rights, as a Virginia Circuit Court opinion has observed:

> Although [art. I, §1] is contained in the Virginia Constitution's Bill of Rights, it neither expressly declares that it is self-executing, as does Article I, §8 [dealing with the rights of criminal defendants], nor does it contain language that supplies a sufficient rule and remedy, as do Article I, §11's guarantees against takings of property. Rather, Article I, §1, merely recites principles, but provides no rules by means of which those principles may be given the force of law. Again, the legislature could have included express self-execution language or language providing a rule and a remedy, as they did for the other two cited sections, but they did not do so for Article I, §1.[50]

Because art. I, §1, does not create judicially enforceable rights, it could not be a source of a right to abortion under the Virginia Constitution.

Common Benefit

Article I, §3, of the Virginia Constitution provides, in part, that "government is, or ought to be, instituted for the common benefit, protection, and security of the people, nation, or community...."[51] In any challenge to a statute prohibiting abortion, abortion advocates may argue that the prohibition violates art. I, §3, because it does not promote the "common benefit." Such an argument would not likely prevail.

Article I, §3, has never been authoritatively construed by the Virginia Supreme Court and has never been cited in support of a decision striking down a statute of the Commonwealth. The use of the precatory phrase, "ought to be," suggests that §3 is aspirational only. This suggestion is confirmed by the

---

48. *Id.* at 64.

49. CCR Report at 87–88.

50. *Gray v. Rhoads*, 55 Va. Cir. 362, 368–69 (Va. Cir. Ct. 2001) (citation and internal quotation marks omitted), *reversed and remanded on other grounds*, 597 S.E.2d 93 (Va. 2004).

51. Va. Const. art. I, §3 (Michie 2005).

Commission on Constitutional Revision which characterized § 3 (along with §§ 1, 2 and 4 of art. I) as "hortatory."[52] Accordingly, § 3 could not serve as a source of an abortion right under the Virginia Constitution.

Fundamental Principles

Article I, § 15, of the Virginia Constitution provides:

> That no free government, nor the blessings of liberty, can be preserved to any people, but by a firm adherence to justice, moderation, temperance, frugality, and virtue; by frequent recurrence to fundamental principles; and by the recognition by all citizens that they have duties as well as rights, and that such rights cannot be enjoyed save in a society where law is respected and due process is observed.
>
> That free government rests, as does all progress, upon the broadest possible diffusion of knowledge, and that the Commonwealth should avail itself of those talents which nature has sown so liberally among its people by assuring the opportunity for their fullest development by an effective system of education throughout the Commonwealth.[53]

In any challenge to a statute prohibiting abortion, abortion advocates may argue that the prohibition interferes with the "fundamental principles" referenced in art. I, § 15. This argument would not likely prevail.

Referring to the first paragraph of § 15, Professor Howard observed that, "[a]s a hortatory provision, this part of § 15 does not impose enforceable obligations on anyone."[54] And in the only case construing art. I, § 15, the Virginia Supreme Court, referring to the second paragraph, held that its "language ... is aspirational and not mandatory."[55] Given that holding, § 15, by itself, cannot be regarded as a source of judicially enforceable "fundamental principles." Those principles are derived from *other* provisions of the state constitution (principally the guarantees set forth in the Bill of Rights). Section 15, therefore, is not a source of substantive rights. Accordingly, a right to abortion could not be derived from the language of art. I, § 15.

---

52. CCR Report at 88.
53. Va. Const. art. I, § 15 (Michie 2005).
54. Howard, Commentaries at 284.
55. *Scott v. Commonwealth*, 443 S.E.2d 138, 142 (Va. 1994).

Unenumerated Rights

Article I, § 17, of the Virginia Constitution provides: "The rights enumerated in this Bill of Rights shall not be construed to limit other rights of the people not therein expressed."[56] Abortion advocates may be expected to cite § 17 in support of an asserted right to abortion under the state constitution. Section 17, however, has never been authoritatively construed (or even cited) by the Virginia Supreme Court,[57] which is at least some indication that it is not a source of any substantive rights under the Virginia Constitution.

An entirely plausible reading of § 17 is that the enumeration of certain rights in the state constitution should not be construed to "limit" other rights retained by the people under the common law or statutes. But even if § 17 is understood to retain unspecified *constitutional* rights (as opposed to *common law* or *statutory* rights), abortion could not plausibly be considered to be among such rights because, at the time the Virginia Constitution was adopted in 1971, abortion was a crime. The argument that the first clause of § 17 retained as an "unenumerated" right conduct that was criminal when the state constitution was adopted is, at the very least, counterintuitive.

The language of § 17 appears to be based on the Ninth Amendment.[58] In light of that equivalence, § 17 should be given a parallel interpretation. That, in turn, suggests that if no right to abortion exists under the Ninth Amendment, then none would be recognized under art. I, § 17. The Supreme Court, however, has rooted the "abortion liberty" in the liberty language of the Due Process Clause of the Fourteenth Amendment, not in the unenumerated rights language of the Ninth Amendment.[59] Because abortion has not been recognized

---

56. VA. CONST. art. I, § 17 (Michie 2005).

57. "There apparently have been no Virginia cases using this section to assert constitutional rights." Howard, COMMENTARIES at 303. *See also* John Dinan, THE VIRGINIA STATE CONSTITUTION: A REFERENCE GUIDE 70 (Westport, Conn. 2006) (section 17 "has not been the subject of discussion or interpretation by the Virginia courts).

58. "The enumeration in the Constitution of certain rights, shall not be construed to deny or disparage others retained by the people." U.S. CONST. AMEND. IX (West 2006). Section 17, as Professor Howard noted, "closely paraphrases the Ninth Amendment...." COMMENTARIES at 303.

59. *See Roe*, 410 U.S. at 153; *Casey*, 505 U.S. at 846. In any event, the Ninth Amendment, standing alone, is not a source of substantive rights. *Gibson v. Matthews*, 926 F.2d 532, 537 (6th Cir. 1991). Although "[s]ome unenumerated rights may be of [c]onstitutional magnitude," that is only "by virtue of other amendments, such as the Fifth or Fourteenth Amendment. A person cannot claim a right that exists solely under the Ninth Amendment." *United States v. Vital Health Products, Ltd.*, 786 F. Supp. 761, 777 (E.D. Wis. 1992), *aff'd mem.*

as a "retained right" under the Ninth Amendment, it should not be recognized as one under § 17, either.[60]

Conclusion

Based on the foregoing analysis, an argument that the Virginia Constitution protects a right to abortion that is separate from, and independent of, the right to abortion recognized in *Roe v. Wade* would not likely succeed. That, in turn, suggests that if *Roe*, as modified by *Casey*, is ultimately overruled, the Commonwealth of Virginia could enact and enforce a statute *prohibiting* abortion. Moreover, nothing in the Virginia Constitution precludes Virginia from *regulating* abortion within federal constitutional limits in the meantime.

---

op., *sub nom. United States v. LeBeau*, 985 F.2d 563 (7th Cir. 1993). *See also Charles v. Brown*, 495 F. Supp. 862, 863 (N.D. Ala. 1980) (same).

60. "The problems that the courts have had in finding applications for the Ninth Amendment should suggest the hesitancy which a Virginia court might feel in applying § 17 of the Virginia Bill of Rights." Howard, COMMENTARIES at 313.

CHAPTER 50

WASHINGTON

Summary

The Washington Supreme Court has not yet decided whether the Washington Constitution protects a right to abortion separate from, and independent of, the right to abortion recognized under the United States Constitution.[1] A careful examination of the state constitution, in light of its history and interpretation, as well as other relevant legal sources, however, suggests that the state supreme court probably would not recognize a state constitutional right to abortion. Thus, if *Roe v. Wade*,[2] as modified by *Planned Parenthood of Southeastern Pennsylvania v. Casey*,[3] were overruled, Washington could enact a statute prohibiting abortion. Moreover, nothing in the state constitution, properly understood, precludes the State from enacting and enforcing reasonable measures regulating abortion within current federal constitutional limits.

---

1. In *State v. Koome*, 530 P.2d 260 (Wash. 1975), the Washington Supreme Court, in a five-to-four decision, struck down a provision in the State's pre-*Roe* statute requiring a minor to obtain the consent of her parents before obtaining an abortion (the statute had no provision for a judicial bypass mechanism). Although the state supreme court held that the parental consent requirement "unduly infringe[d] upon the right of privacy implicit in the fourteenth amendment to the Constitution of the United States and article I, section 3 of the Washington State Constitution," *id.* at 263, the court's decision rested upon federal precedent only, not on any cases interpreting art. I, §3. *Id.* at 260–66. In a more recent opinion, the court recognized that *Koome* was "decided under federal law," not state law. *Andersen v. King County*, 138 P.3d 963, 987 (Wash. 2006). *Koome* also held that the parental consent law impermissibly discriminated between different classes of pregnant women, in violation of the Equal Protection Clause of the Fourteenth Amendment and "the related principles of article I, section 12 of our state constitution." *Koome*, 530 P.2d at 266. Those principles are discussed later in this analysis *infra*.

2. 410 U.S. 113 (1973).

3. 505 U.S. 833 (1992).

Analysis

Washington had two sets of pre-*Roe* abortion statutes. Older statutes prohibited performance of an abortion upon a woman unless the procedure was "necessary to preserve her life or that of [her unborn] child,"[4] and made a woman's participation in her own abortion a criminal offense (subject to the same exception).[5] In November 1970, however, Washington voters approved by referendum a new abortion act.[6] This act, which by its terms did not expressly repeal the older statutes,[7] allowed abortion on demand of a woman "not quick with child and not more than four lunar months after conception."[8] Washington repealed all of its pre-*Roe* statutes in 1991.[9]

Based upon arguments that have been raised in other States with similar constitutional provisions, possible sources for an asserted abortion right could include provisions of the state constitution guaranteeing personal rights (art. I, §3), privacy (§7), religious freedom (§11), and equality of rights (art. XXXI, §1); prohibiting special privileges and immunities (art. I, §12); recognizing political power in the people (§1); urging frequent recurrence to fundamental principles (§32); and retaining rights (§30).[10] The analysis that follows addresses each of these provisions.

---

4. Wash. Rev. Code Ann. §9.02.010 (West Supp. 1971).

5. *Id.* §9.02.020. No prosecutions were reported under this statute.

6. *Id.* §§9.02.060 to 0.02.090.

7. *Id.* §9.020.060

8. *Id.* §§9.020.060, 9.02.070. A "quick" child refers to "quickening," that stage of pregnancy, usually sixteen to eighteen weeks gestation, when a woman first detects fetal movement. Four lunar months is sixteen weeks. The statutes adopted by referendum imposed other conditions. An abortion could be performed only by a licensed physician in a licensed hospital or approved medical facility. If the abortion was being sought by a married woman, the consent of her husband was necessary and, if she was an unmarried minor, the consent of her legal guardian. *Id.* §9.020.070. The law also required physical domicile in the State for ninety days prior to the performance of the abortion. *Id.*

9. 1992 Wash. Laws, ch. 1, §9, Initiative Measure No. 120, approved Nov. 5, 1991. Initiative Measure No. 120 also enacted the "Reproductive Privacy Act." The Act declares that "every individual possesses a fundamental right of privacy with respect to personal reproductive decisions," including abortions. *Id.* §1, *codified at* Wash. Rev. Code Ann. §9.02.100 (West 2003). Consistent with that declaration, the Act provides further that "[t]he state may not deny or interfere with a woman's right to choose to have an abortion prior to viability of the fetus, or to protect her life or health." *Id.* §2, *codified at* Wash. Rev. Code Ann. §9.02.110.

10. One other more unlikely source of an abortion right under the Washington Constitution-art. I, §5 (guaranteeing freedom of speech)-is discussed generally in Chapter 3, *supra.*

Personal Rights

Article I, § 3, of the Washington Constitution provides: "No person shall be deprived of life, liberty, or property, without due process of law."[11] In any state constitutional challenge to a statute prohibiting abortion, abortion advocates are likely to rely upon art. I, § 3, arguing that the prohibition interferes with a woman's liberty interest in obtaining an abortion. Such an argument probably would not succeed, however.

The Washington reviewing courts have consistently held that art. I, § 3, "offers no greater protection than the federal Due Process Clauses of the Fifth and Fourteenth Amendments."[12] This line of cases suggests that the Washington Supreme Court would not recognize a right to abortion under the liberty language of the *state* due process clause if the Supreme Court ultimately overrules *Roe*, as modified by *Casey*, which recognized a right to abortion under the equivalent language in the *federal* due process clause. Whether the state supreme court would recognize such a right while *Roe* remains the law of the land has not been determined,[13] and, given the almost complete absence of any state regulation of abortion, is unlikely to be determined at any time in the foreseeable future.[14] A more likely source of an independent state right to abortion on which abortion advocates are likely to rely is art. I, § 7.

---

11. WASH. CONST. art. I, § 3 (West 2002).

12. *In re Custody of RRB*, 31 P.3d 1212, 1221 n. 10 (Wash. Ct. App. 2001) (citing *State v. Manussier*, 921 P.2d 473, 486–88 (Wash. 1996)). *See also In re Dyer*, 20 P.3d 907, 912 (Wash. 2001) ("Washington's due process clause does not afford a broader due process protection than the Fourteenth Amendment"); *In re Matteson*, 12 P.3d 585, 591 (Wash. 2000) ("there is no material difference between the state and federal due process clauses").

13. *See* n. 1, *supra*.

14. Consistent with federal substantive due process analysis, *see Wisconsin v. Yoder*, 406 U.S. 205, 232 (1972), "Washington law recognizes that parents have a fundamental liberty and privacy interest in the care, custody and management of their children." *In re Dependency of C.B.*, 904 P.2d 1171, 1174 (Wash. Ct. App. 1995). To the extent that Washington reviewing courts recognize the same fundamental rights under the *state* due process guarantee as the Supreme Court does under the *federal* due process guarantee, abortion would not qualify as a "fundamental" right. Although the Supreme Court characterized the right to choose abortion as "fundamental" in *Roe*, 410 U.S. at 152–53, it tacitly abandoned that characterization in *Casey*, 505 U.S. at 869–79 (Joint Op. of O'Connor, Kennedy and Souter, JJ., replacing *Roe*'s "strict scrutiny" standard of review with the more relaxed "undue burden" standard, allowing for a broader measure of abortion regulation).

Privacy

Article I, §7, of the Washington Constitution provides: "No person shall be disturbed in his private affairs, or his home invaded, without authority of law."[15] In any challenge to a statute prohibiting abortion, abortion advocates probably would rely principally on art. I, §7, arguing that the prohibition interferes with a woman's privacy. Such an argument would not likely prevail.

As an initial matter, it must be noted that art. I, §7, "primarily governs search and seizure."[16] Although "a few cases have considered whether art. I, section 7 confers a right to privacy outside the search-and-seizure context,"[17] none has "attributed to the provision [a] broader scope than federal constitutional privacy law."[18] After a careful review of the precedents, the Washington Court of Appeals concluded that:

> [A]rticle I, section 7 does not provide greater protection for privacy interests than does the U.S. Constitution. The privacy provision of the Washington Constitution is largely concerned with protecting citizens from unreasonable search-and-seizure. And no case has suggested that section 7 was intended to afford greater privacy protection outside the search-and-seizure context than the federal constitution.[19]

Given the reluctance of the Washington reviewing courts to recognize "greater privacy protection outside the search-and-seizure context than the federal constitution," the Washington Supreme Court would probably not recognize an independent right to abortion under the privacy guarantee of art. I, §7, if *Roe v. Wade* is overruled. That conclusion is supported by the methodology the Washington Supreme Court has developed for identifying privacy rights (outside the context of search and seizure) under §7.

"Generally, private affairs," as that term is used in art. I, §7, "are 'those privacy interests which citizens of [Washington] have held, and should be entitled to hold, safe from governmental trespass.'"[20] Whether a privacy interest will be recognized under art. I, §7, the Washington Supreme Court recently ex-

---

15. WASH. CONST. art. I, §7 (West 2002).

16. *In re Custody of RRB*, 31 P.3d at 1220. There is no separate search and seizure provision in the Washington Constitution.

17. *Id.*

18. *Bedford v. Sugarman*, 772 P.2d 486, 489 n. 5 (Wash. 1989) (collecting cases).

19. *In re Custody of RRB*, 31 P.3d at 1221.

20. *State v. McKinney*, 60 P.3d 46, 49 (Wash. 2002) (quoting *State v. Myrick*, 688 P.2d 151, 154 (Wash. 1984)).

plained, depends upon a two-step analysis. First, "a court should ... examine the historical protection afforded, i.e., the inquiry into what interests citizens have held, then [second] ask whether the expectation of privacy is one that citizens should be entitled to hold."[21] There was no "historical protection" afforded abortion in Washington law prior to 1970.

Between 1854, when the first territorial legislature enacted Washington's first abortion statutes, until November 1970, when the people of Washington adopted an abortion-on-demand statute (through four lunar months, or sixteen weeks), abortion was prohibited except to save the life of the pregnant woman or her unborn child. The original abortion statutes were enacted by the first territorial legislature.[22] One statute defined and punished as a serious felony the performance of an abortion upon a woman "pregnant with a quick child" with "intent thereby to destroy such child," unless the procedure was "necessary to preserve the life of such [woman]."[23] Another statute defined and punished as a lesser felony performance of an abortion without regard to whether the child had "quickened" (subject to the same exception).[24] These statutes were replaced by a pair of abortion statutes enacted in 1869,[25] and

---

21. *Andersen v. King County*, 138 P.3d 963, 986 (Wash. 2006) (plurality). In *Andersen*, the state supreme court refused to recognize a privacy interest in same-sex marriage in light of the historical and contemporary reservation of marriage to opposite-sex couples. Although the principal opinion in *Andersen*, representing the views of three justices, seems to suggest that the absence of a history and tradition of protecting an asserted privacy interest does not necessarily defeat recognition of that interest under art. I, §7, *id.* at 986–87, the two concurring justices took a narrower view, implying that both *McKinney* factors (that the interest must be one that the citizens of the State *have* held and *should be entitled* to hold) must be present before an asserted privacy interest will be recognized. *Id.* at 1009 (Johnson, J.M. J., concurring in judgment only). In light of the language of *McKinney*, the concurrence would appear to have the better of the argument. *See State v. Surge*, 156 P.3d 208, 211 (Wash. 2007) (following *McKinney*). Significantly, the state supreme court has never recognized a privacy interest under art. I, §7, that has not enjoyed "historical protection." *Compare In re Colyer*, 660 P.2d 738, 742 (Wash. 1983) (recognizing right to refuse unwanted medical treatment on state, as well as federal, privacy grounds), *with Seeley v. State*, 940 P.2d 604, 612 (Wash. 1997) ("the selection of a particular treatment or medicine is not a constitutionally protected right"), *id.* at 613 (terminally ill patient did not have "a fundamental right to have marijuana prescribed as his preferred treatment over the legitimate objections of the state").

22. Act of Apr. 28, 1854, ch. II, §§37, 38, WASH. (TERR.) STAT, p. 81 (1854).

23. *Id.* ch. II, §37. A "quick" child, for purposes of this statute, was a child who had "quickened." *See* n. 8, *supra*.

24. *Id.* ch. II, §38.

25. Act of Nov. 25, 1869, ch. II, §§39, 40, WASH. (TERR.) STAT., p. 205 (1869), WASH. CODE §§820, 821 (1881), *recodified at* WASH. PENAL CODE §§30, 33 (1891), *recodified at* WASH. CODE ANN. §§7067, 7068 (1897).

again in 1909 with the enactment of a new criminal code.[26] The 1909 act eliminated the quickening distinction, prohibited abortions at any stage of pregnancy,
"unless the same [was] necessary to preserve [the pregnant woman's] life or
that of [her unborn] child," and prohibited a woman from participating in her
own abortion (subject to the same exception).[27] These statutes remained on
the books until after *Roe v. Wade* was decided.[28]

Prior to *Roe v. Wade*, the Washington Supreme Court regularly affirmed
abortion convictions (and convictions for homicide of the mother based on
the performance of an illegal abortion) without any hint that the prosecutions
or convictions were barred by the Washington Constitution.[29] In *State v Cox*,[30]
the Washington Supreme Court held that the principal state abortion statute
had been designed to protect the lives of both the pregnant woman and her
unborn child.[31]

Washington has recognized the rights of unborn children in areas outside
of abortion, including tort law, health care law and property law. In tort law,
a statutory cause of action for wrongful death may be brought on behalf of an
unborn child who was viable (capable of sustained survival outside the mother's
womb, with or without medical assistance) at the time of its death.[32] And a
common law action for (nonlethal) prenatal injuries may be brought on behalf
of a viable unborn child.[33]

---

26. Wash. Laws, ch 249, §§ 196–200, pp. 948–49.

27. *Id.* §§ 196, 197. No prosecutions were reported under the latter statute. Section 198
prohibited the manufacture, sale or distribution of instruments, drugs, medicines or other
substances, knowing or intending that they could be used unlawfully to procure the miscarriage of a woman; section 199 dealt with evidentiary matters; section 200 prohibited an
attempt to conceal the birth of a child by disposing of its dead body.

28. WASH. CODE ANN. §§ 2448, 2449 (1910), *recodified at* WASH. CODE ANN. §§ 2397,
2398 (1932), *recodified at* WASH. REV. CODE ANN. §§ 9.02.010, 9.02.020 (West 1951), *repealed by* 1992 Wash. Laws, ch. 1, § 9, Initiative Measure No. 120, approved Nov. 5, 1991.

29. *State v. Gaul*, 152 P. 1029 (Wash. 1915); *State v. Russell*, 156 P. 565 (Wash. 1916);
State v. Martin, 34 P.2d 914 (Wash. 1934); *State v. De Gaston*, 104 P.2d 756 (Wash. 1940);
State v. Hart, 175 P.2d 944 (Wash. 1946); *State v. Bates*, 324 P.2d 810 (Wash. 1958); *State
v. Goddard*, 447 P.2d 180 (Wash. 1968).

30. 84 P.2d 357 (Wash. 1938).

31. *Id.* at 361.

32. *Moen v. Hanson*, 537 P.2d 266, 267 (Wash. 1975), interpreting WASH. REV. CODE ANN.
§ 4.24.010 (West 2005). The state court of appeals, however, has refused to allow wrongful
death actions to be brought on behalf of *non*viable children who were stillborn. *Baum v. Bur-
rington*, 79 P.3d 456, 458–60 (Wash. Ct. App. 2003).

33. *Seattle-First Nat'l Bank v. Rankin*, 367 P.2d 835 (Wash. 1962).

In health care law, a directive to withhold or withdraw life-sustaining treatment under the Natural Death Act has "no force or effect" during a woman's pregnancy.[34] In property law, subject to certain exceptions, a child born after a person executes a will receives the same share of the testator's estate that he would have received if he had been born before the will was executed.[35]

"In determining if an interest constitutes a 'private affair' [within the meaning of art. I, §7]," the Washington Supreme Court recently explained, "we look at the historical treatment of the interest being asserted, analogous case law, and statutes and laws supporting the interest asserted."[36] Although Washington adopted an abortion-on-demand statute prior to quickening (or four lunar months) in 1970, and subsequently adopted the "Reproductive Privacy Act" in 1991, the unbroken history of prohibiting abortion, except to save the life of the pregnant woman, from 1854 until 1970 would militate against recognition of a state right to abortion under art. I, §7, as would the state supreme court's acknowledgment in *State v. Cox* that the principal abortion statute was intended to protect both pregnant women and their unborn children. Moreover, there is no evidence that the framers or ratifiers of the Washington Constitution intended to limit the Legislature's authority to prohibit abortion.[37] Such an intent would have been remarkable in light of Washington's history of prohibiting abortion which dates back to 1854, forty-five years before the state constitution was adopted, with the first territorial legislature's enactment of a criminal code. In sum, art. I, §7, of the Washington Constitution does not support an independent right to abortion.

Religious Freedom

Article I, §11, of the Washington Constitution provides, in part:

Absolute freedom of conscience in all matters of religious sentiment, belief and worship, shall be guaranteed to every individual, and no one shall be molested or disturbed in person or property on ac-

---

34. WASH. REV. CODE. ANN. §70.122.030(1)(d) (West 2002 & Supp. 2005).

35. *Id.* §11.12.091 (West 1998).

36. *State v. Athan*, 158 P.2d 27, 33 (Wash. 2007).

37. *See* JOURNAL OF THE WASHINGTON STATE CONSTITUTIONAL CONVENTION (1889) 491–518 (Seattle, Washington 1962) (Beverly Paulik Rosenow, ed.). The pages cited refer to the Analytical Index to the Journal prepared by Quentin Shipley Smith. No such intent appears in the contemporary newspaper coverage of the actual debates, either. *See* WASHINGTON STATE CONSTITUTIONAL CONVENTION (1889), CONTEMPORARY NEWSPAPER ARTICLES, 1-51 (*Oregon Statesman Weekly*), 4-57, 4-58 (*Tacoma Daily Ledger*), 5-59, 5-60 (*Tacoma Morning Globe*) (Buffalo, New York 1999).

count of religion; but the liberty of conscience hereby secured shall not be so construed as to excuse acts of licentiousness or justify practices inconsistent with the peace and safety of the state. No public money or property shall be appropriated for or applied to any religious worship, exercise or instructions, or the support of any religious establishment.... [38]

In any challenge to a statute prohibiting abortion, abortion advocates may raise either or both of two arguments under art. I, § 11. First, relying upon the second clause of the first sentence of § 11, they may argue that an abortion prohibition interferes with a woman's "[a]bsolute freedom of conscience in all matters of religious sentiment, belief and worship" by forbidding her from obtaining an abortion that would be allowed by her religion. Second, relying upon the second sentence of § 11, they may argue in the alternative (or in addition) that in prohibiting abortion, the Legislature has, in effect, "support[ed] ... [a] religious establishment" because such prohibition reflects sectarian beliefs regarding when human life begins and the sinfulness of abortion. Neither argument is likely to prevail.

With respect to the former argument (free exercise), the Washington Supreme Court has held that in any case brought under the first sentence of § 11, "the complaining party must first prove [that] the government action has a coercive effect on the practice of religion."[39] "Once a coercive effect is established, the burden of proof shifts to the government to show that the restrictions serve a compelling state interest and are the least restrictive means for achieving the government objective."[40] "If no compelling state interest exist," or if the restrictions are not "the least restrictive means" available to achieve the government objective, "the restrictions are unconstitutional."[41]

The threshold inquiry in a free exercise case under art. I, § 11, is whether the enactment in question has a "coercive effect" upon a person "in the practice of his religion."[42] The challenged state action "must somehow compel or pressure the individual to violate a tenet of his religious belief."[43] A statute pro-

---

38. WASH. CONST. art. I, § 11 (West 2002).

39. *First United Methodist Church of Seattle, Inc. v. Hearing Examiner for the Seattle Landmarks Preservation Board*, 916 P.2d 374, 378 (Wash. 1996).

40. *Id.*

41. *Id.*

42. *First Covenant Church of Seattle v. City of Seattle*, 840 P.2d 174, 187 (Wash. 1992) (citation and internal quotation marks omitted).

43. *Witters v. State Comm'n for the Blind*, 771 P.2d 1119, 1123 (Wash. 1989). In *Witters*, the state supreme court determined that denying vocational assistance funds to a dis-

hibiting abortion except to save the life of the pregnant woman does not "coerce" any woman in the "practice of [her] religion" because there is no doctrine in any religion that *requires* (as opposed to *permits*) a woman to undergo an abortion in circumstances when her life is not in danger. Whether a particular religious doctrine *permits* abortion for reasons which are not recognized by law does not present a justiciable free exercise issue under article I, § 11.[44]

Even assuming, however, that a pregnant woman could establish that an abortion prohibition would compel her to violate a tenet of her religious belief, the prohibition could still withstand the strict scrutiny standard of judicial review. The State has a compelling interest in protecting and preserving the life of the unborn child,[45] and there is no "less restrictive means" available, short of an outright prohibition, that would adequately promote and safeguard that interest. An example, not involving abortion, that illustrates this principle is the line of cases authorizing compulsory blood transfusions on pregnant women (typically, Jehovah's Witnesses) to save the lives of their unborn children.[46] The prohibition of abortion, for the same end, stands on even firmer ground, however, because it does not implicate the federal constitutional right to refuse unwanted medical treatment.[47] Moreover, unlike an order authorizing a blood transfusion of a pregnant woman, which is intended to

---

abled person who wanted to study for the clergy did not require the applicant for such funds "to violate any tenet of his religious beliefs," nor did it deny him any benefits "because of conduct mandated by religious belief." *Id.* (citation and internal quotation marks omitted).

44. Of course, a law that singles out religious practices for regulation would present an entirely different question. *See Church of the Lukumi Babalu Aye, Inc. v. City of Hialeah*, 508 U.S. 520 (1993) (a law that is aimed at specific religious practices must satisfy the "strict scrutiny" standard of judicial review).

45. *See generally, State v. Meacham*, 612 P.2d 795, 797 (Wash. 1980) ("the interest of the State in the welfare of its minor children has long been a compelling and paramount concern").

46. *See Fosmire v. Nicoleau*, 536 N.Y.S.2d 492, 496 (App. Div. 1989) (dictum) (when "a pregnant adult woman refuses medical treatment and, as a result of that refusal, places the life of her unborn baby in jeopardy," "the State's interest, as *parens patriae*, in protecting the health and welfare of the child is determined to be paramount") (citing *In the Matter of Application of Jamaica Hospital*, 491 N.Y.S.2d 898 (Sup. Ct. 1985) (blood transfusion) (18 weeks gestation); and *Crouse Irving Memorial Hospital, Inc. v. Paddock*, 485 N.Y.S.2d 443 (Sup. Ct. 1985) (blood transfusion) (premature delivery)). *See also Raleigh Fitkin-Paul Morgan Memorial Hospital v. Anderson*, 201 A.2d 537 (N.J. 1964) (same with respect to blood transfusion at 32 weeks gestation); *but see In re Brown*, 689 N.E.2d 397 (Ill. App. Ct. 1997) (*contra*) (blood transfusion).

47. *See, e.g., Cruzan v. Director, Missouri Dep't of Health*, 497 U.S. 261, 278–79 & n. 7 (1990); *Washington v. Glucksberg*, 521 U.S. 702, 719–26 & n. 17 (1997).

save the life of the unborn child (and very possibly the mother's life as well), the intent in an abortion is to *destroy* the unborn child's life. A prohibition of abortion would not violate the "free exercise" guarantee of art. I, §11, of the Washington Constitution.

With respect to the latter argument (establishment of religion), the Washington Supreme Court has held that the second sentence of art. I, §11, "prohibits appropriation or application of public money or property for four explicit purposes, religious worship, religious exercise, religious instruction and support of any religious establishment."[48] The issue, in a state "establishment" case, is whether the government "has purposefully transferred, or made available, money or property for" a purpose proscribed by §11.[49] Because an abortion prohibition does not entail an "appropriation or application of public money or property" for any of the four purposes specified by §11, it would not violate the second sentence of §11.

Privileges and Immunities, Equality of Rights

Article I, §12, of the Washington Constitution provides: "No law shall be passed granting to any citizen, class of citizens, or corporation other than municipal, privileges or immunities which upon the same terms shall not equally belong to all citizens, or corporations."[50] And art. XXXI, §1, provides: "Equality of rights and responsibilities under the law shall not be denied or abridged on account of sex."[51]

In any challenge to a statute prohibiting abortion, abortion advocates are likely to argue that because only women are capable of becoming pregnant, the prohibition of abortion both discriminates against women as a class, in violation of art. I, §12, and denies them "equality of rights ... under the law ... on account of sex" in violation of art. XXXI, §1. These arguments probably would not succeed.

Prior to the adoption of the Washington Equal Rights Amendment (art. XXXI), the Washington Supreme Court subjected classifications based upon sex to strict judicial scrutiny under art. I, §12, prohibiting special privileges and immunities.[52] Under that standard, a sex-based classification was presumed to

---

48. *Maylon v. Pierce County*, 935 P.2d 1272, 1278 (Wash. 1997). *See also Washington Health Care Facilities Authority v. Spellman*, 633 P.2d 866, 867 (Wash. 1981) (same).

49. *Maylon*, 935 P.2d at 1282.

50. WASH. CONST. art. I, §12 (West 2002).

51. *Id.* art. XXXI, §1 (West 1998).

52. *See Hanson v. Hutt*, 517 P.2d 599 (Wash. 1973).

be unconstitutional and could be upheld only if it was the least restrictive means of promoting a compelling governmental purpose.[53] In 1972, the people of the State of Washington approved the state Equal Rights Amendment (art. XXXI). The Washington Supreme Court has held that the state ERA "absolutely prohibits discrimination on the basis of sex and is not subject to even the narrow exceptions permitted under [the] traditional 'strict scrutiny' [standard]."[54] Notwithstanding this "absolutist" language, the state supreme court has recognized a limited number of exceptions to the ERA's prohibition of sex-based classifications. For example, "[w]hen differential treatment of the sexes is based upon actual differences between the sexes, the ERA is not violated."[55]

A statute prohibiting abortion quite obviously can affect only women because only women are capable of becoming pregnant.[56] Unlike laws that use women's ability to become pregnant (or pregnancy itself) to discriminate against them in *other* areas (*e.g.*, employment opportunities), abortion prohibitions cannot fairly be said to involve a distinction between men and women that is a "mere pretext[] designed to erect an invidious discrimination against [women]."[57] As one federal district court has observed, "Abortion statutes are examples of cases in which the sexes are not biologically similarly situated" because only women are capable of becoming pregnant and having abortions.[58] The Washington Supreme Court appears to recognize as much. In *City of Seattle v. Buchanan*, the court noted that "a legislative body may enact laws which apply only to the members of one sex, provided that they are based on actual differences between the sexes," and cited laws relating to childbearing as one such example.[59] Because men and women are not "biologically similar situated" with respect to childbearing, a statute prohibiting abortion would not contravene either the privileges and immunities

---

53. *Id.* at 603.

54. *Southwest Washington Chapter, Nat'l Electrical Contractors Ass'n v. Pierce County*, 667 P.2d 1092, 1102 (Wash. 1983).

55. *Guard v. Jackson*, 940 P.2d 642, 644 (Wash. 1997) (citing *City of Seattle v. Buchanan*, 584 P.2d 918, 919–22 (Wash. 1978) (municipal ordinance prohibiting public exposure of female breasts is based upon actual differences between the sexes and does not violate the ERA)). *See also Darrin v. Gould*, 540 P.2d 882, 890 n. 8 (Wash. 1975) (noting "dissimilar treatment on account of a characteristic unique to one sex" as one of three possible exceptions to application of the proposed *federal* equal rights amendment).

56. *Geduldig v. Aiello*, 417 U.S. 484, 496 n. 20 (1974) ("[n]ormal pregnancy is an objectively, identifiable physical condition with unique characteristics").

57. *Id.*

58. *Jane L. v. Bangerter*, 794 F. Supp. 1537, 1549 (D. Utah 1992).

59. 584 P.2d at 919.

provision of the state constitution (art. I, § 12) or the equal rights amendment (art. XXXI, § 1).

Inherent Political Power

Article I, § 1, of the Washington Constitution provides: "All political power is inherent in the people, and governments derive their just powers from the consent of the governed, and are established to protect and maintain individual rights."[60] In any challenge to a statute prohibiting abortions, abortion advocates may argue that the prohibition violates the "individual rights" mentioned in art. I, § 1. Such an argument would not likely prevail.

In an early case interpreting art. I, § 1, the Washington Supreme Court held that § 1 is "[a] statement of a fundamental principle inhering in the formation of the state and federal governments."[61] Section 1, the court explained, "has no application to the distribution of the sovereign powers of the government by the people. The legislature represents this sovereignty of the people, except as limited by the constitution."[62] The clear implication of the last sentence is that § 1 is not itself a source of substantive rights. To the extent that § 1 places *any* limitation on the exercise of the police power "to enact legislation to protect the health, safety, and welfare of the citizens," it merely requires "that the legislation be reasonable and not infringe unduly on individual rights."[63] Those rights, however, must be derived from other sources, not § 1.

Assuming that legislation does not otherwise conflict with individual rights, "the State Legislature may prescribe laws to promote the health, peace, safety, and general welfare of the people of Washington."[64] "A statute is a valid exercise of the police power [under art. I, § 1] if it (1) tends to correct some evil or promote some interest of the state, and (2) bears a reasonable and substantial relationship to accomplish its purpose."[65] A statute prohibiting abortion would satisfy this two-part test. It would have a "reasonable and substantial relationship" to the State's legitimate interest in protecting unborn human life.

---

60. WASH. CONST. art. I, § 1 (West 2002).
61. *State v. Clark*, 71 P. 20, 21 (Wash. 1902).
62. *Id.*
63. *City of Seattle v. McConahy*, 937 P.2d 1133, 1137–38 (Wash. Ct. App. 1997).
64. *State v. Brayman*, 751 P.2d 294, 299 (Wash. 1988).
65. *Id.*

Fundamental Principles

Article I, §32, of the Washington Constitution provides:

A frequent recurrence to fundamental principles is essential to the
security of individual right and the perpetuity of free government.[66]

In any challenge to a statute prohibiting abortion, abortion advocates may
argue that the prohibition interferes with the "fundamental principles" referenced in art. I, §32. That argument would not likely prevail.

Section 32 "has primarily been viewed as an interpretative mechanism in
connection with individual rights, and has also been used to define principles of state and local government."[67] Although §32 "emphasizes the importance of [the] individual rights provided in ... §§1-31," it "has not been
interpreted as providing substantive rights in and of itself."[68] Accordingly, if
a statute "does not otherwise violate the [state] constitution," the Washington Supreme Court "will not apply art. I, §32 to overturn the measure."[69]
Section 32 "is not in any sense an inhibition on legislative power," but is simply "an admonition" to both the legislature and the courts "to constantly keep
in mind the fundamentals of our republican form of government...."[70] In
light of the foregoing, §32 could not provide the basis for a right to abortion
under the Washington Constitution.

Retained Rights

Article I, §30, of the Washington Constitution provides: "The enumeration in this Constitution of certain rights shall not be construed to deny others retained by the people."[71] Abortion advocates may be expected argue that
abortion is a "retained right" under §30. Such an argument would not likely
succeed. Section 30 has seldom been cited by the Washington Supreme Court
and never in support of a unenumerated retained right, which is at least some

---

66. WASH. CONST. art. I, §32 (West 2002).

67. *Brower v. State*, 969 P.2d 42, 56 (Wash. 1998) (citing *Seeley v. State*, 940 P.2d 604,
620–22 (Wash. 1997)).

68. *Id.* at 56.

69. *Id.*

70. *Wheeler School District No. 152 of Grant County v. Hawley*, 137 P.2d 1010, 1015
(Wash. 1943).

71. WASH. CONST. art. I, §30 (West 2002).

indication that it is not a source of any substantive rights under the Washington Constitution.[72]

An entirely plausible reading of § 30 is that the enumeration of certain rights in the state constitution should not be construed to "deny" other rights retained by the people under the common law or statutes. But even if § 30 is understood to retain unspecified *constitutional* rights (as opposed to *common law* or *statutory* rights), abortion could not plausibly be considered to be among such rights because, at the time the Washington Constitution was adopted in 1889, abortion was a crime except to save the life of the pregnant woman (or her unborn child). The argument that § 30 retained as an "unenumerated" right conduct that was criminal when the state constitution was adopted is, at the very least, counterintuitive.[73]

The language of § 30 appears to be based on the Ninth Amendment.[74] In light of that equivalence, § 30 should be given a parallel interpretation. That, in turn, suggests that if no right to abortion exists under the Ninth Amendment, then none would be recognized under art. I, § 30. The Supreme Court, however, has rooted the "abortion liberty" in the liberty language of the Due Process Clause of the Fourteenth Amendment, not in the unenumerated rights language of the Ninth Amendment.[75] Because abortion has not been recognized

---

72. In an early case interpreting this provision, the Washington Supreme Court stated that § 30 "is apparently the expression that the declaration of certain fundamental rights belonging to all individuals and made in the bill of rights shall not be construed to mean the abandonment of others not expressed, which inherently exist in all civilized and free states." *State v. Clark*, 71 P. 20, 21 (Wash. 1902). "Consistent with the affirmative declaration of rights, it has been universally recognized by the profoundest jurists and statesmen that certain fundamental, inalienable rights under the laws of God and nature are immutable, and cannot be violated by any authority founded in right." *Id.* Whether the state supreme court would still subscribe to *Clark's* "natural law" interpretation of § 30 is doubtful. In any event, it would seem unlikely that the court would regard a right to abortion as a "fundamental, inalienable right[] under the laws of God and nature," when, for most of the history of the State of Washington and the United States, abortion was a crime.

73. To prevail in a claim based on the reserved rights provision of the Washington Constitution, a party must demonstrate that the asserted right "is or ever was considered a right retained under ... art. I, § 30." *Halquist v. Dep't of Corrections*, 783 P.2d 1065, 1066 n. 4 (Wash. 1989) (journalist had no right to videotape execution).

74. "The enumeration in the Constitution of certain rights, shall not be construed to deny or disparage others retained by the people." U.S. CONST. AMEND. IX (West 2006).

75. *See Roe*, 410 U.S. at 153; *Casey*, 505 U.S. at 846. In any event, the Ninth Amendment, standing alone, is not a source of substantive rights. *Gibson v. Matthews*, 926 F.2d 532, 537 (6th Cir. 1991). Although "[s]ome unenumerated rights may be of [c]onstitutional magnitude," that is only "by virtue of other amendments, such as the Fifth or Fourteenth

as a "retained right" under the Ninth Amendment, it should not be recognized as one under § 30, either.

Conclusion

Based on the foregoing analysis, an argument that the Washington Constitution protects a right to abortion that is separate from, and independent of, the right to abortion recognized in *Roe v. Wade* would not likely succeed. That, in turn, suggests that if *Roe*, as modified by *Casey*, is ultimately overruled, the State of Washington could enact and enforce a statute *prohibiting* abortion. Moreover, nothing in the Washington Constitution precludes Washington from *regulating* abortion within federal constitutional limits in the meantime.

Amendment. A person cannot claim a right that exists solely under the Ninth Amendment." *United States v. Vital Health Products, Ltd.*, 786 F. Supp. 761, 777 (E.D. Wis. 1992), *aff'd mem. op., sub nom. United States v. LeBeau*, 985 F.2d 563 (7th Cir. 1993). *See also Charles v. Brown*, 495 F. Supp. 862, 863 (N.D. Ala. 1980) (same).

CHAPTER 51

WEST VIRGINIA

Summary

The West Virginia Supreme Court of Appeals has not yet decided whether the West Virginia Constitution protects a right to abortion separate from, and independent of, the right to abortion recognized under the United States Constitution.[1] A careful examination of the state constitution, in light of its history and interpretation, as well as other relevant legal sources, however, suggests that the state supreme court of appeals probably would not recognize a state constitutional right to abortion. Thus, if *Roe v. Wade*,[2] as modified by *Planned Parenthood of Southeastern Pennsylvania v. Casey*,[3] were overruled, West Virginia could enforce its pre-*Roe* abortion statute (or enact a new statute prohibiting abortion). Moreover, nothing in the state constitution, properly understood, precludes the State from enacting and enforcing reasonable measures regulating abortion within current federal constitutional limits.

---

1. In *Women's Health Center of West Virginia, Inc. v. Panepinto*, 446 S.E.2d 658 (W.Va. 1993), the state supreme court struck down, on the basis of the "common benefit" provision of the state constitution, art. III, §3, restrictions on public funding of abortion. In *Women's Health Center*, which is discussed below in the text, the supreme court declined to decide whether there is a *state* constitutional right to abortion: "Because there is a *federally-created right of privacy* that we are required to enforce in a non-discriminatory manner, it is inconsequential that no prior decision of this Court expressly determines the existence of an analogous right" under the state constitution. 446 S.E.2d at 664 (emphasis added). *See also, id.* at 667 ("for an indigent woman, the state's offer of subsidies for one reproductive option and the imposition of a penalty for the other necessarily influences her *federally-protected choice*") (emphasis added); *id.* (abortion funding limitations "constitute undue government interference with the exercise of the *federally-protected right to terminate a pregnancy*") (emphasis added).

2. 410 U.S. 113 (1973).

3. 505 U.S. 833 (1992).

Analysis

The pre-*Roe* statute prohibited performance of an abortion upon a pregnant woman unless the procedure was done "in good faith, with the intention of saving the life of [the] woman or [her] child."[4] Pursuant to *Roe*, the statute was declared unconstitutional (on federal, not state, grounds) by a federal court of appeals in *Doe v. Charleston Area Medical Center, Inc.*[5] The statute has not been repealed.[6]

Based upon arguments that have been raised in West Virginia and other States with similar constitutional provisions, possible sources for an asserted abortion right could include provisions of the Bill of Rights guaranteeing religious freedom (art. III, §15), a remedy by due course of law (§17) and due process of law and equal protection (§10); recognizing inherent rights (§1); reserving rights to the People (§3); and emphasizing the importance of frequent recurrence to fundamental principles (§20).[7] The analysis that follows shall consider each of these provisions.

Religious Freedom

Article III, §15, of the West Virginia Constitution provides:

No man shall be compelled to frequent or support any religious worship, place or ministry whatsoever; nor shall any man be enforced, restrained, molested or burthened, in his body or goods, or otherwise suffer, on account of his religious opinions or belief, but all men shall be free to profess, and by argument, to maintain their opinions in matters of religion; and the same shall, in no wise, affect, diminish or enlarge their civil capacities; and the Legislature shall not prescribe any religious test whatever, or confer any peculiar privileges or advantages on any sect or denomination, or pass any law requiring or authorizing any religious society, or the people of any district within this State, to levy on themselves, or others, any tax for the erection or repair of any house for public worship, or for the support of any

---

4. W.Va. Code §61-2-8 (1966).

5. 529 F.2d 638 (4th Cir. 1975).

6. W.Va. Code §61-2-8 (2000).

7. Two other more unlikely sources of an abortion right under the West Virginia Constitution-art. III, §6 (prohibiting unreasonable searches and seizures) and § (guaranteeing freedom of speech)-are discussed generally in Chapter 3, *supra*.

church or ministry, but it shall be left free for every person to select his religious instructor, and to make for his support, such private contract as he shall all be secured, and no inhabitant of the State shall ever be molested in person or property on account of his or her mode of religious worship; and no religious test shall be required for the exercise of civil or political rights.[8]

In any challenge to West Virginia's pre-*Roe* abortion statute (or any other statute prohibiting abortion the State may enact), abortion advocates may raise either or both of two arguments under art. III, § 15. First, relying upon the second clause of § 15, they may argue that the prohibition of abortion interferes with a woman's "religious opinions or belief" by forbidding her from obtaining an abortion that would be allowed by her religion. Second, relying upon the fourth clause of § 15, they may argue in the alternative (or in addition) that an abortion prohibition "confer[s]" a "peculiar privilege[] or advantage[]" on a "sect or denomination" because it reflects sectarian beliefs regarding when human life begins and the sinfulness of abortion. Neither argument would likely prevail.

The West Virginia Supreme Court of Appeals has stated that "[b]y its specification of the rights incident to the free exercise of religion and the prohibition of the establishment of any church or religious belief to the detriment to another," art. III, § 15, is "even more stringently protective than the corresponding federal provision [referring to the Free Exercise and Establishment Clauses of the First Amendment]."[9] Notwithstanding this statement, neither in *Brady* nor in any other decision has the West Virginia Supreme Court deliberately departed from United States Supreme Court precedents interpreting the Religion Clauses of the First Amendment in deciding cases brought under § 15 of the West Virginia Bill of Rights. Indeed, the court has construed § 15 consistently with the First Amendment.[10] This should not be surprising because § 15 was based on Thomas Jefferson's Virginia Statute of Religious Freedom which,

---

8. W.Va. Const. art. III, § 15 (1991).

9. *Brady v. Reiner*, 198 S.E.2d 812, 835 (W.Va. 1973), *overruled on other grounds, Board of Church Extension v. Eads*, 230 S.E.2d 911, 918, n. 6 (W.Va. 1976). *See also State v. Everly*, 146 S.E.2d 705, 707 (W.Va. 1966) (art. III, § 15, is "much broader [than the First Amendment to the United States Constitution]").

10. *See, e.g., Brady*, 198 S.E.2d at 827–35, 843–44 (resolving church property dispute consistently under the First Amendment and art. III, § 15); *Matter of Kilpatrick*, 375 S.E.2d 794, 795 n. 2 (W.Va. 1988) (rejecting state and federal free exercise challenge to statute requiring applicants for marriage licenses to obtain a blood test for syphilis); *State v. Riddle*, 285 S.E.2d 359, 365 (W.Va. 1981) (same with respect to compulsory school attendance law); *State v. Everly*, 146 S.E.2d at 706–07 (recognizing free exercise right to refuse to serve on grand jury); *Janasiewicz v. Board of Education of the County of Kanawa*, 299 S.E.2d 34, 36 (W.Va.

in turn, "was the genesis for the drafting of the First Amendment to the United States Constitution."[11]

Given the equivalency in their interpretation by the West Virginia Supreme Court of Appeals, it would appear that a challenge to an abortion statute that would not succeed under the Free Exercise and Establishment Clauses of the First Amendment would not succeed under art. III, § 15, either. For the reasons set forth in Chapter 2, *supra*, an abortion statute could not be successfully challenged on First Amendment grounds. Accordingly, a similar challenge under art. III, § 15, would not likely be successful.[12]

Remedy by Due Course of Law

Article III, § 17, of the West Virginia Constitution provides, in part, that "every person, for an injury done to him, in his person, property or reputation, shall have remedy by due course of law...."[13] Abortion advocates might argue that any statute prohibiting abortion interferes with a woman's control over her own body, and that such interference challenge an "injury" to her "person," as those terms are used in § 17, for which there must be a "remedy by due course of law." That "remedy," in turn, would be invalidation of the statute. This argument assumes that art. III, § 17, confers substantive rights. The case law is clear, however, that it does not.

The West Virginia Supreme Court of Appeals held that the "remedy by due course of law" language of art. III, § 17, is not implicated unless "a legislative enactment either substantially impairs vested rights or severely limits existing procedural remedies permitting court adjudication of cases...."[14] A "vested

---

1982) ("providing bus transportation for parochial school children does not violate our First Amendment establishment clause or ... art. III, § 15").

11. *Brady*, 198 S.E.2d at 834.

12. Entirely apart from the state supreme court's reliance on federal precedent in interpreting art. III, § 15, an argument challenging an abortion prohibition on the basis that it confers a "privilege" or "advantage" on a religious "sect or denomination," by embodying sectarian views regarding the sinfulness of abortion, would appear to be foreclosed by a decision of the West Virginia Supreme Court of Appeals rejecting a challenge to a Sunday closing law. *See State v. Gates*, 141 S.E.2d 369, 380–85 (W.Va. 1965). If a law enforcing a "day of rest" does not violate art. III, § 15, of the West Virginia Constitution, even though it may coincide with sectarian beliefs regarding the Christian Sabbath, then neither would a law prohibiting abortion, regardless of whether the law coincides with religious views regarding the sinfulness of abortion.

13. W.Va. Const. art. III, § 17 (1991).

14. *Gibson v. West Virginia Dep't of Highways*, 406 S.E.2d 440, 451 (W.Va. 1991). "Even if such impairment or limitation is shown, however, the measure will not violate the 'cer-

right," in turn, "means that an actual cause of action which was substantially affected existed at the time of the legislative enactment."[15] In other words, while art. III, § 17, may *preserve* existing causes of action that have accrued, it does not *create* them; the causes of action are created by other sources of law, typically statutes and the common law. Section 17 does not confer substantive rights and, therefore, could not be a source of a right to abortion under the state constitution.

Inherent Rights and Due Process of Law

Article III, § 1, of the West Virginia Constitution provides:

> All men are, by nature, equally free and independent, and have certain inherent rights, of which when they enter into a state of society, they cannot, by any compact, deprive or divest their posterity, namely: the enjoyment of life and liberty, with the means of acquiring and possessing property, and of pursuing and obtaining happiness and safety.[16]

Article III, § 10, provides: "No person shall be deprived of life, liberty, or property, without due process of law."[17]

In any state constitutional challenge to West Virginia's pre-*Roe* abortion statute (or any other statute prohibiting abortion the State may enact) abortion advocates are most likely to rely upon the "liberty" clauses of art. III, §§ 1 and 10, arguing that the prohibition interferes with a woman's liberty in obtaining an abortion. Such an argument probably would not prevail, however.[18]

---

tain remedy' provision of our constitution if 'the purpose of the alteration or repeal of the existing cause of action or remedy is to eliminate [or curtail] a clear social or economic problem and the repeal or alteration ... is a reasonable method of achieving such purpose.'" *O'Dell v. Town of Gauley Bridge*, 425 S.E.2d 551, 561 (W.Va. 1992) (quoting *Lewis v. Canaan Valley Resorts*, 408 S.E.2d 634, 636 (W.Va. 1991)). *See, e.g., Wallace v. Wallace*, 184 S.E.2d 327, 332–33 (W.Va. 1971) (art. III, § 17, did not preclude legislature from abolishing common law actions for alienation of affections and breach of promise to marry).

15. *Gibson*, 406 S.E.2d at 451. Needless to say, there can be no "vested right" to engage in conduct that the legislature has classified as criminal in an otherwise constitutional statute.

16. W.Va. Const. art. III, § 1 (1991).

17. *Id.* art. III, § 10.

18. Although the analysis in the text focuses on the due process guarantee of art. III, § 10, that analysis also applies to the "inherent rights" guarantee of art. III, § 1, insofar as both secure individual "liberty." The West Virginia Supreme Court of Appeals has not given the liberty language of art. III, § 1, a broader reading than it has to the liberty language of art. III, § 10. *See, e.g., State v. Morrison*, 127 S.E. 75, 79–80 (W.Va. 1925) (con-

The West Virginia Supreme Court of Appeals has recognized that the due process guarantee of the West Virginia Constitution has a substantive, as well as a procedural, component, protecting individual liberties.[19] Although "there can be no fixed definition of due process of law, which is an inherently elusive concept,"[20] the state supreme court has warned that "courts must proceed with the greatest caution when identifying and defining non-enumerated constitutional rights."[21] That "caution" requires " 'continual insistence upon respect for the teaching of history, solid recognition of the basic values that underlie our society, and wise appreciation of the great role[] that the doctrine[] of ... separation of powers ha[s] played in establishing and preserving American freedoms.' "[22] Accordingly, "[m]erely identifying that a law affects an individual liberty is not the end of the matter; our doctrines permit the State to intrude upon liberties protected by the Due Process Clause when reasonably necessary to accomplish a goal of countervailing importance."[23] Even assuming, therefore, that there is an "individual liberty" interest in obtaining an abortion (which is discussed below), a prohibition of abortion would be "reasonably necessary" to promote the State's important objective of protecting unborn human life. The State, after all, "must preserve human life, a concern at the very core of civilization."[24]

The West Virginia Supreme Court of Appeals has held that statutes that affect *fundamental* state liberty interests (as opposed to *non*-fundamental liberty interests) are subject to a more rigorous standard of review.[25] The only

---

struing art. III, § 1, and art. III, § 10, together in decision holding that a chiropractor could be required to obtain a license to practice medicine).

19. *State ex rel. Harris v. Calendine*, 233 S.E.2d 318, 324 (W.Va. 1977).

20. *Id.* at 324 n. 3.

21. *State ex rel Allen v. Stone*, 474 S.E.2d 554, 563 (W.Va. 1996).

22. *Id.* (quoting *Griswold v. Connecticut*, 381 U.S. 479, 501 (1965) (Harlan, J., concurring)).

23. *Id. See also State ex rel. Harris*, 233 S.E.2d at 324 n. 4 (statute that affects the exercise of a recognized liberty interest will generally satisfy substantive due process requirements under art. III, § 10, if it bears "a reasonable relationship to a proper legislative purpose and [is] neither arbitrary nor discriminatory") (citation and internal quotation marks omitted); *Major v. DeFrench*, 286 S.E.2d 688, 697 (W.Va. 1982) (liberty interest in pursuing a lawful occupation is protected against "arbitrary state interference").

24. *State ex rel. White v. Narick*, 292 S.E.2d 54, 58 (W.Va. 1982) (otherwise healthy prison inmate had no constitutional right to starve himself to death).

25. *See Lindsie D.L. v. Richard W.S.*, 591 S.E.2d 308 (W.Va. 2003) (applying strict scrutiny). To the extent that the West Virginia Supreme Court of Appeals considers federal precedent in determining whether an asserted liberty interest (or right) is "fundamental" under the state due process guarantee, abortion would not qualify as a "fundamental" right. Although the Supreme Court characterized the right to choose abortion as "fundamental" in *Roe*, 410

such interest the court has recognized to date, however, is the "interest that parents have in the care of their children."[26] That interest, of course, has a long and distinguished pedigree in the law.[27] The same cannot be said of abortion.

West Virginia separated from Virginia when Virginia seceded from the Union in 1861. At the time, West Virginia adopted the laws of Virginia, including an 1848 statute that prohibited abortion at any stage of pregnancy except "to pre-serve the life of [the pregnant] woman.[28] West Virginia was admitted to the Union in 1863 and enacted a new abortion statute in 1868. This statute also prohibited abortion throughout pregnancy, except when the procedure was performed "in good faith, with the intention of saving the life of [the preg-nant woman] or [her unborn] child."[29] The 1868 statute, substantially un-changed, has remained on the books for one hundred forty years.[30]

Prior to *Roe*, the West Virginia Supreme Court of Appeals affirmed abortion convictions without any hint or suggestion that either the prosecutions or con-victions violated the state constitution.[31] In *State v. Lilly*, the court stated that in an abortion there are "two victims," adding that "[t]here is no crime more heinous against humanity or the Creator."[32] Subsequent to *Roe*, the West Vir-ginia Legislature enacted both a parental notice statute[33] and an informed con-

---

U.S. at 152–53, it tacitly abandoned that characterization in *Casey*, 505 U.S. at 869–79 (Joint Op. of O'Connor, Kennedy and Souter, JJ., replacing *Roe's* "strict scrutiny" standard of review with the more relaxed "undue burden" standard, allowing for a broader measure of abortion regulation).

26. *Lindsie D.L.*, 591 S.E.2d at 313 n. 5. *See also In re Willis*, 207 S.E.2d 129, 130–31 (W.Va. 1973) ("the right of a natural parent to the custody of his or her infant child is ... a fundamental personal liberty protected and guaranteed by the Due Process Clauses of the West Virginia and United States Constitutions").

27. "The liberty interest ... of parents in the care, custody, and control of their chil-dren ... is perhaps the oldest of the fundamental liberty interests recognized by this Court." *Troxel v. Granville*, 530 U.S. 57, 65 (2000) (citing, among other cases, *Meyer v. Nebraska*, 262 U.S. 390 (1923)).

28. Act of March 14, 1848, ch. 120, tit. II, ch. III, §9, 1847–48 Va. Acts 96, codified at Va. Code tit. 54, ch. 191, §8 (1849).

29. W.Va. Code Ann. ch. 144, §8 (1868).

30. W.Va. Code Ann. ch. 144, §8 (1868), *recodified at* W.Va. Code Ann. ch. 118, §8 (1882), *recodified at* W.Va. Code Ann. ch. 144, §8 (1923), *recodified at* W.Va. Code Ann. §5923 (1955), *recodified at* W.Va. Code §61-2-8 (1966).

31. *State v. Lilly*, 35 S.E. 837 (W.Va. 1900); *State v. Evans*, 66 S.E.2d 545 (W.Va. 1951).

32. 35 S.E. at 838.

33. W.Va. Code §16-2F-1 *et seq.* (2006). The requirement that a parent be given twenty-four hours actual notice or forty-eight hours constructive notice is undermined, however, by a provision in the law that allows notice to be waived if a physician, other than the physi-cian who is to perform the abortion, "finds that the minor is mature enough to make the

sent statute that includes a twenty-four hour waiting period.[34] West Virginia has recognized the rights of unborn children in a variety of contexts outside of abortion, including criminal law, tort law and property law.

In criminal law, the "Unborn Victims of Violence Act" recognizes, for purposes of the homicide and battery statutes, that "a pregnant woman and the embryo or fetus she is carrying in the womb constitute separate and distinct victims."[35] In tort law, a statutory cause of action for wrongful death may be brought on behalf of an unborn child without regard to the stage of pregnancy when the injuries causing death were inflicted.[36] A common law action for (nonlethal) prenatal injuries may be brought without regard to the stage of pregnancy when the injuries were inflicted.[37] And the state supreme court of appeals has refused to recognize a cause of action for wrongful life.[38]

In property law, a posthumous heir of a person who dies intestate (without a will) "shall be capable of taking inheritance in the same manner as if such child were in being at the time of such death."[39] And, subject to certain exceptions, a child born after a person executes a will receives the same share of the testator's estate that he would have received if he had been born before the will was executed.[40]

In light of West Virginia's unbroken tradition of prohibiting abortion except to preserve the life of the pregnant woman, as well as the State's solicitude for

---

abortion decision independently or that notification would not be in the minor's best interest." *Id.* § 16-2F-3(c).

34. *Id.* § 16-2I-1 *et seq.*

35. *Id.* § 61-2-30(c) (2005).

36. *Farley v. Sartin*, 466 S.E.2d 522, 532–35 (W.Va. 1995), interpreting W.Va. CODE § 55-7-2 (2000).

37. *Id.* at 532.

38. *James G. v. Caserta*, 332 S.E.2d 872, 879–81 (W.Va. 1985). A "wrongful life" cause of action is a claim brought on behalf of a child who is born with a physical or mental disability or disease that could have been discovered before the child's birth by genetic testing, amniocentesis or other medical screening. The gravamen of the action is that, as a result of a physician's failure to inform the child's parents of the child's disability or disease (or at least of the availability of tests to determine the presence of the disability or disease), they were deprived of the opportunity to abort the child, thus resulting in the birth of a child suffering permanent physical or mental impairment. The court has recognized wrongful birth actions, however. *Id.* at 881–83. A "wrongful birth" cause of action, on the other hand, is a claim, based on the same facts, brought by the parents of the impaired child on their own behalf.

39. W.Va. CODE § 42-1-8 (2004). A "posthumous" heir is an heir who was conceived before but born after the death of the intestate.

40. *Id.* §§ 41-4-1, 41-4-2.

the rights of the unborn child in other areas of law, it cannot reasonably be said that the liberty guaranteed by either art. III, § 1, or art. III, § 10, encompasses a right to abortion-fundamental or otherwise. In the words of Justice Harlan, recognition of such a right would not be consistent with "the teaching of history," "the basic values that underlie our society" or the "doctrine[] of ... separation of powers."[41]

Equal Protection

The West Virginia Constitution does not contain express equal protection language, as such. Nevertheless, the West Virginia Supreme Court of Appeals has held that the concept of equal protection is inherent in art. III, § 10, of the state constitution, which guarantees due process of law.[42] The state supreme court has recognized three standards of equal protection review: "First, when a suspect classification, such as race, or a fundamental, constitutional right, such as speech, is involved, the legislature must survive 'strict scrutiny,' that is, the legislative classification must be necessary to obtain a compelling state interest."[43] "Second, a so-called intermediate level of protection is accorded certain legislative classifications, such as those which are gender-based [and those based on illegitimacy], and the classifications must serve an important governmental objective and must be substantially related to the achievement of that objective."[44] "Third, all other legislative classifications, including those which involve economic rights, are subjected to the least level of scrutiny, the

---

41. *Griswold v. Connecticut*, 381 U.S. at 501 (Harlan, J., concurring).

42. *Israel v. West Virginia Secondary Schools Activities Comm'n*, 388 S.E.2d 480, 486–87 (W.Va. 1989). To the extent that the court had previously interpreted other provisions of the Bill of Rights to secure equal protection, *e.g.*, art. III, §§ 1, 3, 17 and 20, they are effectively discussed herein. *See Allen v. State of West Virginia, Human Rights Comm'n*, 324 S.E.2d 99, 109 (W.Va. 1984) (art. III, §§ 1, 3, 10, 17 and 20 "mandate equal opportunity").

43. *Lewis v. Canaan Valley Resorts*, 408 S.E.2d at 641 (citation omitted).

44. *Id.* (citations omitted). Previously, the state supreme court had stated, in dictum, that strict scrutiny, the most stringent test used in equal protection analysis, applied to gender-based classifications. *See State ex rel. Longanacre v. Crabtree*, 350 S.E.2d 760, 763–64 (W.Va. 1986). In modifying this standard to conform to the federal standard set forth in *Craig v. Boren*, 429 U.S. 190, 197 (1976) (intermediate scrutiny), the court in *Israel* stated that the two standards (strict scrutiny and intermediate scrutiny) "are substantially equivalent," and, therefore, that the modified test adopted therein does not "provide any less protection." 388 S.E.2d at 488. The two standards, of course, are *not* "substantially equivalent." Nevertheless, for the reasons set forth in the text, neither standard applies to laws prohibiting or regulation abortion.

traditional equal protection concept that the legislative classification will be upheld if it is reasonably related to the achievement of a legitimate state purpose."[45]

Strict scrutiny review would not apply to a statute prohibiting abortion (either §61-2-8 or another prohibition) because, for the reasons set forth in the preceding section of this analysis, the state constitution does not confer a "fundamental, constitutional right" to abortion. Nor would the prohibition of abortion classify persons on the basis of race or any other suspect personal characteristic. Abortion advocates may argue in the alternative, however, that a statute prohibiting abortion discriminates against women and is subject to intermediate scrutiny because only women are capable of becoming pregnant.

An abortion prohibition would appear to satisfy this level of scrutiny because the prohibition would be "substantially related" to the "important governmental objective" of protecting unborn human life. Nevertheless, the standard applicable to sex-based discrimination should not apply to an abortion prohibition. Abortion laws do not discriminate on the basis of sex.

First, the United States Supreme Court has reviewed restrictions on abortion funding under a rational basis standard of review, *not* under the heightened scrutiny required of gender-based classifications.[46] Indeed, the Court has held that "the disfavoring of abortion ... is not *ipso facto* sex discrimination," and, citing its decisions in *Harris* and other cases addressing abortion funding, stated that "the constitutional test applicable to government abortion-funding restrictions is not the heightened-scrutiny standard that our cases demand for sex discrimination, ... but the ordinary rationality standard."[47]

---

45. *Lewis*, 408 S.E.2d at 641.

46. *Harris v. McRae*, 448 U.S. 297, 321–26 (1980).

47. *Bray v. Alexandria Women's Health Clinic*, 506 U.S. 263, 273 (1993). Several state supreme courts and individual state supreme court justices have recognized that abortion regulations and restrictions on abortion funding are not "directed at women as a class" so much as "abortion as a medical treatment, which, because it involves a potential life, has no parallel as a treatment method." *Bell v. Low Income Women of Texas*, 95 S.W.3d 253, 258 (Tex. 2002) (upholding funding restrictions) (citing *Harris*, 448 U.S. at 325). *See also Fischer v. Dep't of Public Welfare*, 502 A.2d 114, 125 (Pa. 1985) ("the basis for the distinction here is not sex, but abortion") (upholding funding restrictions); *Moe v. Secretary of Administration & Finance*, 417 N.E.2d 387, 407 (Mass. 1981) (Hennessey, C.J., dissenting) (funding restrictions were "directed at abortion as a medical procedure, not women as a class"); *Right to Choose v. Byrne*, 450 A.2d 925, 950 (N.J. 1982) (O'Hern, J., dissenting) ("[t]he subject of the legislation is not the person of the recipient, but the nature of the claimed medical service"). Both *Moe* and *Right to Choose* were decided on other grounds. The dissenting justices were addressing alternative arguments raised by the plaintiffs, but not reached by the majority opinions.

Second, even assuming that an abortion prohibition differentiates between men and women on the basis of sex, and would otherwise be subject to a higher standard of review, the Supreme Court has held that biological differences between men and women may justify different treatment based on those differences. In upholding a statutory rape statute that applied only to males, the Supreme Court noted, "this Court has consistently upheld statutes where the gender classification is not invidious, but rather realistically reflects the fact that the sexes are not similarly situated in certain circumstances."[48] The West Virginia Supreme Court of Appeals concurs, stating that intermediate scrutiny does not apply to a classification that is based upon "the physical condition of pregnancy," rather than gender, as such.[49] Rather, the appropriate standard is whether the classification is "a rational one and bears a reasonable relationship to a proper governmental purpose."[50] As one federal district court observed: "Abortion statutes are examples of cases in which the sexes are not biologically similarly situated" because only women are capable of becoming pregnant and having abortions.[51]

A statute prohibiting abortion quite obviously can affect only women because only women are capable of becoming pregnant.[52] Unlike laws that use women's ability to become pregnant (or pregnancy itself) to discriminate against them in *other* areas (*e.g.*, employment opportunities), abortion prohibitions cannot fairly be said to involve a distinction between men and women that is a "mere pretext[] designed to erect an invidious discrimination against [women]."[53]

Because a prohibition of abortion would not infringe upon a fundamental state constitutional right and would not impermissibly classify on the basis of a suspect or quasi-suspect class, it would need to satisfy only the rational basis test. Under that test, the classification must be "reasonably related to the achieve-

---

48. *Michael M. v. Superior Court*, 450 U.S. 464, 469 (1981). In a pre-*Michael M.* case, the West Virginia Supreme Court of Appeals upheld the constitutionality of a state statute that imposed life imprisonment upon a male over sixteen years of age "who carnally knew a previously chaste female, not his wife, who was under sixteen or any female not his wife who was less than ten years old," but punished as a misdemeanor conduct of a female over sixteen years of age "who carnally knew a male not her husband who was less than sixteen." *Moore v. McKenzie*, 236 S.E.2d 342, 343 (W.Va. 1977).

49. *State ex rel. West Virginia Dep't of Health & Human Resources v. Carpenter*, 564 S.E.2d 173, 178–79 & n. 7 (W.Va. 2002).

50. *Id.* at 179.

51. *Jane L. v. Bangerter*, 794 F. Supp. 1537, 1549 (D. Utah 1992).

52. *Geduldig v. Aiello*, 417 U.S. 484, 496 n. 20 (1974) ("[n]ormal pregnancy is an objectively, identifiable physical condition with unique characteristics").

53. *Id.* In *Carpenter*, the West Virginia Supreme Court of Appeals cited both *Geduldig* and *Jane L. v. Bangerter* with approval. 564 S.E.2d at 179 n. 3.

ment of a legitimate state purpose."[54] A prohibition of abortion would be "reasonably related" to the "legitimate state purpose" in protecting unborn human life. Accordingly, West Virginia could enact an abortion prohibition without violating the equal protection principle that inheres in art. III, §10, of the West Virginia Constitution.

Reserved Rights

Article III, §3, of the West Virginia Constitution provides, in part: "Government is instituted for the common benefit, protection and security of the people, nation or community."[55] In any state constitutional challenge to West Virginia's pre-*Roe* abortion statute (or any other statute prohibiting abortion the State may enact), abortion advocates may be expected to rely upon *Women's Health Center of West Virginia, Inc. v. Panepinto*,[56] in which a bare majority of the West Virginia Supreme Court of Appeals relied upon the "common benefit" language of art. III, §3, to invalidate restrictions on public funding of abortion. That reliance, however, would be misplaced.

At issue in *Women's Health Center* was the constitutionality of the State's recently enacted statute restricting public funding of abortion for poor women. The statute prohibited Medicaid funds from being used to pay for the performance of an abortion unless, on the basis of the physician's "best clinical judgment," there was a medical emergency "that so complicate[d] a pregnancy as to necessitate an immediate abortion to avert the death of the mother or for which a delay [would] create grave peril of irreversible loss of major bodily function or an equivalent injury to the mother," or there was "[c]lear clinical medical evidence that the fetus ha[d] severe congenital defects or [a] terminal disease or [was] not expected to be delivered...."[57] The statute also permitted funding when the pregnant woman was "a victim of incest or ... of rape when the rape [was] reported to a law-enforcement agency."[58]

In *Women's Health Center*, the state supreme court refused to postulate a *state* (as opposed to a *federal*) constitutional right to abortion.[59] Rather, the

---

54. *Lewis v. Canaan Valley Resorts, Inc.*, 408 S.E.2d at 641.

55. W.Va. Const. art. III, §3 (1991).

56. 446 S.E.2d 658 (W.Va. 1993).

57. W.Va. Code §9-2-11(a)(1) (2007).

58. *Id.* §9-1-11(a)(2).

59. 446 S.E.2d at 664 (not deciding whether state constitution contains an "analogous right" to the one recognized in *Roe v. Wade*). *See also* Robert M. Bastress, The West Vir-

basis for the decision striking down § 9-2-11 was that, under the "common benefit" language of art. III, § 3, "once a government chooses to dispense funds, it must do so in a nondiscriminatory fashion, and it certainly cannot withdraw benefits for no reason *other* than that a woman chooses to avail herself of a *federally-granted constitutional right*."[60] The majority opinion's emphasis on the *federal* source of the abortion right (*see* n. 1, *supra*) leaves little doubt that the decision ultimately rests upon the continued viability of *Roe v. Wade*.[61]

Women's Health Center would not preclude West Virginia from enforcing its pre-*Roe* abortion prohibition (or enacting a new one) if *Roe*, as modified by *Casey*, were overruled. If *Roe* is ultimately overruled, there would no longer be a federal constitutional right to obtain an abortion, thus removing the underlying jurisprudential basis for the state supreme court's decision (interference with the exercise of a federal constitutional right).

Fundamental Principles

Article III, § 20, of the West Virginia Constitution provides: "Free government and the blessings of liberty can be preserved to any people only by a firm adherence to justice, moderation, temperance, frugality and virtue, and by a frequent recurrence to fundamental principles."[62] In a challenge to West Virginia's pre-*Roe* statute prohibiting abortion, abortion advocates might argue that the statute interferes with the "fundamental principles" referenced in art. III, § 20. Such an argument would not likely prevail.

Article III, § 20, simply "urges the people to preserve free government and the blessings of liberty by, *inter alia*, 'a frequent recurrence to fundamental principles.' "[63] It is also an "admonish[ment]" to the courts to "adhere[] to jus-

---

GINIA STATE CONSTITUTION[:] A REFERENCE GUIDE 86 (Westport, Conn. 1995) (*Women's Health Center* "did not ... develop any concept of a state-protected right to privacy").

60. *Women's Health Center*. 446 S.E.2d at 666 (second emphasis added).

61. The reasoning of the majority opinion in *Women's Health Center* is curious. Without holding that the *state* constitution confers a right to abortion, the majority held that the state "common benefit" provision requires public funding of *all* therapeutic abortions where *some* therapeutic abortions are funded. The court arrived at this holding in order to vindicate a *federal*, not a *state*, constitutional right, even though the Supreme Court itself had previously held that the federal constitution does *not* require the government to pay for all therapeutic abortions. *Harris v. McRae*, 448 U.S. 297 (1980).

62. W.Va. Const. art. III, § 20 (1991).

63. *Graf v. Frame*, 352 S.E.2d 31, 35 (W.Va. 1986).

tice," and to have a "'frequent recurrence to fundamental principles.'"[64] Thus, "under the state constitution, it is our sworn duty to support the fundamental principles upon which our legal institutions are founded."[65] Those principles, however, are derived from *other* provisions of the state constitution. Section 20 is not a source of substantive rights.[66] Accordingly, a right to abortion could not be derived from the language of art. III, §20.

Conclusion

Based on the foregoing analysis, an argument that the West Virginia Constitution protects a right to abortion that is separate from, and independent of, the right to abortion recognized in *Roe v. Wade* would not likely succeed.[67] That, in turn, suggests that if *Roe*, as modified by *Casey*, is ultimately overruled, the State of West Virginia could enforce its pre-*Roe* statute *prohibiting* abortion (or enact a new statute prohibiting abortion). Moreover, nothing in the West Virginia Constitution precludes West Virginia from *regulating* abortion within federal constitutional limits in the meantime. Under the West Virginia Supreme Court of Appeals' decision in *Women's Health Center, Inc.*, however, the State's restrictions on public funding of abortion are unconstitutional.

---

64. *Cooper v. Gwinn*, 298 S.E.2d 781, 784 (W.Va. 1981). *See also State v. Young*, 311 S.E.2d 118, 130 (W.Va. 1983) (same).

65. *State ex rel. Miller v. Smith*, 285 S.E.2d 500, 504 (W.Va. 1981) (citing art. III, §20).

66. *See, e.g., G.M. Crossin, Inc. v. West Virginia Board of Regents*, 355 S.E.2d 32, 35 (W.Va. 1987) (by implication in case decided on state due process grounds); *State ex rel. Starr v. Halbritter*, 395 S.E.2d 773, 777 (W.Va. 1990) (citing art. III, §20, in support of decision to enforce the state constitutional right to indictment by a grand jury); *State v. Huber*, 40 S.E.2d 11, 24 (W.Va. 1946) (citing art. III, §20, in support of a decision based on state separation of powers grounds).

67. The foregoing analysis of the West Virginia Constitution does not include any references to the proceedings of the 1872 Constitutional Convention because "[t]here is no record of the debates at the second [1872] convention." Bastress, THE WEST VIRGINIA STATE CONSTITUTION at 301.

CHAPTER 52

WISCONSIN

Summary

The Wisconsin Supreme Court has not yet decided whether the Wisconsin Constitution protects a right to abortion separate from, and independent of, the right to abortion recognized under the United States Constitution.[1] A careful examination of the state constitution, in light of its history and interpretation, as well as other relevant legal sources, however, suggests that the state supreme court probably would not recognize a state constitutional right to abortion. Thus, if *Roe v. Wade*,[2] as modified by *Planned Parenthood of Southeastern Pennsylvania v. Casey*,[3] were overruled, Wisconsin could enforce its pre-*Roe* abortion statute (or enact a new statute prohibiting abortion). Moreover, nothing in the state constitution, properly understood, precludes the State from enacting and enforcing reasonable measures regulating abortion within current federal constitutional limits.

Analysis

The pre-*Roe* statute prohibited performance of an abortion upon a pregnant woman unless the procedure was "necessary to save the life of the mother."[4]

---

1. The Wisconsin Supreme Court has referred to the right to abortion solely as a matter of *federal*, not *state*, constitutional law. *See State v. Horn*, 377 N.W.2d 176, 180 (Wis. Ct. App. 1985) ("[t]he United States Supreme Court has held that a woman's right to choose abortion is constitutionally protected") (quoted with approval in *State v. Migliorino*, 442 N.W.2d 36, 47 (Wis. 1989)).

2. 410 U.S. 113 (1973).

3. 505 U.S. 833 (1992).

4. Wis. Stat. Ann. § 940.04 (1971). Under subsection (3), "[a]ny pregnant woman who intentionally destroy[ed] the life of her unborn child or who consents to such destruction by another" was guilty of a misdemeanor. No prosecutions were reported under this statute.

In *Babbitz v. McCann*,[5] a pre-*Roe* decision, a three-judge federal district court declared the statute unconstitutional (on federal, not state, grounds), insofar as it prohibited abortions before quickening.[6] The same court thereafter permanently enjoined enforcement of the statute.[7] The injunction, however, was subsequently vacated by the Supreme Court.[8] The pre-*Roe* statute, which is not currently enforceable, has not been repealed.[9]

Based upon arguments that have been raised in other States with similar constitutional provisions, possible sources for an asserted abortion right could include provisions of the state constitution guaranteeing a "certain remedy" for injuries (art. I, §9), freedom of worship and liberty of conscience (§18), and due process of law (§8(1)); recognizing inherent rights and equality (§1); and emphasizing the importance of frequent recurrence to fundamental principles (§22).[10] The analysis that follows addresses each of these provisions.

Certain Remedy for Injuries

Article I, §9, of the Wisconsin Constitution provides:

> Every person is entitled to a certain remedy in the laws for all injuries, or wrongs which he may receive in his person, property, or character; he ought to obtain justice freely, and without being obliged to purchase it, completely and without denial, promptly and without delay, conformably to the laws.[11]

Abortion advocates might argue that any statute prohibiting abortion interferes with a woman's control over her own body, and that such interference challenge an "injury" to her "person," as those terms are used in §9, for which

5. 310 F. Supp. 203 (E.D. Wis. 1970), *appeal dismissed*, 400 U.S. 1 (1970).

6. "Quickening" refers to the stage of pregnancy, usually sixteen to eighteen weeks gestation, when a woman first detects fetal movement.

7. *Babbitz v. McCann*, 320 F. Supp. 219 (E.D. Wis. 1970).

8. *McCann v. Babbitz*, 402 U.S. 903 (1971).

9. WIS. STAT. ANN. §940.04 (West 2004). The Wisconsin Supreme Court has recognized that §940.04 is unenforceable on *federal* constitutional grounds only. *State v. Black*, 526 N.W.2d 132, 135 n. 2 (Wis. 1994). In the same case, the state supreme court held that §940.04 has not been repealed by implication by enactment of post-*Roe* statutes regulating abortion. *Id.* at 134–35.

10. Two other more unlikely sources of an abortion right under the Wisconsin Constitution-art. I, §3 (guaranteeing freedom of speech) and §11 (prohibiting unreasonable searches and seizures)-are discussed generally in Chapter Three, *supra*.

11. WIS. CONST. art. I, §9 (West 2002).

there must be a "certain remedy." That "remedy," in turn, would be invalidation of the statute. This argument assumes that art. I, §9, confers substantive rights. The case law is clear, however, that it does not.

The Wisconsin Supreme Court has held that art. I, §9, "confers no legal rights."[12] "Rather, it preserves access to the courts for redress of rights as those rights may either be created by the legislature, or, of rights recognized by the common law, and not modified or suspended by it under the authority granted to it by … art. XIV, §13."[13] Because art. I, §9, "confers no legal rights," it could not be a source of a right to abortion under the Wisconsin Constitution.

Freedom of Worship, Liberty of Conscience

Article I, §18, of the Wisconsin Constitution provides:

> The right of every person to worship Almighty God according to the dictates of conscience shall never be infringed; nor shall any person be compelled to attend, erect or support any place of worship, or to maintain any ministry, without consent; nor shall any control of, or interference with, the rights of conscience be permitted, or any preference be given by law to any religious establishments or modes or worship; nor shall any money be drawn from the treasury for the benefit of religious societies, or religious or theological seminaries.[14]

In any challenge to Wisconsin's pre-*Roe* abortion statute, abortion advocates may raise either or both of two arguments under art. I, §18. First, relying upon the first and third clauses of §18, they may argue that the prohibition of abortion interferes with both a woman's right "to worship Almighty God according to the dictates of [her] conscience" and her "rights of conscience" by forbidding her from obtaining an abortion that would be allowed by her religion. Second, relying upon other language in the third clause of §18, they may

---

12. *Aicher v. Wisconsin Patients Compensation Fund*, 613 N.W.2d 849, 863 (Wis. 2000). *See also Mulder v. Acme-Cleveland Corp.*, 290 N.W.2d 276, 284 (Wis. 1980) (same); *Deegan v. Jefferson County*, 525 N.W.2d 149, 155 (Wis. Ct. App. 1994) (same).

13. *Guzman v. St. Francis Hospital, Inc.*, 623 N.W.2d 776, 787 (Wis. Ct. App. 2000). Article XIV, §13, provides: "Such parts of the common law as are now in force in the territory of Wisconsin, not inconsistent with this constitution, shall be and continue part of the law of this state under altered or suspended by the legislature." WIS. CONST. art. XIV, §13 (West 2002).

14. WIS. CONST. art. I, §18 (West 2002).

argue in the alternative (or in addition) that an abortion prohibition gives a "preference" to a "religious establishment[]" because it reflects sectarian beliefs regarding when human life begins and the sinfulness of abortion. Neither argument would likely prevail.

With respect to the latter argument (establishment of religion), Wisconsin reviewing courts "interpret and apply art. I, § 18 in light of the United States Supreme Court cases interpreting the Establishment Clause."[15] Given this consistency of interpretation, a challenge to an abortion statute that would not succeed under the Establishment Clause of the First Amendment would not succeed under art. I, § 18, either. For the reasons set forth in Chapter 2, *supra*, an abortion statute could not be successfully challenged on Establishment Clause grounds. Accordingly, a similar challenge under art. I, § 18, would not likely be successful.[16]

With respect to the former argument (rights of conscience), the Wisconsin Supreme Court has developed its own methodology for evaluating free exercise and freedom of conscience claims. To challenge a statute on free exercise and/or freedom of conscience grounds, a party must prove "(1) that he or she has a sincerely held religious belief, (2) that is burdened by application of the state law at issue. Upon such proof, the burden shifts to the State to prove: (3) that the law is based on a compelling state interest, (4) which cannot be served by a less restrictive alternative."[17]

A prohibition of abortion except to save the life of the pregnant woman would not "burden[]" a "sincerely held religious belief" because there is no doctrine in any religion that *requires* (as opposed to *permits*) a woman to un-

---

15. *King v. Village of Waunakee*, 499 N.W.2d 237, 245 (Wis. Ct. App. 1993), *aff'd*, 517 N.W.2d 671, 683–84 (Wis. 1994); *Jackson v. Benson*, 578 N.W.2d 602, 620–21 & n. 21 (Wis. 1998); *American Motors Corp. v. Dep't of Industry, Labor & Human Relations*, 286 N.W.2d 847, 854 (Wis. Ct. App. 1979), *rev'd on other grounds*, 305 N.W.2d 62 (Wis. 1981); *State ex rel. Holt v. Thompson*, 225 N.W.2d 678, 687–89 (Wis. 1975).

16. This conclusion is supported by the Wisconsin Supreme Court's decision in *State ex rel. Wisconsin Health Facilities Authority v. Lindner*, 280 N.W.2d 773 (Wis. 1979). In *Lindner*, the state supreme court held that state aid to private hospitals under a statute providing a mechanism for financing improvements though the sale of tax-exempt bonds did not violate either the Establishment Clause of the First Amendment or art. I, § 18, of the Wisconsin Constitution even though some hospitals qualifying for financing prohibited abortion and sterilization as a contraceptive measure. *Id.* at 776–83. If state aid to religious hospitals providing health care for the public on a non-denominational basis does not violate art. I, § 18, even though the hospitals may not allow their facilities to be used for the performance of abortions, then it is difficult to see how a law prohibiting abortion would violate § 18, either.

17. *State v. Miller*, 549 N.W.2d 235, 240 (Wis. 1996).

dergo an abortion in circumstances when her life is not in danger,[18] an exception which is recognized in Wisconsin's pre-*Roe* abortion statute. Even assuming, however, that a pregnant woman could satisfy the first two elements of the *Miller* test, it would seem that she could not satisfy the last two elements. The State has a compelling interest in protecting and preserving the life of the unborn child and there is no "less restrictive alternative" available to the State, short of an outright prohibition, that would adequately promote and safeguard that interest. An example, not involving abortion, that illustrates this principle is the line of cases authorizing compulsory blood transfusions on pregnant women (typically, Jehovah's Witnesses) to save the lives of their unborn children.[19] The prohibition of abortion, for the same end, stands on even firmer ground, however, because it does not implicate the federal constitutional right to refuse unwanted medical treatment.[20] Moreover, unlike an order authorizing a blood transfusion of a pregnant woman, which is intended to *save* the life of the unborn child (and very possibly the mother's life as well), the intent in an abortion is to *destroy* the unborn child's life. The prohibition of abortion would not violate art. I, § 18, of the Wisconsin Constitution

Inherent Rights, Due Process of Law

Article I, § 1, of the Wisconsin Constitution provides, in part, that "[a]ll people ... have certain inherent rights; among these are life, liberty and the

---

18. Whether a particular religious doctrine *permits* abortion under certain circumstances does not present a justiciable free exercise issue because, to have the standing necessary to raise such an issue (with respect to a law that does not single out religious practices for regulation), one must allege that one seeks an abortion "under compulsion of religious belief." *Harris v. McRae*, 448 U.S. 297, 320 (1980).

19. *See Fosmire v. Nicoleau*, 536 N.Y.S.2d 492, 496 (App. Div. 1989) (dictum) (when "a pregnant adult woman refuses medical treatment and, as a result of that refusal, places the life of her unborn baby in jeopardy," "the State's interest, as *parens patriae*, in protecting the health and welfare of the child is determined to be paramount") (citing *In the Matter of Application of Jamaica Hospital*, 491 N.Y.S.2d 898 (Sup. Ct. 1985) (blood transfusion) (18 weeks gestation); and *Crouse Irving Memorial Hospital, Inc. v. Paddock*, 485 N.Y.S.2d 443 (Sup. Ct. 1985) (blood transfusion) (premature delivery)). *See also Raleigh Fitkin-Paul Morgan Memorial Hospital v. Anderson*, 201 A.2d 537 (N.J. 1964) (same with respect to blood transfusion at 32 weeks gestation); *but see In re Brown*, 689 N.E.2d 397 (Ill. App. Ct. 1997) (*contra*) (blood transfusion).

20. *See, e.g., Cruzan v. Director, Missouri Dep't of Health*, 497 U.S. 261, 278–79 & n. 7 (1990); *Washington v. Glucksberg*, 521 U.S. 702, 719–26 & n. 17 (1997).

pursuit of happiness."[21] Article I, §8(1), provides, in that "[n]o person may be held to answer for a criminal offense without due process of law ..."[22]

In any state constitutional challenge to Wisconsin's pre-*Roe* abortion statute (or any other statute prohibiting abortion the State may enact) abortion advocates are most likely to rely upon the "liberty" and "due process" language of art. I, §§1 and 8(1), arguing that the prohibition interferes with a woman's liberty in obtaining an abortion and her right to due process of law.[23] Such an argument probably would not prevail, however.

The Wisconsin Supreme Court has held that art. I, §1, and art. I, §8(1), confer substantive due process guarantees.[24] Those guarantees, whether derived from art. I, §1, or art. I, §8(1), are "similar" to or the "substantial equivalent" of the Due Process Clauses of the Fifth and Fourteenth Amendments.[25] In determining whether an asserted liberty interest (or right) should be regarded as "fundamental" under the federal constitution, the United States Supreme Court applies a two-prong test. First, there must be a "careful description" of the asserted fundamental liberty interest.[26] Second, the interest, so described, must be firmly rooted in "the Nation's history, legal traditions, and practices."[27] Wisconsin reviewing courts employ the same test in evaluating state substantive due process claims.[28] An asserted interest will qualify as a "liberty interest" only "if it is both fundamental and traditionally protected by our society."[29]

---

21. WIS. CONST. art. I, §1 (West 2002).

22. *Id.* art. I, §8(1).

23. Although §8(1), along with the rest of §8 would appear to be concerned only with criminal procedure, it has been interpreted to have a substantive component as well, as the discussion following in the text indicates.

24. *Dowhower v. West Bend Mutual Ins. Co.*, 613 N.W.2d 557, 560–61 (Wis. 2000) (art. I, §1); *In the Interest of Reginald D.*, 533 N.W.2d 181, 184–85 (Wis. 1995) (same); *In re Commitment of Laxton*, 647 N.W.2d 784, 789 & nn. 7, 8 (Wis. 2002) (art. I, §8); *State v. Post*, 541 N.W.2d 115, 122 n. 10 (West 1995) (same). *See also Guzman v. St. Francis Hospital, Inc.*, 623 N.W.2d at 788–89 (art. I, §1).

25. *State v. Post*, 541 N.W.2d at 122 n. 10 ("similar"); *State v. McManus*, 447 N.W.2d 654, 660 (Wis. 1989) ("substantial equivalent"); *State v. Greenwold*, 525 N.W.2d 294, 298 (Wis. Ct. App. 1994) ("substantial equivalent"); *Dowhower*, 613 N.W.2d at 560 ("no substantial difference"); *Reginald D.*, 533 N.W.2d 181, 184 (Wis. 1995) ("no substantial difference").

26. *Washington v. Glucksberg*, 521 U.S. at 721 (citation and internal quotation marks omitted).

27. *Id.* at 710.

28. *Dowhower*, 613 N.W.2d at 560–61 (following *Glucksberg*); *Larson v. Burmaster*, 720 N.W.2d 134, 151 (Wis. Ct. App. 2006) (same); *State v. Radke*, 647 N.W.2d 873, 877 (Wis. Ct. App. 2002) (same).

29. *In the Interest of Angel Lacy M.*, 516 N.W.2d 678, 685 (Wis. 1994). Legislation that

The state supreme court has recognized liberty interests in the right of parents "to the care, custody and management of [their children],"[30] in choosing "whether or not to accept medical treatment,"[31] and in the right of persons to be free "from physical restraint."[32] All of these interests have long been recognized in English and American law.[33] By way of contrast, a liberty interest in (or right to) an abortion cannot be regarded as "fundamental" under art. I, § 1 or art. I, § 8(1), because such an interest (or right) is not firmly rooted in Wisconsin's "history, legal traditions, and practices."[34]

---

restricts a fundamental liberty interest is subject to the "strict scrutiny" standard of review. *State v. Post*, 541 N.W.2d at 122. Under this standard, "the challenged statute must further a compelling state interest and be narrowly tailored to serve that interest." *Id.* (citation omitted). If, however, no fundamental liberty interest is implicated, then the challenged statute "will generally survive a substantive due process challenge if it is rationally related to a legitimate government interest." *State v. Radke*, 647 N.W.2d at 877, citing *Washington v. Glucksberg*, and *State v. McManus*, 447 N.W.2d 654, 660 (Wis. 1989). "Due process requires that the means chosen by the legislation bear a reasonable relationship to the purpose or object of the enactment; if it does, and the legislative purpose is a proper one, the exercise of the police power is valid." *Id.*

30. *In the Interest of J.L.W.*, 306 N.W.2d 46, 53 (Wis. 1981). In *J.L.W.*, the court held that "the due process protections of the State and Federal Constitutions prohibit the termination of a natural parent's rights, unless the parent is unfit." *Id.* at 55.

31. *Matter of Guardianship of L.W.*, 482 N.W.2d 60, 65 (Wis. 1992). In *L.W.*, the court held that "an individual's right to refuse unwanted medical treatment emanates from the common law right of self-determination and informed consent, the personal liberties protected by the Fourteenth Amendment, and from the guarantee of liberty in Article I, section 1 of the Wisconsin Constitution." *Id.*

32. *State v. Post*, 541 N.W.2d at 122. In *Post*, the court held that "[f]reedom from physical restraint is a fundamental right that 'has always been at the core of the liberty protected by the Due Process Clause from arbitrary governmental action." *Id.* (quoting *Foucha v. Louisiana*, 504 U.S. 71, 80 (1992)).

33. *See Troxel v. Granville*, 530 U.S. 57, 65 (2000) ("[t]he liberty interest ... of parents in the care, custody, and control of their children ... is perhaps the oldest of the fundamental liberty interests recognized by this Court"); *Glucksberg*, 521 U.S. at 719–26 & n. 17 (recognizing liberty interest in refusing unwanted medical treatment); *Cruzan v. Director, Missouri Dep't of Health*, 497 U.S. 261, 278–79 & n. 7 (1990) (same); *Union Pacific Railway Co. v. Botsford*, 141 U.S. 250, 251 (1891) ("[n]o right is held more sacred, is more carefully guaranteed by the common law, than the right of every individual to the possession and control of his own person, free from all restraint or interference of others, unless by clear and unquestioned authority of law").

34. To the extent that the Wisconsin Supreme Court considers federal precedent in determining whether an asserted liberty interest (or right) is "fundamental" under the state due process guarantee, abortion would not qualify as a "fundamental" right. Although the Supreme Court characterized the right to choose abortion as "fundamental" in *Roe*, 410 U.S. at 152–53, it tacitly abandoned that characterization in *Casey*, 505 U.S. at 869–79

Wisconsin enacted its first statutes prohibiting abortion and protecting the lives of unborn children in 1849, one year after the State adopted its constitution and was admitted to the Union. One statute provided that the "wilful killing of an unborn quick child, by any injury to the mother of such child, which would be murder if it resulted in the death of such mother, shall be deemed manslaughter in the first degree."[35] Another statute prohibited the performance of an abortion upon a woman "pregnant with a quick child ... with intent thereby to destroy such child, unless the same shall have been necessary to preserve the life of [the] mother, or shall have been advised by two physicians to be necessary for such purpose."[36] The statute defined the offense as manslaughter in the second degree if the death of either the quick child or the pregnant woman resulted.[37] Less than ten years later, the Wisconsin Legislature eliminated the "quickening" requirements in these statutes, making them applicable throughout pregnancy,[38] and added two more statutes prohibiting abortion (a misdemeanor) and making a pregnant woman's participation in her own abortion a criminal offense (also a misdemeanor).[39] These statutes, renumbered from time to time and ultimately consolidated into a single, multi-part statute,[40] have not been repealed.[41]

Prior to *Roe v. Wade*, the Wisconsin Supreme Court regularly affirmed abortion convictions (and convictions for homicide of the mother based on the performance of an illegal abortion) without any hint that either the prosecutions or convictions violated the state constitution.[42] In 1959, the state supreme

---

(Joint Op. of O'Connor, Kennedy and Souter, JJ., replacing *Roe's* "strict scrutiny" standard of review with the more relaxed "undue burden" standard, allowing for a broader measure of abortion regulation).

35. Wis. Rev. Stat. ch. 133, § 10 (1849). A "quick" child, as that word is used in this statute, meant a child who had "quickened." "Quickening" is that stage of pregnancy, usually sixteen to eighteen weeks gestation, when the woman first detects fetal movement.

36. *Id.* ch. 133, § 11.

37. *Id.*

38. *Id.* ch. 164, §§ 10, 11 (1858).

39. *Id.* ch. 169, §§ 58, 59. No prosecutions were reported under the latter statute.

40. Wis. Rev. Stat. ch. 164, §§ 10, 11, ch. 169, §§ 58, 59 (1858), *recodified at* Wis. Rev. Stat. §§ 4347, 4352, 4583, 4584 (1878), *recodified at* Wis. Stat. §§ 340.11, 340.16, 351.22, 351.23 (1925), *recodified at* Wis. Stat. §§ 340.095, 340.11, 351.22, 351.23 (1949), *consolidated and recodified at* Wis. Stat. § 940.04 (1955).

41. Wis. Rev. Stat. § 940.04 (West 2004).

42. *Hatchard v. State*, 48 N.W. 380 (Wis. 1891); *State v. Law*, 137 N.W. 457 (Wis. 1912); *Rotermund v. State*, 168 N.W. 390 (Wis. 1918); *Werner v. State*, 206 N.W. 898 (Wis. 1926); *State v. Henderson*, 274 N.W. 266 (Wis. 1937); *State v. Cohen*, 142 N.W.2d 161 (Wis. 1966); *State v. Mac Gresens*, 161 N.W.2d 245 (Wis. 1968); *State v. Harling*, 170 N.W.2d 720 (Wis. 1969).

court explained that the public policy of prohibiting abortion through the criminal law was "based on the belief that it is wrong to deprive a living fetus of its right to be born."[43] Subsequent to *Roe*, the Wisconsin General Assembly enacted a comprehensive scheme of abortion regulation.[44]

Wisconsin has recognized the rights of unborn children in a variety of contexts outside of abortion, including criminal law, tort law, property law, health care law and guardianship law. In criminal law, causing death or harm to an unborn child at any stage of gestation is a crime.[45]

In tort law, a statutory cause of action for wrongful death may be brought on behalf of an unborn child who was viable (capable of sustained survival outside the mother's womb, with or without medical assistance) at the time of its death.[46] A common law action for (nonlethal) prenatal injuries may be brought without regard to the stage of pregnancy when the injuries were inflicted.[47] And Wisconsin does not recognize wrongful life causes of action.[48]

---

43. *Puhl v. Milwaukee Automobile Ins. Co.*, 99 N.W.2d 163, 170 (Wis. 1959), *overruled on other grounds*, *In re Estate of Stromsted*, 299 N.W.2d 226 (Wis. 1980).

44. Wis. Rev. Stat. §253.10 (West Supp. 2007) (mandating informed consent and a twenty-four hour waiting period); §48.375 (West 2008) (requiring parental consent and a twenty-four hour waiting period); §§253.04 (West 2004), 448.03(5) (West 2005) (recognizing individual and institutional rights of conscience and prohibiting discrimination against persons who object to abortion); §§20.927, 20.9275 (West 2003) (restricting public funding of abortion for indigent women and funding for abortion-related activities).

45. Wis. Rev. Stat. §939.75; §939.24(1) (criminal recklessness); §939.25(1) (criminal negligence); §940.01(1)(b) (first-degree intentional homicide); §940.02(1m) (first-degree reckless homicide); §940.05(2g) (second-degree intentional homicide); §940.06(2) (second-degree reckless homicide); §940.08(2) (homicide by negligent handling of dangerous weapon, explosives or fire); §§940.09(1)(c)-(e), - (1g)(c), -(cm), -(d) (homicide by intoxicated use of vehicle of firearm); §940.10(2) (homicide by negligent operation of a vehicle); §940.195 (battery to an unborn child); §§940.23(1)(b), -(2)(b) (reckless injury); §940.24(2) (injury by negligent handling of dangerous weapon, explosives or fire); §§940.25(1)(c)-(e) (injury by intoxicated use of a vehicle) (West 2004).

46. *See Kwaterski v. State Farm Mutual Automobile Ins. Co.*, 148 N.W.2d 107, 112 (Wis. 1967), interpreting Wis. Rev. Stat. §895.03 (West 2006).

47. *Puhl v. Milwaukee Automobile Ins. Co.*, 99 N.W.2d at 169–81 (dictum).

48. *Dumer v. St. Michael's Hospital*, 233 N.W.2d 372, 374–75 (Wis. 1975). *See also Slawek v. Stroh*, 215 N.W.2d 9, 21–22 (Wis. 1974). A "wrongful life" cause of action is a claim brought on behalf of a child who is born with a physical or mental disability or disease that could have been discovered before the child's birth by genetic testing, amniocentesis or other medical screening. The gravamen of the action is that, as a result of a physician's failure to inform the child's parents of the child's disability or disease (or at least of the availability of tests to determine the presence of the disability or disease), they were deprived of the opportunity to abort the child, thus resulting in the birth of a child suffering permanent physical or mental impairment. Very few courts recognize "wrongful life" causes of

In health care law, a living will may not direct the withholding or withdrawal of life-sustaining medical treatment from a woman who is known to be pregnant.[49] And a physician may not enter a DNR ("do not resuscitate") order for a patient who is known to be pregnant.[50] In property law, heirs conceived before but born after the death of an intestate (a person who dies without a will) may inherit from a decedent if they live 120 or more hours (five days) after birth.[51] Subject to certain exceptions, the same rule applies to afterborn heirs (heirs conceived before the death of a decedent but after the decedent executes a will).[52] Finally, a court may appoint a guardian *ad litem* to represent the interests of an unborn child.[53] Enactment of the foregoing statutes fully justifies the Wisconsin Court of Appeals' observation that "the legislature is in the practice of considering and protecting the rights of unborn children in this state."[54]

A right to abortion cannot be found in the text or structure of the Wisconsin Constitution. There is no evidence that the framers or ratifiers of the state constitution intended to limit the Legislature's authority to prohibit abortion.[55] Such an intent would have been remarkable in light of the contemporaneous prohibition of abortion except to save the life of the pregnant woman. Moreover, recognition of an abortion right would be manifestly inconsistent with the precedents of the Wisconsin Supreme Court. Taken together, these factors militate against recognition of a right to abortion under the inherent rights and due process guarantees of the Wisconsin Constitution.

In light of Wisconsin's unbroken tradition of prohibiting abortion except to preserve the life of the pregnant woman, as well as the State's solicitude for the rights of the unborn child in other areas of law, it cannot reasonably be said that the liberty guaranteed by art. I, §1, or the due process guaranteed by art. I, §8(1), encompasses a right to abortion.

---

action because an assessment of damages requires the courts to compare the value of life, albeit with some degree of physical or mental impairment, to nonexistence. The Wisconsin Supreme Court has recognizes wrongful birth actions, however. *Dumer*, 233 N.W.2d at 376–77. A "wrongful birth" cause of action is a claim, based on the same facts, brought by the parents of an impaired child on their own behalf.

49. Wis. Rev. Stat. §154.03 (West 2006).

50. *Id.* §154.19(1)(e).

51. *Id.* §854.21(5) (West 2002).

52. *Id.*

53. *Id.* §§48.235(1)(f) (West 2008), 757.52 (West 2001).

54. *State v. Deborah J.Z.*, 596 N.W.2d 490, 493 (Wis. Ct. App. 1999).

55. *See* Journal of the Convention to Form a Constitution for the State of Wisconsin 50–51 (first and second readings), 92–96, 100–10, 120–28 (debate on Declaration of Rights in Committee of the Whole); 143 (third reading); 452–53, 455 (final passage) (Madison, Wisconsin 1848).

Equality

Article I, §1, of the Wisconsin Constitution provides, in part, that "[a]ll people are born equally free and independent...."[56] The Wisconsin Supreme Court has held that "[t]he equal protection clause in the Wisconsin Constitution [art. I, §1] requires the identical interpretation as that given to the parallel provision of the United States Constitution [the Equal Protection Clause of the Fourteenth Amendment]."[57]

Consistent with federal equal protection analysis, Wisconsin recognizes three levels of judicial review. Classifications that are based on a suspect class (*e.g.*, race, alienage or national origin) or that interfere with the exercise of a fundamental right (*e.g.*, voting) are subject to strict scrutiny review "and must be shown to be necessary to promote a compelling government interest in order to be found constitutional."[58] "Classifications based on gender are subject to an elevated level of scrutiny."[59] Under that level of scrutiny ("intermediate" or "heightened" scrutiny), a gender-based classification must be "substantially related" to the achievement of "important governmental objectives."[60] All other classifications are subject to rational basis review. Under that level of review, a classification will be upheld "if there is a rational relationship between the disparity of treatment and some legitimate governmental purpose."[61]

Strict scrutiny review would not apply to a statute prohibiting abortion (either §940.04 or another prohibition) because, for the reasons set forth in the preceding section of this analysis, the state constitution does not confer a fundamental right to abortion. Nor would the prohibition of abortion classify persons on the basis of race or any other suspect personal characteristic. Abortion advocates may argue in the alternative, however, that a statute prohibiting abortion discriminates against women and is subject to intermediate scrutiny because only women are capable of becoming pregnant.

---

56. WIS. CONST. art. I, §1 (West 2002).

57. *State v. Heft*, 517 N.W.2d 494, 497 n. 3 (Wis. 1994). *See also State v. Post*, 541 N.W.2d at 128 n. 21 (same); *Treiber v. Knoll*, 398 N.W.2d 756, 760 (Wis. 1987) (same).

58. *State v. Post*, 541 N.W.2d at 129.

59. *Phillips v. Wisconsin Personnel Comm'n*, 482 N.W.2d 121, 129 (Wis. Ct. App. 1992).

60. *Craig v. Boren*, 429 U.S. 190, 197 (1976). Classifications based on illegitimacy are subject to a similar standard. *See Mills v. Habluetzel*, 456 U.S. 91, 96 (1982) (classification must be "substantially related to a legitimate state interest").

61. *Post*, 541 N.W.2d at 129 (citation and internal quotation marks omitted).

An abortion prohibition would appear to satisfy this level of scrutiny because the prohibition would be "substantially related" to the "important governmental objective" of protecting unborn human life. Nevertheless, the standard applicable to sex-based discrimination should not apply to an abortion prohibition. Abortion laws do not discriminate on the basis of sex.

First, the United States Supreme Court has reviewed restrictions on abortion funding under a rational basis standard of review, *not* under the heightened scrutiny required of gender-based classifications.[62] Indeed, the Court has held that "the disfavoring of abortion ... is not *ipso facto* sex discrimination," and, citing its decisions in *Harris* and other cases addressing abortion funding, stated that "the constitutional test applicable to government abortion-funding restrictions is not the heightened-scrutiny standard that our cases demand for sex discrimination, ... but the ordinary rationality standard."[63]

Second, even assuming that an abortion prohibition differentiates between men and women on the basis of sex, and would otherwise be subject to a higher standard of review, the Supreme Court has held that biological differences between men and women may justify different treatment based on those differences. In upholding a statutory rape statute that applied only to males, the Supreme Court noted, "this Court has consistently upheld statutes where the gender classification is not invidious, but rather realistically reflects the fact that the sexes are not similarly situated in certain circumstances."[64] "Abortion statutes," as one federal district court has observed, "are examples of cases in

---

62. *Harris v. McRae*, 448 U.S. at 321–26 (1980).

63. *Bray v. Alexandria Women's Health Clinic*, 506 U.S. 263, 273 (1993). Several state supreme courts and individual state supreme court justices have recognized that abortion regulations and restrictions on abortion funding are not "directed at women as a class" so much as "abortion as a medical treatment, which, because it involves a potential life, has no parallel as a treatment method." *Bell v. Low Income Women of Texas*, 95 S.W.3d 253, 258 (Tex. 2002) (upholding funding restrictions) (citing *Harris*, 448 U.S. at 325). *See also Fischer v. Dep't of Public Welfare*, 502 A.2d 114, 125 (Pa. 1985) ("the basis for the distinction here is not sex, but abortion") (upholding funding restrictions); *Moe v. Secretary of Administration & Finance*, 417 N.E.2d 387, 407 (Mass. 1981) (Hennessey, C.J., dissenting) (funding restrictions were "directed at abortion as a medical procedure, not women as a class"); *Right to Choose v. Byrne*, 450 A.2d 925, 950 (N.J. 1982) (O'Hern, J., dissenting) ("[t]he subject of the legislation is not the person of the recipient, but the nature of the claimed medical service"). Both *Moe* and *Right to Choose* were decided on other grounds. The dissenting justices were addressing alternative arguments raised by the plaintiffs, but not reached by the majority opinions.

64. *Michael M. v. Superior Court*, 450 U.S. 464, 469 (1981). *See also State v. Fisher*, 565 N.W.2d 565, 569 (Wis. Ct. App. 1997) (citing *Michael M.* with approval).

which the sexes are not biologically similarly situated" because only women are capable of becoming pregnant and having abortions.[65]

A statute prohibiting abortion quite obviously can affect only women because only women are capable of becoming pregnant.[66] Unlike laws that use women's ability to become pregnant (or pregnancy itself) to discriminate against them in *other* areas (*e.g.*, employment opportunities), abortion prohibitions cannot fairly be said to involve a distinction between men and women that is a "mere pretext[] designed to erect an invidious discrimination against [women]."[67]

Because a prohibition of abortion would not infringe upon a fundamental state constitutional right and would not impermissibly classify on the basis of a suspect or quasi-suspect class, it would need to satisfy only the rational basis test. Under that test, as previously noted, the classification must be reasonably related to the achievement of a legitimate state purpose. A prohibition of abortion would be "reasonably related" to the "legitimate state purpose" in protecting unborn human life. Accordingly, Wisconsin could enact an abortion prohibition without violating the equal protection clause of art. I, § 1, of the Wisconsin Constitution.

Fundamental Principles

Article I, § 22, of the Wisconsin Constitution provides: "The blessings of a free government can only be maintained by a frequent recurrence to fundamental principles."[68] In a challenge to Wisconsin's pre-*Roe* statute prohibiting abortion (or any other statute prohibiting abortion the State may enact), abortion advocates might argue that the statute interferes with the "fundamental principles" referenced in art. I, § 22. Such an argument would not likely prevail.

Article I, § 22, "contains no reference to law and no express limitations on state action."[69] In an old case, however, the Wisconsin Supreme Court referred

---

65. *Jane L. v. Bangerter*, 794 F. Supp. 1537, 1549 (D. Utah 1992).

66. *Geduldig v. Aiello*, 417 U.S. 484, 496 n. 20 (1974) ("[n]ormal pregnancy is an objectively, identifiable physical condition with unique characteristics").

67. *Id.*

68. WIS. CONST. art. I, § 22 (West 2002).

69. *Jacobs v. Major*, 390 N.W.2d 86, 106 (Wis. Ct. App. 1986), *aff'd*, 407 N.W.2d 832 (Wis. 1987). One commentator referred to art. I, § 22, as "a civics lesson rather than a constitutional provision." Jack Stark, THE WISCONSIN STATE CONSTITUTION[:] A REFERENCE GUIDE 71 (Westport, Conn. 1997).

to "the implied inhibition" that §22 imposes on legislation.[70] The court did not explain what that "inhibition" might be and has never struck down a law on the basis that it violated §22. The "fundamental principles" mentioned in §22 are derived from *other* provisions of the state constitution. Section 22 is not a source of substantive rights. Accordingly, a right to abortion could not be derived from the language of art. I, §22.[71]

Conclusion

Based on the foregoing analysis, an argument that the Wisconsin Constitution protects a right to abortion that is separate from, and independent of, the right to abortion recognized in *Roe v. Wade* would not likely succeed. That, in turn, suggests that if *Roe*, as modified by *Casey*, is ultimately overruled, the State of Wisconsin could enforce its pre-*Roe* statute *prohibiting* abortion (or enact a new statute prohibiting abortion). Moreover, nothing in the Wisconsin Constitution precludes Wisconsin from *regulating* abortion within federal constitutional limits in the meantime.

70. *State ex rel. Milwaukee Medical College v. Chittenden*, 107 N.W. 500, 517–18 (Wis. 1906).

71. Occasionally, the Wisconsin Supreme Court has cited art. I, §22, along with other provisions of the state constitution, as guaranteeing "inherent rights of due process and liberty interests." *Peppies Courtesy Cab Co. v. Kenosha*, 475 N.W.2d 156, 157 (Wis. 1991). *See also Chicago & Northwestern Ry. Co. v. La Follette*, 169 N.W.2d 441, 445 (Wis. 1969). To the extent that §22 guarantees such rights and interests, they are discussed in the section of this analysis addressing art. I, §§1 and 8(1), *supra*.

CHAPTER 53

WYOMING

Summary

The Wyoming Supreme Court has not yet decided whether the Wyoming Constitution protects a right to abortion separate from, and independent of, the right to abortion recognized under the United States Constitution.[1] A careful examination of the state constitution, in light of its history and interpretation, as well as other relevant legal sources, however, suggests that the state supreme court probably would not recognize a state constitutional right to abortion if *Roe v. Wade*,[2] as modified by *Planned Parenthood of Southeastern Pennsylvania v. Casey*,[3] were overruled. Thus, Wyoming could prohibit abortion. Moreover, nothing in the state constitution, properly understood, precludes the State from enacting and enforcing reasonable measures regulating abortion within current federal constitutional limits.

---

1. In *Wyoming NARAL v. Karpan*, 881 P.2d 281 (Wyo. 1994), the Wyoming Supreme Court considered a pre-election challenge to a citizen-sponsored ballot initiative that would have prohibited abortion except to save the life of the mother and banned public funding of abortion (subject to the same exception). The court determined that the abortion ban would run afoul of *Roe*, as reaffirmed in part by *Casey*, but allowed the initiative to remain on the ballot because it was not unconstitutional *in toto* (the ban on public funding of abortion would have been valid). Referring to the abortion prohibition, the court stated that "the initiative is contrary to the ruling of the Supreme Court of the United States in *Roe*." 881 P.2d at 287. "Both the federal and state constitutions require our compliance with federal constitutional law on issues preserved within the federal domain. *Id.* at 288 (citing U.S. Const. art. VI, cl. 2, and Wyo. Const. art. 1, §37 (which recognizes the supremacy of the federal constitution)). Significantly, none of the justices suggested that the initiative would have violated the *state* constitution. The initiative was subsequently defeated at the polls.

2. 410 U.S.113 (1973).

3. 505 U.S.833 (1992).

Analysis

The principal pre-*Roe* abortion statute prohibited performance of an abortion upon a pregnant woman unless the procedure was "necessary to preserve her life."[4] Another statute prohibited a woman from soliciting an abortion or allowing an abortion to be performed upon her (subject to the same exception).[5] Pursuant to *Roe*, §6-77 was declared unconstitutional (on federal, not state, grounds) by the Wyoming Supreme Court in *Doe v. Burk*,[6] and both §6-77 and §6-78 were later repealed.[7]

Based upon arguments that have been raised in other States with similar constitutional provisions, possible sources for an asserted abortion right could include provisions of the Declaration of Rights recognizing inherent power in the people (art. 1, §1); guaranteeing due process of law (§6), equal protection (§§2, 3 and 34), open courts (§8), and religious freedom (§18); prohibiting arbitrary power (§7); and retaining rights (§36).[8] The analysis that follows addresses each of these provisions.

Inherent Power

Article 1, §1, of the Wyoming Constitution provides:

> All power is inherent in the people, and all free governments are founded on their authority, and instituted for their peace, safety and happiness; for the advancement of these ends they have at all times an inalienable and indefeasible right to alter, reform or abolish the government in such manner as they may think proper.[9]

In any challenge to a Wyoming statute prohibiting abortion, abortion advocates might argue that the statute interferes with the "inherent" power of the people because it does not promote their "peace, safety and happiness...." Given the purpose of §1, this argument is not likely to prevail.

Section 1 secures to the people themselves, through the amendment process, the right to decide whether, how and to what extent the organic instrument of

---

4. WYO. STAT. §6-77 (1957).

5. *Id.* §6-78. No prosecutions were reported under this statute.

6. 513 P.2d 643 (Wyo. 1973).

7. 1977 Wyo. Sess. Laws 11, 14, ch. 11, §2.

8. Two other more unlikely sources of an abortion right under the Wyoming Constitution-§4 (prohibiting unreasonable searches and seizures) and §20 (guaranteeing freedom of speech)-are discussed generally in Chapter 3, *supra*.

9. WYO. CONST. art. 1, §1 (2007).

government should be changed.[10] For that reason, §1 cannot be regarded as a source of substantive rights. Whether a given law promotes the "peace, safety and happiness" of the people, within the meaning of art. 1, §1, presents a political question for the legislature (and, ultimately, the people) to decide, not a constitutional question for the judiciary.

Due Process of Law

Article 1, §6, of the Wyoming Constitution provides: "No person shall be deprived of life, liberty or property without due process of law."[11] In any challenge to a statute prohibiting abortion, abortion advocates are most likely to rely upon art. 1, §6, arguing that the statute interferes with a pregnant woman's "liberty" in obtaining an abortion. Such an argument probably would not succeed.

Article 1, §6, has been recognized to have a substantive aspect, as well as a procedural one.[12] With respect to *non*fundamental rights, "the exercise of the state police power must promote a legitimate public objective with reasonable means."[13] Phrased somewhat differently, substantive due process (with respect to *non*fundamental rights) is satisfied if a statute is "rationally related to a legitimate state objective,"[14] a test which an abortion prohibition would easily satisfy. But what determines whether an asserted right is "fundamental" or "non-fundamental"? "A fundamental right," the Wyoming Supreme Court has explained, is a right which is guaranteed explicitly or implicitly by the constitution."[15] The Wyoming Constitution does not contain an explicit guarantee of an abortion right. Nor can it fair be said that such a right is implicitly guaranteed.

First, in its opinion striking down the state abortion statutes on the authority of *Roe v. Wade*, the Wyoming Supreme Court stated that, subject to the Supreme Court's pronouncements interpreting the United States Constitution, "[t]he regulation of abortions in this State is beyond the power of the

---

10. *See Cathcart v. Meyer*, 88 P.3d 1050, 1067 (Wyo. 2004) (art. 1, §1, "recognizes the ultimate right of the people to 'alter, reform or abolish' government, through peaceful means or otherwise").

11. Wyo. Const. art. 1, §6 (2007).

12. *Cheyenne Airport Board v. Rogers*, 707 P.2d 717, 727 (Wyo. 1985), *appeal dismissed*, 476 U.S. 1110 (1985) (citing *State v. Langley*, 84 P.2d 767, 770 (Wyo. 1938)).

13. *Moreno v. State Dep't of Revenue & Taxation*, 775 P.2d 497, 500 (Wyo. 1989).

14. *White v. State*, 784 P.2d 1313, 1315 (Wyo. 1989).

15. *In re Honeycutt*, 908 P.2d 976, 979 (Wyo. 1995) (citing *Mills v. Reynolds*, 837 P.2d 48, 53–54 (Wyo. 1992)).

courts and is solely a matter for the legislature...."[16] This language suggests that an abortion statute could not be successfully challenged on *state*, as opposed to *federal*, grounds.[17]

Second, the Wyoming Supreme Court has held that "if a statute does not violate the Due Process Clause of the Fourteenth Amendment, it does not violate Wyoming's Due Process Clause."[18] If the Supreme Court overrules *Roe*, as modified by *Casey*, and holds that the federal Due Process Clause does not confer a right to abortion, then no such right would exist under art. 1, §6, either.[19]

Third, although the Wyoming Supreme Court has not expressly formulated a methodology for determining whether a right is "implicitly [guaranteed] by the constitution," the court's treatment of other fundamental rights under the state constitution strongly suggests that abortion would not qualify as one. The court has recognized a "right to associate with one's family" as "a fundamental liberty interest" under both the state and federal constitutions.[20] In *DS*, the court remarked on how "deeply seated the child-parent relationship is in

---

16. *Doe v. Burk*, 513 P.2d at 645.

17. That suggestion is reinforced by the court's opinion in *Wyoming NARAL v. Karpan*, *see* n. 1, *supra*. In that case, the court determined that a ballot initiative that would have prohibited abortion throughout pregnancy would violate the *federal* constitution, without any hint that the initiative would also violate any substantive provision of the *state* constitution. More generally, the court has held that the liberty envisioned in art. 1, §6, "is not alone a liberty of person such as is offended by enslavement, imprisonment or other restraint," but "contemplates a person's liberty to do *all that is not made unlawful*." *Bulova Watch Co. v. Zale Jewelry Co. of Cheyenne*, 371 P.2d 409, 417 (Wyo. 1962) (emphasis added).

18. *State v. Laude*, 654 P.2d 1223, 1228 (Wyo. 1982) (citing *McGarvey v. Swan*, 96 P. 697, 714 (Wyo. 1908)).

19. Whether the Wyoming Supreme Court would recognize a right to abortion under art. I, §6, while *Roe*, as modified by *Casey*, remains the law of the land has not been determined. *See* n. 1, *supra*. It should be noted, however, that to the extent that the state supreme court recognizes the same fundamental rights under the *state* due process guarantee as the Supreme Court does under the *federal* due process guarantee, abortion would not qualify as a "fundamental" right. Although the Supreme Court characterized the right to choose abortion as "fundamental" in *Roe*, 410 U.S. at 152–53, it tacitly abandoned that characterization in *Casey*, 505 U.S. at 869–79 (Joint Op. of O'Connor, Kennedy and Souter, JJ., replacing *Roe's* "strict scrutiny" standard of review with the more relaxed "undue burden" standard, allowing for a broader measure of abortion regulation).

20. *In re Adoption of KJD*, 41 P.3d 522, 530 (Wyo. 2002) (citing *Matter of GP*, 679 P.2d 976, 981 (Wyo. 1984), and *DS v. Dep't of Public Assistance & Social Services*, 607 P.2d 911, 918 (Wyo. 1980)). The court cited art. 1, §§2 (equality of all), 6 (due process), 7 (prohibition of arbitrary power), and 36 (retained rights), in support of this fundamental right. Sections 2, 7 and 36 are discussed later in this analysis.

the warp and woof of the American fabric."[21] The court expressed the view that "the rearing of our children might be one example of the pursuit of happiness that the founding fathers envisioned" in the Declaration of Independence.[22] Proceeding on that assumption, the court added that "the rights described in both the state and federal constitutions were formulated to protect the Declaration of Independence."[23]

The Wyoming Supreme Court's emphasis on the antiquity of the "right to associate with one's family," and its association of that right with the "pursuit of happiness" set forth in the Declaration of Independence, indicates that a right will not be considered implicitly guaranteed by the state constitution and, therefore, "fundamental," unless there is an historical basis for recognizing such a right. There is no *historical* basis for recognizing a right to abortion in Wyoming, however.

Wyoming enacted its first abortion statute in 1876, thirteen years before it adopted its present constitution and was admitted to the Union. The statute prohibited the performance of an abortion upon a pregnant woman at any stage of pregnancy unless the procedure was "procured or attempted by, or under advice of a physician or surgeon, with intent to save the life of such woman, or to prevent serious and permanent bodily injury to her."[24] Only fourteen years later, the 1876 statute was repealed and replaced by new statutes that eliminated the exception for "serious and permanent bodily injury," changed the exception for the life of the woman from a subjective standard ("under advice of a physician or surgeon") to an objective standard ("necessary to preserve [the pregnant woman's] life"), increased the criminal penalties,[25] and prohibited a woman from soliciting an abortion or allowing an abortion to be performed upon her (subject to the same exception).[26] These statutes remained on the books until after *Roe v. Wade* was decided.[27]

---

21. 607 P.2d at 919.

22. *Id.*

23. *Id.*

24. Wyo. (Terr.) Laws 1st Sess., ch. 3, §25 (1869), *codified at* Wyo. (Terr.) Comp. Laws, ch. 35, §25 (1876).

25. Wyo. Laws, ch. 73, §31 (1890), *codified at* Wyo. Rev. Stat. §4969 (1899), *recodified at* Wyo. Comp. Stat. §5808 (1910), *recodified at* Wyo. Comp. Stat. §7086 (1920), *recodified at* Wyo. Rev. Stat. §32-222 (1931), *recodified at* Wyo. Comp. Stat. §9-223 (1945), *recodified at* Wyo. Stat. §6-77 (1957).

26. Wyo. Laws, ch. 73, §32 (1890), *codified at* Wyo. Rev. Stat. §4970 (1899), *recodified at* Wyo. Comp. Stat. §5809 (1910), *recodified at* Wyo. Comp. Stat. §7087 (1920), *recodified at* Wyo. Rev. Stat. §32-223 (1931), *recodified at* Wyo. Comp. Stat. §9-224 (1945), *recodified at* Wyo. Stat. §6-78 (1957). No prosecutions were reported under this statute.

27. *See* n. 5, *supra.*

Following *Roe*, Wyoming enacted numerous statutes regulating abortion.[28] Unborn children are protected in other areas of the law, as well. For example, a woman convicted of a capital offense may not be executed while she is pregnant.[29] Posthumous heirs (heirs conceived before but born after the death of a decedent who dies without a will) "inherit as if they had been born in the lifetime of the decedent."[30] And Wyoming does not allow wrongful life causes of action.[31] There is no evidence in the debates of the Wyoming Constitutional Convention of 1889 that the framers of the Declaration of Rights intended to recognize a right to abortion, which was a crime under the territorial laws in force at the time.[32]

In light of Wyoming's longstanding tradition of prohibiting abortion, which goes back more than one hundred years before *Roe v. Wade* was decided and antedates the 1889 Wyoming Constitution, the absence of any indication that the framers intended to recognize a right to abortion, and the State's continuing interest in protecting the rights of unborn children, it cannot plausibly be said that the due process guarantee of the Wyoming Constitution, or any other provision of the Declaration of Rights, secures a right to abortion.

Equal Protection

The Wyoming Constitution "does not contain ... an express 'equal protection' clause," as such.[33] Rather, "it contains a variety of equality provisions, *viz.*, Article 1, §§ 2, 3, and 34; and Article 3, § 27."[34] Article 1, § 2, provides: "In

---

28. *See* Wyo. Stat. §§ 35-6-118 (requiring parental consent); 35-6-117 (restricting public funding of abortion for indigent women); 35-6-102 (restricting post-viability abortions); 35-6-105, 35-6-106 (recognizing individual and institutional rights of conscience); 35-61-114 (prohibiting discrimination against persons who object to abortion) (2007).

29. Wyo. Stat. §§ 7-13-912, 7-13-913 (2007).

30. Wyo. Stat. § 2-4-103 (2007).

31. *Beardsley v. Wierdsma*, 650 P.2d 288, 289-90 (Wyo. 1982). A "wrongful life" cause of action is a claim brought on behalf of a child who is born with a physical or mental disability or disease that could have been discovered before the child's birth through genetic testing, amniocentesis or other medical screening. The gravamen of the action is that, as a result of a physician's failure to inform the child's parents of the child's disability or disease (or at least of the availability of tests to determine the presence of the disability or disease), they were deprived of the opportunity to abort the child, thus resulting in the birth of a child suffering permanent physical or mental impairment.

32. *See* Journal & Debates of the Constitutional Convention of the State of Wyoming of 1889 157, 167, 718–21 (debate on Declaration of Rights in Committee of the Whole); 723–29 (debate on Declaration of Rights in Convention) (Cheyenne, Wyoming 1893).

33. *Greenwalt v. RAM Restaurant Corp.*, 71 P.3d 717, 730 (Wyo. 2003).

34. *Id.*

their inherent right to life, liberty and the pursuit of happiness, all members of the human race are equal."[35] Article 1, §3, provides:

> Since equality in the enjoyment of natural and civil rights is only made sure through political equality, the laws of this state affecting political rights and privileges of its citizens shall be without distinction of race, color, sex, or any circumstances or condition whatsoever other than individual incompetency, or unworthiness duly ascertained by a court of competent jurisdiction."[36]

Article 1, §34 provides: "All laws of a general nature shall have a uniform operation."[37] And art. 3, §27, which is not part of the Declaration of Rights, prohibits the Legislature from enacting "local" or "special" laws in a variety of enumerated cases, including laws "for punishment of crimes," as well as in "all other cases where a general law can be made applicable...."[38]

An "equal protection" challenge to an abortion statute is most likely to be brought under art. 1, §2. Article 1, §3, would have no application because it deals only with "political rights and privileges."[39] Article 1, §34, and its corollary, art. 3, §27, would not be implicated because an abortion statute would be a law of a "general nature" that would have "a uniform operation" through the State upon the persons affected.[40]

Despite language in earlier cases suggesting that the Wyoming Supreme Court would apply a somewhat different equal protection standard under the state constitution than the United States Supreme Court applies under the federal constitution,[41] more recent authority indicates that the state supreme court

---

35. Wyo. Const. art. 1, §2 (2007).

36. *Id.* art. 1, §3.

37. *Id.* art. 1, §34.

38. *Id.* art. 3, §27.

39. In *Hansen v. State*, 904 P.2d 811 (Wyo. 1995), the Wyoming Supreme Court remarked that art. 1, §3, "clearly seems to touch only upon political rights and privileges as distinguished from other personal rights or privileges." *Id.* at 816–17 n. 4. *See, e.g., Cathcart v. Meyer*, 88 P.3d 1050, 1068 (Wyo. 2004) (striking down citizen-sponsored ballot initiative that would have imposed legislative term limits.).

40. The state supreme court has held that art. 3, §27 (and by extension, art. 1, §34) is satisfied if "the classification contained in the statute [is] reasonable, and ... operate[s] alike upon all persons ... in like or the same circumstances and conditions." *Mountain Fuel Supply Co. v. Emerson*, 578 P.2d 1351, 1356 (Wyo. 1978).

41. *See, e.g., Allhusen v. State Mental Professions Licensing Board*, 898 P.2d 878, 885–86 (Wyo. 1995) (citing *Johnson v. State Hearing Examiner's Office*, 838 P.2d 158, 166–67 (Wyo. 1992) (plurality)).

has reformulated that standard in compliance with federal precedent.[42] Under the current state equal protection doctrine, the court must "[i]dentify the legislative classification at issue," "[i]dentify the legislative objectives," and "[d]etermine whether the legislative classification is rationally related to the achievement of an appropriate legislative purpose."[43] "When a 'suspect class' or a 'fundamental right' is involved," however, the court applies "a strict scrutiny test" which requires a demonstration that "the classification is necessary to achieve a compelling state interest."[44]

Strict scrutiny review would not apply to an abortion prohibition because, for the reasons set forth in the preceding section and in the last section of this analysis, the Wyoming Constitution does not confer a "fundamental right" to abortion. Nor would the prohibition of abortion classify persons on the basis of a "suspect" personal characteristic.

Abortion advocates may argue in the alternative, however, that a statute prohibiting (or regulating) abortion discriminates against women, a "quasi-suspect" class for purposes of state and federal equal protection analysis, and therefore is subject to heightened scrutiny, because only women are capable of becoming pregnant. That argument, however, would not likely succeed.

First, the United States Supreme Court has reviewed restrictions on abortion funding under a rational basis standard of review, *not* under the heightened scrutiny required of gender-based classifications.[45] Indeed, the Court has held that "the disfavoring of abortion ... is not *ipso facto* sex discrimination," and, citing its decisions in *Harris v. McRae* and other cases addressing abortion funding, stated that "the constitutional test applicable to government abortion-funding restrictions is not the heightened-scrutiny standard that our cases demand for sex discrimination, ... but the ordinary rationality standard."[46]

---

42. *See Greenwalt v. RAM Restaurant Corp.*, 71 P.3d 717, 729–32 (Wyo. 2003).

43. *Id.* at 732.

44. *Kautza v. City of Cody*, 812 P.2d 143, 147 (Wyo. 1991) (citations omitted).

45. *Harris v. McRae*, 448 U.S. 297, 321–26 (1980).

46. *Bray v. Alexandria Women's Health Clinic*, 506 U.S. 263, 273 (1993). Several state supreme courts and individual state supreme court justices have recognized that abortion regulations and restrictions on abortion funding are not "directed at women as a class" so much as "abortion as a medical treatment, which, because it involves a potential life, has no parallel as a treatment method." *Bell v. Low Income Women of Texas*, 95 S.W.3d 253, 258 (Tex. 2002) (upholding funding restrictions) (citing *Harris*, 448 U.S. at 325). *See also Fischer v. Dep't of Public Welfare*, 502 A.2d 114, 125 (Pa. 1985) ("the basis for the distinction here is not sex, but abortion") (upholding funding restrictions); *Moe v. Secretary of Administration & Finance*, 417 N.E.2d 387, 407 (Mass. 1981) (Hennessey, C.J., dissenting) (funding restrictions were "directed at abortion as a medical procedure, not women as a

Second, even assuming that an abortion prohibition differentiates between men and women on the basis of sex, and would otherwise be subject to a higher standard of review, the Supreme Court has held that biological differences between men and women may justify different treatment based on those differences. In upholding a statutory rape statute that applied only to males, the Supreme Court noted, "this Court has consistently upheld statutes where the gender classification is not invidious, but rather realistically reflects the fact that the sexes are not similarly situated in certain circumstances."[47] As one federal district court observed: "Abortion statutes are examples of cases in which the sexes are not biologically similarly situated" because only women are capable of becoming pregnant and having abortions.[48]

A statute prohibiting abortion quite obviously can affect only women because only women are capable of becoming pregnant.[49] Unlike laws that use women's ability to become pregnant (or pregnancy itself) to discriminate against them in *other* areas (*e.g.*, employment opportunities), abortion prohibitions cannot fairly be said to involve a distinction between men and women that is a "mere pretext[] designed to erect an invidious discrimination against [women]."[50]

Because a prohibition of abortion would not infringe upon a fundamental state constitutional right and would not impermissibly classify on the basis of a suspect or quasi-suspect class, it would need to satisfy only the rational basis test. Under that test, the classification must be "rationally related to the achievement of an appropriate purpose."[51] A prohibition of abortion would be "rationally related" to the "appropriate purpose" of protecting unborn human life. Accordingly, Wyoming could enact an abortion prohibition without violating the equal protection guarantees of the Wyoming Constitution.

---

class"); *Right to Choose v. Byrne*, 450 A.2d 925, 950 (N.J. 1982) (O'Hern, J., dissenting) ("[t]he subject of the legislation is not the person of the recipient, but the nature of the claimed medical service"). Both *Moe* and *Right to Choose* were decided on other grounds. The dissenting justices were addressing alternative arguments raised by the plaintiffs, but not reached by the majority opinions.

47. *Michael M. v. Superior Court*, 450 U.S. 464, 469 (1981). The Wyoming Supreme Court has acknowledged this principle in upholding the different treatment accorded men and women under the State's parentage statutes. *See A. v. X, Y & Z*, 641 P.2d 1222, 1224–26 (Wyo. 1982).

48. *Jane L. v. Bangerter*, 794 F. Supp. 1537, 1549 (D. Utah 1992).

49. *Geduldig v. Aiello*, 417 U.S. 484, 496 n. 20 (1974) ("[n]ormal pregnancy is an objectively, identifiable physical condition with unique characteristics").

50. *Id.*

51. *Greenwalt*, 71 P.2d at 732.

Open Courts

Article 1, §8, of the Wyoming Constitution provides, in part: "All courts shall be open and every person for an injury done to person, reputation or property shall have justice administered without sale, denial or delay."[52] Abortion advocates might argue that a statute prohibiting abortion interferes with a woman's control over her own body, and that such interference constitutes an "injury" to her "person," as those terms are used in §8. The remedy for such interference would be invalidation of the statute. This argument assumes that art. 1, §8, confers substantive rights. The case law is clear, however, that it does not.

As is apparent from its text and structure, §8 is concerned with access to the courts for tortiously inflicted injuries-it does not establish what *constitutes* an injury to anyone's "person, reputation or property." Whether there is a remedy for an injury is determined by sources of law extrinsic to the constitution, not §8.[53] Moreover, the remedies themselves redress injuries recognized by the common law and statutory law, not constitutional "injuries." Although the right to access to the courts is a fundamental right,[54] §8 "is not a limitation on lawmakers who, in the proper exercise of the legislative power, may alter or abolish common law causes of action as long as that legislative action does not violate some other provision of our constitution."[55] "The open courts provision was included in our constitution to insure equal administration of justice by the judiciary and did not intend application to the legislature nor to create a fundamental right to full legal redress. No one has a vested right to any rule of common law."[56] Indeed, the Wyoming Legislature "has the power to abolish substantive common law rights, including those traced to the common law of England, in order to attain a permissible legislative object."[57]

Article 1, §8, limits the Legislature in only one respect-the Legislature may not destroy vested rights. Thus,

> [w]here an injury has already occurred for which the injured person has a right of action, the legislature cannot deny a remedy; but the remedies recognized by the common law in this class of cases, together

---

52. Wyo. Const. art. 1, §8 (2007).
53. Indeed, unlike similar provisions in other state constitutions, §8 does not even use the word "remedy."
54. *Robinson v. Pacificorp*, 10 P.3d 1133, 1136 (Wyo. 2000) (citing *Mills v. Reynolds*, 837 P.2d 48, 54 (Wyo. 1992)).
55. *Greenwalt v. RAM Restaurant Corp.*, 71 P.3d at 728.
56. *Id.*
57. *Id.*

with all rights of action that may arise in the future may be altered or abolished to the extent of destroying actions for injuries or death arising from negligent accident, so long as there is no impairment of rights already accrued.[58]

Under §8, "the courts are to afford remedies not for every wrong but for every wrong *recognized by law*."[59] To establish an "open courts" violation, "a litigant must satisfy a two-part test: first, he must show that he has a well-recognized common-law cause of action that is being restricted; and second, he must show that the restriction is unreasonable or arbitrary when balanced against the purpose and basis of the statute."[60] Abortion advocates could not satisfy either prong of this two-part test. First, the common law did not recognize a cause of action when a pregnant woman was denied an abortion because abortion itself was a crime. Second, an abortion prohibition would be reasonably related to the legitimate state interest in protecting unborn human life.

Taken as a whole, §8 is concerned with reasonable access to the courts. It places no limitation on the State's authority to define and punish crimes and has never been so interpreted.

Religious Liberty

Article 1, §18, of the Wyoming Constitution provides, in relevant part: "The free exercise and enjoyment of religious profession and worship without discrimination or preference shall be forever guaranteed in this state...."[61]

In any challenge to a statute prohibiting abortion, abortion advocates may raise either or both of two arguments under art. 1, §18. First, they may argue that an abortion prohibition interferes with the "free exercise and enjoyment" of a woman's "religious profession" by forbidding her from obtaining an abortion that would be allowed by her religion. Second, they may argue in the alternative (or in addition) that an abortion prohibition gives a "preference" to a religion because it reflects sectarian beliefs regarding when human life begins and the sinfulness of abortion. Neither argument would likely prevail.

The Wyoming Supreme Court has not determined whether analysis under the Establishment Clause and under art. 1, §18, of the Wyoming Constitution are

---

58. *Id.* at 729.

59. *Id.* (emphasis added).

60. *Id.*

61. Wyo. Const. art. 1, §18 (2007). *See also* art. 21, §25: "Perfect toleration of religious sentiment shall be secured, and no inhabitant of this state shall ever be molested in person or property on account of his or her mode of religious worship."

the same. Nevertheless, the paucity of case law under §18 (which has been cited in only two decisions, neither of which dealt with the "preference" language) may suggest that the court does not view §18 as embodying a more rigorous standard than is required by the Establishment Clause. In interpreting the "free exercise" language of §18, the state supreme court has followed Supreme Court precedent interpreting the federal Free Exercise Clause.[62] In light of the foregoing, a challenge to an abortion statute that would not succeed under the Religion Clauses of the First Amendment would not succeed under art. 1, §18, either. For the reasons set forth in Chapter 2, *supra*, an abortion statute could not be successfully challenged on First Amendment grounds. Accordingly, a similar challenge under art. 1, §18, would not likely be successful.

Prohibition of Arbitrary Power

Article 1, §7, of the Wyoming Constitution provides: "Absolute, arbitrary power over the lives, liberty and property of freemen exists nowhere in a republic, not even in the largest majority."[63] Although, as previously noted, art. 1, §7, has been cited (along with other provisions of the Declaration of Rights) in support of the "fundamental right" of family association,[64] it has more commonly been cited in equal protection challenges to statutes.[65] There is no indication in the case law, however, that §7 places any more restrictions on legislation than do other provisions of the Declaration of Rights. Accordingly, if a statute does not violate other provisions of art. 1, it is not likely to violate §1, either.

Retained Rights

Article 1, §36, of the Wyoming Constitution provides: "The enumeration in this constitution, of certain rights shall not be construed to deny, impair, or

---

62. *Trujillo v. State*, 2 P.2d 567, 575–77 & n. 4 (Wyo. 2000) (statutes criminalizing drug possession with intent to deliver do not violate either the Free Exercise Clause or art. 1, §18, of the Wyoming Constitution) (following *Employment Division, Dep't of Human Resources of Oregon v. Smith*, 494 U.S. 872 (1990)).

63. WYO. CONST. art. 1, §7 (2007).

64. *See* the cases cited in n. 20, *supra*.

65. *See, e.g., Bell v. Gray*, 377 P.2d 924, 926 (Wyo. 1963); *Mountain Fuel Supply Co. v. Emerson*, 578 P.2d at 1354–56. The condemnation in §7 of *arbitrary* power indicates that the provision is concerned with measures that are *unreasonable*, either in the means employed or the end sought. The Legislature's decision to enact a statute that is reasonably related to a legitimate state purpose, however, cannot be said to be an exercise of "arbitrary" power, and no case interpreting §7 suggests otherwise.

disparage others retained by the people."[66] In any challenge to a statute prohibiting abortion, abortion advocates may be expected to rely upon § 36, arguing that abortion is a "retained right" under the state constitution. A proper
interpretation of § 36, however, would not support a right to abortion as a retained right.

As previously noted, the Wyoming Supreme Court has cited art. 1, § 36,
along with §§ 2, 6 and 7, in support of a "right to associate with one's family,"
which the court has described as "a fundamental liberty interest" under both
the United States and Wyoming Constitutions.[67] That right, however, as the
court has observed, predates both the adoption of the Wyoming Constitution
and the United States Constitution.[68] The court's emphasis of the antiquity of
the "right to associate with one's family" suggests that only those rights that
were recognized at the time the federal and state constitutions were adopted may
be regarded as "retained rights" under § 36. There was no "right" to abortion
at the time the United States Constitution was adopted in 1787, however; abortion was a common law crime. And by the time the Wyoming Constitution
was adopted in 1889, abortion was a statutory crime in every State, including
Wyoming, except Kentucky, where it was a common law crime.

Apart from the "right to associate with one's family," the Wyoming Supreme
Court has not recognized any other "retained right" under art. 1, § 36. Although § 36 has been mentioned in dictum or in plurality opinions as a source
of a state right of privacy,[69] a majority of the court has never held that § 36 confers a right of privacy.[70] The leading advocate of a broad reading of § 36 on the
Wyoming Supreme Court-former Chief Justice Urbigkit-was never able to
persuade a majority of the court to adopt his approach to interpreting the
provision.[71]

---

66. WYO. CONST. art. 1, § 34 (2007).

67. *In re Adoption of KJD*, 41 P.3d at 530.

68. *Matter of Adoption of Voss*, 550 P.2d 481, 584 (Wyo. 1976) ("the earliest and most
hallowed of the ties that bind humanity, in all countries considered sacred, is the relationship of parent and child").

69. See *Employment Security Comm'n of Wyoming v. Western Gas Processors*, Ltd., 786 P.2d
866, 872 n. 11 (Wyo. 1990) (dictum); *Johnson v. State of Wyoming Hearing Examiner's Office*, 838 P.2d 158, 165 (Wyo. 1992) (plurality).

70. Apart from § 36, the court has referred to a state right of privacy only in dictum. *See
White v. State*, 784 P.2d 1313, 1315 (Wyo. 1989).

71. *See Martin v. State*, 780 P.2d 1354, 1367 & n. 20 (Wyo. 1989) (Urbigkit, J., dissenting); *Jandro v. State*, 781 P.2d 512, 523–28 (Wyo. 1989) (Urbigkit, J., dissenting); *State v.
Sullivan*, 798 P.2d 826, 830 (Wyo. 1990) (Urbigkit, C.J., concurring generally and with special concurrence); *Swazo v. State*, 800 P.2d 1152, 1154–55 (Wyo. 1990) (Urbigkit, C.J., dis-

Conclusion

Based on the foregoing analysis, an argument that the Wyoming Constitution protects a right to abortion that is separate from, and independent of, the right to abortion recognized in *Roe v. Wade* would not likely succeed. That, in turn, suggests that if *Roe*, as modified by *Casey*, is ultimately overruled, the State of Wyoming could enact and enforce a statute *prohibiting* abortion. Moreover, nothing in the Wyoming Constitution precludes Wyoming from *regulating* abortion within federal constitutional limits in the meantime.

---

senting); *A.P. v. State of Wyoming, Dep't of Health & Human Services, Div. of Public Assistance & Social Services ex rel. B.L.S.*, 849 P.2d 703, 711 (Wyo. 1993) (Urbigkit, J. (ret.), dissenting).

CONCLUSION

Of the twelve state supreme courts that have recognized a state constitutional right to abortion, ten have grounded their decisions in state privacy theory.[1] The decision of an eleventh state supreme court is difficult to classify because of the opacity of the court's decision.[2] Only one state supreme court has derived a right to abortion from a source other than an express or implied right of privacy.[3] In light of the predominance of privacy theory in the decisions that have recognized a state right to abortion, it is natural to ask how many other States recognize a right to privacy and how likely is it that their supreme courts would follow the lead of the decided cases.

Ten States contain express privacy language in their Declaration (or Bill) of Rights. In addition to Alaska, California, Florida and Montana, those States are Arizona, Hawaii, Illinois, Louisiana, South Carolina and Washington. Based on the constitutional history of its privacy provision,[4] the Hawaii Supreme Court most likely would recognize a state right to abortion. It is unlikely, however, that the supreme court of any of the other States with express privacy language in their constitutions would follow suit.

In its decision striking down state restrictions on public funding of abortion, the Arizona Supreme Court specifically declined to address whether the Arizona Constitution confers a right to abortion.[5] Moreover, recognizing a right

---

1. *State of Alaska v. Planned Parenthood of Alaska,* 35 P.3d 30 (Alaska 2001); *State of Alaska, Dep't of Health & Human Services v. Planned Parenthood of Alaska, Inc.,* 28 P.3d 904 (Alaska 2001); *Valley Hospital Ass'n v. Mat-Su Coalition for Choice,* 948 P.2d 963 (Alaska 1997); *Committee to Defend Reproductive Rights v. Myers,* 625 P.2d 779 (Cal. 1981); *In re T.W.,* 551 So.2d 1186 (Fla. 1989); *Moe v. Secretary of Administration & Finance,* 417 N.E.2d 387 (Mass. 1981); *Women of the State of Minnesota v. Gomez,* 542 N.W.2d 17 (Minn. 1995); *Pro-Choice Mississippi v. Fordice,* 716 So.2d 645 (Miss. 1998); *Armstrong v. State,* 989 P.2d 364 (Mont. 1999); *Right to Choose v. Byrne,* 450 A.2d 925 (N.J. 1982); *Hope v. Perales,* 634 N.E.2d 183 (N.Y. 1994) (by implication); *Planned Parenthood of Middle Tennessee v. Sundquist,* 38 S.W.3d 1 (Tenn. 2000).

2. *Beacham v. Leahy,* 287 A.2d 836 (Vt. 1972).

3. *New Mexico Right to Choose/NARAL v. Johnson,* 975 P.2d 841 (N.M. 1998) (state equal rights amendment).

4. *See* Chapter 14 (Hawaii), nn. 6–18 and accompanying text, *supra.*

5. *Simat Corp. v. Arizona Health Care Cost Containment System,* 56 P.3d 28, 37 (Ariz. 2002) ("[w]e reach no conclusion about whether the Arizona Constitution provides a right of choice, let alone one broader than that found in the federal constitution").

---

to abortion (a positive right) would not be required by the kind of (negative) privacy interests (*e.g.,* refusing unwanted medical treatment) that the court *has* recognized.[6] The constitutional history of the privacy guarantee in the Illinois Constitution leaves no doubt that it was not intended to secure a right to abortion.[7] The reasoning of the Louisiana Supreme Court's decision in *State v. Smith,*[8] rejecting a state privacy right to engage in acts of homosexual sodomy, strongly suggests that the court would not recognize a right to abortion, either. Although the South Carolina Supreme Court has held that the state constitution protects a right to privacy,[9] it is not at all clear that the privacy language in the constitution, which is part of a provision dealing with search and seizure,[10] has any application to privacy of conduct, as opposed to informational privacy.[11] Finally, the methodology the Washington Supreme Court employs for determining whether given conduct is protected by the state right to privacy would not favor recognition of a state right to abortion.[12]

At least fourteen state constitutions have been interpreted to protect a state right of privacy by implication. In addition to Massachusetts, Minnesota, Mississippi, New Jersey, New York and Tennessee, the highest courts of which have already recognized a state right to abortion, those States are Connecticut, Georgia, Kentucky, Michigan, Missouri, Nebraska, Pennsylvania and Texas. The reviewing courts of Connecticut, Michigan, Missouri and Nebraska have held or implied that their privacy protections are no broader than that afforded by the United States Supreme Court under the Due Process Clause of the Fourteenth Amendment,[13] which suggests that none of those courts would recognize a right to abortion if *Roe v. Wade,* as modified by *Planned Parenthood of Southeastern Pennsylvania v. Casey,* were overruled.[14] The supreme courts of Geor-

---

6. *See* Chapter 6 (Arizona), nn. 37–49 and accompanying text, *supra.*

7. *See* Chapter 16 (Illinois), nn. 39–49 and accompanying text, *supra.*

8. 766 So.2d 501 (La. 2000).

9. *Hendrix v. Taylor,* 579 S.E.2d 320, 323 n. 12 (S.C. 2003).

10. S.C. Const. art. I, § 10 (1997).

11. *See* Chapter 43 (South Carolina), n. 26, *supra.*

12. *See* Chapter 50 (Washington), nn. 15–37 and accompanying text, *supra.*

13. *See* Chapter 10 (Connecticut), nn. 21–65 and accompanying text, Chapter 25 (Michigan), nn. 19–43 and accompanying text, Chapter 28 (Missouri), nn. 1, 22, and Chapter 30 (Nebraska) n. 11, *supra.*

14. Even in the absence of an overruling decision, the Michigan Court of Appeals has concluded that the Michigan Constitution does not protect a right to abortion, *Mahaffey v. Attorney General,* 564 N.W.2d 104 (Mich. Ct. App. 1997), the Missouri Supreme Court has declined to state whether the Missouri Constitution protects a right to abortion in a case in which state abortion rights were advanced, *Reproductive Health Services of Planned Parenthood of the St. Louis Region, Inc. v. Nixon,* 185 S.W.3d 685, 692 (Mo. 2006), and the

gia and Kentucky have held that their (implied) right of privacy *is* broader than the federal right of privacy, but both courts have qualified that right by noting that it does not extend to conduct that harms third parties.[15] Abortion, of course, does harm (and is intended to harm) third parties (unborn children).[16] The historical treatment of abortion in both States, as well as the recognition each State continues to give to unborn children in areas of law outside of abortion, suggests that neither court would extend its right of privacy to embrace abortion.[17]

Both the Pennsylvania Supreme Court and the Texas Supreme Court have rejected state constitutional challenges to statutes and regulations restricting public funding of abortion.[18] Although neither case decided whether the state constitution protects a right to abortion, the courts' opinions, as well as each State's historical treatment of abortion and its contemporary treatment of the rights of unborn children outside the context of abortion,[19] tend to indicate that neither court would recognize a state right to abortion.

In addition to Alaska, Hawaii, Massachusetts, Montana and New Mexico, the supreme courts of which have already recognized (or, in the case of Hawaii, likely would recognize) a state right to abortion, twelve other States—Colorado, Connecticut, Illinois, Louisiana, Maryland, New Hampshire, Pennsylvania, Texas, Utah, Virginia, Washington and Wyoming—have adopted equal rights amendments (or constitutions containing equal rights provisions). Unlike the New Mexico Supreme Court's decision in *New Mexico Right to Choose/NARAL v. Johnson*,[20] however, the supreme courts in other States with equal rights guarantees generally recognize that a classification based upon the

---

Nebraska Supreme Court has referred to the right to abortion solely as a matter of federal, not state, constitutional law, *In re Petition of Anonymous I*, 558 N.W.2d 784, 789 (Neb. 1997).

15. *Powell v. State*, 510 S.E.2d 18, 22 (Ga. 1998) (right of privacy does not extend to conduct that "'interfer[e] with the rights of another or of the public'") (quoting *Pavesich v. New England Life Ins. Co.*, 50 S.E. 68, 70 (Ga. 1905)); *Commonwealth v. Wasson*, 842 S.W.2d 487, 496 (Ky. 1993) (drawing the line at "harmful consequences to others").

16. *See Cabinet for Human Resources v. Women's Health Services, Inc.*, 878 S.W.2d 806, 809 (Ky. Ct. App. 1994) (McDonald, J., concurring) ("[a]n abortion ends the life of a developing child").

17. *See* Chapter 13 (Georgia), nn. 11–39 and accompanying text, Chapter 20 (Kentucky), nn. 13–65 and accompanying text, *supra*.

18. *Fischer v. Dep't of Public Welfare*, 502 A.2d 114 (Pa. 1985); *Bell v. Low Income Women of Texas*, 95 S.W.3d 253, 265 (Tex. 2002).

19. *See* Chapter 41 (Pennsylvania), nn. 16–38 and accompanying text, Chapter 46 (Texas), nn. 28–59 and accompanying text, *supra*.

20. *See* n. 4, *supra*.

unique physical characteristics of a particular sex does not deny either sex equal rights under the law.[21]

Apart from privacy theory and equal rights amendments, other likely sources of an asserted abortion right under state constitutions would include provisions guaranteeing due process of law, recognizing inalienable or inherent (natural) rights and guaranteeing equal protection of the law. It is questionable, however, whether any of these sources would support a state right to abortion if the issue is litigated in a legal environment in which *Roe*, as modified by *Casey*, has been overruled.

The supreme courts of at least ten States have held that the protection afforded by their state due process guarantee is the same or no broader than that afforded by the Due Process Clause of the Fourteenth Amendment.[22] Several other state supreme courts employ a due process methodology (either one that has been expressly developed in its decisions or one that is implicit in the relevant case law) that would not likely lead to recognition of an abortion right.[23]

---

21. The cases have upheld rape statutes, *State v. Fletcher*, 341 So.2d 340, 348 (La. 1976), *Brooks v. State*, 330 A.2d 670, 672–73 (Md. Ct. Sp. App. 1975), *Finley v. State*, 527 S.W.2d 553, 555–57 (Tex. Crim. App. 1975); statutory rape statutes, *People v. Salinas*, 551 P.2d 703, 705–06 (Colo. 1976), *State v. Bell*, 377 So.2d 303 (La. 1979); an aggravated incest statute, *People v. Boyer*, 349 N.E.2d 50 (Ill. 1976); statutes governing the means of establishing maternity and paternity, *People v. Morrison*, 584 N.E.2d 509 (Ill. App. Ct. 1991), *A v. X, Y & Z*, 641 P.2d 1222, 1224–25 (Wyo. 1982); statutes and rules barring female nudity in bars, *Dydyn v. Dep't of Liquor Control*, 531 A.2d 170, 175 (Conn. App. Ct. 1987); *Messina v. State*, 904 S.W.2d 178, 181 (Tex. App.-Dallas 1995, *no pet.*); an ordinance prohibiting public exposure of female breasts, *City of Seattle v. Buchanan*, 584 P.2d 918, 919–21 (Wash. 1978); and limitations on public funding of abortion, *Fischer v. Dep't of Public Welfare*, 502 A.2d at 124–26, *Bell v. Low Income Women of Texas*, 95 S.W.3d at 257–64. *See also Redwood Gym v. Salt Lake County Comm'n*, 624 P.2d 1138, 1147 (Utah 1981) ("[i]n the matter of pregnancy there is no way to find equality between men and women") (upholding county ordinance prohibiting opposite-sex massages in commercial massage parlors). The anti-discrimination provision in the Virginia Constitution (art. I, § 11) "is no broader than the equal protection clause of the Fourteenth Amendment"). *Archer v. Mays*, 194 S.E.2d 707, 711 (Va. 1973). There is no case law on this point from New Hampshire.

22. *See* Chapter 11 (Delaware), n. 23 and accompanying text, Chapter 19 (Kansas), nn. 19–20 and accompanying text, Chapter 22 (Maine), n. 38 and accompanying text, Chapter 36 (North Carolina), nn. 22–23 and accompanying text, Chapter 38 (Ohio), n. 21 and accompanying text, Chapter 39 (Oklahoma), n. 23, Chapter 44 (South Dakota), n. 23, Chapter 47 (Utah), n. 30 and accompanying text, Chapter 52 (Wisconsin), nn. 24–25 and accompanying text, Chapter 53 (Wyoming), n. 17 and accompanying text, *supra*.

23. *See* Chapter 9 (Colorado), nn. 25–42 and accompanying text, Chapter 15 (Idaho), nn. 11–51 and accompanying text, Chapter 18 (Iowa), nn. 26–45 and accompanying text,

Of the thirty-eight States whose supreme courts have not yet decided whether there is a state constitutional right to abortion, twenty-two have constitutional provisions recognizing inalienable or inherent (natural) rights. The Georgia, Kentucky, Missouri, Nebraska and Pennsylvania Constitutions have been discussed above. The reviewing courts of Alabama, Idaho, Illinois, Indiana, Ohio and Oregon have all held or implied that, standing alone, these provisions do not create judicially enforceable rights.[24] The Iowa Supreme Court has held that "[b]oth the inalienable rights clause [art. I, §1] and the unenumerated rights clause [art. I, §25] secure to the people of Iowa *common law rights that pre-existed Iowa's Constitution*."[25] Of course, there was no "right" to abortion at common law. In a similar vein, the North Dakota Supreme Court has suggested that only those rights that were recognized at the time the state constitution was adopted may be regarded as "inalienable" rights.[26] Once again, abortion could not be counted among such rights. The Supreme Courts of Colorado, New Hampshire, West Virginia and Wisconsin have recognized only those "inherent" rights which are firmly rooted in English and American legal traditions and history,[27] which would not include abortion. The inalienable (or inherent) rights provisions in other state constitutions have received little attention and have seldom been invoked in support of a decision to invalidate a state statute or local ordinance.[28]

State equal protection guarantees offer a weak foundation on which to base a right to abortion. Most (although not all) state courts construe their state equal protection provisions consistently with the Supreme Court's construction of the Equal Protection Clause of the Fourteenth Amendment. The Equal Pro-

---

Chapter 23 (Maryland), nn. 22–46 and accompanying text, Chapter 37 (North Dakota), nn. 14–37 and accompanying text, and Chapter 49 (Virginia), nn. 13–31 and accompanying text, *supra*.

24. *Sheppard v. Dowling*, 28 So. 791, 795 (Ala. 1900); *Nelson v. Boundary County*, 706 P.2d 94, 100 (Idaho Ct. App. 1985); *Kunkel v. Walton*, 689 N.E.2d 1047, 1056–57 (Ill. 1998); *Doe v. O'Connor* 790 N.E.2d 985, 990–91 (Ind. 2003); *State v. Williams*, 728 N.E.2d 342, 354 (Ohio 2000); *State v. Ciancanelli*, 121 P.3d 613, 628 (Or. 2005).

25. *Atwood v. Vilsack*, 725 N.W.2d 641, 651 (Iowa 2006) (emphasis added).

26. *See* Chapter 37 (North Dakota), nn. 13–18 and accompanying text, *supra*.

27. *See* Chapter 9 (Colorado), nn. 25–35 and accompanying text, Chapter 32 (New Hampshire), nn. 13–18 and accompanying text, Chapter 51 (West Virginia), nn. 18–28 and accompanying text, Chapter 52 (Wisconsin), nn. 24–29 and accompanying text, *supra*.

28. *See* Chapter 22 (Maine), nn. 7–12 and accompanying text, Chapter 31 (Nevada), nn. 10–11 and accompanying text, Chapter 36 (North Carolina), n. 23, Chapter 44 (South Dakota), nn. 12–17 and accompanying text, Chapter 47 (Utah), n. 10 and accompanying text, *supra*.

tection Clause, however, is not a source of substantive rights,[29] and neither are equivalent provisions in state constitutions. Although statutes regulating and prohibiting abortion directly affect only women, it is "simplistic" to argue that such statutes use "sex as a basis for distinction."[30] "[T]he basis for the distinction ... is not sex, but abortion...."[31] Abortion statutes are not "directed at women as a class" so much as "abortion as a medical treatment, which, because it involves a potential life, has no parallel as a treatment method."[32] Unlike laws that use women's ability to become pregnant (or pregnancy itself) to discriminate against them in *other* areas (*e.g.*, employment opportunities), abortion prohibitions cannot fairly be said to involve a distinction between men and women that is a "mere pretext[] designed to erect an invidious discrimination against [women]."[33] If none of the foregoing theories (privacy, substantive due process, inalienable or inherent rights, equal rights and equal protection) would support a state right to abortion, it is not likely that more unconventional theories (*e.g.*, arguing that pregnancy is a form of involuntary servitude) would, either.

Whether any state supreme court that has not already recognized a state constitutional right to abortion would recognize such a right while *Roe* remains the law of the land is open to question, even in those States whose supreme courts purportedly follow Supreme Court precedents in interpreting their own constitutions.[34] And if *Roe*, as modified by *Casey*, were overruled, it is unlikely that any additonal state supreme court, other than the Supreme Court of Hawaii, would recognize such a right.

---

29. *San Antonio Independent School District v. Rodriguez*, 411 U.S. 1, 33 (1973).

30. *Fischer v. Dep't of Public Welfare*, 502 A.2d at 125 (citation and internal quotation marks omitted).

31. *Id.*

32. *Bell v. Low Income Women of Texas*, 95 S.W.3d at 258 (upholding funding restrictions) (citing *Harris v. McRae*, 448 U.S. 297, 325 (1980)).

33. *Geduldig v. Aiello*, 417 U.S. 484, 496 n. 20 (1974).

34. At least eight state supreme courts have declined to postulate a state right to abortion that is separate from, and independent of, the right to abortion recognized in *Roe*, in cases in which the courts were squarely presented with state abortion rights claims. *See Simat Corp. v. Arizona Health Care Cost Containment System*, 56 P.3d 28, 37 (Ariz. 2002); *Clinic for Women, Inc. v. Brizzi*, 837 N.E.2d 973, 978 (Ind. 2005); *Alpha Medical Clinic v. Anderson*, 128 P.3d 364, 376–77 (Kan. 2006); *Reproductive Health Services of Planned Parenthood of the St. Louis Region, Inc. v. Nixon*, 185 S.W.3d 685, 692 (Mo. 2006); *In re Initiative Petition No. 349*, 838 P.2d 1, 12 n. 29 (Okla. 1992); *Wood v. University of Utah Medical Center*, 67 P.3d 436, 447–48 (Utah 2003);*Women's Health Center of West Virginia, Inc. v. Panepinto*, 446 S.E.2d 658, 664, 667 (W.Va. 1993); *Wyoming NARAL v. Karpan*, 881 P.2d 281, 287 (Wyo. 1994).